Visions of Unity

Visions of Unity

The Golden Paṇḍita Shakya Chokden's New Interpretation of Yogācāra and Madhyamaka

Yaroslav Komarovski

SUNY PRESS

Published by State University of New York Press, Albany

Printed in the United States of America

For information, contact State University of New York Press, Albany, NY
www.sunypress.edu

Production by Diane Ganeles
Marketing by Anne M. Valentine

Library of Congress Cataloging-in-Publication Data

Komarovski, Yaroslav.
Visions of unity : the golden pandita Shakya Chokden's new interpretation of yogacara and madhyamaka / Yaroslav Komarovski.
p. cm.
Includes bibliographical references and index.
ISBN 978-1-4384-3909-9 (hardcover : alk. paper)
1. Sakya-mchog-ldan, Gser-mdog Pan-chen, 1428–1507. 2. Yogacara (Buddhism) 3. Madhyamaka (Buddhism) I. Title.

BQ7471.K66 2011
294.3'92—dc22 2011005362

10 9 8 7 6 5 4 3 2 1

Contents

List of Tables ix

Acknowledgments xi

Introduction 1

1. Introducing the Visions of Unity 6
2. Introducing the Chapters 11

Chapter One: Life and Works of the Golden Paṇḍita 17

1. Political and Religious Landscape of Fifteenth-Century Tibet 17
2. Life of the Golden Paṇḍita 23
   Early Years and Education 25
   Becoming a Prolific Writer and Famous Scholar 31
   Settling in the Golden Monastery and Exploring New Horizons 35
   Becoming a Tantric Master and Crystallizing Novel Views 44
3. Writings of Shakya Chokden 51
   Chronological List of Shakya Chokden's Works 51
   Topical Divisions of Shakya Chokden's Works Addressed in This Book 59

Chapter Two: The Intellectual Background of Shakya Chokden's Interpretation of Yogācāra and Madhyamaka 71

1. Two Tendencies in Yogācāra and Niḥsvabhāvavāda Writings 71
2. Basic Elements of Shakya Chokden's Approach to Mahāyāna Systems 84

3. Pointed Disappointments: Shakya Chokden's Personal Reflections 91

4. Broadening Empty Horizons: A Note on Changes in Shakya Chokden's Views 102

Chapter Three: Readjusting Rungs of the Ladder: Revisiting Doxographical Hierarchies 109

1. Key Features of Shakya Chokden's Approach to the Buddhist Tenets 109

2. Demarcating the Middle: On the Valid Divisions of Madhyamaka and Great Madhyamaka 116

3. Self-Emptiness and Other-Emptiness 122
Self-Emptiness 124
Other-Emptiness 127

4. Bidding Farewell to the Prāsaṅgika/Svātantrika Division? 136

5. Are There Two Types of Yogācāra Madhyamaka? 141

6. Are There Any Cittamātra Followers Around? 145

7. Expanding the Mādhyamika Camp 150

Chapter Four: Through Broken Boundaries to New Enclosures: Reconciling Yogācāra and Madhyamaka 157

1. Differences between Alīkākāravāda and Satyākāravāda 157

2. The Heart of the Matter: Probing the Alīkākāravāda/Niḥsvabhāvavāda Distinction 168

3. A New Look at the Old Origins: Distinctions of Madhyamaka Stemming from Interpretations of the Second and Third Dharmacakras 183
Looking at the Second and Third Dharmacakras through the Eyes of the Madhyamaka Founders 183
Position of Alīkākāravāda 186
Position of Niḥsvabhāvavāda 191
Positions of Later Mādhyamikas 201

4. Steering the Middle Way between the Two Conflicting Middle Ways: The Art of Not Taking Sides 207

Chapter Five: Explorations in Empty Luminosity: Shakya Chokden's Position on Primordial Mind 213

1. Facing the Reality of Primordial Mind 213
   Primordial Mind and the Question of Existence 213
   The Question of Withstanding Analysis 220
   Does True Existence Have to Be Negated in Order to Abandon Grasping at It? 223
2. Primordial Mind as an Impermanent Phenomenon 228
3. (Un)linking the Self-Cognizing Primordial Mind and Dualistic Consciousness 238
4. Does Self-Cognition Cognize Itself? 242
5. Primordial Mind as the Bridge between Yogācāra and Tantra 249
   Primordial Mind as the Focus of All Mahāyāna Paths 249
   Different but Concordant Approaches to Primordial Mind in Alīkākāravāda and Tantra 252
   A Powerful Ally: Using the Tantric View of Reality for Support 264

Conclusion: The Grand Unity—Shakya Chokden's Middle Way 269

Glossary of Buddhist Terms: English-Tibetan with Sanskrit Parallels 279

Spellings of Tibetan Names and Terms 299

Notes 307

Bibliography 391

Index 423

Tables

Acknowledgments

I want to express my deepest gratitude to everyone who directly or indirectly helped bring this book project to completion. First and foremost, I acknowledge my indebtedness to Shakya Chokden himself. Although this remarkable thinker lived five centuries ago, his life and ideas have been the focus of my research for more than twelve years, providing continuing inspiration for my own life and thinking.

I am also highly indebted to all those who provided me with the intellectual background and skills indispensable for this project: the late Khenchen (*mkhan chen*) Künga Wangchuk (*kun dga' dbang phyug*) and my other teachers at Dzongsar Institute for Advanced Studies of Buddhist Philosophy and Research in Bir, India, with whom I spent several years studying teachings of the Sakya tradition; Khenpo (*mkhan po*) Tsewang Sönam (*tshe dbang bsod nams*) at Pelyül Chökhor Ling (*dpal yul chos 'khor gling*) in Bir, under whose guidance I explored teachings of the Nyingma tradition as well as various interpretations of Madhyamaka and Yogācāra; the late Lopzang Gyamtso (*blo bzang rgya mtsho*) and other teachers at the Institute of Buddhist Dialectics in Dharamsala, India, who for six years taught me Buddhist philosophy, logic, epistemology, and other subjects of traditional Tibetan scholarship; and the late Khetsün Zangpo Rinpoché (*mkhas btsun bzang po rin po che*), the late Kirti Tsenzhap Rinpoché (*kirti mtshan zhabs rin po che*), the late Khenchen Tupten Özer (*thub bstan 'od zer*), and other teachers with whom I studied Buddhist tantric systems. It is only due to the training under these and other outstanding scholars that my studies of Buddhism eventually resulted in a modest understanding and deep appreciation of the richness, complexity, and interconnectedness of the multiple elements comprising the Buddhist universe, inspiring my lasting interest in the thought of Shakya Chokden, thought which embodies those qualities.

I am extremely grateful to my instructors at the University of Virginia, and especially Professors Jeffrey Hopkins and David

Germano—my graduate advisors during the coursework and dissertation research on the writings of Shakya Chokden—who provided me with the intellectual stimulation, challenges, and advice that proved indispensable for transforming my long-term interest in the writings of Shakya Chokden into a work of academic research.

I also strongly benefited from discussing Shakya Chokden's ideas and other topics pertinent to this manuscript with Anne Burchardi, Dr. Alberto Todeschini, Khenpo Ngakwang Dorjé (*ngag dbang rdo rje*), Dr. Cyrus Stearns, Professor Kevin Vose, Professor José Cabezón, and other fellow scholars and friends whose skills and knowledge greatly helped me strengthen the manuscript.

I am also very thankful to Professor Beata Grant and my colleagues at the Washington University in St. Louis where I continued my research as a Mellon postdoctoral fellow, as well as my current colleagues at the University of Nebraska–Lincoln, who provided me with support and advice during the final stages of my work on this book.

Last, but not least, I want to thank all those who helped me with proofreading and polishing the manuscript at its different stages, especially Scott Leigh who carefully read its final version and offered many helpful suggestions on how to improve its style and readability.

If there are any benefits and virtues in this study, I want to dedicate them to my teachers, to a deeper understanding of the treasure trove of Buddhist thought, and to an increasing awareness and lasting preservation of the Tibetan culture.

Introduction

During the long history of growth, transformation, and spread of Buddhist traditions across various cultures of Asia, their followers developed a wide variety of worldviews, contemplative techniques, and ritual practices. Of special interest are the diversity of Buddhist ideas about reality and the methods of incorporating those ideas in contemplative practice. For centuries Buddhists have been exploring and contesting such fundamental issues as the nature of reality, the means of accessing it, the connection between its intellectual understanding and direct realization, the ways of its articulation, and the relationship between its realization and other elements of Buddhist thought and practice.

As Buddhism grew and diversified, Buddhists articulated multiple theories of reality and the contemplative techniques intended to achieve its realization. Those theories saturate the voluminous philosophical and contemplative literature that originated in South Asia and was later translated into Chinese, Tibetan, and other languages. They also play a crucial role in numerous systems and traditions that have continuously been evolving in Buddhist cultures until the present day. In contrast to early followers of the Buddha, subsequent generations of Buddhist thinkers faced the additional problem of organizing the theories of reality inherited from their predecessors, selectively matching them with the views of specific traditions, lineages, and schools with which they increasingly came to identify themselves. As a result, in the growing and expanding Buddhist world, the questions of accessing, realizing, and articulating reality were rarely limited to the philosophical, contemplative, or soteriological dimensions of Buddhism. In the Tibetan cultural area—as well as elsewhere—they came to be intricately linked with such issues as sectarian identity, faithfulness to one's lineage, and the struggle for power in religious and political spheres.

The process of organizing, interpreting, transforming, and refining the Mahāyāna systems of thought and practice inherited by Tibetans from their Indian predecessors played a crucial role in the formation of the distinctively Tibetan form of Buddhism. This process started during the last centuries of the first millennium, and gained momentum during the first half of the second. By the fifteenth century, Tibetan thinkers were almost universally addressing the questions of the nature of reality and its realization in terms of Yogācāra (*rnal 'byor spyod pa*, Yogic Practice), Madhyamaka (*dbu ma*, Middle), and several tantric systems of Mahāyāna Buddhism. The general tendency was to valorize Madhyamaka, showing its superiority over Yogācāra while retaining epistemological ideas developed by Yogācāra thinkers and matching the Madhyamaka view of reality with that of Buddhist tantras that came to be unquestionably treated as the highest teachings of the Buddha. By the fifteenth century, many Tibetan traditions had produced distinctive interpretive approaches to reality that came to be accepted as standard. Challenging those positions, or articulating views that appeared to run contrary to them, was tantamount to challenging the very traditions that produced those positions and consequently enmeshing oneself in inter- and intrasectarian controversies. Nevertheless, one would also hear powerful alternative voices whose messages were clearly received by contemporaries, and whose echoes are still resounding today.

This book brings back to light one such voice—that of the seminal Tibetan thinker Serdok Penchen Shakya Chokden[1] (*gser mdog paṇ chen shākya mchog ldan*, 1428–1507), a thinker who occupies a special place in the intellectual history of Mahāyāna Buddhism. Working during one of the most formative but least explored periods in Tibetan history, he was deeply involved in the inter- and intrasectarian polemics of his time, and articulated a startlingly new reconsideration of the core areas of Buddhist thought and practice, in particular Yogācāra and Madhyamaka.

While this study focuses on Shakya Chokden's unique interpretation of the nature and relationship of Yogācāra and Madhyamaka, it goes beyond that. Shakya Chokden's thought provides an invaluable base to challenge and expand our understanding of such seminal topics as epistemology, contemplative practice, the relationship between intellectual study and meditative experience, and other key questions that occupy contemporary scholarship on Buddhism and religion in general. The interpretive strategies he offers are particularly valuable when applied to rival positions on reality and its contemplation held by Buddhist thinkers.[2] Exploring his ideas in the context of these and related topics, this study seeks to enrich our understanding of the religious life of fifteenth-century Tibet, as well as several intellectual developments in Buddhism spanning more than fifteen centuries and culminating in transformations of Tibetan religious thought during the past two centuries.

Although Shakya Chokden was one of the most influential fifteenth-century scholars of the Sakya (*sa skya*) tradition, his works were largely neglected by later generations of Tibetan thinkers. This was caused by a number of factors, such as his controversial questioning of the views of Sakya Pendita Künga Gyeltsen (*sa skya paṇḍita kun dga' rgyal mtshan*, 1182–1251), the supreme authority of the Sakya tradition; his support of the views of other-emptiness (*gzhan stong*) that was rejected by the mainstream Sakya thinkers who saw those views as contradicting the views of self-emptiness (*rang stong*) they advocated; and his severe criticism of the views of Tsongkhapa Lopzang Drakpa (*tsong kha pa blo bzang grags pa*, 1357–1419), the "founder" of the Geluk (*dge lugs*) tradition that eventually became the "government religion" in Central Tibet. Despite the fact that Shakya Chokden was clearly producing sophisticated original work and commentaries, within his own Sakya tradition he was not held in the same high esteem as his contemporary and rival, Gowo Rapjampa Sönam Senggé (*go bo rab 'byams pa bsod nams seng ge*, also known as Gorampa, *go rams pa* 1429–1489). Gorampa's views were more consonant with those of the Sakya mainstream, and he eventually became the most influential Sakya philosopher. His works—unlike those of Shakya Chokden—still comprise an important part of the curricula in Sakya monastic institutions.[3] It also appears that Shakya Chokden's attacks on Geluk literally sealed the fate of his writings: according to some accounts, in the seventeenth century, powerful Geluk supporters sealed the printery where the blocks for his works were kept, and confiscated copies of his writings.[4] Shakya Chokden's works were largely unavailable until recent times, and it was not until 1975 that his collected works in twenty-four volumes were published by Kunzang Tobgey in Thimphu, Bhutan.[5] As a result of those events, Shakya Chokden still occupies a controversial position in the Tibetan Buddhist world in general and the Sakya tradition in particular.

Despite this controversial standing, Shakya Chokden is remembered as an honorable member of a group known as the Six Ornaments Beautifying the Snowy Land (*gangs can mdzes pa'i rgyan drug*). This group consists of Yaktön Sanggyepel (*g.yag ston sangs rgyas dpal*, 1348–1414, also known as Yakpa, *g.yag pa*) and Rongtön Mawé Senggé (*rong ston smra ba'i seng ge*, also known as Rongtön Sheja Künrik, *rong ston shes bya kun rig*, 1367–1449) who excelled in sūtras (i.e., non-tantric Buddhist systems), Ngorchen Künga Zangpo (*ngor chen kun dga' bzang po*, also known as Dorjechang Künga Zangpo, *rdo rje 'chang kun dga' bzang po*, 1382–1456) and Dzongpa Künga Namgyel (*rdzong pa kun dga' rnam rgyal*, 1432–1496) who excelled in tantras, and Gorampa Sönam Senggé and Shakya Chokden who excelled in both sūtras and tantras.[6] Together they are considered to be the most important masters of the Sakya tradition after its Five Foremost Venerable Founders (*rje btsun gong ma lnga*): Sachen Künga Nyingpo (*sa chen kun dga' snying po*, 1092–1158), Sönam Tsemo (*bsod nams rtse mo*, 1142–1182), Drakpa Gyeltsen (*grags pa rgyal mtshan*, 1147–1216), Sakya Pendita Künga Gyeltsen, and Pakpa Lodrö Gyeltsen (*'phags pa blo gros rgyal mtshan*, 1235–1280).[7] Even among the Six Ornaments Shakya Chokden occupies a unique place. He was a student of both Rongtön and Künga Zangpo, and studied under the former for twelve years and under the latter for six years.[8] In addition, he is also recognized by the Sakya tradition as a reincarnation of Yaktön Sanggyepel, Rongtön's teacher. It is not an exaggeration that, along with Gorampa, he is treated as a master of *both* sūtric and tantric systems. Shakya Chokden's mastery is reflected in his encyclopedic knowledge of both systems. He also often makes multiple cross-references between tantric approaches to ultimate reality and contemplative practice on the one hand, and sūtric views of emptiness and epistemological theories on the other.

The complexity and integration of Shakya Chokden's thought can be understood only with the help of the cross-references between his different writings, especially when in later texts he offers refined clarifications of his positions. I was often puzzled by seeming discrepancies and contradictions found in some of his works, only to later encounter passages where he clarifies his positions or gives explanations that together with his other statements complement each other and thereby provide a broader and clearer picture of his system. Gradually, I became convinced that to adequately understand Shakya Chokden in general and his approach to Yogācāra and Madhyamaka in particular, I must deal with a variety of compositions scattered throughout the twenty-four volumes of his collected works. As a result, in this study I have utilized multiple sources—about fifty of his works altogether—including specifically the texts he wrote from his early fifties on, during the period of crystallization of his own unique views on Mahāyāna:[9] independent writings summarizing essentials of particular topics or the whole body of texts; commentaries on Indian texts; letters of replies to particular questions, qualms, and objections raised by other Tibetan thinkers regarding his views; and expressions of realizations (*rtogs pa brjod pa, avadāna*) of Indian masters.

Similar to Tsongkhapa, Gorampa, Dölpopa Sherap Gyeltsen (*dol po pa shes rab rgyal mtshan*, 1292–1361) and other influential Tibetan thinkers, Shakya Chokden developed his ideas as an integrated system that is best appreciated on its own terms. In my explaination of this system, therefore, I adopt the centuries-old method favored by Tibetan writers, namely a sympathetic detailed study of a particular thinker's views as an integrated whole. I do acknowledge the evolution of Shakya Chokden's ideas over time,[10] as he himself does.[11] But I also argue that similar to other seminal thinkers, at a certain point in his life he started focusing on organizing his mature views into an interrelated network of ideas while simultaneously solving problems they raised. This period started in his early fifties, if not earlier, and it is characterized by the crystallization of his unique approach to the nature and relationship of Yogācāra and Madhyamaka—the main topic of this study. In my analysis of his works written during that period, I approach them as mutually complementary and comprising a developing and crystallizing, yet coherent, system.

In the following chapters I also demonstrate how Shakya Chokden's interpretation of Yogācāra and Madhyamaka is related to other areas of his thought and the broader intellectual context of Indian and Tibetan Buddhism. When useful, I make comparative statements, although I am not attempting a general comparison of Shakya Chokden's views with those of other thinkers. It is true that no system of ideas can be formed without an ongoing dynamic relationship with its intellectual environment, absorbing and modifying some views and rejecting others. One cannot fully appreciate Geluk philosophy, for example, without acquaintance with the views of early thinkers that Geluk writers were rejecting or influenced by. Likewise, Gorampa's views can be fully understood only if one is acquainted with the system of Tsongkhapa that was the main focus of Gorampa's criticisms. Shakya Chokden's ideas were also formed in reaction to the views of his predecessors and contemporaries. Therefore, in my explanation of his views, I will be touching upon systems of other thinkers that he was critically responding to. But overall, I will refer to those views only as an intellectual background to Shakya Chokden's own positions.

In order to better explain Shakya Chokden's system, I will also be addressing several criticisms he leveled at Dölpopa, Tsongkhapa, and other thinkers. Analysis of those criticisms and responses to them, especially by Geluk thinkers, is an important topic, as is the comparison of Shakya Chokden's and Tsongkhapa's views.[12] Nevertheless, such analysis and comparison are not relevant in the present context and will only distract readers from the main trajectory of this book. As the following discussion of Shakya Chokden's life and works demonstrates, by the time he started articulating his unique approach to Mahāyāna systems, he already had completed major refutations of Tsongkhapa's version of Madhyamaka, and pursued very different objectives in his novel interpretation of Yogācāra and Madhyamaka. His criticisms of Dölpopa, on the other hand, are much milder and are not as numerous as those of Tsongkhapa. I will selectively address only those criticisms that are relevant to the current study, such as those of Tsongkhapa and Dölpopa's approaches to self- and other-emptiness. Readers interested in comparative study of rival Tibetan philosophies in general, and those of Shakya Chokden and his opponents in particular, are advised to consult the relevant scholarly literature.[13]

I want to reiterate that the ideas of Tsongkhapa, Dölpopa, Gorampa, and other seminal Tibetan thinkers are best understood and appreciated when treated as parts of integrated intellectual systems those thinkers developed. Shakya Chokden's ideas addressed in this book—such as ultimate reality being impermanent, for example—also can be understood only as parts of his broader intellectual project. In the analysis of that project, I see myself not as a critic or apologist, but as someone who unpacks Shakya Chokden's approach to Yogācāra and Madhyamaka within the broader context of his system. I further hope that this study will contribute to our understanding of the intellectual history of fifteenth-century Tibet, although writing such a history per se is clearly beyond the scope of the current project. I will see my mission accomplished if, as a result of reading this book, my readers grasp the inner dynamic of Shakya Chokden's system and acquire a nuanced understanding of his unique worldview, which in turn hinges upon his novel interpretation of the nature and relationship of Yogācāra and Madhyamaka.

1. Introducing the Visions of Unity

The history of Tibetan Buddhist philosophical writings is the story of complex and often uneasy alliances between epistemology, logic, theories of emptiness, tantric views, and other elements that derive from divergent sources, different times, and dissimilar contexts. Possible combinations of those elements and their subdivisions are virtually inexhaustible, and together they inspired remarkably creative interpretive endeavors by generations of Tibetan thinkers. Those thinkers rarely saw themselves as creators of new philosophies or synthesizers of otherwise incompatible systems of thought and practice. Instead, they almost unanimously understood their work as a process of retrieval of original and true intents of the authors of texts they dealt with,[14] and tended to treat their sources as parts of an interconnected and often harmonious whole.

In particular, writings in the style of doxography (*grub mtha'*, *siddhānta*)[15] attempt to bring together, organize, and give structure to multifarious elements of the Buddhist universe. But precisely because of this organizational impulse, doxographical writings tend to be delimiting, bringing into the same discourse such elements as epistemology, Madhyamaka dialectics, contemplative techniques, and tantric rituals that otherwise are highly diverse in terms of their origins, style, and content. Despite its problematic nature, doxographical genre is particularly favored by Shakya Chokden and other Tibetan thinkers who focus on contents and divisions of Buddhist systems. The doxographical structure they commonly use is the fourfold hierarchical division of Buddhist tenet systems into those of Vaibhāṣika (*bye brag smra ba*, Proponents of Particulars), Sautrāntika (*mdo sde pa*, Sūtra Followers), Cittamātra (*sems tsam*, Mind-Only), and Madhyamaka. In this doxographical approach, each preceding system is treated as lower than the succeeding one in terms of its views and practices. Furthermore, Vaibhāṣika and Sautrāntika are treated as Hīnayāna, and Cittamātra and Madhyamaka as Māhayāna systems. Despite its apparent limitations and artificiality, such doxographical discourse extends not only to philosophical, but also ethical, contemplative, ritual, and political dimensions. Far from being an abstraction removed from "real life," doxography is manipulated by actual historical agents and brings about tangible results in areas as seemingly remote from each other as contemplation and politics.

Studying in Tibetan monastic universities, one often hears such statements as "buddhahood cannot be achieved without putting the Madhyamaka view into contemplative practice," "the real Sakya, Geluk, etc., Madhyamaka view of ultimate reality is such and such," and so forth. These and other statements indicate that in the Tibetan Buddhist world, adopting a particular doxographical position is often dictated by and bears on one's sectarian standing. When a particular doxographical stance is considered to be too radical, its author is very likely to be treated as controversial and unorthodox. Alternatively, the organizational coherence and other virtues of the author's doxographical approach might be so appealing that he can acquire a substantial following and his heterodoxy might eventually turn into a new orthodoxy, at least within certain circles. Such was the fate of several important doxographies whose authors (e.g., Tsongkhapa and Dölpopa) remained well-known figures in the Tibetan intellectual world; on the other hand, Shakya Chokden and Taktsang Lotsawa Sherap Rinchen's (*stag tshang lo tsā ba shes rab rin chen*, b.1405) bodies of work receded into relative obscurity. My task in the present book is to bring one such thinker—Shakya Chokden—back to light, place his life and works within the broader context of Tibetan Buddhism, and present the full richness and uniqueness of his writings on the Mahāyāna systems.

One of the most complicated areas of Buddhist thought explored by Shakya Chokden in minute detail is the nature and relationship of Yogācāra and Madhyamaka. In Tibet, the two systems are nearly universally viewed as the two most important Buddhist philosophical traditions. Nevertheless, from their very inception, there has never been consensus on the meaning of Madhyamaka and Yogācāra, and for more than fifteen centuries the question of correct identification and interpretation of these systems has remained unsolved. Below are highly simplified descriptions that contemporary students of Buddhist philosophy in Tibetan monastic institutions or European and American universities are most likely to encounter. I use these descriptions here only in order to introduce the subject and highlight Shakya Chokden's unique position. Greatly expanded versions of these descriptions are presented later in this text.

Madhyamaka and Yogācāra systems are usually viewed as mutually exclusive. Madhyamaka is treated as synonymous with Niḥsvabhāvavāda (*ngo bo nyid med par smra ba*, Proponents of Entitylessness) and Yogācāra[16] as synonymous with Cittamātra. The Madhyamaka view is understood as the negation of nature or "entity" (*ngo bo, bhāva*) of all phenomena, including the entity of negation or emptiness itself. The Yogācāra view, on the other hand, is understood as the affirmation of reality of mind (*sems, citta*) qualified by negation of other phenomena, such as external objects (*phyi rol gyi don, bahirdhārtha*). Although Yogācāra denies the existence of external objects, depending on whether appearances or "aspects" (*rnam pa, ākāra*) of those objects in mind are treated as true (*bden pa, satya*) or false (*rdzun pa, alīka*), Yogācāra is further subdivided into two systems of Alīkākāravāda (*rnam rdzun pa*, False Aspectarians) and Satyākāravāda (*rnam bden pa*, True Aspectarians).[17]

In contrast to that approach, Shakya Chokden accepts that neither Yogācāra and Cittamātra are the same system nor that Madhyamaka is limited only to the system of Niḥsvabhāvavāda. Although he accepts the twofold division of Yogācāra into Alīkākāravāda and Satyākāravāda, he identifies Satyākāravāda as synonymous exclusively with Cittamātra, and Alīkākāravāda as a subdivision of Madhyamaka on an equal footing with Niḥsvabhāvavāda and surpassing Cittamātra. In his opinion, Alīkākāravāda is *both* Yogācāra and Madhyamaka. While seemingly simple, this approach in fact consists of an intricate web of ideas, such as the structure and meaning of Buddhist philosophical and contemplative systems, continuities and discontinuities between tantric and non-tantric forms of Buddhism, reality of self-cognition, transition from conceptual to nonconceptual understanding of emptiness, and disparate approaches to abandoning obscurations, to mention just a few. By placing the system of Alīkākāravāda on the level of Madhyamaka, and showing its important differences, compatibility, and interdependence with the system of Niḥsvabhāvavāda, Shakya Chokden attempts nothing less than a thorough reconsideration and reconfiguration of the fundamental Buddhist categories. His key innovation is to elevate Alīkākāravāda Yogācāra to a position that is comparable, if not superior, to that of Niḥsvabhāvavāda Madhyamaka.

Shakya Chokden's approach to Alīkākāravāda and Niḥsvabhāvavāda is a unique attempt to reconcile the views of these two important Mahāyāna systems. Nevertheless, this reconciliation is far from the much more common Tibetan attempt to integrate Yogācāra presentations of the stages of the path (with some unavoidable modifications) with the Niḥsvabhāvavāda view of emptiness.[18] Rather, Shakya Chokden struggles to accept Alīkākāravāda and Niḥsvabhāvavāda on their own terms as compatible systems, despite their considerable divergences and reciprocal critiques. A dominant theme in the works he composed from his early fifties is a reconciliation of the two systems based upon an acknowledgment of their differences. He provides a detailed analysis of their mutual polemical refutations, yet goes on to argue for their fundamental compatibility and shared vision. He concentrates specifically on this issue in the *Profound Thunder amidst the Clouds of the Ocean of Definitive Meaning: Differentiation of the Two Systems of the Great Madhyamaka Deriving from the Two Great Chariot Ways*[19] and its auto-commentary the *Rain of Ambrosia: Extensive [Auto-] Commentary on the 'Profound Thunder amidst the Clouds of the Ocean of Definitive Meaning.'*[20] Another important text addressing this topic is the *Great Path of Ambrosia of Emptiness: Explanation of Profound Pacification Free from Proliferations*.[21] The question of the meaning and relationship of Alīkākāravāda and Niḥsvabhāvavāda is also addressed by Shakya Chokden in other works used in this study.

Shakya Chokden's techniques are simultaneously constructive and deconstructive. By questioning tenet boundaries that he deems unimportant or wrong, he releases the giants of Yogācāra thought from the confines of the Cittamātra classification into the open space of Madhyamaka. To this end, he sets out to solve problematic questions left unanswered by other systems of thought; reconsider Buddhist intellectual histories; and defend important tantras, practice lineages (*sgrub brgyud*), and their practitioners from polemical attacks. His main objective is clear: to bring Yogācāra back from obscurity, present it in a positive light, and correct its misinerpretations by Tibetan thinkers.[22] Despite the polemical tone he often assumes, Shakya Chokden appears to be primarily motivated by his genuine interest in Yogācāra philosophy.[23]

Shakya Chokden is thus a major resource for scholarly research on the historical and philosophical development of Yogācāra and Madhyamaka. His interpretations of different Yogācāra systems are particularly refreshing and enriching. His explanatory approach clarifies the most intricate elements of Yogācāra, particularly in juxtaposition with other forms of Mahāyāna thought. As a result, his writings serve as an invaluable tool for illuminating Yogācāra theory and practice in ways that transcend the more stereotypical approaches found in most Tibetan corpora. Indeed, a half millennium later, at the end of the 1990s, they sparked a lasting interest in my own mind, when by sheer chance I encountered Shakya Chokden's writings in a library of the Dzongsar Institute in Bir, India, where I was studying with the late senior abbot (*mkhan chen*) Künga Wangchuk (*kun dga' dbang phyug*) and my other Tibetan teachers from the Sakya tradition.

Many of Shakya Chokden's ideas addressed in this book sparkle with an aura of novelty and originality, especially when considered against the background of fifteenth-century Tibet or looked at through the lenses of twentieth- and twenty-first-century traditional Tibetan or academic scholarship. These ideas include the view that ultimate reality according to Madhyamaka is an impermanent phenomenon; conventional existence entails nonexistence, and if something exists it has to exist in reality; no genuine ultimate truth was taught in most of the main Niḥsvabhāvavāda works, and yet Niḥsvabhāvavāda teachings outlined in those works are sufficient for achieving buddhahood; the Yogācāra system of Alīkākāravāda is Madhyamaka while Satyākāravāda is not; Niḥsvabhāvavāda is much more remote from the Tantric approach to reality than Alīkākāravāda; and so forth. These and other ideas analyzed below show clearly that Shakya Chokden is a unique thinker, and indeed they provoked controversies during his life. Nevertheless, I would argue that Shakya Chokden's thought is a coherent system, as compelling and important as systems developed by such original Tibetan thinkers as Tsongkhapa, Gorampa, and Dölpopa. It is not my intention to explain Shakya Chokden's views in general. Nevertheless, because many of his ideas are built on his unique approach to Yogācāra and Madhyamaka, my explanation of this approach also attempts to shed light on his intellectual world as a whole.

2. Introducing the Chapters

The five chapters of this book proceed from a broad, general, overarching discussion to an increasingly focused and detailed analysis. I gradually unpack and explain Shakya Chokden's ideas by discussing (1) the historical, cultural, and biographical elements that formed the background for development of his views, (2) the intellectual milieu from which his ideas grew and to which he dynamically responded in his writings, (3) his (re)positioning of Yogācāra and Madhyamaka within the overall structure of the Buddhist systems, (4) his presentation of Alīkākāravāda and Niḥsvabhāvavāda as involved in a tense but mutually complementary relationship, and (5) his exploration of primordial mind (*ye shes, jñāna*), which in his view is the ultimate reality in all Mahāyāna systems.

The first chapter forms a background for an in-depth analysis of Shakya Chokden's interpretation of Madhyamaka and Yogācāra in the following four chapters. *(1.1)* In its first section I argue that there are clear connections between the style and character of Shakya Chokden's intellectual output and the nature of institutional, political, and intellectual features of his time. To shed light on those connections, I provide a brief sketch of the political and religious climate of fifteenth-century Tibet. *(1.2)* Next, I turn to Shakya Chokden's biography, focusing on those elements of his life that are relevant to the discussion in the following chapters: his education, teachers and patrons, people who influenced his thinking, his connections with other important intellectuals of the time, as well as his activities as a prolific writer and influiential teacher. *(1.3)* I then provide chronological and topical lists of his writings, presenting his works in historical sequence and showing the main foci of his scholarship.

The second chapter puts Shakya Chokden's views into the broader context of Indian and Tibetan approaches to Madhyamaka and Yogācāra. *(2.1)* First, I highlight two tendencies in the development of

Madhyamaka and Yogācāra thought: the tendency toward separating and distancing the two systems from each other and the tendency toward bringing them close to each other and harmonizing. I specifically focus on the works of several influential Indian and Tibetan Buddhist thinkers who despite coming from different backgrounds, traditions, and times, share the common position that the systems of Madhyamaka and Yogācāra are very close to each other—if they do not actually overlap. *(2.2)* I then provide a brief outline of Shakya Chokden's own approach to Madhyamaka and Yogācāra. *(2.3)* In order to further clarify the nature, objectives, and context of his writings, I focus on those passages in his own works where he describes various changes in the religious and intellectual climate of his time as he perceived them. *(2.4)* Shakya Chokden's sympathetic approach to Alīkākāravāda and Niḥsvabhāvavāda naturally raises the question about what his *own* view is, and whether it falls under any one of the categories he explores, such as the system of "self-emptiness" (*rang stong*) or "other-emptiness" (*gzhan stong*). I argue that his views were heavily misinterpreted by subsequent thinkers, and demonstrate that for the last thirty years of his life, when he clearly articulated his unique position with regard to the Mahāyāna systems, Shakya Chokden embraced both views equally.

The third chapter focuses on the key elements of Shakya Chokden's thought that are crucial for an in-depth understanding of his interpretation of Yogācāra and Madhyamaka. It places his thought within the broader perspective of Buddhist doxographical writings, and suggests a new look at philosophical classifications and their advocates. *(3.1)* I show how Shakya Chokden not only reconsiders the meaning of Buddhist systems, but also develops a unique approach to the tenet categories themselves, distancing Alīkākāravāda from Satyākāravāda, presenting Alīkākāravāda as Madhyamaka, and arguing that the Alīkākāravāda system is as soteriologically efficient as Niḥsvabhāvavāda. *(3.2)* I introduce his argument that there are two ways of identifying the Madhyamaka view: one originating from the works of Maitreya with his followers that teach Yogācāra, and the other originating from the treatises of Nāgārjuna with his followers that teach Niḥsvabhāvavāda. *(3.3)* Because the views of Alīkākāravāda and Niḥsvabhāvavāda are distinguished as those of "other-emptiness" and "self-emptiness," respectively, I clarify the meaning of these important categories, and show that Shakya Chokden's interpretation of self- and other-emptiness dramatically differs from the positions of other seminal Tibetan thinkers, such as Dölpopa and Tsongkhapa. *(3.4)* I further explain why, in his overall approach, differences between *Svātantrika (*rang rgyud pa*, Autonomists) and *Prāsaṅgika (*thal 'gyur ba*, Consequentialists)—commonly accepted as the two main if not only types of Madhyamaka—lose their relevance. Arguing that their final views are identical, he denies that these two categories are unproblematic subdivisions of Madhyamaka. *(3.5)* I also address a problematic issue entailed by his system: whether Shakya Chokden accepts two types of Yogācāra Madhyamaka, one based on Niḥsvabhāvavāda and the other on Yogācāra writings. *(3.6)* Given the fact that he treats most well-known Yogācāra thinkers as Alīkākāravādins, I also explain how he handles a conspicuous absence in his system of any works that can be identified as writings of Satyākāravādins. *(3.7)* Finally, I explain how Shakya Chokden augments his view of the compatibility of Alīkākāravāda and Niḥsvabhāvavāda by placing all key Indian Mahāyāna thinkers into the same Madhyamaka camp and arguing that they all explicitly or implicitly agree that the systems of Alīkākāravāda and Niḥsvabhāvavāda come down to the same point.

The fourth chapter explores in detail the main topic of this book: Shakya Chokden's unique approach to Yogācāra and Madhyamaka based on reinterpretation of their nature and subcategories. *(4.1)* I show how making a sharp distinction between Alīkākāravāda and Satyākāravāda enables him to argue that Satyākāravāda cannot belong to Madhyamaka and Alīkākāravāda cannot be subsumed under the category of Cittamātra. *(4.2)* I likewise explain how his interpretation of Alīkākāravāda and Niḥsvabhāvavāda allows him to claim that Alīkākāravāda should be treated as a legitimate category of Madhyamaka alongside Niḥsvabhāvavāda. In this context, I elaborate on his main argument: despite different approaches to, and descriptions of, reality by Niḥsvabhāvavādins and Alīkākāravādins on the conceptual level, they realize the same ultimate reality through direct meditative experience. *(4.3)* I explain in detail how Shakya Chokden supports this position by referring back to different sets of teachings of the Buddha and their interpretations by influential Indian writers such as Nāgārjuna and Asaṅga, as well as later thinkers who further shaped and modified Yogācāra and Madhyamaka systems. *(4.4)* The last section of this chapter demonstrates that despite the mutual efforts at polemical refutations of Niḥsvabhāvavāda and Alīkākāravāda, Shakya Chokden himself does not side with either system but argues for their compatibility as equally valid subdivisions of Madhyamaka, choosing to follow what I call the "middle way between the two conflicting middle ways."

The fifth chapter explores the nature of ultimate reality described by Shakya Chokden as the self-cognizing primordial mind. *(5.1)* He argues that the main point of disagreement between Alīkākāravādins and Niḥsvabhāvavādins is their approach to primordial mind: the former believe it is real and existent, while the latter see it as unreal and nonexistent. In that context, I explore such problematic issues as whether the nonexistence of primordial mind in the face of reasoning necessarily fills the role of nonexistence, what the meaning of "ultimate existence" of primordial mind is, and whether the true existence of ultimate reality has to be negated in order to abandon grasping at that reality. *(5.2)* I further focus on one of the most controversial elements of Shakya Chokden's system that stands in sharp contrast to the positions of other Tibetan thinkers: his argument that primordial mind, ultimate reality, is an *impermanent* phenomenon, and that as such it is accepted not only in the Yogācāra system but in other systems of sūtras and tantras as well. *(5.3)* Shakya Chokden's approach to primordial mind as the self-cognizing ultimate reality of consciousness raises the following question: will it not absurdly follow that this ultimate mind itself experiences sufferings, dualistic appearances, afflictions, and all other factors that pertain to dualistic consciousness? I address in detail his sophisticated response based on a sharp distinction between the self-cognizing primordial mind and dualistic consciousness. *(5.4)* Shakya Chokden's position entails yet another problematic question: because everybody has the self-cognizing primordial mind, will it not also absurdly follow that everybody realizes ultimate reality? I explain his response based on subtle distinctions between self-cognizing, self-realizing, and self-experiencing, and the argument that self-cognition does not necessarily entail realization of itself by itself. *(5.5)* In the final section, I explain how Shakya Chokden uses primordial mind as the bridge between Yogācāra and Tantra, treating it as the quintessence of yogic contemplative practices in all sūtric and tantric Mahāyāna systems. Arguing that the Alīkākāravāda view of ultimate reality as primordial mind agrees with that of Tantra, he utilizes the authoritative view of tantric Madhyamaka to support, augment, and legitimize his presentation of Alīkākāravāda as a valid Madhyamaka system. Thereby, Shakya Chokden further strengthens his claim of compatibility of direct meditative experience of reality in all forms of Madhyamaka—the very foundation of his conciliatory approach to Mahāyāna systems.

Based on the analysis of the multifarious web of interrelated elements of Shakya Chokden's views addressed in the five chapters of this book, I conclude that his works articulate nothing less than the grand unity of Mahāyāna systems, all of which—if we take Yogācāra as a single unit with the Alīkākāravāda view as its final view—provide valid and complete means of achieving buddhahood. I also explain why Shakya Chokden's thought has remained so controversial and underexplored for more than five centuries, and what contributions I hope my analysis of his thought makes to the broader field of Buddhist studies.

Chapter 1

Life and Works of the Golden Paṇḍita

1. Political and Religious Landscape of Fifteenth-Century Tibet

This chapter provides an historical and biographical background for the analysis of Shakya Chokden's philosophical views. Exploring this background is as crucial as exploring Shakya Chokden's interpretive writings themselves. As soon will become clear, although his thought tends to transcend the boundaries of fifteenth-century Tibet and is not confined to some narrow trend in Buddhist philosophical discourse, it is thoroughly embedded in the social, political, and intellectual milieu of his time and Tibetan Buddhist culture in general. In order to contextualize the style and character of Shakya Chokden's intellectual output, I start with a brief sketch of the political and religious climate of fifteenth-century Tibet.

Shakya Chokden's life and activities fall within the broader period of "Post-Sakya Tibet" (1337–1565),[1] a relatively little documented historical period. They are also subsumed under the wider period described as "classical" (mid-13th to 16th century),[2] characterized by the process of systematizing and organizing the materials received from India. This period is also marked by a progressive solidification of teaching lineages and academic establishments into religious sects in the absence of a strong central authority, and related political rivalries.

Sakya rulers lost their political power over Tibet in 1350,[3] when Tai Situ Jangchup Gyeltsen (*tā'i si tu byang chub rgyal mtshan*, 1302–1364) seized power in the entire Ü (*dbus*, "Central Tibet") and Tsang (*gtsang*). Jangchup Gyeltsen and his descendants ruled those regions for more than eighty years under the dynastic name of Pakmo Drupa (*phag mo gru pa*). The Pakmodru (*phag mo gru*)[4] capital was Neudong (*sne'u gdong*)/Neudzong (*sne'u rdzong*) located in Yarlung (*yar klungs*), south of the Tsangpo (*gtsang po*) river in Ü. Having abolished the administrative system used by the Sakya government supported by the Mongol Yuan dynasty (1271–1368),[5] Jangchup Gyeltsen and his successors reinstituted an older Tibetan administrative system of "fortresses" (*rdzong*) that was used before the Sakya period, and invested a number of families from their domains with the title and office of "prefect" (*rdzong dpon*). That office became hereditary, and was passed down from father to son. In this way, a new hereditary aristocracy was created.[6] The system posed a serious danger to centralized authority, because the newly emerging aristocratic families started fighting for independence from the central government, while engaging in conflict and intrigue with each other.

Pakmo Drupa rulers started gradually losing power, while the chiefs of Rinpung (*rin spungs*)—former vassals and allies of Pakmo Drupa—grew in power. The growing conflict between Pakmo Drupa and Rinpungpa (*rin spungs pa*) escalated, and in 1435 the prefect of Rinpung Norzang (*nor bzang*, d. 1466) was able to seize control over the whole of Tsang, making Samdruptsé (*bsam grub rtse*) near Zhikatsé (*gzhis ka rtse*) his residence. This marked the end of Pakmo Drupa centralized rule, and the beginning of more than 100 years of constant struggle between Ü and Tsang. Pakmo Drupa leaders in Ü were patrons of Geluk at the time, while Rinpungpa in Tsang were supporting Karma Kagyü (*karma bka' brgyud*).[7] In this way, political rivalry between Tsang and Ü eventually led to clashes between Karma Kagyü monasteries and rapidly growing Geluk monasteries. The following passage by Guru Trashi (*guru bkra shis*) in Dan Martin's translation illustrates well the shift of political power in that period:

> For eighty-seven years, from the Earth Ox (1349) to the Wood Hare (1435), most of the interior parts of Central Tibet and Gtsang were governed by the Phag-mo-gru-pa Heads (Sde-pa). Some parts (khol-bu) such as Byang and Rgya-mkhar-rtse were governed by their own chiefs. In the Wood Hare year (1435), Rin-spungs Nor-bzang seized Bsam-'grub-rtse. Starting from that time, the governing of Gtsang was mostly done by the Rin-spung-pa. The Head Ring-spung-pa, Field Commander (Sgar-pa) Don-yod-rdorje, took the government of Ü as well.[8]

By the end of the fifteenth century, Pakmo Drupa were sharing political power with Rinpungpa, and by the beginning of the sixteenth century Rinpungpa became the dominant party.[9]

Political struggle was intricately linked with the religious lives and events of the time. For example, the above-mentioned Dönyö Dorjé (*don yod rdo rje*), who was the son of Rinpung Norzang (*rin spungs nor bzang*), wanted to build a Karma Kagyü monastery in Lhasa, but was refused permission by the Lhasa administrator, who supported Geluk. Dönyö Dorjé then built the monastery outside of Lhasa, but monks from neighboring Geluk monasteries descended on it one night and destroyed it. Even the Seventh Karmapa (*karma pa*) Chödrak Gyamtso (*chos grags rgya mtsho*, 1454–1506) had to flee. In retaliation, Dönyö Dorjé led troops against Ü in 1480, captured some districts under the jurisdiction of the Lhasa administrator, marched to Neudong, and there removed from office the deputy minister Könchok Rinchen (*dkon mchog rin chen*), his father's rival. In 1498, Dönyö Dorjé captured Lhasa, and Rinpung forces remained there until 1517.[10] During that period, Geluk monks were forbidden to participate in the Great Aspirational Prayers (*smon lam chen mo*)—the major Lhasa festival established by Tsongkhapa in 1409. The festival was conducted under Karma Kagyü and Sakya sects.[11]

Shakya Chokden's life and work were directly affected by those political changes. He was educated and taught in the famous Sangpu Neutok (*gsang phu ne'u thog*) monastery in Ü, which at the time hosted both Geluk and Sakya communities. Because of Pakmo Drupa's favoritism toward Geluk, early in his life he had problems with education and monastic ordination, and later with handling the affairs of the Nego (*gnas sgo*) college of Sangpu Neutok where he taught. At the same time, when he moved to Serdokchen monastery in Tsang, he was receiving the support of Rinpungpa and became their lama, giving teachings and tantric empowerments (*dbang, abhiṣeka*) to the above-mentioned Dönyö Dorjé and others.[12]

Weakening of a centralized state power structure, constant conflicts among rival political groups, and struggle for centralization during the course of the fifteenth century provided a fertile ground for the flourishing of sects and religious figures whose legitimization and support were sought by political leaders.[13] It comes as no surprise, then, that in tandem with political clashes, the fifteenth century also witnessed an explosion of intra- and inter-sectarian polemics on the questions of perception, scriptural authority, and other topics concerning authority, validity, and reality with clear parallels to political affairs and disputes. Rivalry in the political arena was thus accompanied by rivalry in the religious sphere, and inter- and intra-sectarian polemics became a distinguishing feature of the intellectual landscape of fifteenth-century Tibet.

Sectarian disputes in Tibet were already developing at the time of Sakya Pendita, as reflected in his *Thorough Differentiation of the Three Types of Vows*[14] and other texts. But in the fifteenth century they became much more refined and complex.[15] The strongest and most intricate disputes were going on between Geluk and Sakya thinkers. This was partly caused by the fact that they developed a more or less common technical language, focused on similar philosophical issues, but provided strikingly different interpretations of such key subjects as logic, epistemology, Yogācāra, Madhyamaka, and Tantra. The fact that Tsongkhapa and his two chief disciples, Gyeltsap Darma Rinchen (*rgyal tshab dar ma rin chen*, 1364–1432) and Khedrup Gelek Pelzang (*mkhas grub dge legs dpal bzang*, 1385–1438), studied with Sakya scholars further contributed to the sophistication and subtlety of debates between Sakya and Geluk. Anti-Geluk polemics occupied an important part in the writings of Shakya Chokden and other fifteenth-century Sakya opponents of Geluk, which was rapidly gaining power in the intellectual and political domains. After all, the two schools were competing for the possession of knowledge that in intricate ways was linked with the possession of power.[16]

Rongtön Sheja Künrik, one of Shakya Chokden's main teachers, was the first scholar of wide reputation who questioned and criticized Tsongkhapa's views.[17] Severe criticism of Tsongkhapa and his disciples' views on logic, epistemology, the nature of reality, and other issues was continued by Shakya Chokden and other influential Sakya scholars such as Gorampa and Taktsang Lotsawa.[18]

Disputes were developing both between and within sects. For example, in 1475, Shakya Chokden posed more than 100 critical questions about Sakya Pendita's *Thorough Differentiation of the Three Types of Vows* when he wrote the *Good Questions about the 'Thorough Differentiation of the Three Types of Vows.'*[19] He specifically requested answers from the famous Sakya scholar Jamchen Rapjampa Sanggyepel (*byams chen rab 'byams pa sangs rgyas 'phel*, 1411–1485), the main teacher of Gorampa. These questions provoked considerable controversy among Sakya scholars, and quite a few of them attempted to provide answers, including Gorampa[20] and another famous Sakya scholar, Lowo Khenchen Sönam Lhündrup (*glo bo mkhan chen bsod nams lhun grub*, 1456–1532).[21] In 1481 Shakya Chokden answered his own questions in the *Golden Lancet: Resolved Abundant Discourse on the 'Thorough Differentiation of the Three Types of Vows' Treatise*.[22] In this way, Shakya Chokden managed to get involved in both inter- and intrasectarian disputations and rivalry.

The fifteenth century also witnessed construction of some of the most important new monasteries of different traditions—a process that further contributed to the sectarian separatism and rivalry. The interdependence of political and religious elements in this area too is well illustrated by the construction of the major Geluk monasteries which were built in the fifteenth century, mostly in Ü. Ganden (*dga' ldan*), the main Geluk monastery, was founded by Tsongkhapa in 1409. In 1416, Drepung (*'bras spungs*) monastery was founded by Tsongkhapa's disciple Jamyang Chöjé (*'jam dbyangs chos rje*). Sera monastery was founded in 1419 by another disciple of Tsongkhapa, Jamchen Chöjé (*byams chen chos rje*, 1352–1435). In 1433, another disciple of Tsongkhapa, the foremost venerable Sherap Senggé (*rje btsun shes rab seng ge*, 1383–1445), established Gyümé (*rgyud smad*), and in 1474 Sherap Senggé's own disciple, the foremost venerable Künga Döndrup (*rje btsun kun dga' don grub*, 1419–1486), established Gyütö (*rgyud stod*)—the two main Geluk tantric colleges. All five monasteries were located in Ü. The territorial placement of the monasteries founded by Tsongkhapa and his disciples in Ü reinforced the Geluk connection with Pakmo Drupa leaders in that area. On the other hand, although in 1447 Tsongkhapa's disciple Gendündrup (*dge 'dun grub*, 1391–1474)—posthumously considered the First Dalai Lama (*tā la'i bla ma*)—founded an important monastery, Trashi Lhünpo (*bkra shis lhun po*), in Tsang, the Geluk tradition there did not gain much influence at the time because of the predominance of the rival Karma Kagyü sect that enjoyed the Rinpung patronage.

Of special importance is the establishment of seminal Sakya monasteries in the fifteenth century. Ngor monastery was established in 1429 by the founder of the Ngor (*ngor*) branch of Sakya, Ngorchen Künga Zangpo, one of the main tantric teachers of Shakya Chokden and Gorampa.[23] Nalendra (*nā lendra*) monastery in Penyül (*'phan yul*)[24] was established in 1436[25] by Rongtön Sheja Künrik, who was one of the most influential Sakya scholars of the time. Dreyül Kyetsel (*'bras yul skyed tshal*) was established in 1449 by Jamchen Rapjampa Sanggyepel. In 1474, Gorampa himself established Tanak Tupten Namgyelling (*rta nag thub bstan rnam rgyal gling*) monastery. Zilung (*gzi lung*) monastery in Tsang was established in 1452 by the great paṇḍita (*paṇ chen*) Dönyö Pelwa (*don yod dpal ba*, 1398–1484),[26] one of Shakya Chokden's main teachers. This monastery was later renamed Serdokchen (*gser mdog can*) or "Golden Colored" by Shakya Chokden[27] when it became his own seat. Shakya Chokden thereby came to be known as Serdok Penchen (*gser mdog paṇ chen*) or "Great Paṇḍita from the Golden Colored [Monastery]."

The inter- and intrasectarian polemics and rivalry went side by side with reevaluation and systematization of the Buddhist heritage. In the fifteenth century, Tibetan contacts with India diminished, eventually almost ceasing. By then Buddhism had disappeared in northern India, few erudite scholars traveled to Tibet, and even the greatest translator of the time, Zhalu Lotsawa Chökyong Zangpo (*zha lu lo tsā ba chos skyong bzang po,* 1441–1528), had to work alone on all of his translations (with the exception of only one text that he translated in collaboration with an Indian monk Dīpaṃkara).[28] Having few contacts with India, the fifteenth-century Tibetan thinkers had the opportunity to look inward, evaluate, systematize, and solidify Buddhist teachings in general and their own sectarian traditions in particular. Many influential scholars of the time, such as Gyeltsap Darma Rinchen, Khedrup Gelek Pelzang, Gendündrup, Rongtön, Gorampa, and Shakya Chokden, composed commentaries on the major subjects of Buddhist learning: Madhyamaka, Prajñāpāramitā (*shes rab kyi pha rol tu phyin pa,* Perfection of Wisdom), Abhidharma (*mngon pa,* Higher Knowledge), Pramāṇa (*tshad ma,* Epistemology-Logic), Vinaya (*'dul ba,* Moral Discipline), and Tantra. Many of those texts are still studied in Tibetan monasteries today. They are also the source of the most important polemical issues contested by different Tibetan sectarian traditions for the last 600 years.

In spite of its polemical mood, the fifteenth century also produced inter-sectarian openness that helped the cross-pollination of different traditions. Many intellectuals of the period, including Shakya Chokden himself, were also open to inter-sectarian exchanges. For example, translator Gö Lotsawa Zhönnupel (*'gos lo tsā ba gzhon nu dpal,* 1392–1481), the author of a celebrated masterpiece of Tibetan historical writing, the *Blue Annals,*[29] studied with most of the great teachers of the different traditions of his time, mastered both "old" and "new" tantras, became a master of the Nyingma (*rnying ma*) school, and transmitted Nyingma teachings to the Seventh Karmapa, Chödrak Gyamtso, and the Fourth Zhamarpa (*zhwa dmar pa*), Chödrak Yeshé (*chos grags ye shes,* 1453–1524). At the same time, he also served as a tutor of three Pakmodru princes: Drakpa Jungné (*grags pa 'byung gnas,* 1414–1445), Künga Lekpa (*kun dga' legs pa,* 1433–1483), and Chennga Ngakgi Wangpo (*spyan snga ngag gi dbang po,* 1439–1491).[30] The Sixth Karmapa Tongwa Dönden (*mthong ba don ldan,* 1416–1453) actively engaged in the process of solidifying his own Karma Kagyü tradition, developing its unique liturgical system (previously largely borrowed from other traditions) and sādhana (*sgrub thabs,* "means of accomplishment") rituals,[31] and developed a new style of recitation and chanting. At the same time, he also had a connection with the Sakya tradition, had visions of Sachen Künga Nyingpo, and received multiple teachings on the textual systems (*gzhung lugs*) from Rongtön Sheja Künrik.[32] He also received teachings and initiations from Tangtong Gyelpo (*thang stong rgyal po*, 1361–1485). The Seventh Karmapa Chödrak Gyamtso possessed huge estates, and enjoyed a special patronage of the ruling Rinpung family. He was perhaps the most powerful religious leader of his day, and used his influence for such beneficial activities as protection of animals (he himself was a vegetarian), construction of iron bridges, pacification of conflicts, and repair of Kagyü monasteries. A famous teacher and consummate scholar, Chödrak Gyamtso composed many texts on Vinaya, Madhyamaka, Pramāṇa, Tantra, and other topics.[33] Being open to different traditions, he received various empowerments and transmissions of Pema Lingpa's (*padma gling pa*, 1450–1521) Treasure (*gter ma*) teachings from Pema Lingpa, one of the Five Great Treasure Revealers (*gter chen lnga*).[34]

In sum, Shakya Chokden lived in one of the most important formative periods in Tibetan history, a period characterized by political decentralization, instability, and conflicts; close connection between political and religious rivalry; solidification, reevaluation, and crystallization of sects and lineages; rapid growth and development of the newly emerged Geluk tradition; debates between sects and within them; the proliferation of scholastic literature; inter-sectarian openness and cross-pollination. Together, these factors formed an intricate pattern that gave a creative impetus to Tibetan cultural and religious life for centuries to come. Many essential elements of this life, such as the monastic educational system, inter-sectarian relationships, and important monasteries and lineages were formed and/or were developing during this period, and their influence is still felt nowadays.

In the context of the religious and political climate of fifteenth-century Tibet, Shakya Chokden's major philosophical writings while very innovative intellectually, are "typical" in their form and intent. By this I refer to his works being politically charged with respect to others' positions and saturated with nuanced details that reflect the polemics of his time.

2. Life of the Golden Paṇḍita

To better understand Shakya Chokden's thought, it is important to look closer at his biography, from which we learn that he engaged in writing for two-thirds of his life—from age twenty-seven until age eighty—while at the same time being actively involved in tantric contemplative practice, study, teaching, and travel. His biography also helps clarify why politically charged sectarian dispute became such an important issue in his life, and why some Sakya followers thought that he was attacking their tradition despite the fact that Shakya Chokden clearly saw himself as a faithful Sakyapa.

Discussing Shakya Chokden's life and works, I will be looking in particular at the elements whose examination can tell us more about his intellectual development: what influences he was exposed to early in his life, his education, and the topics he focused on in his writings and teachings. In my description of his life I will be primarily relying on the *Detailed Analysis of the Liberation Story of the Great Paṇḍita Shakya Chokden*[35] by Künga Drölchok (*kun dga' grol mchog*, 1507–1565/1566). As Drölchok himself informs us, he studied with the twelve best disciples of Shakya Chokden and four disciples of disciples—holders of his lineage—receiving from them tantric empowerments, transmissions through reading (*lung*), instructions (*gdams pa*), and so forth.[36] In particular, he received a reading transmission of Shakya Chokden's collected works that were printed (*phyag bzhengs*) after the latter's death in eighteen-volume sets by each of the three brothers, the Lords of Dharma from Tingkyé (*gting skyes chos rje sku mched rnam pa gsum*).[37]

Writing the *Detailed Analysis*, Drölchok relied on his own fieldwork and information he acquired from people who knew Shakya Chokden personally or knew people who knew him. He clearly tried to analyze and provide *additional* information rather than simply organize or paraphrase what had been already said in other biographical accounts. Drölchok himself mentions that he did not merely repeat what already had been said in the three biographies that were available to him.[38] Those three biographies, known as *Dorjé Gyelma* (*rdo rje rgyal ma*), *Jewönma* (*rje dbon ma*), and *Matima* (*ma ti ma*), are no longer available to us. The *Detailed Analysis* therefore is the main source of information about Shakya Chokden's life.[39]

It should be noted that despite his interest in and deep respect for Shakya Chokden's life and work, apparently Drölchok was not very interested in reading colophons of works written by Shakya Chokden himself. As a result, the dates of composition of some of Shakya Chokden's texts provided by Drölchok at times disagree considerably with dates given in the colophons.[40] When addressing such dates, I follow the colophons, but when no dates are provided in the colophons, if available I rely on dates provided by Drölchok. Apart from that, when discussing different events in Shakya Chokden's life—other than the composition of texts—I follow the *Detailed Analysis*. I am aware that it is impossible to verify most of the elements of Shakya Chokden's biography, especially descriptions of his meditative experiences and visions. At the same time, I take those descriptions as neither more nor necessarily less trustworthy than descriptions of other events of his life. With these introductory remarks, I turn now to the biography of the Golden Paṇḍita.

Early Years and Education

As the *Detailed Analysis* tells us, Shakya Chokden was born in 1428[41] in Sangda Bangrim (*gsang mda' bang rim*) in the vicinity of the famous monastic university Sangpu Neutok in Central Tibet.[42] The identity of his father is unclear. His mother, Shakya Zangmo (*shākya bzang mo*), was an ex-nun from a retreat monastery (*dben dgon*) named Pangkha Chöding (*spang kha chos sdings*), to the south of the monastic university Kyormolung (*skyor mo lung*).[43] In 1431, Shakya Chokden's mother passed away, and he was taken from Sangda Bangrim to Pangkha Chöding, where he stayed until 1434.

Shakya Chokden started studying reading, writing, and other basic subjects under his maternal uncle Geshé[44] Döndrup Pelzang (*dge bshes don grub dpal bzang*), and then continued under Sönam Tsültrim (*bsod nams tshul khrims*), a master from Gakhang (*'ga' khang*) college of Kyormolung. He studied at Kyormolung for two years (1435–1436), but during the years 1442–1443 he would visit it again to receive from Sönam Tsültrim transmissions through reading and teachings on Vinaya, Abhidharma, Maitreya's *Ornament of Mahāyāna Sūtras*[45] and *Sublime Continuum of Mahāyāna*,[46] Śāntideva's *Engaging in the Bodhisattva Deeds*,[47] and other texts. During that later time he also received transmissions of Vinaya teachings from the senior abbot (*mkhan chen*) Chökyap Pelzang (*chos skyabs dpal bzang*). The sectarian affiliation of Kyormolung at that time is not entirely clear; apparently it was either a Sakya or a mixed Sakya/Geluk institution.[48] According to Drölchok, this monastic university enjoyed universal respect at the time, and Chökyap Pelzang was highly honored by all affiliates of the Neudong ruling faction.[49]

On the Tibetan New Year of 1437, Rongtön came to Kyormolung. From the first time they met, Shakya Chokden felt a very deep faith in this master. During Rongtön's visit Shakya Chokden received the intermediate renunciate (*bar ma rab byung*, that is, the pre-novice) vows[50] and the name "Shakya Chokden" that would stay with him his whole life. Rongtön also recognized him as a reincarnation of a teacher from Kham (*khams*)—and his own close associate—Baktön

Zhönnu Gyeltsen (*bag ston gzhon nu rgyal mtshan*)/Baktön Shakya Özer (*bag ston shākya 'od zer*).[51]

In 1437, Shakya Chokden entered Nego (*gnas sgo*) college at Sangpu Neutok—the seat of the great paṇḍita Dönyö Pelwa, who became one of his main teachers. He thereby embarked on extensive training in all major subjects of Tibetan scholasticism, including Prajñāpāramitā commentaries (especially Maitreya's *Ornament of Clear Realizations*[52]), logic and epistemology, works on Madhyamaka by Nāgārjuna and his followers, Abhidharma, Vinaya, Yogācāra works, and later tantric theory, rituals, and meditative techniques.[53] In particular, he studied Prajñāpāramitā on the basis of the famous *Rongtön's Commentary*,[54] and Pramāṇa on the basis of oral teachings (*ngag sgros*) of Dönyö Pelwa himself.[55]

Shakya Chokden's studies were not limited to Sangpu Neutok only. As he later told his students in Serdokchen, in order to study those various subjects he had to visit different monastic institutions (49). His mobility during those studies is worth noticing. Reading his biography also creates an overall impression that traveling from place to place to receive teachings from specialists of different subjects was a part of the fifteenth-century Sakya monastic education, at least for those students who like Shakya Chokden were aspiring to master all fields of Buddhist learning available at that time in Tibet.

Drölchok reports that during the course of his studies, Shakya Chokden generated an illusion-like meditative concentration (*sgyu ma lta bu'i ting nge 'dzin*) in which he had an experience of his whole body appearing like a vessel filled with stainless water, transparent and unobstructed, so that one could pass hands through it. At times, his body would feel immaterial, so that he would question what his body actually was, searching for one hand with the other, and moving them through each other without touching, like fingers passing through sunrays. Experiencing the moonlike appearance of luminosity, Shakya Chokden could continue reading his textbooks at night with no need for external light. When fellow students asked what he was doing, he said that it did not make the slightest difference whether it was day or night, then to everyone's surprise demonstrated that he could easily read at night as if it were daytime.[56]

In 1438, he visited Nalendra monastery, the monastic seat of Rongtön. From Rongtön he received numerous Prajñāpāramitā teachings stemming from Maitreya and Asaṅga and transmitted to Rongtön through Yakpa; Pramāṇa teachings coming from Dignāga and Dharmakīrti and also transmitted to Rongtön directly by Yakpa; as well as all textual systems of Prāsaṅgika and Svātantrika.[57] From that time on and until Rongtön passed away, he received from him multiple teachings and reading transmissions of treatises on Prajñāpāramitā, Pramāṇa, Vinaya, and Madhyamaka, including writings of Nāgārjuna, Maitreya, Asaṅga, Haribhadra, Kamalaśīla, as well as all instructional writings (*khrid yig*) of Rongtön himself.

Shakya Chokden developed a very strong connection with the teachings of Rongtön as well as Yakpa. Later in his life, after having studied under Rongtön for many years, he transmitted Rongtön's teachings to his own students.[58] When he became a teacher at Sangpu Neutok, he also revived there studies of Yakpa's writings on Prajñāpāramitā. (Apparently, studies of those writings had gone into decline due to the popularity of Rongtön's, Gyeltsap Darma Rinchen's, and other commentaries on the subject.[59]) Because of that, studies of Yakpa's Prajñāpāramitā teachings continued at Sangpu while everywhere else they virtually disappeared.[60] Zilung monastery, which later became Shakya Chokden's own seat, also apparently maintained Rongtön and Yakpa's teachings (36).

Shakya Chokden also grew very close to his teacher Dönyö Pelwa, and received teachings and transmissions from this important Sakya master for more than thirty years.[61] They included Vinaya, Asaṅga's *Summary of Higher Knowledge*,[62] Sakya Pendita's *Thorough Differentiation of the Three Types of Vows*, and other texts. When Shakya Chokden matured as a scholar, Dönyö Pelwa was greatly impressed with his knowledge, and eventually passed down to him his monastic seat in Tsang named "Zilung" that Shakya Chokden renamed into "Serdokchen."[63]

His other teachers with whom at different times he studied Kadam (*bka' gdams*) teachings, Pramāṇa, Abhidharma, Vinaya, *Five Dharmas of Maitreya*,[64] and other non-tantric systems were Sanggyé Chökyongwa (*sangs rgyas chos skyong ba*), Martön Gyamtso Rinchen (*smar ston rgya mtsho rin chen*), Dröpa Özer Gyelpo Pelwa (*gros pa 'od zer rgyal po dpal ba*), Zangpa Lodrö Gyamtso (*bzang pa blo gros rgya mtsho*), Gewa Gyeltsen (*dge ba rgyal mtshan*, 1387–1462), and many others. While in Ü, Shakya Chokden mostly stayed at Sangpu, but would also travel to different monasteries to receive teachings.

In 1439 at Sangpu, he took the beginner's monastic examinations (*blo gsar grwa skor*) on the subjects of Prajñāpāramitā and Pramāṇa. Around that time, he also gave pointing-out instructions (*mdzub khrid*) on two chapters of the *Rongtön's Commentary* and on Chapa Chökyi Senggé's (*phya pa chos kyi seng ge*, 1109–1169) *Collected Topics* (*phya / cha bsdus*). While teaching the latter text, Shakya Chokden showed where its topics were misinterpreted by later commentators. As he himself later said, it was at that point in his life when for the first time he had the courage to differentiate between his own tenet system and those of others. From that time on he would write on slate, paper, and whatever else he had at hand, the words scornful of other systems. As these words make clear, the "other systems" were Geluk teachings.[65] As has been mentioned earlier (19), at the time Sangpu hosted both Geluk and Sakya communities. The growing influence and popularity of the Geluk system, together with its support by Pakmodru rulers, contributed to the bitterness with which Shakya Chokden approached its philosophical positions.

In 1440 at Nalendra he received the novice monk's (*dge tshul, śrāmaṇera*) vows from Rongtön. With the new name "Drimé Lekpé Lodrö" (*dri med legs pa'i blo gros*) affixed to his previous name, his full name now was "Shakya Chokden Drimé Lekpé Lodrö." Thereafter he would memorize a page a day of the *Sūtra on Moral Discipline*,[66] was tested by Dönyö Pelwa every day without interruption, and also would clarify with him difficult points of Vinaya and other subjects.[67]

In 1441, he already could give pointing-out instructions on Sakya Pendita's *Treasure of the Science of Valid Cognition*[68] and Vasubandhu's *Treasury of Higher Knowledge*.[69] Because he was so young, monks would have to lift him to the Dharma-throne on their backs. Thus, he became known as a "master kid" (*slob dpon bu chung*). He himself would say that from the very time of his apprenticeship everybody would treat him as a future master and ask him questions about complicated topics of Pramāṇa and other textual teachings.[70]

In spring of 1442, due to orders issued from Neudong regarding Sakya and Geluk followers, Shakya Chokden had to go to Sera monastery to receive extensive teachings on Candrakīrti's *Clear Words*[71] given by Gungru Gyeltsen Zangpo (*gung ru rgyal mtshan bzang po*, 1383–1450).[72] In the summer of the same year in Tsel Chökhorling (*tshal chos 'khor gling*) Shakya Chokden received from the Lord of Dharma Namgyel (*chos rje rnam rgyal*) complete teachings on Tsongkhapa's commentaries on Nāgārjuna's *Wisdom: Root Stanzas on Madhyamaka*[73] and Candrakīrti's *Engaging in Madhyamaka*.[74] According to Künga Drölchok, he went to receive teachings in Sera and Tsel Chökhorling not because he wanted to, but because orders were issued by the Pakmo Drupa rulers from Neudong. As has been mentioned above (18), the Pakmo Drupa rulers at the time were supporting Geluk. It seems, therefore, that those orders effectively forced Sakya monks to study Geluk teachings.[75] It comes as no surprise, then, that such a sectarian politicized atmosphere would play an important role in Shakya Chokden's strong anti-Geluk agenda.

Tsongkhapa's interpretation of Madhyamaka made a negative impression on Shakya Chokden, and later he would refute it in multiple commentaries, such as the *Smaller Summarized Exposition [of Madhyamaka] Called 'Vajra of the Lord [of Gods]' Pleasing Clear-Minded Ones*[76] and the *Ocean of Scriptural Statements and Reasoning: Treasury of Ascertainment of Mahāyāna Madhyamaka*.[77] When he told Sönam Tsültrim of Gakhang college about his study with Gelukpas, Sönam Tsültrim became very upset with this sectarian agenda and strongly encouraged Shakya Chokden to go to Nalendra and keep studying with Rongtön.[78]

Starting from 1445, by which time he had already learned numerous treatises of his own and others' traditions, Shakya Chokden officially became a Zurchepa (*zur 'chad pa*, "Adjunct Teacher") at Sangpu. In 1446 he was elevated to the status of a Loppön (*slob dpon*, "Master") teacher at Nego college.[79] It is difficult to judge what kind of knowledge these two positions required, and whether he had to take any formal examinations as a prerequisite to holding them. It is also unclear whether the two titles had any weight outside Sangpu, unlike the status of a Geshé mentioned below (32).

In 1447 and 1448 Shakya Chokden undertook an extensive study of various treatises on Sanskrit grammar and composition, as well as poetry and Tibetan grammar. For that purpose he went to Nyetang Chödzong (*snye thang chos rdzong*) to study with the great paṇḍita Loten the Fourth (*blo brtan bzhi pa*)/Lodrö Tenpa (*blo gros brtan pa*), a Bodongpa (*bo dong pa*) master.[80] Eventually, Shakya Chokden learned Sanskrit so well that he was able to converse in it, translate from and into Sanskrit, and even give a Kālacakra empowerment in Sanskrit.[81]

From 1449 on, he began receiving the tantric teachings and empowerments of different traditions, primarily Sakya and various Kagyü lineages. From Nenang (*gnas nang*) master Drakpa Özer (*grags pa 'od zer*), for example, he received many empowerments of the Karma Kagyü tradition, such as Cakrasaṃvara and Vajravārāhī, teachings on the *Hevajra* and other tantras, instructions on ritual dance, maṇḍala measurements, ritual singing, and so forth.[82] It is important to note that besides Shakya Chokden's primary involvement in his own Sakya tradition, he maintained connection with Kagyü traditions throughout his life, and would receive teachings of the Karma, Shangpa (*shangs pa*), Taklung (*stag lung*), and other Kagyü lineages. There is no doubt that this connection extended beyond a mere intellectual understanding of different Kagyü systems, and greatly contributed to his sympathetic attitude to the various practice lineages addressed below (87, 96–97).

Apparently, the Sakya/Kagyü sectarian divide in the middle of the fifteenth century was not as rigid and antagonistic as the Sakya/Geluk or Karma Kagyü/Geluk divides. Even the latter would be transcended or at least downplayed by some masters, including one of Shakya Chokden's main teachers Changlung Rinpoché (*spyang lung rin po che*)/Changlung Chödingpa Zhönnu Lodrö (*spyang lung chos sdings pa gzhon nu blo gros*, 1372–1476), from whom he received multiple Kagyü teachings (31). As Shakya Chokden's biography of him demonstrates, although this great scholar and yogin was affiliated with Sakya, he was truly a non-sectarian master who studied under teachers of different traditions—including Rendawa Zhönnu Lodrö (*red mda' ba gzhon nu blo gros*, 1349–1412) and Tsongkhapa—and also held virtually all practice lineages surviving in Tibet.[83] Indeed, Changlung Rinpoché embodied that very non-sectarian ideal which was later cherished by leaders of the nineteenth-century ecumenical movement who emphasized a harmonizing approach to different practice lineages and downplayed sectarian divisions into such schools as Nyingma, Sakya, Kagyü, and Geluk.[84] Furthermore, it seems that it was not uncommon in the fifteenth century to be a member of one tradition, and receive and transmit tantric instructions passed down through other traditions—not unlike what more recent non-sectarian masters of the past two centuries have done. In particular, one could be a Sakya intellectual and at the same time hold Shangpa and other Kagyü tantric instructions without unnecessary qualms about mixing sectarian identities. This is because many practice lineages were not *owned by* sects; rather, they were *transmitted through* sects—the fact that remains true today.

During 1449–1450, Shakya Chokden visited Kam (*kam/ skam*) monastery where he received multiple Highest Yoga Tantra (*bla med kyi rgyud, anuttarayogatantra*) teachings and empowerments from Lodrö Chökyongwa (*blo gros chos skyong ba*), a close student of the renowned tantric master Künga Trashi (*kun dga' bkra shis*, 1349–1425). Those teachings included Hevajra, Vajrabhairava, Cakrasaṃvara, Tārā of the Highest Yoga Tantra, Mañjuśrīvajra Guhyasamāja, Kālacakra, Raktayamāri, and other systems transmitted through the lineage of Künga Trashi.[85] During the teachings on the tantric ritual dance Pañjara in 1449, Shakya Chokden was able to differentiate between Sanskrit and Prakrit languages, greatly pleasing Lodrö Chökyongwa, who kept calling him "paṇḍita." According to Shakya Chokden, it is from that time that he first received the name "penchen" (*paṇ chen, mahāpaṇḍita*), that is, the "great paṇḍita."[86] This name too would stay with him his whole life. (Apparently, such a name was reserved for only very learned individuals. At the same time, the context in which it was given to Shakya Chokden also implies that by the middle of the fifteenth century detailed knowledge of Sanskrit was a rarity.)

At different times from different teachers, Shakya Chokden would receive many more tantric teachings, empowerments, transmissions, and instructions. One of his main tantric teachers was Changlung Rinpoché—a prominent immediate disciple of Künga Trashi—whom Shakya Chokden met at Changlung at the age of twenty-three. Later, he received from Changlung Rinpoché the complete Path and Result (*lam 'bras*) teachings in the lineage of Künga Trashi, multiple Kālacakra teachings from different lineages, the Six Dharmas of Nāro (*nā ro chos drug*), Great Seal (*phyag chen, mahāmudrā*), and other teachings of different Kagyü lineages such as Karma, Drigung (*'bri gung*), Taklung, and Druk (*'brug*). He also received from him all teachings of Shangpa Kagyü (*shangs pa bka' brgyud*): the instructions of the Four Golden Dharmas of Shangpa (*shangs pa'i gser chos bzhi*), such as the Great Seal Amulet Box (*phyag chen ga'u ma*), as well as empowerments, and so forth. Besides that, he received from him about sixty different types of the Mind Training (*blo sbyong*), Rendawa's guiding instructions on the Madhyamaka view (*dbu ma'i lta khrid rnams*), and other teachings. Shakya Chokden held a deep respect for Changlung Rinpoché and always remembered his kindness. Zhönnu Chödrup (*gzhon nu chos grub*)—a reincarnation of that lama—later became his disciple and eventually Künga Drölchok's teacher.[87]

In 1451, he went to Ngor monastery, and for the first time met another important tantric teacher—Dorjechang Künga Zangpo. Shakya Chokden received from him various tantric teachings and empowerments of the Path and Result, Akṣobhya Guhyasamāja, Cakrasaṃvara, Kurukullā and other deities, as well as some auxiliary transmissions related to the Path and Result. Until Künga Zangpo passed away Shakya Chokden received from him many more tantric teachings, such as guiding instructions on the Vajrayoginī Central Channel (*rtsa dbu ma, avadhūtī*), Path and Result, *One Hundred Means of Accomplishment* (*sgrub thabs brgya rsa*) collection, and so forth.[88]

In 1452, Shakya Chokden received the full monastic ordination from Künga Zangpo.[89]

Becoming a Prolific Writer and Famous Scholar

In 1454, Shakya Chokden composed his first major treatises: the *Garlands of Waves of Assertions: Investigation of Connections of Former and Later [Elements in] the 'Ornament of Clear Realizations' Treatise of*

Quintessential Instructions on the Perfection of Wisdom Together with Its Commentaries, and Placement of the Army of Good Explanations on Difficult Points of Explicit Teachings[90] and other commentaries and supplementary writings on Maitreya's *Ornament of Clear Realizations* in which he followed the *Rongtön's Commentary.*[91] This marked the beginning of more than fifty years of writing on all major topics of Buddhist scholarship—the period that ended only when he passed away in 1507. This also marked the beginning of a long process of writing on the *Five Dharmas of Maitreya,* including several commentaries on the *Ornament of Clear Realizations.* He would keep composing commentaries on the *Ornament of Clear Realizations* up until 1499 when he wrote the *Great Path Compressing the Two Chariot Ways into One: Explanation of [Maitreya's] 'Ornament of Clear Realizations' Together with [Haribhadra's] 'Clear Meaning' Commentary.*[92] Also, the very year he passed away Shakya Chokden composed the *Opening Doors of a Chest of Gems: Treatise Elucidating Stages of the Path of the 'Five Dharmas of Maitreya.'*[93] It is clear that his interest in the *Dharmas of Maitreya*—all of which he eventually classified as Madhyamaka works—persisted from the beginning to the very end of his writing career spanning over half a century.

Although Shakya Chokden wanted to focus on receiving teachings, Künga Zangpo urged him to take monastic examinations (*grwa skor,* literally "going on monastic rounds"), saying that it was a tradition for becoming a Sakya Geshé (*sa skya pa'i dge bshes*) to give scholarly discourses at great monastic seats. He advised Shakya Chokden to stay in a closed retreat studying texts (*phyag dpe gzigs pa'i sku mtshams dam pa*) in preparation. Because Shakya Chokden knew the texts very well, he did not even have to study while in retreat, and instead engaged in tantric practice, apparently meditating on Yamāntaka.[94]

In 1455, he went to Sakya monastery, and following an established tradition took the examinations starting on the auspicious day of summer solstice. The examinations consisted of giving explanations of about fifty[95] different texts of sūtras, tantras, and sciences that included, but were not limited to works on Prajñāpāramitā, Pramāṇa, works of Maitreya, Asaṅga, and Vasubandhu, treatises on poetry, ritual dance, crafts, Sanskrit, synonymics, Sönam Tsemo's *General Presentation of Tantras,*[96] the *Three Hevajra Tantras,*[97] and the *Three Bodhisattva Commentaries.*[98] The examinations were successful, and especially remarkable was his reasoning.[99] The *Detailed Analysis* does not mention any formal title received by Shakya Chokden at the time. Nor does the term "Sakya Geshé" mentioned above seem to be a particular title, although it does convey a high status. At the same time, the number of texts Shakya Chokden was tested in greatly exceeded those required for receiving titles of "Kazhipa" (*bka' bzhi pa*, "Master of Four Texts"), "Kachupa" (*bka' bcu pa / ka bcu pa*, "Master of Ten Texts"), and even "Rapjampa" (*rab 'byams pa*, "Master of Numerous [Texts]").[100] None of those titles requires knowledge of Sanskrit, poetry, rituals, or detailed knowledge of Tantra. Shakya Chokden's examination in effect was a declaration of his mastery of all subjects of learning available in monastic institutions of his day, which was a rare feat, as is clear from the impression he made on his teacher Künga Zangpo (see following paragraph).

After the examinations were over, Shakya Chokden returned to Ngor monastery. Künga Zangpo was extremely pleased and offered him such priceless things as a statue given to Sakya Pendita by a Kashmiri paṇḍita he studied with, and the ceremonial robe that Pakpa Lodrö Gyeltsen wore for twenty-five years. (Later, a year after Künga Zangpo passed away, Chesa Dakchen Lodrö Wangchuk (*che sa bdag chen blo gros dbang phyug*, 1402–1481) from Chumik (*chu mig*), told Shakya Chokden that although he had spent more than thirty years inseperable from Künga Zangpo, he had never seen him as happy and making such outstanding offerings as the ones he gave to Shakya Chokden and his assistants.) On that occasion, in a special empowerment room Künga Zangpo gave Shakya Chokden empowerments of Cakrasaṃvara, Vajrayoginī, and other transmissions in a one-on-one fashion, and told him to make them the essence of his tantric practice. He also gave him transmissions through reading of different tantric scriptures translated by Sakya Pendita, and asked him to give explanations of and write about differences between interpretations of the *Secret Assembly Tantra*[101] by their own Sakya and others' systems. Later, when Shakya Chokden settled in Serdokchen, he wrote such a text, printed it, and sent its copy wrapped in a white ceremonial scarf to Ngor monastery as an offering to Künga Zangpo's statue.[102] The "others' systems" targeted in that text are Geluk interpretations of Tantra in general, of the relationship of tantric and non-tantric views and practices, and of the *Secret Assembly Tantra* in particular.

In 1465 Shakya Chokden was elevated to the position of a Chenpo (*chen po*, "Great One") that was held in high respect by both Geluk and Sakya monastic communities of Sangpu Neutok.[103] Thus, the order of Shakya Chokden's promotions at Sangpu was that of a Zurchepa, Loppön, and finally Chenpo, which was the final step before becoming a Khenpo (*mkhan po*, "Abbot") mentioned below (34). It is possible that the examinations at Sakya that earned him the status of a Sakya Geshé helped his promotion as a Chenpo at Sangpu, but they were not necessarily a part of Sangpu educational process, unlike the beginnner's monastic examinations he took at Sangpu earlier.

Shakya Chokden was already writing refutations of Geluk views on Madhyamaka at the early age of thirty-two, as is clear from the colophon of the *Smaller Summarized Exposition*.[104] Nevertheless, according to Künga Drölchok, it was in 1467 at Sangpu that Shakya Chokden for the first time conceived the idea of writing the *Big and Small Ascertainments of Madhyamaka*[105] where with the aid of scriptural statements and reasonings he would differentiate between his own and others' systems.

Shakya Chokden knew that the next step after acquiring the Chenpo position was that of Khenpo.[106] Nevertheless, it appears that he was dissatisfied with the intellectual climate and state of scholarship at Sangpu. According to Drölchok, Sangpu monks were greatly respected as the best scholars in the land and had excellent understanding of the different points of their own and others' traditions. Nevertheless, it was hard to find anyone at Sangpu at the time who would advocate a coherent textual system, rather than just taking whatever positions would fit at any particular moment. A standpoint they would immediately accept in discussion, etc., would be dictated not by attempts to follow a coherent system but by whatever came to their mind at the time as more suitable.[107]

Thus, Shakya Chokden appointed a top scholar—Trapuwa Sanggyé Zangpo (*phra phu ba sangs rgyas bzang po*)—as his representative at Nego college, and left the majority of his students with him.[108] From the end of the summer of 1468 through the spring of 1469, for nine months Shakya Chokden stayed in a strict retreat on Hevajra approximation-accomplishment (*bsnyen bsgrub*) at Öseltsé (*'od gsal rtse*)/ Ösel Tsemo (*'od gsal rtse mo*). In nine months he came to the stage of the replenishing burnt offerings ritual.[109] Shakya Chokden gave the following description of his experiences in retreat:

> As soon as I had left the responsibilities of being the Chenpo of Sangpu, I stayed in a strict nine month retreat on Hevajra approximation-accomplishment at Öseltsé. At that time there were signs that sorts of evils had been purified. At dawn, some variegated doors of appearance of luminosity emerged. "Ösel Tsemo" [that is, "Luminosity Peak"] is a meaningful name.[110]

In his early forties, during 1468–1470—right before, during, and after the Hevajra retreat—he wrote commentaries on Candrakīrti's

Engaging in Madhyamaka, Nāgārjuna's *Wisdom: Root Stanzas on Madhyamaka*, and some other texts.[111]

It is notable that although Shakya Chokden would at times call himself a "dry dialectician" (*mtshan nyid pa skam po*),[112] his interests were clearly not limited to logic and philosophy. It is also notable that his writing on the Niḥsvabhāvavāda could go hand in hand with tantric retreats. It suggests that he took the ritual and contemplative practices as complementary, not contradictory to his philosophical studies and teachings. As this and other examples demonstrate, during one and the same period in his life Shakya Chokden could engage in philosophical study and writing, receive tantric empowerments, and also have different meditative experiences. Later, he would teach and emphasize in his writings the unity of different aspects of Buddhist thought and practice, and maintain a reconciliatory attitude to diverse conceptual approaches that trigger similar meditative experiences of ultimate reality. This implies that his harmonizing approach to different systems of Mahāyāna thought and practice emphasized in this study was incorporated into his own life as well. I would speculate that his statement that different conceptual approaches can lead to similar experiences of ultimate reality described as luminous primordial mind in both sūtric and tantric forms of Mahāyāna[113] was more than a rhetoric; it is possible that he actually had in mind his experiences of tantric practice similar to the one mentioned above.

It appears that after this time, Shakya Chokden stopped writing texts focused purely on the Niḥsvabhāvavāda system, although as late as in 1501, by request of Ünyönpa (*dbus smyon pa*, "Madman from Ü")/Ünyönpa Künga Zangpo (*dbus smyon pa kun dga' bzang po*), he wrote the *Garlands of Wondrous Ornaments of the Union of Calm Abiding and Special Insight: Guiding Instructions on the Madhyamaka View*,[114] focusing primarily on the Niḥsvabhāvavāda approach to meditation on reality, and that of Candrakīrti in particular.[115]

Settling in the Golden Monastery and Exploring New Horizons

On the 15th day of the first lunar month of 1471, Shakya Chokden arrived at Serdokchen. At the time of the abbacy of Dönyö Pelwa, this monastic university was called "Zilung." According to Drölchok, from the time Shakya Chokden placed his feet (*zhabs bkod*) in that monastery, he gave it a new name: "Serdokchen."[116] Back in 1468, Dönyö Pelwa showed him great respect as his best disciple, and Dönyö Pelwa's monks insisted on Shakya Chokden inheriting this monastic seat because they treated him as the best disciple of Dönyö

Pelwa. That same year at Chumik, Chesa Dakchen Lodrö Wangchuk also insisted that Shakya Chokden should take care of Zilung because it had such special features as maintaining the uncommon teachings of Yakpa and Rongtön, and so forth. In addition he promised to add his Chumik estate as a part of its monastic estate.[117]

Monastic discipline in Serdokchen was not very strict, and not all monks studied monastic rules in depth. So, during the annual monastic summer retreat (*dbyar gnas*), Shakya Chokden again established in Serdokchen the tradition of the Vinaya rites of the three bases (*gzhi gsum cho ga*)[118] that had not been strictly followed before, even at the time of Dönyö Pelwa's abbacy.[119]

On the fifth lunar month of 1472, Shakya Chokden left Serdokchen, traveling to Ngari Lowo (*mnga' ris glo bo*),[120] where he had been invited a few years previously by the Buddhist king (*chos rgyal*) Trashigön (*bkra shis mgon*)/Lowo Depa Tsangchen Trashi Gönpo (*glo bo sde pa tshang chen bkra shis mgon po, c.* 1440–1489). Shakya Chokden was accompanied by an impressive group of 300 people that consisted of 100 scholars and 200 students. In Lowo, they settled in Namgyel monastic university (*rnam rgyal chos sde*). Shakya Chokden's party would stay there together with 500 other monks, and their sustenance, provision, and all other necessities would be completely covered by the ruler Trashigön himself. The monks only had to care about an intensive study day and night. Following the rules set earlier by Dorjechang Künga Zangpo,[121] who determined what texts should be used in Namgyel curriculum, Shakya Chokden taught Abhidharma on the basis of Rongtön's commentary, the *Treasure of the Science of Valid Cognition* on the basis of Yakpa's commentary, and so forth. Otherwise, all explanations of general meaning, consequences, and syllogisms related to different subjects were his own.[122]

Shakya Chokden was very active during his stay in Lowo. Although he gave almost no tantric teachings and transmissions at the time, he taught extensively on sūtric subjects. He gave bodhisattva vows to crowds, and novice and full ordination vows to some individuals. During that period he also composed texts on Vinaya, Pramāṇa, the buddha-essence (*sangs rgyas kyi snying po, buddhagarbha*), and other topics, printed various great scriptures (*gzhung chen*) and composed their postscripts (*par byang*).[123]

Drölchok reports that in 1474, Shakya Chokden generated a deep contemplative realization of selflessness (*bdag med, nairātmya,* that is, emptiness, *stong pa nyid, śūnyatā*), and at the moment of reading the *Summarized Exposition of Madhyamaka* (*Dbu ma'i stong thun*) by Mapcha Jangchup Tsöndrü (*rma bya byang chub brtson 'grus,* d. 1185), he remembered his previous incarnation as Mapcha and had a very vivid vision of smiling White Mañjuśrīvajra (*'jam pa'i rdo rje dkar po*). From that time on the words "Jampel Gepé Shenyen" (*'jam dpal dges pa'i bshes gnyen*, literally meaning "Spiritual Friend—Delighted Mañjuśrī") were affixed to his name.[124]

At the end of Shakya Chokden's stay in Lowo an event happened that changed the course of his life forever. In 1475, many visitors came to Lowo, in particular monks from Dreyül Kyetsel monastery of Jamchen Rapjampa. In the midst of a big assembly, when everybody was sitting together, Shakya Chokden asked: "What does omniscient Jamchen Rapjampa mainly teach nowadays?" Knowing that Lowo people were particularly attached to Sakya views, the visitors answered that he was focusing on Sakya Pendita's *Thorough Differentiation of the Three Types of Vows* and *Treasure of the Science of Valid Cognition*, especially on the former. Shakya Chokden then asked more specifically about how Jamchen Rapjampa explained certain passages in the text, but could not get any clear answer at all—only "yes, yes" (*lags lags*) and nothing more. This became an occasion for the ruler Trashigön to purposefully request Shakya Chokden to put his questions in writing. Shakya Chokden then composed the *Good Questions* previously mentioned (20), as well as some other questions, such as the *Defeater of Flower Arrows: Questions on the 'Bhaiśajyaguru Sūtra' Ritual*.[125]

It seems obvious that both the ruler's and Shakya Chokden's intention was to clarify Sakya teachings, not to criticize them. At the end of the *Good Questions* Shakya Chokden explicitly states his devoted attitude to the *Three Types of Vows*, and explains that if people who lack a solid understanding of the points of questioning and refutation (*dri ba dang ni sun 'byin gyi// gnas rnams*) say that these questions were intended to refute Sakya Pendita's text, it is their own problem.[126] He addressed the *Good Questions* to scholars of Ü, Tsang, and Kham, and in particular sent it through the visitors from Dreyül Kyetsel monastery to Jamchen Rapjampa Sanggyepel—whom he respectfully called "Ancestor of the Teachings" (*bstan pa'i mes bo*).[127]

As has been mentioned before (20), the *Good Questions* initiated a considerable controversy, and different scholars attempted to reply, although Jamchen Rapjampa himself did not write an answer.[128] Most importantly and unfortunately, it does seem that those questions were taken as an attack on Sakya Pendita, and therefore on the Sakya tradition itself. According to the ruler Trashigön's younger brother, Lowo Khenchen Sönam Lhündrup, who studied Vinaya, Prajñāpāramitā, and Pramāṇa under Shakya Chokden, the composition of the *Good Questions* made Shakya Chokden a controversial figure in the Sakya scholarly world.[129] Sönam Lhündrup himself later came to the conclusion that although Shakya Chokden was an outstanding master or "treasure holder" (*mdzod 'dzin pa*), his views deviated from the authentic Sakya tradition.[130]

Shakya Chokden's party left Lowo in 1475. Shakya Chokden decided to go back to Serdokchen through Jang Ngamring (*byang ngam rings*), being invited there by the ruler of that area, Namgyel Drakpa Zangpo (*rnam rgyal grags pa bzang po*, also known as Rikden Namgyel Drakzang, *rigs ldan rnam rgyal grags bzang*, 1395–1475), who was a famous scholar of Kālacakra, medicine, and other subjects. Earlier that year Shakya Chokden had sent him the *Questions to the Jang Ruler Namgyel Drakpa about Three [Topics of] the Sugata-Essence, [Four Tantras of] Medical Analysis, and Kālacakra*.[131]

Upon Shakya Chokden's arrival, Namgyel Drakzang discussed with him multiple Buddhist subjects and was very pleased, saying that he had met both of Shakya Chokden's main teachers—Rongtön and Künga Zangpo—and discussed with them various Buddhist topics, but those discussions would not match even a small part of his conversation with Shakya Chokden. During that meeting, he also gave Shakya Chokden an empowerment of the Mahāsaṃvara form of Kālacakra (*dus kyi 'khor lo sdom pa chen po'i dbang*).[132] In his *Thunder of Melodious Praise: Liberation Story of the Dharma King Rikden Namgyel Drakpa Zangpo*, Drölchok also writes that Shakya Chokden greatly pleased Namgyel Drakzang by answering in detail his continuous questions about Asaṅga's *Five Treatises on Grounds* (*Sa sde lnga*), while the ruler clarified all doubts Shakya Chokden had earlier about Kālacakra teachings, and Shakya Chokden venerated Namgyel Drakzang as the supreme vajra master (*mchog gi rdo rje slob dpon chen po'i yul du bkur bar mdzad*).[133]

Importantly, the *Thunder of Melodious Praise* sheds some light on what possibly influenced Shakya Chokden's interest in the definitive meaning of the *Five Dharmas of Maitreya*, all of which he later treated as expressing the ultimate view of Alīkākāravāda and Madhyamaka. Drölchok quotes Shakya Chokden as saying:

> When I myself was a child, I once accompanied the Lord Dönyö Pelwa on a visit to a senior abbot Pema Zangpowa (*padma bzang po ba*). At that time, the senior abbot asked [Dönyö Pelwa]: "Master, what are you teaching about where the intent (*dgongs pa*) of the three intermediate *Dharmas of Maitreya* lies?" The Lord Dönyö Pelwa replied: "I am teaching that it lies in Cittamātra (*sems tsam*)."[134] [Pema Zangpowa asked:] "What is the reason for that?" [In reply, Dönyö

> Pelwa] quoted the passage [from the *Ornament of Mahāyāna Sūtras*:] "Having cognized by intellect that there is nothing apart from mind . . ." [Pema Zangpowa countered:] "Well then, what about the following words appearing right after that passage: 'Having realized the nonexistence of both, the intelligent one . . .', etc.? As for us, at all times and on all occasions we interpreted the intended meaning (*dgongs don*) of the *Dharmas of Maitreya* as the faultless chariot [way of] the Great Madhyamaka (*dbu ma chen po*).[135]

This passage demonstrates that Dönyö Pelwa, one of the most important teachers of Shakya Chokden, treated the three intermediate *Dharmas* as Cittamātra writings—the most popular position by Shakya Chokden's time, as the latter himself admitted.[136] In contrast to that view, Pema Zangpowa argued that the Great Madhyamaka was taught in all the *Five Dharmas of Maitreya* without exception: the *Ornament of Clear Realizations, Ornament of Mahāyāna Sūtras, Differentiation of the Middle and Extremes, Differentiation of Phenomena and the Nature of Phenomena,* and *Sublime Continuum of Mahāyāna.*[137] The passage that the two scholars were referring to is found in the *Ornament of Mahāyāna Sūtras*:

> Having well amassed limitless transcendent collections
> Of merits and primordial mind,
> Because [his] mind thoroughly ascertains dharmas,
> The bodhisattva realizes that the aspects of [external] objects have verbalization [as their] cause.
> Having cognized [external] objects as only verbalizations,
> [He] immaculately dwells in mind-only appearing as those [external objects].
> [He] then directly realizes the dharma-sphere
> Devoid of characteristics of both [external things and minds causing their appearances].
> Having cognized by intellect that there is nothing apart from mind,
> [The bodhisattva] then realizes the mind also as exclusively nonexistent.
> Having cognized the nonexistence of both, the intelligent one
> Dwells in the dharma-sphere (*chos kyi dbyings, dharmadhātu*) devoid of them.[138]

By showing that the mind-only (*sems tsam*) is not the final realization intended by the passage, Pema Zangpowa demonstrated that the intended meaning of the *Dharmas of Maitreya* transcends Cittamātra. Later in his writings, Shakya Chokden would use the same technique to demonstrate that the meaning of this and similar passages transcends Cittamātra and lies in the Alīkākāravāda form of Madhyamaka.[139]

Similar to the meaning of "Madhyamaka," the meaning of "Great Madhyamaka" varies from author to author and from context to context, and it is unclear what Pema Zangpowa meant by "Great Madhyamaka" on that particular occasion. As I explain below (119), in his later works Shakya Chokden treated both Niḥsvabhāvavāda and Alīkākāravāda systems as the Great Madhyamaka. Nevertheless, it is remarkable that in one of his latest works, the *Wish Fulfilling Meru: Discourse on the History of Madhyamaka,* he makes a statement very similar to Pema Zangpowa's:

> [S]ome of the later Tibetans say that all of the *Five* [*Dharmas*] are ascertained as Cittamātra. Others say that all of them are ascertained as Madhyamaka. In these later times it is unanimously taught that the first and the last [*Dharmas*] are ascertained as Madhyamaka and the three intermediate ones as Cittamātra. Nevertheless we accept that [from looking at] the explanatory style of the scriptures themselves it is established by direct perception that [along with the intermediate three] both the first and last scriptures of Maitreya also make their main topic the Madhyamaka which is that very interpretation of the intent of the *Perfection of Wisdom* sūtras by the third dharmacakra.[140]

Shakya Chokden's approach to different sets of the Buddha's teachings known as dharmacakras (*chos 'khor,* "wheel of teachings") is explained in the third section of Chapter 4. As I explain there, he argues that the third dharmacakra interprets the meaning of the *Perfection of Wisdom* sūtras, i.e., the second dharmacakra, in the Alīkākāravāda style, as the non-dual primordial mind (*gnyis su med pa'i ye shes, advayajñāna*). What inspired Shakya Chokden to develop this approach? In the passage from the *Thunder of Melodious Praise* that immediately follows the one translated above, Drölchok quotes Shakya Chokden saying:

> [Pema Zangpowa] looked at me and said, "Wise young nephew, closely investigate topics such as this!" and also gave me a gift of tea.
>
> After that time I closely investigated the definitive meaning, but did not really record it in great detail in treatises strictly devoted to the works of the philosophical tenets. I just spoke of it a little bit in conversation. Later,

> because I received the command of the great Rikden [Namgyel Drakzang], I have specially emphasized it.[141]

Künga Drölchok adds that Shākya Chokden himself frequently mentioned this episode in the assembly, and that the differences will become clear if one analyzes his works written before and after his trip to Ngari Lowo.[142] The first such text appears to be the above-mentioned (29) *Ocean of Scriptural Statements and Reasoning* written in 1477.

In sum, Drölchok's *Thunder of Melodious Praise* demonstrates that Shakya Chokden's interest in searching for the definitive meaning of Yogācāra teachings—that he later interpreted as Madhyamaka and Great Madhyamaka—was inspired initially by Pema Zangpowa, and that later his meeting with Namgyel Drakzang inspired him to write actual treatises exploring that meaning. How much Pema Zangpowa and Namgyel Drakzang's actual views Shakya Chokden shared remains unclear. I will return to the issue of shift in Shakya Chokden's views in the last section of Chapter 2.

In fall of 1475 Shakya Chokden and his monks returned to Serdokchen. Shakya Chokden missed the annual monastic summer retreat because he was traveling back from Lowo. As he remarked later, this was the only time he missed the summer retreat—another indication of how seriously he took the monastic discipline. To make up for the missed summer retreat, in seclusion he composed the *Chariot of the Sun Illuminating the 'Sūtra': Explanation of Difficult Points of the 'Sūtra on Moral Discipline.'*[143]

From the end of 1475 until 1478 Shakya Chokden stayed in Tsang, mostly in Serdokchen. In 1476 he expanded the monastery, laying out a monastic garden with thirty-six pillars, and erecting in the shrine room a life-size statue of Dönyö Pelwa, and invited Dönyö Pelwa himself to consecrate it.[144] According to a nameless text written by Shakya Chokden, 1476 was the actual time when he gave the monastery the new name "Serdokchen."[145]

In 1477 he composed the monumental *Ocean of Scriptural Statements and Reasoning*, a work that marked the beginning of an open articulation, crystallization, and polishing of his unique views on Madhyamaka and Yogācāra. In that text, not only did Shakya Chokden differentiate between his own and others' systems on the level of Niḥsvabhāvavāda, as he did earlier, but he also started formulating his novel interpretation of the systems of Alīkākāravāda and Niḥsvabhāvavāda as two forms of Madhyamaka. During the next few years he wrote two further commentaries on the *Ornament of Clear Realizations*, as well as a commentary on Nāgārjuna's *Praise of the Dharma-Sphere*[146] and a commentary on Asaṅga's *Summary of Higher*

Knowledge.[147] In 1481[148] he composed the above-mentioned *Golden Lancet* (20) where he answered his own *Good Questions*. He wrote it at the request of a senior abbot (*mkhan chen*) from Ü Nyimedrung (*nyi ma'i drung*) and a senior abbot from Chölung (*chos lung*) on the West Renakara (*ratna ka ra*). Drölchok reports that he himself later saw twelve initial replies to the *Good Questions*—including the *Golden Lancet* itself—and four further replies based on those initial replies. King Trashigön copied the *Golden Lancet* three times with golden ink and sponsored the carving of its woodblocks that was completed in 1483.[149]

In 1478,[150] with a group of more than 500 scholars, Shakya Chokden set out on an extensive trip from Tsang to Ü, visiting holy places and giving teachings. All teachers and students accompanying him were provided with a generous allowance and travel supplies from Rinpung.

Upon his return to Tsang, Shakya Chokden made it customary from the eleventh until the first lunar month to give explanations of the *Perfection of Wisdom* sūtras, *Compendium of Higher Knowledge*, and *Treasury of Higher Knowledge* in alternation. During the second and third lunar months, he would teach in their entirety Nāgārjuna's *Wisdom: Root Stanzas on Madhyamaka* and Candrakīrti's *Engaging in Madhyamaka*. During the annual monastic summer retreat, he would teach extensively on the subjects of Vinaya and Pramāṇa. Besides that, he would give multiple teachings on specific topics, such as various summaries—the Seventy Meanings (*don bdun cu*) based on the Prajñāpāramita writings, the Types of Minds (*blo rigs*) and Types of Reasons (*rtags rigs*) based on the Pramāṇa writings, and so forth. In general, during the daytime he would concentrate on teaching great Buddhist texts and commentaries, while in the evenings he would teach even such minor subjects as a reasoning application from *Collected Topics* (*bsdus sbyor*).[151] As this teaching approach demonstrates, Shakya Chokden tried to maintain studies of major subjects of sūtric learning (he did not extensively teach Tantra at that time), and even though he was already articulating the Alīkākāravāda view as Madhyamaka, neither then nor later did he downplay the importance of Niḥsvabhāvavāda teachings. On the other hand, he clearly distinguished between major and minor subjects of Buddhist learning, and even when teaching on minor topics he was cautious to avoid new interpretations that he deemed incorrect. He himself said, for example, that even when he would merely hear words of later Tibetan treatises on substance and isolates (*rdzas dang ldog pa'i bstan bcos*), he would cover his ears—not to mention upholding those teachings.[152]

In 1482 he composed the *Enjoyment Ocean of the Speech of the 'Seven Works': Explanation of the 'Treasure of the Science of Valid Cognition.'*[153] The same year he became a lama of the great Tsang ruler (*sde pa gtsang chen pa*),[154] Hor Shakya (*hor shākya*), and other powerful rulers. Around that time he was also offered different estates by the great Tsang ruler, Hor Shakya, Chesa Dakchen from Chumik, and other influential individuals.[155] It appears that he developed a very good connection both with Gyama (*rgya ma*) rulers in Ü and first and foremost with the Rinpung rulers in Tsang.

At the end of the annual monastic summer retreat of 1483, Shakya Chokden was called from Gönpa Shar (*dgon pa shar*) by Dönyö Pelwa. When they met, Dönyö Pelwa told him that he was extremely pleased with his success as a scholar. But he also mentioned that some people were spreading rumors that Shakya Chokden was not a real Sakyapa, and advised him on what prayers to recite when monks get together in order to show otherwise. Dönyö Pelwa died a few months later.[156] Thus, by 1484, Shakya Chokden's four closest teachers have passed away: Rongtön, Künga Zangpo, Changlung Rinpoché, and finally Dönyö Pelwa—the teacher with whom he was connected for the longest period of time.

This same year in Namtseden (*gnam rtse ldan*) for the first time he met with Karmapa Chödrak Gyamtso. Together with 500 monks for seven days he received from Chödrak Gyamtso guiding instructions on the *Great Reasons of Madhyamaka* (*Dbu ma'i gtan tshigs chen mo*)[157] by the Fourth Karmapa Rölpé Dorjé (*rol pa'i rdo rje*, 1340–1383).[158]

It is worth noticing that works written by Shakya Chokden before his early fifties—the time when he established himself in Tsang in general and in Serdokchen monastery in particular—reflect a more or less "standard" Sakya interpretation of the system of Niḥsvabhāvavāda and polemics against Geluk, although in those works he does appear as an inquisitive thinker able to compare multiple standpoints and assert his own. On the other hand, works written in Serdokchen in Tsang tend to increasingly emphasize the importance of the Alīkākāravāda view—that he also described as the view of other-emptiness—and present that view as Madhyamaka on a par with the Niḥsvabhāvavāda view of self-emptiness. This expansion of Shakya Chokden's view of reality was a result of multiple factors such as his personal growth as a thinker and his genuine and growing interest in Yogācāra philosophy. Nevertheless, correspondence between the expansion of his views, the expansion of his influence in Tsang, and the expansion of the political power of Tsang itself in the last quarter of the fifteenth century is worth noticing. It appears that in Tsang Shakya Chokden found a suitable niche for exploring, expanding, and asserting his own unique system of thought.

Becoming a Tantric Master and Crystallizing Novel Views

In his late fifties, Shakya Chokden started giving increasingly numerous tantric teachings. In 1484, after the annual monastic summer retreat he went to Khartsé Langtang (*mkhar rtse glang thang*) and stayed there for some time. There he gave such tantric teachings as a subsequent permission[159] of Vajrapāṇi and teachings of the Niguma cycle. In 1485, in Chumik he gave subsequent permissions of deities of the *Ocean of Means of Accomplishment* (*sgrub thabs rgya mtsho*) to a thousand lay and ordained people.[160]

In 1485 he started construction of a Maitreya statue in Serdokchen that was completed in 1487. During that time, he further expanded the monastery, making more cells, most of the temple, and so forth. Later, in 1491–1493, he made images of Mañjuśrī and Avalokiteśvara on the two sides of the Maitreya statue, appliqué images (*gos sku*) of Sixteen Arhats (*'phags pa'i gnas brtan bcu drug*), images of the Thirty-Five Buddhas of Confession (*ltung bshags kyi sangs rgyas so lnga*), Bhaiśajyaguru sugatas with retinue (*sman bla'i bde gshegs 'khor bcas*), completed a new assembly hall, and so forth.[161]

While in Serdokchen, Shakya Chokden kept producing important works on Abhidharma, *Ornament of Clear Realizations*, and other subjects. In 1488, he composed the *Enjoyment Ocean of the Entirely Good Dharma: Explanation of the Extensive Treatise 'Commentary on Valid Cognition.'*[162] He said that he taught more than fifty times Prajñāpāramitā relying on the *Rongtön's Commentary* and Pramāṇa relying on Dönyö Pelwa's commentary. From that time on, he decided to teach the latter on the basis of his own *Enjoyment Ocean of the Entirely Good Dharma.* Most importantly for our subject, in 1489, he composed the *Rain of Ambrosia*[163] mentioned earlier (9) in which he most clearly articulated his unique approach to the systems of Yogācāra and Madhyamaka.

Throughout the 1490s, Shakya Chokden was actively involved in teaching Tantra and passing down tantric empowerments and transmissions. In 1490 he was invited to Rinpung where he gave numberless empowerments and blessings to the ruler and his relatives (*sde bdag sku mched*). On that occasion many people came from Shang (*shangs*) and Rong (*rong*) to receive from him lay Buddhist, novice, and full ordination vows, and bodhisattva vows. At that time he also composed songs of contemplative experience (*gsung mgur*)[164] at the request of his followers.[165] That same year, Shakya Chokden with students visited Kelden Shingté Podrang Gyama Trikhang (*skal ldan shing rta'i pho brang rgya ma khri khang*)—the seat of the Gyama rulers, where they stayed for two months. To his followers headed by Gyama leaders, he gave all the Four Golden Dharmas of Shangpa in connection with Niguma's empowerment, Innate Union (*lhan cig skyes sbyor*), Nāro's Great Seal, and other teachings. (He also taught at Gyama in 1497, giving many monastic ordinations, the Path and Result, Innate Union Great Seal (*phyag chen lhan cig skyes sbyor*) teachings, and so forth.[166] (He would visit and teach there again in 1502.) The fact that among other tantric systems he also gave various Kagyü teachings indicates the point I made above: a person with a distinct Sakya identity could transmit teachings of different practice lineages without sectarian restraints. This also suggests that Shakya Chokden incorporated into his own teaching style the aforementioned unity of different instruction lineages (29–30).

Notably, during that 1490 visit to Gyama, in a group of ten monks (himself included) he gave vows of a fully ordained nun (*dge slong ma, bhikṣuṇī*) to Chödrup Pelmotso (*chos grub dpal mo 'tsho*)—a Buddhist practitioner from the Gyama ruling family who came to be known as a "fully ordained nun from Gyama" (*rgya ma dge slong ma*).[167] This interesting episode shows that even in the matters of monastic ordination Shakya Chokden held uncommon ideas. A strict follower of monastic rules who knew Vinaya inside and out, he nevertheless found it possible to give a full ordination to a woman—almost an impossible feat during his time in Tibet.

For the annual monastic summer retreat Shakya Chokden went to Langtang (*glang thang*) where he gave the Assembly Dharma (*tshogs chos*)[168] of the Path and Result teachings in the Ngor tradition to about 300 monks. To Gyama leaders and to the young reincarnation of Changlung Rinpoché he gave the complete Path and Result teachings transmitted through Künga Trashi, saying that these were the teachings of Changlung Rinpoché.[169]

In winter at the end of 1490 Shakya Chokden went to Nalendra where he taught both resident and visiting monks Sakya Pendita's *Thorough Clarification of Muni's Intent*[170] and *Thorough Differentiation of the Three Types of Vows*. Also in the assembly hall he gave subsequent permissions of the *One Hundred Means of Accomplishment* (*sgrub thabs brgya rtsa*). Nalendra monks earnestly requested him to become an abbot, but he declined.[171] It is interesting to note that at least as Drölchok presents it, there does not appear to have been any problem with Shakya Chokden teaching the text he "criticized" in the *Good Questions*. The fact that he was requested to become an abbot of one of the main Sakya monastic universities of the time also demonstrates his high standing in the Sakya tradition in general, despite the earlier controversies.

In 1494 in Serdokchen, he was visited by Ünyönpa to whom he gave a week-long Path and Result instruction, *Hevajra in Two Chapters*, and other teachings. Ünyönpa attained high realizations, became a famous master, and was later venerated by Shakya Chokden's students as their guru. By his request Shakya Chokden wrote such texts as the *Guiding Instructions on the Madhyamaka View* mentioned above (35) and the *Abbreviated Meaning of the '[Hevajra in] Two Chapters': Transmission Stages of the Explanatory Lineage.*[172] Later, when Shakya Chokden was seventy-five, Ünyönpa came to visit him in Langtang, and received from him the *Abbreviated Meaning of the '[Hevajra in] Two Chapters'* and the *Drop of Ambrosia: Clarification of the Eight Path Cycles,*[173] also written by his request.[174]

It is important to note that the *Guiding Instructions on the Madhyamaka View* was composed in 1501—many years after Shakya Chokden had developed and clearly articulated his unique approach to Mahāyāna systems. In this text—which primarily focuses on the Niḥsvabhāvavāda view, and more specifically Candrakīrti's approach to realization of reality—Shakya Chokden follows his usual reconciliatory approach to the systems of self-emptiness and other-emptiness, and calls Niḥsvabhāvavādins:

> Followers of the Great Madhyamaka
> Advocating entitylessness—the pinnacle
> Of the four types of proponents of tenets.[175]

As this passage and the text overall demonstrate, he neither despises Niḥsvabhāvavāda, nor stops appreciating its views, nor treats the other-emptiness approach as superior to self-emptiness. This is just one indication among many that Shakya Chokden never changed his view from "self-emptiness" to "other-emptiness," if by that "change" we mean abandoning the former to uphold the latter.[176]

In 1494, Shakya Chokden sent messengers with appeals to many monastic institutions, inviting leading scholars of the time to Serdokchen where he planned extensive teachings on the Tibetan New Year of 1495. A large number of people arrived: about 1,800. Among them there were many scholars, hundreds of students from famous monastic universities, and independent thinkers. Different teachers delivered talks during the day, followed by discussions at night. For about ten days, Shakya Chokden taught on Pramāṇa, Vinaya,

Abhidharma, and other systems, refuting what he saw as their erroneous interpretations. He also taught on different dharmacakras, the differences between interpretations of sūtric and tantric systems by earlier and later Tibetans, and so forth. When teaching on Prāsaṅgika and Svātantrika Madhyamaka, he particularly emphasized separating one's own and others' systems, because in his opinion later Tibetans committed significant mistakes in their interpretations of that subject. When teaching the *Five Dharmas of Maitreya* with Asaṅga's treatises, he tried to bring them back to the level of high standing they deserved, because he believed those works were smeared by those who treated the systems of Prāsaṅgika and Svātantrika as the highest. Also, in contrast to Geluk's explanations of interpretive and definitive (*drang nges*), he elaborated on the way in which the two chariot ways of Niḥsvabhāvavāda and Yogācāra were not contradictory.[177] Shakya Chokden describes those teachings in his *Letter Pleasing Impartial Wise Ones on How Presentations of Turning Dharmacakras have been Accomplished* composed the same year.[178]

The following episode successfully demonstrates Shakya Chokden's general attitude toward his own Sakya tradition around that time and, in particular, his attitude toward his teachers' systems. In 1496, a master Trangpowa (*'phrang po ba*) came from Ü especially in order to receive the Path and Result teachings in the lineage of Künga Trashi. Shakya Chokden told him that he had received a transmission of this Path and Result lineage from Changlung Rinpoché who in turn received it from Künga Trashi himself. He also said that when he expressed worries about practicing this type of Path and Result system after he had received the Path and Result teachings in Künga Zangpo's system, Künga Zangpo told him that he did not see a problem, and that indeed he himself practiced it. Thus, Shakya Chokden continued practicing that system personally. Nevertheless, said Shakya Chokden, since he established the monastic university of Serdokchen, he made it a rule and even sealed a document ordering that in his institution sūtric systems have to be taught on the basis of Rongtön's teachings, and tantric systems on the basis of Ngor teachings of Künga Zangpo. Thus, for two weeks he refused to give Künga Trashi's Path and Result teachings to Trangpowa. After another master Ramdopa (*rab mdo pa*) joined in earnestly requesting him again and again to grant those teachings, Shakya Chokden finally conceded and in secret quickly transmitted only limited instructions of that system.[179]

This episode shows that while freely exploring the depths of Yogācāra teachings, developing his own unique views, and maintaining, practicing, and transmitting outside Serdokchen a variety of tantric teachings, in his own monastic university, Shakya Chokden focused on promoting what he saw as an orthodox Sakya tradition consisting of Künga Zangpo's Path and Result tantric system and Rongtön's sūtric system. In other words, he did not want to jeopardize any part of the mainstream Sakya tradition by teaching something in even mild disagreement with it in his own monastery. Possibly he saw the teachings of Rongtön and Künga Zangpo as the best expression of the Sakya tradition, despite his respect for its other lineages. This suggests an interesting "paradox": despite the fact that Shakya Chokden was open to different lineages of contemplative practice, tantric instructions, and so forth, he had preferences when it came to choosing between different approaches to the *same* tantric system, such as Künga Zangpo's and Künga Trashi's approaches to the Path and Result. He did it possibly, in part, because Künga Zangpo's system was formed as an alternative to earlier approaches to the Path and Result. To downplay the difference between this and earlier approaches would, in effect, contradict the very reason for accepting it. On the other hand, as Shakya Chokden's writings and teachings during the 1495 New Year and at other times demonstrate, he saw *his own* views as a part of the mainstream Sakya system and not conflicting with the teachings of either Rongtön or Künga Zangpo.

By 1501, Shakya Chokden had written most of his sūtric treatises, with the exception of such texts as the histories of Madhyamaka and Pramāṇa and the aforementioned (32) *Opening Doors of a Chest of Gems*, and gave their reading transmission and explanations. The printing of texts was at different times sponsored by the king Trashigön and other sponsors, and Shakya Chokden himself wrote their postscripts (*par byang*). Besides that, when teaching on Yogācāra, Madhyamaka, Mind Training, Vinaya, Chapa's *Collected Topics*, and other systems, he would orally explain different points that had not found their way into his written commentaries.[180]

Around that time Shakya Chokden received a letter from Chödrak Gyamtso informing him that the Karmapa was coming to Ütsang (*dbus gtsang*), requesting him to come quickly to Ü for a consultation on important Buddhist topics, and asking that he compose and send histories of Madhyamaka and Pramāṇa.[181] In 1502, when Shakya Chokden visited Ü with some students, he met the Karmapa in Lhasa and taught on many elements pertaining to the definitive meaning of the two systems. After meeting with the Karmapa, he went to Langtang and Gyama, where he gave empowerments and blessings. Apparently it was the last time he gave teachings in Ü.[182]

In 1503, after the end of the summer retreat, he went to visit Chödrak Gyamtso at Rinpung. He stayed there for a month, acting as a witness to debates between different scholars. The Karmapa also requested that Shakya Chokden correct his *Ocean of Textual Systems of Reasoning Entirely Condensing Streams of All Good Explanations of Valid Cognition*.[183] Shakya Chokden was very busy and asked a scholar Dönyöpa (*don yod pa*) who attended with him to read the text and mark pages that showed either an admixture of other systems or some unusual details. When Dönyöpa finished, Shakya Chokden quickly glanced at the text one morning, and then for some days delivered talks only in relation to that *Ocean of Textual Systems of Reasoning*. Then in the midst of a big gathering, for about a month Shakya Chokden gave discourses on the histories of Madhyamaka and Pramāṇa, which he composed by the Karmapa's request, and on related issues.[184] According to Pawo Tsuklak Trengwa's (*dpa' bo gtsug lag phreng ba*, 1504–1564/1566) *Feast for Scholars: Buddhist History*—which dates the Karmapa's visit to Rinpung to 1502—Shakya Chokden was highly impressed with the Karmapa, received from him many profound teachings, and accepted the Karmapa as his root guru (*rtsa ba'i bla ma, mūlaguru*).[185]

From 1504, Shakya Chokden composed such important tantric treatises as the *Sevenfold Treasury of Gems: Explanation of the Glorious 'Secret Assembly' [Tantra]*,[186] the *Thorough Establishment of the Glorious Original Buddha That Condenses the Essence of All Sūtras and Tantras of the Pronouncement of the Third Dharmacakra*,[187] and so forth.[188]

In 1505, he continuously gave tantric teachings to his disciples and different rulers, and engaged in tantric meditative practices without even minute omissions. He continued giving tantric teachings in 1506: a causal empowerment of Hevajra (*kyee rdo rje'i rgyu dbang*), Nāro Ḍākiṇī (*nāro mkha' spyod*) blessing, and so forth. He ordered the making of Rongtön's statue, as well as images of Tārā and the gurus of the Path and Result. That year he had persistent memories of Dönyö Pelwa and saw him in dreams many times. In 1507 he gave transmissions through reading of the aforementioned (44) *Enjoyment Ocean of the Entirely Good Dharma* and *Opening Doors of a Chest of Gems*; the latter written also in 1507.[189]

On the first day of the sixth lunar month of 1507, from the Dharma throne Shakya Chokden delivered a talk telling Serdokchen monks how fortunate they were: when he himself had studied in his youth, he had to go to various places to learn different systems, while now teachings of all subjects including sciences were readily available in one and the same place—Serdokchen.[190] He passed away a few days later.[191]

Nourished by Shakya Chokden's teachings, multiple scholars and practitioners appeared in the regions of Ngari (*mnga' ris*) in Upper Tibet (*stod*), Dokham (*mdo khams*) in Lower Tibet (*smad*), and Ütsang Ruzhi (*dbus gtsang ru bzhi*) in Middle Tibet (*bar*).[192]

From his early years until his last days, Shakya Chokden actively taught, wrote about, and practiced Buddhism. His remarkable life and teachings made his personality appear unique to many people, including Shakya Chokden. Both he and those around him saw his life as a link in a chain of many rebirths spent in devoted study, practice, and the spreading of Buddhist teachings. He said that he remembered his previous reincarnations as Ngok Lotsawa Loden Sherap (*rngog lo tsā ba blo ldan shes rab*, 1059–1109) and Mapcha Jangchup Tsöndrü. He was also known as a reincarnation of both Yakpa and Baktön—teacher and student. When the Seventh Karmapa and Shakya Chokden saw verses of praise to Shakya Chokden offered to him by Ngodro Rapjampa Wangchuk Pelwa (*ngo gro rab 'byams pa dbang phyug dpal ba*),[193] who implied that Shakya Chokden was a reincarnation of the Karmapa since it was known that Baktön and the Fourth Karmapa Rölpé Dorjé had one mental continuum (*thugs rgyud gcig*), they said that "it did not occur that we were not united in the sphere of thought" (*dgongs pa'i dbyings su mi 'byor ba ma byung*).[194] At another time, Chödrak Gyamtso himself said: "Because I and the great Lord of Dharma have one mind, whichever one [of us you] venerate, [your] wishes will be fulfilled."[195] Nyangtö Rapjampa Lhündrup Pel Zangpo (*nyang stod rab 'byams pa lhun grub dpal bzang po*) perceived Shakya Chokden as a reincarnation of Dignāga, Dharmakīrti, and Ratnākaraśānti. Other people also saw him as an incarnation of different exalted beings.

Shakya Chokden is a fine example of a scholar who underwent a thorough and rigorous scholastic training, learned different systems of thought, and with his own intelligence developed a novel approach to Buddhist systems. When dealing with Madhyamaka in his early works, he concentrated on exploring Niḥsvabhāvavāda, and later turned to Yogācāra writings. Starting in his early fifties, he began explicitly articulating and crystallizing his interpretation of Alīkākāravāda as a legitimate form of Madhyamaka, and working out the ways to reconcile it with Niḥsvabhāvavāda. This crystallization process ended only with his death in 1507.

Notably, in his personal life too, Shakya Chokden's approach to different systems of theory and practice displayed a remarkable encompassing tendency. Turning to tantric meditations did not divert him from writing on Niḥsvabhāvavāda; writing texts on Buddhist logic did not diminish the importance of meditative experience that he would emphasize in those texts, and his emphasis on what he saw as the best approach to his own Sakya system did not divert him from transmitting different practice lineages. The development of Shakya Chokden's views was a continuous life-long project, and his collected works embody a unique, transforming and expanding, but coherent vision.

3. Writings of Shakya Chokden

In this section I provide two lists of Shakya Chokden's works—chronological and topical—in order to demonstrate the breadth of his scholarship, present his works in historical sequence, and point out the main areas that he focused on in his writings. The first list contains only those works whose dates are provided in their colophones and/or the *Detailed Analysis*. The second list contains all Shakya Chokden's works addressed in this book, classifying them on the basis of their main emphases. Because topics addressed in those works are often overlapping, these classificatory categories should not be treated as mutually exclusive.

Chronological List of Shakya Chokden's Works

1447 (fire-female-hare)

Necklace for Clear-Minded Ones: Description of Parts of Realizations of the Lord of Reasoning Gewa Gyeltsen and His Veneration (*Rigs pa'i dbang phyug dge ba rgyal mtshan gyi rtogs pa'i cha shas brjod cing 'dud pa blo gsal gyi mgul rgyan*), vol. 16, 258–260.

1454 (wood-male-dog)

Garlands of Waves of Assertions: Investigation of Connections of Former and Later [Elements in] the 'Ornament of Clear Realizations' Treatise of Quintessential Instructions on the Perfection of Wisdom Together with Its Commentaries, and Placement of the Army of Good Explanations on Difficult Points of Explicit Teachings (*Shes rab kyi pha rol tu phyin pa'i man ngag gi bstan bcos mngon par rtogs pa'i rgyan 'grel pa dang bcas pa'i snga phyi'i 'brel rnam par btsal zhing/ dngos bstan gyi dka' ba'i gnas la legs par bshad pa'i dpung tshogs rnam par bkod pa/ bzhed tshul rba rlabs kyi phreng ba*), vol. 11, 157–587.

Ocean of Meaning of Scriptural Statements: Extensive Explanation of the Body and Branches of the 'Perfection of Wisdom' Sūtras and the 'Ornament of

Clear Realizations' Together with Commentaries (*Shes rab kyi pha rol tu phyin pa'i mdo dang mngon par rtogs pa'i rgyan 'grel dang bcas pa'i lus dang yan lag rgyas par bshad pa lung don rgya mtsho*), vol. 3, 1–161.

Beautifying Ornament of the Lord of Speech: Decisive Analysis in Consequences of the Twenty Kinds of Saṅgha (*Dge 'dun nyi shu'i mtha' rnam par dpyad pa'i thal 'gyur ngag gi dbang po'i mdzes rgyan*), vol. 13, 1–111.

1455 (wood-female-pig)

Feast for the Lord of Speech: Praise to Glorious Places and Persons of Sakya Issuing from [Meanings Expressed by] the Sound [of Its First Letter "Sa"] (*Dpal ldan sa skya'i gnas dang gang zag la sgra las drangs pa'i bstod pa ngag gi dbang po'i dga' ston*), vol. 17, 28–30.

1456 (fire-male-rat)

Drop of Ambrosia: Differentiation of Classes of Tantras (*Rgyud sde'i rnam par phye ba bdud rtsi'i thig pa*), vol. 13, 467–478.

Drumming Sounds amidst Wondrous Clouds: Liberation Story of Glorious Holy Lama Kumāramati (*Dpal ldan bla ma dam pa ku ma ra ma ti'i rnam thar ngo mtshar sprin gyi rnga sgra*), vol. 16, 379–401.

1457 (fire-female-ox)

Explanation of the First Level—[Vows of] Individual Liberation; from Extensive Explanation of the Presentation of the Three Types of Vows (*Sdom gsum gyi rnam par bzhag pa rgya cher bshad pa las/ so sor thar pa'i rim pa dang po rnam par bshad pa*), vol. 6, 285–342.

1459 (earth-female-hare)

Smaller Summarized Exposition [of Madhyamaka] Called 'Vajra of the Lord [of Gods]' Pleasing Clear-Minded Ones (*Stong thun chung ba dbang po'i rdo rje zhes bya ba blo gsal mgu byed*), vol. 4, 433–605.

1468 (earth-male-rat)

Commentary on Essentials of Definitive Meaning: Explanation of [Candrakīrti's] 'Engaging in Madhyamaka' (*Dbu ma la 'jug pa'i rnam par bshad pa nges don gnad kyi ṭī ka*), vol. 5. 281–457.

Necklace for Clear-Minded Ones: Presentation of Time Periods (*Dus tshigs kyi rnam par bzhag pa blo gsal gyi mgul rgyan*), vol. 6, 231–283.

1470 (iron-male-tiger)

Harbor for Fortunate Ones: Explanation of [Nāgārjuna's 'Wisdom:] Root [Stanzas] on Madhyamaka' (*Dbu ma rtsa ba'i rnam bshad bskal bzangs kyi 'jug ngogs*), vol. 5, 1–280.

1471 (iron-female-hare)

Garland of White Lotuses: Agreeing with Sūtras Description of the Array of Positive Qualities of the Land of Bliss and Pure Aspirational Prayers (*Bde ba can gyi zhing gi yon tan gyi bkod pa dang smon lam rnam par dag pa mdo dang 'thun par brjod pa padma dkar po'i phren ba*), vol. 7, 284–301.

Intensive Expansion of Fortune: Praise of the Wondrous Outstanding Munīndra (*Ngo mtshar rmad du byung ba'i thub pa'i dbang po'i bstod pa bkra shis rab rgyas*), vol. 16, 491-494.
Wondrous Divine Drum Melody: Exposition of the Bodhisattva Dwelling in the Land of Tuṣita (*Byang chub sems dpa' dga' ldan gyi gnas na bzhugs pa'i bkod pa ngo mtshar lha'i rnga dbyangs*), vol. 7, 265–284.
Sounds of Brahma's Drum: Praise to the Lord of Dharma [Sakya Pendita] Himself as Superior to Other Teaching Holders (*Chos kyi rje nyid la bstan 'dzin gzhan las khyad par du 'phags par bstod pa tshangs pa'i rnga sgra*), vol. 17, 23–28.
Entrance into Scholarship (*Chos la 'jug pa'i sgo*), vol. 24, 309–320.

1472 (water-male-dragon)

Mirror Captivating Clear-Minded Ones That Clarifies Ornaments of Meaning: Praise to the Teacher Munīndra (*Ston pa thub pa'i dbang po la bstod pa don rgyan gsal ba'i me long blo gsal yid 'phrog*), vol. 16, 495–500.
Moon Chariot: Treatise Clarifying Individual Meanings of Difficult Points of Hundred and One Activities [of Moral Discipline] (*Las brgya rtsa gcig gi dka' gnas so so'i don gsal bar byed pa'i bstan bcos zla ba'i shing rta*), vol. 22, 311–525.

1473 (water-female-snake)

Appearance of Reasoning Defeating Bad Systems: Commentary on Difficult Points of the Extensive Treatise 'Commentary on Valid Cognition' (*Rgyas pa'i bstan bcos tshad ma rnam 'grel gyi dka' 'grel rigs pa'i snang ba lugs ngan pham byed*), vol. 19, 169–445.

1474 (wood-male-horse)

Essence of Sūtras and Tantras: Explanation of the Buddha-Essence (*Sangs rgyas kyi snying po'i rnam bshad mdo rgyud snying po*), vol. 13, 124–136.
Treasury of Immortality: Praise to the Teacher Munīndra in Agreement with His Teachings (*Ston pa thub pa'i dbang po la bstan pa dang mthun par bstod pa 'chi med kyi mdzod*), vol. 16, 487–490.
Drumming Sounds of the Melodious Voice of Brahma: Refutation of Mistakes About Meditative Stages of the Great Madhyamaka and Explanation of the Tenets and Topics of the Views of Prāsaṅgika and Svātantrika (*Dbu ma chen po'i sgom rim la 'khrul pa spong shing thal rang gi grub pa'i mtha' dang lta ba'i gnas rnam par bshad pa tshangs pa'i dbyangs kyi rnga sgra*), vol. 4, 249–373.
Ornament of Intent of the 'Treasure of the Science of Valid Cognition' [Called] 'Defeater of Bad Systems with the Wheel of Scriptural Statements and Reasonings'; Also Called 'Great Destroyer of Mistakes about Logic' (*Tshad ma rigs pa'i gter gyi dgongs rgyan lung dang rigs pa'i 'khor los lugs ngan pham byed pa'am/ ming gzhan rtog ge'i 'khrul 'joms chen mo*), vol. 9, 1–vol. 10, 587.

Ocean of Ambrosia: Treatise Clarifying Words of the Three Bases [of Moral Discipline] (*Gzhi gsum gyi tshig gsal bar byed pa'i bstan 'chos bdud rtsi'i rol mtsho*), vol. 22, 267–302.

Enjoyment Ocean of Faith: Wondrous Liberation Story of the Foremost Venerable Omniscient Spiritual Friend Rongtön Shakya Gyeltsen (*Rje btsun thams cad mkhyen pa bshes gnyen shākya rgyal mtshan gyi rnam thar ngo mtshar dad pa'i rol mtsho*),vol. 16, 299–377.

Sarasvatī's Enjoyment Ocean: Commentary on [Daṇḍin's] 'Mirror of Poetry' (*Snyan ngag me long gi 'grel ba dbyangs can gyi rol mtsho*), vol. 24, 1–67.

Register of Printing [Dharmakīrti's] 'Commentary on Valid Cognition' Text (*Rnam 'grel gyi gzhung par du bsgrub pa'i dkar chag*), vol. 17, 216–220.

Register of Printing [Sakya Pendita's] 'Thorough Differentiation of the Three Types of Vows' Text (*Sdom gsum rab dbye'i gzhung par du bsgrub pa'i dkar chag tu gnang ba*), vol. 17, 222–226.

Register of Printing [Sakya Pendita's] 'Treasure of the Science of Valid Cognition' Text (*Rigs gter gyi gzhung par du sgrub pa'i dkar chag*), vol. 17, 220–222.

Register of Printing the 'Litany of [Ultimate] Names [of Mañjuśrī] (*Mtshan brjod kyi par sgrub pa'i dkar chag*), vol. 17, 226–227.

Register of Printing the 'Perfection of Wisdom' [Sūtra] in Lowo (*Glo bo phar phyin gyi par bzhengs pa'i dkar chag tu gnang ba*), vol. 17, 213–214.

1475 (wood-female-sheep)

Defeater of Flower Arrows: Questions on the 'Bhaiśajyaguru Sūtra' Ritual (*Sman bla'i mdo chog gi dri ba me tog mda' 'joms*), vol. 17, 319–324.

Questions to the Jang Ruler Namgyel Drakpa about Three [Topics of] the Sugata-Essence, [Four Tantras of] Medical Analysis, and Kālacakra (*Byang pa bdag po rnam rgyal grags pa la bde gshegs snying po sman dpyad dus 'khor gsum gyi dri ba*), vol. 17, 325–329.

Good Questions about the 'Thorough Differentiation of the Three Types of Vows' (*Sdom gsum rab dbye la dri ba legs pa*), vol. 17, 448–462.

Drumming Sounds from the Treasury of Immortality: Explanation of the Texts of the 'Extensive Sūtra on Differences between Former Aspirational Prayers of Seven Tathāgatas' and [Related] Rituals (*De bzhin gshegs bdun gyi sngon gyi smon lam gyi khyad par rgyas pa'i mdo dang cho ga'i gzhung gi rnam bshad 'chi med mdzod kyi rnga sgra*), vol. 8, 426–445.

Essence of Logic: Condensed Thatness of [Dignāga's] 'Sūtra on Valid Cognition' and [Dharmakīrti's] Textual System of 'Seven Works' (*Tshad ma'i mdo dang gzhung lugs sde bdun gyi de kho na nyid bsdus pa rtog ge'i snying po*), vol. 18, 1–187.

Chariot of the Sun Illuminating the 'Sūtra': Explanation of Difficult Points of the 'Sūtra on Moral Discipline' (*'Dul ba mdo'i dka' ba'i gnas rnam par bshad pa mdo'i snang byed nyi ma'i shing rta*), vol. 22, 1–265.

1477 (fire-female-bird)

Ocean of Faith: Ascertainment of the Akaniṣṭhaghanavyūha Realm (*'Og min stug po bkod pa'i zhing khams kyi rnam par nges pa dad pa'i rgya mtsho*), vol. 7, 231–264.

Ocean of Scriptural Statements and Reasoning: Treasury of Ascertainment of Mahāyāna Madhyamaka (*Theg pa chen po dbu ma rnam par nges pa'i bang mdzod lung dang rigs pa'i rgya mtsho*), vol. 14, 341–vol. 15, 695.

Praise to Mañjuśrī Which Agrees with Clear Realizations [of the 'Litany of Ultimate Names of Mañjuśrī'] (*'Jam dpal gyi bstod pa mngon rtogs dang mthun pa*), vol. 16, 501–503.

Quintessential Instructions on the Correct Reading of the 'Litany of Ultimate Names of the Foremost Venerable [Mañjuśrī]jñānasattva' (*Rje btsun ye shes sems dpa'i don dam pa'i mtshan yang dag par brjod pa tshul bzhin du klag pa'i man ngag*), vol. 8, 275–320.

Stanzas for Offering Seven Royal Attributes and Seven Gems (*Rgyal srid sna bdun dang/ rin chen sna bdun 'bul ba'i tshigs bcad*), vol. 17, 314–317.

Enjoyment Ocean of Scriptural Statements and Reasoning Differentiating One's Own and Others' Tenets: Explanation of Difficult Points of the 'Ornament of Clear Realizations' Treatise of Quintessential Instructions on the Perfection of Wisdom Together with Its Commentaries (*Shes rab kyi pha rol tu phyin pa'i man ngag gi bstan bcos mngon par rtogs pa'i rgyan 'grel pa dang bcas pa'i dka' ba'i gnas rnams rnam par bshad pa rang gzhan gyi grub mtha' rnam par dbye ba lung rigs kyi rol mtsho*), vol. 1–vol. 2, 1–469.

1478 (earth-male-dog)

Entrance into the 'Dharmas of Maitreya': Explanation of the Aspirational Prayer Made by Ārya Maitreya (*'Phags pa byams pas btab pa'i smon lam gyi rnam par bshad pa byams pa'i chos la 'jug pa'i sgo*), vol. 8, 403–426.

Harbor of the Ocean of Faith: Extensive Explanation of the 'King of Aspirational Prayers of Deeds of Ārya Samantabhadra' (*'Phags pa kun tu bzangs po'i spyod pa'i smon lam gyi rgyal po'i rgya cher bshad pa dad pa rgya mtsho'i 'jug ngogs*), vol. 8, 352–403.

1479 (earth-female-pig)

Ascertainment of the Dharma-Sphere: Explanation of [Nāgārjuna's] Treatise 'Praise of the Dharma-Sphere' (*Chos kyi dbyings su bstod pa zhes bya ba'i bstan bcos kyi rnam par bshad pa chos kyi dbyings rnam par nges pa*), vol. 7, 303–346.

Garlands of Waves of the Ocean of Yogācāras' Scriptures: Explanation of the Holy Dharma of [Asaṅga's] 'Summary of Higher Knowledge' (*Dam pa'i chos ngon pa kun las btus pa'i rnam par bshad pa rnal 'byor spyod gzhung rgya mtsho'i rlabs kyi phreng ba*), vol. 14, 1–339.

Music of a Wondrous Discourse: Summary of the Ways of Maintaining the Teachings by the Great Ngok Lotsawa [Loden Sherap] (*Rngog lo tsā ba chen pos bstan pa ji ltar bskyangs tshul mdo tsam du bya ba ngo mthsar gtam gyi rol mo*), vol. 16, 443–456.

1480 (iron-male-rat)

Essence of the Ocean of Scriptural Teachings: Condensation of Desiderata of General Meaning of the 'Ornament of Clear Realizations' with Its Commentaries (*Mngon par rtogs pa'i rgyan 'grel pa dang bcas pa'i spyi'i don nyer mkho bsdus pa lung chos rgya mtsho'i snying po*), vol. 3, 163–561.

1481 (iron-female-ox)

Golden Lancet: Resolved Abundant Discourse on the 'Thorough Differentiation of the Three Types of Vows' Treatise (*Sdom gsum gyi rab tu dbye ba'i bstan bcos kyi 'bel gtam rnam par nges pa legs bshad gser gyi thur ma*), vol. 6, 439–vol. 7, 229.

1482 (water-male-tiger)

Enjoyment Ocean of the Speech of the 'Seven Works': Explanation of the 'Treasure of the Science of Valid Cognition' (*Tshad ma rigs pa'i gter gyi rnam par bshad pa sde bdun ngag gi rol mtsho*), vol. 19, 447–749.

Thorough Clarification of Definitive Commitments: Answers to Objections to [Drakpa Gyeltsen's] 'Elimination of Mistakes [Regarding Root Downfalls]' (*'Khrul spong gi brgal lan rnam par nges pa'i dam tshig rab tu gsal ba*), vol. 23, 105–295.

Ascertainment of Secrecy of the Three Tantras: Extensive Explanation of the 'Sūtra on Taking the Result as the Path' (*'Bras bu lam byed kyi mdo'i rgya cher bshad pa rgyud gsum gyi gsang ba rnam nges*), vol. 13, 485–521.

1485 (wood-female-snake)

Enjoyment Ocean of the Altruistic Melody: Explanation of [Parahitaghoṣāraṇyaka's] Treatise Called 'Seventy Stanzas on Aspirational Prayers' (*Smon lam bdun cu pa zhes pa'i bstan bcos kyi rnam par bshad pa gzhan phan pa'i dbyangs kyi rol mo*), vol. 24, 151–232.

1486 (fire-male-horse)

Divine Drum Melody: Praise of the Great Kashmiri Paṇḍita Śākyaśri (*Kha che paṇ chen shākya shri'i bstod pa lha'i rnga dbyangs*), vol. 16, 556–557.

Beautifully Woven Garlands of Wondrous Deeds of Glorious Atiśa with His [Spiritual] Sons and Lineage (*Dpal ldan a ti sha sras dang brgyud par bcas pa'i ngo mtshar mdzad pa'i phreng ba spel legs*), vol. 16, 538–550.

Great Ocean of Particularized Explanations: Treatise Explaining Difficult Points of [Vasubandhu's] 'Treasury of Higher Knowledge' (*Chos mngon pa'i mdzod kyi dka' ba'i gnas rnam par bshad pa'i bstan bcos bye brag tu bshad pa'i mtsho chen po*), vol. 20, 1–vol. 21, 355.

1488 (earth-male-monkey)

Enjoyment Ocean of the Entirely Good Dharma: Explanation of the Extensive Treatise 'Commentary on Valid Cognition' (*Rgyas pa'i bstan bcos tshad ma rnam 'grel gyi rnam bshad kun bzang chos kyi rol mtsho*), vol. 18, 189–693.

1489 (earth-female-bird)

Rain of Ambrosia: Extensive [Auto-]Commentary on the 'Profound Thunder amidst the Clouds of the Ocean of Definitive Meaning' (*Nges don rgya mtsho sprin gyi 'brug sgra zab mo'i rgyas 'grel bdud rtsi'i char 'bebs*), vol. 2, 471–616.

[Nameless], vol. 17, 111–113.

1491 (iron-female-pig)

Key to Essential Points of Definitive Meaning: Modes of Identification of Individual Views—Answers to the Questions of the Great Meditator Yeshé Zangpo (*Sgom chen ye shes bzang po'i dris lan lta ba so so'i ngos 'dzin tshul nges don gnad kyi lde mig*), vol. 23, 99–104.

1495 (wood-female-hare)

Letter Pleasing Impartial Wise Ones on How Presentations of Turning Dharmacakras have been Accomplished (*Chos kyi 'khor lo bskor ba'i rnam gzhag ji ltar grub pa'i yi ge gzu bor gnas pa'i mdzangs pa dga' byed*), vol. 16, 457–482.

Liberation Story of the Foremost Venerable Holy Amoghaśrībhadra That Induces Devotion of All Fortunate Beings (*Rje btsun dam pa a mo gha shrī bha tra'i rnam par thar ba skal bzang skye rgu'i dang ba 'dren byed*), vol. 17, 43–62.

1496 (fire-male-dragon)

[Nameless], vol. 17, 116–117.

1499 (earth-female-sheep)

Ornament of Intents of Quintessential Instructions: Answers to the Questions from [Tsongkhapa's] 'Questions [Based on] Purely White Supreme Motivation' (*Dri ba lhag bsam rab dkar gyi dris lan man ngag gi dgongs rgyan*), vol. 23, 297–358.

Great Path Compressing the Two Chariot Ways into One: Explanation of [Maitreya's] 'Ornament of Clear Realizations' Together with [Haribhadra's] 'Clear Meaning' Commentary (*Mngon par rtogs pa'i rgyan 'grel pa don gsal ba dang bcas pa'i rnam par bshad pa shing rta'i srol gnyis gcig tu bsdus pa'i lam po che*), vol. 12, 1–319.

1500 (iron-male-monkey)

Garland of Trees Fulfilling All Wishes: Explanation of [Ngok Loden Sherap's] Letter 'Drop of Ambrosia' (*Spring yig bdud rtsi'i thigs pa'i rnam bshad dpag bsam yongs 'du'i ljon phreng*), vol. 24, 320–348.

1501 (iron-female-bird)

Appearance of the Sun Pleasing All Thinkers: Discussion of the History of the Chariot Ways of [Dignāga's] 'Sūtra on Valid Cognition' and [Its] Treatises (*Tshad ma'i bstan bcos kyi shin rta'i srol rnams ji ltar 'byung ba'i tshul gtam du bya ba nyin mor byed pa'i snang bas dpyod ldan mtha' dag dga' bar byed pa*), vol. 19, 1–137.

Garlands of Wondrous Ornaments of the Union of Calm Abiding and Special Insight: Guiding Instructions on the Madhyamaka View (*Dbu ma'i lta khrid/ zhi gnas dang lhag mthong zung du 'jug pa ngo mtshar rgyan gyi phreng ba*). In *'Hundred and Eight Dharma Sections' Treatise* (*Chos tshan brgya dang brgyad pa zhes bya ba'i bstan bcos*), vol. 13. 190–202.

1502 (water-male-dog)

'Hundred and Eight Dharma Sections' Treatise (*Chos tshan brgya dang brgyad pa zhes bya ba'i bstan bcos*), vol. 13, 159–462.

[Nameless], vol. 17, 204–207.

1503 (water-female-pig)

Seventeen Wondrous Answers to the Questions of the Whole Monastic Community of Zi Samdrupling (*Gzi bsam 'grub gling pa'i dge 'dun spyi'i dris lan ya mtshan bcu bdun pa*), vol. 23, 418–473.

Sun Benefiting Others That Dispels External and Internal Darkness: Notes Thoroughly Clarifying the Five Stages of the Glorious 'Secret Assembly' [Tantra] (*Dpal gsang ba 'dus pa'i rim pa lnga rab tu gsal bar byed pa'i brjed byang phyi nang gi mun pa sel byed gzhan la phan pa'i nyi ma*), vol. 23, 496–518.

Ascertainment of Intents of Supreme Accomplished Ones: Treatise on Differentiation of the Great Seal (*Phyag rgya chen po'i shan 'byed kyi bstan bcos grub pa mchog gi dgongs pa rnam nges*), vol. 17, 346–355.

1504 (wood-male-rat)

Sevenfold Treasury of Gems: Explanation of the Glorious 'Secret Assembly' [Tantra] (*Dpal gsang ba 'dus pa'i rnam bshad rin po che'i gter mdzod bdun pa*), vol. 7, 405–612.

Continuous Meter Praise of the Gathering of Deities of the Support and Supported [Maṇḍala] of Cakrasaṃvara (*Rten dang brten par bcas pa'i 'khor lo bde mchog gi lha tshogs la rgyun chags pa'i sdeb sbyor gyi sgo nas bstod pa*), vol. 8, 1–10.

Threefold Precious Treasury: Treatise of Quintessential Instructions Combining the Three [Types of Kālacakra]—External, Internal, and Alternative (*Phyi nang gzhan gsum sbyor ba'i man ngag gi bstan bcos rin chen gter mdzod gsum pa*), vol. 8, 219–226.

Fifty-One Sections of Definitive Meaning: Abbreviated Meaning of the 'Thorough Establishment of the Glorious Original Buddha' Treatise (*Dpal dang po'i sangs rgyas rab du grub pa zhes bya ba'i bstan bcos kyi bsdus pa'i don nges don gyi tshoms lnga bcu rtsa gcig zhes bya ba*), vol. 8, 187–193.

1505 (wood-female-ox)

Thorough Establishment of the Glorious Original Buddha: [Treatise] Condensing the Essence of All Sūtras and Tantras of the Pronouncement of the Third Dharmacakra (*Dpal dang po'i sangs rgyas rab tu grub pas bka' 'khor lo gsum pa'i mdo dang rgyud sde kun gyi snying po bsdus pa*), vol. 8, 10–183.

1506 (fire-male-tiger)

Answer to the Inquiry Regarding Identification of the Support and Supported [Maṇḍala] of Raktayamāri (*Gshed dmar gyi rten dang brten par bcas pa'i ngos 'dzin gyi zhus lan*), vol. 17, 606–608.

1507 (fire-female-hare)

Opening Doors of a Chest of Gems: Treatise Elucidating Stages of the Path of the 'Five Dharmas of Maitreya' (*Byams chos lnga'i lam gyi rim pa gsal bar byed pa'i bstan bcos rin chen sgrom gyi sgo 'byed*), vol. 11, 39–149.

[Nameless], vol. 17, 471–472.

Topical Divisions of Shakya Chokden's Works Addressed in This Book

BIOGRAPHIES AND HISTORIES

Appearance of the Sun Pleasing All Thinkers: Discussion of the History of the Chariot Ways of [Dignāga's] 'Sūtra on Valid Cognition' and [Its] Treatises (*Tshad ma'i bstan bcos kyi shin rta'i srol rnams ji ltar 'byung ba'i tshul gtam du bya ba nyin mor byed pa'i snang bas dpyod ldan mtha' dag dga' bar byed pa*), vol. 19, 1–137.

Beautifully Woven Garlands of Wondrous Deeds of Glorious Atiśa with His [Spiritual] Sons and Lineage (*Dpal ldan a ti sha sras dang brgyud par bcas pa'i ngo mtshar mdzad pa'i phreng ba spel legs*), vol. 16, 538–550.

Drumming Sounds amidst Wondrous Clouds: Liberation Story of Glorious Holy Lama Kumāramati (*Dpal ldan bla ma dam pa ku ma ra ma ti'i rnam thar ngo mtshar sprin gyi rnga sgra*), vol. 16, 379–401.

Music of a Wondrous Discourse: Summary of the Ways of Maintaining the Teachings by the Great Ngok Lotsawa [Loden Sherap] (*Rngog lo tsā ba chen pos bstan pa ji ltar bskyangs tshul mdo tsam du bya ba ngo mthsar gtam gyi rol mo*), vol. 16, 443–456.

Liberation Story of the Foremost Venerable Holy Amoghaśrībhadra That Induces Devotion of All Fortunate Beings (*Rje btsun dam pa a mo gha shrī bha tra'i rnam par thar ba skal bzang skye rgu'i dang ba 'dren byed*), vol. 17, 43–62.

Letter Pleasing Impartial Wise Ones on How Presentations of Turning Dharmacakras have been Accomplished (*Chos kyi 'khor lo bskor ba'i rnam gzhag ji ltar grub pa'i yi ge gzu bor gnas pa'i mdzangs pa dga' byed*), vol. 16, 457–482.

Enjoyment Ocean of Faith: Wondrous Liberation Story of the Foremost Venerable Omniscient Spiritual Friend Rongtön Shakya Gyeltsen (*Rje btsun thams cad mkhyen pa bshes gnyen shākya rgyal mtshan gyi rnam thar ngo mtshar dad pa'i rol mtsho*), vol. 16, 299–377.
Wish Fulfilling Meru: Discourse on the History of Madhyamaka (*Dbu ma'i byung tshul rnam par bshad pa'i gtam yid bzhin lhun po*), vol. 4, 209–248.

DESCRIPTIONS OF PURE LANDS AND THEIR INHABITANTS

Garland of White Lotuses: Agreeing with Sūtras Description of the Array of Positive Qualities of the Land of Bliss and Pure Aspirational Prayers (*Bde ba can gyi zhing gi yon tan gyi bkod pa dang smon lam rnam par dag pa mdo dang 'thun par brjod pa padma dkar po'i phren ba*), vol. 7, 284–301.
Ocean of Faith: Ascertainment of the Akaniṣṭhaghanavyūha Realm (*'Og min stug po bkod pa'i zhing khams kyi rnam par nges pa dad pa'i rgya mtsho*), vol. 7, 231–264.
Wondrous Divine Drum Melody: Exposition of the Bodhisattva Dwelling in the Land of Tuṣita (*Byang chub sems dpa' dga' ldan gyi gnas na bzhugs pa'i bkod pa ngo mtshar lha'i rnga dbyangs*), vol. 7, 265–284.

DEVOTIONAL WRITINGS, POETRY, AND COMMENTARIES ON DEVOTIONAL WRITINGS

Continuous Meter Praise of the Gathering of Deities of the Support and Supported [Maṇḍala] of Cakrasaṃvara (*Rten dang brten par bcas pa'i 'khor lo bde mchog gi lha tshogs la rgyun chags pa'i sdeb sbyor gyi sgo nas bstod pa*), vol. 8, 1–10.
Divine Drum Melody: Praise of the Great Kashmiri Paṇḍita Śākyaśri (*Kha che paṇ chen shākya shri'i bstod pa lha'i rnga dbyangs*), vol. 16, 556–557.
Drumming Sounds from the Treasury of Immortality: Explanation of the Texts of the 'Extensive Sūtra on Differences between Former Aspirational Prayers of Seven Tathāgatas' and [Related] Rituals (*De bzhin gshegs bdun gyi sngon gyi smon lam gyi khyad par rgyas pa'i mdo dang cho ga'i gzhung gi rnam bshad 'chi med mdzod kyi rnga sgra*), vol. 8, 426–445.
Enjoyment Ocean of the Altruistic Melody: Explanation of [Parahitaghoṣāraṇyaka's] Treatise Called 'Seventy Stanzas on Aspirational Prayers' (*Smon lam bdun cu pa zhes pa'i bstan bcos kyi rnam par bshad pa gzhan phan pa'i dbyangs kyi rol mo*), vol. 24, 151–232.
Entrance into the 'Dharmas of Maitreya': Explanation of the Aspirational Prayer Made by Ārya Maitreya (*'Phags pa byams pas btab pa'i smon lam gyi rnam par bshad pa byams pa'i chos la 'jug pa'i sgo*), vol. 8, 403–426.

Harbor of the Ocean of Faith: Extensive Explanation of the 'King of Aspirational Prayers of Deeds of Ārya Samantabhadra' (*'Phags pa kun tu bzangs po'i spyod pa'i smon lam gyi rgyal po'i rgya cher bshad pa dad pa rgya mtsho'i 'jug ngogs*), vol. 8, 352–403.

Feast for the Lord of Speech: Praise to Glorious Places and Persons of Sakya Issuing from [Meanings Expressed by] the Sound [of Its First Letter "Sa"] (*Dpal ldan sa skya'i gnas dang gang zag la sgra las drangs pa'i bstod pa ngag gi dbang po'i dga' ston*), vol. 17, 28–30.

Intensive Expansion of Fortune: Praise of the Wondrous Outstanding Munīndra (*Ngo mtshar rmad du byung ba'i thub pa'i dbang po'i bstod pa bkra shis rab rgyas*), vol. 16, 491–494.

Mirror Captivating Clear-Minded Ones That Clarifies Ornaments of Meaning: Praise to the Teacher Munīndra (*Ston pa thub pa'i dbang po la bstod pa don rgyan gsal ba'i me long blo gsal yid 'phrog*), vol. 16, 495–500.

[Nameless], vol. 17, 471–472.

Necklace for Clear-Minded Ones: Description of Parts of Realizations of the Lord of Reasoning Gewa Gyeltsen and His Veneration (*Rigs pa'i dbang phyug dge ba rgyal mtshan gyi rtogs pa'i cha shas brjod cing 'dud pa blo gsal gyi mgul rgyan*), vol. 16, 258–260.

Treasury of Immortality: Praise to the Teacher Munīndra in Agreement with His Teachings (*Ston pa thub pa'i dbang po la bstan pa dang mthun par bstod pa 'chi med kyi mdzod*), vol. 16, 487–490.

Praise to Mañjuśrī Which Agrees with Clear Realizations [of the 'Litany of Ultimate Names of Mañjuśrī'] (*'Jam dpal gyi bstod pa mngon rtogs dang mthun pa*), vol. 16, 501–503.

Praise to the Great Paṇḍita Loten the Fourth (*Paṇ chen blo brtan bzhi pa la bstod pa*), vol. 16, 266–267.

Prayers and Numerous Songs of Contemplative Experience (*Gsol 'debs dang mgur 'bum gyi skor*), vol. 17, 463–472.

Quintessential Instructions on the Correct Reading of the 'Litany of Ultimate Names of the Foremost Venerable [Mañjuśrī]jñānasattva' (*Rje btsun ye shes sems dpa'i don dam pa'i mtshan yang dag par brjod pa tshul bzhin du klag pa'i man ngag*), vol. 8, 275–320.

Shakwangma (*Shāk dbang ma*), vol. 8, 448–450.

Sounds of Brahma's Drum: Praise to the Lord of Dharma [Sakya Pendita] Himself as Superior to Other Teaching Holders (*Chos kyi rje nyid la bstan 'dzin gzhan las khyad par du 'phags par bstod pa tshangs pa'i rnga sgra*), vol. 17, 23–28.

White Lotus Garland of Ascertainment of Oral Instructions of the Pervasive Lord Vajrasattva: [Treatise Providing] an Easy Understanding of the 'Praise of Nairātmyā''s Commentary (*Bdag med bstod 'grel gyi go sla khyab bdag rdo rje sems dpa'i zhal lung rnam par nges pa padma dkar *po'i 'phreng ba*). In *'Hundred and Eight Dharma Sections' Treatise* (*Chos tshan brgya dang brgyad pa zhes bya ba'i bstan bcos*), vol. 13, 345–386.

LOGIC AND EPISTEMOLOGY

Appearance of Reasoning Defeating Bad Systems: Commentary on Difficult Points of the Extensive Treatise 'Commentary on Valid Cognition' (*Rgyas pa'i bstan bcos tshad ma rnam 'grel gyi dka' 'grel rigs pa'i snang ba lugs ngan pham byed*), vol. 19, 169–445.

Dispelling Mental Darkness: Abridgement of the Modes of Inducing Ascertainment by Valid Cognition (*Tshad mas nges pa 'dren pa'i tshul nyung ngur bsdus pa yid kyi mun sel*), vol. 19, 146–155.

Enjoyment Ocean of the Entirely Good Dharma: Explanation of the Extensive Treatise 'Commentary on Valid Cognition' (*Rgyas pa'i bstan bcos tshad ma rnam 'grel gyi rnam bshad kun bzang chos kyi rol mtsho*), vol. 18, 189–693.

Enjoyment Ocean of the Speech of the 'Seven Works': Explanation of the 'Treasure of the Science of Valid Cognition' (*Tshad ma rigs pa'i gter gyi rnam par bshad pa sde bdun ngag gi rol mtsho*), vol. 19, 447–749.

Essence of Logic: Condensed Thatness of [Dignāga's] 'Sūtra on Valid Cognition' and [Dharmakīrti's] Textual System of 'Seven Works' (*Tshad ma'i mdo dang gzhung lugs sde bdun gyi de kho na nyid bsdus pa rtog ge'i snying po*), vol. 18, 1–187.

Great Ocean of Particularized Explanations: Treatise Explaining Difficult Points of [Vasubandhu's] 'Treasury of Higher Knowledge' (*Chos mngon pa'i mdzod kyi dka' ba'i gnas rnam par bshad pa'i bstan bcos bye brag tu bshad pa'i mtsho chen po*), vol. 20, 1–vol. 21, 355.

Ornament of Intent of the 'Treasure of the Science of Valid Cognition' [Called] 'Defeater of Bad Systems with the Wheel of Scriptural Statements and Reasonings'; Also Called 'Great Destroyer of Mistakes about Logic' (*Tshad ma rigs pa'i gter gyi dgongs rgyan lung dang rigs pa'i 'khor los lugs ngan pham byed pa'am/ ming gzhan rtog ge'i 'khrul 'joms chen mo*), vol. 9, 1–vol. 10, 587.

MISCELLANEOUS TOPICS

Answers to Three Universally Known Questions from the 'One Hundred and Eight Questions on the 'Thorough Differentiation of the Three Types of Vows'' (*Sdom pa gsum gyi rab dbye'i dri ba brgya dang brgyad las kun la grags che ba'i dri ba gsum gyi lan gdabs pa*), vol. 17, 381–401.

Discourse Eliminating Mistakes with Regard to Teachings of Scriptural Collections: Fourteen Dharma Sections (*Sde snod kyi chos la 'khrul pa *sel ba'i gtam chos tshan bcu bzhi pa*). In *'Hundred and Eight Dharma Sections' Treatise* (*Chos tshan brgya dang brgyad pa zhes bya ba'i bstan bcos*), vol. 13, 202–229.

Explanation of [Sakya Pendita's] 'Entrance into Scholarship' Together with Answers to Questions (*Mkhas pa la 'jug pa'i sgo'i rnam bshad dri lan dang bcas pa*), vol. 24, 67–149.

Golden Lancet: Resolved Abundant Discourse on the 'Thorough Differentiation of the Three Types of Vows' Treatise (*Sdom gsum gyi rab tu dbye ba'i bstan bcos kyi 'bel gtam rnam par nges pa legs bshad gser gyi thur ma*), vol. vol. 6, 439–vol. 7, 229.

Good Questions about the 'Thorough Differentiation of the Three Types of Vows' (*Sdom gsum rab dbye la dri ba legs pa*), vol. 17, 448–462.

'Hundred and Eight Dharma Sections' Treatise (*Chos tshan brgya dang brgyad pa zhes bya ba'i bstan bcos*), vol. 13, 159–462.

Meaningful to Behold: Answers to the Questions of Spiritual Friend Müpa Rapjampa (*Bshes gnyen mus pa rab 'byams pa'i dri lan mthong ba don ldan*), vol. 23, 297–418.

Mirror Clarifying Individual Texts: Presentation of the Views, Meditations, and Actions of Earlier and Later Great Beings of the Land of Snows (*Gangs can gyi chen po snga phyir byon pa'i lta sgom spyod pa'i rnam bzhag rang gzhung gsal ba'i me long*), vol. 23, 78–99.

Key to Essential Points of Definitive Meaning: Modes of Identification of Individual Views—Answers to the Questions of the Great Meditator Yeshé Zangpo (*Sgom chen ye shes bzang po'i dris lan lta ba so so'i ngos 'dzin tshul nges don gnad kyi lde mig*), vol. 23, 99–104.

Ornament of Intents of Quintessential Instructions: Answers to the Questions from [Tsongkhapa's] 'Questions [Based on] Purely White Supreme Motivation' (*Dri ba lhag bsam rab dkar gyi dris lan man ngag gi dgongs rgyan*), vol. 23, 297–358.

Questions to the Jang Ruler Namgyel Drakpa about Three [Topics of] the Sugata-Essence, [Four Tantras of] Medical Analysis, and Kālacakra (*Byang pa bdag po rnam rgyal grags pa la bde gshegs snying po sman dpyad dus 'khor gsum gyi dri ba*), vol. 17, 325–329.

Precious Treasury of the Condensed Essence of the Profound and Extensive in Eight Dharma Sections (*Zab rgya'i snying po bsdus pa rin chen gter mdzod chos tshan brgyad pa*). In *'Hundred and Eight Dharma Sections' Treatise* (*Chos tshan brgya dang brgyad pa zhes bya ba'i bstan bcos*), vol. 13, 166–190.

Seventeen Wondrous Answers to the Questions of the Whole Monastic Community of Zi Samdrupling (*Gzi bsam 'grub gling pa'i dge 'dun spyi'i dris lan ya mtshan bcu bdun pa*), vol. 23, 418–475.

NON-TANTRIC RITUALS

Defeater of Flower Arrows: Questions on the 'Bhaiśajyaguru Sūtra' Ritual (*Sman bla'i mdo chog gi dri ba me tog mda' 'joms*), vol. 17, 319–324.

Stanzas for Offering Seven Royal Attributes and Seven Gems (*Rgyal srid sna bdun dang/ rin chen sna bdun 'bul ba'i tshigs bcad*), vol. 17, 314–317.

POSTSCRIPTS AND SHORT MESSAGES

[Nameless], vol. 17, 111–113.

[Nameless], vol. 17, 116–117.

[Nameless], vol. 17, 204–207.

[Nameless], vol. 17, 307–309.

Register of Printing [Dharmakīrti's] 'Commentary on Valid Cognition' Text (*Rnam 'grel gyi gzhung par du bsgrub pa'i dkar chag*), vol. 17, 216–220.

Register of Printing [Sakya Pendita's] 'Thorough Differentiation of the Three Types of Vows' Text (*Sdom gsum rab dbye'i gzhung par du bsgrub pa'i dkar chag tu gnang ba*), vol. 17, 222–226.

Register of Printing [Sakya Pendita's] 'Treasure of the Science of Valid Cognition' Text (*Rigs gter gyi gzhung par du sgrub pa'i dkar chag*), vol. 17, 220–222.

Register of Printing the 'Litany of [Ultimate] Names [of Mañjuśrī]' (*Mtshan brjod kyi par sgrub pa'i dkar chag*), vol. 17, 226–227.

Register of Printing the 'Perfection of Wisdom' [Sūtra] in Lowo (*Glo bo phar phyin gyi par bzhengs pa'i dkar chag tu gnang ba*), vol. 17, 213–214.

PRAJÑĀPĀRAMITĀ WRITINGS

Beautifying Ornament of the Lord of Speech: Decisive Analysis in Consequences of the Twenty Kinds of Saṅgha (*Dge 'dun nyi shu'i mtha' rnam par dpyad pa'i thal 'gyur ngag gi dbang po'i mdzes rgyan*), vol. 13, 1–111.

Enjoyment Ocean of Scriptural Statements and Reasoning Differentiating One's Own and Others' Tenets: Explanation of Difficult Points of the 'Ornament of Clear Realizations' Treatise of Quintessential Instructions on the Perfection of Wisdom Together with Its Commentaries (*Shes rab kyi pha rol tu phyin pa'i man ngag gi bstan bcos mngon par rtogs pa'i rgyan 'grel pa dang bcas pa'i dka' ba'i gnas rnams rnam par bshad pa rang gzhan gyi grub mtha' rnam par dbye ba lung rigs kyi rol mtsho*), vol. 1, 9–vol. 2, 469.

Essence of the Ocean of Scriptural Teachings: Condensation of Desiderata of General Meaning of the 'Ornament of Clear Realizations' with Its

Commentaries (*Mngon par rtogs pa'i rgyan 'grel pa dang bcas pa'i spyi'i don nyer mkho bsdus pa lung chos rgya mtsho'i snying po*), vol. 3, 163–561.

Garlands of Waves of Assertions: Investigation of Connections of Former and Later [Elements in] the 'Ornament of Clear Realizations' Treatise of Quintessential Instructions on the Perfection of Wisdom Together with Its Commentaries, and Placement of the Army of Good Explanations on Difficult Points of Explicit Teachings (*Shes rab kyi pha rol tu phyin pa'i man ngag gi bstan bcos mngon par rtogs pa'i rgyan 'grel pa dang bcas pa'i snga phyi'i 'brel rnam par btsal zhing/ dngos bstan gyi dka' ba'i gnas la legs par bshad pa'i dpung tshogs rnam par bkod pa/ bzhed tshul rba rlabs kyi phreng ba*), vol. 11, 157–587.

Great Path Compressing the Two Chariot Ways into One: Explanation of [Maitreya's] 'Ornament of Clear Realizations' Together with [Haribhadra's] 'Clear Meaning' Commentary (*Mngon par rtogs pa'i rgyan 'grel pa don gsal ba dang bcas pa'i rnam par bshad pa shing rta'i srol gnyis gcig tu bsdus pa'i lam po che*), vol. 12, 1–319.

Ocean of Meaning of Scriptural Statements: Extensive Explanation of the Body and Branches of the 'Perfection of Wisdom' Sūtras and the 'Ornament of Clear Realizations' Together with Commentaries (*Shes rab kyi pha rol tu phyin pa'i mdo dang mngon par rtogs pa'i rgyan 'grel dang bcas pa'i lus dang yan lag rgyas par bshad pa lung don rgya mtsho*), vol. 3, 1–161.

TANTRIC WRITINGS

Abbreviated Meaning of the '[Hevajra in] Two Chapters': Transmission Stages of the Explanatory Lineage (*Brtag gnyis kyi bsdus don// bshad rgyud kyi rgyud pa'i rim pa rnams*), vol. 13, 463–467.

Answer to the Inquiry Regarding Identification of the Support and Supported [Maṇḍala] of Raktayamāri (*Gshed dmar gyi rten dang brten par bcas pa'i ngos 'dzin gyi zhus lan*), vol. 17, 606–608.

Ascertainment of Intents of Supreme Accomplished Ones: Treatise on Differentiation of the Great Seal (*Phyag rgya chen po'i shan 'byed kyi bstan bcos grub pa mchog gi dgongs pa rnam nges*), vol. 17, 346–355.

Ascertainment of Secrecy of the Three Tantras: Extensive Explanation of the 'Sūtra on Taking the Result as the Path' (*'Bras bu lam byed kyi mdo'i rgya cher bshad pa rgyud gsum gyi gsang ba rnam nges*), vol. 13, 485–521.

Ascertainment of Intents of Mighty Lords: [Treatise in] Eleven Dharma Sections Eliminating Mistakes Regarding Hidden Meanings of Oral Lineages (*Snyan rgyud gyi sbas don la 'khrul pa spong ba mthu stobs dbang phyug gi dgongs pa rnam nges chos tshan bcu gcig pa*). In *'Hundred and Eight*

Dharma Sections' Treatise (*Chos tshan brgya dang brgyad pa zhes bya ba'i bstan bcos*), vol. 13, 274–300.

Clarification of Acceptance and Rejection Regarding the Profound Path: [Treatise in] Thirteen Dharma Sections on Differentiation of Incorporation into Experience of Mantra by Outsiders [non-Buddhists] and Insiders [Buddhists] (*Phyi nang gi sngags kyi nyams len so sor phye ba zab lam blang dor gsal byed chos tshan bcu gsum*). In *'Hundred and Eight Dharma Sections' Treatise* (*Chos tshan brgya dang brgyad pa zhes bya ba'i bstan bcos*), vol. 13, 428–458.

Drop of Ambrosia: Clarification of the Eight Path Cycles (*Lam skor brgyad kyi gsal byed bdud rtsi'i thig pa*), vol. 13, 630–640.

Drop of Ambrosia: Differentiation of Classes of Tantras (*Rgyud sde'i rnam par phye ba bdud rtsi'i thig pa*), vol. 13, 467–478.

Fifty-One Sections of Definitive Meaning: Abbreviated Meaning of the 'Thorough Establishment of the Glorious Original Buddha' Treatise (*Dpal dang po'i sangs rgyas rab du grub pa zhes bya ba'i bstan bcos kyi bsdus pa'i don nges don gyi tshoms lnga bcu rtsa gcig zhes bya ba*), vol. 8, 187–193.

Lamp of Dharma Eliminating Obscurity with regard to Engaging in Mantra: Seventeen Textual Sections (*Sngags la 'jug pa'i mun pa sel bar byed pa'i chos kyi sgron me gzhung tshan bcu bdun pa*). In *'Hundred and Eight Dharma Sections' Treatise* (*Chos tshan brgya dang brgyad pa zhes bya ba'i bstan bcos*), vol. 13, 229–274.

Precious Harbor of Definitive Meaning [for] Entering into the Wish Fulfilling Ocean of the Highest Secret Mantra upon Analysis of Doubts Regarding Difficult Points of Explicit Teachings of [Drakpa Gyeltsen's] 'Precious Tree: Clear Realizations [of Tantras]' (*Mngon par rtogs pa rin po che'i ljon shing zhes bya ba'i dngos bstan gyi dka' gnas la som nyi'i mtha' rnam par dpyad nas/ gsang sngags bla na med pa'i yid bzhin gyi rgya mtshor 'jug pa/ nges don rin po che'i 'jug ngogs*), vol. 17, 432–448.

Sevenfold Treasury of Gems: Explanation of the Glorious 'Secret Assembly' [Tantra] (*Dpal gsang ba 'dus pa'i rnam bshad rin po che'i gter mdzod bdun pa*), vol. 7, 405–612.

Sun Benefiting Others That Dispels External and Internal Darkness: Notes Thoroughly Clarifying the Five Stages of the Glorious 'Secret Assembly' [Tantra] (*Dpal gsang ba 'dus pa'i rim pa lnga rab tu gsal bar byed pa'i brjed byang phyi nang gi mun pa sel byed gzhan la phan pa'i nyi ma*), vol. 23, 496–518.

Thorough Clarification of Definitive Commitments: Answers to Objections to [Drakpa Gyeltsen's] 'Elimination of Mistakes [Regarding Root Downfalls]' (*'Khrul spong gi brgal lan rnam par nges pa'i dam tshig rab tu gsal ba*), vol. 23, 105–295.

Thorough Clarification of Vajradhara's Intent: Ascertainment of Profound and Extensive Points of the Mantra System in Twenty-One Dharma Sections (*Sngags lugs kyi zab rgya'i gnad rnam par gtan la dbab pa rdo rje 'chang gi dgongs pa rab gsal chos mtshan nyi shu rtsa gcig pa*). In *'Hundred and Eight Dharma Sections' Treatise* (*Chos tshan brgya dang brgyad pa zhes bya ba'i bstan bcos*), vol. 13, 301–345.

Thorough Establishment of the Glorious Original Buddha: [Treatise] Condensing the Essence of All Sūtras and Tantras of the Pronouncement of the Third Dharmacakra (*Dpal dang po'i sangs rgyas rab tu grub pas bka' 'khor lo gsum pa'i mdo dang rgyud sde kun gyi snying po bsdus pa*), vol. 8, 10–183.

Vajra Shortcut: Disputes about Common Appearances of Ordinary Beings and Āryas in Seventeen Dharma Sections (*Skye 'phags snang ba 'thun pa la brtsad pa rdo rje'i gseng lam chos tshan bcu bdun pa*). In *'Hundred and Eight Dharma Sections' Treatise* (*Chos tshan brgya dang brgyad pa zhes bya ba'i bstan bcos*), vol. 13, 386–428.

TIME CALCULATIONS

Necklace for Clear-Minded Ones: Presentation of Time Periods (*Dus tshigs kyi rnam par bzhag pa blo gsal gyi mgul rgyan*), vol. 6, 231–283.

TREATISES ON GRAMMAR AND POETRY

Entrance into Scholarship (*Chos la 'jug pa'i sgo*), vol. 24, 309–320.

Sarasvatī's Enjoyment Ocean: Commentary on [Daṇḍin's] 'Mirror of Poetry' (*Snyan ngag me long gi 'grel pa dbyangs can gyi rol mtsho*), vol. 24, 1–67.

VINAYA

Chariot of the Sun Illuminating the 'Sūtra': Explanation of Difficult Points of the 'Sūtra on Moral Discipline' (*'Dul ba mdo'i dka' ba'i gnas rnam par bshad pa mdo'i snang byed nyi ma'i shing rta*), vol. 22, 1–265.

Explanation of the First Level—[Vows of] Individual Liberation; from the Extensive Explanation of the Presentation of the Three Types of Vows (*Sdom gsum gyi rnam par bzhag pa rgya cher bshad pa las/ so sor thar pa'i rim pa dang po rnam par bshad pa*), vol. 6, 285–342.

Ocean of Ambrosia: Treatise Clarifying Words of the Three Bases [of Moral Discipline] (*Gzhi gsum gyi tshig gsal bar byed pa'i bstan 'chos bdud rtsi'i rol mtsho*), vol. 22, 267–302.

Moon Chariot: Treatise Clarifying Individual Meanings of Difficult Points of Hundred and One Activities [of Moral Discipline] (*Las brgya rtsa gcig gi dka' gnas so so'i don gsal bar byed pa'i bstan bcos zla ba'i shing rta*), vol. 22, 311–525.

WRITINGS FOCUSING ON THE *COLLECTION OF REASONINGS* AND MAIN TYPES OF PRĀSAṄGIKA AND SVĀTANTRIKA

Beautiful Garland of Water-Lilies: Explanation of Several Difficult Points of [Candrakīrti's] 'Engaging in Madhyamaka' (*Dbu ma la 'jug pa'i dka' ba'i gnas 'ga' zhig rnam par bshad pa ku mud kyi phreng mdzes*), vol. 5, 459–497.

Clear Identification of the Presence of the String of One Hundred and Eight Beads of Mistakes Conceived by [Wrong] Logic in Madhyamaka of the System of Others (*Gzhan lugs kyi ni dbu ma la// rtog ges brtags pa'i nor ba'i phreng// brgya dang rtsa brgyad yod pa yi// ngos 'dzin gsal po*), vol. 4, 407–419.

Commentary on Essentials of Definitive Meaning: Explanation of [Candrakīrti's] 'Engaging in Madhyamaka' (*Dbu ma la 'jug pa'i rnam par bshad pa nges don gnad kyi ṭī ka*), vol. 5. 281–457.

Drop of Ambrosia of Definitive Meaning: Entering Essential Points of the Two Truths (*Bden pa gnyis kyi gnad la 'jug pa nges don bdud rtsi'i thigs pa*), vol. 4, 375–381.

Drumming Sounds of the Melodious Voice of Brahma: Refutation of Mistakes About Meditative Stages of the Great Madhyamaka and Explanation of Tenets and Topics of the Views of Prāsaṅgika and Svātantrika (*Dbu ma chen po'i sgom rim la 'khrul pa spong shing thal rang gi grub pa'i mtha' dang lta ba'i gnas rnam par bshad pa tshangs pa'i dbyangs kyi rnga sgra*), vol. 4, 249–373.

Great Ship of Discrimination that Sails into the Ocean of Definitive Meaning: Treatise Differentiating the Tenets of Prāsaṅgika and Svātantrika Madhyamaka (*Dbu ma thal rang gi grub pa'i mtha' rnam par dbye ba'i bstan bcos nges don gyi rgya mtshor 'jug pa'i rnam dpyod kyi gru chen*), vol. 4, 399–407.

Harbor for Fortunate Ones: Explanation of [Nāgārjuna's 'Wisdom:] Root [Stanzas] on Madhyamaka' (*Dbu ma rtsa ba'i rnam bshad bskal bzangs kyi 'jug ngogs*), vol. 5, 1–280.

Smaller Summarized Exposition [of Madhyamaka] Called 'Vajra of the Lord [of Gods]' Pleasing Clear-Minded Ones (*Stong thun chung ba dbang po'i rdo rje zhes bya ba blo gsal mgu byed*), vol. 4, 433–605.

YOGĀCĀRA AND MADHYAMAKA WRITINGS *NOT* FOCUSING ON THE *COLLECTION OF REASONINGS* AND MAIN TYPES OF PRĀSAṄGIKA AND SVĀTANTRIKA

Answers to Questions Issuing from the 'Differentiation of the Two Modes' (*Tshul gnyis rnam 'byed las 'phros pa'i dris lan*), vol. 17, 414–416.

Ascertainment of the Dharma-Sphere: Explanation of [Nāgārjuna's] Treatise 'Praise of the Dharma-Sphere' (*Chos kyi dbyings su bstod pa zhes bya ba'i bstan bcos kyi rnam par bshad pa chos kyi dbyings rnam par nges pa*), vol. 7, 303–346.

Condensed Essence of Madhyamaka: Explanation of [Nāgārjuna's] 'Commentary on the Ultimate Mind of Enlightenment' (*Don dam byang chub sems 'grel gyi bshad pa dbu ma'i snying po bsdus pa*), vol. 7, 346–391.

Essence of Sūtras and Tantras: Explanation of the Buddha-Essence (*Sangs rgyas kyi snying po'i rnam bshad mdo rgyud snying po*), vol. 13, 124–136.

Garland of Trees Fulfilling All Wishes: Explanation of [Ngok Loden Sherap's] Letter 'Drop of Ambrosia' (*Spring yig bdud rtsi'i thigs pa'i rnam bshad dpag bsam yongs 'du'i ljon phreng*), vol. 24, 320–348.

Garlands of Waves of the Ocean of Yogācāras' Scriptures: Explanation of the Holy Dharma of [Asaṅga's] 'Summary of Higher Knowledge' (*Dam pa'i chos ngon pa kun las btus pa'i rnam par bshad pa rnal 'byor spyod gzhung rgya mtsho'i rlabs kyi phreng ba*), vol. 14, 1–339.

Garlands of Wondrous Ornaments of the Union of Calm Abiding and Special Insight: Guiding Instructions on the Madhyamaka View (*Dbu ma'i lta khrid/ zhi gnas dang lhag mthong zung du 'jug pa ngo mtshar rgyan gyi phreng ba*). In *'Hundred and Eight Dharma Sections' Treatise* (*Chos tshan brgya dang brgyad pa zhes bya ba'i bstan bcos*, vol. 13, 190–202.

[Nameless], vol. 17, 416–417.

Ocean of Scriptural Statements and Reasoning: Treasury of Ascertainment of Mahāyāna Madhyamaka (*Theg pa chen po dbu ma rnam par nges pa'i bang mdzod lung dang rigs pa'i rgya mtsho*), vol. 14, 341–vol. 15, 695.

Opening Doors of a Chest of Gems: Treatise Elucidating Stages of the Path of the 'Five Dharmas of Maitreya' (*Byams chos lnga'i lam gyi rim pa gsal bar byed pa'i bstan bcos rin chen sgrom gyi sgo 'byed*), vol. 11, 39–149.

Previously Unseen Sun: The Definitive Meaning of the 'Sublime Continuum' Treatise (*Rgyud bla ma'i bstan bcos kyi nges don sngon med nyi ma*), vol. 13, 113–124.

Profound Thunder amidst the Clouds of the Ocean of Definitive Meaning: Differentiation of the Two Systems of the Great Madhyamaka Deriving from the Two Great Chariot Ways (*Shing rta'i srol chen gnyis las 'byung ba'i dbu ma chen po'i lugs gnyis rnam par dbye ba/ nges don rgya mtsho'i sprin gyi 'brug sgra zab mo*). In *Two Controversial Mādhyamika Treatises*, 301–318. Bir, India: Yashodhara Publications, 1996.

Rain of Ambrosia: Extensive [Auto-]Commentary on the 'Profound Thunder amidst the Clouds of the Ocean of Definitive Meaning' (*Nges don rgya mtsho sprin gyi 'brug sgra zab mo'i rgyas 'grel bdud rtsi'i char 'bebs*), vol. 2, 471–616; also in *Two Controversial Mādhyamika Treatises*, 319–499. Bir, India: Yashodhara Publications, 1996.

Snatching Away the Heart's Torments with the Garland of the White Moon-rays of Definitive Meaning: Expression of Realizations of Honorable Ārya Asaṅga (*'Phags pa thogs med zhabs kyi rtogs pa brjod pa nges don zla zer dkar po'i phreng bas snying gi gdung ba 'phrog byed*), vol. 16, 566–573.
Thorough Clarification of Definitive Meaning of the 'Five Dharmas of Maitreya' (*Byams chos lnga'i nges don rab tu gsal ba zhes bya ba'i bstan bcos*), vol. 11, 1–37.

Chapter 2

The Intellectual Background of Shakya Chokden's Interpretation of Yogācāra and Madhyamaka

1. Two Tendencies in Yogācāra and Niḥsvabhāvavāda Writings

In this chapter I address those elements in the intellectual history of Mahāyāna Buddhism that facilitate a better understanding of Shakya Chokden's views. I start with the developments in the Madhyamaka and Yogācāra systems that anticipated the formation of his ideas. I then move to Shakya Chokden's own descriptions of various changes in the religious and intellectual climate of his time. Next, I explain key elements of his system that comprise the framework in which his interpretation of Madhyamaka and Yogācāra is embedded. I close this chapter by addressing the question of how his views developed and changed—a question that was given conflicting answers by later Tibetan writers. While the first chapter was designed to provide the socio-historical and biographical background, this chapter puts Shakya Chokden's views into the broader intellectual context of Buddhist philosophy.

When explaining Shakya Chokden's views, I often use the paired terms "Niḥsvabhāvavāda" and "Yogācāra," instead of a more widely used "Madhyamaka" and "Yogācāra" pair. I do this for two reasons. First, although the system of Nāgārjuna (between the 2nd and 4th centuries CE) and his followers is known variously as "Madhyamaka," "Niḥsvabhāvavāda," and "Śūnya(tā)vāda" (Proponents of Emptiness),[1] not all thinkers agree that the first term is synonymous with the latter two.[2] As we have already seen, Shakya Chokden's unique approach to Mahāyāna systems is built on the view that one of the two subdivisions of Yogācāra falls under the category of Madhyamaka but is distinct from Niḥsvabhāvavāda. Second, it seems that the term "Madhyamaka" was first applied to Nāgārjuna's system of thought by Bhāviveka[3] (*c.* 500–570?).[4] It appears that neither the "founder" of the Niḥsvabhāvavāda "school," Nāgārjuna, nor the "founders" of the Yogācāra "school," Maitreya and Asaṅga, applied the term "Madhyamaka" to their own system. At the same time, they applied the term "middle" (*dbu ma, madhyama*) to the *views* they advocated—one of the facts used by Shakya Chokden for justifying *both* systems as Madhyamaka. (His task was further eased by the fact that in Tibetan both *madhyama* and *madhyamaka* are translated by the same word *dbu ma*.)

Niḥsvabhāvavāda and Yogācāra developed side by side for centuries, stimulating each other's growth through mutual polemics and refutations, as well as mutual borrowings and cross-pollination. It is impossible, therefore, to fully appreciate either one of these systems without understanding the other—a fact that writers of doxographies acknowledge, but rigid doxographical categories often obscure.

It is widely accepted that the development of the Niḥsvabhāvavāda system began with the works of Nāgārjuna, who is considered by most historians and Niḥsvabhāvavādins themselves as the originator of Niḥsvabhāvavāda.[5] This system is outlined in Nāgārjuna's *Collection of Reasonings*[6] and his disciple Āryadeva's *Four Hundred*.[7] According to the majority of Buddhist thinkers, Niḥsvabhāvavāda concentrates on the emptiness of all phenomena in and of themselves. This type of emptiness later came to be known in Tibet as "self-emptiness."

The introduction of Niḥsvabhāvavāda stimulated the development of Yogācāra, as found in the works of Asaṅga (3rd–4th century CE), his teacher Maitreya,[8] and his younger brother Vasubandhu.[9] According to the key Yogācāra texts, such as the middle three of the *Five Dharmas of Maitreya*, Asaṅga's *Summary of Mahāyāna*[10] and *Grounds of Yogācāra*,[11] Vasubandhu's *Commentary on [Asaṅga's] 'Summary of Mahāyāna'*[12] and *Commentary on [Maitreya's] 'Differentiation of the Middle and Extremes,'*[13] and other works, external phenomena do not exist, but certain mental states[14] are real and exist in reality. Because in the Yogācāra system emptiness is described as mental states empty of other, nonexistent types of phenomena, some Tibetan thinkers—Shakya Chokden included—call it "other-emptiness."[15]

Because neither Yogācāras nor Niḥsvabhāvavādins accept that the external material world exists in reality, the main point of their disagreement lies in their views on the reality of mental states. It was up to doxographers, therefore, to decide how substantial the disagreement between the two systems was, and whether it should be used as the reason for emphasizing an unbridgeable gap between them.

With the flow of time, Yogācāras and Niḥsvabhāvavādins developed different ways of explaining their own systems. These interpretive differences eventually became labels for new subcategories and subdivisions of Yogācāra and Niḥsvabhāvavāda. Importantly, some categories—such as Prāsaṅgika and Svātantrika—that are often taken for granted were either nonexistent for centuries, or assigned very little importance in general. It was again up to later doxographers to decide which divisions to emphasize and which to deemphasize or ignore.

Two distinctions known to virtually all students of Indian and Tibetan Buddhist thought are the division of Niḥsvabhāvavāda into Prāsaṅgika and Svātantrika, and the division of Yogācāra into Alīkākāravāda and Satyākāravāda. The Prāsaṅgika/Svātantrika distinction did not exist from the very inception of Niḥsvabhāvavāda. It is rooted in a debate about whether on the conceptual level the ultimate view can be arrived at through consequences (*thal 'gyur, prasaṅga*) or only through autonomous reasons (*rang rgyud kyi gtan tshigs, svatantrahetu*). This debate started with Bhāviveka's refutation of Buddhapālita's (*c.* 470–540?) usage of consequences, and was followed by Candrakīrti's (*c.* 600–650) defense of Buddhapālita and his refutation of Bhāviveka's usage of autonomous reasons.[16]

The twofold division of Yogācāra into Satyākāravāda and Alīkākāravāda—also called "Aspectarians" (*rnam bcas pa, sākāra*) and "Non-Aspectarians" (*rnam med pa, nirākāra / anākāra*), respectively[17]—did not exist from the inception of Yogācāra either. It developed much later, although in the views of such early Yogācāras as Dharmapāla (*c.* 530–561?) and Sthiramati (*c.* 510–570?) one finds differences similar to those between Satyākāravāda and Alīkākāravāda. That allows both early and contemporary scholars to package Yogācāra thinkers, as well as such Buddhist logicians as Dignaga (*c.* 480–540) and Dharmakīrti (7th century), into either of these Yogācāra camps.[18] Like the Prāsaṅgika/Svātantrika distinction, the Satyākāravāda/Alīkākāravāda distinction is very subtle and ultimately boils down to the question of the reality of mental appearances. Although Yogācāras in general do not accept the existence of an external material world, according to Satyākāravāda its appearances or "aspects" (*rnam pa, ākāra*) reflected in consciousness have a real existence, because they are of one nature with the really existent consciousness, their creator. According to Alīkākāravāda, neither external phenomena nor their appearances and/in the minds that reflect them really exist. What exists in reality is only primordial mind (*ye shes, jñāna*), described as self-cognition (*rang rig, svasaṃvedana/svasaṃvitti*) or individually self-cognizing primordial mind (*so so(r) rang gis rig pa'i ye shes*).[19]

For the purposes of this study, I highlight two contradictory tendencies in the development of Niḥsvabhāvavāda and Yogācāra thought: the tendency toward separating and distancing the two systems from each other and the tendency toward bringing them close to each other and harmonizing them. The first tendency is prominent in the works of such authors as Bhāviveka and Candrakīrti on the Niḥsvabhāvavāda side, and Dharmapāla on the Yogācāra side. The second tendency is prominent in the works of such authors as Śāntarakṣita (8th century) and Kamalaśīla (*c.* 740–795) on the Niḥsvabhāvavāda side, and Ratnākaraśānti (*c.* 1000) on the Yogācāra side.[20] Thinkers of the former group were explicitly accusing each other's systems of having fallen into extremes, while those in the latter group tried to bring the two systems as close to each other as possible. On the Niḥsvabhāvavāda side, these two tendencies are further related to the number of epistemological ideas developed by Yogācāras that Niḥsvabhāvavādins were willing to include in their system as steps toward realizing ultimate reality. On the Yogācāra side, they depend on how much reality is allowed to the mental states: the less that mental states are seen as really existent, the closer their system is to Niḥsvabhāvavāda.

Writers of doxographies play on these two tendencies in different ways, depending on their personal objectives in organizing Buddhist systems, such as bringing them closer to each other, distancing them from one another, and/or synthesizing them on various levels. Shakya Chokden too makes full use of these options. His works show that he understands the fragility of seemingly rigid doxographical categories, and he tries to break through them in order to uncover new meanings and connections. As a result, he elevates one type of Yogācāra—Alīkākāravāda—to the same level as Niḥsvabhāvavāda, emphasizing their compatibility as two main subdivisions of Madhyamaka. At the same time he retains the second type of Yogācāra—Satyākāravāda—below Madhyamaka, and treats it as a stepping stone toward realization of the Alīkākāravāda view.

For centuries Buddhist thinkers displayed either the distancing or harmonizing tendency in their writings. Buddhapālita, Bhāviveka, and Candrakīrti, who maintained primarily the first tendency, did not attempt to bring the Niḥsvabhāvavāda and Yogācāra views of reality close to each other.[21] Bhāviveka criticized Yogācāras in his *Stanzas on the Heart of Madhyamaka* and its autocommentary, *Blaze of Reasoning:*

Commentary on the 'Heart of Madhyamaka,'[22] as Candrakīrti did in his *Engaging in Madhyamaka* with its autocommentary, *Explanation of the 'Engaging in Madhyamaka.'*[23] Yogācāras who chose the distancing approach would also criticize Niḥsvabhāvavāda views and/or comment on the works of founding Niḥsvabhāvavādins (Nāgārjuna and Āryadeva) in the Yogācāra fashion, refuting explanations of those works by Niḥsvabhāvavādins. For example, Sthiramati commented on Nāgārjuna's *Wisdom: Root Stanzas on Madhyamaka*, and Dharmapāla wrote a commentary on Āryadeva's *Four Hundred*. Both were critics of Bhāviveka.[24]

Arguably, germs of the harmonizing tendency were already present in the works of Nāgārjuna. As Shakya Chokden points out, Nāgārjuna's description of ultimate reality in the *Collection of Praises*[25] agrees with the Yogācāra description.[26] In addition, Nāgārjuna's *Commentary on the Mind of Enlightenment*[27] contains ideas that agree with both Niḥsvabhāvavāda and Yogācāra.[28] In that text, Nāgārjuna describes the view determined by reasoning in the Niḥsvabhāvavāda way. Nevertheless, his description of the view of meditative equipoise is in agreement with the ultimate view of Yogācāra.[29] To claim that Nāgārjuna's authentic view is only the one expressed in his *Collection of Reasonings*, and particularly in the *Wisdom: Root Stanzas on Madhyamaka*, is problematic, to say the least.[30]

The harmonizing tendency is prominent in the works of Śāntarakṣita and Kamalaśīla, whose approach to the two systems was clearly reconciliatory, albeit hierarchical. They kept Yogācāra on the level below Madhyamaka, but used Yogācāra philosophy as a step toward realization of the ultimate view of Niḥsvabhāvavāda. Śāntarakṣita and Kamalaśīla were the first Indian thinkers who introduced Niḥsvabhāvavāda to Tibet. Their system was called "Yogācāra Madhyamaka" (*rnal 'byor spyod pa'i dbu ma*) by Tibetan scholars of the early dissemination of Buddhism in Tibet. The system of Bhāviveka and his followers also received attention, and became known as "Sautrāntika Madhyamaka" (*mdo sde spyod pa'i dbu ma*). The Sautrāntika Madhyamaka/Yogācāra Madhyamaka distinction sprang from two different ways of approaching the ultimate view on the conceptual level. The former system uses the ultimate view of Sautrāntika as a step toward determining the ultimate view of Niḥsvabhāvavāda. The latter adds the ultimate view of Yogācāra as an additional step before positing the ultimate Niḥsvabhāvavāda view.[31]

The "Yogācāra Madhyamaka" and "Sautrāntika Madhyamaka" appellations were current among Tibetan scholars by the end of the eighth century,[32] and used by both Yeshé Dé (*ye shes sde, c.* 800) in his *Differences of the Views*[33] and Peltsek (*dpal brtsegs*, end of the 8th century) in his *Quintessential Instructions on the Stages of the Views: Seventeen Visions*[34] and the *Explanation of the Stages of the Views*.[35] When the Prāsaṅgika/Svātantrika distinction became established in Tibet in the twelfth century,[36] both Yogācāra Madhyamaka and Sautrāntika Madhyamaka were subsumed under the category of Svātantrika Madhyamaka.[37]

The interpretive difference between Prāsaṅgika and Svātantrika mentioned above was the germ for a full-blown distinction between the Prāsaṅgika and Svātantrika "schools" and "tenet systems" which gradually developed in Tibet, culminating in Tsongkhapa's position that the Prāsaṅgika view is indispensable for the attainment of not only buddhahood but even the liberation from cyclic existence. Such a claim was possible only when the works of Candrakīrti—who came to be classified as a Prāsaṅgika—were translated into Tibetan.[38] And even then, Candrakīrti's works were not accepted by Tibetans immediately.[39] Doxographical texts of the early dissemination do not mention him at all, and those written during the late dissemination also ignore him up until the close of the first millennium.[40] The Prāsaṅgika/Svātantrika distinction is found in the twelfth century in the writings of Jayānanda and Sönam Tsemo,[41] and even then some time had to pass before it became an acknowledged fact for Tibetan doxographers. For example, the *Lamp Demonstrating Great Tenets: Buddhist History Clearly Teaching Texts Asserted by Individual Tenets* by Sherap Ö (*shes rab 'od*, 1166–1244) mentions neither Candrakīrti nor Prāsaṅgika in its description of Madhyamaka systems and their advocates.[42]

Prāsaṅgika's superiority over Svātantrika was already asserted by such early thinkers as Patsap Nyimadrak (*pa tshab nyi ma grags*, 1055–1145?), who might have been the first Tibetan thinker to do so.[43] While some Tibetan thinkers also followed Patsap's lead,[44] it is no doubt Tsongkhapa who has to be credited with making the hierarchical distinction between the *final* views of Prāsaṅgika and Svātantrika the focal point of interpretation of Madhyamaka.[45]

Afterward, only Tsongkhapa's followers accepted this position, while non-Geluk writers were purposefully reiterating that the ultimate views of the two systems are equally valid and come to the same point.[46] For example, in his *Vision of Profound Thatness: Explanation of [Nāgārjuna's 'Wisdom:] Root [Stanzas on] Madhyamaka'* Rongtön writes:

> The differentiation of Prāsaṅgika and Svātantrika in terms of particulars of good/bad views—without realizing the meaning of the explanation that they branched because of

> the particulars of explaining the intent of the '*[Wisdom:] Root [Stanzas on] Madhyamaka*' in a way of consequences and autonomous [reasons]—is the description of the views of the great Madhyamaka proponents of the Land of Āryas [i.e., India] in ways of superimposition (*sgro 'dogs, samāropa*) and deprecation (*skur 'debs, apavāda*). Thus, it has to be discarded as spittle.[47]

If the Svātantrika/Prāsaṅgika distinction was relatively unimportant even to the alleged founders of Svātantrika/Prāsaṅgika,[48] it comes as no surprise that in Tibet too, both Shakya Chokden and Gorampa insisted that there is no difference in the final views of Prāsaṅgika and Svātantrika,[49] as did the Eighth Karmapa Mikyö Dorjé (*mi bskyod rdo rje*, 1504–1557).[50] The fact that the Prāsaṅgika/Svātantrika distinction received such a widespread attention in Tibet testifies to its importance in the world of Geluk philosophy and the crucial role it played in refutations of that philosophy by Geluk opponents. It seems that this focus on the Prāsaṅgika/Svātantrika distinction was at least partly responsible for a relatively limited interest among Tibetans in the Alīkākāravāda/Satyākāravāda distinction.

As later Indian and Tibetan scholars were organizing Buddhist tenets, the differences between Satyākāravāda and Alīkākāravāda became more pronounced and refined. As happens so often, explanations developed by different thinkers became classificatory tools for subsequent generations of doxographers to include those thinkers in particular "schools" or "systems of thought." Similarly to Prāsaṅgika and Svātantrika, Alīkākāravāda and Satyākāravāda were shaped into subcategories of one and the same Yogācāra system.

Shakya Chokden is not alone in drawing clear distinctions between Alīkākāravāda and Satyākāravāda, while treating the final views of Svātantrika and Prāsaṅgika as the same, or ignoring the latter division altogether. After all, the distinction into Sākāravāda/Nirākāravāda had already been made by Indian scholars at the time when the Prāsaṅgika/Svātantrika distinction was not yet pronounced.[51] He is also similar to other Tibetan thinkers in claiming the superiority of Alīkākāravāda over Satyākāravāda. It appears that all Tibetan doxographers, regardless of their sectarian affiliations, placed Alīkākāravāda above Satyākāravāda. The main reason, I would argue, is that in its negation of the reality of the dualistic consciousness asserted by Satyākāravāda, Alīkākāravāda is closer to Niḥsvabhāvavāda that negates everything, and therefore it appears to be superior to Satyākāravāda from that perspective. (It is also interesting to note that unlike the Prāsaṅgika/Svātantrika distinction, this hierarchical distinction between Alīkākāravāda and Satyākāravāda has not been contested in Tibet.) However, Shakya Chokden is unique in arguing that *the only genuine division* of non-tantric Madhyamaka[52] is the Alīkākāravāda/Niḥsvabhāvavāda division.[53] He also appears to be the only Tibetan thinker who explicitly[54] treated the Alīkākāravāda and Niḥsvabhāvavāda systems as *equally valid and compatible* divisions of Madhyamaka.

Whether taken as a "higher" system than Svātantrika or not, the Prāsaṅgika approach was favored by Tibetan thinkers by the time of Shakya Chokden. The fact that the increasingly influential Candrakīrti maintained the distancing tendency with respect to Niḥsvabhāvavāda and Yogācāra affected the course chosen by most Tibetan doxographers in subsequent centuries. Eclipsed by Prāsaṅgika views, the harmonizing tendency did not take hold in the Snowy Land, and the majority of Tibetan thinkers tended to favor the distancing approach to Niḥsvabhāvavāda and Yogācāra. How many Yogācāra ideas are (re) admitted into the Niḥsvabhāvavāda system without acknowledging it, and what is meant by Yogācāra and Madhyamaka in each case, is a controversial question that would require further detailed analysis. What is clear is that advocates of the distancing approach themselves believe that the ultimate view of Niḥsvabhāvavāda they side with is distant from and incompatible with that of Yogācāra—all branches of Yogācāra. In the Sakya tradition in particular, such a distancing approach was maintained by Shakya Chokden's contemporary and rival Gorampa.[55]

As a result of the distancing tendency becoming a dominant feature of the Tibetan approach to the systems of Yogācāra and Niḥsvabhāvavāda, they ended up being separated from each other by a seemingly impenetrable wall. Nevertheless, early thinkers who maintained the harmonizing tendency, such as Śāntarakṣita, Kamalaśīla, and Ratnākaraśanti—all of whom treated the Alīkākāravāda view as the highest Yogācāra position—did not fail to notice how thin the wall between the two systems really is: mind, devoid of dualistic appearances, exists in reality according to the Alīkākāravāda view, but not according to the Niḥsvabhāvavāda view. Śāntarakṣita and Kamalaśīla's approach is well known both in the Tibetan and the contemporary scholarly world. I also address its explanation by Shakya Chokden in Chapter 3. Ratnākaraśānti is relatively less known, but importantly, it is Ratnākaraśānti whose authority Shakya Chokden often evokes in support of his approach to the Yogācāra and Niḥsvabhāvavāda systems.[56]

Ratnākaraśānti was a famous paṇḍita of the Indian monastic university Vikramaśīla. He was a follower of Alīkākāravāda and at the same time treated his view as Madhyamaka.[57] He explicitly argued that the views of Yogācāras and Niḥsvabhāvavādins are very close, as the following passage from one of his major works, the *Quintessential Instructions on the Perfection of Wisdom*, testifies:

> Thus, Yogācāras accept the primordial nature of phenomena (*chos rnams kyi rang bzhin gnyug ma*), a mere clarity (*gsal ba tsam*), as substantially existent (*rdzas su yod pa*). Mādhyamikas (*dbu ma pa*, Followers of the Middle), on the other hand, do not accept even that substance (*rdzas*), and realize this feature also as a mere name. Thus, [those] Yogācāras and Mādhyamikas who rootlessly debate together [are] individuals [in] extremely bad condition.[58]

A few pages earlier in the same text, Ratnākaraśānti also argues that the Yogācāra and Madhyamaka tenets are concordant, and the only feature that makes them different is the fact that Yogācāra accepts as truth the primordial nature (*gnyug ma'i rang bzhin*) described as self-cognition (*rang rig pa*) or individual self-cognition (*so so rang gis rig pa*), while Madhyamaka treats it as neither existent nor nonexistent due to the fact that it cannot withstand very subtle analysis (*shin tu phra ba brtags pa*).[59] In other words, the difference between Yogācāras and Mādhyamikas lies in whether they accept that self-cognition underlying all phenomena as real or not. If, argues Ratnākaraśānti, the only substantial difference lies in just that, and otherwise the two systems are concordant, is it not indeed a bad thing for Mādhyamikas and Yogācāras to engage in mutual debates?

Such a harmonizing and reconciliatory approach resonated across the Tibetan intellectual world, attracting its advocates throughout centuries. Mipam Gyamtso (*mi pham rgya mtsho*)/Ju Mipam Jamyang Namgyel Gyamtso (*'ju mi pham 'jam dbyangs rnam rgyal rgya mtsho*, 1846–1912), a Nyingma thinker who played an important role in the ecumenical movement of the nineteenth century, is a good example of such an advocate. In his commentaries and independent treatises, Mipam accepts the doxographical hierarchy wherein Niḥsvabhāvavāda reigns supreme, while both Satyākāravāda and Alīkākāravāda are treated as subdivisions of Cittamātra, which he understands as synonymous with Yogācāra, thus inferior to Madhyamaka.[60] Yet, similar to Ratnākaraśānti and Shakya Chokden, Mipam argues that the fundamental difference between Yogācāra and Niḥsvabhāvavāda—which he treats as Madhyamaka—is not a big one. As Mipam explains in his *Differentiation of Primordial Mind and Appearances: Commentary on Maitreya's Stanzas of 'Differentiation of Phenomena and the Nature of Phenomena'*:

> Thus, if even Cittamātra Followers (*sems tsam pa*) have to realize mere inexpressible, naturally luminous cognition (*rig pa rang bzhin gyis 'od gsal ba*) free from all aspects of the apprehended and apprehender and devoid of object and subject, which is not different from the thoroughly established nature empty of the two selves, then what need is there to mention that Mādhyamikas [also have to realize it]? According to Cittamātra Followers, that cognition is accepted as free from proliferations, because the meaning of the sixteen [types of] emptiness is perfectly complete in its nature, and [it can] not be thought of or expressed as any external, internal, etc., phenomena of the apprehended and apprehender. Nevertheless, it is a pure Madhyamaka [approach] if one refutes by reasoning those remaining subtle tenets of the way of positing as truly established the entity of that inexpressible knowing (*brjod med kyi shes pa*), and accepts that very knowing devoid of the apprehended and apprehender (*gzung 'dzin med pa'i shes pa*) also as the originally pure luminosity (*gdod ma nas dag pa'i 'od gsal*) itself [described as] one's own mind in union with empti[ness] devoid of truth. Thus, apart from severing [versus] not severing [this] subtle essential point of clinging, the two Mahāyāna [systems of] Madhyamaka and Cittamātra seem to be similar in the practice of meditative equipoise and subsequent attainment. It is because of such a fact that great paṇḍitas and accomplished practitioners of the Land of Āryas also treated these two as not different for Mahāyāna practice.[61]

In this passage Mipam argues that both Cittamātra Followers and Mādhyamikas realize naturally luminous cognition, primordially pure luminosity. While Cittamātra Followers simply see it as the inexpressible thoroughly established nature, Mādhyamikas realize it in union with the emptiness of its nature, as empty of truth, and thus sever the subtle clinging to it not severed by Cittamātra Followers. With that exception, both Cittamātra Followers and Mādhyamikas approach the practice of the path similarly. For the above reasons, great Indian scholars and yogis also treated them as not different for the practice of Mahāyāna. In his *Oral Instructions of Delighted Guru Mañjughoṣa: Explanation of [Śāntarakṣita's] 'Ornament of Madhyamaka,'* Mipam further specifies that a genuine (*mtshan nyid pa*) Cittamātra is only the Satyākāravāda system, and the Alīkākāravāda position is very close to Madhyamaka.[62]

Perhaps the thinker whose approach to Yogācāra and Madhyamaka is closest to Shakya Chokden's is the Seventh Karmapa Chödrak Gyamtso. In his *Ocean of Textual Systems of Reasoning*, Chödrak Gyamtso argues that the final intent (*mthar thug gi dgongs pa*) of Dignāga's *Sūtra on Valid Cognition*[63] and Dharmakīrti's *Seven Works on Valid Cognition*[64] lies in Madhyamaka transmitted from Maitreya to Asaṅga with Vasubandhu, and it also agrees with Madhyamaka texts of Nāgārjuna and his followers.[65] He further explains that Mādhyamikas in the lineage stemming from Asaṅga determined reality primarily from the mind side (*sems phyogs*), while scholars in the lineage stemming from Nāgārjuna did it primarily from the emptiness side (*stong phyogs*).[66] Then he makes the following statement:

> Thus, through limitless scriptural statements and reasonings one should understand that the profound important points and intents of the final views of the two founders of chariot ways are one.[67]

Although on the surface Chödrak Gyamtso's approach appears to be very close to Shakya Chokden's position as discussed in this book, it is uncertain whether Chödrak Gyamtso treats either Yogācāra in general or the Alīkākāravāda system in particular as a valid subdivision of Madhyamaka—this is because according to the Eighth Karmapa, Mikyö Dorjé, it is not the case. Notably, as Mikyö Dorjé himself says, he "correctly edited the words and meaning" (*tshig don gyi zhu dag yang dag par bgyis*) of the version of the *Ocean of Textual Systems of Reasoning* from which I quoted the above passage.[68] However, in his addendum to the text Mikyö Dorjé states that it is feasible to refute the tenets of cognizance (*rnam rig grub pa'i mtha'*, i.e., Vijñaptivāda, *rnam rig smra ba*, Proponents of Cognizance)—that he treats as synonymous with Cittamātra/Yogācāra[69]—because by following them one *cannot* realize the lack of nature of the self of phenomena (*chos kyi bdag rang bzhin med pa*). Apparently, he thinks that misinterpretations of Chödrak Gyamtso's position are caused by misunderstanding the views of the Third Karmapa Rangjung Dorjé (*rang byung rdo rje*, 1284–1339).[70] He thereby gives the following explanation of Rangjung

Dorjé's statement that Asaṅga and Nāgārjuna's intents are not contradictory: Asaṅga emphasized the mind's clarity factor (*sems kyi gsal cha*) from which all phenomena of cyclic existence and nirvāṇa emerge, while Nāgārjuna emphasized the mind's empty factor (*sems kyi stong cha*) which is devoid of all proliferations of cyclic existence and nirvāṇa. Assuming a more general tone, Mikyö Dorjé objects to those who say that according to the Karmapa even Nāgārjuna did not teach a system of Madhyamaka higher than the Alīkākāravāda system. His argument is that if such were the case, it would follow that the Vijñaptivāda system advocates both true existence and the lack of true existence, and that such contradictory false words are not suitable for the Karmapa. Finally, he warns the reader about the danger of erroneous interpretations of the Kagyü (*bka' brgyud*) system by those who pretend to understand it but lack proper instructions transmitted through the lineage of high lamas.[71] His interpretation of Chödrak Gyamtso's position is further corroborated by Pawo Tsuklak Trengwa, who in his *Feast for Scholars* describes the Seventh Karmapa's approach in the aforementioned *Ocean of Textual Systems of Reasoning* and the *Lamp of the Three Worlds*[72]—Chödrak Gyamtso's commentary on Maitreya's *Ornament of Clear Realizations*:

> [Chödrak Gyamtso] explained the view [of] these two [systems of] Prajñāpāramitā and Pramāṇa (*phar tshad*) primarily as other-emptiness. Nevertheless, he did not explain it in accordance with assertions of some Tibetans who gave the name of "other-emptiness" to the Cittamātra view. Rather, this Lord [Chödrak Gyamtso] in general asserted that the two chariot ways have one intent because the lineage of profound view primarily teaches the empty character of mind and the lineage of extensive deeds primarily teaches the luminous nature, and the profundity and clarity of mind [they teach] are inseparable into two.[73]

Among Tibetan thinkers, it is Shakya Chokden who *unequivocally* argues that Alīkākāravāda is not just close to Madhyamaka, but *is* Madhyamaka. In that way, Shakya Chokden completely demolishes the wall separating Niḥsvabhāvavāda and Yogācāra and lets both of them share the same Madhyamaka space.

Overall, Shakya Chokden is less interested in the standard doxographical walls than in what is happening behind those walls. Most Tibetan doxographers tend to focus more on the fact that sūtric Mahāyāna thinkers—other than Mādhyamikas—describe themselves as "Yogācāras," differentiating between themselves and Niḥsvabhāvavādins, who in turn call themselves "Mādhyamikas." This, together with statements of existence of the four Buddhist systems of Vaibhāṣika, Sautrāntika, Yogācāra, and Madhyamaka made in authoritative texts of sūtras and tantras creates an impression that Yogācāra and Madhyamaka are two mutually exclusive categories. In contrast, Shakya Chokden prefers to focus on how Yogācāras describe their *view*. Based on statements made in Maitreya's *Differentiation of the Middle and Extremes* and other key Yogācāra texts that posit their ultimate view as the "middle," he explains the views of Maitreya, Asaṅga and other Alīkākāravādins as Madhyamaka, and by extension treats the holders of that view—Alīkākāravādins—as Mādhyamikas. Shakya Chokden is less interested in whether Alīkākāravādins put their system into the highest of the four doxographical categories, Madhyamaka, although he does argue that the division of Yogācāra into Cittamātra and Madhyamaka was made in India but did not catch on in Tibet.[74] Furthermore, he openly objects to the doxographical partisanship wherein Yogācāra is not treated as Madhyamaka primarily because Niḥsvabhāvavādins do not want it treated that way.[75]

Shakya Chokden extends his harmonizing approach to the "lower" Buddhist systems as well, assigning them more weight than most Tibetans. All Tibetan thinkers, Shakya Chokden included, share a common opinion that one can attain buddhahood only by cultivating the Madhyamaka view. In the non-tantric context, according to Tsongkhapa this view has to be specifically that of Prāsaṅgika. According to Gorampa it can be either the Svātantrika or Prāsaṅgika view. According to Shakya Chokden it can be the view of Prāsaṅgika, Svātantrika, or Alīkākāravāda. The majority of Tibetan thinkers, including Shakya Chokden's contemporary Gorampa, also believe that the Madhyamaka view is indispensable, even if one just aims at personal liberation from cyclic existence. Shakya Chokden disagrees, arguing that even the "lowest" view of Vaibhāṣika is sufficient for the purpose of individual liberation.[76]

In spite of the emphasis on the harmonizing approach mentioned above, by placing Alīkākāravāda on the level of Madhyamaka Shakya Chokden automatically distances it from Satyākāravāda and creates a sharper hierarchical distinction between Satyākāravāda and Alīkākāravāda than do other Tibetan doxographers. In Shakya Chokden's system, this sharp distinction is crucial, because it is the main tool for rearranging the philosophical divisions and showing the compatibility of Alīkākāravāda and Niḥsvabhāvavāda. Also, by placing the Alīkākāravāda system within the category of Madhyamaka,

Shakya Chokden secures its support for his own unique view of reality, presented in that light as the "mainstream" interpretation of Madhyamaka.

In sum, while choosing a highly reconciliatory approach to Niḥsvabhāvavāda and Yogācāra, Shakya Chokden did not simply erase their differences. Rather, recognizing and maintaining minute distinctions between the two systems, he was able to show their compatibility and complementarity, and bring them closer to each other than any Tibetan thinker before or after him. This approach in turn is based on a sharp distinction between conceptual and direct understanding of ultimate reality that I will explain in the next section.

2. Basic Elements of Shakya Chokden's Approach to Mahāyāna Systems

What is the correct view of ultimate reality and its realization? This is the central question Shakya Chokden deals with in his innovative efforts to (re)interpret the relationship of Madhyamaka and Yogācāra. Addressing this question, he focuses on the fundamental issue of the relationship between "conceptual" and "experiential" approaches to understanding reality.[77] In particular, he concentrates on the relationship between the view of reality determined by reasoning and the view of reality directly experienced in meditation. Arguing that the two are *different*, he agrees with the majority of Tibetan thinkers, such as Rendawa, Gorampa, and Mipam.[78] For example, in the *Lamp Illuminating Thatness: Explanation of [Candrakīrti's] 'Engaging in Madhyamaka,'* Rendawa discusses the process of realizing reality according to the Niḥsvabhāvavāda system as follows: one starts investigating the nature of phenomena by conceptual analysis that leads to not finding any nature of phenomena at all. Then one proceeds to placing one's mind within meditative equipoise (*mnyam gzhag, samāhita*) on that state of non-findability. Afterward one rises from that state during subsequent attainment (*rjes thob, pṛṣṭhalabdha*) and manifests the correct view: thinking that all phenomena are entirely free from proliferations. Through alternating such meditative equipoise and subsequent attainment, the practitioner eventually achieves the direct realization of reality. That realization, which is the nature of the perfection of wisdom (*shes rab kyi pha rol tu phyin pa, prajñāpāramitā*), does not realize any object. Nevertheless, on the conventional level that very nonrealization is given the name of realization of reality. Having no object, such perfection of wisdom is also not a knowing (*shes pa*), because knowing is characterized by cognition of objects (*yul rig pa*). Nevertheless, it is a nonconceptual primordial mind (*rnam par mi rtog pa'i ye shes, nirvikalpajñāna*).[79] Thereby Rendawa shows that the difference between conceptual and nonconceptual realization of reality lies not just in the presence/absence of concepts, but in what is taken as reality itself, in the presence of realization, and in the type of subject that realizes it.

Not all Tibetan thinkers agree that direct realization of reality is accepted by Mādhyamikas "in name only." Admitting positive qualities to ultimate reality, they describe it as the inseparability of clarity and emptiness (*gsal stong dbyer med*), as the buddha-essence endowed with qualities of a buddha, and so forth, and approach its direct realization in a positive way too, such as the realization of the inseparability of clarity and emptiness.[80] Nevertheless, those very thinkers—Shakya Chokden included—also maintain that "reality" determined conceptually and reality realized directly in meditative experience are very different, the first being a reality in name only, and the second being the only possible reality. What makes Shakya Chokden's position unique is that unlike most other thinkers he uses this conceptual/experiential difference as a basis for his explanation of Alīkākāravāda and Niḥsvabhāvavāda as two equally valid and compatible forms of Madhyamaka. Below is a brief summary of Shakya Chokden's position, which I unpack in the following chapters.

According to Shakya Chokden, there is only one type of reality directly realized on the sūtric or non-tantric path of Mahāyāna, and it is the same for all practitioners.[81] Both Alīkākāravāda and Niḥsvabhāvavāda systems provide valid tools for directly realizing that ultimate reality, and their differences pertain only to the conceptual level, not to the level of the direct realization of reality. While many Niḥsvabhāvavādins do not go beyond saying that not realizing anything within meditative equipoise is merely given the name of realization of emptiness, Alīkākāravādins describe that realization as individually self-cognizing primordial mind.

The view of reality directly realized in meditative equipoise while following the Mahāyāna path is accepted by all Mahāyāna thinkers as the highest ultimate view, because its cultivation serves as a direct antidote of ignorance obstructing achievement of buddhahood. Mahāyāna thinkers are also in agreement that as long as a system provides sufficient means for direct and complete realization of that ultimate reality, this system *is* Madhyamaka in terms of being the system of the middle free from extremes. Shakya Chokden goes a step further and argues that *both* Niḥsvabhāvavāda and Alīkākāravāda provide such tools, and therefore both should be treated as valid forms of Madhyamaka. Furthermore, he insists that the two systems are not only compatible, but even complementary, because Niḥsvabhāvavāda provides the most powerful reasonings for severing conceptual proliferations, while Alīkākāravāda focuses on reality directly realized in meditative equipoise.

In particular, he argues that Alīkākāravāda's description of the ultimate as the non-dual primordial mind is valid, explaining why neither deconstructive nor constructive reasoning can ever reach this reality. First, reasoning is conceptual by definition. Therefore, it can access only that which is within the scope of conceptuality. Whatever is affirmed or negated by reasoning cannot be a genuine ultimate reality, even if the label of ultimate reality is attached to it. Reasoning can neither affirm nor negate the non-dual primordial mind, because the non-dual primordial mind is beyond the reach of concepts. Second, it is possible to eliminate all obscurations to buddhahood, regardless of whether one negates primordial mind and its true existence by reasoning or not. The deconstructive reasoning of Madhyamaka does not have to be applied to primordial mind, and even when it is applied, it negates primordial mind and its true existence within the scope of that reasoning only, not in general. Third, no matter how one describes a direct meditative experience of reality in the post-meditative state, what one directly experiences within meditative equipoise when following the Mahāyāna path necessarily has to be primordial mind.[82] Finally, reasoning is not absolutely necessary for getting access to the direct realization of primordial mind.

Although Alīkākāravādins and Niḥsvabhāvavādins have different types of reasoning, different approaches to primordial mind, and describe meditative equipoise on ultimate reality differently, what they arrive at in direct meditative experience is one and the same thing—primordial mind, and its cultivation brings about the same final result—buddhahood. Therefore, their systems are compatible, and despite mutual disagreements, they are in agreement on the very deep level of direct meditative experience of ultimate reality. Although they verbalize that ultimate reality differently, its direct realization is the same.

Arguing that both Alīkākāravāda and Niḥsvabhāvavāda are equally valid types of Madhyamaka, Shakya Chokden reconsiders labels attached to different Indian thinkers and systems of thought. He argues that similar to Niḥsvabhāvavādins, Alīkākāravādins are also Mādhyamikas due to the following complementary reasons: they treat their own view as Madhyamaka;[83] the Buddha himself prophesied that pioneers of the two systems would be teaching ultimate reality non-mistakenly; there are no valid reasons that can refute as invalid the view of reality developed by either system; the views of reality of both systems are sufficient for attaining the highest Buddhist goal of buddhahood.

Shakya Chokden does acknowledge that most Niḥsvabhāvavādins and Yogācāras see faults in each other's views, do not see each other as Mādhyamikas, and see only their own views as Madhyamaka. Nevertheless, in his opinion, although Niḥsvabhāvavādins criticize Alīkākāravādins, their criticisms make Alīkākāravādins no less Mādhyamikas than Alīkākāravādins' criticisms of Niḥsvabhāvavādins make Niḥsvabhāvavādins non-Mādhyamikas.

Scrutinizing the nature and relationship of Niḥsvabhāvavāda and Alīkākāravāda, Shakya Chokden also reconsiders labels attached to ideas developed *within* the two systems. He openly addresses such sensitive questions as whether true existence has to be negated in order to negate grasping at true existence, whether ultimate reality is permanent or impermanent, whether the Niḥsvabhāvavāda view is suitable for tantric practice or not, and whether both the self-emptiness and other-emptiness views are equally valid, to mention just a few. His answers to these and other questions are far-reaching and refreshing due to their novelty and ingenuity.

Shakya Chokden's reconciliatory approach to Niḥsvabhāvavāda and Alīkākāravāda is unique in the Tibetan intellectual world. Arguing that despite mutual accusations of not being Madhyamaka both systems *are* Madhyamaka, he sides with neither one of them, and explains that either system is sufficient by itself. This point is usually missed by those who package Shakya Chokden himself into the narrow category of "Followers of Other-Emptiness" (*gzhan stong pa*) and by those who think that according to him either of the two systems of Madhyamaka is incomplete without the other.[84]

Shakya Chokden's approach to Mahāyāna systems reveals him as a Mādhyamika who values all forms of Madhyamaka deriving from India, and who works on clarifying the subtleties and complexities of their nature and relationship. This position, in combination with his general non-sectarian attitude to various practice lineages, such as the Great Perfection (*rdzogs chen*), Great Seal, and Path and Result,[85] might be the reason why the key figure in the ecumenical movement (*ris med*) of the nineteenth century, Kongtrül Yönten Gyamtso (*kong sprul yon tan rgya mtsho*)/Lodrö Tayé (*blo gros mtha' yas*, 1813–1899), when discussing Madhyamaka systems in his monumental *Limitless Ocean of Knowables*,[86] either cited verbatim or paraphrased a number of crucial passages from Shakya Chokden's two main texts on the nature and relationship of Yogācāra and Niḥsvabhāvavāda mentioned above:[87] the *Rain of Ambrosia* and the *Great Path of Ambrosia of Emptiness*. One of the reasons why Shakya Chokden was concerned with preserving practice lineages, meditative instructions and rare teachings was that in his opinion they were endangered by the spread of Geluk views. This also brings him closer to the nineteenth-century ecumenical movement that in large part started as a response to the Geluk dominance in political and religious spheres.

In spite of his reconciliatory approach to Mahāyāna systems, Shakya Chokden is also one of the most polemically-oriented authors to appear in Tibet. His polemical slant is prominent in those very works in which he tries to reconcile Niḥsvabhāvavāda and Alīkākāravāda, despite their mutual polemics and refutations. When writing on these two systems, he is often more inclined to state his opinions through lengthy arguments against his opponents—real or imaginary—rather than through definitions, categorizations, and classifications. The polemical arguments he uses are invaluable for those who wish to understand differences between the views of different Tibetan thinkers and traditions. Until recent times, research on Tibetan forms of Madhyamaka was mostly informed and dominated by Geluk-oriented explanations, many of which—such as the establishment of relative phenomena by valid cognition—were often taken for granted as the view of Madhyamaka itself. Shakya Chokden's critical approach to Tsongkhapa's views is therefore invaluable as a healthy alternative, and greatly contributes to our understanding of a rich diversity of Buddhist systems in general, and Tibetan thought of the fifteenth century in particular.

Shakya Chokden's emphasis on the paramount importance of the view of reality directly experienced in meditation and the subservient role of reasoning makes him sympathetic to the meditative techniques that ended up on the periphery of the Tibetan religious world, not forming a significant part of most sūtric or tantric systems.[88] Such techniques as inquiring whether the mind has color, shape, and so forth in order to realize the nature of mind were underestimated due to their apparently simplistic approach. Arguing that these techniques are also valid means for realizing ultimate reality, Shakya Chokden absolves from blame those meditators and yogins—not necessarily skilled in scholastic discourses and the syllogisms of Madhyamaka—who were criticized by later Tibetans for not having formed a correct conceptual view of reality and therefore cultivating mistaken views of reality in meditation.

Emphasizing the sameness of meditative experience of reality by followers of different Madhyamaka systems, Shakya Chokden claims that the same direct realization of reality can be accessed through different types of reasoning, or even without any reasoning whatsoever. But this emphasis on meditative experience by no means implies that he treats reasoning lightly or sees conceptuality in general as unimportant. On the contrary, as we have learned already, he himself wrote a large number of commentaries, summaries, and polemical texts on logic, and used intricate *reasoning* to negate the views of his opponents, debating about which *conceptual* descriptions of the view of reality—including descriptions of its nonconceptual realization—are correct and which are not. Nevertheless, it is clear that the conceptual/experiential polarity, and the way Shakya Chokden approaches it, plays a crucial role in his overall system. It is this very polarity that he uses as the foundation of his own unique approach to the doxography of Mahāyāna systems.

Like the majority of Tibetan thinkers, Shakya Chokden presents his position as an elaboration on the views of long-standing traditions transmitted to Tibet from India and initiated by early Indian masters, with roots ultimately going back to the teachings of the Buddha himself. By creating overarching connections, distinguishing between different systems of thought, lineages, and schools, and organizing them in ladder-like hierarchical structures, Shakya Chokden joins a vast number of Tibetan thinkers who engage in building what I call "doxographical pyramids." Tibetan scholastic writers believe that these massive buildings are grounded in the soil of the original teachings of the Buddha, their foundations are made of the views of Indian forerunners, their layers are cemented by the systems of successive Indian and Tibetan followers, and their tops are sharpened with subsequent explanations developed by sectarian Tibetan traditions and lineages.

As far as their "shape" is concerned, these doxographical pyramids look much the same as each other. They include similar systems with similar types of divisions filled with similar thinkers with similar labels attached to them, such as "Mādhyamikas" and "Cittamātra Followers." Nevertheless, *how* contents of the lower pyramidal layers are explained depends on who their observers standing on top are. In other words, although Tibetan doxographers believe that their views are rooted in systems of early Indian thinkers, within "reasonable limits"—as long as the pyramids do not collapse—they allow themselves to explain the views of those early thinkers differently.

Divisions into tenet systems originally developed in India, and many Buddhist authors had a distinct sense of "schools" and "tenet systems," as is clear from the works of Candrakīrti, Bhāviveka, and other thinkers, as well as in such teachings attributed to the Buddha himself as the *Hevajra Tantra*. These divisions performed a great service to Tibetans, especially during the second dissemination of Buddhism in Tibet starting in the eleventh century, because they helped organize the immense flow of Buddhist writings from India into Tibet. Yet, as happens so often in so many areas, means would become ends in themselves, and divisions of systems would be taken as rigid labels to attach to virtually every thinker, including doxographers themselves. Defending a system which was most valorized at the time would be seen as an act of promoting the most subtle and profound Buddhist view, and would obviously help in promoting oneself and one's own sectarian tradition. Doxography therefore became a polemical tool to maintain, reinforce and protect one's sectarian identity. Eventually, doxographical approaches and sectarian affiliations became so intertwined that changing doxographical outlook would be taken as tantamount to betrayal of one's own tradition, as Shakya Chokden's own example so aptly demonstrates.

In the Tibetan intellectual world, doxography came to be widely used as a tool for looking at the past and organizing the Indian-based material, but at the same time it could be profoundly creative. With a certain amount of ingenuity one could even rearrange contents of the whole doxographical pyramid without openly admitting it. Paradoxically, it is this creative and novel outlook presented as a "traditional" and "the only correct" position, that could turn its creator into a founder of a new movement that would quickly become an old orthodoxy. A good example is Tsongkhapa and his students who bypassed the views of "early Tibetans" (*bod snga rabs pa*) and claimed that their system was in agreement with the views of exalted Indian thinkers of the past. They were severely attacked by their Sakya critics for virtually rewriting the Buddhist canon. Nevertheless, it is their views that in centuries to come would be elevated to the level of orthodoxy, and it is the views of their critics that would be treated as heterodox by the advocates of the Geluk sect that secured the support of the Central Tibetan government in the seventeenth century.

Shakya Chokden chose another way to present his novel position. By placing the Alīkākāravāda system on the level of Madhyamaka, he rearranged the traditionally accepted pyramidal layers themselves, thereby affecting their contents. In order to justify his position, he also worked through multiple doxographical layers all the way down to the bottom of the pyramid, demonstrating that his position was in agreement with the systems of early Sakya masters, exalted Indian thinkers, and ultimately the Buddha himself. Despite his novel outlook, Shakya Chokden himself clearly had the sense of orthodoxy, and did not present his view as heterodox.

He started openly expressing this unique view only in his early fifties, once he had become an established teacher and settled in his own monastic seat of Serdokchen. By that time, he had absorbed and processed an impressive amount of Indian and Tibetan materials, having found important "pressure points" in Mahāyāna systems that he used for recirculating the flow of intellectual energy saturating "canonical" texts, removing doctrinal blocks obstructing his vision, and creating new connections between multiple elements of the Buddhist universe. As a result, he managed to present his system as a coherent and integrated whole. Such was possible only due to his encyclopedic learning embracing virtually all aspects of Buddhist scholarship.

3. Pointed Disappointments: Shakya Chokden's Personal Reflections

To better understand Shakya Chokden's views, it is also helpful to look at passages in his works where Shakya Chokden himself describes various changes in the religious and intellectual climate of his time. His predominant attitude to those changes was clearly negative, expressing feelings of disappointment and longing for an apparent unity of various systems of Buddhist thought and practice which had been disrupted by the emergence of new ideologies. His feelings were obviously affected by such elements as the institutional and political rivalry mentioned in Chapter 1. But being a refined thinker, he was strongly interested in the intellectual basis for those changes.

When Shakya Chokden became established as an independent thinker, he found—or put—himself in a situation characterized by pointed disappointments in the following areas: newly emerged philosophical views were rapidly spreading and affecting even those who considered themselves to be Sakyapas; the views of Niḥsvabhāvavāda were misunderstood; the views of Yogācāra that he increasingly cherished were frequently being misinterpreted; the views of Tantra—which are closely linked with those of Yogācāra—were either being deprecated because the view of some tantras was explained as that of Yogācāra, and—by an erroneous extension—Cittamātra, or they were erroneously seen as those of Prāsaṅgika; lineages of contemplative practice and their instructions were deprecated as inferior and not providing a valid means for realizing ultimate reality; and Tibetan thinkers were treating teachings of the third dharmacakra less and less seriously, overemphasizing the importance of the Niḥsvabhāvavāda teachings deriving from the second dharmacakra.

One of the developments Shakya Chokden reacted to with great bitterness was the rapid spread of Geluk views on Madhyamaka, epistemology, Tantra, meditation, and other subjects of Tibetan Buddhist study and practice. Many of his writings contain vehement refutations of this new ideology. In Shakya Chokden's opinion, the system developed by Tsongkhapa and his followers undermined the long-standing tradition of Buddhist thought and practice stemming from India and practiced in Tibet. On the other hand, despite differences in opinions of various non-Geluk masters, their positions on the key points of Buddhist thought and practice displayed a remarkable unanimity, in contrast to the Geluk system which according to Shakya Chokden disagreed with virtually all of them. As he sarcastically put it in the *Letter Pleasing Impartial Wise Ones*:

> These [thinkers—Tsongkhapa, Darma Rinchen and Gelek Pelzang] are known as the "three, the father Tsongkhapa and sons." First, they initiated a great chariot way of both Sūtra and Tantra separate from all previous followers of explanatory and practice lineages (*bshad rgyud pa dang sgrub rgyud pa*). In the middle, they upheld it, and finally perfected it by great discourses that despised previous traditions.[89]

Shakya Chokden's attitude toward Geluk stands in sharp contrast to his approach to earlier Indian and Tibetan systems of thought and practice. In the same text Shakya Chokden accepts the validity of various Indian traditions, despite their mutual differences and disagreements, and says that multiple writers of indisputable (*rtsod bral*) treatises on Mahāyāna teachings appeared starting from Nāgārjuna and Asaṅga through to Ratnākaraśānti and Abhayākāragupta (11th century).[90] Likewise, Shakya Chokden presents as concordant the views of multiple teachings and lineages transmitted to Tibet from India. In the *Seventeen Wondrous Answers to the Questions of the Whole Monastic Community of Zi Samdrupling*, he gives a list—not exhaustive in itself—of Buddhist systems whose transmission lineage is pure (*brgyud pa rnam par dag pa*): the unbroken lineage of vows of individual liberation (*so thar gyi sdom brgyud*) transmitted from Śāntarakṣita; the unbroken lineage of bodhisattva vows (*byang sems kyi sdom brgyud*) transmitted from Atiśa (972/982–1054); the unbroken lineage of Secret Mantra vows (*gsang sngags kyi sdom brgyud*) transmitted from translators

Drokmi Lotsawa (*'brog mi lo tsā ba*, 11th century) and Marpa Lotsawa Chökyi Lodrö (*mar pa lo tsā ba chos kyi blo gros*, 1002/1012–1097); the explanatory traditions of Mantra (*sngags kyi bshad srol*): one translated from the originals kept in the heart of Master Padmasambhava (8th century) and known as the Old Tradition (*rnying ma*), and the others translated from Indian texts and known as the New Traditions (*gsar ma*); the explanatory traditions of dialecticians (*mtshan nyid pa'i bshad srol*) transmitted from translator Ngok Lotsawa Loden Sherap and Sakya Pendita; the lineage transmitted from Padampa Sanggyé (*pha dam pa sangs rgyas*, 11th century); and the lineage transmitted from Shangpa Dubupa (*shangs pa gdu bu pa*), i.e., Khyungpo Neljor (*khyung po rnal 'byor*, 978/990–1127).[91] Shakya Chokden further explains that all those systems are in agreement on the most important points of philosophy and practice, contrasting them with the teachings that spread in Tibet later that disagree with them all:

> Those [traditions have] an unbroken lineage of accomplished yogis (*grub thob*) [stemming] from the Land of Āryas; the roots of their ways of positing the two truths (*bden gnyis, satyadvaya*), the view and meditation (*lta sgom*), and calm abiding and special insight (*zhi lhag, śamatha-vipaśyanā*) are exclusively in agreement. [Nevertheless,] in later times in the Snowy Land there newly emerged collections of books that in their presentations of those [topics] one-sidedly disagree with all followers of explanatory lineages and followers of practice lineages appeared in the Tibetan land previously. Their multiple advocates completely polluted minds of teachers and students who came later claiming to be followers of those former Dharma lineages (*chos brgyud*), and they scorn (*zur za*) those who advocate as Dharma terminology (*chos skad*) discourses that do not exist in their own lineages. What are those [books]? They are mainly collections of books issuing from those who planted as the life pillar [of their views] the tenet systems of excessive attachment to relative truth.[92]

What Shakya Chokden negatively describes as the "excessive attachment to relative truth" (*kun rdzob kyi bden pa la lhag par zhen pa*) derives from what Tsongkhapa and his followers describe as the "establishment of conventions by valid cognition" (*tha snyad tshad grub*); that is, the establishment of conventional or relative phenomena by conventional valid cognitions[93]—the position that was criticized by many critics of Geluk. Shakya Chokden's own position is the direct opposite of Tsongkhapa's. As I demonstrate below, throughout his life, starting from early writings,[94] Shakya Chokden emphasized that whatever exists has to exist truly and really, and relative or conventional truth simply does not exist. The mind that establishes it cannot be a valid cognition, because valid cognitions establish only what exists in reality.[95]

Reading the passage cited above, one should not be misled into thinking that Shakya Chokden does not see differences between various systems of thought and practice other than Geluk, or that he agrees with all of them. For example, he is critical of Ngok Loden Sherap's explanations of the buddha-essence,[96] and does not unquestionably accept his approach to epistemology and views on reality. He differentiates it from the view of Sakya Pendita, but still treats Ngok's system as valid.[97] Importantly, discussing what he sees as incorrect explanations of self-emptiness and other-emptiness, Shakya Chokden often criticizes Tsongkhapa in tandem with Dölpopa,[98] calling them "Tibetan proponents of self-emptiness and other-emptiness," respectively, and arguing that both their systems run contrary to the correct views developed by influential Indian and Tibetan thinkers. But although Shakya Chokden rejects Dölpopa's explanation of the view of other-emptiness, he holds Dölpopa in high esteem and likens him and thinkers in his lineage—such as Mati Penchen (*ma ti paṇ chen*, 1294–1376) and Jonang Choklé Namgyel (*jo nang phyogs las rnam rgyal*, 1306–1386)—to a garland of pearls (*mu tig gi phreng ba*).[99] In contrast, Shakya Chokden berates Tsongkhapa and his disciples, and neither esteems them nor treats their views as valid.

There is another important reason for his disappointment with Tsongkhapa and his followers. According to Shakya Chokden, not only did Geluk views become popular in general, but what is even worse, they affected the minds of followers of *his own* Sakya tradition. And not only did those views infiltrate Sakyapas' minds, but they infiltrated them in such a subtle way that Sakyapas themselves were not even aware of that influence! (It is hardly surprising, especially in the case of Sangpu monastery where Sakya and Geluk monks interacted on a daily basis.) Thus, the spread of Geluk views, as Shakya Chokden perceived it, meant unwelcome changes in the views of his fellow Sakya thinkers and practitioners. This situation was combined with the disturbing fact that the Geluk tradition was attracting more and more followers—a fact that he acknowledged. In a word, the Sakya system was endangered by Geluk both from without and within, and the fact that Sakyapas would not always acknowledge it, being unable to differentiate between the two, only added to his disappointment.

Shakya Chokden embraced the task of distinguishing Sakya views from the increasingly popular views of "later Tibetans" (*bod phyi ma*) in multiple writings penned both before and after he developed his novel approach to the Mahāyāna systems. The following passage from the *Seventeen Wondrous Answers* is a good example of how he distinguishes Geluk and Sakya views. His description of the latter's position is in agreement with his own position outlined in this book. Thus, by supporting the authentic Sakya view as he sees it, Shakya Chokden kills two—or actually three—birds with the same stone: he refutes Tsongkhapa's view, reinforces the Sakya view, and legitimizes his own view:

> Later [thinkers] assert that no object of the final view of sūtras and tantras can be identified other than that emptiness explained by the master Candrakīrti, and no identification of the illustration of ultimate truth other than that [can be provided] either. Those assertions nowadays became blended into [the views of] all advocates of our side (*rang phyogs pa*). [In contrast to that, authentic] Sakyapa [thinkers] assert that no efficient ultimate truth (*don dam bden pa go chod*) was taught in Niḥsvabhāvavāda texts. They assert the emptiness of that [Niḥsvabhāvavāda] system as a general meaning (*spyi don*), a mere metaphorical ultimate (*rnam grangs pa'i don dam, paryāyaparamārtha*), and the view understood through listening and explanation. They do not assert a final and meditatively experienced view other than the self-arisen innate primordial mind (*rang byung lhan cig skyes pa'i ye shes*).[100]

Elaborating on distinctions between the views of different traditions, Shakya Chokden explains that the majority of early Tibetan tantric masters of the New and Old Traditions,[101] as well as all followers of the practice lineages such as Pacification, Great Seal and Great Perfection (*zhi phyag rdzogs gsum*),[102] asserted that only the view deriving from the third dharmacakra has the definitive meaning, and explained it exclusively in agreement with the subsequent *Dharmas of Maitreya* (*byams chos phyi ma*).[103] Sakya thinkers approached the view of reality in two stages, explaining that "having determined [the view] as freedom from extremes (*mtha' bral du gtan la phab*), one incorporates [the view] into experience in union (*zung 'jug tu nyams su len*)."[104] In the former context they primarily relied on the explicit teachings of the second dharmacakra, in the latter—the third dharmacakra with its commentaries. Thereby, Shakya Chokden demonstrates that the view taught in the third dharmacakra was explained by most tantric masters as definitive, and even when Sakya thinkers divided the view into two, the one experienced in meditative equipoise was taught as the non-dual primordial mind—the definitive meaning of the third dharmacakra. He contrasts this approach with the Geluk position that accepts neither the meaning nor the terminology of the "Mantric Madhyamaka" (*sngags kyi dbu ma*) superseding Madhyamaka of Svātantrika and Prāsaṅgika.[105]

In general, Shakya Chokden was sympathetic to the practice lineages, and his defense of those lineages was not directly related to protecting the Sakya system from Geluk influence and criticisms. He received numerous tantric teachings, empowerments, and transmissions of Sakya and different Kagyü lineages, had meditative experiences based on tantric practice, stayed in retreats on such tantric deities as Hevajra, and later himself transmitted Sakya and Kagyü tantric teachings. Thus, maintaining teachings stemming from those lineages was a part of maintaining his own religious heritage. At the same time, this also provided ample opportunity for criticizing and distancing Geluk thinkers from the mainstream systems of Tibetan Buddhism as Shakya Chokden perceived them. In his opinion, Tsongkhapa taught that followers of practice lineages at best meditate just on calm abiding (*zhi gnas, śamatha*) and do not have the view of reality necessary for achieving genuine special insight (*lhag mthong, vipaśyanā*). In the *Precious Treasury of the Condensed Essence of the Profound and Extensive in Eight Dharma Sections*, Shakya Chokden summarizes and refutes the main elements of Tsongkhapa's system,[106] saying that Tsongkhapa was refuting all old traditions from the past (*sngon gyi lugs rnying kun*) and treating the identifications of special insight by all Tibetan followers of quintessential instructions merely as a stagnant calm abiding (*ltengs po yi zhi gnas tsam*).[107]

In the *Ocean of Scriptural Statements and Reasoning*, Shakya Chokden objects to criticisms leveled at followers of early practice lineages by later Tibetans who argued that instructions on inquiring whether the mind has color and shape or not, where it comes from, where it abides, and where it goes to are not valid techniques for realizing the mind's non-findability, its ultimate nature.[108] He argues that such criticisms entail deprecation of Nāgārjuna's scriptures, because in the *Commentary on the Mind of Enlightenment* Nāgārjuna taught that the mind cannot be found outside, inside, or in between, has no color or shape, and so forth.[109] Similarly, those criticisms are self-contradictory for Geluk thinkers who esteem Atiśa's teachings as highly as the Buddha's. This is because in his *Quintessential Instructions on Madhyamaka*,[110] explaining the means of realizing the Madhyamaka view, Atiśa also instructed trainees to think that the past mind has ceased, future mind is not produced yet, and the present mind is difficult to analyze because it has neither shape nor color, is neither one nor many, and so forth.[111] Likewise, Shakya Chokden cites the *Last Stage of Meditation* (*Sgom rim mtha' ma*)[112] by Kamalaśīla, who also says that when one analyzes the nature of mind, one realizes that it is not findable inside or outside, has no form, and so forth. He continues with a defense of instructions coming from translator Drokmi on determining appearances as mind (*snang ba sems su thag gcod*), establishing mind as illusion (*sems sgyu ma[r sgrub]*), and establishing illusion as naturelessness (*sgyu ma rang bzhin med par sgrub*), arguing that those are also efficient reasonings analyzing the ultimate and that they are justified by the *Intermediate Stage of Meditation* (*Sgom rim bar ma*)[113] by Kamalaśīla and the progression of the four stages of yoga (*rnal 'byor sa bzhi'i rim pa*) explained by Haribhadra.[114] In other words, Shakya Chokden takes the texts, highly esteemed by Geluk thinkers, and shows that those very texts teach what Geluk thinkers refute.

Shakya Chokden's sympathetic approach to those contemplative instructions might have been influenced by his teacher Rongtön—one of the greatest intellectuals of the fifteenth century thoroughly engaged in composition of voluminous writings and teaching scholastic literature—who treated such instructions as a valid means of realizing reality.[115] In general, Shakya Chokden's interest in practice lineages was most probably inspired by the above-mentioned Changlung Rinpoché, who, according to Shakya Chokden, received without exception all lineages of quintessential instructions surviving in Tibet (30).

But Geluk thinkers were not the only source of disappointment for Shakya Chokden. The views of Rendawa,[116] an influential Sakya thinker who was a teacher of Tsongkhapa and his disciples Gyeltsap Darma Rinchen and Khedrup Gelek Pelzang, were also problematic. In the *Meaningful to Behold: Answers to the Questions of Spiritual Friend Müpa Rapjampa*, Shakya Chokden takes the spread of Rendawa's views as one of the reasons for the decline of the ways of cultivating the definitive meaning taught by all followers of earlier practice lineages:

> The reason for the decline is as follows. The foremost venerable Rendawa said: "There appear no other [thinkers] who know Cittamātra tenet systems correctly," and "In this Snowy Land there appear no other [thinkers] who correctly identified the [stage of] luminosity (*'od gsal, prabhāsvara*)

> asserted by the father Ārya [Nāgārjuna and his spiritual] son Āryadeva."[117] These statements [incorrectly] establish as Cittamātra the view of the three [systems]—Pacification, Great Seal, and Great Perfection—and the Path and Result. They also incorrectly establish as Cittamātra the self-cognizing purity (*rang rig pa'i dag pa*) explained in the *Hevajra*. They also incorrectly negate a common locus (*gzhi mthun*) of ultimate truth and knowing. Because [Rendawa] gave explanations having asserted [the above points], it is important to differentiate between our own and others' tenet systems.[118]

According to Shakya Chokden, Rendawa misinterpreted Cittamātra and even criticized as Cittamātra the views of such tantric teachings as *Hevajra*. Acknowledging the influence of Rendawa's views on the Sakya tradition, Shakya Chokden admonishes Sakyapas to be discriminative and not to fall under the spell of this new position. As will be explained in detail below, Shakya Chokden's own position is that ultimate truth *must* have a common locus (*gzhi mthun*) with knowing, because it is necessarily the latter of the two types of knowing or mind: dualistically appearing knowing (*gnyis snang gi shes pa*) and non-dual primordial mind (*gnyis su med pa'i ye shes, advayajñāna*).[119] (Shakya Chokden distinguishes between two types of knowing: consciousness (*rnam shes, vijñāna*) and primordial mind (*ye shes, jñāna*). As he puts it in his *Appearance of the Sun Pleasing All Thinkers: Discussion of the History of the Chariot Ways of [Dignāga's] 'Sūtra on Valid Cognition' and [Its] Treatises*, "it is contradictory for that which is explained as primordial mind to be consciousness.")[120]

In the *Seventeen Wondrous Answers*, Shakya Chokden addresses those views of Rendawa and Tsongkhapa (along with his followers) that became blended with the authentic Sakya views after its earlier teachings had declined:

> Nowadays, everybody is pervaded by many errors of extensive blending of the lately emerged Dharma terminology [with authentic views. The errors are] as follows: having accepted ultimate truth (*don dam pa'i bden pa, paramārthasatya*), to say that it is not truly established (*bden par ma grub*); to assert that relative existence (*kun rdzob tu yod pa*) fills the role of existence, while ultimate non-being and ultimate nonexistence (*don dam du ma yin pa dang med pa*) do not fill the role of that [non-being] and that [nonexistence];

> lama Rendawa's explanation: having accepted all knowing—[such as] omniscience, innate primordial mind, and so forth—as relative truth only, [to argue] that if primordial mind free from the duality of the apprehended and apprehender itself is explained as the mode of being (*gnas lugs*) and ultimate truth, such would not transcend Cittamātra. [What provides] the support for this [claim of Rendawa] comes down to [Candrakīrti's] *Engaging in Madhyamaka*. Because later [thinkers] of our own and other [traditions] (*rang gzhan gyi phyi rabs pa*) do not provide identifications of ultimate truth apart from that which is explained in the *Engaging in Madhyamaka*, [their views] degenerate from all systems of Vajrayāna (*rdo rje theg pa*, Vajra Vehicle) path. This is because there are no texts of sūtras or tantras that do not explain each and every relative truths as mistaken appearances [arisen from] ignorance exclusively, and there are not any early Tibetan [thinkers] who do not explain so. Therefore, one should not be afraid of true establishment (*bden grub*). This is because if something exists, it has to be true (*bden*). At the same time, there are no textual systems of Madhyamaka or Tantra that do not assert conceptual consciousnesses grasping at existence as objects of abandonment.[121]

Shakya Chokden thereby explains that it was Rendawa who taught that if primordial mind free from the apprehended and apprehender is explained as the mode of being and ultimate truth, such a view will not transcend Cittamātra. He gives Rendawa credit, while admitting that this claim in turn is supported by Candrakīrti's *Engaging in Madhyamaka*. Shakya Chokden thinks that in his criticisms of Yogācāra, Candrakīrti emphasized the Satyākāravāda view, and this became the basis for later Tibetan interpretations of all forms of Yogācāra as being synonymous with Cittamātra, and therefore inferior to Madhyamaka.[122] As a result of following Candrakīrti's view too narrow-mindedly, later followers of Sakya and other traditions do not provide identifications of ultimate truth—other than the one from the *Engaging in Madhyamaka*. Thereby they diverge from all tantric systems because, in Shakya Chokden's opinion, all early Sakya masters agreed that no actual (i.e., efficient, non-metaphorical) ultimate truth was taught in the Niḥsvabhāvavāda texts.[123]

Furthermore, as the above passage demonstrates, later Tibetans did not even seem to understand Candrakīrti—one of their most cherished Niḥsvabhāvavādins. They inverted what Shakya Chokden sees as the correct view of Niḥsvabhāvavāda by treating existence in a conventional or relative way as equal to existence in general, and thereby argued that nonexistence in a true or ultimate way did not necessarily imply nonexistence. Shakya Chokden sees exactly the opposite as Candrakīrti's opinion: to exist means to exist truly, and conventional existence entails nonexistence.

Such were the interrelated elements of religious and intellectual life that Shakya Chokden was responding to in his writings. It is important to note that his views were not formed simply as a response to those new developments. For example, although in many respects Shakya Chokden's approach to reality and related topics is the direct opposite of Tsongkhapa's, his unique approach to Mahāyāna systems should *not* be seen just as a reaction to Tsongkhapa. It is rather an attempt to augment what Shakya Chokden saw as authentic views of earlier Sakya thinkers that were endangered by the Geluk "heterodoxy" gaining popularity right in front of his eyes. In this respect, he is similar to Rongtön and other critics of Geluk views such as Gorampa. After all, despite explanatory differences within the Sakya tradition itself, it developed a distinct flavor of "orthodoxy" going back to the founding Sakya masters, while the newly emerged but aggressively self-assertive system of Tsongkhapa and his followers only started taking hold by the fifteenth century.

This being said, Shakya Chokden's unique interpretation of the nature and relationship of Alīkākāravāda and Niḥsvabhāvavāda—the main topic of this book—was mainly the result of his personal philosophical quest. It was not of much help in refuting Geluk views on Madhyamaka per se, because Geluk thinkers mostly focused on their novel interpretation of the system of Prāsaṅgika and legitimizing Prāsaṅgika's superiority over Svātantrika. Furthermore, many criticisms of Tsongkhapa's views, especially those on the Niḥsvabhāvavāda system, were written by Shakya Chokden *prior* to the time when he started promoting the Alīkākāravāda view as Madhyamaka.[124] This is not surprising, because one of his main esteemed teachers was Rongtön—arguably the first open Sakya critic of Tsongkhapa.[125] Nor was it helpful for bringing his own position closer to the mainstream Sakya tradition that seemed to have been content with the "Madhyamaka = Niḥsvabhāvavāda" formula.

Indeed, Shakya Chokden was already contrasting the existence of differences between the views of Satyākāravāda and Alīkākāravāda with the nonexistence of the difference between the final views of Prāsaṅgika and Svātantrika in one of his earliest treatises, the above-mentioned *Garlands of Waves of Assertions* written in 1454.[126] This seems to have been a widely accepted Sakya position at the time. On the other hand, as Shakya Chokden's works written in the 1470s demonstrate, he became genuinely interested in the deeper meaning of Yogācāra philosophy. Drawing on the internal evidence from Yogācāra texts, the Buddha's prophesies, and multiple reasons he himself adopted or developed, he became convinced that the views expressed in those texts were neither Cittamātra nor Niḥsvabhāvavāda. In 1477[127] Shakya Chokden wrote the monumental *Ocean of Scriptural Statements and Reasoning* where he started addressing the system of Alīkākāravāda as a form of Madhyamaka. By that time, he had already completed his major commentaries on two fundamental Niḥsvabhāvavāda texts popular in Tibet—Nāgārjuna's *Wisdom: Root Stanzas on Madhyamaka* and Candrakīrti's *Engaging in Madhyamaka.*[128] He was never to write *complete* commentaries on Niḥsvabhāvavāda texts again (although he did continue writing texts addressing Niḥsvabhāvavāda views).[129] He had also written Pramāṇa commentaries, commentaries on Maitreya's *Ornament of Clear Realizations,*[130] and some other topics of Maitreya's corpus such as the buddha-essence,[131] and briefly addressed Tantra.[132] Nevertheless, from his early fifties and ending only in 1507—the year he passed away—Shakya Chokden would come back to the topic of Yogācāra and the nature of its relation to Niḥsvabhāvavāda again and again, both in independent writings and multiple commentaries on the *Ornament of Clear Realizations*, as well as on other works of Maitreya, Asaṅga, Dharmakīrti, and other authors, taking his analysis to increasingly deeper and more sophisticated levels.[133]

Shakya Chokden complained that his interest in Yogācāra teachings was not shared by the majority of Tibetans of his time who stopped studying Yogācāra works seriously. As he put it in the *Seventeen Wondrous Answers*, during his lifetime, the discourse of the third dharmacakra was not even heard of—let alone read or studied. It was like a sky lotus—not even stars on the daytime sky. Only he alone was working hard on this system.[134] When he undertook a thorough reconsideration of categories of Mahāyāna systems and their contents, he knew perfectly well that his understanding of the Alīkākāravāda views as belonging to Madhyamaka entailed many problems, as can be judged from the letters of replies to his critics and other texts. Nonetheless, he certainly tried to align himself with the views of early Tibetans and important Indian thinkers as well. This can be seen in his efforts to prove that the approach he followed was also accepted—whether explicitly or implicitly—by the founding Sakya masters and such Indian thinkers as Ratnākaraśānti, Śāntarakṣita, and even Atiśa.

One might surmise that in his criticisms of the newly-emerged views of later Tibetans Shakya Chokden felt himself in a position similar to that of Sakya Pendita more than two centuries earlier.[135] In the same way as Sakya Pendita felt that Buddhist views were polluted by later misunderstandings, Shakya Chokden felt that authentic views coming from India were polluted by later innovations. At the same time, Shakya Chokden felt more freedom to level criticisms at his opponents, partly because polemical writings were better established by his time than at the time of Sakya Pendita, and partly because his opponents—whether dead or alive "later Tibetans"—criticized the traditions of "early Tibetans," including his own.

4. Broadening Empty Horizons: A Note on Changes in Shakya Chokden's Views

One of the important problems involved in the reception of Shakya Chokden's writings by later thinkers is that his unique views were categorized as "other-emptiness" and contrasted to the views of "self-emptiness" held by mainstream Tibetan thinkers. Such a perception was often accompanied by confusion regarding the development or change in his views. In my final remarks in this chapter I want to look at this question of change, which is often mistakenly perceived as a dramatic discontinuity in his thought.

The issue of the extent to which Shakya Chokden changed his views throughout his lifetime was addressed by a number of scholars, both Tibetan and non-Tibetan.[136] When his system of thought is discussed, it is almost inevitably described as that of "other-emptiness"; by extension, Shakya Chokden is treated as an advocate of other-emptiness. In the Tibetan intellectual world, whenever the label "other-emptiness" is attached to Shakya Chokden and his view, it is used as a loosely defined floating category with more sectarian implications than content—a perfect example of a label which itself carries more significance than the meaning it signifies. Consequently, in a context where the other-emptiness view is favored, admitting him into the "other-emptiness camp" helps boost its numbers and prestige. When other-emptiness is treated negatively, labeling him a "Follower of Other-Emptiness" (*gzhan stong pa*) automatically excludes him from the category of thinkers who hold the valid view of "Followers of Self-Emptiness" (*rang stong pa*).

As an outcome of either approach, the next "logical" step is to find out when and why Shakya Chokden became an advocate of other-emptiness. The most common answer is that he changed his views at a certain point from those of self-emptiness, and became an advocate of other-emptiness only later in his life. Another answer is that he always advocated the view of other-emptiness. While there is no need to address all possible ideas about that change or lack thereof, I want to look at two different approaches to this question—one held by a famous Geluk thinker, Tuken Lopzang Chökyi Nyima (*thu'u bkwan blo bzang chos kyi nyi ma*, 1737–1802), and another by an important Sakya thinker Ngakwang Chödrak (*ngag dbang chos grags*, 1572–1641).

In his *Crystal Mirror of Good Explanations: Presentation of the Origins and Assertions of All Tenet systems*, Tuken wrote that first Shakya Chokden adhered (*zhen*) to the view of Madhyamaka, then Cittamātra, and finally Jonangpa (*jo nang pa*).[137] In the same text Tuken also wrote that late in his life Shakya Chokden treated Asaṅga and Vasubandhu as Great Mādhyamikas (*dbu ma pa chen po*), while treating the emptiness accepted by Candrakīrti and other Niḥsvabhāvavādins as a nihilistic emptiness which is not an object of meditative experience.[138] Clearly, Tuken was either misinformed or purposefully distorted Shakya Chokden's views. As I explain in the following chapters, Shakya Chokden's presentation of the self-emptiness taught by Niḥsvabhāvavādins is much more subtle. Also, depending on the context, he treated both Niḥsvabhāvavāda and Alīkākāravāda as the Great Madhyamaka.[139] Apparently, Tuken did not get a chance to glance at the self-explanatory title of Shakya Chokden's major work mentioned above: *Profound Thunder amidst the Clouds of the Ocean of Definitive Meaning: Differentiation of the Two Systems of the Great Madhyamaka Deriving from the Two Great Chariot Ways*, not to mention lengthy discussions of *different* views of the Great Madhyamaka in that root text and its autocommentary—the *Rain of Ambrosia*. Tuken's assessment of Shakya Chokden's views therefore is not trustworthy. Numerous criticisms of Dölpopa in both Shakya Chokden's early and later writings, on the one hand, and the existence of such late texts as the aforementioned *Guiding Instructions on the Madhyamaka View* (35, 46) supportive of Niḥsvabhāvavāda, on the other, further disqualify the model of change of Shakya Chokden's views suggested by Tuken.

In contrast to Tuken, Ngakwang Chödrak, in his *Abundant Discourse on Distinguishing and Decisive Analysis of Tenets of Early and Late Tibetan Scholars*, says that Shakya Chokden *always* advocated the view of other-emptiness.[140] If we take into account Shakya Chokden's words cited in Drölchok's *Thunder of Melodious Praise* (40–41), it is indeed possible that from an early age Shakya Chokden became interested in and started exploring the view that he later came to describe as "other-emptiness." But neither those words nor Shakya Chokden's works written before his journey to Lowo provide any support for the claim that he always advocated that view. For example, in 1474—just a few years before he started addressing the Alīkākāravāda view as Madhyamaka—Shakya Chokden wrote the *Drumming Sounds of the Melodious Voice of Brahma: Refutation of Mistakes About Meditative Stages of the Great Madhyamaka and Explanation of Tenets and Topics of the Views of Prāsaṅgika and Svātantrika*, in which he still counted the Alīkākāravāda system as Cittamātra. In that text he objected to interpretations of the third dharmacakra by "those who accept other-emptiness" (*gzhan stong khas len pa dag*), adding: "What you accept does not surpass the view of Alīkākāravāda even a little."[141] Then, summarizing his refutations of erroneous systems, he wrote:

> In brief, in this Land of Snows there are two [erroneous traditions]: those known as Proponents of Other-Emptiness, who assert the Alīkākāravāda Cittamātra (*sems tsam rnam rdzun [pa]*, False Aspectarian Mind-Only) view as Madhyamaka, and those who in disagreement with all four [Buddhist] tenets assert as the middle (*dbu ma*) a mind which apprehends emptiness as signs, claiming that [such is] the system of self-emptiness.[142]

In the same text he provided arguments refuting both Satyākāravāda and Alīkākāravāda,[143] and narrowed the meaning of Madhyamaka to Prāsaṅgika and Svātantrika when he said that the explanation of emptiness developed by later Tibetans is outside the four Buddhist systems: "[It is] nonexistent in [the systems of] Mādhyamikas, because it exists in neither Prāsaṅgika nor Svātantrika."[144]

Therefore, it is difficult to accept Ngakwang Chödrak's claim. An excellent scholar, he had outstanding knowledge of and devotion to Gorampa's system, but his description of Shakya Chokden's views in the *Abundant Discourse on Distinguishing and Decisive Analysis* seems to indicate that Ngakwang Chödrak did not study Shakya Chokden's works very carefully. For example, he attempts to simultaneously refute what he sees as Shakya Chokden's and Dölpopa's explanation of the buddha-essence, mistakenly assuming that they shared the same view on that issue.[145] He also writes that according to Shakya Chokden, passages from Nāgārjuna's *Praise to the Dharma-Sphere* indicate that the mental continua of sentient beings from the beginning have the buddha-essence ornamented with major and minor marks of a buddha.[146] This statement directly contradicts Shakya Chokden's own *Ascertainment of the Dharma-Sphere: Explanation of [Nāgārjuna's] Treatise 'Praise of the Dharma-Sphere,'*[147] in which he explicitly states it is impossible for sentient beings to have the essence and yet not to see it. Thus, I do not take Ngakwang Chödrak as a reliable source.

In their search for "reasons" for the change in Shakya Chokden's views, some point in the direction of the Seventh Karmapa, assuming that the Karmapa held the view of other-emptiness—an opinion contested by the Eighth Karmapa.[148] Chödrak Gyamtso's influence on Shakya Chokden's view change is problematic, even if we agree that Chödrak Gyamtso *did* hold the view of other-emptiness in one or another form and that his explanation of other-emptiness was similar to Shakya Chokden's—a notion also contested already in the sixteenth century, as we have seen above.[149] Drölchok's *Detailed Analysis* describes three actual meetings between Shakya Chokden and Chödrak Gyamtso. Only during the first meeting in 1484—which lasted for one week—did Shakya Chokden, together with 500 monks he was leading, act as a recipient of the Karmapa's teachings. As for the meetings in 1502 and 1503, Drölchok presents Shakya Chokden in the role of an advisor to the Karmapa. It is true that Pawo Tsuklak Trengwa in his *Feast for Scholars*, focusing on the figure of the Karmapa, writes that Shakya Chokden received many teachings from the Karmapa during the Rinpung visit. The two descriptions are not necessarily contradictory. Nevertheless, it seems that the latter one is sometimes taken as the "reason" for Shakya Chokden's changing his views.[150] Such a theory can hardly stand, as has been rightly noticed by Stearns.[151] We know that by 1502/1503, Shakya Chokden already had written most of his main treatises dealing with Alīkākāravāda/Niḥsvabhāvavāda and self-emptiness/other-emptiness.[152] Therefore, it was simply too late for Shakya Chokden to change his views on emptiness at that time.

Whatever scarce information we have on meetings and relations between Shakya Chokden and the Karmapa, it does not provide more foundation for assuming that he was converted or influenced by the Karmapa than that the Karmapa was converted or influenced by him—an option not at all impossible considering Shakya Chokden's advisory role described in the *Detailed Analysis*. Also, although according to Pawo Tsuklak Trengwa's description of their meeting at Rinpung, Shakya Chokden was impressed by the Karmapa and accepted him as his root guru, Pawo Tsuklak Trengwa does not make the claim of influence or conversion in that description either. According to the *Detailed Analysis*, the Seventh Karmapa and Shakya Chokden said that they were of one mind, but that too does not add any proofs to the conversion version. Is it possible that the fifty-six-year-old Shakya Chokden was somehow influenced by the thirty-year-old Karmapa during their first meeting in 1484? I see no reason to accept that option. By that time Shakya Chokden had already composed such texts as the *Ocean of Scriptural Statements and Reasoning* and the *Ascertainment of the Dharma-Sphere* where he treated the Alīkākāravāda view of other-emptiness as Madhyamaka. Thus, until evidence to the contrary is found, it is preferable to dismiss all claims of conversion or influence exercised on Shakya Chokden by the Karmapa as unjustified and unnecessary. Rather, it appears that that the mutual affinity Shakya Chokden and the Karmapa developed during their meetings was part of the broader intertwined processes of Tsang getting more political power, the Karmapa being one of the most powerful religious leaders of the time, Shakya Chokden becoming popular as a teacher, and both of them being recipients of the generous support of Rinpung rulers. It is even possible that Shakya Chokden met the Karmapa *because* of Rinpung connections.

I would also note that quite early in his life, in 1456, Shakya Chokden wrote the *Drop of Ambrosia: Differentiation of Classes of Tantras*.[153] According to its colophon, he wrote it in a "mountain retreat of Nenang Gyelwa, a place of utter solitude at glorious Tsurpu" (*dpal mtshur phu'i yang dben gnas snang rgyal ba'i ri khrod*). In that text, when addressing the number of lifetimes required for attaining buddhahood by practicing different classes of tantras, Shakya Chokden mentions separately—without rejection or approval—the approach of the *Profound Inner Meaning*,[154] written by the Third Karmapa Rangjung Dorjé, and that of Sakyapa.[155] Together with the fact that Shakya Chokden had received various empowerments and transmissions of Karma Kagyü in his early twenties (29), it demonstrates that he was familiar with Karma Kagyü systems long before meeting the Seventh Karmapa.

I want to reiterate that while Drölchok never talks about the Karmapa converting Shakya Chokden, Drölchok's *Thunder of Melodious Praise* indicates that Shakya Chokden's interest in the definitive meaning of Yogācāra teachings was initially inspired by Pema Zangpowa, and his meeting with Namgyel Drakzang inspired him to write texts openly treating Alīkākāravāda as Madhyamaka. Given Drölchok's unmatched knowledge of Shakya Chokden's life and works, it only makes sense to accept that the primary influences on the development and change in Shakya Chokden's views were Pema Zangpowa and Namgyel Drakzang, although it remains unclear how many of their views he actually shared.

Why is the question of change of Shakya Chokden's views so confusing? I would argue that the confusion is caused primarily by the question itself rather than the material it deals with. In my opinion, the discussion of change in Shakya Chokden's views from self-emptiness to other-emptiness is inherently flawed because it assumes that self- and other-emptiness are defined doxographical categories. It also assumes that it is possible to have only a "monogamous marriage" with them, i.e., that it is not possible to hold self-emptiness and other-emptiness views at the same time—precisely what Shakya Chokden himself objects to. Furthermore, what is inevitably *not* addressed in such discussion is whether Shakya Chokden ever calls his view "other-emptiness" and describes himself as its advocate, and whether in his opinion espousing that view implies divorcing the view of self-emptiness. Even if we leave aside the fact that there exist different explanations of self- and other-emptiness, such an approach is destined to failure precisely because Shakya Chokden in his works written from 1477 to 1507 embraced *both* Alīkākāravāda and Niḥsvabhāvavāda views as valid, thereby advocating a "polygamous marriage" to the two systems and the two types of emptiness they teach. As his own works demonstrate, Shakya Chokden *never* became an exclusive proponent of other-emptiness in the first place, because he never abandoned the view of self-emptiness. Rather, for more than thirty years (from 1477 until his death) he equally embraced both views, being a proponent of other-emptiness no more and no less than self-emptiness. As I emphasize throughout this book, Shakya Chokden treated *both* views as Madhyamaka.

Clear as it is, his approach seems to have been too complex or too broad to fit the narrow outlook of those who treat self-emptiness and other-emptiness as mutually contradictory, like water and fire. This is understandable, because the majority of Tibetan thinkers in general, and Shakya Chokden's critics in particular, can imagine only a monogamous marriage to either of the two types of emptiness. The polygamous relationship with self-emptiness and other-emptiness espoused by him seems to have been prohibited by the unwritten law of the Tibetan intellectual world, and for violating that law Shakya Chokden paid the worst penalty a thinker of his caliber can pay—his views were misunderstood and largely neglected.

If we look at the process of development of Shakya Chokden's thought from the open perspective he himself proposes, we will also understand the change of his views differently. This change did not imply the abandonment of the Niḥsvabhāvavāda view of self-emptiness.

Rather than discarding self-emptiness in favor of other-emptiness, he expanded the horizons of emptiness to fit both types of emptiness into the category of valid Madhyamaka views. Therefore, when we talk about his growth as a thinker, it is preferable to use the term "development" or "expansion" of views rather than "change," if the latter is meant to imply a dramatic discontinuity in his thought. On the other hand, if by "change" we mean exploration, development, and expansion, with some unavoidable adjustments of the views, then there is no problem in saying that he—as have many other important Tibetan thinkers—changed his views. Indeed, no thinkers would ever develop intellectually if they were simply repeating what their teachers taught them and/or what they themselves said in their youth.

In a nutshell, the answer to the question of change in Shakya Chokden's views—an answer suggested by his own works—is: he did not *convert* to the other-emptiness view, but rather *expanded* his view of Madhyamaka to include the Alīkākāravāda version of other-emptiness into the category of Madhyamaka on a par with the Niḥsvabhāvavāda version of self-emptiness.

Chapter 3

Readjusting Rungs of the Ladder

Revisiting Doxographical Hierarchies

1. Key Features of Shakya Chokden's Approach to the Buddhist Tenets

This chapter focuses on key elements of Shakya Chokden's approach that are crucial for an in-depth understanding of his interpretation of Yogācāra and Madhyamaka. It places that interpretation within the broader context of Buddhist doxographical writings and provides a new perspective on philosophical classifications and their advocates as it is put forward by Shakya Chokden.

In his interpretation of Buddhist tenets, Shakya Chokden not only reconsiders the meaning of the Buddhist systems, but also develops a unique approach to the tenet categories themselves, as well as their interrelationship. His approach is particularly powerful due to the intricate relationship between the "vessel" of the tenet categories and the "content" of the views they contain.

He accepts the standard fourfold hierarchical division of Buddhist systems into Vaibhāṣika, Sautrāntika, Cittamātra, and Madhyamaka that had already been introduced from India to Tibet by the time of the early dissemination of Buddhism. Each preceding system in this hierarchical structure is seen as "lower" than the next in terms of accuracy, comprehensiveness, and profundity.[1] He also agrees with the placement of Cittamātra below Madhyamaka in this four-runged hierarchical ladder of tenets.[2] This being said, his approach to the interpretation of tenets has two unique features that can be described as follows. First, he holds that what has been negated by followers of the lower tenets is not reintroduced and not affirmed by followers of the higher tenets. Second, he argues that complete realizations of the selflessness of persons (*gang zag gi bdag med, pudgalanairātmya*) and partial realizations of the selflessness of phenomena (*chos kyi bdag med, dharmanairātmya*) based on the teachings of the lower tenets are genuine from the point of view of the higher tenets as well. Based upon this, Shakya Chokden draws two important conclusions: it is possible to abandon all afflictions and become an arhat even by contemplating the selflessness of persons taught in the Vaibhāṣika system, without relying on the views of higher tenets; and starting from the level of Satyākāravāda (i.e., Cittamātra), the existence of external phenomena is not accepted by *any* proponents of the Buddhist tenets, including Prāsaṅgika.

As a result, in Shakya Chokden's system, the views of lower Buddhist tenets are assigned substantial weight as self-sufficient soteriological tools. In particular, the higher the tenets are placed in the four-runged ladder of tenets, the closer they come to each other, the more subtle their differences with each other become, and the more those differences pertain to the reality of mental states. When one accepts—as Shakya Chokden does—that the self of persons (*gang zag gi bdag, pudgalātman*) is completely refuted even by Vaibhāṣikas, and external existence is not accepted by anyone starting from the level of Cittamātra, then the main points of disagreement left between proponents of Mahāyāna tenets about ultimate reality come down to which aspects of mind are real and which are not, which mental aspects should be maintained as true and which should be discarded as illusory and obstructive. Shakya Chokden explains his position in the *Ocean of Scriptural Statements and Reasoning*:

> When one engages in the Teachings through the stages of the four tenets, with respect to the modes of proving objects being proven (*bsgrub bya sgrub pa'i tshul*), there are [cases when] those very [elements] that were established by preceding [tenets] have to be refuted by succeeding ones. Nevertheless, with respect to the modes of negating objects of negation (*dgag bya 'gog pa'i tshul*), those very negations that were made by preceding [tenets] also have to be posited straight as they are (*thad sor 'jog*) by the succeeding ones. This is like, for example, the negation of the self of persons by the śrāvaka schools (*nyan thos sde pa*) and the negation of the self of the apprehended-phenomena (*gzung ba chos kyi bdag*) by Cittamātra Followers.[3]

In other words, certain claims of lower systems, such as the existence of partless atoms accepted by Vaibhāṣika and Sautrāntika, are negated by followers of Mahāyāna systems. Nevertheless, the views refuted by followers of lower systems do not have to be refuted anew by followers of higher ones. Those refutations made by followers of lower tenets—as long as they are not aimed at assertions made by followers of higher tenets—are accepted as they are by the latter, because such refutations are complete from the point of view of followers of higher tenets as well. Therefore, there is no need to develop a more intricate reasoning for negating what has been already negated; otherwise—to use an analogy—it will be like shooting a victim who has already been killed with a knife. What has been negated by followers of lower tenets will never sneak back into the views of followers of higher ones; otherwise—to use another analogy—it will be like pebbles that could not get through a sieve with bigger holes but manage somehow to get through a sieve with smaller holes. This approach presupposes that followers of lower tenets do not have sufficient tools for refuting assertions made by followers of higher tenets. For example, although followers of non-Mahāyāna Buddhist systems refute the emptiness of all phenomena asserted by Mahāyāna systems, such refutations are not asserted by Mahāyāna thinkers as valid or efficient.

Buddhist thinkers are in consensus that a certain system of thought is valid only if it can contribute to the soteriological objective of enlightenment, and yet, typically these standard systems are themselves understood to have differing soteriological capacities. Shakya Chokden takes this approach a step further, and argues that the view of the selflessness of persons developed by proponents of *all four* Buddhist tenets is a valid means of liberation. It is non-mistaken not only in and of itself, but also as the antidote of that ignorance which causes rebirth in cyclic existence. This is why he not only argues that "there is no disagreement between the four [types of] proponents of tenets with regard to the meaning of the selflessness of persons,"[4] but also explains how the selflessness of persons taught even by the śrāvaka schools (Vaibhāṣika and Sautrāntika) is sufficient for the attainment of liberation from cyclic existence. From the *Great Path of Ambrosia of Emptiness*:

> If the selflessness of persons is explained in its entirety even by Vaibhāṣika texts, it goes without saying that it is accepted by Sautrāntika [as well]. Hence, by accustoming [one's mind] to that selflessness of persons determined by texts of Vaibhāṣika and Sautrāntika, it is possible to see it directly, and by further accustoming oneself to that very

> [direct realization], it is possible to manifest nirvāṇa [in which] the seeds of grasping at the self of persons have been abandoned.[5]

When Shakya Chokden correlates views of proponents of different tenets with the presentation of the three vehicles (*theg pa, yāna*)—Śrāvakayāna, Pratyekabuddhayāna, and Mahāyāna—he treats the views of Vaibhāṣika and Sautrāntika as sufficient for attaining the nirvāṇa of Śrāvakayāna, and the view of Cittamātra as sufficient for attaining the nirvāṇa of Pratyekabuddhayāna. In the *Rain of Ambrosia,* he explains:

> Thus, it is possible to accept the explanation of the views of both Vaibhāṣika and Sautrāntika as filling the role of the view of followers of Śrāvakayāna (within the three vehicles), and this view of Cittamātra as filling the role of the view of followers of Pratyekabuddhayāna. This is because it is explained that uninterrupted paths of meditative equipoise (*mnyam par gzhag pa'i bar chad med lam*) on the meaning of those views are able to eradicate the seeds of what is treated as their respective objects of abandonment by the paths of these two vehicles: afflictive obscurations (*nyon mongs pa['i sgrib pa]*) and those obscurations of knowables which are conceptions of the apprehended (*shes bya'i sgrib pa gzung rtog*).[6]

This approach is supportive of lower tenets as valid tools of liberation, but is also delimiting. Not only Vaibhāṣika and Sautrāntika, but Cittamātra too is relegated to the level of those systems that cannot bring about the attainment of buddhahood. This approach also helps Shakya Chokden to increase the distance between Satyākāravāda and Alīkākāravāda, and cement the wall separating the two systems.

Similarities between the views on reality held by proponents of the four tenets are not limited to the selflessness of persons. Shakya Chokden extends his approach to the selflessness of phenomena, arguing that "apart from cognitions appearing as matter (*gzugs, rūpa*), no matter is accepted in Mahāyāna teachings."[7] More specifically, he explains:

> With regard to the reasoning establishing the truthlessness of external objects (*phyi rol gyi don bden med*), there is no difference at all between Madhyamaka and Cittamātra; with regard to the reasoning establishing the truthlessness

> of the apprehended-aspects (*gzung rnam bden med*), there is no difference at all in the profundity of [the view of] Alīkākāravāda and Niḥsvabhāvavāda.[8]

Cittamātra's negation of external material things is complete, and Madhyamaka is not required to posit additional deeper arguments negating external matter. The negation of the apprehended-aspects by Alīkākāravāda and Niḥsvabhāvavāda is treated in the same way: both systems refute them completely.

The passages cited thus far suggest that Shakya Chokden is trying to reconcile different tenets by stressing their commonalities. From this perspective, the four Buddhist tenets resemble four matryoshka dolls, the smaller or lower ones fitting perfectly into the bigger or higher ones. But if this is such a perfect fit, then why would the advocates of higher tenets so persistently critique and polemically refute the arguments of the lower tenet systems?

According to Shakya Chokden, the elements of lower tenets refuted by advocates of higher ones are primarily those asserted to be true or real. In other words, in the context of negations of the two types of self (of persons and phenomena), advocates of the higher tenets are in perfect harmony with the negations made by advocates of the lower tenets, but disagree with their affirmative positions. For example, the negation by Vaibhāṣika and Sautrāntika of phenomena extended in space and time, or the negation by Cittamātra of all external phenomena, is accepted and assimilated by followers of the higher systems. In contrast, advocates of those higher systems refute the positive assertions by Vaibhāṣika and Sautrāntika of partless atoms and by Cittamātra of true existence of the apprehended-aspects.

Judged from this perspective, advocates of lower systems can achieve nirvāṇa, while at the same time making philosophical mistakes with respect to details concerning the nature of external phenomena, mind, and so on. This is because the achievement of nirvāṇa depends primarily on what is negated rather than what is asserted. From among the three possible nirvāṇas—of śrāvakas, pratyekabuddhas, and buddhas—the former two are achieved through abandoning afflictive obscurations (*nyon sgrib, kleśāvaraṇa*) and do not require the complete abandonment of obscurations of knowables (*shes sgrib, jñeyāvaraṇa*),[9] but the latter one does. Philosophical misunderstandings do not necessarily block the abandonment of afflictions that is a precondition for achieving nirvāṇa. Only a buddha's nirvāṇa is unattainable if one has lingering areas of ignorance, since a buddha in Mahāyāna thought is omniscient by definition, and therefore free from all sorts of ignorance.

More specifically, according to the widely accepted Buddhist view, the path (*lam, mārga*) has to be practiced by alternating meditative equipoise and subsequent attainment. During the former, one cultivates the view of reality; during the latter, one cultivates views and practices that allow further advance on the path. The way one sees the world in these two contexts also changes: in meditative equipoise, one observes and meditates on selflessness or emptiness, described as a negation. Cultivation of the view directly realizing selflessness results in abandonment of obscurations; the extent of the abandonment correlates directly to the extent of the negation of the two types of self. However, when one engages in various virtuous practices during subsequent attainment, mistaken visions and perspectives are not only unavoidable, but can even be helpful for further progress on the path. For example, in order to achieve results of the path, it is permissible to cultivate compassion to other beings while knowing at the same time that "sentient beings" is an imputation based on ignorance. As Śāntideva puts it in his *Engaging in the Bodhisattva Deeds*:

> - If sentient beings do not exist,
>   Whom will one generate compassion to?
> - Those who are imputed by delusion [and]
>   Accepted for the sake of [achieving] the result.
> - Without sentient beings, whose result is it?
> - True, but [such is] asserted out of delusion.[10]

Utilizing this feature of the Buddhist worldview, in the *Rain of Ambrosia* Shakya Chokden splits the views pertaining to each of the four tenets into separate views relating to meditative equipoise and subsequent attainment, respectively. The meditative equipoise views are presented in terms of negations by the system in question, and the subsequent attainment views are presented in terms of its positive assertions. From this perspective, Shakya Chokden argues that advocates of the higher tenets develop their view of meditative equipoise by expanding the view of meditative equipoise of advocates of the lower tenets,[11] but in no way are required to accept the assertions made by advocates of the lower systems in the context of subsequent attainment.

Because negations made by advocates of the higher systems are broader than the corresponding negations made by advocates of the lower systems, advocates of the higher tenets not only absorb negations made by advocates of the lower tenets, but unavoidably negate specific affirmations made by advocates of the lower tenets as well.

Disagreements between proponents of different systems stem from this fundamental dynamic, including the contexts in which advocates of higher tenets try to refute and surpass advocates of lower ones.

According to Shakya Chokden, certain tenets are not accepted as belonging to Madhyamaka because their negations are not extensive enough to abandon obscurations of knowables. At the same time, to be a Mādhyamika, one does not have to make the broadest negation possible either. Here lies an important difference between Shakya Chokden's approach to Cittamātra and Madhyamaka on the one hand, and Alīkākāravāda and Niḥsvabhāvavāda subdivisions of Madhyamaka on the other. Madhyamaka is placed above Cittamātra because it negates more than Cittamātra (in particular, the apprehended-aspects), and such negation *is necessary* to achieve buddhahood. On the other hand, although Niḥsvabhāvavāda negates more than Alīkākāravāda (i.e., it negates the apprehender-aspects that Alīkākāravāda retains), such negation *is not necessary* even for the achievement of buddhahood. This is why in Shakya Chokden's system, both Niḥsvabhāvavāda and Alīkākāravāda are located at the same level as equal subdivisions of Madhyamaka.

Finally, it should be noted that even in his early texts where he was still considering Alīkākāravāda as a subdivision of Cittamātra, Shakya Chokden explicitly disagreed with those Tibetan thinkers whose position was that systems from Alīkākāravāda on downward lack both the reasoning establishing external things and the apprehended-aspects as empty and the valid cognition realizing that emptiness. For example, in his *Enjoyment Ocean of Scriptural Statements and Reasoning Differentiating One's Own and Others' Tenets: Explanation of Difficult Points of the 'Ornament of Clear Realizations' Treatise of Quintessential Instructions on the Perfection of Wisdom Together with Its Commentaries*, he explained that the "reason of the lack of being one or many" (*gcig dang du bral gyi gtan tshigs, ekānekaviyogahetu*) is the same nominally and functionally in the various contexts in which it is deployed, whether by both Madhyamaka and Cittamātra in their negation of external things or by Alīkākāravāda and Niḥsvabhāvavāda in their negation of the apprehended-aspects:

> The "reason of the lack of being one or many" is taught as a reasoning establishing [both] external objects and the apprehended-aspects appearing [as] those [external objects] to be without truth. In the mode of it[s positing,] there is not observed even the slightest difference in profundity between the two, Madhyamaka and Cittamātra.[12]

This and similar statements in other early texts written by Shakya Chokden demonstrate that even before he worked out his own unique classification of Mahāyāna systems, he already was pursuing approaches that lay fertile ground for the later, more radical interpretative frameworks. In fact, the later works are quite continuous with the earlier works, with the major shift being that he reclassified Alīkākāravāda as belonging to Madhyamaka. Of course, this shift of contextualization involved multiple other issues, such as distancing Alīkākāravāda from Satyākāravāda, legitimizing Alīkākāravāda as Madhyamaka, and proving that the Alīkākāravāda view is as soteriologically efficient as that of Niḥsvabhāvavāda. These in turn are intricately linked with his revised understanding of the nature of the Madhyamaka category itself.

2. Demarcating the Middle: On the Valid Divisions of Madhyamaka and Great Madhyamaka

Shakya Chokden admits that thinkers of each of the four Buddhist systems treat their own view of selflessness as the Madhyamaka view (*dbu ma'i lta ba*)[13]—literally, "view of the Middle"—because they see it as the middle between the two extremes (*mtha' gnyis, antadvaya*) of eternalism (*rtag mtha', śāśvatānta*) and nihilism (*chad mtha', ucchedānta*) as they are defined by their tenets. Nevertheless, not all of those thinkers see their view as Madhyamaka in the sense of one of the four systems traditionally discussed in Buddhist scholasticism.[14] Furthermore, none of the advocates of Buddhist tenet systems accepts the existence of other tenets higher than one's own.[15] Shakya Chokden does not therefore argue that all four systems can be equally accepted as Madhyamaka in the sense of the fourth and highest system:

> As long as the mode of eliminating the two extremes with respect to phenomena [i.e., the self of phenomena (*chos kyi bdag, dharmātman*), as contrasted to the self of persons] is not completely perfected, [such systems can] not be posited as Madhyamaka.[16]

As I explained above, according to Shakya Chokden, all four tenet systems provide a comprehensive presentation of the selflessness of persons. He further argues that with respect to their presentation of the selflessness of persons, views of all four tenets *have* to be posited as Madhyamaka.[17] Nevertheless, with respect to the view of the selflessness of phenomena, Shakya Chokden is more selective, arguing that only some systems have the ability to eliminate the two extremes, which is necessary to be classified as Madhyamaka. Even though Vaibhāṣikas and Sautrāntikas claim that one can abandon all obscurations and attain buddhahood by following their own respective tenets, Shakya Chokden agrees with the Mahāyāna critique of this as impossible. At the same time, he parts ways with the majority of Tibetan doxographers who claim that only Niḥsvabhāvavādins have the ability to eliminate all extremes. He does not believe that the only valid Madhyamaka is a system of thought with the most efficient reasoning aimed at abandoning all extremes and refuting all other systems of thought. As we have learned already, although Alīkākāravāda does not negate the apprehender-aspect and Niḥsvabhāvavāda does, Shakya Chokden treats both of them equally as Madhyamaka. What then does he posit as the valid divisions of Madhyamaka?

The following statement from his *Thorough Clarification of Definitive Meaning of the 'Five Dharmas of Maitreya'* is a good starting point for the discussion of which systems he sees as valid subdivisions of Madhyamaka, which arguments he puts forward to prove his position, and how he correlates those divisions with other categories:

> In brief, the division of Cittamātra into Satyākāravāda and Alīkākāravāda and [the division of] Madhyamaka into Prāsaṅgika and Svātantrika do not exist in the divisions of tenets in the Land of Āryas [India]. This is because they are not observed in scriptural statements, and also because [they are proved to be] unsuitable through reasoning: divisions of tenets are made on the basis of *views*, but no difference is apparent between the views of Prāsaṅgika and Svātantrika Madhyamaka. In contrast, the division of Madhyamaka into the two systems of methods of Followers of Self-Emptiness and Other-Emptiness (*rang gzhan stong pa'i tshul lugs*) is well clarified in the texts of the two great chariot ways [opened by Nāgārjuna and Maitreya, respectively].[18]

It is worth noticing that neither the "Prāsaṅgika/Svātantrika" nor the "Followers of Self-Emptiness/Followers of Other-Emptiness" paired terms existed in India. At the same time, in his rejection of substantial differences between Svātantrika and Prāsaṅgika and his assertion of important differences between Niḥsvabhāvavāda and Alīkākāravāda, Shakya Chokden agrees with the majority of Indian and Tibetan thinkers. By extension, when he treats Niḥsvabhāvavāda and Alīkākāravāda views as those of Self-Emptiness and Other-Emptiness, respectively, Shakya Chokden presents the Self-Emptiness/Other-Emptiness distinction as more "authentic" than that of Prāsaṅgika/Svātantrika.

Note also that in the above passage Shakya Chokden does not deny the categories of Satyākāravāda and Alīkākāravāda per se. Instead, he is against subsuming both of them under the category of Cittamātra. He preserves the category of Yogācāra with its two subdivisions, but places Alīkākāravāda into the category of Madhyamaka, equating Satyākāravāda with Cittamātra. To support his interpretation, he appeals to Yogācāra texts themselves, as in the following passage from the same text:

> There is no valid source explaining these Alīkākāravādins as Cittamātra Followers. As for the scriptural statement demonstrating them as Mādhyamikas, there is this *Differentiation of the Middle and Extremes* [by Maitreya].[19]

Likewise, in the *Answers to Questions Issuing from the 'Differentiation of the Two Modes,'* Shakya Chokden appeals to the authority of Maitreya and Indian commentators on Maitreya's texts in order to support his explanation of the tenet divisions. He contrasts it to the approach of Tibetan thinkers who treat both Satyākāravāda and Alīkākāravāda as subdivisions of Cittamātra:

> In the textual system of Yogācāra, the division into the two [systems of] Cittamātra Followers and Mādhyamikas exists in the texts of Maitreya with their commentaries. Cittamātra Followers [as they are] renowned in Tibet are explained as "Satyākāravāda" and "Alīkākāravāda."[20]

Shakya Chokden also acknowledges that the terms "Satyākāravāda" and "Alīkākāravāda" themselves are mostly used by Tibetans. In the *Ocean of Scriptural Statements and Reasoning*, he explains that what was known to past Tibetan thinkers as the differences between Satyākāravāda and Alīkākāravāda was in fact conceptualized in India as differences between Yogācāra Cittamātra Followers and Mādhyamikas (*rnal 'byor spyod pa'i sems mtsam pa dang dbu ma pa*).[21] Nevertheless, he does not discard the terms "Satyākāravāda" and "Alīkākāravāda," and uses them in different contexts and combinations (such as "Alīkākāravāda Mādhyamika," etc.[22]), possibly because these terms explicitly express one of the most important differences between the two systems as he sees them: accepting the apprehended-aspects as true versus treating them as false.[23]

Shakya Chokden never disputes the idea that the Niḥsvabhāvavāda system should be classified as Madhyamaka. Nevertheless, as the passage from the *Thorough Clarification of Definitive Meaning of the 'Five Dharmas of Maitreya'* cited above shows, he does think that the categories of Svātantrika and Prāsaṅgika are insignificant as divisions of Madhyamaka.[24] Thus, according to him, the only two valid subdivisions of Madhyamaka are instead Alīkākāravāda and Niḥsvabhāvavāda.[25] A good example of this approach is his *Wish Fulfilling Meru*, where Alīkākāravāda Yogācāra and Niḥsvabhāvavāda Madhyamaka are presented as subdivisions of Madhyamaka, while Cittamātra is put into the category of Vastusatpadārthavāda (*dngos por smra ba*, Proponents of Phenomenal Existence) together with the two śrāvaka schools: Vaibhāṣika and Sautrāntika.

Importantly, Shakya Chokden treats both Alīkākāravāda and Niḥsvabhāvavāda as the Great Madhyamaka (*dbu ma chen po*), as is clear from the title of his major work on the two systems: *Profound Thunder amidst the Clouds of the Ocean of Definitive Meaning: Differentiation of the Two Systems of the Great Madhyamaka Deriving from the Two Great Chariot Ways*, and other writings. Shakya Chokden provides details of his position in the *Rain of Ambrosia*, where he comments on the meaning of the "Differentiation of the Two Systems of the Great Madhyamaka" (*dbu ma chen po'i lugs gnyis rnam par dbye*). It is worth citing this important passage at length, because it well illustrates his reconciliatory and context-oriented approach to Niḥsvabhāvavāda and Alīkākāravāda:

> In general, it is universally known that the Lesser Madhyamaka (*dbu ma chung ngu*) is explained as the view of definitive meaning of the śrāvaka schools. The Great Madhyamaka is that very Madhyamaka which is on the upper end of the four [types of] proponents of tenets. There are two dissimilar [approaches] to its identification: [the one] derives from the Yogācāra texts, and [the other one] derives from the Niḥsvabhāvavāda texts. Are both [of them] posited exclusively as the Great [Madhyamaka]? There are two contexts there: the level of Pāramitāyāna (*phar phyin theg pa*, Perfection Vehicle) alone, and the time [when it is] combined with Mantrayāna (*sngags kyi theg pa*, Mantra Vehicle). In terms of the first one, only Niḥsvabhāvavāda Madhyamaka is the Great [Madhyamaka]. This is because [its] reasoning negating elaborations apprehending signs (*mtshan 'dzin gyi spros pa 'gog byed kyi rigs pa*) is much more profound than [that of] the former one [i.e., Yogācāra

> Madhyamaka]. At that time, the other one [i.e., Yogācāra Madhyamaka] is posited as the Intermediate Madhyamaka (*dbu ma 'bring po*). In terms of the second one [i.e., the approach incorporating Mantrayāna as well], there are two further [types: the one] connected with the explicit teachings of the last pronouncement (*bka' tha ma'i dngos bstan*), and [the other one] connected with the explicit teachings of the middle pronouncement (*bka' bar pa'i dngos bstan*). The first one is ascertained as exclusively the Great Madhyamaka, because of being Madhyamaka where that very primordial mind free from the duality of the apprehended and apprehender (*gzung 'dzin gnyis su med pa'i ye shes*) is ascertained as the object of meditative experience (*sgom pas nyams su myong bya*). The connection [between the parts] of that [reasoning is established], because in this [Mantra] Vehicle, the analysis by the wisdom of individual analysis (*so sor rtog pa'i shes rab kyi dpyad pa*) preceding [the meditative experience] is not main[ly stressed]; what is main[ly stressed] is the meditative experience (*sgom pas nyams su myong ba*) [itself]. By implication (*de'i shugs la*), the explicit teachings of [Nāgārjuna's] *Collection of Reasonings* are established as the Intermediate Madhyamaka. If that Madhyamaka explicitly taught by the *Collection of Reasonings* is also combined with the object of experience (*nyams su myong bya*) [taught] by [Nāgārjuna's] *Collection of Praises*, [it] is ascertained in this Mantrayāna as the Great Madhyamaka. Therefore, both [chariot] ways also have to be posited as the Great Madhyamaka. This is because here [i.e., in Mantrayāna], ceasing elaborations apprehending signs does not depend exclusively on the reasoning of listening and thinking (*thos bsam gyi rigs pa*).[26]

As this passage demonstrates, Shakya Chokden agrees with what he understands as the widespread Mahāyāna interpretation of the śrāvaka schools of Vaibhāṣika and Sautrāntika as the Lesser Madhyamaka. On the other hand, his identification of the Great Madhyamaka is not as clear-cut, because he has to take into account divergent opinions of Mahāyāna thinkers that clash and contradict each other. Instead of siding with just one of those opinions, he chooses a more nuanced approach and argues that the meaning of the "Great Madhyamaka" is contextually dependent on whether one interprets it from the point of view of Pāramitāyāna (i.e., non-tantric Mahāyāna teachings) alone or from the point of view of the Mahāyāna teachings that include Mantrayāna (i.e., tantric teachings) as well. He further argues that both approaches derive from the authentic teachings of the Buddha himself: his middle and last pronouncements or dharmacakras.[27]

Note that in the above passage, Shakya Chokden does not give preference to Alīkākāravāda over Niḥsvabhāvavāda or to Niḥsvabhāvavāda over Alīkākāravāda. His objective in that passage—as well as in the *Profound Thunder* and the *Rain of Ambrosia* as a whole—is to demonstrate that both Alīkākāravāda and Niḥsvabhāvavāda are equally valid types of Madhyamaka. They are therefore "great" in specific contexts that allow their greatness to shine forth, although they are far from treating each other as great. In this way, Shakya Chokden avoids taking sides,[28] and thereby presents both systems not only as Madhyamaka but as the Great Madhyamaka—the approach that distinguishes him from other thinkers such as Taranatha (*tā ra nā tha*, 1575–1634), who limit the category of Great Madhyamaka to a more narrowly defined type of Madhyamaka, such as the system of Other-Emptiness.[29]

Shakya Chokden's reference to tantric teachings is also significant, and will be discussed separately below.[30] Overall, by weaving the discussion of tantric views into his presentation of Buddhist tenets, he resorts to the authority of Buddhist tantras in order to support his interpretation of Alīkākāravāda as an authentic type of Madhyamaka and the Great Madhyamaka. As we will see below (254 ff.), he treats tantric views themselves as the third type of Madhyamaka, and argues for a very close proximity of Alīkākāravāda and Tantra. He also follows this approach in such texts as the *Precious Treasury of the Condensed Essence*. The first section of that text[31] is dedicated specifically to the exploration of the question of the Great Madhyamaka, and its rhetoric is similar to the one in the passage cited above. It also posits tantric views taught in Buddhist tantras, their commentaries, and quintessential instructions on tantric practice as the Great Madhyamaka alongside the other two types of the Great Madhyamaka—Niḥsvabhāvavāda and Alīkākāravāda.

As these and other texts we will be dealing with demonstrate, Shakya Chokden's approach to categorizations of Buddhist systems as Madhyamaka and Great Madhyamaka is context-dependent, and the identifications he provides shift depending on which system he uses as his interpretive standpoint. Nevertheless, precisely because of this shifting approach he manages to firmly hold the ground of his basic position that there are two and only two valid subdivisions of the non-tantric (Great) Madhyamaka: Niḥsvabhāvavāda and Alīkākāravāda.

3. Self-Emptiness and Other-Emptiness

When comparing Alīkākāravāda and Niḥsvabhāvavāda, Shakya Chokden also uses the terms "other-emptiness" and "self-emptiness," because they clearly highlight major differences between these two forms of Madhyamaka. In the *Ocean of Scriptural Statements and Reasoning*, he explains that there are two ways to identify the Madhyamaka view: one originating from the three intermediate treatises of Maitreya[32] with his followers that teach the Yogācāra view, and the other originating from the treatises of Nāgārjuna with his followers that teach the Niḥsvabhāvavāda view. One of the differences between the views of emptiness they posit is expressed as the former's other-emptiness versus the latter's self-emptiness. Shakya Chokden writes:

> In general, the presentation of other-emptiness originates from the texts of Yogācāra, while the presentation of self-emptiness originates from the texts of Niḥsvabhāvavāda.[33]

He thereby treats Yogācāras as Proponents of Other-Emptiness (*gzhan stong smra ba*) and Niḥsvabhāvavādins as Proponents of Self-Emptiness (*rang stong smra ba*).[34] To understand his explanation of Yogācāra and Niḥsvabhāvavāda tenets, therefore, it is important to clarify the meaning of other-emptiness and self-emptiness.

It appears that the terms "other-emptiness" and "self-emptiness" came to be treated as indicators of distinct systems only after the term "other-emptiness" had been made popular by Dölpopa.[35] Such influential contemporaries of Dölpopa as Longchen Rapjam (*klong chen rab 'byams*)/Longchenpa (*klong chen pa*, 1308–1364) do not seem to have attached any significant weight to the self-emptiness/other-emptiness distinction.[36] For example, in his *Great Chariot: [Auto-]Commentary on the 'Mind Nature Revitalization of the Great Perfection,'* Longchen Rapjam mentions three types of emptiness: self-emptiness (*rang gis stong pa*), other-emptiness (*gzhan gyis stong pa*), and emptiness of both (*gnyis kas stong pa*) as a matter of fact, without treating them as related to distinct systems of thought or as being contradictory.[37] By the fifteenth century the situation has changed, possibly due to the increasing popularity of Dölpopa's views in the fourteenth century followed by their criticisms by Tsongkhapa, Gorampa, Shakya Chokden, and other thinkers, that more firmly entrenched the self-emptiness/other-emptiness distinction. Shakya Chokden himself treats "self-emptiness" and "other-emptiness" as indicating both two distinct systems of thought and two types of emptiness. Nevertheless, in his opinion self-emptiness systems also teach certain types of other-emptiness, while other-emptiness systems teach certain types of self-emptiness.

According to Shakya Chokden, self-emptiness and other-emptiness are taught in the sūtras, tantras, and their commentaries. The distinction between these two types of emptiness pertains to the selflessness of phenomena only, because all four Buddhist tenets are similar in presenting the selflessness of persons exclusively as other-emptiness.[38] In the *Great Path of Ambrosia of Emptiness*, Shakya Chokden explains how Niḥsvabhāvavādins interpret the selflessness of persons:

> Proponents of Self-Emptiness . . . explain the mode of positing the selflessness of persons in terms of other-emptiness. This is because as the meaning of the selflessness of persons, they explain that the basis of negation (*dgag gzhi*), the five appropriated aggregates (*nyer len gyi phung po, upādāna-skandha*), is empty of the object of negation (*dgag bya*), the self of persons. That very [approach] is not the mode of explanation of self-emptiness.[39]

In contrast to the selflessness of phenomena, which Niḥsvabhāvavādins describe as phenomena being empty of themselves, the selflessness of persons is not described as self being empty of self. Instead, it is described as the *aggregates* being empty of self. This type of emptiness is other-emptiness, because it is understood as the basis of negation, aggregates, being empty of the object of negation, self of persons, which is *other* than that basis of negation.

Yogācāras split all existent and nonexistent phenomena into three natures (*ngo bo nyid gsum, trisvabhāva*). Explaining the selflessness of persons, they subsume the object of negation, self of persons, under the category of the imaginary natures (*kun btags/ kun brtags, parikalpita*), and the basis of negation, mind, under the category of the dependent natures (*gzhan dbang, paratantra*). They describe the thoroughly established nature (*yongs grub, pariniṣpanna*)[40] as the dependent natures being empty of the imaginary natures. Because this type of emptiness is other-emptiness, the selflessness of persons in the Yogācāra system too falls under the category of other-emptiness. In other words, Yogācāras explain both types of selflessness in terms of other-emptiness. Thus, Yogācāras and Niḥsvabhāvavādins posit the selflessness of persons exclusively as other-emptiness, despite their dramatically different approaches to the seflessness of phenomena. (As we will learn below, according to Shakya Chokden, the imaginary natures themselves are self-empty. Therefore, Yogācāras do not present *all* the three natures in terms of other-emptiness.[41])

Interpretations of the selflessness of phenomena by Niḥsvabhāvavādins and Yogācāras vary from text to text. Some texts, such as Candrakīrti's *Engaging in Madhyamaka*, teach only self-emptiness, while others, such as Maitreya's *Differentiation of the Middle and Extremes*, focus on other-emptiness. Some other texts, such as Nāgārjuna's *Commentary on the Mind of Enlightenment*, shift focus, and describe the emptiness accessed conceptually (i.e., determined by reasoning) in terms of self-emptiness, and the emptiness realized in the meditative equipoise of Mahāyāna āryas in terms of other-emptiness.

Both Yogācāras and Niḥsvabāvavādins use reasoning related to self-emptiness as well as other-emptiness. Nevertheless, because of the type of emptiness they emphasize, Shakya Chokden describes Niḥsvabhāvavāda—including Prāsaṅgika and Svātantrika—as the system of Proponents of Self-Emptiness, and Yogācāra as the system of Proponents of Other-Emptiness.

In Shakya Chokden's perspective, the majority of thinkers he classifies as Niḥsvabhāvavādins composing texts on self-emptiness, also teach other-emptiness in other sūtric texts and/or tantric commentaries.[42] For example, according to him, Nāgārjuna taught self-emptiness in the *Collection of Reasonings*, but also taught other-emptiness in the *Praise of the Dharma-Sphere* and the *Five Stages*;[43] Candrakīrti taught self-emptiness in his *Engaging in Madhyamaka*, and other-emptiness in the *Clear Lamp*.[44]

Self-Emptiness

Shakya Chokden interprets the terms "self-emptiness" and "other-emptiness" literally: "self-emptiness" means being empty of itself, while "other-emptiness" means being empty of something other than itself. In the *Great Path of Ambrosia of Emptiness*, plugging in the terminology of the basis of negation or the basis of emptiness (*stong gzhi*),[45] the object of negation, and the way of being empty (*ji ltar stong pa'i tshul*), he provides a clear and succinct explanation of the two types of emptiness. The Niḥsvabāvavāda view of self-emptiness is as follows:

> The basis which is empty is all phenomena as many as they may be that exist as knowables. The object of negation of which [phenomena] are empty is the same as the basis of negation; in brief, [it is all] persons and phenomena.[46] The way in which [phenomena] are empty is as follows: whatever

> phenomenon is taken as the basis of negation, that very [phenomenon] is empty of that very [phenomenon]. This is because that very [phenomenon] is not established as that very [phenomenon] when analyzed by reasoning analyzing the ultimate (*don dam dpyod byed kyi rigs pa*). For example, a pot is not established as a pot at the time of analyzing whether it is established as one or many.[47]

The self-emptiness of a pot is the pot being empty of itself, that is, the pot being empty of the pot. What is negated in this type of emptiness is the pot itself, and what it is empty of is the pot itself. This is why, in the context of the presentation of self-emptiness, there is no difference between what is negated and the basis of negation. Niḥsvabāvavādins apply this reasoning to all phenomena.

The above approach is the only interpretation of self-emptiness that Shakya Chokden accepts as correct. In the *Rain of Ambrosia,* he addresses two different approaches to self-emptiness:

> Regarding the mode of explaining self-emptiness, there emerged two systems in Tibet. [One] system explains that whatever subjects [of emptiness] are, all of them are empty of themselves. [According to the other] system, if such an explanation is given, it turns into a nihilistic emptiness. Therefore, [this system] explains as self-emptiness [the state of being] empty of the object of negation, a non-established base, with respect to the subject established by valid cognition. Nevertheless, the latter [approach] is unfeasible in the system of Niḥsvabhāvavādins, [as demonstrated] by scriptural statements and reasoning.[48]

The first approach is the one I addressed above. It is the self-emptiness view that Shakya Chokden himself accepts: all phenomena being empty of themselves. The second one is the approach of Tsongkhapa.[49] In his *Great Path of Ambrosia of Emptiness,* Shakya Chokden provides further details of what he sees as problems in Tsongkhapa's view:

> Later [scholars, who] emerged in the Land of Snows and see [themselves as] Proponents of Self-Emptiness, explain:
>
> > The meaning of self-emptiness is not the negation of all those phenomena within the two truths (*bden pa gnyis, satyadvaya*)[50] being those very [phenomena]. If it were so, it would turn out to undercut each and

> every [instance of] the two truths. For example, the following faults would emerge: if a sprout were not a sprout, a sprout would have to be accepted as nonexistent; and if the emptiness of true [existence] of a sprout also were not itself, it will follow that that [emptiness] does not exist. Therefore, positing self-emptiness, [one has to proceed as follows]: with respect to the subject[-basis of emptiness] established by valid cognition (*tshad mas grub pa*), one has to identify the measure (*tshad*) of the object of negation, "true establishment" (*bden grub*), and the boundaries of positing (*'jog mtshams*) the two types of self, and then negate those very [objects of negation only].[51]

In contrast to Shakya Chokden, Tsongkhapa explains self-emptiness not as phenomena being empty of themselves, but as phenomena being empty of objects of negation other than themselves. According to Tsongkhapa, both conventional phenomena and emptiness are established by valid cognition. Therefore, to negate phenomena would entail the view of nihilism. What should be negated then is a very specific object of negation—expressed by such terms as "true establishment"—that has to be first correctly identified and then negated. Furthermore, what is identified as the object of negation in this context has to be nonexistent. Thus, the basis of negation, existent phenomena, is different from the object of negation, nonexistent "true establishment."[52]

Shakya Chokden criticizes this approach by appealing to the scriptural authority of Niḥsvabhāvavāda writers, such as Candrakīrti:

> [There are no proofs] because in such passages as "since [their nature is that], eyes are empty of eyes,"[53] the meaning of self-emptiness is explained as any subject-basis for dispute (*rtsod gzhi'i chos can*) being empty of that very [subject] itself. It is not explained as a negation of something that does not even bear any relation to [that subject] itself, not to mention being its own entity.[54]

He also argues that what Tsongkhapa means by self-emptiness indeed is nothing other than other-emptiness:

> While you assert that the explanatory mode of other-emptiness is incorrect, in actuality [you yourself] explain

> [emptiness] having accepted that very meaning [of other-emptiness] and [simply] given it the name of "self-emptiness." This is because the Followers of Other-Emptiness explain that the basis of negation, the dependent natures established by valid cognition, is empty of the object of negation, the imaginary natures not established by valid cognition. Then they accept as the final ultimate truth the emptiness in which those [dependent natures] are empty of those [imaginary natures], and state that if this emptiness were accepted as nonexistent, [such] would be the view of deprecation. [This is what they] accept, and [this is exactly] what you also accept.[55]

With the help of the terminology of the three natures, Shakya Chokden demonstrates the similarity between the interpretive approaches of Tsongkhapa and Proponents of Other-Emptiness. In his unwillingness to take at face value the meaning of self-emptiness, Tsongkhapa develops an interpretation of emptiness similar to Yogācāra interpreters of the *Perfection of Wisdom* sūtras, who feel that the acceptance of all phenomena as being empty of themselves would entail the view of nihilism, that is, literal nonexistence of phenomena. Accepting that relative phenomena are established by valid cognition, Tsongkhapa is similar to those Yogācāras who assert that the dependent natures are established by valid cognition.[56] Accepting that such phenomena are empty of objects of negation that are not established by valid cognition, Tsongkhapa is again similar to Yogācāras who explain emptiness as the dependent natures being empty of the imaginary natures that are not established by valid cognition. Finally, although Tsongkhapa presents his interpretation as typifying the position of self-emptiness, in his assertion that phenomena are empty of objects of negation other than themselves, he again is similar to Yogācāras who assert that bases of negation, the dependent natures, are empty of objects of negation, the imaginary natures that are other than those bases of negation. This approach does not count as a valid interpretation of self-emptiness according to Shakya Chokden.

Other-Emptiness

When Shakya Chokden contrasts the Yogācāra position of other-emptiness with the Niḥsvabhāvavāda position of self-emptiness, he prefers to rely on the presentation of the three natures given in the system of Asaṅga:

> The bases that are empty are dependent natures: all knowing that has dualistic appearance of the apprehended and apprehender (*gzung 'dzin gnyis snang can gyi shes pa*). The objects of negation are the imaginary natures. They are of two types, due to the division into the apprehended (*gzung ba, grāhya*) and apprehender (*'dzin pa, grāhaka*). Each of these two, the apprehended and apprehender, also has two [subdivisions]: in terms of persons and in terms of phenomena . . . The way in which [phenomena] are empty is [as follows:] the bases of negation are empty of the objects of negation in terms of other-emptiness, not in terms of self-emptiness. This is because in relation to the bases of negation, i.e., the two types of dualistically appearing knowing (*gnyis snang gi shes pa*), the objects of negation, i.e., the two types of the apprehended and apprehender, are other entities (*gzhan gyi ngo bo*); they are not posited as the own entities (*rang gyi ngo bo*) of those [bases of negation].[57]

From this perspective of other-emptiness, the dependent natures, i.e., consciousnesses with dualistic appearances, are taken as the bases of emptiness/bases of negation. The imaginary natures, i.e., all dualistic appearances of persons and phenomena appearing as objects and subjects apprehending those objects, are taken as the objects of negation. In other words, consciousnesses with dualistic appearances both project or appear as the imaginary natures and are empty of them at the same time. According to the Yogācāra system, the bases of negation—the dependent natures—are empty of the objects of negation—the imaginary natures—in terms of other-emptiness, not self-emptiness. This is because with respect to the dependent natures, the imaginary natures are other entities; they are not the own entities of the dependent natures.

This position is characteristic of both Satyākāravāda and Alīkākāravāda, and Shakya Chokden makes extensive use of it in his discussion of the two systems, while acknowledging their differences in the identification of the three natures.[58] Nevertheless, it is important to note that in the above passage, he is not arguing that the dependent natures are empty of the imaginary natures simply because they are different from them. Rather, he emphasizes that their *entities* are different. This emphasis on the entities of the dependent and imaginary natures has a special significance in the Alīkākāravāda system. As will be explained below (166), in that system as Shakya Chokden understands it, no dependent natures can be identified apart from the imaginary and thoroughly established natures. Nevertheless, the entity of the dependent natures exists, and that entity is none other than the throughly established nature (166, 171). That real and truly existent entity is different from the unreal and nonexistent entities of the imaginary natures. This is why the possessors of that entity—the dependent natures—are empty of the imaginary natures in terms of other-emptiness, not self-emptiness.

Nevertheless, this is not the only interpretation of other-emptiness discussed by Shakya Chokden. He also addresses other interpretations of other-emptiness that originate from Indian Mahāyāna texts, which are improvised on by Tibetan thinkers. In the *Rain of Ambrosia*, he contrasts those interpretations with the approach outlined above:

> There emerged two dissimilar [approaches] regarding the mode of identifying the subject-basis of other-emptiness (*gzhan stong gi gzhi chos can*). In the Yogācāra texts, the reality, [understood as] the bases of emptiness, the dependent natures, being empty of the objects of negation, the imaginary natures, is explained as the thoroughly established nature. In the *Sublime Continuum*[59] and the *Conquest over Objections about the [Three] Mother Scriptures*,[60] the reality, the thoroughly established nature, is explained as empty of the imaginary natures. [These] two also [stem] from [interpretive] differences: including all knowables into two, the imaginary and thoroughly established natures, or dividing them into three: [the imaginary, thoroughly established] and dependent natures. They are not contradictory.[61]

The first approach described in this passage is the same as the Yogācāra position mentioned above: the dependent natures are taken as the basis of emptiness, the imaginary natures are negated on that basis, and that negation is explained as the thoroughly established nature. According to the second approach, the thoroughly established nature itself is explained as being empty of the imaginary natures.

In this particular passage, Shakya Chokden simply acknowledges the existence of interpretive differences, and without criticism links them with the two ways of classifying phenomena: into the three and the two natures. Thereby, he accepts the two interpretations of other-emptiness both as legitimate and noncontradictory. In another section of the *Rain of Ambrosia*, he also admits that in the *Sublime Continuum* and its commentary by Asaṅga,[62] the subject-basis of emptiness (*stong gzhi'i chos can*) is explained as the reality-limit (*yang dag pa'i mtha'*, *bhūtakoṭi*, i.e., ultimate reality), in contrast to other Yogācāra texts where the subject-basis of emptiness is explained as the dependent natures.[63] (Note that the *Sublime Continuum* and its commentary by Asaṅga do not utilize the terms "imaginary" and "thoroughly established natures." Therefore, the reference to the two natures in the *Sublime Continuum* should be understood not in terms of those categories per se but rather in terms of the translation of the *Sublime Continuum*'s approach into those categories.)

It should be noted that in general Shakya Chokden never criticizes the *Sublime Continuum*. Throughout his life, both in early and later writings, he showed tremendous respect for this text, and viewed it as a treatise of definitive meaning (*nges don, nītārtha*).[64] I think that in this particular context the *Sublime Continuum* is spared criticism also because it makes no attempt to reinterpret or restructure the key Yogācāra interpretive tools of the three natures, as the *Conquest over Objections* does; rather, it simply does not address them.

Although the *Conquest over Objections* is spared criticism in the *Rain of Ambrosia*, Shakya Chokden is more critical when he discusses it in the *Great Path of Ambrosia of Emptiness*. In the latter text, he actually acknowledges that the *Conquest over Objections* talks about *three* natures.[65] (I think the reason why he said in the *Rain of Ambrosia* that the *Conquest over Objections* addresses two natures is because the *Conquest over Objections* treats both dependent and the imaginary natures as the same in terms of being objects of negation.) He feels uncomfortable about this interpretive approach, because it does not agree with his understanding of the mainstream Yogācāra way of positing emptiness.

It is important to note that the problem Shakya Chokden addresses in the *Great Path of Ambrosia of Emptiness* is not that the thoroughly established nature cannot be seen as empty of the other natures, but that it should not be taken as the basis of emptiness *in the context of addressing the three natures*. Otherwise, Shakya Chokden himself argues that Alīkākāravāda asserts all conventional phenomena as self-empty. In the *Seventeen Wondrous Answers*, he describes the Alīkākāravāda identification of emptiness as follows: "having determined all relative truths as self-empty, one posits as remaining only the ultimate primordial mind (*don dam pa'i ye shes*)."[66] According to him, this approach stems from the explicit teachings (*dngos bstan*) of the third dharmacakra and the *Dharmas of Maitreya* interpreted by Asaṅga and Vasubandhu.[67]

As I explain below (166), Shakya Chokden argues that the dependent nature does not exist separately from the other two natures, although it is used as a temporary basis for determining emptiness.

According to him, when Yogācāra describes the final ultimate reality experienced in meditative equipoise (i.e., the final Alīkākāravāda view), it describes it as the non-dual primordial mind (which is the thoroughly established nature). It is empty of all other phenomena because no other phenomena exist. In other words, while taking the dependent natures as the bases of emptiness is the starting point of determining emptiness by reasoning in terms of other-emptiness, what one arrives at as a result of that process—and what one incorporates into meditative experience—is none other than the thoroughly established nature, the non-dual primordial mind.

In the *Great Path of Ambrosia of Emptiness*, Shakya Chokden quotes and comments on a lengthy passage from the *Conquest over Objections* which deals with three types of form: the imaginary form (*kun brtags pa'i gzugs*; corresponds to the imaginary natures), the imputational form (*rnam par brtags pa'i gzugs*; corresponds to the dependent natures), and the reality-form (*chos nyid kyi gzugs*; corresponds to the thoroughly established nature).[68] His explanation is that there is no fault in interpreting the reality-form as being empty of the other two forms. Nevertheless, if one takes the reality-form as the basis of emptiness, that will contradict Yogācāra scriptures in general, and in particular it will contradict the textual system of Vasubandhu, the author of the *Conquest over Objections*. It has to be further analyzed, he says, whether the *Conquest over Objections*'s statement that the imputational form is empty of its entity agrees with the intent of Yogācāra scriptures or not. Because the *Conquest over Objections* states that the reality-form exists by its own entity, it is also incorrect to claim that it teaches the Niḥsvabhāvavāda view. As a result, Shakya Chokden decides that the mode of emptiness explained in the *Conquest over Objections* does not agree with either of the two systems of Madhyamaka.[69] Nevertheless, he stops short of criticizing the text itself. Instead, he argues that further analysis is required.[70]

Shakya Chokden does not agree with other scholars' interpretations of the *Conquest over Objections*, and in the same text directs an explicit criticism at Dölpopa in this regard. He reveals what he sees as Dölpopa's mistakes by juxtaposing Dölpopa's interpretation with the first approach to other-emptiness explained above. It is worth quoting this passage at length, because it demonstrates which arguments Shakya Chokden uses to buttress his own view of other-emptiness, and which Indian Buddhist authorities he cites in support of his position:

> Proponents of Other-Emptiness who emerged in the Land of Snows say:

> This explanation of all relative compounded phenomena (*kun rdzob 'dus byas kyi dngos po*) in terms of self-emptiness and the uncompounded ultimate (*don dam 'dus ma byas*) in terms of other-emptiness is intended by the great Mādhyamika Vasubandhu because he gave such an explanation in the *Conquest over Objections about the [Three] Mother Scriptures.*

This explanation is not correct, because it does not agree with the root texts of the foremost venerable [Maitreya], and contradicts the modes of explanation of other-emptiness clearly taught in the unquestionable treatises of brothers Asaṅga [and Vasubandhu] and in the textual tradition of Dignāga as well as [his spiritual] son [Dharmakīrti]. How is it [incorrect]? In your case, when you explain the meaning of other-emptiness, you do not explain it as the dependent natures (the possessors of reality, *chos can, dharmin*) being empty of the imaginary natures (the objects of negation). Rather, as the meaning of other-emptiness you accept the thoroughly established nature (reality, *chos nyid, dharmatā*), being empty of the dependent natures and the imaginary natures (the possessors of reality). Such an explanatory method does not exist in those textual systems [of Asaṅga and others].[71]

According to Shakya Chokden, Dölpopa's mistake lies in describing other-emptiness as the thoroughly established nature being empty of both the dependent natures and the imaginary natures. In contrast to Dölpopa, all other thinkers mentioned in the passage are presented as sharing the same other-emptiness view of the dependent natures being empty of the imaginary natures. This is true for Yogācāras Asaṅga and Vasubandhu, as well as for Dignāga and Dharmakīrti, whom Shakya Chokden brings together into the same group of Proponents of Other-Emptiness. That position is further reinforced when it is linked with the authoritative writings of Maitreya. Shakya Chokden continues:

What [explanatory method] exists [in those textual systems]? [The following explanatory method] exists [in Maitreya's *Differentiation of the Middle and Extremes*]:

> Unreal ideation (*yang dag ma yin kun rtog, abhūtaparikalpa*) exists.

The two do not exist in it.[72]

> According to this passage, the dependent natures are described as subject-bases of emptiness; two types of the imaginary natures, the apprehended and apprehender, are described as objects of negation of which [subject-bases of emptiness] are empty; and primordial mind of non-duality of the apprehended and apprehender is described as the empty phenomenon (*stong pa'i dngos po*).[73]

As I explain in the following chapters, the interpretation of ultimate reality as primordial mind is not a general Yogācāra position, but is more specifically the position of Alīkākāravāda. The above-mentioned thinkers, therefore, share the same Alīkākāravāda view according to Shakya Chokden.

A mere reference to a scriptural authority is not the strongest argumentative tool. Therefore, next he turns to reasoning:

> [The thoroughly established nature, that is, primordial mind] is not posited as a subject-basis of emptiness, because there is no proof and there are factors damaging to it. There is no proof, because [valid] scriptures providing such explanation do not exist. The damaging factors are as follows: if the reasoning establishing emptiness had to establish the thoroughly established nature [taken as] the subject[-basis of emptiness], as being empty of [both] the imaginary and dependent natures [taken as] negated phenomena, it would follow that at the time of ascertaining the subject-basis for dispute, the probandum (*bsgrub bya*, *sādhya*) would have been proved. Otherwise, there could exist a correct reason that establishes the probandum without [initially] ascertaining the subject-basis for dispute.[74]

Here, Shakya Chokden appeals to the following reasoning: the basis of dispute has to be ascertained *before* the mechanism of a correct syllogism is triggered and its probandum is proved. For example, a sound—when it is taken as the subject-basis for dispute about whether a sound is permanent or impermanent—has to be ascertained prior to establishing the probandum "sound is impermanent." If "impermanent sound" itself is taken as the subject-basis for dispute about sound being impermanent, the syllogism will be defective, because it will imply that the impermanence of a sound is or has already been established by the time of ascertaining the subject-basis for dispute. (If the subject-basis for dispute is not ascertained, the syllogism also will be defective; therefore, that is not an option either.) The same problem is entailed if the thoroughly established nature—that in the opponent's view is understood as the thoroughly established nature empty of the other two natures—is taken as the subject-basis for dispute about whether the thoroughly established nature is empty of the other two natures or not: the probandum, "the thoroughly established nature is empty of the other two natures," will be ascertained at the same moment that the subject-basis for dispute is ascertained. The syllogism will simply prove what has already been ascertained, and therefore will be defective.

Shakya Chokden proceeds with criticizing the interpretation of the dependent natures as self-empty in the context of the three natures:

> Also, there is no proof and there are factors damaging to the description of the dependent natures in terms of self-emptiness. There is no proof, because no such explanation is given in those scriptures [of Asaṅga, Maitreya, and others]. Damaging factors exist: if the entity of the dependent natures (*gzhan dbang gi ngo bo*) were not truly established, the entity of the thoroughly established nature, reality (*chos nyid yongs grub kyi ngo bo*), would not be truly existent. This is because thatness free from the duality of the apprehended and apprehender (*gzung 'dzin gnyis med kyi de kho na nyid*) is asserted [in valid scriptures presenting other-emptiness] as the entity of dualistically appearing knowing (*gnyis snang gi shes pa'i ngo bo*). That [thatness] is explained as the entity of that [dualistically appearing knowing] by the text [of Dharmakīrti's *Commentary on Valid Cognition*: "Thus,] that [emptiness of duality] is the thatness of that.[75]

This informative passage once again focuses on the view of Alīkākāravāda: although dualistically appearing minds are unreal and nonexistent, nevertheless they are not lacking their own entity or nature. This is because their own entity is not themselves, but the thoroughly established nature.[76] Therefore, to treat them as self-empty in this context would imply the nonexistence of their entity, which in turn would imply the nonexistence of the thoroughly established nature. This is why the dependent natures cannot be treated as self-empty in the context of the three natures.

I want to emphasize at this point that Shakya Chokden's view of other-emptiness dramatically differs from Dölpopa's. Far from agreeing with Dölpopa, he openly criticizes Dölpopa's interpretation of the *Conquest over Objections*, and allies himself with what he understands to be the mainstream Alīkākāravāda interpretations. Therefore, to put Shakya Chokden together with Dölpopa into the same camp of Followers of Other-Emptiness makes no more sense than placing him into the camp of Followers of Self-Emptiness together with Tsongkhapa.[77] Instead, we should acknowledge that in his interpretation of self-emptiness and other-emptiness, Shakya Chokden clearly differentiates the two systems as well as different approaches to them. He supports his explanations with the writings of mainstream Niḥsvabhāvavāda and Yogācāra thinkers, while distancing himself from Tsongkhapa's and Dölpopa's interpretations of self-emptiness and other-emptiness, respectively. In fact, he often criticizes Tsongkhapa's and Dölpopa's views in the same text and section in order to highlight his own interpretation of self-emptiness and other-emptiness.[78]

Before closing this section, I should reiterate that according to Shakya Chokden, the basis of emptiness not only need not be existent in the case of self-emptiness, but does not even have to be existent in the context of other-emptiness. This is because in the Niḥsvabhāvavāda system, as he understands it, all relative, conventional phenomena do not exist, and in the Alīkākāravāda system too, dualistic consciousness, i.e., the dependent nature, does not exist.[79] Nevertheless, as has been previously explained, these nonexistent phenomena *do* serve as the bases of emptiness. This being said, Niḥsvabhāvavāda and Alīkākāravāda differ in their approaches to those nonexistent bases of emptiness: the former describes them as self-empty, while the latter describes them as other-empty. Therefore, according to Proponents of Other-Emptiness, it is possible to be nonexistent and not to be self-empty at the same time. As Shakya Chokden explains in the *Great Path of Ambrosia of Emptiness*:

> [T]he non-contradictory explanation of dependent [natures] as existent by nature and [at the same time] being truthless like an illusion should be understood as the key that opens the [treasury of] thatness of the texts of Proponents of Other-Emptiness.[80]

According to Shakya Chokden, having a truly established entity or nature does not entail being itself truly established. This is similar to the case when the emptiness of a pot is described as the ultimate reality of a pot, but the pot itself is not accepted as ultimate reality. As he puts it in the *Rain of Ambrosia*:

> The dependent natures being truly established is not a tenet of honorable Asaṅga, because in his texts those [dependent natures] were explained as [being] like an illusion. Those [dependent natures] do not become truly established [simply] because their entity was explained as truth. This is like the case of explaining the entity of a pot, etc., as reality [while not accepting a pot, etc., as reality].[81]

In summary, Shakya Chokden accepts only one interpretation of self-emptiness that derives from the works of Indian Niḥsvabhāvavādins: all phenomena being empty of themselves. On the other hand, he accepts two interpretations of other-emptiness. One is given in the *Sublime Continuum* and its commentary by Asaṅga; it addresses other-emptiness in the context of only two natures (i.e., the imaginary and thoroughly established natures). The other is given in texts of Asaṅga and Maitreya other than Maitreya's *Sublime Continuum* and its commentary by Asaṅga; it addresses other-emptiness in the context of the three natures (i.e., the dependent, imaginary, and thoroughly established natures). Shakya Chokden objects to the interpretation of the second type of other-emptiness in terms of the first type, which he attributes to Dölpopa's explanation that the thoroughly established nature is empty of both the dependent natures and the imaginary natures. He also objects to the concealed interpretation of self-emptiness in terms of other-emptiness, which he attributes to Tsongkhapa's explanation that phenomena established by valid cognition are empty of objects of negation other than themselves.

Emphasizing the self-emptiness/other-emptiness distinction, Shakya Chokden shifts focus from distinctions between other types of Madhyamaka, such as Prāsaṅgika and Svātantrika, to the differences between Yogācāra and Niḥsvabhāvavāda. In his overall approach, differences between Prāsaṅgika and Svātantrika lose their relevance as he himself explicitly acknowledges. In the next section I explain how he justifies his approach to those subdivisions of Madhyamaka, and what place they occupy in his system.

4. Bidding Farewell to the Prāsaṅgika/Svātantrika Division?

Shakya Chokden does not reject the categories of Prāsaṅgika and Svātantrika, even commenting on their differences in various works, including some of his latest compositions.[82] At the same time, he does not acknowledge any difference in the ultimate views of Prāsaṅgika and Svātantrika. He explains that although their positions leading to the final view of ultimate reality differ temporarily, the final view itself is identical.[83] In addition, he argues that Prāsaṅgika and Svātantrika do not hold different views on conventional phenomena posited by wordly minds. For these two reasons, he denies that these two categories are unproblematic subdivisions of Madhyamaka.

In the *Ocean of Scriptural Statements and Reasoning*, Shakya Chokden explains where similarities and differences between Prāsaṅgika and Svātantrika lie:

> The masters renowned as Prāsaṅgika and Svātantrika Mādhyamikas do not appear to be different at all in the mode of positing without analysis by reasoning the relative truth of the world (*'jig rten pa'i kun rdzob bden pa*).[84] This is because they agree in presenting it in accordance with how it appears to and is renowned in the innate worldly mind (*'jig rten gyi blo lhan skyes*), without [resorting to] analysis by the reasonings of the proponents of tenets. Those masters also do not appear to be even slightly dissimilar in the way of identifying the final ultimate truth. This is because they are in accord in applying the term "ultimate truth" to what is beyond objects of sounds and concepts (*sgra rtog gi yul*), being divested from all collections of proliferations. Nevertheless, the reasonings determining that ultimate truth and the initial entrance into those reasonings [as explained by those masters] are different. This is because the modes of determining [the ultimate] by autonomous reasoning (*rang rgyud kyi rigs pa*) and by consequence reasoning (*thal 'gyur gyi rigs pa*) are ascertained as distinct. In addition, at the time of entering into ultimate truth without discarding relative truth, two modes are observed: the mode of entering into Madhyamaka having [first] gradually entered the lower tenets, and the mode of entering into Madhyamaka from the [level of] worldly renown (*'jig rten gyi grags pa*) itself, without having [first] entered the lower tenets. The former [mode] also has two [subdivisions]: the mode of initially entering Sautrāntika, without [subsequently] entering the tenets of Vijñaptimātra (*rnam par rig pa tsam*, Cognizance-Only) as well, and then entering Madhyamaka itself; the mode of gradually entering the two, Sautrāntika and Cittamātra, and then entering Madhyamaka. The first [approach] originates from

> the *Differentiation of the Two Truths*[85] by master Jñānagarbha. The second [approach] originates from the *Ornament of Madhyamaka*[86] by Bodhisattva Śāntarakṣita.[87]

As this passage demonstrates, the main distinction between Prāsaṅgika and Svātantrika lies first in the type of reasoning they use to determine ultimate truth: Svātantrika uses autonomous reasoning or reasons, while Prāsaṅgika uses consequences. Second, they are different in the way of proceeding from the conventional level to the level of realization of ultimate reality: plunging into the ultimate directly from the relative level by Prāsaṅgika or proceeding gradually by Svātantrika, either via the Sautrāntika level only, or via both Sautrāntika and Vijñaptimātra (i.e., Yogācāra)[88] levels. Despite the different types of logical tools used by the two systems, they arrive at the same identification of emptiness.[89] Therefore, the former distinction based on their application of autonomous reasons versus consequences cannot serve as the basis for distinguishing between their ultimate views.

The latter distinction can be understood as the Niḥsvabhāvavādins' exploration of three different options for moving from the relative level to the level of realization of ultimate reality. The first is a one-step option, accepted by Prāsaṅgikas: when inquiring into the ultimate, one negates the reality of all phenomena without any exception, and thereby plunges from the level of worldly conventions straight into ultimate reality. The second is a two-step option, accepted by some Svātantrikas: the ultimate is approached gradually, such that first one accesses the ultimate as it is posited in the Sautrāntika system, then transcends it and reaches Madhyamaka's own ultimate. The third is a three-step option, accepted by the rest of Svātantrikas: the ultimate is approached gradually; first, one accesses the Sautrāntika ultimate, transcends it, moves to the Yogācāra ultimate, and then, having transcended it as well, reaches the ultimate posited by Niḥsvabhāvavāda. As we can see, both the ultimate reality one is trying to reach and the conventional level serving as the departure point are the same in all three cases; only what happens on the way is different. Therefore, this distinction cannot be used either as the basis for claiming there are any substantial differences between Svātantrika and Prāsaṅgika.

Shakya Chokden further elaborates on these features when he addresses Niḥsvabhāvavāda divisions, explaining that there are two ways of distinguishing different Mādhyamikas. Their divisions can be made in terms of the mode of introducing students to Madhyamaka tenets and the mode of positing the ultimate after they have been introduced. In the first case, Mādhyamikas are divided into three types: Mādhyamikas Utilizing Worldly Renown (*'jig rten grags sde spyod pa'i dbu ma pa*), represented by Candrakīrti with his followers; Sautrāntika Mādhyamikas (*mdo sde spyod pa'i dbu ma pa*, Followers of the Middle of Sūtra Followers), represented by such thinkers as Bhāviveka and Jñānagarbha; and Yogācāra Mādhyamikas (*rnal sbyor spyod pa'i dbu ma pa*, Followers of the Middle of Yogic Practice), represented by Śāntarakṣita and Kamalaśīla.[90] These three types correspond to the three types of Niḥsvabhāvavādins addressed above in the same order.

In the way the ultimate is posited, the divisions are made into "what Tibetans termed 'Prāsaṅgika' and 'Svātantrika.' "[91] Their differences come from disagreements between Buddhapālita, Bhāviveka, and Candrakīrti regarding the way of accessing the ultimate through the autonomous reasons or consequences.[92] As Shakya Chokden explains in the *Rain of Ambrosia*, when positing the view of reality, Svātantrikas temporarily establish their own position through autonomous reasons, while Prāsaṅgikas do not establish their own position even temporarily, negating the positions of others only through consequences.[93]

In other words, the original distinction between Prāsaṅgika and Svātantrika lies in their different modes of determining the ultimate.[94] When different ways of introducing students to the ultimate are outlined, Niḥsvabhāvavādins are further subdivided into three groups: Mādhyamikas Utilizing Worldly Renown are counted as advocates of Prāsaṅgika; while Sautrāntika Mādhyamikas and Yogācāra Mādhyamikas are subsumed under the category of Svātantrika.[95] None of these features affect the way Svātantrika and Prāsaṅgika systems treat ultimate reality and conventional phenomena posited by wordly minds. Therefore, their mutual debates are of little relevance in the overall approach chosen by Shakya Chokden.

By erasing internal distinctions between the two types of Niḥsvabhāvavāda, Shakya Chokden created a fertile ground for introducing those distinctions between Madhyamaka tenets that he saw as valid: Alīkākāravāda and Niḥsvabhāvavāda.

Table 1 provides two charts that visually represent his approach to the divisions of tenets, in contrast to the one that became predominant in the Tibetan Buddhist world. The first two categories (starting from the bottom up) in the hierarchical ladder of tenets are left intact. The main differences come from his (re)interpretation of the categories of Yogācāra and Madhyamaka.

Table 1

Common Doxographical Subdivisions

Madhyamaka = Niḥsvabhāvavāda	Prāsaṅgika	
	Svātantrika	Yogācāra Svātantrika Madhyamaka Sautrāntika Svātantrika Madhyamaka
Cittamātra = Yogācāra	Alīkākāravāda Satyākāravāda	According to the majority of Tibetan Buddhist thinkers, all non-tantric Madhyamaka systems share the same final view of ultimate reality; no hierarchical distinction is made in that context
Sautrāntika		
Vaibhāṣika		

Shakya Chokden's Alternative Doxographical Subdivisions

Madhyamaka	Niḥsvabhāvavāda	Prāsaṅgika	
		Svātantrika	Yogācāra Madhyamaka Sautrāntika Madhyamaka
	Yogācāra Madhyamaka which is equal to Alīkākāravāda Yogācāra	All non-tantric Madhyamaka systems, including Alīkākāravāda Yogācāra, share the same final view of ultimate reality	
Cittamātra = Satyākāravāda Yogācāra			
Sautrāntika			
Vaibhāṣika			

5. Are There Two Types of Yogācāra Madhyamaka?

Placing Alīkākāravāda into the category of Madhyamaka, Shakya Chokden also calls its followers "Yogācāra Mādhyamika" (*rnal 'byor spyod pa'i dbu ma pa*),[96] "Alīkākāravāda Yogācāra" (*rnal 'byor spyod pa'i rnam rdzun pa*, False Aspectarians of Yogic Practice),[97] and *"Alīkākāravāda Mādhyamika" (*rnam rdzun/ brdzun dbu ma pa*, False Aspectarian Followers of the Middle).[98] In some texts he calls this system *"Vijñaptivāda Madhyamaka" (*rnam rig smra ba'i dbu ma*, Middle of Proponents of Cognizance),[99] and even applies such descriptive terms as "Madhyamaka Advocating Interiority of Knowables" (*shes bya nang gir smra ba['i dbu ma]*), and "Madhyamaka Advocating Cognizance-Only" (*rnam par rig pa tsam du smra ba'i dbu ma*).[100] Most of these terms simply address the same category of tenets and their followers from slightly different angles. Nevertheless, the term "Yogācāra Mādhyamika" makes one wonder how many kinds of Yogācāra Mādhyamikas Shakya Chokden accepts, and what kind he has in mind every time he uses this term.

On the one hand, he calls the Niḥsvabhāvavādins Śāntarakṣita, Kamalaśīla, and Haribhadra "Yogācāra Mādhyamika." Thereby, he downplays the importance of the label "Svātantrika" attached to their system by later doxographers, and allies himself with Yeshé Dé and other early doxographers who called it just "Yogācāra Madhyamaka."[101] On the other hand, he also applies the term "Yogācāra Mādhyamika" to those thinkers whom he sees as Alīkākāravādins: Asaṅga, Maitreya, Dharmakīrti, and others. "Yogācāra Mādhyamika" is of course a pertinent rubric to use for thinkers whom he sees as both Yogācāras and Mādhyamikas, especially because he wants to emphasize that one type of Yogācāra is in fact a type of Madhyamaka, despite the common polarization of Yogācāra and Madhyamaka. Shakya Chokden solves this ambiguity in the *Meaningful to Behold*:

> Thus, there are two [types of] Yogācāra Madhyamaka: the one explained in the *Dharmas of Maitreya*, and the other one asserted by Bodhisattva Śāntarakṣita and [his spiritual] son [Kamalaśīla]. Their differences are [based on] dissimilar reasonings [used] to negate concepts apprehending signs with respect to the mode of being (*gnas lugs la mtshan 'dzin gyi rtog pa 'gog byed kyi rigs pa*). There is no difference in [what they accept as] the ultimate way of being (*don dam gyi gnas tshul*) and the object of experience (*nyams su myong bya*) . . . Although in this system [of Śāntarakṣita and Kamalaśīla], emptiness in the face of reasoning (*rigs ngo'i*

> *stong nyid*) is explained as a non-affirming negation (*med dgag, prasajyapratiṣedha*), emptiness experienced through meditation (*nyams su myong bya'i stong nyid*) is not explained as a non-affirming negation. Therefore, [the view of this system] has to be distinguished from precisely [those] main [types of] Prāsaṅgika and Svātantrika (*thal rang gi gtso bo*) [that are advocated by Candrakīrti and Bhāviveka, respectively].[102]

This passage clearly demonstrates that Shakya Chokden accepts two types of Yogācāra Madhyamaka: one is based on Niḥsvabhāvavāda and the other on Yogācāra writings. Their differences stem from different ways of positing emptiness through reasoning, not from their different approaches to ultimate reality experienced in meditative equipoise.

Interestingly, he uses this feature as the reason for suggesting that Śāntarakṣita's system should be distinguished from the mainstream or "main" types of Prāsaṅgika and Svātantrika. As will be demonstrated below, Shakya Chokden argues that one way or another virtually all Mādhyamikas accept the view of emptiness experienced in meditative equipoise in accordance with the ultimate view of Yogācāra. Nevertheless, such key Niḥsvabhāvavāda figures as Candrakīrti do not *explicitly* do it in their writings focusing on the view of emptiness posited through reasoning. Rather, they explicitly accept the view of emptiness experienced in meditative equipoise in their tantric writings, while only implicitly accepting it in their sūtric commentaries. What makes Śāntarakṣita and his followers' system distinct is that they explicitly posit both views in the same texts. In that way the distinction between Yogācāra and Niḥsvabhāvavāda is problematized, so their writings must be distinguished from those of the "founders" of Prāsaṅgika and Svātantrika, Cāndrakīrti, and Bhāviveka, who keep those systems strictly separate.

Note that Shakya Chokden is not saying that Śāntarakṣita and his followers only provisionally accept primordial mind as it is explained in Yogācāra, but do not accept its reality on the ultimate level. Rather, he argues that on the level of meditative experience, Śāntarakṣita and his followers posit the ultimate view itself in agreement with the ultimate view of Yogācāra, i.e., as primordial mind. This position is reiterated in the *Rain of Ambrosia*:

> This explanation of the final [view] of definitive meaning as primordial mind is [accepted] not only in this Madhyamaka [system] asserted by Ārya Asaṅga, but it is also

> asserted by Yogācāra Mādhyamikas within [the system of] Niḥsvabhāvavāda such as, for example, masters Āryavimuktisena and Haribhadra.[103]

Regarding Haribhadra in particular, Shakya Chokden writes in the *Wish Fulfilling Meru*:

> One of the followers of Śāntarakṣita is the master Haribhadra. Everybody in the Land of Snows agrees that he interpreted the meaning of the *Mother [Perfection of Wisdom* sūtras*]* according to the Yogācāra approach. Thus, he used the Niḥsvabhāvavāda reasoning (*ngo bo nyid med pa'i rigs pa*) in his method of refutation of grasping at signs, while he explained the object of meditative experience in accordance with the Yogācāra system.[104]

In other words, in the system of Śāntarakṣita and his followers, it is not contradictory to accept the non-dual primordial mind as the ultimate view experienced in meditative equipoise, and at the same time, when positing the view of emptiness through reasoning, to refute that non-dual primordial mind. This interpretation is not surprising given the fact that according to Shakya Chokden, the Niḥsvabhāvavāda position of self-emptiness entails the negation of all phenomena in the face of reasoning.[105] Nevertheless, in this context we should distinguish between refutations of Satyākāravāda and Alīkākāravāda views in the face of reasoning: Shakya Choken's interpretation of Śāntarakṣita and his followers' position entails that while the Satyākāravāda view of reality is only provisionally accepted[106] and then refuted without being carried into meditation on ultimate reality, the Alīkākāravāda view of reality is refuted through reasoning but then is accepted as the object of meditation on ultimate reality.

Understanding Shakya Chokden's classification of the two types of Yogācāra Mādhyamika helps clarify otherwise confusing statements, such as the following passage from the *Rain of Ambrosia*:

> There are two types of Mādhyamikas: Yogācāra Mādhyamikas and Niḥsvabhāvavāda Mādhyamikas (*ngo bo nyid med par smra ba'i dbu ma pa*, Followers of the Middle of Proponents of Entitylessness). Among the first [type], there are Proponents of Self-Emptiness and Proponents of Other-Emptiness. Among those Niḥsvabhāvavādins also, there are Prāsaṅgikas and Svātantrikas. Among that [latter type],

> there are also those who provisionally make assertions in accordance with Sautrāntika and those who [provisionally] make assertions in accordance with Cittamātra.[107]

Based on what has been explained above, the passage reads as saying that in general, there are two types of Mādhyamikas: Yogācāra Mādhyamikas and Niḥsvabhāvavāda Mādhyamikas. The first type contains categories of both Proponents of Self-Emptiness, i.e., Niḥsvabhāvavādins Śāntarakṣita and his followers, and Proponents of Other-Emptiness, i.e., Alīkākāravādins Asaṅga and others. Niḥsvabhāvavādins too are subdivided into Prāsaṅgikas and Svātantrikas, and the latter type is further subdivided into those who provisionally make assertions in accordance with Sautrāntika and those who provisionally make assertions in accordance with Cittamātra. The latter category is once again occupied by Śāntarakṣita and his followers. To grasp the meaning of passages like this one, it is crucial to understand that in Shakya Chokden's approach, Yogācāra Madhyamaka and Niḥsvabhāvavāda Madhyamaka categories are overlapping. I had struggled with this passage until discovering the *Meaningful to Behold*, which proved very meaningful to behold indeed.

Clarifying Shakya Chokden's approach to the two types of Yogācāra Madhyamaka also helps in understanding why, in the above passage, he uses the term "Cittamātra" and not "Yogācāra." The Cittamātra (i.e., Satyākāravāda) view is used by Śāntarakṣita and his followers *only* provisionally (i.e., it is first asserted and then negated by reasoning without being reasserted on any other level). The Alīkākāravāda view, in contrast, is used by them provisionally with respect to positing emptiness through reasonings, but it is asserted as the final view when describing the reality experienced in meditative equipoise. Usage of the term "Cittamātra" in that passage serves the purpose of identifying a specific category of Niḥsvabhāvavādins. If the term "Yogācāra" were applied, that could create confusion as to whether all Yogācāra views are only used provisionally by Śāntarakṣita and his followers.

Because Śāntarakṣita and his followers share such important features of the final view of reality with Yogācāras, Shakya Chokden goes as far as admitting that they too can be described as Yogācāras. Arguing against those who call Vasubandhu and other Yogācāra thinkers "Cittamātra Followers" on the grounds that those thinkers are Yogācāras, he says:

> If [someone] is established as a Cittamātra Follower merely by virtue of being described as a Yogācāra, then it will follow

> that the master Śāntarakṣita with his disciple [Kamalaśīla] and all other Yogācāra Mādhyamikas are [those] Cittamātra Followers themselves.[108]

When addressing the Alīkākāravāda Yogācāra system, Shakya Chokden himself prefers to use the term "Yogācāra Madhyamaka." Nevertheless, when I describe that system in the present book, I am mostly using the term "Alīkākāravāda," in order to avoid confusion concerning the two types of Yogācāra Madhyamaka.

6. Are There Any Cittamātra Followers Around?

At this point, I should address another puzzling issue. As we have seen, not only does Shakya Chokden accept the existence of all four Buddhist tenet systems, including Cittamātra, but he builds his unique approach to Mahāyāna systems on the basis of a sharp distinction between Satyākāravāda and Alīkākāravāda.[109] We also have learned that he treats the most well-known Yogācāra thinkers as both Alīkākāravādins and Mādhyamikas. This leads us to the following question: whom does he identify as Satyākāravādins and Cittamātra Followers, and in what texts do they express a view so radically different from Alīkākāravāda? Shakya Chokden's own contemporaries challenged him with this very question, as can be seen from the following objections addressed in the *Meaningful to Behold*: "If one accepts the Alīkākāravāda view as Madhyamaka, then no Cittamātra masters and texts will be found."[110] In the *Seventeen Wondrous Answers*, he also writes: "They say: 'If the chariot way of the *Dharmas of Maitreya* and Asaṅga is Madhyamaka, then what is an illustration of Cittamātra texts and masters [who wrote them]?' "[111]

Shakya Chokden's answer is simple and provocative at the same time. Rather than trying to identify separate Satyākāravāda thinkers and their texts as other doxographers do,[112] he says that the tenets of both Satyākāravāda and Alīkākāravāda were authored by *identical* thinkers. Thus, in the *Meaningful to Behold*,[113] he explains that Cittamātra texts and masters can be identified because both Satyākāravāda and Alīkākāravāda views derive from identical textual sources, such as Maitreya's *Differentiation of the Middle and Extremes*. As a precedent for such position, he cites well-known examples of texts belonging to dual traditions with their respective authors understood to advocate tenets belonging to both—the *Treasury of Higher Knowledge* as a text common to both Vaibhāṣika and Sautrāntika (*bye mdo mthun mong ba['i gzhung]*), and Dharmakīrti's *Commentary on Valid Cognition* and

Asaṅga's *Summary of Higher Knowledge* as texts common to both Sautrāntika and Cittamātra (*mdo sems mthun mong ba'i gzhung*).[114] Likewise, he says, both Satyākāravāda and Alīkākāravāda views were taught in the *Dharmas of Maitreya*, the *Commentary on Valid Cognition*, Vasubandhu's *Thirty Stanzas*,[115] and other texts.[116] Throughout his writings, Shakya Chokden provides detailed illustrations of this approach, as in the following passage from his *Appearance of the Sun*:

> Also, [those who] say that the final [view] of the *Seven Works [on Valid Cognition]* lies in Cittamātra do not differentiate between individual divisions of the great chariot ways. Explanations in these texts of Maitreya together with [the texts of his] followers[117] are given in reliance upon a twofold division of [philosophical] systems: [the system described by] the passages teaching Cittamātra, and the system above it, in which that [Cittamātra system] has been refuted. In that context, one cannot show even a single letter explaining that the latter system belongs to Cittamātra and that there exist Madhyamaka tenets above it. The way of making the twofold division is illustrated [by the passages] from [Maitreya's] *Ornament of Mahāyāna Sūtras*:
>
>> [He] immaculately dwells in the mind-only which appears as those [external objects . . .]
>
> and [a few lines later]:
>
>> [The bodhisattva] then realizes the mind also as exclusively nonexistent.[118]
>
> and [Maitreya's] *Differentiation of the Middle and Extremes*:
>
>> Unreal ideation exists.
>
> and [immediately in the next line]:
>
>> The two do not exist in it.[119]
>
> There are numerous [passages like these]. Thereby, the first line [in each of the above citations is] the passage on mind-only devoid of the apprehended (*gzung ba med pa*). The second [line], having negated mind-only, [describes]

> the middle (*dbu ma*) as that which is left in remainder of negation of both the apprehended and apprehender (*gzung 'dzin gnyis po bkag pa*), [namely] primordial mind which is the mode of being. [Such mind] is asserted as the final suchness which is not taken as an object by reasons and expressive sounds.[120]

Shakya Chokden makes three important points in this passage. First, Cittamātra and Alīkākāravāda tenets are taught by the same authors in the same texts, and even the same passages. Second, those authors treat only the latter system as their own final view that transcends the mind-only view of Cittamātra, and do not posit any middle, i.e., Madhyamaka view higher than that. Third, they do not discard the Cittamātra view as useless, but use it as a step toward realization of their final Madhyamaka view.

Shakya Chokden clearly treats Cittamātra as a temporary view that has to be transcended by those Yogācāras who fully grasp the meaning of their own scriptures. He argues that this approach is shared by sūtric and tantric authors of important Indian writings. In the *Rain of Ambrosia*, he quotes one and the same passage simultaneously from three different texts: Puṇḍarīka's *Stainless Light*,[121] Āryadeva's *Summary of Primordial Mind's Essence*,[122] and Jetāri's *Differentiation of Sugata's Texts*:[123]

> "Free from the apprehended and apprehender
> Consciousness exists [as] the ultimate"—
> Proclaim those who crossed
> The ocean of Yogācāras' texts.[124]

Shakya Chokden comments:

> The first line [describes] the way of [being] empty of both the apprehended and apprehender. The second line [describes] that primordial mind existing in the remainder of that [emptiness] as ultimate truth. Then the [last] two lines explain that such interpretation is the system of the latter of the two [types] of Yogācāras: those who are provisionally Cittamātra Followers (*gnas skabs sems tsam pa*) and ultimately Mādhyamikas (*mthar thug dbu ma pa*). What is called "consciousness" (*rnam par shes pa*) in this [passage] is not something contrasted to primordial mind. Were it so, it would contradict its being free from the apprehended and apprehender.[125]

The overall impression we get from reading Shakya Chokden's works is that he does not want to allow Cittamātra an independent existence on a par with Alīkākāravāda and other such higher order systems, and instead treats it as a transitory and incomplete system created by followers of other tenets only as a stepping-stone toward realization of the final view of Alīkākāravāda. In this way, it is different from other tenets that were created by their own authors as freestanding systems in separate texts, even though later they might have been turned into a part of another multilayered system (such as Sautrāntika in the Sautrāntika Madhyamaka system mentioned above). Unlike such systems, Cittamātra lacked any autonomous and self-sufficient existence from its very inception.

It is not surprising, therefore, that at times Shakya Chokden makes strong statements that sound self-contradictory if taken out of context. The following passage from the *Explanation of [Sakya Pendita's] 'Entrance into Scholarship' Together with Answers to Questions* deserves attention:

> What is called "Satyākāravāda" and "Alīkākāravāda" are only rungs of the ladder to enter the ocean of definitive meaning of Yogācāras' [texts; they] are not separate tenets.[126]

If we read this passage out of context, it sounds as if Shakya Chokden were undercutting his own basis, because his entire approach to philosophical divisions of Mahāyāna is based on the differentiation between Alīkākāravāda and Satyākāravāda. Yet, if we plug in the elements discussed above and understand this statement contextually, we will see that it is expressive of his overall approach. The statement that Alīkākāravāda and Satyākāravāda are not "separate tenets" (*grub mtha' so so ba*) is a part of a broader point, namely that *unlike Prāsaṅgika and Svātantrika*, Alīkākāravāda and Satyākāravāda are not separate tenets authored by different authors and originating from different scriptures.[127] However, Alīkākāravāda and Satyākāravāda *are* separate tenets in the sense of divergent philosophical positions, as Shakya Chokden himself makes clear in multiple passages.[128]

In my opinion, Shakya Chokden chose this approach to strike a balance between two important elements. First, it enables him to emphasize the Alīkākāravāda/Satyākāravāda distinction, which is crucial for bringing the Alīkākāravāda Yogācāra system to the level of Madhyamaka. Second, it allows him to promote as many Yogācāra thinkers as possible to the Alīkākāravāda Mādhyamika "rank" in order to support that distinction. As a result, Cittamātra in Shakya

Chokden's system became like a trampoline, never intended as a permanent residence, but only as a temporary means to jump high into the space of ultimate reality of the Alīkākāravāda view.

We have already seen the importance of the Alīkākāravāda/ Satyākāravāda distinction to Shakya Chokden. However the second issue is equally important. Its importance can be seen in cases where he is willing to admit the existence of the Alīkākāravāda view even where he *himself* cannot see it clearly. This is why he disagrees with those Tibetans who treat Dignāga as a Satyākāravādin,[129] and argues that Dignāga produced the Alīkākāravāda view in his mind, although he did not present it clearly in the *Sūtra on Valid Cognition*.[130]

Such statements are indicative of yet another important feature of Shakya Chokden's approach to the Alīkākāravāda/Satyākāravāda distinction. If a person accepts the Satyākāravāda view as the highest rather than a stepping-stone to the Alīkākāravāda view, it entails a merely partial understanding of Yogācāra system. As he puts it in the *Rain of Ambrosia*: "Although Cittamātra Followers *are* Yogācāras, they have not crossed the ocean of those [Yogācāras'] texts."[131] This explains why he is hesitant to put such important thinkers as Dignāga into the category of Cittamātra Followers: it would imply that Dignāga did not fully grasp the meaning of Yogācāra writings.

Shakya Chokden's interpretation of Yogācāra tenets still allows for the possibility of thinkers fixated on the Cittamātra view as supreme, and thereby drifting in the ocean of Yogācāras' texts instead of crossing it. But notably, this issue is not important for him: he does not identify those thinkers even when addressing the direct challenge of vanishing Cittamātra Followers in the *Meaningful to Behold* and the *Seventeen Wondrous Answers*. In that context, instead of providing at least a couple of names of Cittamātra thinkers or titles of their texts, he prefers to discuss well-known Yogācāra thinkers and present all of them as Alīkākāravādins. He is no doubt aware of later Indian writers who interpreted the works of such thinkers as Dignāga and Dharmakīrti in the Satyākāravāda way,[132] presumably because they held the Satyākāravāda view themselves. Nevertheless, he clearly prefers to focus on the seminal Yogācāra thinkers, not later interpreters of their works.

At the same time, further analysis demonstrates that according to Shakya Chokden's own system, there should exist practitioners who accept the Satyākāravāda view as the highest. However, such figures are only identified as nameless followers of the path to the nirvāṇa of pratyekabuddhas. As we remember, Shakya Chokden argues that with the view of Satyākāravāda, one can become a pratyekabuddha, even though that view is not sufficient for attaining complete buddhahood.[133] These practitioners have to transcend the views of Vaibhāṣika or Sautrāntika, because those views are not sufficient for attaining the pratyekabuddha nirvāṇa. At the same time, they cannot directly realize Madhyamaka view, because that would absurdly entail their realization of the buddha-essence characterized by the purity from adventitious stains (*glo bur rnam dag*), which is open only to Mahāyāna āryas according to Shakya Chokden.[134] Therefore, the only view they can possibly cultivate to attain the highest goal of their chosen path is Satyākāravāda.

In summary, Shakya Chokden argues that both Alīkākāravāda and Satyākāravāda views were authored by Alīkākāravādins, namely individuals who held the Alīkākāravāda position as supreme. These authors utilized the Satyākāravāda view as a provisional step toward understanding the Alīkākāravāda view. For Shakya Chokden, complete understanding and acceptance of the Yogācāra system implies the acceptance of the Alīkākāravāda view of reality as the highest view.[135] One context where maintaining the Satyākāravāda view can be useful is the application of that view as a practical means of achieving nirvāṇa via one of the three Buddhist paths.[136]

7. Expanding the Mādhyamika Camp

It is impossible to imagine a Tibetan doxographer who does not appeal to the authority of Indian Buddhist thinkers in order to support his interpretations of Buddhist tenets. Shakya Chokden is no exception, as he too seeks and finds support for his innovative views on Mahāyāna systems in the writings of major Indian Yogācāra and Niḥsvabhāvavāda figures. These thinkers include those who themselves openly claim (in his view) that the Alīkākāravāda and Niḥsvabhāvavāda systems are compatible, and those who do not directly address the issue of compatibility, but accept both the Alīkākāravāda and Niḥsvabhāvavāda views (either in separate texts or in the same text).

The first group on the Niḥsvabhāvavāda side includes such thinkers as Atiśa and Śāntarakṣita, and on the Yogācāra side, Ratnākaraśānti.[137] The second group on the Niḥsvabhāvavāda side includes Haribhadra, and on the Yogācāra side, Dharmakīrti. I make this twofold division to distinguish between the two ways in which Shakya Chokden resorts to Indian thinkers for support: either by using their statements that explicitly claim the compatibility of the two systems or by using their statements that only imply it. As will be seen in the passages addressed below, he himself does not make this division, and often shifts between the two approaches in the same context.

In the *Rain of Ambrosia*, Shakya Chokden suggests the following approach to the Niḥsvabhāvavāda and Alīkākāravāda systems:

> It is good [to approach them] in accordance with the explanations that the two systems agree in their intent, [as taught by] Bodhisattva Śāntarakṣita, master Haribhadra, and Ratnākaraśānti, Omniscient One of the Age of Conflicts. Therefore, one should not fall into partiality.[138]

Haribhadra can serve as a good example of an Indian thinker who accepts both Niḥsvabhāvavāda and Alīkākāravāda views without explicitly discussing their compatibility. As I have mentioned above (143), Shakya Chokden explains that although Haribhadra did refute the reality of primordial mind, he did it only in the context of positing the view through reasoning; he identified the object of meditative experience as primordial mind. Shakya Chokden provides more details in the *Rain of Ambrosia*:

> *Question:* Did this master [Haribhadra] not establish the non-dual primordial mind as self-empty, [when he wrote]: "because that [non-dual primordial mind] is also dependently arisen. . . ?"
>
> *Answer:* [Yes, he] did explain so on the level of severing superimpositions by reasoning arisen from thinking (*bsam byung gi rigs pas sgro 'dogs gcod pa'i tshe*). Nevertheless, on the level of incorporation into experience by [wisdom] arisen from meditation (*sgom byung gis nyams su len pa'i tshe*), [Haribhadra] explained that very primordial mind as the object of experience. This is because [a few lines later in the same text he] explained: ". . . if there has been precisely, perfectly produced the individually self-cognizing nonconceptual mind appearing as the illusion-like selfness (*sgyu ma lta bu'i bdag nyid du snang ba'i blo rnam par mi rtog pa so sor rang gis rig pa*) . . ." If that very primordial mind is not experienced, there will be no ground for arising of that self-cognition in that context.[139]

It is worth citing the passage by Haribhadra at length, because it demonstrates how Haribhadra incorporates Yogācāra and Niḥsvabhāvavāda views into his system and how Shakya Chokden uses Haribhadra's approach in support of his own position. The passage in question is found in Haribhadra's commentary on the *Ornament of Clear Realizations* known as the *Clear Meaning*.[140] In the Clear Realization of the Peak (*rste mo'i mngon rtogs, mūrdhābhisamaya*) chapter of that text, Haribhadra outlines the fourfold progression of practice that Shakya Chokden identifies as the "four stages of yoga (*rnal 'byor gyi sa bzhi*)": the stage of yoga realizing the selflessness of persons (*gang zag gi bdag med rtogs pa'i rnal 'byor gyi sa*), the stage of yoga realizing the selflessness of the apprehended-phenomena (*gzung ba chos kyi bdag med rtogs pa'i rnal 'byor gyi sa*), the stage of yoga realizing the selflessness of the apprehender-phenomena (*'dzin pa chos kyi bdag med rtogs pa'i rnal 'byor gyi sa*), and the stage of yoga not realizing any extremes of proliferations (*spros pa'i mtha' gang yang ma rtogs pa'i rnal 'byor gyi sa*).[141] Of crucial interest here are the second, third, and fourth stages that are described in the *Clear Meaning* as follows:

> One considers: "because it is ascertained that blue and mind [apprehending] that [blue] are observed simultaneously, this [world] is mind-only; external objects do not exist," and without having completely discarded manifest clinging to mind possessing the aspect of the apprehender (*'dzin pa'i rnam pa can gyi sems*), one abandons manifest clinging to external objects. Then, thinking with certainty, "if the apprehended does not exist, the apprehender does not exist [either]," [the yogin] also eliminates that mere cognizance characterized by the aspect of the apprehender (*'dzin pa'i rnam pa'i mtshan nyid rnam par rig pa tsam*),[142] and ascertains: "this sole non-dual primordial mind is a really existent entity" (*yang dag par yod pa'i ngo bo*). After that, [the yogin] meditates: "because that [non-dual primordial mind] is also dependently arisen, it lacks [that] very entity, like an illusion. In reality, [it is] devoid of entities imputed solely as a thing, a no-thing, and so forth." Thereby, with the power of meditation being accomplished, if there has been correctly, perfectly produced the individually self-cognizing nonconceptual mind appearing as the illusion-like selfness (*sgyu ma lta bu'i bdag nyid du snang ba'i blo rnam par mi rtog pa so so rang gis rig par bya ba*)[143] [in which] there have been abandoned all characteristics of mistakes similar to [those of mistaken] knowing [apprehending] some [objects such as shells, etc.] as jewels, silver, and so forth, the yogin [eventually] completely abandons obscurations of knowables.[144]

According to this passage, Mahāyāna yogis progressively negate through reasoning increasingly subtle levels of conceptualization. This process is described as negating the external world but retaining the apprehension of mind appearing as that external world (stage two) with the help of what is known as the "reason of ascertainment of simultaneous observation" (*lhan cig dmigs nges pa'i rtags*), negating that subjective mind as well but retaining the reality of primordial mind devoid of subjective-objective duality (stage three), and finally establishing even that non-dual primordial mind as entityless like an illusion (stage four). Because this last negation is the final stage in the fourfold progression, it is tempting to conclude—as Shakya Chokden's opponent does in the preceding passage—that what one is left to meditate on is that very negation of all entities including primordial mind. Nevertheless, Haribhadra continues—and Shakya Chokden is quick to mention it—what one uses in meditation as the antidote to the obscurations of knowables (i.e., the main tool of achieving buddhahood) is none other than the individually self-cognizing nonconceptual mind that Shakya Chokden treats as the non-dual primordial mind and self-cognition. In this way, splitting the ultimate view addressed by Haribhadra into the dimension determined by reasoning and the dimension realized in meditation, Shakya Chokden argues that even when Haribhadra himself refutes the reality of primordial mind, he does so only on the level of severing superimpositions by reasoning. This does not run contrary to the fact that in the same passage Haribhadra also asserts that self-cognizing primordial mind is the object of meditative experience.

Shakya Chokden demonstrates that other Niḥsvabhāvavāda thinkers also treat Niḥsvabhāvavāda and Yogācāra systems as non-contradictory. According to him, Śāntarakṣita and Atiśa openly state that the two systems' views of emptiness are in agreement:

> This explanation of the identification of thatness which is an object of experience (*nyams su myong bya'i de kho na nyid*) as the non-dual primordial mind is asserted by both Bodhisattva Śāntarakṣita and Lord Atiśa. The [following verse] appears in both the *Ornament of Madhyamaka* [composed by Śāntarakṣita] and the *Song of the View of the Dharma-Sphere* composed by Lord [Atiśa]:
>
> > Those who hold the reins of reasoning,
> > Riding the chariot of the two approaches,
> > Attain therefore the state of
> > True Mahāyāna followers.[145]

> The two approaches are the approach of Yogācāras and the approach of Niḥsvabhāvavādins.[146]

In this way, Shakya Chokden argues that even Atiśa, who taught that Candrakīrti's instructions should be used in order to realize ultimate reality,[147] identified ultimate reality directly experienced in meditative equipoise in accordance with Yogācāra teachings. Thus, according to Shakya Chokden, even such well-known Niḥsvabhāvavādins as Atiśa, who later came to be identified by Tibetans as a Prāsaṅgika, share the same ultimate view with Alīkākāravādins.

Shakya Chokden extends his inclusion of Indian scholars in the Madhyamaka camp via the classification of famous Buddhist logicians too as Alīkākāravādins. In the *Appearance of the Sun*, he argues that the views of Dignāga and Dharmakīrti are identical,[148] and that their ultimate view is Yogācāra Madhyamaka (i.e., Alīkākāravāda). He also highly praises Prajñākaragupta, the author of the *Ornament of [Dharmakīrti's] 'Commentary on Valid Cognition,'*[149] and says that his ascertainment of the final view lies in Madhyamaka.[150] He and Sūryagupta identified the ultimate valid cognition as primordial mind free from the duality of the apprehended and apprehender, and identified the ultimate intent of Dharmakīrti as Madhyamaka.[151] Śākyabuddhi also interpreted the non-dual primordial mind as the main topic of the *Commentary on Valid Cognition*, although he is not known to have explained Dharmakīrti's view as Madhyamaka explicitly.[152]

Shakya Chokden explains that an important feature of Dharmakīrti's approach that distinguishes him from Dignāga is that he posits the apprehended and apprehender as self-empty by the reasoning of the lack of being one or many (*gcig dang du bral gyi rigs pa*).[153] Because Dharmakīrti accepted the emptiness of the apprehended and apprehender, some Indian thinkers, such as Jetāri, saw him as a Mādhyamika; nevertheless, Shakya Chokden argues that Dharmakīrti does not accept a non-affirming negation as the ultimate view.[154] Thus, he is not a Mādhyamika in the Niḥsvabhāvavādin sense. Rather, Dharmakīrti shares the same view of reality with Maitreya,[155] and thereby also agrees on the final view with Alīkākāravāda.

In a word, Shakya Chokden argues that the same Alīkākāravāda view of ultimate reality is shared by all famous Yogācāras, and that it is a valid view of Madhyamaka. He explains in the *Ocean of Scriptural Statements and Reasoning*:

> To summarize: in the texts of brothers Asaṅga [and Vasubandhu], and father Dignāga with [his spiritual] son

[Dharmakīrti], no other Madhymaka approach emerged apart from the one explained above. According to the great chariot, the glorious honorable Dharmapāla, as reported in the commentary on the *Four Hundred* [by Candrakīrti],[156] the intent of honorable Nāgārjuna is also like that. This is also what Ratnākaraśānti [meant when he] said in the treatise called the *Ornament of Madhyamaka*:

> Herein, I will explain the two truths
> Endowed with valid scriptural statements
> Taught by Maitreya and Asaṅga
> And also accepted by Nāgārjuna.[157]

Lord Dīpaṃkara [Atiśa also] taught:

> Ratnākaraśānti says that
> The tenets of Nāgārjuna and
> Asaṅga too are concordant as well.[158]

He continues, arguing that when Prajñākaragupta, Śāntarakṣita, and Ngok Loden Sherap said that the final intent of the treatises of Dignāga and Dharmakīrti was Madhyamaka, they were pointing to this very type of Madhyamaka, i.e., the Alīkākāravāda Yogācāra, and not to the system of Niḥsvabhāvavāda. Likewise for the early Sakya masters, who taught that the intent of the three intermediate *Dharmas of Maitreya* is Madhyamaka.[159]

In summary, Shakya Chokden argues that there are Niḥsvabhāvavādins who disagree with Yogācāras in the context of determining the view through reasoning, but agree with them on the level of positing the view which is directly experienced in meditation. The main points of disagreement between such Niḥsvabhāvavādins and Alīkākāravādins therefore lie in different ways of identifying the Madhyamaka view posited by reasoning. The view experienced in meditative equipoise is explained by both of them as identical. In this way, Shakya Chokden uses the ultimate view experienced in meditation like glue to join together the views of Niḥsvabhāvavādins and Yogācāras, including Buddhist logicians.

By placing key Yogācāra and Niḥsvabhāvavāda thinkers into the same Mādhyamika camp, and arguing that they explicitly or implicitly agree that Alīkākāravāda and Niḥsvabhāvavāda come down to the same point, Shakya Chokden seeks to authenticate *his own* view of the compatibility of these two systems. Against the background of this greatly expanded Madhyamaka camp, his approach becomes a part of the mainstream position shared and supported by numerous Madhyamaka thinkers on both the Alīkākāravāda and the Niḥsvabhāvavāda sides. In the next chapter we will look more closely at details of this approach and explore some specific techniques Shakya Chokden uses in presenting Alīkākāravāda and Niḥsvabhāvavāda as equally valid and compatible Madhyamaka systems.

Chapter 4

Through Broken Boundaries to New Enclosures

Reconciling Yogācāra and Madhyamaka

1. Differences between Alīkākāravāda and Satyākāravāda

To put forward and defend his own unique structuring of Mahāyāna tenets, Shakya Chokden advances on two different but interdependent fronts: reworking the subcategories of Yogācāra and reworking the subcategories of Madhyamaka, respectively. In the first case, he demonstrates clear differences between Alīkākāravāda and Satyākāravāda and explains why Satyākāravāda cannot belong to the Madhyamaka system and Alīkākāravāda cannot be subsumed under the category of Cittamātra. In the second case, which will be discussed in the following sections, he explains why Alīkākāravāda should be treated as a legitimate category of Madhyamaka alongside Niḥsvabhāvavāda.

Discussing differences between Alīkākāravāda and Satyākāravāda, Shakya Chokden is primarily concerned with the question of what each system categorizes as real and unreal. In the *Ocean of Scriptural Statements and Reasoning*, he puts Satyākāravāda and Alīkākāravāda side by side and outlines the following differences: Satyākāravāda accepts consciousness as truly established (*bden grub*), while Alīkākāravāda only accepts primordial mind as truly established; the two systems are similar in not accepting the apprehended and apprehender with different substances with respect to external objects (*phyi rol gyi don la ltos pa'i gzung 'dzin rdzas gzhan*), but they differ in accepting (Satyākāravāda) and not accepting (Alīkākāravāda) the apprehended and apprehender with different substances with respect to internal knowing (*nang shes pa la ltos pa'i gzung 'dzin rdzas gzhan*); Satyākāravāda accepts unreal ideation (*yang dag pa ma yin pa'i kun tu rtog pa, abhūtaparikalpa*) or the apprehended-aspect (*gzung rnam, grāhyākāra*) as truly established, while Alīkākāravāda treats it as an illusion; Satyākāravāda accepts all appearances as mind (*sems, citta*), while Alīkākāravāda instead reduces appearances to the dharma-sphere (*chos dbyings, dharmadhātu*).[1]

Unpacking these differences, Shakya Chokden draws a sharp distinction between the Alīkākāravāda and Satyākāravāda approaches to knowing and primordial mind. He argues that Satyākāravāda does not posit a separate category of primordial mind, and accepts the reality of knowing with and without dualistic appearances. Alīkākāravāda, on the other hand, denies the reality of dualistically appearing knowing or consciousness. It only accepts the reality of knowing free from dualistic appearances, and classifies it as primordial mind.

Elaborating on the Alīkākāravāda position, Shakya Chokden explains that in general, the term "mind" (*sems, citta*) designates two types of phenomena: the possessor of reality, the relative mind (*kun rdzob pa'i sems*); and reality itself, the ultimate mind (*don dam pa'i sems*). The former is the consciousness dualistically appearing as the apprehended and apprehender (*gzung 'dzin gnyis su snang ba'i rnam shes*). The latter is the non-dual primordial mind (*gnyis su med pa'i ye shes, advayajñāna*). The former, being a relative truth, is not the mode of being, luminosity (*'od gsal, prabhāsvara*), and is not established by valid cognition.[2] Thus, it is only the dharma-sphere, identified with luminosity and the mode of being, that Alīkākāravāda accepts as established by valid cognition in its own system. According to Alīkākāravāda, all knowables are the dharma-sphere, because nothing else exists apart from the dharma-sphere, which is primordial mind.[3] In other words, knowables in this system are not different from the knower, primordial mind. No other phenomena exist.

In contrast to Alīkākāravāda, Satyākāravāda accepts as ultimate truth consciousness empty of the apprehended and apprehender with different substances with respect to external objects (*phyi rol gyi don la ltos pa'i gzung 'dzin rdzas gzhan gyis stong pa'i rnam par shes pa*). Satyākāravāda asserts this type of ultimate reality because it does not accept the existence of the apprehended (*gzung ba, grāhya*), i.e., external objects, *not* because it accepts the lack of substantial existence of the mind that appears as those external objects.[4] (As an analogy to the Satyākāravāda position, we can imagine someone who thinks that a dreamer and dreams are not different because dreams do not actually exist, while at the same time believing in the real existence of a dreamer.)

In other words, the reason why Satyākāravāda does not accept that the apprehended and apprehender have different substances is just because it treats the apprehended, i.e., external objects, as non-existent. Nevertheless, it accepts the reality of the apprehender, i.e., consciousness with dualistic appearances. Alīkākāravāda, on the other hand, negates both the apprehended and apprehender, because it does not accept the reality of either external objects or consciousness with dualistic appearances. The unique position of Alīkākāravāda is the assertion that only primordial mind really exists. This primordial mind is self-cognition free from both the apprehended and apprehender.

Shakya Chokden provides further details about the differences and similarities between the two systems in the *Meaningful to Behold*:

> Those who accept all relative appearances as mind (*sems, citta*) and do not accept the primordial mind free from the duality of the apprehended and apprehender (*gzung 'dzin gnyis med kyi ye shes*) are given the name "Cittamātra Followers." Those who do not accept any ultimate truth apart from the non-dual primordial mind are called "Alīkākāravāda Mādhyamikas" (*rnam rdzun dbu ma pa*). Both of them do not differ in advocating interiority of knowables (*shes bya nang gir smra ba*) and advocating cognizance-only (*rnam par rig pa tsam du smra ba*).[5]

Satyākāravāda and Alīkākāravāda are similar in asserting that whatever appears to perception does not pass beyond the internal boundaries of mind, since nothing exists outside the mind. Nevertheless, they are different first in whether or not they accept relative, dualistic appearances as mind, and second in whether they accept dualistically appearing mind as real (Satyākāravāda), or reject any real existence of dualistically appearing mind, and view only primordial mind as really existent (Alīkākāravāda). Based on that distinction, Shakya Chokden also argues that it is only Satyākāravāda, not Alīkākāravāda, that accepts the two key Yogācāra syllogisms—the reason of ascertainment of simultaneous observation mentioned above (153) and the reason of clarity and cognition (*gsal zhing rig pa'i rtags*)[6]—because these reasons establish dualistic appearances as mind. While both systems are advocating the interiority of knowables, only Alīkākāravāda is subtle enough to be treated as Madhyamaka, because it accepts the non-dual primordial mind alone as real.

The non-dual primordial mind is the middle way according to Alīkākāravāda. From Shakya Chokden's point of view, the acceptance of the reality of this primordial mind combined with the nonacceptance of the reality of anything else is what makes the Alīkākāravāda system so distinct from Satyākāravāda. Alluding to such passages from Maitreya's corpus as

> Because there are no phenomena
> Except for the dharma-sphere . . .

from the *Ornament of Mahāyāna Sūtras*,[7] and

> Thus, except for the dharma-sphere
> There are no phenomena.[8]

from the *Differentiation of the Middle and Extremes*, he writes in the *Wish Fulfilling Meru*:

> "The middle" in this system is that which is free from the two extremes of the apprehended and apprehender, the self-illuminating self-cognition (*rang rig rang gsal ba*). Because no phenomena except the dharma-sphere are accepted in this system, it is greatly distinguished from Cittamātra.[9]

Given the above distinctions, Shakya Chokden argues that the two systems also identify the two truths differently. In the *Discourse Eliminating Mistakes*, he addresses this distinction in terms of cognizance (*rnam par rig pa, vijñapti*), arguing that both systems accept the existence of only cognition, but interpret it differently:

> In general, [the term] "cognizance"
> [Means that] the two truths are not posited
> Apart from cognizance, and
> All knowables are contained within the two [truths].
> There are two types of Vijñaptivādins (*rnam rig smra ba*, "Proponents of Cognizance")
> Due to their division into Cittamātra Followers and Mādhyamikas.
> Cittamātra Followers explain external objects
> As nonexistent and as relative truths.
> [On the other hand, they interpret] the consciousness that appears as those [objects] by the power of predispositions (*bag chags, vāsana*)

As existent and ultimate truth. . . .
Vijñaptivāda Mādhyamikas (*rnam rig smra ba'i dbu ma pa*)
[Argue that] both external objects and the consciousness that appears
As those [external objects] are relative truths.
[They argue that] primordial mind empty of duality is the ultimate meaning (*dam pa'i don, paramārtha*).[10]

According to Shakya Chokden, the category of cognizance encompasses both primordial mind and other types of mind. This explains why he calls both Alīkākāravādins and Satyākāravādins "Vijñaptivādins," which is similar to calling both of them "Yogācāras." He treats the categories of Vijñaptivāda and Yogācāra as synonymous.

This passage provides an additional clarification of the primary difference between Satyākāravāda and Alīkākāravāda: while both systems view external phenomena as nonexistent and relative truths, Satyākāravāda asserts that the consciousness appearing as external phenomena is existent and ultimate truth. Alīkākāravāda, on the other hand, subsumes even this dualistically appearing consciousness under the category of relative truth and nonexistent phenomena. The only phenomenon asserted as real and existent by Alīkākāravāda is the non-dual primordial mind. (This passage also demonstrates the important feature of Shakya Chokden's interpretation of the Buddhist tenets mentioned above (99): the equation of existence with ultimate truth and the description of relative truth as nonexistent.)

Shakya Chokden discusses further differences between Satyākāravāda and Alīkākāravāda in terms of the "apprehended-aspect" (*gzung rnam, grāhyākāra*) and the "apprehender-aspect" (*'dzin rnam, grāhakākāra*). The apprehended-aspect/apprehender-aspect pair is not synonymous with the apprehended (*gzung ba, grāhya*)/apprehender (*'dzin pa, grāhaka*) pair mentioned above. The latter pair deals with external objects (the apprehended) versus consciousness appearing as external objects (the apprehender). In contrast to that, the former pair deals exclusively with the mind. According to both Satyākāravāda and Alīkākāravāda, the part of mind which deceptively appears as the external world is called the "apprehended-aspect," while the part of mind which appears as the mind itself is called the "apprehender-aspect." The former is dualistically appearing consciousness, unreal ideation. The latter is self-cognition.

Satyākāravāda and Alīkākāravāda differ in *how* they treat the apprehended-aspect. Both systems accept that the apprehended-aspect is the apprehender, i.e., the dualistically appearing consciousness. Nevertheless, according to Satyākāravāda, it is real and true. According to

Alīkākāravāda, it is unreal and false. As for the apprehender-aspect, both Satyākāravāda and Alīkākāravāda treat it as true, although they differ with respect to its meaning due to their dissimilar interpretations of self-cognition.[11]

Alīkākāravāda in particular equates the apprehended-aspect with the dualistic consciousness and the apprehender-aspect with primordial mind. Shakya Chokden emphasizes that although primordial mind is the apprehender-aspect, it should not be confused with the apprehender: "[T]he word 'apprehender' is explained as [referring] to that very mind which appears as the apprehended[-phenomena] and apprehends that [appearance]; the term 'apprehender' does not appear in the excellent sayings [of the Buddha and Indian Buddhist masters as referring] to the non-dual primordial mind."[12] On the other hand, he argues that "[a]ccording to Alīkākāravāda, there can exist no knowing apart from the apprehender-aspect."[13]

The above-mentioned differences based on the apprehended-aspect/apprehender-aspect distinction are given a detailed treatment in the following passage from the *Previously Unseen Sun: The Definitive Meaning of the 'Sublime Continuum' Treatise*:

> Mahāyāna followers do not explain as their tenets an existence of pleasures and sufferings apart from cognition, that is, an appearance as worldly pleasures and sufferings to consciousness. In that context, there are two [types of] cognition: the factor of the outward-looking apprehended-aspect (*kha phyir blta gzung rnam gyi cha*) and the factor of the inward-looking apprehender-aspect (*kha nang blta 'dzin rnam gyi cha*). The acceptance of the first one as knowing and cognition (*shes rig*) [belongs] to Cittamātra tenets. This is like, [for example,] when explaining [the process of] seeing a form by the eye consciousness apprehending a form, [Cittamātra Followers] accept that although there is no form, the seer [of form] is the mind itself. Starting from Alīkākāravāda Mādhyamikas (*rnam brdzun dbu ma pa*), [all Mādhyamikas] have to explain the "non-duality of the apprehended and apprehender"[14] as [their own] tenets. Therefore, [in that context] the apprehender is not accepted even as a functional thing (*dngos po*), how much less as knowing.[15]

Thus, while Satyākāravāda treats the apprehended-aspect—the part of knowing that projects appearances of external phenomena—as real and having a truly existent nature of mind, Alīkākāravāda treats the apprehended-aspect as false and nonexistent, does not accept it as mind at all, and sees only primordial mind, the apprehender-aspect, as true, real, and ultimate.

Due to these differences, the two systems also interpret the meaning of self-cognition differently. In the *Enjoyment Ocean of the Speech of Seven Treatises: Explanation of the 'Treasure of the Science of Valid Cognition,'* Shakya Chokden explains that Satyākāravāda accepts the direct self-cognition of the outward-looking [mind] (*kha phyir lta'i rang rig mngon sum*), while Alīkākāravāda accepts the self-cognition of the non-dual knowing (*gnyis med kyi shes pa*) only.[16] In the *Enjoyment Ocean of the Entirely Good Dharma*, he also says:

> According to Alīkākāravāda, there can exist no knowing apart from the apprehender-aspect. Therefore, the apprehender-aspect experiencing the apprehended-aspect cannot exist. According to Satyākāravāda, it can exist. [Therefore,] it is clear that in that context, one has to make a slight distinction between the apprehender-aspect and self-cognition being turned exclusively inward [according to Alīkākāravāda] or not [according to Satyākāravāda].[17]

He further explains in the *Enjoyment Ocean of the Speech of the 'Seven Works'*:

> According to Satyākāravāda, precisely because the outward-looking types of knowing (*kha phyir blta'i shes pa*) also are non-mistaken with respect to their own apprehended-aspects, they are direct self-cognitions (*rang rig pa'i mngon sum, svasaṃvedanapratyakṣa*) . . . According to Alīkākāravāda, because such [types of knowing] also are mistaken like a [distorted] sensory consciousness with appearances of falling hair, they are unsuitable as direct perceptions (*mngon sum, pratyakṣa*). Therefore, self-cognition is exclusively the non-dual knowing.[18]

Satyākāravāda does acknowledge that the outward-looking consciousness is mistaken with respect to external appearances, because it apprehends them as external phenomena "out there" rather than as its own mental projections. Nevertheless, it is non-mistaken with respect to its appearance as those phenomena. This appearance is none other than the outward-looking consciousness itself. Therefore, even this dualistically appearing consciousness is accepted as self-cognition by Satyākāravāda. Alīkākāravāda, on the other hand, argues that precisely because the outward-looking consciousness is mistaken with respect to external phenomena, it has simply no non-mistaken modality that might engage in genuine self-cognition. This is why, according to Alīkākāravāda, self-cognition is only the non-dual primordial mind which is distinct from other types of knowing. Because this non-dual mind is non-mistaken with respect to its appearance, it is also non-mistaken when it cognizes itself.[19] In this way, Shakya Chokden presents the non-dual primordial mind as immaculate in all respects. There is simply no other way to go: according to him, in the Alīkākāravāda system, the non-dual primordial mind is the only phenomenon that exists, exists truly, and exists as ultimate truth.[20]

Put differently, because Satyākāravāda accepts the apprehended-aspect as existent, the meaning of self-cognition in that system is taken more broadly: it extends to the self-cognition of dualistically appearing consciousness as well. In contrast to that, because Alīkākāravāda accepts the non-dual primordial mind only, self-cognition is limited exclusively to the apprehender-aspect, the non-dual primordial mind itself. It is only the non-dual primordial mind which is termed "self-illuminating self-cognition" in the Alīkākāravāda system.

Consequently, the effect of valid cognition (*tshad 'bras, pramāṇaphala*), according to Satyākāravāda, is the self-cognition experiencing the apprehended-aspect (*gzung rnam nyams su myong ba'i rang rig*), i.e., the apprehender-aspect comprehending that apprehended-aspect (*gzung rnam de 'jal ba'i 'dzin rnam*). According to Alīkākāravāda, on the other hand, the effect of valid cognition is the self-cognition devoid of the duality of the apprehended and apprehender (*gzung 'dzin gnyis med kyi rang rig*), i.e., the apprehender-aspect of that [very self-cognition] (*de'i 'dzin rnam*).[21] In other words, it is the apprehender-aspect of self-cognition which itself is the apprehender-aspect devoid of the apprehended and apprehender.[22]

These dissimilar interpretations of mental phenomena by Satyākāravāda and Alīkākāravāda are reflected in their approaches to the three natures as well. In the *Snatching Away the Heart's Torments with the Garland of the White Moonrays of Definitive Meaning: Expression of Realizations of Honorable Ārya Asaṅga*,[23] Shakya Chokden explains that according to Satyākāravāda, the imaginary nature is not truly existent, the dependent nature is truly existent, and the emptiness in which the apprehended and apprehender with different substances are negated (*gzung 'dzin rdzas gzhan khegs pa'i stong nyid*) is described as the thoroughly established nature. Alīkākāravāda, on the other hand, accepts as the ultimate meaning the emptiness of duality of the apprehended and apprehender (*gzung 'dzin gnyis stong*), which is more profound. It treats both external objects and their apprehended-aspects as the imaginary apprehended and apprehender (*gzung 'dzin kun btags*) respectively, and by the reason of the lack of being one or many (*gcig dang du mar med pa'i gtan tshigs*) proves that the apprehended-aspect is not truly existent.

According to Satyākāravāda, although the imaginary nature, the apprehended, does not exist, the dependent nature, the apprehender, does truly exist. Because of that, the thoroughly established nature cannot be described as the emptiness of the duality of the apprehended and apprehender; Satyākāravāda negates only their existence as different substances. To put it differently, according to Satyākāravāda, external phenomena that are included in the category of the imaginary natures do not exist at all, but minds that are included in the category of the dependent natures substantially exist. Therefore, external phenomena and minds are not different substances: the former are nonexistent while the latter substantially exist.

Alīkākāravāda, on the other hand, does not accept the reality of the dependent natures, i.e., minds projecting appearances of external phenomena, either, because it places the apprehended-aspects into the category of the imaginary natures. It negates both the apprehended and the apprehender, and thereby arrives at the emptiness, or negation, of the two. This affects its approach to the thoroughly established nature as well. In the Alīkākāravāda system, it is understood only as the primordial mind devoid of duality of the apprehended and apprehender.

Shakya Chokden further argues that as long as one accepts that the dependent nature is truly established (*bden grub*), one has no chance to affirm the emptiness of duality of the apprehended and apprehender. Without that, in turn, one cannot access the essence of the final definitive meaning of the ocean of Yogācāras' texts (*rnal 'byor spyod gzhung rgya mtsho yi nges don mthar thug snying po*).[24] As we already know, this means that one cannot realize the Alīkākāravāda view. By understanding the emptiness in which the apprehended and apprehender with different substances are negated, one can realize the self-emptiness of the imaginary natures. Nevertheless, to fully understand Yogācāras' texts, one has to realize that the dependent natures are like an illusion in their not being truly established. Such is possible only if one realizes the emptiness of the duality of the apprehended and apprehender.[25]

This harks back to the discussion of other-emptiness in the previous chapter. As I mentioned there (134 ff.), the statement that the dependent nature does not exist and yet has the entity of the thoroughly established nature pertains to the Alīkākāravāda view only. Here too, Shakya Chokden explains that according to Alīkākāravāda, even though the entity (*ngo bo, bhāva*) of the dependent nature is truly existent, the dependent nature itself does not truly exist: the entity of the dependent nature is not the dependent nature, but the thoroughly established nature. What truly exists is only the non-dual primordial mind, ultimate truth, the thoroughly established nature.[26]

Because in his interpretation of Alīkākāravāda, Shakya Chokden treats the apprehender—the dualistically appearing consciousness—as the imaginary nature,[27] his position raises an obvious question about the status of the dependent nature in the Alīkākāravāda system. In the *Ocean of Scriptural Statements and Reasoning*, Shakya Chokden makes a statement that helps clarify this point. Invoking the authority of Asaṅga's *Summary of Mahāyāna*, he explains that the dependent nature "belongs to both parts" (*gnyis ka'i char gtogs*), i.e., it is split into the imaginary and thoroughly established natures. The part of dualistic appearance (*gnyis snang gi cha*) is subsumed under the category of the imaginary natures, while the part of clarity and cognition (*gsal rig gi cha*) is subsumed under the thoroughly established nature.[28] By itself, the dependent nature does not have a separate entity. In the *Snatching Away the Heart's Torments* too, he explains that according to Alīkākāravāda, both the apprehended and apprehender are the imaginary natures, only the non-dual primordial mind is the ultimate, and apart from them, no dependent nature can be identified at all.[29] The dependent nature, therefore, is like a vehicle that provisionally transports the mind to the cosmic expanse of the ultimate view, but is itself shattered into pieces when the final Alīkākāravāda view is asserted.

Satyākāravāda and Alīkākāravāda approaches to ultimate reality can be summarized as follows. Satyākāravāda negates the apprehended and apprehender with different substances with respect to external objects; it accepts as ultimate truth the consciousness empty of the apprehended and the apprehender with different substances, or the emptiness in which the apprehended and apprehender with different substances are negated. Alīkākāravāda negates what Satyākāravāda negates, but also goes further and negates the apprehended and apprehender with different substances with respect to internal knowing; it accepts as ultimate truth the non-dual primordial mind, or the emptiness of duality of the apprehended and apprehender. Emphasis on these distinctions helps Shakya Chokden authenticate his interpretation of Alīkākāravāda as Madhyamaka, distance Alīkākāravāda from

Satyākāravāda, and equate the Satyākāravāda system with Cittamātra. It also allows him to leave intact the standard fourfold hierarchical division of the Buddhist tenets into Vaibhāṣika, Sautrāntika, Cittamātra, and Madhyamaka, and simultaneously relocate the thinkers usually associated with the third category into the fourth category.

The above distinctions between Satyākāravāda and Alīkākāravāda, and the placement of Alīkākāravāda into the Madhyamaka category, would not be valid unless the Alīkākāravāda view is presented as sufficient for attaining buddhahood. This is because, as mentioned earlier, Shakya Chokden argues that cultivation of only the Madhyamaka view can result in the attainment of the nirvāṇa of a buddha. Thus, he differentiates the Satyākāravāda and Alīkākāravāda systems in terms of the Buddhist paths and their fruits as well, insisting that from among the two, only cultivation of the Alīkākāravāda view can result in the attainment of buddhahood. In contrast, with the Satyākāravāda (i.e., Cittamātra) view one can attain only a lower result, such as the nirvāṇa of a pratyekabuddha. Furthermore, when treated in the context of the Mahāyāna path, the Satyākāravāda view cannot take one higher than the path of preparation (*sbyor lam, prayogamārga*). In the *Discourse Eliminating Mistakes*, Shakya Chokden gives the following description of the cultivation of the Cittamātra view:

> By using clarity and cognition (*gsal rig*) empty of external objects
> As the object of observation (*dmigs pa, ālambana*) and accustoming oneself with [that object],
> One acquires the view of pratyekabuddhas
> And eliminates grasping at the self of the apprehended-phenomena (*gzung ba chos kyi bdag 'dzin*).[30]
> It is taught that by uniting that view with the mind of enlightenment (*byang chub sems, bodhicitta*),
> One attains the partial concordance with definite discrimination (*nges 'byed cha mthun, nirvedhabhāgiya*) of Mahāyāna.[31]

Thus, the Satyākāravāda view can be used either to achieve a goal of the path other than Mahāyāna or merely as a step in the five paths, not even reaching the first of the ten grounds (*sa bcu, daśabhūmi*) of the Mahāyāna path. In contrast to that, by following the Alīkākāravāda view, one can cover all the five paths and ten grounds, and achieve the highest Buddhist goal of buddhahood:

> Using the primordial mind empty of duality (*gnyis stong ye shes*) as the purificatory object of observation (*rnam dag gi dmigs pa, viśuddhālambana*)
> And accustoming oneself with [that object],
> Through uniting [that view] with the mind of enlightenment,
> One perfects the ten grounds.[32]

In summary, Shakya Chokden demonstrates sharp differences between Satyākāravāda and Alīkākāravāda in various contexts, focusing on their treatment of the divisions of mind, the apprehended/apprehender, the apprehended-aspect/apprehender-aspect, the two truths, the three natures, and self-cognition. These differences boil down to the question of what the two systems see as real, and whether their respective views of reality are practically useful as tools for achieving the objective of enlightenment. By showing that from among the two systems, only the Alīkākāravāda view of the reality of the non-dual primordial mind and of the unreality of all other phenomena is sufficient for the attainment of buddhahood, Shakya Chokden asserts the superiority of Alīkākāravāda over Satyākāravāda, and justifies his treatment of only the former as Madhyamaka.

2. The Heart of the Matter: Probing the Alīkākāravāda/Niḥsvabhāvavāda Distinction

As demonstrated by Shakya Chokden's writings from around 1477 onward, starting from his early fifties he became increasingly occupied with the nature of the relationship between the two systems that he saw as valid subdivisions of Madhyamaka: Alīkākāravāda and Niḥsvabhāvavāda. Exploring those systems, he tried to clarify their differences and at the same time prove their compatibility in the light of both of them being Madhyamaka. In the *Rain of Ambrosia*—the text that most extensively treats this issue—he explains his major analytical point regarding the relationship of Alīkākāravāda and Niḥsvabhāvavāda:

> I wish to explain the way in which there is a difference between the two systems in the modes of temporarily positing [their views] through reasoning (*rigs pas gtan la 'bebs tshul*), but no difference in their modes of upholding [the ultimate view] in the context of identification of the definitive meaning experienced through meditation (*sgom pas nyams su myong bya'i nges don*).[33]

Shakya Chokden's objective is clear: to demonstrate that differences between Niḥsvabhāvavāda and Alīkākāravāda pertain to the view determined through reasoning on the conceptual level, but not to the ultimate view directly realized through meditative experience.[34] Consequently, by following different conceptual approaches to ultimate reality, both Niḥsvabhāvavādins and Alīkākāravādins can access the same direct realization of it.

Shakya Chokden also explains that it is not the views realized on the level of meditative equipoise of Mahāyāna āryas, but descriptions of those views on the level of its subsequent attainment that are distinct in the two systems of Niḥsvabhāvavāda and Alīkākāravāda.[35]

He thus claims both difference and compatibility between the views of Niḥsvabhāvavāda and Alīkākāravāda. Both systems are equally valid divisions of Madhyamaka, because both have the capacity to dispel the most subtle obscurations and thereby enable the achievement of buddhahood. In his *Thorough Clarification of Definitive Meaning of the 'Five Dharmas of Maitreya,'* Shakya Chokden explains:

> Both [systems] are also similar in asserting that on the level of severing proliferations by the view within meditative equipoise (*mnyam gzhag tu lta bas spros pa gcod pa*), one does not take to mind any characteristics, and even the wisdom of individual analysis (*so sor rtog pa'i shes rab*) itself only has to be consumed by the fire of primordial mind. Nevertheless, on [the level of] subsequent attainment, when they present tenets in their own systems, [they differ in] accepting non-dual primordial mind or not accepting it. Therefore, due to that lack of difference in their modes of severing proliferations within meditative equipoise, it is not possible to distinguish between ability and non-ability to abandon predispositions (*bag chags*, *vāsana*) of obscurations of knowables by the views of the two systems.[36]

Thus, the views realized in meditative equipoise are differentiated from the views conceptually determined by reasoning prior to meditative equipoise, or described during subsequent attainment following meditative equipoise. This distinction allows Shakya Chokden to bring the two systems together on the level of direct realization of ultimate reality, while keeping them distinct on the level of conceptual approach to it. An interesting outcome of this method is that the more differences between the two systems are highlighted, the more dramatic and convincing their compatibility looks. That in turn allows their differences to be downplayed when contrasted with his position that both Niḥsvabhāvavāda and Alīkākāravāda are equally efficient systems of Madhyamaka. Therefore, the key to Shakya Chokden's interpretation of the two systems lies in understanding precisely how he manipulates different comparisons to demonstrate both difference and compatibility.

There is not a single form of Buddhism that prioritizes a conceptual understanding of reality over its direct, nonconceptual realization. Conceptual understanding, when properly relied upon, can serve as a step toward nonconceptual realization, even though the correspondence between the two is understood differently by different Buddhist thinkers. Conceptually formed views are treated as less powerful than directly realized views mainly because they cannot serve as direct antidotes to obscurations. Furthermore, they must be discarded when final nirvāṇa is achieved, and indeed even prior to that culminating moment. From this perspective, differences between conceptual views outlined by the two systems of Madhyamaka appear to be less important than the identity of their nonconceptual realizations. It is especially clear in Shakya Chokden's own interpretive system, where the view realized through reasoning is not always deemed necessary for gaining access to the view directly experienced in meditation, and where the connection between the two views is not straightforward.[37]

Contrasting conceptual descriptions of reality with the direct realization of reality, Shakya Chokden argues that the latter has to be preferred over the former. He explains that because meditative equipoise is primordial mind separated from corruption of ignorance, it engages its object in agreement with the object's way of being (*yul gyi gnas tshul dang mthun par 'jug*). Conventions of subsequent attainment (*rjes thob kyi tha snyad*),[38] on the other hand, cannot take as their object the meaning of the mode of being (*gnas lugs kyi don*), because they do not go beyond sounds and concepts (*sgra rtog*).[39] This line of argument also augments the importance of the view of meditative equipoise, which is the same in the two systems, but leaves enough space for keeping their subsequent conventions distinct, thereby maintaining the difference between the two systems on the level of conceptual descriptions of emptiness.

To reiterate: according to Shakya Chokden, because the views of Alīkākāravāda and Niḥsvabhāvavāda realized directly during the meditative equipoise of Mahāyāna āryas are the same, the fundamental differences between the two systems lie not in what their practitioners experience in meditative equipoise, but in the different reasonings they use to access the view experienced in meditative equipoise and different conceptual descriptions of that view during subsequent attainment. Other than that, Alīkākāravāda and Niḥsvabhāvavāda views are compatible and equally valid in the sense of being equally efficacious with regard to dispelling all obscurations and achieving buddhahood. This is what makes both of them Madhyamaka systems.

At the same time, it should be noted that the differences between their conceptual approaches to ultimate reality are significant enough for Shakya Chokden to treat Alīkākāravāda and Niḥsvabhāvavāda as distinct systems of Madhyamaka, unlike Prāsaṅgika and Svātantrika. Otherwise, according to his own approach, what would make the Alīkākāravāda/Niḥsvabhāvavāda distinction more legitimate than the Svātantrika/Prāsaṅgika distinction? Therefore, preserving distinctions on the conceptual level is as crucial for him as emphasizing their oneness on the level of direct realization. This is why in his analysis of Niḥsvabhāvavāda and Alīkākāravāda Shakya Chokden tries to strike a balance between their substantial differences and compatibility.[40]

Comparing the two systems in the context of the self-emptiness/other-emptiness distinction, Shakya Chokden explains that Niḥsvabhāvavādins determine reality in terms of the self-emptiness of all phenomena, while Alīkākāravādins do it in terms of other-emptiness.[41] Applying that distinction to the discordant interpretations of the three natures by the two systems, he elaborates on their differences. From the *Rain of Ambrosia*:

> Concerning the modes of severing superimpositions (*sgro 'dogs gcod pa'i tshul*) by the views originating from the texts of the two [types of] Mādhyamikas (*dbu ma smra ba*), there is a very big difference in the extensiveness of the subject-basis [of emptiness]. Niḥsvabhāvavādins, having determined as empty of entity [all] the three natures—the imaginary, dependent, and thoroughly established—do not accept in remainder of that [negation] even the phenomenon (*chos, dharma*) called "emptiness," because they explain that that [emptiness] also is empty of its own entity. [Alīkākāravāda] Yogācāras, [on the other hand,] explain that the imaginary natures are empty of their own entities, the dependent natures are empty of other entities, and what is left in remainder of that [emptiness] as not being empty of one's own entity is that very entity of the dependent natures which is otherwise called the "the thoroughly established nature." Or, in other words, they explain that the subject-basis of emptiness is the dependent natures; the object of negation of which it is empty is the imaginary natures; the

> phenomenon [which is characterized as] that subject [of emptiness] being empty of that object of negation is the thoroughly established nature.[42]

When determining reality on the conceptual level, or, as Shakya Chokden puts it here, severing proliferations by the views deriving from their respective texts,[43] followers of the two systems posit emptiness very differently. Niḥsvabhāvavādins treat it as a total negation of the entities of all phenomena, including emptiness itself. In contrast to that, Alīkākāravādins selectively negate some phenomena (the imaginary natures) on the basis of other phenomena (the dependent natures), and preserve the entity of the non-dual primordial mind, the thoroughly established nature, left in remainder of that negation. Highlighting this sharp distinction between Niḥsvabhāvavāda and Alīkākāravāda views of emptiness on the conceptual level, he demonstrates that they *are* different systems of Madhyamaka.

In spite of that, Shakya Chokden argues that this difference itself does not go beyond conceptually determined views. Even though on the conceptual level the two types of Mādhyamikas sever proliferations differently, i.e., determine emptiness differently, both of them sever the same proliferations and access the same direct realization of the view of reality within the meditative equipoise of Mahāyāna āryas. He continues:

> [Nevertheless,] when both of those [Proponents of] Madhyamaka also accept an object of meditation or incorporation into experience by the meditative equipoise of āryas, their modes of identifying it are in agreement. [Alīkākāravāda] Yogācāras apply conventions of the actual ultimate truth (*don dam pa'i bden pa dngos*), true self (*bdag dam pa*), permanence (*rtag [pa], nitya*), stability (*brtan [pa], dhruva*), peace (*zhi ba, śānta*), eternity (*g.yung drung, śāśvatā*), and true establishment (*bden par grub pa, satyasiddhi*) itself to that very primordial mind of the dharma-sphere (*chos dbyings ye shes, dharmadhatujñāna*), non-dual primordial mind, that bears the name of the "unchangeable thoroughly established nature" (*'gyur ba med pa'i yongs grub*).[44] The others [i.e., Niḥsvabhāvavādins] explain that because on the level of subsequent attainment of the final view[45] the object of negation, true establishment, does not exist, truthlessness does not exist either. Thus, both Mādhyamikas are also in agreement on the mode of the view (*lta tshul*) within meditative equipoise. This is because

> according to the [Alīkākāravāda] Yogācāra system as well, in the face of the view (*lta ba'i ngor*), that dharma-sphere which is observed by that [view] is not apprehended as existent or nonexistent, true or false, or anything else. [Not only that:] as it is not apprehended, [in the face of the view] it is not established as this or that [either].[46]

Shakya Chokden admits that not only the views determined through listening and thinking in the two systems are different, but their descriptions of the ultimate reality are virtually contradictory. Nevertheless, he argues that what the advocates of those systems actually experience in the meditative equipoise of Mahāyāna āryas is the same. In his opinion, the divergence of accepting or rejecting the really existent primordial mind experienced on the level of meditative equipoise does not prevent both of them from acquiring the same direct meditative experience. What they experience is inexpressible. Nonetheless, it is called the "primordial mind" by one of the two systems and not called anything at all by the other. (The only exception from this "rule," as we already know, is Yogācāra Madhyamaka on the Niḥsvabhāvavāda side: its description of the view realized within meditative equipoise agrees with that of Alīkākāravāda.)

Shakya Chokden applies the conceptual/experiential distinction to emptiness itself. In the *Wish Fulfilling Meru*, he describes two types of emptiness that he calls "the pinnacle of all tenets, Madhyamaka which is the meaning expressed [by Madhyamaka teachings]" (*grub mtha' kun gyi rtse mor gyur ba'i brjod bya don gyi dbu ma*): the nonanalytical Madhyamaka experienced through meditation (*rnam par ma brtags pa sgom pas nyams su myong bya'i dbu ma*) and the analytical Madhyamaka accessed by severing superimpositions apprehending signs (*rnam par brtags pa mtshan 'dzin gyi sgro 'dogs gcod pa'i dbu ma*).[47] Each is accompanied by multiple synonyms (*mtshan gyi rnam grangs*). Synonyms of the first one include "vajra of ultimate bodhicitta" (*don dam pa byang chub sems kyi rdo rje*), "element of sugata-essence" (*khams bde bar gshegs pa'i snying po*), "object of functioning of individually self-cognizing primordial mind" (*so so rang rig pa'i ye shes kyi spyod yul*), "object experienced by wisdom produced from meditation" (*sgom pa las byung ba'i shes rab kyis nyams su myong bya*), "primordial mind of the dharma-sphere" (*chos kyi dbyings kyi ye shes*), and "emptiness endowed with the supreme of all aspects" (*rnam pa kun gyi mchog dang ldan pa'i stong pa nyid*). Synonyms of the second type include "emptiness [arrived at] through severing superimpositions by listening and thinking" (*thos bsam gyi sgro 'dogs bcad pa'i stong pa nyid*), "emptiness related to searching for and not finding terminologically imputed meanings" (*tha snyad kyis btags don btsal bas ma rnyed pa'i stong pa nyid*), "emptiness which is beyond objects of mind" (*blo yi yul las 'das pa'i stong nyid*), "emptiness which is a non-affirming negation" (*med par dgag pa'i stong nyid*), "emptiness in which the aggregates are excluded" (*phung po rnam bcad kyi stong pa nyid*).[48]

I should reiterate that Shakya Chokden presents *both* types of emptiness as valid Madhyamaka views, as is clear from the context and the word "pinnacle of all tenets, Madhyamaka." He further links these two types of emptiness with the teachings of the two last dharmacakras and tantric teachings, thereby demonstrating their origins in the words of the Buddha himself:

> The former set of synonyms is taught in the sūtras of the pronouncement of the third dharmacakra and tantras which are the pinnacle of all vehicles. The second set of synonyms is taught primarily in the explicit teachings of the *Perfection of Wisdom* sūtras known as the pronouncement of the middle dharmacakra. It is also taught not [just] once in many [other] sūtras.[49]

Furthermore, Shakya Chokden argues that both types of emptiness are important in particular contexts, and insists on a harmonizing approach to them. He uses the following reasons:

> Both are taught in authentic scriptural sources, and for them to be the basis of limitless positive qualities, the first one is indispensable. Also, if the first type of emptiness is accepted to be relative truth, it will follow that it is a phenomenon polluted by ignorance. On the other hand, if emptiness which is the non-affirming negation is not established by reasons explained in the *Collection of Reasonings*, it will be difficult to abandon conceptual minds apprehending signs. As it is said [by Nāgārjuna in his *Sixty Stanzas of Reasoning*]:
>
> When suchness is not known,
> Thoughts fancying cyclic existence and nirvāṇa arise.
> If suchness is seen,
> There are no thoughts fancying cyclic existence and
> nirvāṇa.
>
> Here, the first Madhyamaka approach removes the extreme of deprecation (*skur 'debs kyi mtha'*) and the second approach

> removes the extreme of superimposition (*sgro 'dogs kyi mtha'*).[50]

We know already that Shakya Chokden does not insist on using both views of Madhyamaka in combination, precisely because they are views of Madhyamaka, and therefore should be sufficient in themselves as valid tools for achieving buddhahood. Nevertheless, he does think that on the level of directly experiencing emptiness within meditative equipoise, the former view is needed (although it does not have to be explicitly articulated), while on the level of severing proliferations through reasoning the latter view is preferable. (Note that this approach is virtually identical to that of Yogācāra Madhyamaka on the Niḥsvabhāvavāda side as he understands it.)

It is crucial to note that Shakya Chokden emphasizes the importance of the two types of the view of emptiness for *different* reasons. The former type is absolutely indispensable and cannot be avoided. As will be demonstrated below, no matter how one describes the direct realization of emptiness, what one actually experiences in the meditative equipoise of Mahāyāna āryas is the same non-dual primordial mind. The second type of view of emptiness (self-emptiness determined by reasonings) is the most powerful tool for getting rid of proliferations in order to gain access to the meditative equipoise directly realizing emptiness. Nevertheless, it is not the *only* valid tool: the view of other-emptiness determined by reasonings is equally valid, albeit less powerful. In my opinion, understanding this distinction is the key to understanding Shakya Chokden's harmonizing approach to Alīkākāravāda and Niḥsvabhāvavāda systems.

Furthermore, as the following passage from the *Rain of Ambrosia* demonstrates, although both conceptually approached and directly experienced types of emptiness are valid views of Madhyamaka, they are not necessarily equally valid on all levels. In this passage too, Shakya Chokden explains that there are two types of emptiness: one is the object of sounds and concepts, while the other is the object of direct yogic experience:

> There are two types of that which bears the name of emptiness: the emptiness imputed by sounds and concepts which is renowned in tenets (*sgra dang rtog pas btags pa'i stong nyid grub mtha' la grags pa*) and the natural emptiness established as the mode of being which is experienced by yogis (*gnas lugs su grub pa'i rang bzhin stong nyid rnal 'byor pas nyams su myong ba*).[51] Precisely because the first one has to be posited as a non-affirming negation, a mental phenomenon

> (*blo chos*), an exclusion of other isolates (*ldog pa gzhan sel*), and a generally characterized [phenomenon] (*spyi mtshan, sāmānyalakṣaṇa*), it is unsuitable as ultimate truth, since it is also unreasonable for it to be an object of experience of yogic direct perception (*rnal 'byor mngon sum gyi myong bya*). The second [type of emptiness] has to be posited as ultimate truth. The reasons are as follows. Because even a buddha's primordial mind sees that very actuality (*don, artha*), it is the actual phenomenon (*don chos*); because it cannot be destroyed by conceptuality, it is vajra; because it is able to perform a function ultimately (*don dam par don byed nus pa*), it is a self-characterized [phenomenon] (*rang mtshan, svalakṣaṇa*); because it is non-deceptive (*mi slu ba, avisaṃvādin*), it is the truth itself (*bden pa nyid*).[52]

This passage clearly illustrates that only the emptiness directly experienced by yogic direct perception is the actual ultimate truth. The emptiness which is cognized conceptually is not. This is because it is a non-affirming negation and a generally characterized phenomenon that according to Shakya Chokden can be objects of conceptual minds only, and cannot serve as objects of yogic direct perception. He succinctly puts it in the *Appearance of the Sun* as well:

> Non-affirming negations do not go beyond [being] exclusively generally characterized [phenomena]. Minds that take them as actual objects are none other than conceptual minds apprehending sounds as meaning (*sgra don 'dzin pa'i rtog pa*). Therefore, [being a non-affirming negation] contradicts [being] an object of functioning of individually self-cognizing primordial mind.[53]

Such an approach gives an additional weight to the view directly realized in the meditative equipoise of Mahāyāna āryas, because that view is none other than emptiness directly experienced by yogic direct perception (*rnal 'byor mngon sum, yogipratyakṣa*).

While such a directly realized view of emptiness is one and the same for both Alīkākāravāda and Niḥsvabhāvavāda, their views of emptiness determined through reasoning vary. The direct realization of the view of emptiness can be accessed either through the reasoning of self-emptiness or other-emptiness. Besides that, this direct realization does not necessarily have to be preceded by conceptual understanding of the view determined by reasoning. Tantric practitioners can access that realization in alternative ways. Shakya Chokden continues:

> There are two methods of realizing that way of being (*gnas tshul*): followers of Pāramitāyāna [realize it] through listening and thinking; followers of the Secret Mantra [realize it] through self-blessings (*rang byin rlabs*), binding bodily functioning (*lus kyi byed bcings*),[54] empowerment stages (*dbang gi rim pa*), and so forth. The first one also is of two types: Yogācāras [realize it] through determining the two, the apprehended and apprehender, as empty of their own entities, and non-dual primordial mind as empty of other [entities]; Niḥsvabhāvavādins [realize it] through determining all knowables as empty of their own entities. Both of those methods are also non-deceptive with regard to the object of engagement (*'jug yul, pravṛttiviṣaya*), ultimate truth. This is because by having determined and engaged in [the ultimate] in that way, [one can] manifest yogic direct perception incorporating into experience that very ultimate.[55]

According to Shakya Chokden, there are two approaches to the actual ultimate truth: sūtric and tantric. Only the former approach requires conceptual analysis for eventually accessing the direct realization of emptiness. In the tantric approach, it is possible to access the direct realization of reality through empowerments, and so forth, without requiring recourse to preliminary conceptual reasoning. Also, even when reasons are used, both self-emptiness reasoning and other-emptiness reasoning are sufficient for getting rid of proliferations in order to access the direct realization of the same ultimate reality.

In Shakya Chokden's system, the Niḥsvabhāvavāda view of self-emptiness entails the view of non-affirming negation, because it entails negation of all phenomena without positing anything in its stead. On the other hand, the Alīkākāravāda view of other-emptiness entails the view of affirming negation (*ma yin dgag, paryudāsa*), because it casts the non-dual primordial mind in remainder of negation of the object of negation. As he puts it in the General Identification of Emptiness (*stong nyid kyi dngos 'dzin spyir bstan pa*) section of the *Great Path of Ambrosia of Emptiness*:

> According to Yogācāras, [emptiness] is interpreted only as a functional thing [qualified by] negation of the objects of

> negation, the two [types of] self. According to Proponents of Self-Emptiness (*rang stong du smra ba*), [emptiness] is the factor of non-affirming negation (*med par dgag pa'i cha*) which is a mere negation of the two [types] of self.[56]

Note that unlike the non-affirming negation, the affirming negation can be a functional thing, according to Shakya Chokden. For example, in the *Ocean of Scriptural Statements and Reasoning*, he explains that the "sugata-essence" (*bde gshegs snying po, sugatagarbha*) is the luminous mind and an affirming negation: "Here, [in the last dharmacakra,] the final definitive meaning is what has the name of the 'sugata-essence,' that very mind luminous by nature. It is also an affirming negation, not a non-affirming negation. . ."[57] In the *Appearance of the Sun*, he also explains that the final definitive meaning presented in Dharmakīrti's *Commentary on Valid Cognition*, as well as in Maitreya's *Differentiation of the Middle and Extremes*, is the "functional thing which is an affirming negation" (*ma yin par dgag pa'i dngos po*).[58]

The distinction between Niḥsvabhāvavāda and Alīkākāravāda in terms of the two types of negation is also reflected in different interpretations of the dharma-sphere by the two systems. In the *Ocean of Scriptural Statements and Reasoning*, Shakya Chokden explains that according to Niḥsvabhāvavāda the dharma-sphere is the space-like non-affirming negation of all extremes of proliferations (*spros pa'i mtha' thams cad bkag pa'i med dgag nam mkha' lta bu*), while according to Alīkākāravāda it is the mind luminous by nature (*sems rang bzhin gyis 'od gsal ba*).[59] (In the same passage, he explains that "mind" (*sems, citta*) in this case is understood as the ultimate mind, i.e., the non-dual primordial mind.[60])

Although Shakya Chokden accepts two types of emptiness, we have just seen that a non-affirming negation in his opinion is an object of concepts only, and therefore cannot be directly experienced in the meditative equipoise of Mahāyāna āryas. An affirming negation can be experienced directly in meditative equipoise, because the self-cognizing primordial mind is both an affirming negation and a functional thing. What it entails in turn is that Niḥsvabhāvavāda does not teach the actual ultimate reality that can be directly experienced in the meditative equipoise of Mahāyāna āryas *unless* it identifies it in agreement with Alīkākāravāda. (We know already that Yogācāra Mādhyamikas on both Alīkākāravāda and Niḥsvabhāvavāda sides agree in their identification of the emptiness directly experienced in meditative equipoise as the non-dual primordial mind.)

In a word, Shakya Chokden argues that in both Alīkākāravāda and Niḥsvabhāvavāda systems, the genuine view of reality cannot be a subject of a non-affirming negation. Were it so, it would follow that it is a conceptual mind (*rtog pa*).[61] When determining emptiness by reasoning, Alīkākāravādins treat it as an affirming negation, primordial mind. Because primordial mind can be an object of direct experience, Alīkākāravādins have no problem with describing the emptiness directly realized in meditative equipoise also as a primordial mind and an affirming negation. Niḥsvabhāvavādins, on the other hand, posit the emptiness determined by reasoning as a non-affirming negation. Nevertheless, because this negation is the object of conceptual minds only, neither can it be directly realized in meditative equipoise nor can the emptiness directly realized in meditative equipoise be described as a non-affirming negation. Therefore, during subsequent attainment, Niḥsvabhāvavādins on the Prāsaṅgika and Sautrāntika Madhyamaka side cannot provide any descriptions of what has been directly realized within meditative equipoise, and simply use the convention of "realization of emptiness" without accepting that anything has been realized within meditative equipoise. Niḥsvabhāvavādins on the Yogācāra Madhyamaka side, on the other hand, ally themselves with Alīkākāravādins on the level of descriptions given in subsequent attainment.

The above distinction contributes to further contrasts between Niḥsvabhāvavāda and Alīkākāravāda without undermining their unity on the level of direct realization. As has been mentioned already, Shakya Chokden believes that although their descriptions of ultimate reality are different, their actual realizations of that reality are the same.

The differences and similarities between Alīkākāravāda and Niḥsvabhāvavāda on the three levels addressed above can be depicted as shown in Table 2.

Because the distinction between the conceptual description of emptiness and its direct realization plays such a crucial role in Shakya Chokden's system, the question of correspondence between the two is also highly important to him. Contrary to what one might expect based on the above discussion, in the *Rain of Ambrosia* he explains that in the Niḥsvabhāvavāda system, the meditative equipoise and subsequent attainment modes of positing the final view are concordant, while in the system of Alīkākāravāda, conventions of meditative equipoise and subsequent attainment are discordant.[62] It is Niḥsvabhāvavāda, not Alīkākāravāda, that approaches in the same manner the meditative equipoise and subsequent attainment modes of

Table 2

The View	Alīkākāravāda	Niḥsvabhāvavāda: Prāsaṅgika and Sautrāntika Madhyamaka	Niḥsvabhāvavāda: Yogācāra Madhyamaka
Determined by reasoning	Other-emptiness, affirming negation, primordial mind	Self-emptiness, non-affirming negation	Self-emptiness, non-affirming negation
Experienced in meditative equipoise	Non-dual primordial mind	Non-dual primordial mind (experienced but not subsequently described)	Non-dual primordial mind
Described in subsequent attainment	Non-dual primordial mind	No actual description; not realizing anything is merely given the name of "realizing emptiness"	Non-dual primordial mind

positing the final view. This is because in the Alīkākāravāda system, ultimate reality is presented *as if* it could be described by sounds and concepts, since it is described as the non-dual primordial mind. In the Niḥsvabhāvavāda system, ultimate reality is not presented as anything at all (the emptiness posited through reasoning is not ultimate reality according to Niḥsvabhāvavāda). In meditative equipoise no concepts function, and it is impossible to apprehend reality as this or that. Because Niḥsvabhāvavāda does not attempt such a description while Alīkākāravāda does, their approaches on the two levels are, respectively, concordant and discordant.

Note that neither the fact that Alīkākāravāda describes ultimate reality as primordial mind nor that Niḥsvabhāvavāda describes it as indescribable makes ultimate reality the object of sounds and concepts in either system. As Shakya Chokden explains in the *Rain of Ambrosia*:

> In brief, in the systems of both types of Madhyamaka also, their own treatises clarify that the ultimate is necessarily ineffable, inconceivable, and inexpressible. Because it is clarified in that way, [it can be said that] although something recognized as ultimate truth (*don dam pa'i bden pa yin ngo shes pa zhig*) is experienced by the self-cognizing primordial mind of āryas (*'phags pa rnams kyi rang rig pa'i ye shes*), it is impossible to identify that something as "this" or "that" by expressive sounds and concepts (*rjod byed kyi sgra dang rtog pa*) [in either system].[63]

However, this approach does not run contrary to the fact that it is indeed Alīkākāravāda, not Niḥsvabhāvavāda, which is more consistent in terms of describing the final view as primordial mind and experiencing it as primordial mind in meditative equipoise. He continues:

> Nevertheless, [ultimate truth] cannot be realized without relying on conventions. Therefore, if at the time of [applying] conventions one identifies an illustration of that truth which does not contradict scriptural statements and reasoning, it has to be identified as that very primordial mind free from the duality of the apprehended and apprehender. The Prāsaṅgika and Svātantrika Mādhyamikas' own texts do not identify an illustration of that genuine ultimate truth. [On the other hand,] the *Dharmas of Maitreya* with [the treatises of their] followers [do provide such an illustration, as can be

> seen] from scriptural statements that clearly explain a recognized (*yin ngo shes pa*) illustration of that [ultimate truth] as that very primordial mind; and reasoning [that proceeds as follows]: without being comprehended by valid cognition, no [phenomenon] is suitable as ultimate truth. Furthermore, [there are two types of] valid cognition: [direct perception (*mngon sum, pratyakṣa*) and inference (*rjes dpag, anumāna*)]. That which is comprehended by inference is explained as a generally characterized [phenomenon]. Therefore, it is unsuitable as an ultimate truth. The object of comprehension (*gzhal bya, prameya*) by direct perception is necessarily a self-characterized [phenomenon]. Thus, [ultimate truth] is only [the non-dual primordial mind described] above.[64]

I would argue, therefore, that according to Shakya Chokden, Niḥsvabhāvavādins are more faithful to *how* reality is realized within meditative equipoise. This is why they do not posit any actual view of reality on the level of subsequent attainment. Alīkākāravādins, on the other hand, are more faithful to *what* experiences that reality and what that reality is. This is why on the level of subsequent attainment they posit primordial mind as the actual view. Approached in this way, the differences between the two systems only contribute to their compatibility: on the one hand, adherents of both systems agree that ultimate reality is beyond sounds and concepts. On the other hand, both of them directly realize the same primordial mind.

In summary, although according to Shakya Chokden both the reasoning of self-emptiness that posits emptiness as a non-affirming negation and the reasoning of other-emptiness that posits it as an affirming negation are efficient means of accessing the direct realization of the ultimate view, nevertheless, because the object of meditative experience is by definition primordial mind, the ultimate view realized by followers of both systems is that of other-emptiness and affirming negation. This is why, when Niḥsvabhāvavādins stick to the non-affirming negation of the self-emptiness approach only, they do not provide any descriptions of the real ultimate view at all. Alīkākāravādins do, and their identification of the view as the non-dual primordial mind, as well as descriptions that agree with such identification (given by Yogācāra Mādhyamikas on the Niḥsvabhāvavāda side) are the only valid descriptions when descriptions are given at all. Yet, descriptions pertain to the conceptual level only; both systems accept that the ultimate view transcends sounds and concepts. Thus, no matter which of the two systems one chooses, or whether one mixes them (as Yogācāra Mādhyamikas on the Niḥsvabhāvavāda side do), it is possible to negate all proliferations, access the direct realization of ultimate reality, and eventually, through its cultivation combined with virtuous deeds, achieve buddhahood.

3. A New Look at the Old Origins: Distinctions of Madhyamaka Stemming from Interpretations of the Second and Third Dharmacakras

Looking at the Second and Third Dharmacakras through the Eyes of the Madhyamaka Founders

In his analysis of distinctive features of the two Madhyamaka systems, Shakya Chokden turns to the founders of Yogācāra and Niḥsvabhāvavāda, connecting their views on conceptually determined and directly experienced reality with their different explanations of the second and third dharmacakras. He then shows how the views of those founders were explained differently by later generations of Yogācāras and Niḥsvabhāvavādins.

In the *Rain of Ambrosia*, he identifies Nāgārjuna and Asaṅga as the two masters who upheld Madhyamaka ways initially opened by Mañjuśrī and Maitreya, emphasizing that both Nāgārjuna and Asaṅga were prophesied by the Buddha himself as non-mistaken in their explanations of the definitive meaning, ultimate truth.[65] Thereby, Shakya Chokden shows that it is not only later thinkers, but the Buddha himself who prophetically saw the views expressed by the two systems as definitive, and therefore prophesied that both Nāgārjuna and Asaṅga would accurately identify the ultimate view.

Describing the views of Niḥsvabhāvavāda and Alīkākāravāda, respectively, Shakya Chokden focuses on the writings of Nāgārjuna and the team of Maitreya and Asaṅga.[66] He demonstrates differences in their approaches to the teachings of the second and third dharmacakras, but also explains that both Nāgārjuna and Maitreya (with Asaṅga) identified the final definitive meaning in the same way: as the non-dual primordial mind. It is that ultimate reality which is directly experienced through meditation and explicitly taught in the definitive teachings of the third dharmacakra:

> Both the former and latter system founders, when identifying that utimate truth which is the definitive meaning of the last pronouncement (*bka' tha ma'i nges don*), agree in

> explaining it as that very indestructible mind-vajra (*gzhom du med pa sems kyi rdo rje*)[67] which is the object of experience of primordial mind of the meditative equipoise of Mahāyāna āryas.[68]

The Alīkākāravāda and Niḥsvabhāvavāda founders also do not differ in their identifications of the explicit teachings (*dngos bstan*) of the second dharmacakra: emptiness described as the negation of reality of all phenomena, emptiness temporarily posited through reasoning, or a conceptually understood emptiness. Such emptiness is not the object of direct experience in meditation for the reasons cited above.

Where the two systems differ is in their identifications of the main topic (*bstan bya'i gtso bo*) of the second dharmacakra. According to Nāgārjuna, it is the same as the explicit teachings of the second dharmacakra. Although Nāgārjuna temporarily posited such emptiness as ultimate truth, he finally explained it only as a metaphorical ultimate, and therefore a relative truth. This is why Shakya Chokden argues that in Nāgārjuna's view, no ultimate reality can be identified at all on the level of the second dharmacakra. Consequently, when in that context Nāgārjuna addresses the view realized in meditative experience, he simply applies the term "meditation" to not meditating on anything at all:

> As for the emptiness explicitly taught by the middle dharmacakra, it is finally explained by the first system [i.e., that of Nāgārjuna] only as a relative truth. Therefore, no need to mention explanations as ultimate truth and the object of experience of meditative equipoise: when that system explains the meditation explicitly taught by the middle dharmacakra, the mind-vajra is not explained as the object of meditation itself, and the lack of anything to meditate upon is imputed as meditation (*sgom rgyu ci yang med pa la sgom du btags pa*).[69]

Asaṅga agrees that that emptiness explicitly taught in the second dharmacakra is not a real ultimate truth. Nevertheless, according to Asaṅga, such emptiness is not the main topic of the second dharmacakra. Its main topic (albeit not taught explicitly) is the same as the one which is taught in the definitive teachings of the third dharmacakra: the non-dual primordial mind:

> The second system founder [Asaṅga] in his turn [explained that] the emptiness which is the main topic of the middle

> dharmacakra is that very primordial mind which is determined by the last dharmacakra. On the other hand, that factor of non-affirming negation (*med dgag gi cha*) [described as] the dependent natures being empty of the imaginary natures, which is present in the explicit teachings of the middle [dharmacakra], is not asserted [by Asaṅga] even as a mere ultimate truth (*don dam pa'i bden pa tsam*),[70] and even less so as an object of [meditative] experience. This is because it is a generally characterized [phenomenon] (*spyi mtshan, sāmānyalakṣaṇa*) and is conceptually superimposed through listening and thinking (*thos bsam gyi rtog pas sgro btags pa*). Therefore, when identifying a [real] ultimate truth, the two systems are in agreement.[71]

We are already familiar with the reasoning used by Shakya Chokden to demonstrate why the emptiness taught in the explicit teachings of the second dharmacakra cannot be ultimate reality directly realized in meditative experience. Because the emptiness explicitly taught by the second dharmacakra is a non-affirming negation, it has to be a generally characterized phenomenon; because it is a generally characterized phenomenon, it is an object of concepts only; because it is an object of conceptual minds only, it cannot be directly experienced in meditative equipoise. According to Shakya Chokden, both systems of Madhyamaka agree on this, and this is why neither identifies the actual ultimate reality as a non-affirming negation.

As the above passage demonstrates, Nāgārjuna and Asaṅga differ in their identifications of the non-affirming negation taught in the explicit teachings of the second dharmacakra: Nāgārjuna identifies it as all phenomena being empty of themselves, while Asaṅga identifies it as the dependent natures being empty of the imaginary natures. While Nāgārjuna temporarily accepts his version of the non-affirming negation as an ultimate truth, and then treats it as a relative truth,[72] Asaṅga from the beginning does not posit his version as an ultimate truth at all.[73] Although in the Alīkākāravāda system upheld by Asaṅga, primordial mind qualified by negation of the imaginary natures on the basis of the dependent natures *is* the actual ultimate truth,[74] the mere factor of negation of the imaginary natures on the basis of the dependent natures is not. It implies that according to Shakya Chokden, this type of non-affirming negation is neither self-emptiness nor other-emptiness, because neither Alīkākāravāda nor Niḥsvabhāvavāda accept it as valid.[75]

This distinction does not affect the primary difference between Nāgārjuna's and Asaṅga's approaches. It lies not in their explanation of the definitive meaning of the third dharmacakra, and not in their understanding of the non-affirming negations taught by the explicit teachings of the second dharmacakra as exclusively conceptual objects. Rather, the difference is in their understanding of the main topic of the second dharmacakra and whether the emptiness explicitly taught by the second dharmacakra can be accepted at least temporarily as the ultimate view. In their explanations, the two thinkers eventually come down to the same point: they do not accept that a non-affirming negation can be an ultimate truth, and they identify the real ultimate truth only as non-dual primordial mind.

As has been mentioned, the differences between Alīkākāravāda and Niḥsvabhāvavāda are as important for presenting them as distinct Madhyamaka systems as their similarities that allow Shakya Chokden to claim their compatibility. Below I discuss further details of the views of the Madhyamaka founders in relation to the last two dharmacakras that make the two systems distinct yet compatible.

Position of Alīkākāravāda

The Alīkākāravāda system stemming from the writings of Maitreya and Asaṅga posits the individually self-cognizing primordial mind as both the emptiness determined by reasoning related to listening and thinking, and the emptiness realized in meditative experience. Thus, the crux of the Alīkākāravāda system is primordial mind, the thoroughly established nature. If not realized, primordial mind serves as the cause of cyclic existence; if realized, it becomes the path to nirvāṇa and sparks enlightenment.[76] According to Alīkākāravāda, this primordial mind is the main topic not only of the third dharmacakra, but of the second dharmacakra as well:[77]

> [Alīkākāravāda] Yogācāras explain that the definitive meaning of the explicit teachings of the last pronouncement (*bka' tha ma'i dngos bstan gyi nges don*) is that very primordial mind [characterized by] the dependent natures being empty of the imaginary natures. They also explain that this [primordial mind] itself is taught by the truly perfect Buddha himself as the main topic of the middle pronouncement (*bka' bar pa'i bstan bya'i gtso bo*).[78]

The overall approach of Alīkākāravādins in this light looks very coherent. Unlike Niḥsvabhāvavādins, they treat the main topics of both dharmacakras as the same. This makes explanation of their tenets relatively simple: whether we deal with their presentatation of the main topic of the second or the third dharmacakra, it is the same non-dual primordial mind. According to this system, in the conventions of subsequent attainment of the two last dharmacakras, it is accepted that only reality exists, and that possessors of reality, i.e., the apprehended- and apprehender-phenomena that have that reality as their substratum, do not exist.[79] Thus, what is experienced in meditative equipoise and described in subsequent attainment is the same according to Alīkākāravāda: the non-dual primordial mind. It is the main topic of both dharmacakras, although in the third dharmacakra it is described explicitly, and in the second dharmacakra implicitly. In contrast to Niḥsvabhāvavāda, the Alīkākāravāda system accepts this primordial mind as truly existent, and leaves it as it is (*rang sor 'jog*) without analyzing it by reasoning. (According to Niḥsvabhāvavādins, such would entail falling into the extreme of eternalism;[80] Shakya Chokden argues that Niḥsvabhāvavādins analyze and negate all phenomena, including primordial mind.) From the *Profound Thunder*:

> Honorable Asaṅga explaned as the definitive meaning of
> the [last] two dharmacakras
> The non-dual primordial mind free from all
> proliferations,
> The self-illuminating self-cognition (*rang rig rang gsal ba*),
> The final ultimate [truth], the "buddha-essence."[81]

In his auto-commentary, the *Rain of Ambrosia*, Shakya Chokden adds further details, explaining that in general, in the system initiated by Maitreya and Asaṅga, the definitive meaning and the final ultimate truth are described as the luminous nature of mind free from all proliferations (*spros pa thams cad dang bral ba sems kyi rang bzhin 'od gsal ba*), that persists throughout all levels of the basis, path, and result, transcending sounds and concepts. It is the main topic of the middle dharmacakra, but it was taught there in a nonliteral way (*sgra ji bzhin pa ma yin pa'i sgo nas bstan*). In contrast to that, in the last dharmacakra it was taught literally (*sgra ji bzhin pa nyid du bstan*), and it is the main topic of that dharmacakra as well.[82]

According to Shakya Chokden, Alīkākāravādins do not treat all sūtras of the third dharmacakra as teachings of definitive meaning. Besides the "mainstream" Yogācāra sūtras, such as the *Sūtra Unraveling the Intent*,[83] the final dharmacakra also includes numerous sūtras on the buddha-essence, such as the *Sūtra of the Ornament of Appearances of Primordial Mind*[84] and the *Great Nirvāṇa Sūtra*.[85] Shakya Chokden splits the sūtras of the third dharmacakra into two groups: sūtras explaining that the buddha-essence—inseparable from all positive qualities of a buddha—exists even on the level of sentient beings and sūtras teaching that such an explanation has only an interpretive meaning. Correspondingly, there are two types of Indian and Tibetan treatises. According to him, it is obvious that the *Great Nirvāṇa Sūtra* and the *Sublime Continuum* treatise themselves explained the first type of teachings as nonliteral.[86]

In the *Essence of Sūtras and Tantras: Explanation of the Buddha-Essence*,[87] Shakya Chokden explains that in general, Pāramitāyāna teaches two types of essence, as described in the second and third dharmacakras. The first type is the non-affirming negation of all extremes of proliferations (*spros pa'i mtha'*, *prapañcānta*). It pervades all beings: ordinary sentient beings, ārya bodhisattvas (*byang sems 'phags pa*), and buddhas. This type of essence is not a real buddha-essence, only an imputed one. Therefore, the second dharmacakra, as well as those commentaries that agree with it (such as Candrakīrti's non-tantric writings on Madhyamaka), do not teach the real buddha-essence.

The presentation of the third dharmacakra's teachings on the buddha-essence is divided into those of sūtras and those of their treatises. Sūtras are of two types: some explain that the buddha-essence endowed with all positive qualities of a buddha is present in all sentient beings. Other sūtras take this explanation as having a veiled intent (*dgongs pa can*), as nonliteral. They interpret it by demonstrating three elements of interpretive teachings: the basis of intent (*dgongs gzhi*), the purpose (*dgos pa*), and the damage to the explicit [teaching] (*dngos la gnod byed*). Following *the latter* type of sūtras, Shakya Chokden argues that the basis of intent of the third dharmacakra's teachings on the buddha-essence is the natural luminosity (*rang bzhin 'od gsal*, *prakṛtiprabhāsvara*) free from all extremes of proliferations, the object of experience of individually self-cognizing primordial mind, an affirming negation. According to him, this is precisely how the *Sublime Continuum* interprets the first type of sūtras. By demonstrating the three elements of interpretive teachings, it explains that the teaching of the buddha-essence pervading all sentient beings is to be interpreted and has a veiled intent. In the *Golden Lancet*, he further argues that the *Sublime Continuum*'s explanation of the basis of intent in teaching the buddha-essence by such sūtras was misunderstood by Tibetan thinkers as an explanation of the actual buddha-essence.[88] In the *Essence of Sūtras and Tantras*, he also makes clear that those buddha-essence teachings of the third dharmacakra and their commentaries, such as Nāgārjuna's *Praise to the Dharma-Sphere*, which Shakya Chokden himself approves of, agree with the *Sublime Continuum*. He treats the *Sublime Continuum* itself together with Asaṅga's commentary as teachings of the definitive meaning.

According to the *Sublime Continuum*, as Shakya Chokden understands it, nobody below the first bodhisattva ground (*byang chub sems pa'i sa, bodhisattavabhūmi*) has the buddha-essence—neither a complete nor a partial one. In his explanation of the *Sublime Continuum*, Shakya Chokden utilizes the categories of the three levels found in that text: the impure (*ma dag, aśuddha*), impure-pure (*ma dag dag pa, aśuddhaśuddha*, i.e., partially pure) and very pure (*shin tu rnam dag, suviśuddha*) levels that correspond respectively to the categories of sentient beings, bodhisattvas (understood as ārya bodhisattvas in this context), and tathāgatas. He argues that one becomes a possessor of the buddha-essence free from adventitious stains only on the impure-pure level. In other words, when bodhisattvas enter the Mahāyāna path of seeing (*mthong lam, darśanamārga*), simultaneously with the attainment of the first bodhisattva ground of utmost joy (*rab tu dga' ba, pramuditā*), they become ārya bodhisattvas, directly realize ultimate truth (*don dam bden pa, paramārthasatya*), and thereby for the first time generate an antidote to obscurations of knowables. They start gradually removing them, and thereby actually see at least a partial purification of stains "covering" the buddha-essence, and its inseparability from at least some positive qualities. Such is not possible for anyone below that level, including non-Mahāyāna arhats (i.e., śrāvakas and pratyekabuddhas). Therefore, only Mahāyāna āryas have the buddha-essence characterized by the purity from adventitious stains; ārya bodhisattvas have only a part of it, while buddhas have it completely.[89]

Thus, Alīkākāravādins do not accept *all* teachings of the last dharmacakra as literal, and in this respect, they are similar to Niḥsvabhāvavādins who also treat as nonliteral the teachings which assert that the buddha-essence ornamented with the positive qualities of a buddha is present in all sentient beings. The two types of Mādhyamikas differ, however, in what they think the real buddha-essence is: Alīkākāravādins treat it as a non-dual primordial mind and an affirming negation, while Niḥsvabhāvavādins, not surprisingly, provisionally treat it as a non-affirming negation, but ultimately treat it as being beyond definitions. As Shakya Chokden puts it in the *Rain of Ambrosia*, in their identification of the essence, Bhāviveka and Candrakīrti temporarily explained the buddha-essence as the factor of non-affirming negation, and finally treated it as unidentifiable. He argues that this approach agrees with Nāgārjuna's words in the *Wisdom: Root Stanzas on Madhyamaka*:

That which is the nature of tathāgata
Is the nature of these migrators.
The nature of tathāgata does not exist.[90]

It should also be noted that according to Shakya Chokden, having primordial mind is not equivalent to having the buddha-essence: although everyone, including ordinary beings, has primordial mind, only those who manifest it—that is to say, directly realize ultimate reality, these being Mahāyāna āryas—have the buddha-essence.

Shakya Chokden describes the Alīkākāravāda approach to the view (*lta ba, dṛṣṭi*), meditation (*sgom pa, bhāvanā*), action (*spyod pa, caryā*), and result (*'bras bu, phala*) stemming from the subsequent *Dharmas of Maitreya* (*byams chos phyi ma*)[91] in a verse from the *Profound Thunder*, and unpacks its meaning in the *Rain of Ambrosia*:

The [following verse of the root text] explains that

- having severed superimpositions by the reasoning of other-emptiness, *the view*,
- [in] *meditation* one sets in equipoise on the individually self-cognizing primordial mind,
- and by uniting [that realization] with the collection of merits, *the action*,
- spontaneously accomplishes *the result*, the entity-body (*ngo bo nyid kyi sku, svābhāvikakāya*) with all positive qualities complete, and the two form-bodies (*gzugs kyi sku, rūpakāya*)[92] in the appearances of others (*gzhan snang*):

Having realized that the mere cognition of clarity-emptiness
Free from the apprehended and apprehender is the mode of being of all phenomena,
By the union [of that realization] with the boundless collection of merits
One spontaneously accomplishes the three bodies [—this is taught in] Asaṅga's texts.[93]

In the system of Maitreya and Asaṅga, on the level of determining the view by reasoning, primordial mind is posited through the reasoning of other-emptiness that we are already familiar with: the negation of the imaginary natures on the basis of the dependent natures that leaves primordial mind in its remainder. Thus, the connection between the view posited through reasoning and experienced in meditation in this system is straightforward: determine primordial mind through reasoning, then directly experience it within meditative equipoise.[94]

Note the remarkable unanimity of the Alīkākāravāda "camp": Maitreya and Asaṅga come down to the same ultimate view of the non-dual primordial mind in their different texts; all "fully matured" Yogācāras (the ones who have crossed the ocean of Yogācāras' scriptures) following them also agree on the Alīkākāravāda view as the highest.

Position of Niḥsvabhāvavāda

In comparison to Alīkākāravāda, Niḥsvabhāvavāda views on reality are much more difficult to explain for at least two reasons: Nāgārjuna himself approached ultimate reality differently in different types of texts, and Niḥsvabhāvavādins who followed him also explained ultimate reality differently—with or without an admixture of Yogācāra teachings.

Nāgārjuna identifies the ultimate view differently in his *Collection of Reasonings* and *Collection of Praises*. Linking the view of reality described in the *Collection of Reasonings* with the conceptual approach to emptiness, and the view of reality described in the *Collection of Praises* with the direct realization of emptiness, Shakya Chokden writes:

> In the *Collection of Reasonings*, [explanations are given] in terms of severing superimpositions through listening and thinking, while in the *Collection of Praises*, [they are given] in terms of incorporation into experience through meditation.[95]

These differences in Nāgārjuna's two *Collections* occur because in the *Collection of Reasonings* he explains the second dharmacakra teachings literally, while in the *Collection of Praises* he explains the definitive meaning of the last dharmacakra. Shakya Chokden writes in the *Profound Thunder*:

> The two types of explanatory modes [taught] by that
> best Ārya [Nāgārjuna]
> Are distinguished by way of the literal explanation
> Of the sūtras of the second dharmacakra by the *Collection of Reasonings* [on the one hand],
> And the mode of explaining the definitive meaning of the last dharmacakra in the *Collection of Praises* [on the other hand].[96]

Correspondingly, there are two referents of such terms as "reality," etc., that are discussed by Nāgārjuna separately in the two *Collections*: a non-affirming negation and the non-dual primordial mind. The former is taught in the explicit teachings of the second dharmacakra, and is commented upon in Nāgārjuna's *Collection of Reasonings*. The latter is taught in the third dharmacakra and is commented upon in Nāgārjuna's *Collection of Praises* and other texts. In the *Rain of Ambrosia*, Shakya Chokden comments on the above passage, echoing the explanation dealt with in the previous section:

> There are two bearers of the names "emptiness" (*stong pa nyid, śūnyatā*), "suchness" (*de bzhin nyid, tathatā*), and "reality" (*chos nyid, dharmatā*) that derive from the texts of honorable Nāgārjuna: a non-affirming negation [in which] all collections of proliferations have been negated by reasoning, and primordial mind not apprehending any extremes of proliferations that persists (*rgyun chags pa*) throughout all levels of the basis, path, and result. The first one is [taught in] the explicit teachings of the middle dharmacakra. Limitless reasonings proving it are the explicit teachings of the *Collection of Reasonings*. The second one in its turn is of two types: [primordial mind that has been] preceded by the reasoning negating [all] signs of proliferations and is not grasping [at them], and [primordial mind that] has become free from proliferations by the power of empowerments, blessings, and so forth. These [last] two [types] are explained as the definitive meanings of respectively those parts of the last dharmacakra [which are taught] in terms of Pāramitāyāna and in terms of the Mantra system (*sngags lugs*).[97]

Note the "perfect match" of Nāgārjuna's *Collection of Praises* with the definitive teachings of the third dharmacakra. We already know that the emptiness taught in the explicit teachings of the second dharmacakra is not the real ultimate, while the one taught in the definitive teachings of the third dharmacakra is. As Shakya Chokden explains in the above passage, the latter type of emptiness can be accessed in either a sūtric or a tantric manner: through reasoning or through empowerments, and so forth. As a result of this explanation, the emptiness described as a non-affirming negation is distanced not only from the sūtric but from the tantric teachings as well. On the other hand, the view of emptiness taught in Nāgārjuna's *Collection of Praises* is presented as being in agreement with the definitive meaning of the third dharmacakra, the Alīkākāravāda Yogācāra view, and tantric teachings as well. It is that very non-dual primordial mind described as an affirming negation.[98]

In contrast to the *Collection of Praises*, the view described in Nāgārjuna's *Collection of Reasonings* is very different from Alīkākāravāda. Shakya Chokden argues that according to the approach of the *Collection of Reasonings*, the main topic of the second dharmacakra is "just a non-affirming negation [understood as] all knowable phenomena being empty of their own entities."[99] The *Collection of Reasonings* addresses this view in two ways: in the context of realization within meditative equipoise, and in the context of accepting conventions during subsequent attainment.[100] The first one is described in the *Rain of Ambrosia* as follows:

> Unlike [in the system of] Yogācāra, [in the *Collection of Reasonings*,] a phenomenon called "emptiness" which is an object of experience of yogic direct perception is not accepted even conventionally. The reason is that since non-affirming negations do not pass beyond [being] eliminations of other isolates (*ldog pa gzhan sel*), they are not suitable as objects of even a mere nonconceptual knowing (*rtog med kyi shes pa*), no use to consider them [being objects of] direct perception. This is why [according to this system] the wisdom of meditative equipoise on the meaning of emptiness determined by listening and thinking [preceding it] does not apprehend any signs of being empty, not empty, and so forth.[101]

Once again we learn that the emptiness described as a non-affirming negation is an object exclusively of conceptual minds. According to the *Collection of Reasonings*, the emptiness determined through listening and thinking is a non-affirming negation. This emptiness, therefore, cannot be cognized by yogic direct perception. Since there is no other emptiness determined by listening and thinking in the *Collection of Reasonings*, nothing can be posited even conventionally as an object realized in meditative equipoise either.

Note that Shakya Chokden does not argue that because meditative equipoise is nonconceptual, its object cannot be fully described conceptually. Rather, he argues that the only view posited through listening and thinking in the *Collection of Reasonings* is a non-affirming negation that is by definition an object of concepts only. This is why it cannot be realized in meditative equipoise that by definition is nonconceptual.

On the level of subsequent attainment, one applies conventions to and describes the view of meditative equipoise that has been realized. From the *Rain of Ambrosia*:

> The convention of "seeing the ultimate" is applied to not seeing any signs of an object (*yul gyi mtshan ma*) within meditative equipoise; because according to the [*Collection of Reasonings*'] own final system (*rang gi lugs mthar thug*) even an illustration (*mtshan gzhi*) of "ultimate truth" is not accepted, how can its direct realization exist? It is attested [by the statements that] emptiness, natural nirvāṇa, dharma-sphere and so forth—everything that is suitable to be an object of sounds and concepts is exclusively a relative truth, because of not withstanding the legions of analysis and because of not passing beyond objects of sounds and concepts.[102]

In other words, in the context of the *Collection of Reasonings* Nāgārjuna teaches that realization in meditative equipoise is indescribable, and merely applies the convention of "seeing the ultimate" to not seeing anything at all. This is because according to the *Collection of Reasonings*, no objects of sounds and concepts can be posited as ultimate truth even in subsequent attainment. Therefore, the non-affirming negation view of emptiness determined through listening and thinking also is a relative truth, not the genuine ultimate truth. This is why even during subsequent attainment it is not described as the object realized in meditative equipoise.

Having denied the status of the real ultimate to the metaphorical ultimate, in his *Collection of Reasonings* Nāgārjuna does not grant this status to any other phenomena either, including primordial mind:

> That which is explained as ultimate truth at the time of provisionally presenting the two truths, is also explained as merely a metaphorical [ultimate] and concordant ultimate (*mthun pa['i] don dam*). The "non-metaphorical ultimate" (*rnam grangs ma yin pa'i don dam, aparyāyaparamārtha*) is not explained in the *Collection of Reasonings* with commentaries. Finally, even primordial mind realizing that [ultimate] is not accepted.[103]

How is the view taught in the *Collection of Reasonings* connected with other aspects of Buddhist practice? From the *Rain of Ambrosia*:

The [following verse of the root text of the *Profound Thunder*] explains that

- having severed superimpositions by the reasoning of self-emptiness, *the view*,
- [in] *meditation* one sets in equipoise within the state of non-observation of an object (*yul dmigs med*) and non-apprehension by a subject (*yul can 'dzin med*),
- [during] subsequent attainment one exerts oneself in [*action*, accumulation of] the collection of merits of generosity, and so forth through the stages of the ten grounds,
- and thereby spontaneously accomplishes the *result*, the dharma-body (*chos kyi sku, dharmakāya*) free from all proliferations and the form-body in the appearances of others:

> Without relenting in the extensive collection of merits,
> Through the reasoning of all phenomena being
> empty of [their own] entities
> By setting in equipoise within the state free from
> apprehension,
> One spontaneously accomplishes the three bodies
> [—this is taught in] Nāgārjuna's texts.[104]

Importantly, as this passage demonstrates, Shakya Chokden does not conclude that the view explained in the *Collection of Reasonings* is insufficient. As we know already, whichever of the two types of reasonings is used in determining the ultimate and whichever of the two descriptions is provided during subsequent attainment, ultimate reality realized within the meditative equipoise of Mahāyāna āryas is the same. Therefore, even if the authentic reality is not described in the *Collection of Reasonings*, it is not a problem, because the objective is to access the direct realization of that reality which is beyond descriptions anyway. According to Shakya Chokden, both the explicit teachings of the second dharmacakra and their explanation by the *Collection of Reasonings* are sufficient for this task. If the radical negation of all phenomena by reasoning can eventually bring one to the direct realization of reality, then why should it be worse than the assertion of the non-dual primordial mind qualified by negation of other phenomena?

The explanatory approach of the *Collection of Praises* is very different from the *Collection of Reasonings*. Similar to Alīkākāravādins, in the *Collection of Praises* Nāgārjuna makes a distinction between possessors of reality, relative phenomena, and their ultimate reality, the ultimate primordial mind (*don dam pa'i ye shes*).[105] Furthermore,

> That very [ultimate primordial mind] conventionally has to be accepted as a genuine (*mtshan nyid pa*) ultimate truth, because it is an object of experience of yogic direct perception of foremost āryas, and [also] because it has to be explained exactly as the dharma-sphere, the element of sugata-essence, and the mind-vajra (*sems kyi rdo rje*).[106]

This view is connected with other elements of the Buddhist practice in the way described below:

> The [following verse of the root text] explains that
>
> - after the complete severing of superimpositions by the reasoning of self-emptiness, *the view*,
> - [in] *meditation*, with primordial mind realizing freedom from proliferations, one takes the ultimate mind of enlightenment (*don dam byang chub kyi sems, paramārthabodhicitta*) as the basis of purification of stains (*dri ma sbyang ba'i gzhi*),
> - and by incorporating into experience method and wisdom in union, [*the action*,]
> - one spontaneously accomplishes *the result*, the three bodies
>
> —[this] also is the second [approach] intended by father Nāgārjuna [with his spiritual] son [Āryadeva]:
>
>> Explaining the sphere of mind (*sems kyi dbyings*) as the ultimate mind-vajra
>> To scholars who are not ignorant about the reasoning
>> [Of] all phenomena being free from proliferations—
>> [This] also is the second explanatory mode of honorable Nāgārjuna.[107]

As we can see, both *Collections* of Nāgārjuna teach the reasoning establishing self-emptiness, a non-affirming negation, as the means of accessing the direct realization of ultimate reality. What distinguishes them from each other is their description of ultimate reality experienced within meditative equipoise. No such reality is identified in the

Collection of Reasonings, while in the *Collection of Praises* it is described as the non-dual primordial mind.

Overall, the approach of the *Collection of Praises* stands in between the approaches of the *Collection of Reasonings* and Alīkākāravāda: on the level of the view posited through reasoning, it is the same as the former, while on the level of setting in meditative equipoise, it is the same as the latter.

It should be noted that despite the fact that according to Shakya Chokden the two *Collections* were authored by the same Nāgārjuna, and despite the above-mentioned similarity between the views expressed in the *Collection of Praises* and Alīkākāravāda, Shakya Chokden always identifies Nāgārjuna *himself* as a Niḥsvabhāvavādin. For example, in the *Rain of Ambrosia*, he says:

> . . . treating scriptural statements of Nāgārjuna's *Collection of Praises* as valid, [I will demonstrate that] in the texts of Niḥsvabhāvavādins also, [that] very primordial mind of the dharma-sphere is being established as exactly [that] definitive meaning which is the object of experience of yogic direct perception.[108]

The statement that Niḥsvabhāvavādins' texts also teach the genuine ultimate truth distinguishes Shakya Chokden from his fellow Sakyapas as he presents them, because in the *Seventeen Wondrous Answers* he clearly states: "Sakyapas assert that no efficient ultimate truth was explained in the texts of Niḥsvabhāvavādins,"[109] and attributes to them the same description of the Niḥsvabhāvavāda view as he himself gave with regard to the explicit teachings of the second dharmacakra and the *Collection of Reasonings*. Nevertheless, it should be also noted that sometimes Shakya Chokden applies this generic term "Niḥsvabhāvavāda" to the main types of Prāsaṅgika and Svātantrika (*thal rang gi gtso bo*) mentioned above (142). So, the difference might be not that substantial after all, and perhaps lies in simply how specific Shakya Chokden himself is when he uses the term "Niḥsvabhāvavāda."

An obvious question arises: why, in his two *Collections*, did Nāgārjuna use the same view of emptiness determined by reasoning, but propose two different modes of setting in meditative equipoise? Shakya Chokden's reply is that the differences stem from whether those elements are connected with the definitive meaning of the third dharmacakra (as in the *Collection of Praises*) or not (as in the *Collection of Reasonings*). This is why the *Collection of Reasonings* teaches setting in equipoise within the state of non-findability by reasoning. The

Collection of Praises, in contrast, teaches that with the understanding of non-findability coming first, one sets in equipoise on the non-dual primordial mind.[110]

Another important question addressed by Shakya Chokden is which approach to the ultimate view has to be taken as more authoritative (*dbang btsan par byed*): that of the *Collection of Reasonings*, which does not accept any illustration of ultimate truth, or that of the *Collection of Praises*, which treats it as the non-dual primordial mind? His response is that authority is specific to the system with which one is dealing. Such an approach, he argues, is a general tradition of commentators on textual systems. In other words, the answer depends on which position one assumes when answering the question: that of the *Collection of Reasonings* or the *Collection of Praises*. Nevertheless, he immediately adds that if the two systems are analyzed in general (*spyi tsam nas dpyod*), then the approach of the *Collection of Praises* is more authoritative, because it agrees with the tantric teachings that describe the ultimate mind of enlightenment exclusively as the indestructible vajra.[111] This is also because from among the two types of "freedom from proliferations" (*spros bral, aprapañca*)—the emptiness described as negation of all phenomena and the non-dual primordial mind—the former cannot serve as an object of yogic direct perception:

> From among the two, the freedom from proliferations as the factor of non-affirming negation (*spros bral med dgag gi cha*) and the naturally luminous mind free from proliferations (*spros pa dang bral ba'i sems rang bzhin gyis 'od gsal ba*), the first is [taught in] the explicit teachings of the middle dharmacakra, while the second is the main topic taught by the final dharmacakra. Thus—to leave aside the case of not upholding (*'dzin pa*) an illustration of the ultimate, [such as in the *Collection of Reasonings*]—as long as it is upheld, it is ascertained exclusively as the latter [type of freedom from proliferations]. This is because the first [type of freedom from proliferations] is ascertained only as an exclusion of other isolates, a generally characterized [phenomenon], and an object realized by mind in an exclusionary way (*blos rnam bcad du rtogs bya*), and therefore it is not directly seen by the primordial mind of buddhas.[112]

This statement leads to yet another challenging question: will it not follow then that contradiction will be permissible,[113] since one and the same primordial mind is accepted as relative in the *Collection of*

Reasonings and ultimate in the *Collection of Praises*? Shakya Chokden replies:

> [When] such [phenomena] as natural nirvāṇa (*rang bzhin gyi myang 'das*), are explained in the *Collection of Reasonings* as relative, [what it means is that] although within the scope of presumption (*rlom tshod*) [by conceptual minds it is] presumed to be an actual natural nirvāṇa, their scope of reach (*song tshod*) is only an other-exclusion (*gzhan sel, anyāpoha*) of that [nirvāṇa], because [that nirvāṇa has been] turned into a convention by sounds and concepts. Thus, there is not any contradiction at all between the two: explaining an actual object of sounds and concepts as relative, and explaining an object of direct experience as ultimate. Although such [a word] as "natural nirvāṇa" is one [and the same] term, its meaning is ascertained individually [depending on context].[114]

In this highly ingenious explanation that applies Buddhist epistemological ideas to the Niḥsvabhāvavāda teachings, Shakya Chokden argues that the reason why in the *Collection of Reasonings* Nāgārjuna negates all phenomena is because there he unmasks the fundamental mistake sentient beings make: presuming that what we are conceptualizing and talking about is really out there, i.e., that there is a direct correspondence between words and ideas on the one hand and their referents on the other. Nevertheless, this does not prevent certain things from actually existing in reality. What exists in reality is the genuine ultimate truth, the non-dual primordial mind (called in the passage "natural nirvāṇa"), and it is described by Nāgārjuna in the *Collection of Praises*. Thus, the two explanations that appear to be contradictory on the surface turn out to be only complementary on a deeper level.

Shakya Chokden further emphasizes the complementarity of the teachings of the two *Collections* by arranging them in stages. Although he sees neither as insufficient, he does present the teachings of the *Collection of Praises* as a "natural outcome," so to say, of the teachings of the *Collection of Reasonings*: he links the views taught in the two *Collections* with the practical sequence of first determining emptiness by reasoning and then subsequently setting in equipoise directly realizing the ultimate. Interestingly, he thinks that this temporal progression is also reflected in the very order of composition of the two *Collections* by Nāgārjuna:

> Thus, it is established that Ārya [Nāgārjuna] composed the *Collection of Reasonings* first, and subsequently composed the *Collection of Praises*, because it is reasonable that with the reasoning severing superimpositions with respect to the view coming first, one incorporates into experience the meaning determined by that [reasoning]; the *Collection of Reasonings* determines by reasoning as exclusively literal the explicit teachings of the middle pronouncement, while the *Collection of Praises*, having explained that very definitive meaning that originated from the pronouncement of the last dharmacakra as the basis of accomplishing the dharma-body, explains [that definitive meaning] as the object incorporated into experience by yogis.[115]

Shakya Chokden does agree that what is determined by reasoning in the *Collection of Reasonings* and what is experienced in meditation according to descriptions in the *Collection of Praises* are not identical. Nevertheless, he does not see linking them together as contradictory, because when arranged in stages, the former is needed for accessing the latter, and the latter is the necessary outcome of the former. If superimpositions are not severed, one cannot access the direct realization of the ultimate mind. On the other hand, when superimpositions have been severed, the only thing left to experience is ultimate mind:

> Severing superimpositions by the mind of listening and thinking is [taught] in the *Collection of Reasonings* in order to cease (*'gog*) concepts apprehending signs regarding the object of experience. Having ceased [concepts] in such a way, there is no fault at all in demonstrating the dharma-sphere as an object of experience.[116]

Shakya Chokden does not see this approach as implying a gap between determining emptiness by reasoning and experiencing emptiness within meditative equipoise:

> *Question*: Then, will it not turn out that having determined one thing by the view, one incorporates into experience through meditation something else [entirely different from it]?
>
> *Answer:* No. When one meditates having [initially] negated by the view all collections of proliferations, it is absolutely

> not feasible for the familiarizing mind to experience anything other than primordial mind of the dharma-sphere itself.[117]

What on the surface might seem as a discontinuity between the two sets of teachings, in his explanation turns out to be the only possible continuity: when all concepts have ceased, one is left with ultimate reality beyond concepts, and the only thing that this ultimate reality can ever be is the non-dual primordial mind.

Shakya Chokden disagrees with those who claim that according to Niḥsvabhāvavāda teachings one has to cultivate in meditative experience that very emptiness which has been conceptually determined by reasoning. Such a position contradicts the mainstream Sakya tradition:

> The statement "that very [object] which has been determined by reasoning
> Is to be experienced [in meditation]"
> Does not belong to the system of this [Sakya tradition]
> Because it contradicts all its teachings.[118]

Note also that, technically speaking, in the context of the Niḥsvabhāvavāda reasoning, it cannot be said that primordial mind is *left in remainder of negation*, because on the conceptual level it is negated as well, while on the level of direct experience it simply cannot be reached by reasoning. In other words, although primordial mind is inevitably experienced after all phenomena have been negated by reasoning, it is not experienced *in remainder of that negation*, because non-affirming negations have no remainders.

In sum, whether Shakya Chokden analyzes the teachings of the two *Collections* as two separate systems or as parts of a broader continuous process in which one system is presented as building upon the other, he treats the systems as compatible and mutually complementary.

Positions of Later Mādhyamikas

These explanatory differences of the founding Madhyamaka thinkers are reflected in different readings of their works by later Mādhyamikas, whose explanations depend on whether they focus on the ideas linked with the explicit teachings of the second dharmacakra, the definitive meaning of the third dharmacakra, or their mixture. For example, Shakya Chokden explains that Maitreya's *Ornament of Clear Realizations* was commented upon in two ways, as articulated by such Niḥsvabhāvavādins as Āryavimuktisena and such Yogācāras as Rantākaraśānti. Likewise, Nāgārjuna's works were commented upon in two ways: by the Yogācāra Dharmapāla and by such Niḥsvabhāvavādins as Candrakīrti, to mention just a few. Niḥsvabhāvavādins, in turn, provided explanations in Prāsaṅgika and Svātantrika styles.[119] Addressing those second-order commentators, Shakya Chokden demonstrates that even Niḥsvabhāvavāda works can be explained in Yogācāra fashion, and vice versa. The very lack of criticism of these "cross-explanations" is indicative of his overall position: despite temporary differences on the conceptual level, the final views of the two systems are substantially the same.

Because Shakya Chokden is convinced that ultimate reality directly experienced in the meditative equipoise of Mahāyāna āryas is the same for all Mādhyamikas, he faces relatively little problem with explaining Alīkākāravāda writings that explicitly describe emptiness as the non-dual primordial mind. However, explaining the writings of Niḥsvabhāvavādins who came after Nāgārjuna is more cumbersome, and poses problems similar to the ones that arise from explanations of the two *Collections* of Nāgārjuna. Similar to Nāgārjuna in his *Collection of Reasonings*, such important Niḥsvabhāvavādins as Candrakīrti did not explicitly teach the non-dual primordial mind in their non-tantric writings. Unlike Nāgārjuna—presented by Shakya Chokden as the most diverse Indian Mādhyamika who wrote in both the second and third dharmacakra styles on the level of sūtric teachings, besides composing tantric works—Candrakīrti and Bhāviveka in their sūtric works approached the ultimate view only in accordance with the *Collection of Reasonings*—as a non-affirming negation. As Shakya Chokden writes in the *Rain of Ambrosia*:

> In the explicit teachings of the *Collection of Reasonings*, the definitive meaning is not explained as other than the factor of non-affirming negation. Therefore, [those teachings] explain not meditating on anything as meditation on emptiness and not seeing anything as seeing thatness.[120] There are no explanations [of the meditative experience of reality] as anything other than that. That very [approach] is [made] clear in the texts of Bhāviveka and Candrakīrti, as well as in [Śāntideva's] *Engaging in the Bodhisattva Deeds.*[121]

Similar to Nāgārjuna in the *Collection of Reasonings*, Candrakīrti and Bhāviveka treated all phenomena, including primordial mind and dualistic consciousness, buddhas and sentient beings, as equally existing on the conventional level and nonexisting on the ultimate level. Of special notice is the fact that "both Candra[kīrti] and Bhāviveka zealously refuted the individually self-cognizing primordial mind together with its objects of functioning."[122]

On the other hand, Yogācāra Mādhyamikas on the Niḥsvabhāvavāda side explained the object of meditative experience as the non-dual primordial mind:

> Some Niḥsvabhāvavāda masters, having explained the view as self-emptiness, accept meditation as [the cultivation of] the individually self-cognizing primordial mind. All of them [thereby] have accepted the last pronouncement as the final definitive meaning, because the definitive meaning of the explicit teachings of the middle pronouncement (*bka' bar pa'i dngos bstan gyi nges don*) does not fit as the object of experience of yogic direct perception.[123]

The approach of these Mādhyamikas, therefore, is similar to that of the *Collection of Praises* described above. Also, because they accept the teachings of the last dharmacakra as definitive, they agree with Alīkākāravāda as well:

> This explanation of the final [view] of definitive meaning as primordial mind is [accepted] not only in the [system] of Madhyamaka asserted by Ārya Asaṅga, but it is also asserted by Yogācāra Mādhyamikas among Niḥsvabhāvavādins [such as,] for example, the masters Āryavimuktisena and Haribhadra.[124]

Their approach, therefore, like the approach of the *Collection of Praises*, stands between the approaches of the *Collection of Reasonings* and Alīkākāravāda, or, to put it differently, between the explicit teachings of the second dharmacakra and definitive teachings of the third dharmacakra (that are, according to Shakya Chokden, the same as the implicitly taught definitive meaning of the second dharmacakra). On the level of the view posited through reasoning they agree with the former, while on the level of the view directly realized in meditative experience they agree with the latter:

> Both Āryavimuktisena and Haribhadra also assert the way of determining the view [through reasoning] in accordance with [other] Prāsaṅgikas and Svātantrikas. Nevertheless,

> they explain the definitive meaning implicitly taught by the middle pronouncement (*bka' bar pa'i shugs bstan gyi nges don*) and the definitive meaning incorporated into experience through meditation (*sgom pas nyams len gyi nges don*) as primordial mind.[125]

Putting it differently, Shakya Chokden explains that such thinkers as Śāntarakṣita and Haribhadra asserted the way of severing superimpositions through listening and thinking in accordance with the *Collection of Reasonings* and the object experienced through meditation in accordance with the system of Asaṅga and Vasubandhu.[126]

Furthermore, he links their explanatory approach with that of Maitreya's *Ornament of Clear Realizations*:

> That very [approach] exists as the intent of the foremost venerable [Maitreya], because [in] the *Ornament* [*of Clear Realizations*, he] gave explanations putting together the main topic of the *Perfection of Wisdom* sūtras—that hidden meaning, the level of clear realizations (*sbas don mngon rtogs kyi rim pa*), with its explicit teachings, the level of emptiness (*dngos bstan stong nyid kyi rim pa*).[127]

In this way, he traces even the "hybrid" approach of Āryavimuktisena and Haribhadra to the writings of the Madhyamaka founders, in this case the *Ornament of Clear Realizations*. Unlike the other four *Dharmas of Maitreya* that entirely present the Alīkākāravāda view, this text presents the view determined by reasoning in the Niḥsvabhāvavāda way, but the view directly experienced in meditative equipoise as the non-dual primordial mind. This in turn allows Shakya Chokden to claim that all the *Five Dharmas of Maitreya* present the final ultimate view in the same way, as the non-dual primordial mind.

Note how his explanation of the views expressed in Nāgārjuna's *Collection of Praises*, Maitreya's *Ornament of Clear Realizations*, and writings of later Yogācāra Mādhyamikas on the Niḥsvabhāvavāda side (as a "hybrid" of Alīkākāravāda and Niḥsvabhāvavāda) contributes to his demonstration of the compatibility of Alīkākāravāda and Niḥsvabhāvavāda. It demonstrates that one and the same thinker can harmoniously advocate both views while preserving their unique features, thereby "internalizing" both their distinctions and compatibility.

In the light of the explanation of their views by Shakya Chokden, all later Niḥsvabhāvavādins appear to be faithful to the works of Nāgārjuna himself. The very distinction between the two *Collections* appears to have later manifested in the two types of Nāgārjuna's followers:

Cāndrakīrti and Bhāviveka adhered to the approach of the *Collection of Reasonings*, while Haribhadra and other Yogācāra Mādhyamikas on the Niḥsvabhāvavāda side agree with the *Collection of Praises*.

In summary, we can delineate three groups of Mādhyamikas:

(i) *Yogācāra Mādhyamikas on the Alīkākāravāda side*
This group includes Maitreya, Asaṅga, Vasubandhu, Dignāga, Dharmakīrti, and Dharmapāla.
Their views derive from and/or agree with the last four of the *Five Dharmas of Maitreya* that in turn follow the definitive teachings of the final dharmacakra.

(ii) *Yogācāra Mādhyamikas on the Niḥsvabhāvavāda side*
This group includes Śāntarakṣita, Kamalaśīla, Haribhadra, Āryavimuktisena.
On the level of determining the view through reasoning they follow Nāgārjuna's *Collection of Reasonings*, but describe the view directly realized in meditative equipoise in agreement with Alīkākāravāda, Nāgārjuna's *Collection of Praises*, and Maitreya's *Ornament of Clear Realizations* that in turn describe that view in agreement with the definitive teachings of the third dharmacakra.

(iii) *Prāsaṅgika and Sautrāntika Mādhyamikas*
This group includes Bhāviveka and Candrakīrti.
They faithfully follow Nāgārjuna's *Collection of Reasonings* that in turn follows the explicit teachings of the second dharmacakra.

The correspondence between their views is depicted in Table 3. It can be seen as a progressive development of respective views of Madhyamaka starting from the teachings of the two last dharmacakras through the works of the Madhyamaka founders to the works of later Mādhyamikas (moving from the first column to the third column). One possible exception is the correspondence between the *Collection of Praises* and works of Yogācāra Madhyamaka within Niḥsvabhāvavāda. Although their views are similar, Shakya Chokden does not explicitly present the latter as a development of the former. The reason for that, I think, is that later Mādhyamikas in their works focused primarily on the *Collection of Reasonings*, not the *Collection of Praises*.

Table 3

<table>
<tr><td rowspan="2">Second dharmacakra's explicit teachings</td><td>The *Collection of Reasonings*</td><td>Prāsaṅgika and Sautrāntika Madhyamaka</td></tr>
<tr><td rowspan="2">The *Collection of Praises* and the *Ornament of Clear Realizations*</td><td rowspan="2">Yogācāra Madhyamaka within Niḥsvabhāvavāda</td></tr>
<tr><td rowspan="2">Third dharmacakra's definitive teachings (and second dharmacakra's main topic according to Alīkākāravāda)</td></tr>
<tr><td>Other four of the *Five Dharmas of Maitreya* and Asaṅga's works</td><td>Alīkākāravāda</td></tr>
</table>

4. Steering the Middle Way between the Two Conflicting Middle Ways: The Art of Not Taking Sides

The more we learn about Shakya Chokden's insistence on the compatibility of the two types of Madhyamaka, the more we wonder why Niḥsvabhāvavādins and Alīkākāravādins would attempt to refute each other? Not only does Shakya Chokden accept the two as equally valid systems of Madhyamaka with origins in the second and third dharmacakras, but he also believes that their final views amount to the same thing. Do the debates between adherents of these systems arise from mutual misunderstanding, or do they actually understand each other but not accept certain specific elements of the other system?

Shakya Chokden himself admits that debates took place, and that Yogācāras and Niḥsvabhāvavādins did not see each other equally as Mādhyamikas. In his *Thorough Clarification of Vajradhara's Intent: Ascertainment of Profound and Extensive Points of the Mantra System in Twenty-One Dharma Sections*, he explains:

> Brothers Asaṅga [and Vasubandhu] do not describe as Madhyamaka that system of Prāsaṅgikas and Svātantrikas. Nor do those [Prāsaṅgikas and Svātantrikas] explain that [system of Asaṅga and Vasubandhu] as that [i.e., Madhyamaka].[128]

In the *Wish Fulfilling Meru* too, he admits that in his *Summary of Higher Knowledge*, Asaṅga treated Niḥsvabhāvavādins as nihilists, while Candrakīrti taught that Vasubandhu and others had not realized the Niḥsvabhāvavāda view.[129]

At the same time, Shakya Chokden strongly opposes doxographical favoritism, such as giving preference to the opinions of Bhāviveka and Candrakīrti about Alīkākāravādins over the opinions of Alīkākāravādins themselves about themselves and Niḥsvabhāvavādins. In the *Wish Fulfilling Meru* he writes:

> *Objection:* Although the definitive meaning derived from those textual systems [of the third dharmacakra with its commentaries] was explained by the foremost venerable Maitreya as Madhyamaka, the two explanations of it by Bhāviveka and Candrakīrti as not Madhyamaka are more authoritative.
>
> *Answer:* However, honorable Asaṅga also, having quoted sūtras, described explanations of those [who side with

> Niḥsvabhāvavādins] as a view of deprecation. Also, in Indian texts of quintessential instructions (*man ngag, upadeśa*) and in sūtras, the emptiness explained by Niḥsvabhāvavādins was called the "inanimate emptiness" (*bems po'i stong pa nyid*), "nihilistic emptiness" (*chad pa'i stong pa nyid*) and "overextended emptiness" (*thal byung gi stong pa nyid*). Because partial refutations of both sides of identifications of the definitive meaning were made in valid texts, it is not possible to mutually refute one by the other without analysis of intended profound meanings (*dgongs don zab mo*).[130]

This type of reasoning clearly demonstrates that Shakya Chokden does not want to take sides, and does not want to criticize Alīkākāravāda from the position of Niḥsvabhāvavāda, and vice versa, although he does admit that they themselves did. He furthermore argues that their mutual refutations are only partial, and that rather than siding with either system in those criticisms, one should look for the profound meaning intended by both. Shakya Chokden does precisely that, discovering (for himself at least) that indeed the views of the two systems come down to the same final definitive meaning.

In the *Appearance of the Sun* too, he openly argues that the explanation of one system by another system discordant with it does not necessarily have to be accepted. When he explains that Alīkākāravādins should not be taken as Cittamātra Followers, even though Candrakīrti described them as such, he uses the following arguments:

> [Simply] because a dissimilar, different chariot tradition explains it differently, one does not [necessarily] have to accept it as that. This is because otherwise, separate chariot traditions will be confused. This is also because there are those who say that the mere Mahāyāna (*theg pa chen po tsam*)[131] and Vajrayāna are not the Word of the Buddha (*sangs rgyas kyi bka', buddhavacana*). [Also, Śāntideva] does say that higher yogis invalidate (*gnod*) [the views of] the lower ones. Nevertheless, it is difficult to distinguish features of superiority (*gong 'og gi khyad par*) of these two Madhyamaka systems.[132]

Shakya Chokden's line of argument is as follows. It is true that there are critics who say that Mahāyāna is not an authentic teaching of the Buddha. There are those who doubt the authenticity of the Buddhist tantric teachings too. Nevertheless, does it mean that one has to side with them? Indeed, how many fifteenth-century Tibetans would doubt the authenticity of Mahāyāna in general and Buddhist Tantra in particular? Furthermore, as we already know, it is possible to move progressively through the stages of the view,[133] and this is what Śāntideva had in mind when he wrote in the *Engaging in the Bodhisattva Deeds*:

> There, the ordinary world
> Is invalidated by the yogis' world.
> Due to the distinctive features of their minds,
> Higher yogis also invalidate [the views of] the lower ones.[134]

Nevertheless, it does not mean that the views of *all* tenets have to be approached in the hierarchical way. Niḥsvabhāvavāda and Alīkākāravāda are a paradigmatic example of two systems that cannot be treated hierarchically, although Shakya Chokden himself admits that they have their own strengths that make one system more efficient than the other in some areas.

According to the *Ocean of Scriptural Statements and Reasoning*,[135] later Tibetans' mistakes about the identity and meaning of Alīkākāravāda originate precisely from this problematic doxographical partisanship. The majority of Tibetan thinkers, including Rendawa, Tsongkhapa, and Gorampa, sided with Candrakīrti, who in his criticisms of Yogācāra emphasized the Satyākāravāda view. As a result, his Tibetan followers tended to treat both Satyākāravāda and Alīkākāravāda as inferior to Madhyamaka and synonymous with Cittamātra. In another text too, Shakya Chokden points out that because of their partial readings of Bhāviveka and Candrakīrti's works, most Tibetan thinkers of his time say that Vijñaptivāda and Cittamātra are the same.[136] In a word, in Shakya Chokden's view, later Tibetans sided with Candrakīrti and Bhāviveka in their opinions about Alīkākāravāda.

It is interesting to observe that Shakya Chokden could not simply discard as mistaken certain opinions of such exalted figures as Sakya Pendita. In the *Meaningful to Behold* he himself admits that Sakya Pendita used such terms as Nirākāra Cittamātra (*sems tsam rnam med pa*, Aspectless Mind-Only), that could indicate he treated Alīkākāravāda as Cittamātra.[137] Nevertheless, Shakya Chokden finds a graceful way out of even this sensitive issue by explaining that Sakya Pendita applied such terms *when assuming the position of the textual system of Niḥsvabhāvavādins*, not in general.[138] He further adds that when assuming the position of Alīkākāravādins it is even permissible to call Niḥsvabhāvavādins "nihilists" (*chad par smra ba, ucchedavādin*), because although they did set forth effective reasoning for determining emptiness, they spoke of neither an effective primordial mind that meditates on it nor its object of experience.[139]

Shakya Chokden's approach therefore can be described as follows. It is permissible to use criticisms of one system of Madhyamaka *when* assuming the position of another, especially when one wants to explore one and determine the other's sturdiness. Nevertheless, it is not permissible to assume the position of one system of Madhyamaka *in order to* criticize another, because by definition such a stance is not free from bias.

He proposes the following approach. When it comes to determining the view through reasoning, the Niḥsvabhāvavāda system is more effective, while with regard to the direct experience of emptiness, the Alīkākāravāda system is more effective. In the *Appearance of the Sun*, analyzing a question about which of the two systems is more "profound" and "extensive," he explains:

> *Question:* What are the distinctive features of profundity and extensiveness (*zab rgyas*) of these two [systems] of Madhyamaka?
>
> *Answer:* With regard to the reasoning positing all phenomena as entityless that [Niḥsvabhāvavāda system] is more extensive, while [the description of] the definitive meaning experienced through meditation is more profound in this [Alīkākāravāda system]. Because its explanation of exclusively the non-dual primordial mind as the very object of meditative experience is in strong agreement with the Vajrayāna teachings (*rdo rje theg pa dag*), this system is more profound.[140]

Shakya Chokden understands that mutual attempts at refuting each other's system are unavoidable. He argues that the Niḥsvabhāvavāda view of self-emptiness posited through reasoning is more effective than the Alīkākāravāda view of other-emptiness posited through reasoning. By definition the Niḥsvabhāvavāda view of self-emptiness negates the Alīkākāravāda view of other-emptiness, because it negates primordial mind that Alīkākāravāda treats as truly existent. On the other hand, Alīkākāravāda's description of ultimate reality directly realized in meditative equipoise as primordial mind is the most accurate description available. By definition this approach runs contrary to Niḥsvabhāvavāda's "not realizing anything being called realization of emptiness." At the same time, Shakya Chokden does not see attempts at mutual refutations based on these issues as a significant problem. After all, they do not prevent followers of both Madhyamaka systems from achieving the same realizations within meditative equipoise, and—what is most valuable, of course—achieving the same final goal of buddhahood.

Nevertheless, if according to Shakya Chokden all Mādhyamikas share the same final view of ultimate reality, one still wonders why Candrakīrti would not accept the non-dual primordial mind as ultimate reality? To put it differently, why did Candrakīrti interpret the explanation of the thoroughly established nature by the last dharmacakra as nonliteral? Shakya Chokden gives the following answer in the *Rain of Ambrosia*:

> Such an interpretation of that [last pronouncement as nonliteral] is made [by Candrakīrti] in terms of severing superimpositions by listening and thinking (*thos bsam gyis sgro 'dogs gcod pa*). [In contrast,] the explanation [of the definitive meaning of the last pronouncement] as an object of experience of [wisdom] arisen from meditation (*sgom byung gi nyams su myong bya*) is given in terms of practical incorporation into experience (*spyod pa nyams len*). Thus, the ways of positing the tenets of the view and practice (*lta spyod kyi grub mtha'*) are not concordant.[141]

Although Candrakīrti and other Niḥsvabhāvavādins, with the exception of Yogācāra Mādhyamikas, did not accept the reality of the non-dual primordial mind which is the main topic of the last dharmacakra, they did it only in terms of severing superimpositions through listening and thinking, i.e., as it had been done in the *Collection of Reasonings* that they followed in their writings.[142] Their criticisms therefore are context dependent, and cannot be taken as refutations of the Alīkākāravāda system in general.

Likewise, Shakya Chokden treats Alīkākāravādins' polemics against Niḥsvabhāvavādins as context dependent too. In the *Meaningful to Behold* he writes:

> As for some sūtras and the brothers Asaṅga [with Vasubandhu] calling Niḥsvabhāvavādins "nihilists," [such was done] with the thought that Niḥsvabhāvavādins had not identified the object experienced through meditation. They did not object to [Niḥsvabhāvavādins'] way of determining

> [the view] by reasoning. This is because Dharmakīrti too asserted the same reasoning as Niḥsvabhāvavādins.[143]

In the same way as Candrakīrti was not refuting Asaṅga in general, but in the context of positing the view through listening and thinking, likewise Asaṅga (as well as some sūtras) was not refuting Niḥsvabhāvavādins in general, but focused on criticizing Niḥsvabhāvavādins' lack of identification of the object of meditation. Otherwise, with regard to the reasoning positing selflessness, Dharmakīrti himself presented it in agreement with Niḥsvabhāvavādins, because similar to them he used the reasoning of the lack of being one or many.[144] In Shakya Chokden's opinion, this indicates that other Alīkākāravādins too did not have issues with that.

Following this line of reasoning, Shakya Chokden manages to keep the mutual criticisms of the two systems of Madhyamaka on two distinct levels: determining emptiness by reasoning and describing the object directly experienced in meditative equipoise. He packages refutations leveled by Bhāviveka and Candrakīrti into those made on the level of determining emptiness through reasoning, and refutations leveled by Alīkākāravādins into those related to the issue of identification of the ultimate view experienced in meditation. Neither of these two mutual criticisms undermines his position that the ultimate reality realized in meditative equipoise by followers of both systems is the same.

Reading the passages from Shakya Chokden cited in this section should convince the reader that in his own approach to Madhyamaka he is siding with neither Niḥsvabhāvavāda nor Alīkākāravāda—rather, he embraces them both. It is understandable at the same time how this position might easily have confused those followers of an "either-or" approach who attempted to classify Shakya Chokden himself as a Follower of Other-Emptiness. Were he to learn about this classification, he would doubtlessly say that those "either-or" classifiers *either* did not read his key writings *or* read but ignored them on purpose.

In his reconciliatory approach to the two systems, Shakya Chokden does not agree with those very Mādhyamikas whose views he tries to reconcile. This is because Niḥsvabhāvavādins and Alīkākāravādins accuse each other of not being Mādhyamikas, while he treats both sides equally as Mādhyamikas. Consequently, he chooses to steer the "middle way between the two conflicting middle ways," so to say, and thereby be a Mādhyamika who avoids the extremes of even Madhyamaka itself.

Chapter 5

Explorations in Empty Luminosity

Shakya Chokden's Position on Primordial Mind

1. Facing the Reality of Primordial Mind

Primordial Mind and the Question of Existence

Whether we explore tantric teachings and meditative instructions, address the question of reality contested by Mahāyāna thinkers, or analyze ultimate truth directly experienced in meditative equipoise, we will notice that one of the key themes saturating these issues is the nature, meaning, and status of mind and its relation to other elements of Buddhist thought and practice.

In the Tibetan Buddhist world, the reality of mental phenomena was problematized by those who take the Niḥsvabhāvavāda stance, which rejects the reality of mind, and look down on the explanation of reality offered by Cittamātra, the system which takes mind (*sems, citta*) as the main element of its ultimate view and the object of meditation on ultimate truth. As a result, practically all Tibetan thinkers developed different strategies for separating what they deemed to be ultimate reality and what they saw as the non-ultimate mind asserted in such "lower" tenets as Cittamātra. This task was complicated by the fact that the majority of Buddhist thinkers also admit at least some mental elements to ultimate truth and/or its realization.

Dölpopa, Longchenpa, Shakya Chokden, and other thinkers of various traditions accept as ultimate truth the categories of primordial mind (*ye shes, jñāna*), cognition (*rig pa, vidya*), fundamental mind (*gnyug sems*), and so forth; the names and identifications vary, but the mental "flavor" is easily discernible. At the same time, those thinkers emphasize a fundamental difference between primordial mind and ordinary mentality. Even in the "anti-mental" descriptions of reality provided by Geluk thinkers who treat ultimate reality exclusively as a non-affirming negation—not only in the Niḥsvabhāvavāda system, but in Yogācāra/Cittamātra as well[1]—mind is deemed necessary for realization of that ultimate reality. Although mind is not included *in* ultimate reality, according to the Geluk system mind is indispensable for the realization of ultimate reality because ultimate reality is an object that requires a subject in order to be known.[2]

Tibetan thinkers use different strategies for separating ordinary mentality and primordial mind on the level of both philosophical discourse and contemplative practice. For example, Longchenpa, Mipam, and other important Nyingma thinkers in minute detail explain differences between ordinary types of knowing and ultimate reality understood as cognition (*rig pa*). A big part of the practical instructions of the Great Perfection system too is aimed at differentiating the two in meditative experience and discovering the unique characteristics of the latter. Sakya thinkers tend to take clarity, cognition, and appearances in general as conventional truths, but take the union of clarity and emptiness, appearance and emptiness, and awareness and emptiness as ultimate truth. Such an approach is carried into meditative instructions as well, as evident in Shakya Chokden's teacher Rongtön's writings.[3]

We have seen that Shakya Chokden explains ultimate reality as primordial mind different from consciousness. Nevertheless, his explanation of primordial mind is unusual in many respects. First and foremost, he accepts the explanation of ultimate reality by Alīkākāravāda, and insists that it is not only a valid type of ultimate reality, but it is that very reality which is explicitly accepted and/or meditatively experienced also by Niḥsvabhāvavādins, and definitely asserted in Tantra. As a result, he comes up with the highly unusual ideas that will be discussed in this chapter: although primordial mind is ultimate reality, it is impermanent; although it is a self-cognition, it does not necessarily cognize itself; although grasping at its true existence has to be abandoned, it truly exists, and so forth.

It would be difficult to overestimate the importance of the notion of primordial mind in Shakya Chokden's overall approach to Madhyamaka. As he puts it in the *Rain of Ambrosia*:

> In brief, from among Mahāyāna followers, whoever's system it is—that of [Alīkākāravāda] Yogācāras, Niḥsvabhāvavādins,

> or followers of Vajrayāna—as long as they accept a definitive meaning that is the direct object of cognition (*dngos kyi rig bya*) of the view realizing the selflessness of phenomena, the entity of emptiness is necessarily identified as primordial mind.[4]

Shakya Chokden argues that whenever Mādhyamikas provide an identification of a genuine, non-metaphorical ultimate truth, they identify it exclusively as the non-dual primordial mind. Exploration of the nature of primordial mind, therefore, is the task of paramount importance. Furthermore, primordial mind is the only phenomenon accepted as existent by Madhyamaka—if any existence at all is accepted. Consequently, exploring the nature of primordial mind is tantamount to exploring the ultimate nature of existence.

According to Shakya Chokden, Alīkākāravāda and Niḥsvabhāvavāda are similar in not accepting the existence of any relative, conventional phenomena. As he puts it in the *Answers to Three Universally Known Questions from the 'One Hundred and Eight Questions on the 'Thorough Differentiation of the Three Types of Vows''*:

> *Question:* Does only the Niḥsvabhāvavāda system [accept that] if something exists it necessarily has to be the dharma-sphere?
>
> *Answer:* [Such is accepted] not only in that [system], but [also in] the final system of what is known as Alīkākāravāda Cittamātra (*sems tsam rnam rdzun pa*). This is because in both the *Ornament of Mahāyāna Sūtras* and the *Differentiation of the Middle and Extremes* [Maitreya] taught:
>
>> Thus, except for the dharma-sphere
>> There are no phenomena.[5]

According to both Alīkākāravāda and Niḥsvabhāvavāda, to exist means to exist *in reality* and to exist *as reality* (the dharma-sphere and reality are synonymous). Where the two systems diverge is in their positions on the existence of primordial mind. When a system of Madhyamaka applies the explanatory approach of self-emptiness, it does not accept any existence, any reality, any phenomena, including primordial mind. When a system of Madhyamaka follows the explanatory approach of other-emptiness, it takes primordial mind as the only reality, and therefore the only existent thing. This is explained in the following passage from the *Thorough Clarification of Definitive Meaning of the 'Five Dharmas of Maitreya,'* where Shakya Chokden deals with the question of what the "middle" is according to the systems of Madhyamaka:

> The modes of explaining Mahāyāna Madhyamaka contain two [approaches]: the explanatory mode by way of self-emptiness and the explanatory mode by way of other-emptiness. According to the first one, there is left no thing at all called "center" (*dbus ma*) in the remainder of negation of all extremes of proliferations. The term "middle" is a mere label attached to [that nothing], because knowables not empty of their own entities are impossible. According to the second one, the two—the apprehended and apprehender—do not exist, but the non-dual primordial mind exits. A phenomenon existing in remainder of such elimination of the two extremes of superimposition and deprecation is called "middle."[6]

With the important exception of their views on primordial mind, both approaches are similar in their general rejection of the existence of any phenomena. Nevertheless, according to the first approach, not even a primordial mind is left in remainder of negation of extremes. According to the second approach, primordial mind itself is the only reality, the middle free from extremes which is left in remainder of their negation. When determining emptiness by reasoning, the first approach is followed by all Niḥsvabhāvavādins and partly by Dharmakīrti,[7] while the second is employed by Alīkākāravādins.

We find further details in the *Wish Fulfilling Meru*, where Shakya Chokden addresses different ways of describing what the extremes are and how they are eliminated according to the two systems of Madhyamaka. As the passage demonstrates, the main difference between the ways of eliminating extremes by the two systems of Madhyamaka lies in whether primordial mind is negated together with all other phenomena or not. I am quoting the passage at length, because it shows clearly how Shakya Chokden understands the meaning of existence and nonexistence:

> There are two ways of eliminating the two extremes in [Madhyamaka,] the fourth tenet [system]: that of Yogācāra and that of Niḥsvabhāvavāda. Because according to the first [system] neither the apprehended- nor the apprehender-phenomena have ever existed from the beginning, as taught

in the *Dharmas of Maitreya*, it eliminates the extreme of existence. Also, because [according to that system, phenomena] are not made nonexistent either by pure reasoning or by other causes and conditions, it eliminates the extreme of nonexistence. Its explanation is as follows. If one accepts that a previously existent thing later became nonexistent, one abides in the extreme of nonexistence [as well as the extreme of existence. For example,] when previously existent wealth is later exhausted, worldly individuals accept that it is nonexistent. Thereby they abide in extremes of both eternalism and nihilism. "The middle" in this system is that which is free from the two extremes of the apprehended and apprehender, the self-illuminating self-cognition. Because no phenomena except the dharma-sphere are accepted in this system, it is greatly distinguished from Cittamātra.[8]

Because according to the second [system], no knowables of the mode (*ji lta, yathā*) and multiplicity (*ji snyed, yāvat*)[9] have ever existed from the beginning, it eliminates the extreme of existence. Because previously existent [things] are not made nonexistent either by reasoning or by the knowledge-seeing of āryas (*'phags pa'i shes mthong*), it eliminates the extreme of nonexistence. Because nobody [and nothing] has ever existed, it eliminates the extreme of being both [existent and nonexistent]. The ground of dependence on which to depend (*gang la ltos pa'i ltos sa*), that is, "being both" is impossible. Hence the dependent phenomenon (*bltos chos*), that is, "not being both" also cannot be accepted. [According to this system,] if phenomena which are not dependently established (*ltos grub, apekṣyasamutpāda*) were accepted, they would not go beyond being truly established (*bden grub*).[10]

As this passage demonstrates, Alīkākāravāda and Niḥsvabhāvavāda have different ways of explaining the nonexistence of phenomena, but their underlying arguments are the same. The extreme of existence is eliminated because no existence of phenomena to which this extreme could be attached is accepted. The extreme of nonexistence is eliminated by further reiterating that very lack of existence, and arguing that precisely because phenomena do not exist, they cannot become nonexistent either. Phenomena are free from the other two extremes, because the last two extremes in their turn are derived from the first two.

In a word, neither system accepts the existence of any subjective or objective phenomena, and both use this lack of existence as the foundation for eliminating all extremes. The main point of disagreement that sharply separates the two systems of Madhyamaka is their explanation of whether primordial mind is real and existent or unreal and nonexistent. Shakya Chokden elaborates on details of this difference in the *Meaningful to Behold*:

> This is the system of the main [types of] Prāsaṅgika and Svātantrika [to say that] because [primordial mind] does not exist in the face of that [reasoning analyzing the ultimate, such nonexistence] fills the role of nonexistence (*med pa'i go chod pa*). Nevertheless, [such] is not [accepted] in [the system of] Yogācāras.
>
> *Objection:* Then it will follow that the relative [level] is more authoritative (*dbang btsan*).
>
> *Answer:* No, because it is not ascertained that if [something] does not exist in the face of reasoning analyzing the ultimate, it [necessarily] does not exist as the ultimate.[11]

The two systems of Madhyamaka have different opinions on the question of whether nonexistence in the face of reasoning fills the role of nonexistence. Both systems agree that the reasoning of Madhyamaka negates everything that stands before it. Nevertheless, sūtric works of Candrakīrti, Bhāviveka, and their followers (as well as Nāgārjuna in the *Collection of Reasonings*) do not provide any description of ultimate truth which is beyond the reach of that reasoning. Those works, therefore, teach no reality existing beyond the reach of reasoning that could counterbalance the nonexistence in the face of reasoning. Alīkākāravādins, on the other hand, do provide a description of such reality, describing it as primordial mind which is beyond the reach of concepts, and therefore beyond the reach of reasoning. Although primordial mind does not exist in the face of reasoning, it does ultimately exist, and it exists as the ultimate.

In this context, the following subtle distinction should be made. According to the other-emptiness reasoning used by Alīkākāravāda, primordial mind is left in remainder of negation. Nevertheless, as the above passage shows, Alīkākāravādins also accept that primordial mind does not exist in the face of reasoning analyzing the ultimate. Therefore, being left in remainder of negation does not necessarily imply existence in the face of reasoning, and the nonexistence in the face of reasoning does not necessarily imply not being left in remainder of negation.

Note also that the nonexistence in the face of reasoning does not necessarily entail being an object of negation by that reasoning. As I explained earlier (124, 128), Shakya Chokden argues that although according to the Niḥsvabhāvavāda system of self-emptiness the object of negation of which phenomena are empty is the same as the basis of negation, in the Yogācāra system of other-emptiness the basis of negation and the object of negation are different. Therefore, in contrast to Niḥsvabhāvavāda, the general Yogācāra position is that although primordial mind does not exist in the face of reasoning, it is not an object of negation by that reasoning.[12]

Shakya Chokden makes a statement similar to the one in the previous passage in the *Great Path Compressing the Two Chariot Ways into One*, where he argues that according to Haribhadra too, the nonexistence of primordial mind in the face of reasoning does not entail its nonexistence. He writes:

> [In general, there are two approaches to this issue: the assertion] that because something is not established in the face of reasoning (*rigs ngor*), [such non-establishment] fills the role of non-establishment in the way of being as well; [the assertion] that although something is not established in that [face of reasoning], nevertheless, because it is established in the face of meditative equipoise (*mnyam gzhag gi ngor*), [such establishment] fills the role of establishment [in the mode of being]. These assertions [belong to] the separate systems of Sautrāntika Mādhyamika and Mādhyamika Utilizing Worldly Renown [on the one hand] and Yogācāra Mādhyamika [on the other].[13]

The above distinction, once again, derives from Shakya Chokden's view that the sūtric writings of Candrakīrti, Bhāviveka, and their followers do not provide an identification of ultimate truth experienced in the meditative equipoise of Mahāyāna āryas, which Yogācāra Mādhyamikas on both Niḥsvabhāvavāda and Alīkākāravāda sides identify as the non-dual primordial mind.

The nonexistence of primordial mind in the face of reasoning does not fill the role of nonexistence according to both types of Yogācāra Madhyamaka. It is safe to argue, therefore, that the overall position of Shakya Chokden is that whenever primordial mind is asserted as ultimate truth, its nonexistence in the face of reasoning is not accepted as filling the role of nonexistence.

But if primordial mind does not withstand analysis by reasoning, how can it ultimately exist? If it does ultimately exist, does it follow that it withstands analysis?

The Question of Withstanding Analysis

Shakya Chokden's position is that according to both systems of Madhyamaka the non-metaphorical ultimate can never be reached by analysis or reasoning. It is beyond the scope of reasoning both in terms of what is *determined* by reasoning and what is *negated* by reasoning. The reasoning of Madhyamaka determines ultimate reality through negation, be it an affirming or non-affirming negation. Therefore, similar to everything determined by reasoning not being the actual non-metaphorical ultimate, everything negated by reasoning cannot be the actual ultimate either.

Although Shakya Chokden's position on this issue is clear, nevertheless, when directly dealing with the question whether primordial mind withstands analysis by reasoning (*rigs pas dpyad bzod*), he provides slightly different answers—answers that might sound contradictory if not properly understood. In the following passage from the *Rain of Ambrosia*, linking the description of primordial mind in sūtric and tantric writings, he says:

> *Question:* Is it accepted that [primordial mind] withstands analysis by reasoning?
>
> *Answer:* No, because in the face of reasoning analyzing the ultimate (*don dam dpyod byed kyi rigs pa*), it is not accepted that [primordial mind] is established as any extreme of one, many, etc.
>
> *Objection:* Then it contradicts [the fact that primordial mind] is indestructible (*gzhom du med pa*).
>
> *Answer:* No, it does not, because there is no contradiction between being destructible by conceptuality and not being destructible in the face of primordial mind.[14]

As this passage shows, Shakya Chokden sees no problem in accepting that primordial mind does not withstand analysis by reasoning.

Nevertheless, he immediately clarifies his position by saying that this non-withstanding of analysis happens only in the face of analysis itself. In this passage, the non-withstanding of analysis is explained as destructibility by conceptuality, because analysis and reasoning can be only conceptual. On the other hand, in the face of primordial mind itself primordial mind is indestructible, because both the primordial mind which is experienced and the primordial mind which experiences it comprise the same self-cognizing entity, which is exclusively nonconceptual. Concepts cannot reach this entity which is beyond concepts. Therefore, primordial mind cannot be destroyed or negated by reasoning. The only phenomenon that has access to primordial mind is primordial mind itself, and since its mode of knowing is nonconceptual, it neither negates nor affirms itself.

At the same time, in the *Sevenfold Treasury of Gems*[15] Shakya Chokden makes a statement that might seem to directly contradict the one cited above. He describes ultimate truth as taught in all tantric teachings, and specifically in the *Secret Assembly Tantra*, as none other than the primordial mind of emptiness (*stong pa nyid kyi ye shes*) and the primordial mind of the dharma-sphere (*chos kyi dbyings kyi ye shes*). Thereby he links the tantric description of primordial mind with its description in sūtric systems of Madhyamaka. In this context, Shakya Chokden says that primordial mind necessarily *does* withstand analysis by reasoning (*rigs pas dpyad pa nges par bzod pa*), and adds that the emptiness in terms of non-findability at the time of examination by reasoning (*rigs pas brtags pa'i tshe ma rnyed pa'i stong pa nyid*) is not the reality experienced in meditation, and the subject of that emptiness is necessarily a conceptual mind. In other words, in that passage he argues that the emptiness arrived at through searching for and not finding phenomena under analysis is not the real ultimate truth but only the metaphorical ultimate, while the real ultimate truth, primordial mind itself, *does* withstand analysis.

In both passages, Shakya Chokden addresses sūtric and tantric descriptions of primordial mind together. His statements are meant to be taken generally and address primordial mind which is accepted in both tantric and sūtric teachings. Nevertheless, I do not take the two passages as contradictory, because in the first passage he specifies that primordial mind does not withstand analysis in the face of the analysis, while in the second passage he explains that primordial mind which withstands analysis is the one experienced in meditation, and cannot be reached by reasoning. In other words, the discussion in the two passages is respectively linked with the two approaches to emptiness already familiar to us: conceptual and experiential. Therefore, these passages only complement each other by clarifying Shakya Chokden's overall position: ultimate mind is destructible and does not withstand analysis by reasoning only in the face of that reasoning. Otherwise, it is neither destructible nor non-withstanding analysis, because it is beyond conceptuality, and transcends the scope of reasoning, whether affirming or destructive.

Shakya Chokden does not argue that "withstanding analysis" means that Madhyamaka analysis somehow cannot negate something that is within its reach. Were such the case, this analysis would be ineffective as a tool for cutting through conceptual proliferations and accessing the direct realization of ultimate reality. Madhyamaka analysis has to negate everything it can "put its hands on." Therefore, if it does not negate something, this means that it does not reach it. According to the Niḥsvabhāvavāda systems that do not provide descriptions of the actual ultimate reality, no such unreachable thing exists at all. According to the Alīkākāravāda and tantric systems, as well as the Niḥsvabhāvavāda system of Yogācāra Madhyamaka, all of which *do* provide that description, this thing is primordial mind. To use a boxing analogy: the punches of Madhyamaka reasoning are so deadly that they knock down everything in their way. One cannot withstand Madhyamaka punches by somehow absorbing the impact of the blows. It is not possible. At the same time, when engaged in a fight with objects of negation through reasoning, Madhyamaka boxers never step outside the ring of conceptuality. Thus, the only person who is able to withstand Madhyamaka punches is the person who stays outside the ring.

The statement about primordial mind not being able to withstand analysis in the face of the analysis by reasoning, but not in general, is supported by the following passage from the *Appearance of the Sun*:

> With the reasoning explained by honorable Nāgārjuna, the non-dual primordial mind is negated as existent in the face of that reasoning. It is not negated as existent in general. This is because it is beyond objects of sounds and concepts, and [also] because it is experienced by primordial mind.[16]

Thus, even the deadly Nāgārjunean reasonings outlined in the *Collection of Reasonings*—the reasonings that Shakya Chokden esteems as the most effective tools for eliminating proliferations—negate primordial mind only in the face of the conceptual mind that applies those reasonings. They simply do not reach ultimate reality that transcends all sounds and concepts. The same is true for the Alīkākāravāda system as well: it either does not attempt to negate primordial mind (as in the case of the other-emptiness reasoning), or negates it but accepts that such negation is possible only in the face of reasoning itself (as in the case of the self-emptiness reasoning used by Dharmakīrti).[17]

To reiterate: when Shakya Chokden says that primordial mind does not withstand analysis, it is meant that it does not withstand the analysis by reasoning *in the face of that reasoning*. Nevertheless, when he says that primordial mind does withstand analysis, it means that analysis cannot reach it. The two statements should not be taken as contradictory or mutually exclusive. A good parallel to this approach is how Shakya Chokden handles the question of Nāgārjuna negating and accepting natural nirvāṇa in the context of the *Collection of Reasonings* and the *Collection of Praises* respectively.[18]

Does True Existence Have to Be Negated in Order to Abandon Grasping at It?

It is clear that according to Shakya Chokden, all Mādhyamikas are "destined" to directly realize the same ultimate reality. No matter what system of Madhyamaka one follows, one eventually will break through the thicket of conceptuality and directly experience the non-dual primordial mind. Yogācāra Mādhyamikas on both the Alīkākāravāda and Niḥsvabhāvavāda side, as well as Nāgārjuna in his *Collection of Praises*, reiterate this fact by asserting primordial mind as ultimate reality directly experienced in meditative equipoise. Candrakīrti and Bhāviveka remain silent on this issue in their sūtric writings, but Candrakīrti breaks silence in his tantric writings where he too asserts the existence of primordial mind directly experienced in meditative equipoise. Therefore, all Mādhyamikas who accept primordial mind transcending sounds and concepts agree that it is indestructible, cannot be reached by reasoning, and in this sense withstands analysis.

Shakya Chokden assumes the following position: whether Mādhyamikas negate primordial mind prior to meditative equipoise or not, all of them can access this primordial mind within meditative equipoise. Furthermore, this primordial mind is truly established because it is ultimate truth. Yet, he himself argues that all types of grasping have to be abandoned, including the grasping at the true existence of primordial mind. This position is open to the following challenge. If the reasoning analyzing the ultimate can negate primordial mind, why does it not follow that primordial mind is not truly and ultimately established? If it cannot negate primordial mind, why does it not follow that this reasoning cannot negate true existence, and therefore it is impossible to abandon grasping at true existence based on that reasoning? What is the way out of this trap? Or, is it really a trap?

Shakya Chokden approaches the question of the true existence of primordial mind in a way similar to his approach to primordial mind itself. In the *Appearance of the Sun* he writes:

> The explanation of the ultimate as truthless (*bden min*) also is [given] in the face of that analytical reasoning (*rnam dpyod kyi rigs pa*), not in general. This is because the acceptance of something as the ultimate and the acceptance of it as truthless do not match.[19]

Similar to the negation of primordial mind only in the face of reasoning, the negation of its reality or truth also is done only in the face of reasoning. Otherwise, because primordial mind is ultimate truth, it has to be truly established. The truth cannot be truthless.

Shakya Chokden does not share the view that something can be ultimate truth and yet not be established as truth or not truly established.[20] In the same way as a pot is established as a pot, and primordial mind is established as primordial mind, likewise whatever is truth has to be established as truth, and has to be truly established. Nevertheless, how is it possible to abandon grasping at the true existence of primordial mind if one accepts that primordial mind truly exists?

Shakya Chokden agrees that grasping at the true existence of primordial mind—as well as all other types of grasping—is the object of abandonment from the point of view of *all* Mādhyamikas, not only Niḥsvabhāvavādins. In the *Meaningful to Behold*, he first explains that according to Alīkākāravāda primordial mind is truly established and the reasoning establishing it as truthless is not accepted.[21] He continues:

> It is not [the case that Alīkākāravādins] do not assert that grasping as true (*bden 'dzin*) at that primordial mind is not an object of abandonment. This is because [Alīkākāravādins] accept that the apprehender-imaginary nature (*'dzin pa kun btags*) is empty of [its own] entity, and the dependent nature is the object of abandonment.[22]

In other words, the truly established primordial mind, the thoroughly established nature, is not an object of abandonment, while the other natures are. True existence itself is not an object of abandonment, but the grasping at true existence is.

The issue was as important to Shakya Chokden's contemporaries as it is today, especially to those trained in the Geluk system that treats true establishment exclusively as the object of abandonment by Madhyamaka reasoning. This is why in the *Appearance of the Sun*, Shakya Chokden geared his answer specifically to later Tibetans who were arguing that "if something is truly established, it is impossible to abandon concepts grasping at it as true, and therefore Mādhyamikas accepting true existence are similar to sons of barren women."[23] He reiterated:

> Primordial mind of the dharma-sphere *is* truly established. Nevertheless, because concepts grasping at it as signs are just the dependent natures, they are the objects of abandonment; because they are ascertained as just the imaginary natures, they can be abandoned.[24]

Rather than categorically insisting that everything truly established has to be an object of abandonment, he allows a dose of true establishment, but allows it only for the thoroughly established nature, the non-dual primordial mind. This type of true establishment does not have to be abandoned, nor can it be. However, this fact does not legitimize grasping at true establishment or any other grasping, because *all* grasping is exclusively to be abandoned.

Nevertheless, the question remains: *how* is it possible to negate grasping at the true existence of something without negating the true existence of that something? Shakya Chokden handles this question by arguing that there are two different ways of negating grasping. In the *Precious Treasury of the Condensed Essence* he explains:

> There are two types of reasoning negating
> Adhering minds (*zhen blo*) together with habitual tendencies (*bag chags, vāsana*):
> The reasoning that negates grasping at objects
> By having negated those objects in the face of conceptuality (*rtog ngor*), and
> [The reasoning negating] only the apprehender-imaginary nature
> By the reason of the lack of being one or many.[25]

The first approach is used by Niḥsvabhāvavādins and partly by Alīkākāravādins such as Dharmakīrti; the second, by Alīkākāravādins. Describing the tools that negate all proliferations, Niḥsvabhāvavādins argue that without negating the object, its subject cannot be negated. This is because (as we already saw in the description of abandoning extremes) the Niḥsvabhāvavāda system treats subjects and objects as dependently established. Because they are *established* in mutual dependence, they have to be *negated* in mutual dependence too.

According to the Alīkākāravāda system, on the other hand, it is possible to negate grasping at objects by negating just subjects that grasp. One does not necessarily have to negate the objects those subjects grasp at. In other words, by negating grasping subjects, their grasping function will be cancelled automatically. We might think of cutting off a hand as an analogy: the moment it is cut off its grasping or "grabbing" function stops on its own accord, without removal of objects formerly grabbed at.

In particular, it is possible to negate grasping at the true existence of primordial mind by negating the consciousness that takes primordial mind as its object and grasps at it as truly existent. To put it in Yogācāra terms, by negating the apprehender-imaginary nature it is possible to simultaneously abandon grasping at true existence and all other projections it creates. This is true also when the apprehender-imaginary nature apprehends primordial mind, i.e., the apprehender-aspect, the thoroughly established nature.

Shakya Chokden treats both approaches as valid, and argues that it is possible to abandon all obscurations by following either one. This is how he presents them in the *Rain of Ambrosia*:

> Honorable Candrakīrti and other [Niḥsvabhāvavādins] assert that without determining the object, the dharma-sphere, as self-empty, it is impossible to reverse thoughts that grasp at it as signs. On the other hand, honorable Asaṅga, commenting on Maitreya's scriptures, [asserts that] having determined the apprehender-imaginary nature as self-empty, and accustomed [one's mind to it], due to that very [process] the grasping [at the dharma-sphere] can subside by itself within meditative equipoise.[26]

Grasping can be negated in two ways: either by negating both the subject and its object, or by negating only the subject, and thereby letting grasping at its object subside by itself. As an analogy, we might think of two ways of getting rid of sexual desire toward a beautiful body seen in dreams. Having awakened, in the former case the person tries to get rid of desire by thinking that both the object of desire and its subject are unreal because they exist only in mutual dependence. We desire what we ourselves believe to be beautiful and desirable, but at the same time our thinking about something as beautiful depends on the object to which we relate and respond. In the latter case, by realizing that the very mind that projects dreams is mistaken, one understands that the dream images are nothing more than phantoms lacking reality.[27]

In the *Rain of Ambrosia*, Shakya Chokden explicitly states that even though the direct realization of primordial mind in the Alīkākāravāda system is *not* preceded by reasoning determining primordial mind as truthless, nevertheless one *can* eliminate grasping at it as truth, which is an object of abandonment. In contrast to Niḥsvabhāvavādins, Alīkākāravādins argue that one does not have to determine by reasoning primordial mind's truthlessness in order to abandon grasping at it as true. One simply cannot do that, because primordial mind is beyond either affirmation or negation by reasoning:

> *Objection:* . . . Because that [view eliminating the two extremes] is not preceded by reasoning determining it as truthless, grasping at it as true cannot be reversed.
>
> *Answer:* That reasoning cannot determine [that view] as that [i.e., being truthless], because [that view] transcends the objects of that [reasoning. On the other hand,] grasping at truth cannot grasp at that [view] either, because [that view] transcends the objects of that [grasping]. The object of that conceptual mind which grasps at the thoroughly established [nature] as true does not transcend [being] a meaning-generality (*don spyi, arthasāmānya*) or other-exclusion of that [thoroughly established nature]. Because that [meaning-generality] is just an imaginary [nature], it has already been determined as empty of its entity.[28]

Primordial mind is beyond objects of both grasping at true existence and reasonings negating true existence. From this standpoint, it simply does not have to be negated. Also, even when a consciousness grasping at the true existence of primordial mind presumes that it takes primordial mind as its object, what it actually deals with is only a conceptual image of that primordial mind, not primordial mind itself. To put it in Yogācāra terms: when grasping at true existence attempts to take the thoroughly established nature as its object, what it ends up dealing with is only the imaginary nature.

In the *Rain of Ambrosia*, Shakya Chokden specifies that although primordial mind can be accepted as truly existent, nevertheless one does not hold it to be truly existent at the time of directly realizing it within meditative equipoise. Such acceptance, therefore, does not pose danger to the elimination of extremes through the direct realization of reality within meditative equipoise, because that realization does not apprehend reality as any extreme at all:

> *Objection:* If the thoroughly established [nature] is accepted as truth, will [such an assertion] not turn into the extreme of eternalism? How can this view eliminate the two extremes?
>
> *Answer:* There is no fault, because the view eliminating the two extremes does not have the mode of apprehension [of something] as truly established (*bden grub tu lta ba'i 'dzin stangs*), and because [the statement] "this is true" (*'di bden no*) is [only] a subsequent convention of both the view and meditation.[29]

Shakya Chokden does not see a problem in describing non-dual primordial mind as truly existent, because such a description does not necessarily indicate grasping at true existence. On the contrary, using it can be a convenient way of describing in subsequent attainment the reality one has experienced within meditative equipoise. Although meditative equipoise itself does not apprehend primordial mind as true, there is no contradiction in saying in subsequent attainment that what one has experienced in meditative equipoise is true, real, truly established, established in reality, and established as reality.

In sum, primordial mind does not necessarily have to be determined as truthless in order to reach the direct realization of truly established primordial mind which is free from grasping at primordial mind as true.

2. Primordial Mind as an Impermanent Phenomenon

If the non-dual primordial mind is the only existent thing accepted by Mādhyamikas, the question arises as to what kind of existence it has. Is it permanent or impermanent? Is it created by causes and conditions? Does it change moment by moment or not?

Answering this question is important due to the significance of the categories of permanence (*rtag pa, nitya*) and impermanence (*mi rtag pa, anitya*) in the Buddhist worldview. In general, Buddhist teachings or Dharma have four distinct characteristics called the "four seals" (*phyag rgya bzhi, caturmudrā*). The first Dharma-seal (*chos kyi phyag rgya dang po*) is described as "all compounded phenomena are impermanent" (*'dus byas thams cad mi rtag pa*).[30] At the same time, Niḥsvabhāvavādins argue that ultimately, phenomena do not have any nature, including the nature of impermanence. Treating the Niḥsvabhāvavāda position as the highest, the majority of Tibetan thinkers believe that only the "lower" tenet systems (such as Vaibhāṣika, Sautrāntika, and—for non-Geluk thinkers—Citttamātra) accept that the ultimate nature of phenomena can be impermanent. Tibetan thinkers such as Dölpopa who do *not* accept the superiority of the Niḥsvabhāvavāda view, also do not accept ultimate reality as impermanent. Thus, if any characteristics of ultimate reality taught in Mahāyāna are admitted at all, Tibetan thinkers tend to describe them as *other than* impermanence.

The dominant attitude in the Tibetan intellectual world is to treat ultimate truth either as permanent or as transcending permanence and impermanence. These two descriptions are often taken as synonymous, because the former is usually understood as permanence other than the opposite of impermanence in the permanence/impermanence pair, while the latter is understood as permanence transcending the pair of permanence and impermanence.[31] Even when different types of permanence and impermanence are listed side by side, and ultimate truth is described as primordial mind, the general tendency is to emphasize that the ultimate is permanent. For example, in his *Treatise Called 'Explanation of the Tathāgata-Essence,'* the Third Karmapa Rangjung Dorjé addresses three types of permanence which he ascribes to primordial mind, and three types of impermanence which he ascribes to stains (*dri ma*). He explains that primordial mind is permanent as a natural permanence (*rang bzhin rtag pa*), as a permanence of continuity (*rgyun gyis rtag pa*), and as having a ceaseless continuity (*rgyun mi 'chad pa*). These three are related to the dharma-body (*chos sku, dharmakāya*), the enjoyment-body (*longs sku, saṃbhogakāya*), and the emanation-body (*sprul sku, nirmāṇakāya*), respectively. Primordial mind is free from three types of impermanence: emptiness created by mind (*blo[s] byas stong pa*), fluctuating conceptual mentality (*g.yo ba'i rtog yid*), and the six collections [of consciousness that are] compounded (*tshogs drug 'dus byas*).[32] In this way, Rangjung Dorjé appears to rule out the possibility of ultimate reality being impermanent.

The acceptance of ultimate reality as permanent by Dölpopa, Tāranātha, and other thinkers is often based on a literal reading of multiple statements in the *Dharmas of Maitreya*, such as the *Sublime Continuum* and other texts that describe the ultimate as permanent, stable, and eternal. Although Shakya Chokden wholeheartedly advocates the views expounded in those texts, he does not literally accept their descriptions of reality as permanent. Instead, throughout his writings he emphasizes that primordial mind is *impermanent*. Likewise, he treats primordial mind as compounded (*'dus byas, saṃskṛta*) in the sense of undergoing production, disintegration, and abiding (*skye 'jig gnas gsum*) because of being impermanent.[33]

The explanation of primordial mind as impermanent can be seen as a trademark of Shakya Chokden's approach to reality that stands in sharp contrast to the positions of other Tibetan thinkers. As Tāranātha rightly mentioned in the *Twenty-one Differences Regarding the Profound Meaning*, differences between Shakya Chokden and Dölpopa's systems primarily arise from their approach to primordial mind which, in contrast to Dölpopa, Shakya Chokden treats as manifold (*du ma'i tshul can*) and impermanent.[34]

In my opinion, Shakya Chokden's position demonstrates his dedication to the Yogācāra system as articulated in the works of Dharmakīrti and other Buddhist logicians—another fact rightly noticed by Tāranātha, who wrote that when Shakya Chokden had taught that suchness (*de bzhin nyid*) is only an imputed uncompounded phenomenon (*'dus ma byas btags pa ba*), and so forth, he was largely in harmony with the general vocabulary of the Pramāṇa and Abhidharma texts.[35]

Shakya Chokden's approach is further supported by Sakya Pendita's *Treasure of the Science of Valid Cognition: The Root Text and the [Auto-]Commentary* that focuses on the writings of Dharmakīrti. There, Sakya Pendita explains that while permanence is accepted as substance (*rdzas, dravya*) by followers of such systems as Vaibhāṣika, Dharmakīrti simply applied the term "permanence" to a reverse of impermanence (*mi rtag pa log pa*).[36] Saying that, Sakya Pendita does not imply that permanence is a different type of existent thing that exists on a par with impermanence despite being different from it and not being a substance. Rather, Sakya Pendita's position is that in the context of Dharmakīrti's system permanence does not exist at all, because only impermanent phenomena can be functional things (*dngos po*), and because only functional things exist, as is clear from the following passage:

> What is that existent [phenomenon that is] not a functional thing? If it is able to perform a function, it will be a functional thing. If it is not able [to perform a function] it is nothing at all. Therefore, even though [it might be] named existent, it is exclusively nonexistent.[37]

Shakya Chokden accepts the final views of Dignāga with Dharmakīrti on the one hand, and Maitreya with Asaṅga on the other, as the same Alīkākāravāda system, despite their different approaches to reality. Because of that, he has no choice but to reconcile them by taking some of their statements as literal and others as requiring interpretation. In the *Golden Lancet,* he explains that in the teachings of the last four *Dharmas of Maitreya* with writings of their followers, as well as in the system of Dharmakīrti, the entity of the dharma-sphere is exclusively identified as primordial mind free from the duality of the apprehended and apprehender (*gzung 'dzin gnyis med kyi ye shes*). He continues:

> Because of that, it also has to be accepted as impermanent: because it is a functional thing, it has to be accepted as momentarily disintegrating (*skad cig gis 'jig pa*). Nevertheless, it does not contradict its being explained as permanent in other contexts: it is explained that way with the permanence of continuity (*rgyun gyi rtag pa*) in mind.[38]

Likewise, in the *Previously Unseen Sun,* he argues that when in the teachings of the third dharmacakra, the buddha-essence—which is a primordial mind too—is explained literally as permanent (*rtag pa, nitya*), stable (*brtan pa, dhruva*), and eternal (*g.yung drung, śāśvatā*),

> that is also done in terms of its continuum (*rgyun*). Otherwise, [it should] be [understood as] impermanent precisely because of having an immediately preceding condition [deriving] from [its previous] moment.[39]

Thus, despite the fact that Shakya Chokden separates primordial mind from all other phenomena, including ordinary knowing, he insists that similar to other types of knowing, primordial mind is impermanent. Because primordial mind is ultimate truth, it follows that ultimate truth is impermanent too. Even the fact that it transcends sounds and concepts does not strip it of the characteristics of impermanence. As Shakya Chokden succinctly explains in the *Enjoyment Ocean of the Speech of the 'Seven Works'*:

> *Question:* If both the apprehended and apprehender do not exist, then what remains to exist?
>
> *Answer:* What exists is only the knowing devoid of duality of the apprehended and apprehender that does not have

> momentary parts (*gzung 'dzin gnyis med kyi shes pa skad cig gi cha med*).[40]

Non-dual primordial mind, the only existent thing, is an impermanent, momentary phenomenon in the sense of lasting only for a single moment, disintegrating momentarily, and producing the next moment of a similar type, thereby maintaining the continuity of moments. The moments its continuity consists of do not have temporal parts, i.e., cannot be split into shorter moments.

This approach to primordial mind as impermanent is complicated by several factors. In the *Precious Treasury of the Condensed Essence*, Shakya Chokden himself argues that the teaching on the first Dharma-seal is the very means of establishing the emptiness of all phenomena. By explaining the meaning of impermanence as momentariness (*skad cig ma, kṣaṇika*), and demonstrating that all phenomena are impermanent, one negates their abiding (*gnas pa*) even for a moment, and by demonstrating that they do not abide anywhere proves them to be self-empty.[41] In the same text he further specifies that by this reasoning of impermanence, Dharmakīrti established all phenomena as self-empty, and this self-emptiness is not different from the self-emptiness established by Prāsaṅgika and Svātantrika.[42] Even the three characteristics of production, disintegration, and abiding of phenomena happen simultaneously according to both Dignāga and Dharmakīrti. This is because the abiding and disintegration of phenomena are the results of those very causes that brought them into existence.[43] The fact that phenomena are said to arise, abide, and vanish only supports the statement that they do not abide even for a moment without vanishing at the same time, immediately disintegrating.[44] Permanence on the other hand does not exist on the ultimate level. It is just a convention indicating a mere other-exclusion that is the reverse of impermanence (*mi rtag pa las log [pa]*).[45] When it is said that the unchangeable thoroughly established nature is permanent, stable, and eternal, it is only a way of ascribing permanence to a phenomenon whose continuity is not severed (*rgyun mi 'chad pa yi dngos po*). Otherwise, ultimate truth is doubtlessly impermanent because of being momentary.[46]

Shakya Chokden is well aware that those very texts teaching primordial mind as ultimate reality also describe it as permanent, everlasting, and unchanging. Yet, he insists that even those texts do not mean to say that it is *not* impermanent. According to him, the permanence they address is not the opposite of impermanence or momentariness. Rather, it is the permanence of continuity understood as the persisting, never-ending process of discrete moments of primordial mind produced by preceding moments and producing next moments of similar type. This permanence of continuity is just a conceptual construct imputed on the basis of preceding and succeeding moments of primordial mind. Primordial mind itself is exclusively impermanent.

A very important issue arises out of this reasoning: if, according to the followers of Dharmakīrti's system, all phenomena are established as self-empty by reason of being impermanent and momentary, why does the same not apply to primordial mind? This issue is further complicated by the fact that according to Shakya Chokden both Dharmakīrti and Maitreya are Alīkākāravādins who teach the same type of ultimate truth, the impermanent primordial mind. Is it not a direct contradiction to say that Dharmakīrti proves all phenomena to be self-empty (and therefore unreal, truthless, illusion-like and nonexistent) by reason of their impermanence, yet at the same time say that according to Dharmakīrti the impermanent primordial mind is not self-empty and is truly existent? The following passage from the *Precious Treasury of the Condensed Essence* helps untangle this puzzle:

> *Objection:* Not explaining the thoroughly established nature as true
> Contradicts Maitreya's texts.
>
> *Answer:* Even the mind-vajra does not exist in the face of analysis
> By the reasoning of listening and thinking.
> Nevertheless, it cannot be posited as nonexistent,
> Because it is beyond objects of sounds and concepts.
>
> *Objection*: Then what is the use of emphasizing
> The reasoning of self-emptiness?
> *Answer:* [It is used] in order to abandon adherence (*zhen pa*)
> To the thoroughly established nature, the mind-vajra.[47]

This passage explains that not only Niḥsvabhāvavādins, but even Dharmakīrti himself, agree that primordial mind is negated in the face of reasoning. Nevertheless, unlike Candrakīrti and Bhāviveka in their sūtric works, Dharmakīrti as a faithful Alīkākāravādin accepts the existence of primordial mind beyond sounds and concepts. Therefore, although both primordial mind and other phenomena are similar in being impermanent, no other phenomena transcend sounds and concepts—only primordial mind does so. This difference makes the condition of impermanence sufficient for proving other phenomena self-empty, but insufficient for proving primordial mind self-empty. This is somewhat similar to the difference between movies (the scope of functioning of reasoning) with animated cartoon characters (conventional phenomena) and movies with characters played by real actors (primordial mind). If the first type of character dies in the movie, one can find no "real persons" who played these characters and are still alive in "real life." If the second type of character dies in the movie, one can still find live people who enacted their death in the movie, but did not die in "reality." In other words, as long as one accepts primordial mind in the same body of texts in which he negates it, one also has to accept that such negation does not transcend the conceptual scope of reasoning and does not negate the ultimately existent primordial mind that transcends conceptuality. (This also explains why Candrakīrti and Bhāviveka in their sūtric works treat the nonexistence of all phenomena—including primordial mind—as filling the role of nonexistence. Because in those sūtric works they do not posit primordial mind transcending sounds and concepts, they treat its negation as filling the role of negation.)

This discussion leads to the following question. Primordial mind cannot be proved as self-empty, unreal, and nonexistent by reason of its impermanence. At the same time, impermanence is an inherent and real characteristic of primordial mind. Does it follow then that similar to primordial mind, impermanence itself cannot be proved as unreal and nonexistent even though it is negated in the face of reasoning? What about arguments used by Niḥsvabhāvavādins to negate partless moments of knowing along with partless atoms? This question is very important, because in the same way as primordial mind, itself, is beyond the reach of reasoning, its qualities— including impermanence, etc.—also should be beyond the reach of reasoning. All its qualities comprise a single, truly established, and real entity. If it is accepted that partless moments comprising its continuity are negatable by Madhyamaka reasoning in a manner similar to partless atoms that are "smashed into pieces" by it, then it will follow that primordial mind itself can be destroyed by reasoning.

Shakya Chokden is far from listing different characteristics of primordial mind and then simply saying that they are not negatable because, similar to primordial mind itself, they are beyond reasoning. This approach would be too simplistic. Impermanence is a very specific quality, and if it is accepted, it should be proven to be true. Otherwise, why would he accept it in the first place? In his analysis, therefore, Shakya Chokden resorts to a very subtle argument demonstrating that partless moments cannot be destroyed by the reason of the lack of being one or many.

In the *Enjoyment Ocean of the Speech of the 'Seven Works'* he emphasizes the difference between the negation of partless atoms and the negation of partless moments of knowing. He does so in the context of elaborating on the Alīkākāravāda position that only the knowing devoid of duality of the apprehended and apprehender that does not have momentary parts exists, and Alīkākāravāda's rebuttal of Niḥsvabhāvavāda's objections:

> Here, early Tibetan [thinkers][48] say: "Reasonings negating truly established atoms (*rdul phran bden grub*) and reasonings negating truly established moments (*skad cig bden grub*) are concordant." [However,] they are not concordant. This is because at the time of composing gross objects (*rags pa*), the middle particle turns out to have parts (*cha bcas*) because it is *simultaneously* surrounded by particles on the six sides. In contrast to that, because the three times are not produced simultaneously, the knowing at the present (*da lta'i shes pa*) does not have momentary parts (*skad cig gi cha med*). In that [context, I] say:
>
> It is the way of [proponents of] self-emptiness [to say that] if analyzed by conceptual analysis (*rtog dpyod*),
> The non-dual primordial mind does not remain.
> It is the system of Proponents of Other-Emptiness
> [To say that it] remains beyond [the reach of] conceptual analysis.[49]

In this passage, Shakya Chokden makes a subtle distinction between partless atoms and partless moments of knowing, explaining why the former can be negated by the reasoning of self-emptiness but the latter cannot. Non-Mahāyāna Buddhist thinkers treat partless atoms as real building blocks of external existence, while Mahāyāna thinkers use intricate reasoning for vanquishing these tiny blocks into the sphere of emptiness. Partless atoms do not withstand Madhyamaka analysis, because when they form clusters (as they always do), one and the same atom can be surrounded by neighboring atoms on all six sides. This means that one and the same atom has six different sides or directional parts that are mutually exclusive: its northern side faces only the atom on the north, not on the east, etc., its southern side faces only the southern atom, and so on. No matter how subtle the atoms are, the same reasoning can be applied to all of them. Therefore, partless atoms cannot exist.

At the same time, when dealing with partless moments of knowing, Shakya Chokden advises not to jump to the conclusion that the reasoning negating the existence of partless atoms can also negate the existence of partless moments of knowing. It cannot. This is because in order to negate partless moments of knowing by such reasoning, one has to find some other phenomena these moments are related to in order to show that they have parts. Nevertheless, unlike single atoms that can be surrounded by other atoms simultaneously, single moments of the non-dual primordial mind cannot be simultaneously surrounded by other such moments or by anything else, because the non-dual primordial mind in its present moment is the only thing that exists. Even though single moments of knowing are preceded and succeeded by other such moments, this in itself is not a sufficient reason for saying that a single moment of knowing has temporal parts that face the future and the past, and then conclude on that basis that this moment of knowing is not partless. As we know already, in Dharmakīrti's system, the production, abiding, and disintegration of momentary phenomena happen simultaneously, because they are simultaneously produced from the same preceding cause. Therefore, one cannot argue that the arising part of one moment of knowing is somehow linked with the preceding moment, while its disintegrating part faces the next moment.

Shakya Chokden's approach agrees with that of Sakya Pendita in the *Treasure of the Science of Valid Cognition*. In that text, Sakya Pendita also differentiates between two types of partless phenomena, arguing that while partless atoms can be negated by the reason of the lack of being one or many, partless moments of knowing cannot. He argues that Nāgārjunean reasoning negating temporal partlessness by treating the three moments together can indeed negate assertions of those śrāvakas who assert the three times as substantially existent (*rdzas yod, dravyasat*). Nevertheless, it does not apply to the systems that do not accept the future and past as substantially existent. Sakya Pendita argues that the negation of momentary knowing in that context is similar to destroying a pot (the present moment) between two rabbit horns (future and past moments).[50] It should be noted, however, that Sakya Pendita makes these statements in the context of explaining Cittamātra's rebuttal of objections leveled at it by Niḥsvabhāvavādins, and they do not necessarily reflect his own position.

According to Shakya Chokden, although Niḥsvabhāvavādins argue that on the level of determining emptiness by reasoning they negate even primordial mind through negating partless moments of knowing, Alīkākāravādins do not agree with that. Instead, they show why the non-dual primordial mind is beyond the reach of reasoning that negates indestructible moments of knowing. According to Alīkākāravādins, partless moments of primordial mind are real and ultimately existent, and cannot be negated by demonstrating that they have parts. It is permissible to accept these very subtle partless moments as truly established building blocks of existence. Even more: they *are* existence itself, because nothing else exists.

It should be noted that even though Shakya Chokden says that the reasonings negating partless atoms and partless moments of knowing are not concordant, it does not mean that the reason of the lack of being one or many cannot negate both partless atoms and partless moments of knowing *in the face of that reasoning*. In other words, similar to splitting atoms into spatial parts, it is possible to mentally split moments of knowing into temporal parts, thereby negating those moments as partless. Nevertheless, here lies a very subtle and crucial distinction: according to the Dharmakīrtean system as Shakya Chokden understands it, although moments of knowing can be mentally divided into parts that face the future and the past, in reality such does not happen, because production, abiding, and disintegration of those moments are simultaneous. On the other hand, atoms' parts are not only conceptually conceived but would exist in reality if they were accepted. Similar to tables, mountains, etc., atomic parts too would have sides facing in different directions. Since the spatial qualities of subtle atoms and gross matter are the same, they are only imaginary, because both subtle and gross matter do not exist. Therefore, their falsity can be exposed through the application of the reason of the lack of being one or many, and all of them can be completely negated as unreal. In contrast to that, the temporal qualities of subtle moments of knowing and temporal "chunks" of gross impermanence are not the same. The former are not imaginary, while the latter are. The former do not undergo the imaginary threefold process of *successive* production, abiding and disintegration while the latter do. Therefore, although mental moments, similar to phenomena extended in space and time, can be split into parts through reasoning, this splitting does not render those moments unreal and nonexistent.

In Shakya Chokden's opinion, Dharmakīrti—along with Candrakīrti and Bhāviveka—agrees that everything, including primordial mind, can be negated in the face of reasoning. Nevertheless, he disagrees with them on the question of whether this negation entails the nonexistence of all phenomena including primordial mind and its impermanence. Because in their sūtric works Candrakīrti and Bhāviveka do not accept truly existent primordial mind, its negation through mentally splitting its moments into parts is viewed as an actual negation. Dharmakīrti, on the other hand, accepts primordial mind that transcends sounds and concepts. Therefore, according to Dharmakīrti, as Shakya Chokden understands him, the negation of primordial mind and the negation of its impermanence are adequate in the face of reasoning only. Conceptual reasoning does not reach this truly existent, luminous, and self-cognizing entity that lasts only for a single, partless, but real moment.

3. (Un)linking the Self-Cognizing Primordial Mind and Dualistic Consciousness

One of the most complicated issues involved in Shakya Chokden's description of primordial mind as ultimate reality is his explanation of it as self-cognition. The fact that he treats primordial mind as self-cognition in itself is not surprising, especially in the context of Sakya thinkers' treatment of all minds as self-cognition. As Sakya Pendita explains in the *Treasure of the Science of Valid Cognition*, minds are divided into different types in terms of their objects, modes of engagement in those objects, and other factors; but "in terms of knowing (*shes pa*), [minds are just] one self-cognition."[51] Sakya Pendita further explains that all types of knowing or mind are subsumed under the category of self-cognition.[52] In other words, in the Sakya system articulated by Sakya Pendita, minds do not just *have* self-cognitions distinct from but accompanying and cognizing those minds. Minds *are* self-cognitions.

Shakya Chokden fully embraces this approach, assigning it a special significance in the context of his treatment of primordial mind as the only existent phenomenon: because only primordial mind exists, cognition of primordial mind also has to be performed by primordial mind. Ultimate reality itself, therefore, is self-cognizing. Because its continuity is not created anew and has always existed, *all* beings have this self-cognizing quality inseparable from their mental streams. Ultimate reality has always been and will always be there, both prior to its direct realization by ārya bodhisattvas on the Mahāyāna path of seeing and after that, all the way through to buddhahood.

The following question arises: if self-cognition is both the ultimate nature of everyone's mind and the self-experiencing quality of mind, will it not absurdly follow that this ultimate mind itself experiences sufferings, dualistic appearances, afflictions, and all other factors that pertain to consciousness? Answering this question in the *Previously Unseen Sun*, Shakya Chokden reiterates that according to *all* Mādhyamikas no subjective and objective things exist:

> Starting from Alīkākāravāda Mādhyamikas, [all Mādhyamikas] have to explain the "non-duality of the apprehended and apprehender" as [their own] tenets. Therefore, [in that context] the apprehender is not accepted even as a functional thing (*dngos po*), how much less as knowing.[53]

Because primordial mind is the only existent thing, the possibility of its experiencing sufferings that are projected by dualistic minds does not apply. Dualistic minds appearing as sufferings are unreal and nonexistent, while primordial mind cognizes only what is real and existent. There is simply no chance for primordial mind to cognize sufferings: neither does it cognize sufferings through self-projecting them nor through experiencing consciousness that is their creator.

Although consciousness with its appearances does not exist, it does appear as existent, and it has kept us in cyclic existence from beginningless time. If consciousness and primordial mind are put side by side, how would one describe their relation to each other, imaginary as it is? In the *Previously Unseen Sun*, Shakya Chokden explains their relationship as follows:

> Every phenomenon of a mistaken consciousness has the factor of the inward-looking primordial mind [related with it]. Nevertheless, it is impossible for the clarity factor of primordial mind (*ye shes kyi gsal cha*) to become the entity (*ngo bo*) of consciousness, and it is also impossible for that [entity of consciousness] to become that [clarity factor of primordial mind]. Otherwise, it would follow that primordial mind is an experiencer (*myong ba po*) of worldly pleasures and sufferings. [Also,] it would follow that those unreal ideations (*yang dag pa ma yin pa'i kun tu rtog pa, abhūtaparikalpa*) that bear the name of consciousness, are the very basis of accomplishment of all stainless positive qualities. Without that original primordial mind (*gdod ma'i ye shes*), adventitious consciousness (*blo bur gyi rnam shes*) does not emerge as mistaken appearances. Nevertheless,

> the possibility of a common locus (*gzhi mthun*) of the two is not asserted. [Rather, they are] similar to clouds in the sky, oxide (*g.ya*) on gold, and dirt (*rnyog pa*) in pure water.[54]

The split between primordial mind and consciousness could not have been demonstrated more sharply. Shakya Chokden does not want to allow any mixture of the two.[55] Until the time when all traces of consciousness vanish forever, the two exist side by side as two polarities that never mix to assume the same nature. Clouds and sky never become one, nor rust and gold, nor even dirt and water. They can coexist, but can never completely blend. Even their coexistence is not a coexistence of equals. It is the coexistence of the everlasting entity with unalterable—albeit impermanent—nature and a temporary, adventitious, ephemeral entity. The former continues forever, while the latter is an apparition that is ready to vanish and never reappear when conditions are right. This is similar to clouds disappearing from the sky, rust being removed from gold, and water being purified of dirt.

Note that in the above passage Shakya Chokden says that the clarity factor of primordial mind cannot become or turn into the entity of consciousness, that is, the thoroughly established nature cannot assume the entity of the dependent nature. At the same time, as has been explained previously (134 ff.), he argues that the dependent nature has the entity of the thoroughly established nature, that is, the thoroughly established nature is the entity of the dependent nature. The two statements should not be taken as contradictory, because the former is meant to indicate that the two natures cannot become a single entity, while the latter indicates that one nature has or possesses the other without the two becoming one.

One might object that if primordial mind and consciousness do not assume each other's nature, and the factor of clarity is an exclusive quality of primordial mind only, it will follow that consciousness lacks the first of its two defining characteristics: clarity and cognition (*gsal zhing rig pa*). In that case, its second characteristic will be impossible also. If such is the case, then what makes it different from inanimate matter?

> *Objection:* If consciousness's own entity is not accepted as clarity and cognition (*gsal rig*), then it will not cognize objects because of [having absurdly turned into inanimate] matter.
>
> *Answer:* No [such] absurd consequence will apply [here]: in general, it is accepted that although consciousness is not established by valid cognition, because of a mistake it is

> only superimposed (*sgro btags*) as existent. It is not accepted even as existent—how much less a cognition—precisely because it is a relative truth.[56]

In his answer, Shakya Chokden once again emphasizes that consciousness does not exist. It does not exist because it is a relative truth. Only ultimate truth, the non-dual primordial mind exists. If the dualistic consciousness existed, then without the qualities of clarity and cognition it would indeed become a piece of inanimate matter. Nevertheless, since it does not exist, the question whether it is clear and cognizing simply does not apply. We could say that the opponent's objection therefore is similar to arguing that if a son of a barren woman did not have male organs, he would be no different from his sister.

If primordial mind and consciousness are so sharply separated, then why should we accept any relationship between the two at all? Why do we need to refer back to primordial mind in order to explain the arising of mistaken appearances?

> *Objection:* In that case, since mistakes have no basis, mistaken appearances will be produced even without reliance on primordial mind.
>
> *Answer:* No. This is like, [for example,] if there is no cairn (*mtho yor*), concepts grasping [at it] as a human will not arise. Without the originally established primordial mind (*gdod ma nas grub pa'i ye shes*), mistaken appearances do not arise. The factors of the inward-looking apprehender-aspect (*kha nang blta 'dzin rnam gyi cha*) of mistaken appearances are definitely present as the original primordial mind. . . .[57] [The relationship between the inward-looking and outward-looking factors] is similar to the following example: without space (*nam mkha'*), appearances of pots, houses, etc., do not arise. Yet, space itself has not turned into the entity of pots, etc.[58]

Mistaken appearances, nonexistent as they are, do need some referent. They are not no-things arising out of *no*thing. Rather, they are no-things arising out of *some*thing, and that *some*thing is the space-like primordial mind. Primordial mind does not *create* mistaken appearances, but it is needed for those appearances to take place. Similar to a physical space providing space for material objects, primordial mind too provides space for the arising of consciousness.

4. Does Self-Cognition Cognize Itself?

Shakya Chokden's position that primordial mind is self-cognition and ultimate truth—both of which are self-cognizing—entails yet another problematic question: because everybody has primordial mind, will it not absurdly follow that all of us realize ultimate truth?

Answering this question, he argues that self-cognition does not necessarily imply realization of itself. Although primordial mind is self-cognizing, it does not necessarily realize (*rtogs*) itself. Primordial mind does experience (*myong*) itself. Nevertheless, only when it becomes able to induce ascertainment (*nges pa 'dren pa*) of that experience can one say that it realizes itself. Such is a general answer given by Shakya Chokden, as the passages cited below demonstrate. This distinction helps him explain why all beings experience ultimate reality, but not all of them realize it.

What is the meaning of self-cognition then? Does self-cognition necessarily imply cognizing itself? Shakya Chokden addresses this question in the *Sevenfold Treasury of Gems*:

> *Question:* If ultimate truth on the level of the basis (*gzhi dus kyi don dam bden pa*)[59] is accepted as primordial mind, will it not follow that short-sighted ones (*tshur rol mthong ba*) too directly see ultimate truth and the sugata-essence?
>
> *Answer:* On the level of short-sighted ones, the convention of "self-cognition" is applied to [the mind] itself being merely produced as an entity of clarity (*gsal ba'i ngo bo*). Nevertheless, because [such mind] is not able to induce ascertainment (*nges pa 'dren*) of that [clarity], it is not said that it cognizes itself by itself (*rang gis rang rig pa*). On the other hand, because on the [Mahāyāna] ārya grounds (*'phags pa'i sa*), [the mind] can induce ascertainment of that, it is described as the "object of functioning of individually self-cognizing primordial mind" (*so so rang gis rig pa'i ye shes kyi spyod yul*).[60]

In this passage, Shakya Chokden explains that "self-cognition" does not necessarily mean "cognizing itself by itself." It can be said that primordial mind cognizes itself by itself only when primordial mind itself is able to induce ascertainment of the act of self-cognizing.

It should be noted that according to Sakya Pendita (as well as Shakya Chokden, who follows him), *all* forms of direct perception (*mngon sum, pratyakṣā*)—including self-cognition—by definition cannot ascertain (*nges pa*) their objects. Sakya Pendita, for example, argues against positing "that which has an appearance but does not ascertain it" (*snang la ma nges*) as a separate category of mental phenomena, arguing that all direct perceptions fall into this category. Shakya Chokden shares this view.[61]

Shakya Chokden argues that primordial mind in the mental streams of ordinary beings (the "short-sighted ones") is not able to induce ascertainment of the act of self-cognizing. This is why it is not accepted that those beings realize ultimate truth. Starting from the Mahāyāna path of seeing, primordial mind in the mental streams of Mahāyāna āryas can induce that ascertainment. This is why it is said that Mahāyāna āryas realize ultimate truth, and this is when the term "object of functioning of individually self-cognizing primordial mind" can start being applied to primordial mind. This is also the reason why Shakya Chokden insists that one can see the buddha-essence only starting from the first bodhisattva ground, not earlier.

Similarly, in the *Vajra Shortcut: Disputes about Common Appearances of Ordinary Beings and Āryas in Seventeen Dharma Sections*, Shakya Chokden explains:

> In the great writings of the author of the *Commentary [on Valid Cognition]*
> It is clearly taught that the primordial mind of the basis (*gzhi dus [kyi] ye shes*)
> Is experienced by the apprehender-aspect itself.
> But in the *Sublime Continuum*, [Maitreya] described
> Four types [of individuals]—ordinary beings, etc.—
> Who do not have eyes seeing the sugata-essence.
> [He did it] with the thought that they do not ascertain that [primordial mind].[62]

This passage also shows that self-cognition according to Shakya Chokden is the self-experiencing mind. In his opinion, both Maitreya and Dharmakīrti agree that even primordial mind that exists on the level of the basis is self-cognition that experiences itself. Nevertheless, according to Maitreya, such experience is not counted as cognition, realization, or seeing of the buddha-essence, because it does not induce ascertainment of itself. The buddha-essence is realized only from the first bodhisattva ground. Mahāyāna āryas are able to induce ascertainment of the self-cognition of primordial mind, and this is why the terms "seeing the buddha-essence" and "realizing the buddha-essence" can be applied. They cannot be applied before that level because other beings—including those with great desires (*'dod chen, icchantika*), heretics (*mu stegs, tīrthika*), śrāvakas, and pratyekabuddhas[63]—are not able to induce ascertainment of that self-cognizing primordial mind. To say that primordial mind realizes itself by itself and yet only Mahāyāna āryas see the buddha-essence will be contradictory in that context.

Elaborating on the question of experience versus realization and cognition of primordial mind, Shakya Chokden writes in the *Precious Treasury of the Condensed Essence*:

> *Objection:* Because the luminous nature of mind
> Is cognized by self-experiencing valid cognition (*rang myong tshad ma*),[64]
> It follows that all migrating beings realize
> Their own essence.
>
> *Response:* Nobody but Mahāyāna āryas
> Have the luminous nature of mind that,
> Having experienced itself by itself (*rang gis rang nyid nyams myong*),
> [Can] induce ascertainment of that [experience].[65]

Although luminous mind experiences itself, on the level below the Mahāyāna path of seeing it cannot induce ascertainment of that experience. Therefore, although ordinary beings do experience ultimate reality, they neither cognize nor realize it.[66] Mahāyāna āryas, on the other hand, cognize and realize it, because their experience of ultimate reality also can induce its ascertainment.

The following debate ensues, most probably hypothetically:

> *Objection:* Then it follows that one's own mind
> Is a hidden phenomenon (*lkog (tu) gyur (pa), parokṣa*) for oneself.
>
> *Response:* Because that very luminous mind
> Is direct valid cognition (*mngon sum tshad ma, pratyakṣapramāṇa*) of itself,
> It does not follow that one's own mind
> Is a hidden phenomenon for oneself.

Objection: If [a mind] is a direct valid cognition of something
It contradicts its not realizing that something.

Response: The author of the *Commentary on Valid Cognition* [Dharmakīrti] explained that
Although all direct perceptions (*mngon sum, pratyakṣa*) are valid cognitions (*tshad [ma], pramāṇa*)
Of their own objects of engagement (*'jug pa'i yul*),
There is no certainty that they realize those [objects of engagement].[67]

Using the distinction between hidden phenomena (*lkog gyur, parokṣa*) versus manifest phenomena (*mngon gyur, pratyakṣa*), Shakya Chokden's opponent argues that if the mind does not realize something, that something will be a hidden phenomenon for that mind. Applying this reasoning to primordial mind itself, he argues that if self-cognition does not realize itself, it will absurdly follow that self-cognition is hidden from itself. Shakya Chokden neither agrees with his opponent nor changes his position that self-cognition of ordinary beings does not realize itself. His response is that self-cognition is *not* a hidden phenomenon for itself, because it is the direct valid cognition of itself. This puzzles his opponent even more: he sees as contradictory that a mind can be a valid cognition of something without realizing that something. Disagreeing with him once again, Shakya Chokden appeals to the authoritative position of Dharmakīrti that he describes as follows: although direct perceptions are valid cognitions of their own object of engagement, they do not necessarily have to realize that object. Thereby, he firmly holds the same ground: to be a valid cognition of something, the mind does not have to realize that something, and therefore, to be self-cognition, the mind does not have to realize itself.

The opponent now asks the already familiar question:

Objection: Not cognizing itself by itself
Contradicts being self-cognition.

Response: If luminous mind became (*song*) nonconceptual (*rtog [pa] dang bral [ba], kalpanāpoḍha*)
And non-mistaken (*ma 'khrul ba, abhrānta*) with respect to something,

> [It has to be] a direct perception of that something.
> And that is none other than self-cognition.
> [Nevertheless,] making oneself an object is not feasible
> For self-cognition in general.
> In particular, in [Sakya Pendita's] *Treasure of the Science of Valid Cognition*, it is explained
> That non-dual primordial mind does not have an object.
> Also in general, in Mahāyāna it is explained that
> The [meaning of the] "individual self-cognition"
> Is [the mind] itself being merely born as cognition,
> With nothing else to realize (*rtogs bya*).[68]

Shakya Chokden's opponent believes that it is contradictory to be self-cognition and yet not to cognize itself. Obviously, he takes the term "self-cognition" to necessarily mean "cognition of itself." According to the opponent, this in turn implies that primordial mind has an object, i.e., takes itself as an object.[69] Shakya Chokden disagrees: to accept such an approach would contradict the position of Sakya Pendita that he takes as authoritative.[70] This position is outlined in the *Treasure of the Science of Valid Cognition*, where Sakya Pendita explains that self-cognition does not have an object, and is not split into a subject and an object. Objects of self-cognition are merely imputed (*btags pa ba*).[71] Also in the same text, Sakya Pendita explains:

> Self-cognition also is not a self-cognition in a way of separation into what is cognized and cognizer; being merely produced as cognition through being the reverse of matter is [what is understood as] that very [self-cognition].[72]

Further elaborating on this approach, in the *Enjoyment Ocean of the Speech of the 'Seven Works'* Shakya Chokden explains that according to both Alīkākāravāda and Satyākāravāda, self-cognition does not have an object. In the Alīkākāravāda system in particular, self-cognition does not have an object because it is devoid of both the apprehended and apprehender.[73]

Therefore, according to Shakya Chokden, when it is said that the mind is self-cognition, it means that the mind involves direct perception with respect to itself. What this means in turn is that it is luminous, nonconceptual, and non-mistaken with respect to itself. It does not have to cognize or realize itself to be self-cognition. To put it differently: the mind is self-cognition with respect to something when it is produced as a luminous, nonconceptual, and non-mistaken entity with respect to that. Because only self-cognition exists, self-cognition is self-cognition with respect to itself. Thus, the meaning of "self-cognition" he advocates in this context can be described as "itself as cognition" instead of "cognition of itself."

In Shakya Chokden's opinion, even the individual self-cognition taught in Mahāyāna does not imply cognition of itself. It simply means the bare luminous and cognizing entity totally free from anything else to realize. By extension, even the meaning of the "object of functioning of individually self-cognizing primordial mind" mentioned in the passage from the *Sevenfold Treasury of Gems* above (242) does not mean that primordial mind becomes its own object when one becomes a Mahāyāna ārya. Similar to the object of engagement of primordial mind, its object of functioning does not have to be taken as its object.

It should be noted that according to Shakya Chokden even ordinary beings can *see* (*mthong*) ultimate reality directly on certain occasions. This happens by the power of meditation, tantric empowerments, and so forth. In the *Ornament of Intents of Quintessential Instructions: Answers to the Questions from [Tsongkhapa's] 'Questions [Based on] Purely White Supreme Motivation,'* Shakya Chokden says: "Although in general, ordinary beings do not have yogic direct perception, [they can] have a direct seeing of the mode of being (*gnas lugs mngon sum du mthong ba*)."[74] Shakya Chokden cannot accept that this direct seeing of ultimate reality is yogic direct perception, because it would absurdly follow that ordinary beings who have that seeing are Mahāyāna āryas. (Only Mahāyāna āryas have direct yogic perception realizing ultimate reality according to Shakya Chokden.) At the same time, this direct seeing is more than just an experience of primordial mind that is always open to everyone. The category of direct seeing, therefore, helps accommodate those experiences of primordial mind that exceed its automatic self-experience, but which are neither conceptual understanding of the ultimate nor its direct realization.

To summarize: primordial mind, both on the level before and after the first bodhisattva ground, is ultimate truth and self-cognition. It is valid cognition and direct perception with respect to itself. It also experiences itself. Nevertheless, prior to the first bodhisattva ground, it does not cognize or realize itself, although it can directly see itself on certain occasions. What distinguishes primordial mind on the two levels is the ability to induce ascertainment of itself by itself. One acquires this ability only from the first bodhisattva ground, not earlier. None of these distinctions affects the fact that primordial mind does not take itself as its own object, because it is devoid of the subjective-objective duality of the apprehended and apprehender.

The statement that self-cognition does not necessarily mean "cognition of itself" is somewhat problematized, given that in other texts Shakya Chokden argues that in general minds *do* cognize themselves by themselves. For example, in the *Essence of Logic: Condensed Thatness of [Dignāga's] 'Sūtra on Valid Cognition' and [Dharmakīrti's] Textual System of 'Seven Works,'* he accepts as his own system (*rang lugs*) the approach of early Tibetans who taught that "all minds each have the clarity and cognition part that is not altered by objects; merely because of having it, all minds cognize themselves by themselves."[75] Nevertheless, in this passage he does not include "self-cognition" in the category of "all minds." Furthermore, the statement is made in the context of the Dharmakīrtean system wherein, according to Shakya Chokden, one proceeds through increasingly subtle levels of analysis, accepting cognition of the apprehended-aspect by the apprehender-aspect, but then refuting it and asserting only the apprehender-aspect stripped of everything else. The expression "all minds" implies that Shakya Chokden is not talking about the most subtle level of self-cognition. In other words, in the Dharmakīrtean system it is permissible to accept that all minds cognize themselves *before* moving to the most subtle level of primordial mind per se.

Likewise, in the *Ocean of Scriptural Statements and Reasoning*, Shakya Chokden writes: "In general, if it is not possible for a knowing to cognize itself by itself, it will follow that the omniscient primordial mind (*thams cad mkhyen pa'i ye shes*) is not the object of functioning of only the omniscient primordial mind."[76] In this context, the statement about the omniscient primordial mind cognizing itself is made specifically to demonstrate that even Candrakīrti can accept self-cognition on the conventional level. It does not entail that self-cognition itself necessarily cognizes itself. Nor should the statement be seen as expressing Candrakīrti's own system. As I have mentioned above (203), Shakya Chokden himself argues that "both Candra[kīrti] and Bhāviveka zealously refuted the individually self-cognizing primordial mind together with its objects of functioning."

I conclude, therefore, that according to Shakya Chokden, in the systems of both Candrakīrti and Dharmakīrti the assertion that minds cognize themselves by themselves is made in a context where the ultimate reality of their own systems is *not* posited. When it is posited, Dharmakīrti (and other Alīkākāravādins) accept it as self-cognition, but do not necessarily accept it as the cognition of itself by itself. Candrakīrti does not accept it at all. Depending on context, Shakya Chokden also either focuses on self-cognition as the ultimate nature and rebuttal of objections regarding the ultimate nature cognizing itself, or deals with the question of self-cognition in general. Those context-dependent explanations should not be treated as contradictory.

Despite these contextually-dependent readings of the word "self-cognition," Shakya Chokden makes clear that self-cognition *does* imply experience of itself. He also makes clear that it *does not* necessarily imply realization of itself. He emphasizes the exclusiveness and uniqueness of primordial mind. He presents it as the entity that *is* separated *from* all phenomena other than itself. It is also the entity that is *not* separated *into* other phenomena of subjects and objects.

5. Primordial Mind as the Bridge between Yogācāra and Tantra

Primordial Mind as the Focus of All Mahāyāna Paths

As the preceding discussion has made clear, Shakya Chokden treats the realization of primordial mind as the quintessence of the practice of meditative equipoise in all Mahāyāna systems. This is true for both sūtric and tantric traditions. According to him, primordial mind is the only reality, while everything else does not exist, and appears to exist only due to ignorance. How then can illusionary states of mind rooted in ignorance completely eliminate illusions? Success here, we might say, is about as likely as managing to pull oneself up by one's own bootstraps.[77] It is only primordial mind, therefore, that can serve as the foundation of the path, can become the path, and finally can transform into the result of the path, buddhahood.

Different approaches to utilizing primordial mind in non-tantric Mahāyāna practice have been treated in detail above.[78] In the following passages, I will show how, with the help of the familiar terminology of the apprehended-/apprehender-aspects, Shakya Chokden describes the way of utilizing primordial mind in the practice of the two stages (*rim pa gnyis, dvikrama*) of the Highest Yoga Tantra (*bla med kyi ryud, anuttarayogatantra*)—the generation stage (*bskyed pa'i rim pa, utpattikrama*) and the completion stage (*rdzogs pa'i rim pa, saṃpannakrama*)—and extends it to Mahāyāna practice in general. He writes in the *Previously Unseen Sun*:

> The factors of the inward-looking apprehender-aspect of mistaken appearances are definitely present as the original

> primordial mind. When followers of Secret Mantra [apply] skillful means of utilizing afflictions and concepts as the path, those present [inward-looking factors] initially [serve as] the basis of accomplishment of the generation and completion stages; in the middle, they spontaneously become (*lhun gyis grub*) the very entity (*ngo bo nyid*) of those two [stages; finally,] the outward-looking factors of the objects of abandonment subside by themselves (*rang zhi*) and are purified by themselves (*rang dag*) like clouds dissolving into the sky. The outward-looking factors do not have to be abandoned by utilizing them as the path separately from those inward-looking [factors] that have become the very entity of the generation and completion stages.[79]

Shakya Chokden shows that primordial mind persists throughout all levels of the basis, path, and result. Similar to the way it allows mistaken appearances to arise like clouds appearing in the sky, it also allows them to disappear like clouds disappearing from the sky. It is also the only tool that finally makes them completely vanish, and the only phenomenon left after all mistaken appearances disappear in the state of buddhahood.

Tantric and non-tantric Mahāyāna practices that do not directly focus on primordial mind also "make sense" because they are linked to it in the way of the apprehended-/apprehender-aspects. In the *Thorough Establishment of the Glorious Original Buddha*, Shakya Chokden demonstrates it in the context of practicing the body maṇḍala (*lus kyi dkyil 'khor*) of Cakrasaṃvara that consists of meditation on tantric deities visualized within the practitioner's body. He explains that the mind meditating on the body as the divine maṇḍala is a conceptual mind. Nevertheless, that mind has two aspects: the consciousness factor of the outward-looking apprehended-aspect (*phyir blta gzung rnam rnam shes kyi cha*) and the primordial mind factor of the inward-looking apprehender-aspect (*nang blta 'dzin rnam ye shes kyi cha*). The conventional mind meditating on the body maṇḍala is connected to primordial mind in the way of the apprehended-/apprehender-aspects. Due to this connection, the meditation on the conventional maṇḍala brings about the manifestation of the ultimate maṇḍala that is none other than the apprehender-aspect, primordial mind.[80] When the habituation of the mind to the body maṇḍala has been completed, the following result is achieved:

> [T]he outward-looking stain factor (*phyi blta dri ma'i cha*) subsides by itself, and with the inward-looking primordial

> mind factor (*nang blta ye shes kyi cha*) one manifests that which is described as "having become the ultimate maṇḍala and the [ultimate] buddha." Not only [in] this [context, but in general too], the way of purifying all stains of consciousness is like that.[81]

In this way, Shakya Chokden demonstrates that primordial mind is the very focus of both sūtric and tantric practice. It is what Mahāyāna practice is related to, aimed at, comes down to, and utilizes. This primordial mind exists from beginningless time as the underlying reality of all phenomena. It is the basis of cyclic existence, nirvāṇa, and the path out of cyclic existence into nirvāṇa. Nevertheless, while in the case of cyclic existence it simply provides space for mistaken appearances to occur, in the case of the path it becomes its very entity.

According to Shakya Chokden, the fact that both Alīkākāravāda and Tantra provide similar descriptions of primordial mind and explicitly focus on it in practice brings them close to each other, while distancing them from those Niḥsvabhāvavāda systems that do not do it. This is why in the *Lamp of Dharma Eliminating Obscurity with regard to Engaging in Mantra: Seventeen Textual Sections* he says:

> In the uncommon Mantra texts (*sngags gzhung*),
> There are no any explanations
> Of objects of experience by the view
> That are not in agreement with Maitreya's texts.[82]

As was explained earlier (186 ff.), what is treated as the object of experience in Maitreya's texts and other Yogācāra Madhyamaka writings is none other than the non-dual primordial mind.

Sūtric teachings on primordial mind are far from being mere preliminaries for realizing the tantric view, as Shakya Chokden makes clear in the following passage from the *Appearance of the Sun*:

> These definitive meanings determined by the author of the *Seven Works* [Dharmakīrti] have originated precisely from the chariot way determined by the foremost venerable Maitreya. Also, they are not just an entrance to Mahāyāna in general and Secret Mantra in particular, but are the final root of the central pillar of the Vajrayāna path (*rdo rje theg pa'i lam gyi gzhung shing du gyur pa'i rtsa ba mthar thug pa*).[83]

The Alīkākāravāda view taught in the works of Dharmakīrti and Maitreya is not only the entrance and link to the tantric views and practices, but it is the door to Mahāyāna teachings in general, and it is incorporated into practices of the tantric path as its central element. The pivotal role of primordial mind could not have been expressed more sharply.

Note that Shakya Chokden focuses specifically on the Highest Yoga Tantra when discussing similarities between the views of Alīkākāravāda and Tantra. The discussion below also follows this pattern.

Different but Concordant Approaches to Primordial Mind in Alīkākāravāda and Tantra

Shakya Chokden is not alone in his efforts to bring sūtric and tantric teachings together. Tibetans became interested in the issue of matching sūtric and tantric systems during the period of the early dissemination of Buddhism, no doubt inspired by precedents found in Indian teachings. The reconciliatory approach to sūtras and tantras became a dominant tendency among Tibetan thinkers starting from the eleventh century, after the Indian master Atiśa had been invited to Tibet, allegedly for the very purpose of working out the ways to reconcile the two systems.

In the Sakya tradition in particular, the approach to the views of sūtras and tantras is well articulated by Sakya Pendita in his *Thorough Differentiation of the Three Types of Vows*:

> If there were a view higher than Pāramitā[yāna]
> View of] freedom from proliferations,
> That view would have proliferations.
> If it is free from proliferations, there is no difference [between the two].
> Therefore, the view [arisen from] listening
> Understood through explanation is only one [for both systems].
> Nevertheless, Secret Mantra is superior in terms of
> Means of realizing freedom from proliferations.[84]

Although seemingly straightforward, this passage provides ample space for a creative explanation. An obvious way to comment on the first four lines is to say that they indicate a lack of difference in the "object" realized by followers of sūtras and tantras, because both systems teach it as a total freedom from the proliferations of being/nonbeing, existence/nonexistence, and so forth. Thereby, shifting the focus of the sūtric/tantric distinction away from the "object," one can emphasize that their difference lies in different ways of realizing that "object."[85] Because Tantra—and more specifically Highest Yoga Tantra—teaches an uncommon "subject" such as the great bliss (*bde ba chen po, mahāsukha*) arisen from empowerments (*dbang, abhiṣeka*) that realizes that common "object," Tantra is superior to non-tantric Mahāyāna systems.

Shakya Chokden approaches the issue of superiority of tantric teachings over sūtric from two different angles. In his *Rain of Ambrosia*, providing an explanation similar to the one above, he explains in what way the tantric view surpasses that of both Alīkākāravāda Yogācāra and Niḥsvabhāvavāda Madhyamaka:

> The term "view" is explained as the object, freedom from proliferations (*yul spros bral*), and [it is] explained as the subject, primordial mind (*yul can ye shes*). From among the two, in terms of the former, no view superior to that is explained in Mantra (*sngags*), but in terms of the latter, [the tantric view is] establied as superior to the former [i.e., the Yogācāra view]. This is because [in Tantra] the subject, supremely unchangeable bliss (*yul can mchog tu mi 'gyur ba'i bde ba*), experiences that very object, primordial mind free of proliferations (*yul spros bral gyi ye shes*).[86]

In this passage, Shakya Chokden argues that although the objective view in sūtric and tantric teachings is the same, tantric systems are superior in terms of presenting an uncommon subject, supremely unchangeable bliss. Such subject and the means of its utilization are taught only in Tantra. As has been mentioned above (198), Shakya Chokden distinguishes between two types of freedom from proliferations: non-affirming negation and primordial mind (which is an affirming negation). In the quote above it is the latter, as it is made clear by the passage, its context, and by Shakya Chokden's basic position that non-affirming negations are objects of concepts only.

In the *Wish Fulfilling Meru*, on the other hand, Shakya Chokden draws the reader's attention to the two lines from the *Thorough Differentiation of the Three Types of Vows* passage cited above:

> Therefore, the view [arisen from] listening
> Understood through explanation is only one [for both systems].

He argues that what Sakya Pendita asserts as one is that which is determined by listening and thinking (*thos bsam gyis gtan la dbab bya*), not that which is experienced (*nyams su myong bya*).[87] In other words, that passage shows that it is only the views conceptually formulated on the basis of intellectual study of the Buddhist teachings that are "just one" in sūtras and tantras. The tantric view realized in meditation is different from the sūtric one precisely because this view, and not just the means of realizing it, has to be produced by empowerments and other uncommon tantric means. It is this view that makes Tantra more efficient, resulting in—among other things—the achievement of buddhahood in a single lifetime. Note that freedom from proliferations in this context is treated as the object of concepts only (i.e., the first of the two types of freedom from proliferations mentioned above (198)).

Despite different ways of addressing the views of sūtras and tantras, it is clear that Shakya Chokden treats the tantric view as superior to the sūtric view *both* when the view is artificially split into subjective and objective parts, *and* when it is treated as a single unit. In either way, he achieves the same point of showing the superiority of the tantric view over the sūtric. Due to the special features of this view, he puts it into a separate category of Madhyamaka.

As I have demonstrated in Chapter 3 section 2, he classifies as Madhyamaka only those systems that have the ability to completely eliminate all extremes, thereby providing sufficient means for achieving buddhahood. Because Buddhist tantric teachings provide such means, he also classifies them as Madhyamaka. According to him, sūtras and tantras are overall in agreement regarding the identification of the ultimate view as primordial mind. Nevertheless, he considers the tantric system in general, and its view of primordial mind in particular, superior to the sūtric system. To use the above distinction: although the "objective" primordial mind described in sūtras and tantras is the same, the "subjective" primordial mind taught in tantras is more profound. In other words, although practitioners of both sūtric Madhyamaka and Tantra realize the same primordial mind in meditative equipoise, tantric practitioners realize it with the primordial mind produced through uncommon tantric means, while sūtric practitioners do not.

As a result of this reasoning, Shakya Chokden counts tantric Madhyamaka as a third type of Madhyamaka. As he states in the *Thorough Clarification of Vajradhara's Intent*:

> In general, there are three types of Madhyamaka:
> Two types of Madhyamaka emerged from the two
> chariot ways
> [Opened by Asaṅga and Nāgārjuna], and that of Mantra.[88]

In the *Wish Fulfilling Meru*, he describes these three as "Madhyamaka with the Approach of Entitylessness of All Phenomena" (*chos thams cad ngo bo nyid med pa'i tshul can gyi dbu ma*), "Madhyamaka with the Approach Advocating Thoroughly Established Phenomena as Entityness" (*yongs grub ngo bo nyid du smra ba'i tshul can gyi dbu ma*), and "Madhyamaka of the Highest Secret Mantra" (*gsang sngags bla na med pa'i dbu ma*).[89] In the *Appearance of the Sun*, he calls them, respectively, "Madhyamaka Explained by the *Collection of Reasonings* with [the Texts of Its] Followers" (*rigs tshogs rjes 'brang dang bcas pas bshad pa'i dbu ma*), "Madhyamaka Asserted by Maitreya and Brothers Asaṅga [and Vasubandhu]" (*byams pa dang thogs med mched kyis bzhed pa'i dbu ma*), and "Madhyamaka of the Highest Secret Mantra" (*gsang sngags bla na med pa'i dbu ma*).[90]

When contrasting sūtric and tantric types of Madhyamaka, Shakya Chokden presents the latter as higher than the former, because tantric Madhyamaka has such unique elements as more profound teachings on emptiness, practices of union (*zung 'jug, yuganaddha*), empowerments, and practices of the two stages.[91] He insists on treating tantric Madhyamaka separately, and even dedicates a separate section to this issue in the *Wish Fulfilling Meru* called "Showing the Indispensability of Explaining Tantric Madhyamaka Separately."[92]

It should be further noted that Shakya Chokden views the innate primordial mind (*lhan cig skyes pa'i ye shes*) as the unique feature of the tantric system. Therefore, we should not confuse such interchangeable terms as the "primordial mind," "self-cognizing primordial mind," "individually self-cognizing primordial mind," "non-dual primordial mind," etc., on the one hand, and the "innate primordial mind" on the other. The latter is described in the uncommon tantric teachings only. As Shakya Chokden puts it in the *Thorough Clarification of Vajradhara's Intent*:

> Pāramitā[yāna] has neither
> The method of realization nor the object of realization
> Of the uncommon view of Mantra[yāna]—
> The innate primordial mind.
> The mere freedom from proliferations (*spros bral tsam*) [taught by] Pāramitāyāna followers
> Is not realized by primordial mind [taught in] Mantra;
> The emptiness realized by [the path of] Mantra
> Is subsumed under [the category of] the stainless great bliss (*zag med bde ba chen po*).[93]

Note that the "mere freedom from proliferations" in this passage refers not to the primordial mind free from proliferations, but a mere non-affirming negation of all proliferations. Because it is the object of conceptual minds only, it cannot be realized by primordial mind taught in Tantra (as well as in the sūtric Madhyamaka). On the other hand, as we already know, the freedom from proliferations described as an affirming negation, i.e., the primordial mind free from proliferations, is taught and realized by followers of both Alīkākāravāda and Tantra. This interpretation is supported by the *Precious Treasury of the Condensed Essence* where Shakya Chokden contrasts two types of freedom from proliferations that he calls "mere freedom from proliferations" (*spros pa bral tsam*) and "primordial mind free of proliferations" (*spros bral ye shes*), and argues that the subject of the former is a conceptual mind while the latter is experienced by primordial mind itself.[94]

Note too that the statement that Pāramitāyāna does not have the object of realization of the uncommon view of Mantrayāna does not contradict Shakya Chokden's basic position that the "objective" primordial mind taught in sūtras and tantras is the same. On the one hand, the innate primordial mind falls under the category of primordial mind. On the other hand, because the innate primordial mind is self-cognizing, its "object" too has to be the innate primordial mind. Because such "objective" innate primordial mind is taught only in tantras, it is not the object of realization common to both sūtras and tantras. This innate primordial mind is the object of realization of the uncommon tantric view only. But primordial mind in general is the object of realization of the view common to both sūtras and tantras.

As an example, we can think of descriptions of two individuals drinking water. Let us say that one person "drinks water," while another "drinks sweet water." These statements indicate that both individuals drink water and not, say, gasoline. They also refer to two different categories of water: broader and narrower. But importantly, they do not express two *contradictory* categories, such as sweet water and salty water. Although not everyone who drinks water necessarily drinks sweet water, whoever drinks sweet water *does* drink water. The categories of primordial mind taught in sūtras and tantras are similar to this example. Sūtric practitioners can drink the water of primordial mind, although they cannot drink the sweet water of innate primordial mind. Tantric practitioners can. Nevertheless, they are not drinking waters of two contradictory realities: both of them drink the water of primordial mind.

Despite the sūtric-tantric distinction, the similarity between Alīkākāravāda and tantric explanations of primordial mind is the very reason why Shakya Chokden overall presents tantric Madhyamaka as being much closer to Alīkākāravāda than to Niḥsvabhāvavāda. After all, if primordial mind is the only reality, then reality must in turn be primordial mind. It stands true for the tantric great bliss as well. This is why in the *Meaningful to Behold* he says "the Vajrayāna view appears exclusively within the category of primordial mind free from the duality of the apprehended and apprehender."[95] Despite distinctions in depth, effectiveness, and so forth, the views of both Alīkākāravāda and Tantra do not transcend the boundaries of primordial mind.

Based on these reasons, Shakya Chokden writes about the view of tantric and sūtric Madhyamaka in the *Meaningful to Behold*:

> Thus, the common views of the Mantra system are in agreement with Yogācāra, and not in agreement with Prāsaṅgika and Svātantrika. The uncommon [views] are superior to [the views of all] three types of Madhyamaka of Pāramitā[yāna] Followers (*phar phyin pa'i dbu ma*).[96]

Although in terms of its uncommon view, tantric Madhyamaka is superior to all sūtric forms of Madhyamaka, it shares the view of primordial mind with Alīkākāravāda Yogācāra, but does not share it with those Niḥsvabhāvavāda systems that do not provide its description. This distinction helps Shakya Chokden bring Alīkākāravāda and tantric Madhyamaka closer together, while distancing the tantric view from that of Niḥsvabhāvavāda. In the *Thorough Clarification of Vajradhara's Intent*, he elaborates:

> In particular, it should be known that
> It is impossible to have even a [mere] common locus
> (*gzhi mthun*)
> Of the emptiness of Prāsaṅgika and Svātantrika Mādhyamikas
> And the object of realization of the Mantra system.
> Because there is a common locus of
> The emptiness of Yogācāra and
> The innate nature (*rang bzhin lhan skyes*) of the Mantra
> [system],
> Both are called the "self-cognizing primordial mind."[97]

Shakya Chokden demonstrates further similarity between Alīkākāravāda and Tantra views on primordial mind by arguing that both systems derive from the teachings of the third dharmacakra. In the *Appearance of the Sun*, he admits that for the followers of Pāramitāyāna alone, the reality taught in the second dharmacakra is sufficient to eliminate all obscurations. Nevertheless, he continues, followers of both Yogācāra and Vajrayāna realize that no other reality but a non-affirming negation has been taught in the *Perfection of Wisdom* sūtras, and that the mind taking it as its object is necessarily only conceptual. Thereby they raise the question: what is the object of experience of individually self-cognizing primordial mind? Their answer is that it is the primordial mind free from the duality of the apprehended and apprehender, which is taught in the last dharmacakra.[98] Thus, he argues, "the final definitive meaning to be experienced in meditation by all followers of Vajrayāna originates from this very third dharmacakra of perfect differentiation (*legs par rnam par phye ba dang ldan pa'i chos kyi 'khor lo gsum pa*)."[99] Ultimate reality taught in the third dharmacakra—and also accepted by Alīkākāravādins—is the primordial mind of the dharma-sphere, the basis of cyclic existence and nirvāṇa, the final ultimate truth.[100]

In the *Rain of Ambrosia*, too, Shakya Chokden explains that similar to the Alīkākāravāda view, the tantric view also derives from the teachings of the third dharmacakra. Their similarity, once again, is related to their explanations of primordial mind:

> [I]n reliance on the middle pronouncement as well, sūtras of the pronouncement of the last dharmacakra are established exactly as having the definitive meaning. The reasons are as follows. Having taken as the basis [the fact that] all concepts of superimposition and deprecation (*sgro skur gyi rtog pa*) had already been eliminated by the middle pronouncement, [the last pronouncement] clearly determined as "such-and-such" that very final definitive meaning that is incorporated into experience through meditation. In what sūtras? In the last pronouncements in terms of Pāramitāyāna, such as the *Sūtra Unraveling the Intent*, that very [reality] that bears the name of the natural dharma-body (*rang bzhin chos sku*) and the sugata-essence was elucidated as the object of experience of individually self-cognizing primordial mind (*so sor rang gis rig pa'i ye shes kyi myong bya*). Also, in Mantrayāna in terms of those very last pronouncements, the final definitive meaning was clearly taught [as that] very primordial mind of the dharma-sphere in which all proliferations of the apprehended and apprehender—the objects of abandonment—have ceased. It was not taught in the middle pronouncement literally. [On the other hand,] as long as this dharma-sphere is not realized at least through a mere mental application of belief (*mos pa yid byed, abhimuktimanaskāra*), a

> knowing incorporating into experience the path of the two stages will not emerge.[101]

Shakya Chokden explains that one is prepared for both sūtric and tantric teachings of the third dharmacakra by the teachings of the second dharmacakra that negate conceptual proliferations and thereby clear the way for actual teachings on primordial mind. At the same time, because they do not explicitly teach primordial mind itself, the explicit teachings of the second dharmacakra are not sufficient as the basis of the practice of the generation and completion stages. Primordial mind taught in the third dharmacakra is the object of experience in both sūtric and tantric practice. Not only that—it is not possible to have an actual experience in tantric practice without at least believing in such primordial mind.

Because Alīkākāravāda and tantric Madhyamaka agree in their approaches to primordial mind, they are also similar in rejecting the idea that emptiness determined by reasoning can ever be an actual object of meditative experience. That object can be only primordial mind. Therefore, they are *similar* in treating as *dissimilar* views determined by listening and thinking on the one hand and experienced in meditative equipoise on the other. In the *Lamp of Dharma*, Shakya Chokden explains that unlike in the Niḥsvabhāvavāda system where the views determined by reasoning and experienced in meditation are concordant in the sense of being treated as unobservable (*mi dmigs pa*),[102] in the teachings of both the *Dharmas of Maitreya* and Tantra, the two are dissimilar, being distinguished, respectively, as conceptual and nonconceptual. He puts it as follows:

> The *Dharmas of Maitreya* are in agreement with Mantra,
> Because they assert that non-dual primordial mind alone
> As the object of realization after
> The apprehended-/apprehender-phenomena have been
> realized as empty.[103]

In other words, both Alīkākāravāda and Tantric approaches first determine by listening and thinking all apprehended and apprehender phenomena as empty, and then posit the non-dual primordial mind as the object of meditative experience.

In the *Appearance of the Sun*, Shakya Chokden specifies that according to Vajrayāna followers, it is possible to cease proliferations apprehending signs by using Yogācāra reasoning. Nevertheless, according to those followers, the way of ceasing proliferations by relying on Nāgārjuna's *Collection of Reasonings* is much superior, because all phenomena in that way are posited as self-empty. Shakya Chokden strongly supports that approach, but he also adds that it works only on the level of the view determined by reasoning. Otherwise, Niḥsvabhāvavāda's description of meditative experience is not applicable in the tantric context, because in the Niḥsvabhāvavāda system, not seeing anything is explained as seeing emptiness.[104] Not surprisingly, this position accords with Shakya Chokden's own approach outlined in Chapter 4: the Niḥsvabhāvavāda system is superior in terms of reasoning negating proliferations, while the Alīkākāravāda system is superior in terms of positing the object of meditative experience.

While the view taught in the *Collection of Reasonings* is not suitable as the object of actual tantric meditation of the two stages,[105] the approach of the *Collection of Praises* suits it very well. This is because, as was explained above (196), in that collection Nāgārjuna taught positing all phenomena as self-empty by reasoning and then meditating on primordial mind in meditative equipoise. In the *Rain of Ambrosia* Shakya Chokden writes:

> These stages of the view and meditation [taught in the *Collection of Praises*] connect very well with the systems of both Sūtra and Mantra. This is because when [their practitioners] proceed by the Sūtra path alone, their mode of generating wisdom that ceases concepts apprehending signs is much more profound than even the final system of Yogācāras. When connected to the Mantra system, then on the initial basis of those profoundest reasonings that cease concepts apprehending signs, [practitioners] use that ultimate mind of enlightenment (*don dam byang chub kyi sems, paramārthabodhicitta*) [generated after the concepts have been stopped] as the basis of accomplishment of the special deity (*lhag pa'i lha*) [i.e., *yi dam, iṣṭadevatā*], its cognition, primordial mind of the great bliss (*bde ba chen po'i ye shes*), and so forth.[106]

In other words, the tantric system can use self-emptiness reasoning as a very efficient tool for severing proliferations first, then move to primordial mind and use it as the basis for the unique tantric practice of the two stages, and so forth.

Effective as it is, such self-emptiness reasoning is not absolutely necessary in tantric practice. Similar to Alīkākāravāda, in Tantra, understanding all objects as self-empty does not necessarily have to precede the actual meditative practice of the generation and completion stages.[107] Tantric practitioners have two other options. They might either choose the reasoning of other-emptiness in order to clear away proliferations before proceeding to the actual part of tantric practice, or they might not use conceptual reasoning at all. Conceptual reasoning in general—whether related to self- or other-emptiness—is *not* absolutely necessary for accessing the meditative experience of primordial mind free from proliferations. Primordial mind can be manifested by special tantric techniques, such as the wisdom-primordial mind empowerment (*shes rab ye shes kyi dbang, prajñājñānābhiṣeka*).[108] As Shakya Chokden explains in the *Rain of Ambrosia*:

> For the inexpressible (*brjod bral*) to be experienced, it does not [necessarily] have to be preceded by reasonings determining [the view] as that [i.e., inexpressible]. This is because [the view can] already have been established as unthinkable and inexpressible by that very inexpressible primordial mind (*brjod bral gyi ye shes*) which manifested due to the features of tantric skills in means (*gsang sngags thabs la mkhas pa*). This is like, for example, the primordial mind of the third empowerment (*dbang gsum pa*).[109]

In the *Appearance of the Sun* too, Shakya Chokden explains that it is possible to realize emptiness without reasoning, through the stage of self-blessings (*rang byin gyis brlabs pa'i rim pa*)[110] and other methods. Emptiness realized in that case is the actual ultimate reality described as a self-characterized phenomenon (*rang mtshan, svalakṣaṇa*), not just a conceptual image or an other-exclusion.[111]

The above arguments diminish the necessity of the Niḥsvabhāvavāda reasoning of self-emptiness without at the same time undermining its superiority over the Alīkākāravāda reasoning of other-emptiness. The Niḥsvabhāvavāda reasoning is a very helpful element even in Tantra, because it is the most effective tool for negating conceptual proliferations. Nevertheless, it is limited only to the scope of conceptuality, and it is not what one meditates on in actual tantric practice. In the *Rain of Ambrosia* Shakya Chokden explains:

> In Mantrayāna, if treated from the point of view of merely severing proliferations apprehending signs, that Niḥsvabhāvavāda view explained in the *Collection of Reasonings* is also efficient. Nevertheless, merely that [view] is not sufficient for accomplishing the body of union (*zung 'jug gi sku*).[112]

The Niḥsvabhāvavāda view is useful for doing preliminary work in Tantra, but when it comes down to the cultivation of the actual view that results in accomplishing buddhahood by tantric means, the practice has to focus on primordial mind, as described at the beginning of this section.

In tantric meditation, the Niḥsvabhāvavāda view is not much help any more, while the Alīkākāravāda view is a perfect fit. By accepting the Alīkākāravāda view, one allows for a smooth transition to actual tantric practice. In the *Seventeen Wondrous Answers*, rejecting the idea that the object of meditative equipoise of the generation and completion stages can be self-emptiness, Shakya Chokden argues that primordial mind as explained in the Alīkākāravāda system is highly suitable for entering the tantric practice of accumulating the collection of primordial mind (*ye shes kyi tshogs, jñānasaṃbhāra*).[113]

In a nutshell, in Tantra one can do quite well without the Niḥsvabhāvavāda view, while the Alīkākāravāda view is indispensable, because it comprises an inseparable part of the tantric view of reality.

Because, in Shakya Chokden's opinion, Alīkākāravāda and Tantra share similar views of primordial mind, he treats Alīkākāravāda as the closest sūtric system to Tantra. He argues that even when tantric texts list Niḥsvabhāvavāda after Yogācāra and before Tantra, it implies neither that the Niḥsvabhāvavāda system is higher than Yogācāra nor that it is closer than Yogācāra to Tantra. In the *Wish Fulfilling Meru*, he gives the following comment on the famous passage from the *Hevajra Tantra* where different Buddhist tenets are arranged hierarchically, and Madhyamaka is placed between Yogācāra and Tantra:

> In the *Hevajra* it is said:
>
> > Yogācāra is [to be taught] after that.
> > Madhyamaka is to be taught afterwards.
> > Having learned all stages of Mantra,
> > One [should be] taught Hevajra afterwards.
>
> In that context of explaining a gradual engagement in the views (*lta ba rim 'jug*), three views are explained step by step. They are respectively the primordial mind free from the duality of the apprehended and apprehender, the non-affirming negation [described as] all phenomena being empty of their own entities, and the union of non-observing compassion and emptiness (*dmigs pa med pa'i snying rje dang stong pa nyid zung du 'jug pa*).[114]

Elaborating on the *Hevajra* passage in the *Meaningful to Behold*, Shakya Chokden explains that when one engages in the views gradually,[115] the *Hevajra* statement that Madhyamaka is to be taught after Yogācāra refers to the reasoning severing proliferations. This reasoning is followed by the tantric view, as is taught by the last two lines of the verse.[116] In other words, one first determines the view of Yogācāra, then Niḥsvabhāvavāda, and then Hevajra. In the *Precious Harbor of Definitive Meaning [for] Entering into the Wish Fulfilling Ocean of the Highest Secret Mantra upon Analysis of Doubts Regarding Difficult Points of Explicit Teachings of [Drakpa Gyeltsen's] 'Precious Tree: Clear Realizations [of Tantras]'* [117] too, he explains that in that verse Madhyamaka is said to be taught after Yogācāra in terms of reasoning severing superimpositions, while the statement that afterward one has to meditate on Hevajra eliminates doubts about whether one has to meditate on what has been determined by that reasoning. In the *Appearance of the Sun* he also explains that Madhyamaka is sandwiched between Yogācāra and Tantra according to that verse in order to negate concepts grasping at the extremes of existence, nonexistence, and so forth with respect to the ultimate meaning, the truly existent primordial mind taught by Yogācāra.[118]

In other words, the *Hevajra* passage does not imply that the Niḥsvabhāvavāda system is higher than Yogācāra, but only demonstrates that Niḥsvabhāvavāda reasoning is used for negating concepts with respect to the ultimate reality taught by Yogācāra. The same is true for other tantric texts that place Madhyamaka between Yogācāra and Tantra. For example, in the *Appearance of the Sun* Shakya Chokden quotes the *Stainless Light* passage:

> "Free from the apprehended and apprehender
> Consciousness exists [as] the ultimate"—
> Proclaim those who crossed
> The ocean of Yogācāras' texts.[119]

which after few passages is followed by the words:

> That primordial mind too is not asserted
> By scholars as ultimately existent.[120]

He argues that such a statement only explains the way of negating proliferations with respect to primordial mind realized in meditative equipoise. He thereby resists any attempts to use this passage for showing a hierarchical superiority of Niḥsvabhāvavāda over Yogācāra.[121]

In the *Lamp of Dharma,* he further explains how this approach can be applied in the tantric practice of dissolving all phenomena into the state of reality, identifying oneself with that reality, and then negating proliferations with respect to that reality.[122] Both there and in the *Precious Treasury of the Condensed Essence,*[123] he explains that according to Tantra, primordial mind itself cannot be negated by reasoning, but the attachment to it can—a position we are already familiar with.

In sum, Shakya Chokden argues that whether one uses self-emptiness reasoning as a preliminary stage for actual tantric practice or puts Niḥsvabhāvavāda teaching of self-emptiness between Yogācāra and Tantra, as in the quote from *Hevajra,* the Niḥsvabhāvavāda view of self-emptiness has one and the same function—severing proliferations. In itself, it is not the view meditated upon in either Yogācāra or Tantra. What followers of both systems meditate upon is the nondual primordial mind.

A Powerful Ally: Using the Tantric View of Reality for Support

In the intellectual and religious atmosphere of fifteenth-century Tibet, one could express doubts about the validity of certain forms of Madhyamaka taught in sūtras and their commentaries. Likewise, individual thinkers could criticize some tantric teachings. Nevertheless, overall, one can hardly find an established thinker in that period who would doubt the validity of the view of Highest Yoga Tantra, no matter how he would describe it. Demonstrating that the Alīkākāravāda view of ultimate reality agrees with Tantra, Shakya Chokden is thereby appealing to a virtually unquestionable authority. Using primordial mind as the bridge between the Alīkākāravāda and tantric Madhyamaka, he utilizes the view of tantric Madhyamaka to support, augment, and legitimize the Alīkākāravāda view. In the *Appearance of the Sun,* he writes:

> If it were not possible to eliminate non-afflicted ignorance (*nyon mongs pa can ma yin pa'i ma rig pa*) by the view of the three intermediate *Dharmas of Maitreya,* then how is such possible by the view of Vajrayāna? [This argument is valid] because it is difficult to distinguish the differences between that [view of Maitreya] and that [Vajrayāna view].[124]

This non-afflicted ignorance is the root of obscurations of knowables; it can be eliminated only in the state of buddhahood. In this passage Shakya Chokden argues that if the view of ultimate reality taught in Vajrayāna can eliminate the obscurations of knowables and bring about the achievement of buddhahood, then the same stays true for the Alīkākāravāda view taught by Maitreya's *Ornament of Mahāyāna Sūtras, Differentiation of the Middle and Extremes*, and *Differentiation of Phenomena and the Nature of Phenomena* due to the fundamental similarity of the two views.

Likewise, standing on this bridge between the views of Alīkākāravāda and Tantra, Shakya Chokden claims that the differences between Alīkākāravāda and Cittamātra are accepted even in the texts where Yogācāra is described only as Cittamātra. In the *Precious Harbor of Definitive Meaning*, he explains why in spite of the existence of two types of Yogācāra—Cittamātra and Madhyamaka—Drakpa Gyeltsen did not set forth a Yogācāra view higher than that of Cittamātra in his *Precious Tree: Clear Realizations of Tantras*:[125]

> Yogācāra view has two [divisions]—
> Madhyamaka and Cittamātra.
> Nevertheless, in the *[Precious] Tree* no [Yogācāra view]
> Superseding the view of Cittamātra is explained [because
> Drakpa Gyeltsen] intended that the view renowned as "Alīkākāravāda"
> Is subsumed under the objects of realization of Mantra (*sngags kyi rtogs bya*).[126]

Shakya Chokden argues that although on the sūtric level Drakpa Gyeltsen did not provide an explanation of the Yogācāra view higher than that of Cittamātra, it does not mean that he did not distinguish between the views of Cittamātra and Alīkākāravāda. He made this distinction by treating the Alīkākāravāda view of primordial mind as an object of realization in Tantra. It follows, therefore, that he treated it as Madhyamaka. Shakya Chokden adds that the Alīkākāravāda view of primordial mind free from the duality of the apprehended and apprehender taught in the *Dharmas of Maitreya* is explained as the view realized in Mantra (*sngags kyi rtogs bya'i lta ba*) by both Drakpa Gyeltsen and his brother Sönam Tsemo.[127]

Shakya Chokden also uses the closeness of the tantric and Alīkākāravāda views for demonstrating that even Niḥsvabhāvavādins—both those who did and who did not provide descriptions of primordial mind in their sūtric works—accept primordial mind as the highest reality, and in that respect agree with Alīkākāravādins. This is because, he argues, they provided such descriptions in their tantric works. Shakya Chokden thinks that sūtric and tantric works attributed to Nāgārjuna were written by the same person. It is also true for the works of Āryadeva and Candrakīrti. Nevertheless, instead of using this "fact" for proving that these thinkers teach the same view of Niḥsvabhāvavāda in both sūtric and tantric contexts, Shakya Chokden argues that even though Nāgārjuna, Āryadeva, and Candrakīrti *are* Niḥsvabhāvavādins themselves, the view they teach in their tantric works is *not* that of Niḥsvabhāvavāda. It is different from the Niḥsvabhāvavāda view, and agrees with that of Alīkākāravāda, because it matches the Alīkākāravāda view of primordial mind as ultimate reality. From the *Rain of Ambrosia*:

> In the mantric treatises composed by those Niḥsvabhāvavāda masters, the identification of the subject—the view, and the object of that view—the dharma-sphere and ultimate truth, is exclusively in agreement with that [identification] which originates from the texts of ārya Asaṅga [with his] brother [Vasubandhu] and other Yogācāra masters. This is because [in their mantric treatises] the mind-vajra and the luminous nature of mind (*sems kyi rang bzhin 'od gsal ba*) themselves are described as ultimate truth, and when primordial mind directly realizing that [ultimate truth] is produced, [such realization is] posited as the realization of the view.[128]

In particular, Candrakīrti's tantric view agrees with Asaṅga's Alīkākāravāda view. From the *Meaningful to Behold*:

> There appears no difference at all in [the identification of] that "primordial mind free from the duality of the apprehended and apprehender" realized by honorable Asaṅga and the identification by honorable Candrakīrti himself of the "stage of luminosity"[129] and "mind-vajra" explained in the *Secret Assembly [Tantra]*.[130]

Shakya Chokden shows that even Candrakīrti, who was refuting primordial mind when determining the view by reasoning in his sūtric works, accepts that very primordial mind as ultimate reality in his tantric works. The implication is clear: because the tantric view agrees with Alīkākāravāda, Candrakīrti also agrees with Alīkākāravāda, although he does not admit it in his sūtric treatises.

Shakya Chokden also calls tantric teachings as witness in order to support *his own* reconciliatory approach to Yogācāra and Madhyamaka. In the *Appearance of the Sun*, he argues that even though

Niḥsvabhāvavādins and Alīkākāravādins refute each other, one should rely on the authority of the tantric teachings in order to find which view is correct:

> What turns out to be the definitive meaning should be analyzed having taken tantras and quintessential instructions of Vajrayāna as valid.[131]

In that context, he explains that due to the similarity between the views on reality of Alīkākāravāda and Tantra, the view of primordial mind taught by Alīkākāravāda is supported by the tantric view—despite the fact that it is refuted by Candrakīrti in his non-tantric works.

By showing that the views on primordial mind of Alīkākāravāda and Tantra are compatible, Shakya Chokden assigns additional weight to the Alīkākāravāda view, moving the Niḥsvabhāvavāda view—useful as it is—further to the periphery. By placing the Yogācāra view of ultimate reality on the level closest to Tantra, it becomes a bridge connecting sūtras and tantras. Indeed, in his system, primordial mind is more than the continuity of the mental stream of an individual being; it is the ceaseless continuity that underlies, pervades, and connects multiple layers of Mahāyāna teachings.

Every system attempting to embrace the multifarious elements of Buddhist thought and practice is destined to face and raise problems of reconciling ideas that derive from different sources, have discordant formulations, and express conflicting meanings. At the same time, the treasure-trove world of Buddhist thought offers a virtually inexhaustible variety of ideas that geniuses like Shakya Chokden are able to organize in coherent clusters by building parallels between different categories of ideas, valorizing some, downplaying others, but ultimately aiming at bringing further harmony, lucidity, and meaning to the teachings they are dealing with. Developing their views, different thinkers put stronger emphasis on a particular set of ideas, tending to apply those ideas to an increasingly wider variety of contexts. Those ideas eventually become unique markers of their overall systems. Primordial mind clearly is such a category in Shakya Chokden's system. His claim that primordial mind is accepted as ultimate reality by the majority of Mahāyāna thinkers is doubtlessly related to his overall reconciliatory attitude to Buddhist systems. Furthermore, unlike, for example, the category of cognition (*rig pa*), which is treasured so highly by the Great Perfection followers, he does not treat primordial mind as an objective that all Buddhist teachings lead to but only the highest systems directly address. In contrast, he believes that all Alīkākāravāda, Tantra, and many Niḥsvabhāvavāda teachings address the same primordial mind, and address it in depth, although Tantra does address it more extensively and in more depth than the others.

As we have seen, this approach to primordial mind helps Shakya Chokden justify different statements that he makes in the Alīkākāravāda context by relying on the support of Tantric teachings, and vice versa. It also makes his approach to Tantra more "logical" due to his recourse to writings of Buddhist logicians on primordial mind that he carries into the tantric discourse. This brings a distinct flavor to his writings overall: quite often an excellent discussion of Dharmakīrtean epistemological ideas is embedded in Shakya Chokden's tantric treatises, and alternatively a lucid exposition of the tantric view of reality can be found in his writings focusing on Alīkākāravāda, Pramāṇa, and other subjects. As a person too, Shakya Chokden would call himself a "dry dialectician," and yet be deeply involved in tantric practices and teachings. One can hardly imagine that such would happen were he treating logic and Tantra as two unrelated modalities. In fact, the more time that went by, the more his writings emphasized the relatedness of all categories of Mahāyāna teachings, and the more primordial mind seemed to move to the forefront of his thought. Indeed, Shakya Chokden's whole life journey can be seen as an increasingly deeper immersion into the expanse of empty luminosity of primordial mind—the state into which his temporary bodily appearance finally dissolved in 1507.

Conclusion

The Grand Unity—Shakya Chokden's Middle Way

The multiple strands of Shakya Chokden's thought explored in this study are all in some way related to its main topic: the nature and relationship of Alīkākāravāda Yogācāra and Niḥsvabhāvavāda Madhyamaka. Against a background of different approaches—both distancing and reconciliatory—to the relationship of these two systems his position is unique in terms of his efforts to erase differences between them on the level of the direct realization of ultimate reality. Showing that from this perspective neither one of them can be treated as higher than the other, he argues that "it is difficult to distinguish features of superiority of these two Madhyamaka systems."[1] He further asserts that the Satyākāravāda view is accepted by all key Yogācāra thinkers only temporarily, as a stepping-stone toward the final Yogācāra view of Alīkākāravāda. He also rejects any difference between the views of Prāsaṅgika and Svātantrika on both the ultimate level and the level of worldly conventions. Furthermore, in his opinion the ultimate views of both sūtric and tantric systems of Madhyamaka are subsumed under the category of primordial mind. When all those elements are put together, it becomes clear that, in effect, Shakya Chokden articulates nothing less than a grand unity of Mahāyāna systems, all of which—if we take Yogācāra as a single unit with the Alīkākāravāda position as its final view—provide valid and complete means of achieving buddhahood.

Such an approach is doubtless very appealing, and it is highly regrettable that despite their virtues, Shakya Chokden's views receded into obscurity to only occasionally spark interest in rare thinkers. We can only speculate about possible reasons for this oversight, but would include, of course, at least the above-mentioned ban on his writings and his controversial questioning of Sakya Pendita's views—two factors that jeopardized survival of his system from without and within the Sakya tradition, respectively.

In addition, Shakya Chokden's encompassing approach—sympathetic to apparently conflicting systems of thought—might have required too much reconsideration of established categories, thereby exceeding the threshold of acceptability for most Tibetan thinkers. It is also possible that in the sectarian intellectual world supportive of "taking sides" his approach did not provide sufficient means for its advocates to identify themselves as following "the only one" and/or "the only true" type of doctrinal system originating from India. Furthermore, from his contemporaries' viewpoint he might have assigned too much importance to Yogācāra—a system that most of them treated as inferior to Madhyamaka. As a result, his approach—open, broad, and inclusive as it is—may not have resonated in the minds and hearts of his contemporaries and later generations of Tibetan thinkers.

It appears that from the time Niḥsvabhāvavāda Madhyamaka was assigned by Tibetans the paramount position in the hierarchy of Buddhist tenets, Yogācāra views were largely undervalued, often neglected, and almost unanimously treated as inferior. So by placing Niḥsvabhāvavāda on the same level with Yogācāra, which was treated as a lower system by the majority of Tibetan thinkers, he may have been seen as implicitly—in the eyes of that majority—undermining the status of Niḥsvabhāvavāda. His position that the Alīkākāravāda view explicitly or implicitly—through meditative experience—is shared by all other Mādhyamikas could have created the impression that he was suggesting a reversal of the Yogācāra/Niḥsvabhāvavāda hierarchical standing. Even worse, one could argue that he was suggesting that practioners directly experience that very phenomenon which most Niḥsvabhāvavāda students learned to refute: truly existent and other-empty primordial mind.

If we agree that many already attached a stigma to the other-emptiness views in the fifteenth through sixteenth centuries, then it is also possible that Shakya Chokden's explanation of the ultimate view directly realized in meditative equipoise by *all* Mādhyamikas as other-emptiness heavily jeopardized his credibility as a legitimate thinker. The idea that all advocates of self-emptiness are also "destined" to directly realize other-emptiness was probably confusing in a world of sharp distinctions between the two types of emptiness. To add to that confusion, as a thinker he could not easily be classified in either the self-emptiness or the other-emptiness "camps."

In particular, his description of ultimate reality as impermanent could have sounded very controversial in an intellectual milieu heavily saturated with descriptions of reality as anything *but* impermanent: as permanent, as transcending permanence and impermanence, and so forth—no matter whether judged from the perspective of self-emptiness or other-emptiness.

Besides the fact that neither Shakya Chokden himself nor his system fit easily into dichotomous categories of Yogācāra/Madhyamaka and self-emptiness/other-emptiness, it is possible that *he* was not interested in promoting his own system with an eye on developing a separate movement. As has been mentioned above, in his own monastery of Serdokchen he preferred to focus on teaching what became the "mainstream" Sakya system of Rongtön and Künga Zangpo. Apparently, he never planned to branch off and form a separate sect alongside the Jonangpas, the Bodongpas, the Gelukpas, and so forth. Otherwise, he had all the external conditions necessary for doing just that: powerful supporters, influential allies, multiple disciples, people eager to publish his works, and last but not least—his own Golden Monastery. An impression one gets from studying his works and biography is that articulating the unity of divergent systems of Mahāyāna thought and practice interested him more than uniting his followers into a separate sect or even uniting different elements of his approach for the sake of presenting it as distinct from the "mainstream" Sakya tradition. Rather, Shakya Chokden preferred to invest his energy in articulating and promoting the unity of Mahāyāna systems. And the unity he pointed out remained one of the most remarkable achievements of his thought overall.

As this study demonstrates, the grand unity of Mahāyāna systems articulated by Shakya Chokden is achievable *only* because he insists and clearly shows that conflicting ways of conceptualizing reality and different ways of negating unreality do not result in conflicting direct experiences of the ultimate. His overall system simply would not allow other options. In his opinion, ultimate reality and the mind which directly realizes it are a single entity: the non-dual primordial mind. Thus, he cannot claim that one ultimate can be realized in two conflicting ways. Nor can he accept the existence of two ultimates realized by followers of two conflicting systems of Madhyamaka. It would entail that one of conflicting ultimates is not an ultimate, because a notion of multiple contradictory ultimates is unacceptable in Buddhism. Buddhists can go only as far as admitting different but compatible ultimates, such as the different types of emptiness realized by bodhisattvas and śrāvakas, or the different types of primordial mind realized by bodhisattvas practicing sūtras and tantras. Thus, *the idea of sameness or compatibility of the direct meditative experience of reality in all forms of Madhyamaka is the very foundation of Shakya Chokden's conciliatory and encompassing approach to Mahāyāna systems.*

At the same time, his emphasis on sameness is far from being just a conceptual claim alluding to a nonconceptual experience for its own justification. On the contrary, while admitting that reality directly realized by all Mādhyamikas is beyond concepts, Shakya Chokden uses elaborate reasons, brilliant ideas, and exquisite conceptual constructions in order to demonstrate how and why the direct meditative experience of reality should be the same for all sūtric Mādhyamikas and compatible for sūtric and tantric Mādhyamikas.

Nonetheless, because Shakya Chokden's approach to the systems of Madhyamaka is not syncretic, the grand unity he achieves cannot be called a "synthesis." His approach to Niḥsvabhāvavāda and Alīkākāravāda is inclusionary and harmonizing, and he presents them as complementary; nevertheless he does not view them as incomplete in themselves, and does not propose to synthesize them. Although he admits an additional Madhyamaka category of Alīkākāravāda, he also agrees with other Sakya thinkers in his presentation of Niḥsvabhāvavāda philosophy, treats Niḥsvabhāvavāda as a self-sufficient system, and keeps it on the level of Madhyamaka. In this way he stays in agreement with the "mainstream" Sakya approach to Niḥsvabhāvavāda while at the same time emphasizing that Alīkākāravāda is an equally valid form of Madhyamaka.

Skillful in the art of not taking sides, Shakya Chokden does not side with either of the two systems in their accusations of not being Madhyamaka. At the same time, eager as he is to prove Alīkākāravāda a legitimate system of Madhyamaka on par with Niḥsvabhāvavāda, he recognizes how different their approaches are. Trying to be fair to both systems, he does not attempt to ignore or erase their differences. On the contrary, what makes the proposed compatibility of the two systems look so dramatically impressive is his usage of a masterful technique: sharply distinguishing their unique features on a conceptual level, then explaining how they each lead to—and provide sufficient tools for—the same nonconceptual realization of reality.

I should reiterate that in his reconciliatory approach to the two systems, Shakya Chokden never claims that one is somehow incorrect with regard to its main views and practices while another is not. On the contrary, he tries to show the validity of Niḥsvabhāvavāda and Alīkākāravāda systems by highlighting the strengths of both. Thereby he shows us the possibility of a new direction in approaching Mahāyāna systems: rather than showing how to find *the only correct system*, he suggests the way in which *different conflicting systems* can be conceived of as being correct.

The strongest elements of the two systems stressed by Shakya Chokden are Niḥsvabhāvavāda's reasoning leading to the direct realization of reality and Alīkākāravāda's identification of the view of ultimate reality. When using those elements in order to reconcile the two systems, he does not argue that they identify their ultimate view differently, but rather insists that they either do not identify it at all (as in the case of Candrakīrti in his sūtric writings) or identify it as primordial mind (as in the case of the two types of Yogācāra Mādhyamikas). As far as reasoning goes, Shakya Chokden shows that both self-emptiness reasoning and other-emptiness reasoning lead to the same direct realization of reality; thus, both are valid approaches. He further shows that although Niḥsvabhāvavādins primarily use self-emptiness reasoning, along with all other followers of Buddhist tenets they determine the selflessness of persons as other-emptiness. Also, while Alīkākāravādins use other-emptiness reasoning, such Yogācāra thinkers as Dharmakīrti resort to self-emptiness reasoning as well.

Because Shakya Chokden agrees that self-emptiness reasoning is the most effective tool for dispelling concepts and accessing the direct meditative experience of reality, the virtue and the importance of that reasoning are self-evident in his system. At the same time, overall he does not clearly explain why Yogācāra descriptions of the ultimate view are important. As I understand him, he takes for granted that although descriptions of ultimate reality are not the actual means of realizing it, nevertheless they are much more than *mere* descriptions. Everyone familiar with the "guiding mind instructions" (*sems khrid*) in the Great Seal system, the "empowerment of cognition-display" (*rig pa'i rtsal dbang*) in the Great Perfection system, or the "word empowerment" (*tshig dbang*) in the Highest Yoga Tantra knows that identifications of reality given in those contexts are intended to ground practitioners to the correct ways of cultivating reality by providing for and confirming their experiences through words, symbols, and so forth. Alīkākāravāda's description of the direct meditative experience of the ultimate in Shakya Chokden's system appears to be similar to that. It seems that in his opinion it helps Alīkākāravādins—more effectively than Niḥsvabhāvavādins—keep moving in the right direction after the realization of freedom from proliferations has been achieved. In other words, verbalization of the ultimate is more efficient in terms of adequately expressing what one has experienced. As has been mentioned earlier (182), according to Shakya Chokden, the

Niḥsvabhāvavāda approach is more faithful to *how* reality is realized within meditative equipoise, while the Alīkākāravāda approach is more faithful to *what* experiences that reality and what that reality actually is, i.e., primordial mind. Another virtue of the Alīkākāravāda description of the ultimate as primordial mind is that it provides a convenient bridge for progressing toward the view of tantric Madhyamaka, to which it stays very close—much closer in fact than Niḥsvabhāvavāda.

Although Shakya Chokden called himself a "dry dialectician," his biography and writings show that he was also a highly skilled tantric practitioner, teacher, as well as a visionary. I surmise that in combination with his ecumenical and sympathetic attitude toward a variety of Buddhist meditative and philosophical systems, his personal experience of luminosity mentioned above (34) might have contributed to his lasting interest in primordial mind as the focal point of multifarious Mahāyāna teachings. Presenting this subliminal mind which is realized directly only through meditation as a connecting link between different Mahāyāna systems is highly acceptable in the Tibetan Buddhist world, where a direct meditative experience of reality is always valued over its conceptual descriptions. Also appealing is the idea that this primordial mind—the mystery of mysteries that we all carry within—is accessible to a wide variety of Mahāyāna practitioners, not only to dialecticians trained in Niḥsvabhāvavāda reasoning. Its flavor can be tested even by uneducated meditators, Yogācāras, and followers of unique tantric techniques of realizing reality which do not require any reasoning whatsoever. I presume therefore that Shakya Chokden's position was attractive not only to himself but to other thinkers and practitioners, and especially to those scholar-yogis who, like him and his teachers, were striving to explain various systems of Mahāyāna as equally valid and to personally taste the reality those systems teach.

It should be noted that when Shakya Chokden reconciles Mahāyāna systems, he approaches their similarities in *different* ways. He agrees that Alīkākāravāda and Niḥsvabhāvavāda articulate their views differently, and in that context either refute each other or use each other's views as a step toward what they conceptually outline as their highest views. Nevertheless, according to him their practitioners reach the same view in direct meditative experience. Prāsaṅgika and Svātantrika, on the other hand, approach ultimate reality and worldly conventions in the same way, and debate only about the ways of determining the ultimate view. Thus, he agrees with the majority of Tibetan thinkers in treating even conceptual descriptions of the final view of Svātantrika and Prāsaṅgika as the same, and in treating descriptions of the views of Niḥsvabhāvavāda and Alīkākāravāda as different. Nevertheless, he is unique in arguing that despite that difference the views of both Niḥsvabhāvavāda and Alīkākāravāda directly realized in meditative equipoise are the same.

Based on reconsideration of Mahāyāna philosophical categories and their contents, Shakya Chokden's system makes substantial contributions to Buddhist studies, both traditional and academic. The hierarchical distinction between the final views of Alīkākāravāda and Satyākāravāda had never been contested in Tibet, unlike that of Prāsaṅgika and Svātantrika. Virtually all Tibetans treated the Alīkākāravāda position as more advanced than Satyākāravāda, and partly for that reason the Alīkākāravāda/Satyākāravāda distinction was not explored in any significant detail in contemporary scholarship in contrast to the Prāsaṅgika/Svātantrika distinction. Although Shakya Chokden also agreed with the hierarchical approach to Satyākāravāda and Alīkākāravāda, he took one further step by placing Alīkākāravāda on the level of Madhyamaka, thereby sharpening the distinction between the two forms of Yogācāra. Interestingly, in his demonstration of subtle—but in his opinion vital—differences between Alīkākāravāda and Satyākāravāda, he was similar to Tsongkhapa who emphasized what he saw as subtle but crucial differences between Prāsaṅgika and Svātantrika. Thus, it is my hope that as Tsongkhapa's works sparked interest in in-depth study of the Prāsaṅgika/Svātantrika distinction, Shakya Chokden's works will also provoke interest in more detailed study of the Alīkākāravāda/Satyākāravāda distinction. This in turn will help clarify the Yogācāra/Madhyamaka distinction by suggesting a new angle for looking at it.

It is self-evident that scholarship without any personal interest, preference, and motivation is impossible. Clearly, an attitude to the subject of one's study plays a vital role in research on it. I would argue that Shakya Chokden's system suggests a change and expansion of attitudes toward studies of Buddhist thought, whether in traditional Tibetan or contemporary academic contexts. If we take seriously his argument that major Yogācāra works should be classified as Madhyamaka too, then clearly we will not be able to state in our own writings and teach our students that a genuine Madhyamaka view is contained only in Candrakīrti's *Engaging in Madhyamaka*, a few of Nāgārjuna's texts, and writings of their followers. Research on and teaching of Madhyamaka would involve then an in-depth study of the works of Maitreya, Asaṅga, Dharmakīrti, and other Yogācāra authors, as well as serious study of meditative instructions passed down in little known but vitally important "minor" texts and oral teachings.

In turn, that would likely change the way we discuss ultimate reality and approaches to it. Besides exploring such important conceptual tools as syllogisms and consequences, we might open our perspective to different processes of realizing the view, exploring meditative experience even in the midst of scholastic discourse.

Due to the deep respect Tibetans have for Buddhist teachings originating in India and crystallized in Tibet, the idea that all those teachings could be approached in a noncontradictory way has been very appealing to Tibetan thinkers. At the same time, splitting and separating Buddhist systems into distinct groups helps organize, evaluate, and clarify the nature of those systems. Against that background, siding with a position which is deemed the highest can be used as a tool for promoting the views of one's own system or sectarian tradition and showing the inferiority of opposing systems. Alternatively, one can present one's own position as bringing the views of multiple systems closer together, thereby being supportive of (and, in turn, supported by) those systems. In that light, the views of one's opponents can be presented as separatist and as creating disharmony between different Buddhist systems which agree with each other on a deeper level. Shakya Chokden clearly follows the latter approach.

He attempts to bring back to light the multifarious world of Buddhist thought and practice, vehemently objecting to what he sees as the narrow-mindedness of those who try to focus on only "one true" system. Thus, he suggests appreciating multiple Buddhist teachings in their own right rather than embracing the criticisms and partial readings put forth by followers of other systems. His approach also offers more freedom of choice to Mahāyāna followers: having accepted both Niḥsvabhāvavāda and Alīkākāravāda as legitimate forms of Madhyamaka, they can choose between these systems (perhaps based on their personalities and inclinations) without having to feel uncomfortable about preferring a supposedly "inferior" system.

These are just some of the avenues open to exploration through Shakya Chokden's articulation of the unity of Mahāyāna systems. We are fortunate that his works were rediscovered after years of neglect. I am personally fortunate to rediscover, interpret, translate, and make better known Yogācāra and Madhyamaka views of this outstanding thinker.

This book, based on Shakya Chokden's key works—most of which were never translated into any language or explored in detail in any extant writings both in and outside the Tibetan cultural area—is an effort to contribute to the scholarly study of Shakya Chokden's philosophical vision. By extension, it expands our understanding of fifteenth-century Tibetan Buddhist thought, Yogācāra and Madhyamaka systems, and Mahāyāna Buddhist philosophy in general. It opens a new field of in-depth research on Shakya Chokden's thought by utilizing his system as a key to a fresh perspective on the universe of Buddhist thought and practice. And it is an invitation to appreciate, analyze, and possibly even adopt the grand unity of Mahāyāna systems—Shakya Chokden's Middle Way.

Glossary of Buddhist Terms

English-Tibetan with Sanskrit parallels

(Those Sanskrit terms that I use instead of their English translations are not italicized)

Abbot *mkhan po*
abiding *gnas pa*
able to perform a function ultimately *don dam par don byed nus pa*
accomplished yogi *grub thob*
accusative case *las su bya ba*
action *spyod pa, caryā*
actual phenomenon *don chos*
actual ultimate truth *don dam pa'i bden pa dngos*
actuality *don, artha*
adherence *zhen pa*
adhering minds *zhen blo*
Adjunct Teacher *zur 'chad pa*
adventitious consciousness *blo bur gyi rnam shes*
advocating cognizance-only *rnam par rig pa tsam du smra ba*
advocating interiority of knowables *shes bya nang gir smra ba*
affirming negation *ma yin dgag, paryudāsa*
afflictive obscurations *nyon mongs pa'i sgrib pa, kleśāvaraṇa*
analysis by the wisdom of individual analysis *so sor rtog pa'i shes rab kyi dpyad pa*
analytical Madhyamaka accessed by severing superimpositions apprehending signs *rnam par brtags pa mtshan 'dzin gyi sgro 'dogs gcod pa'i dbu ma*
analytical reasoning *rnam dpyod kyi rigs pa*
appearances of others *gzhan snang*
application of the mode of apprehension in remainder of negation of the object of negation *dgag bya bkag shul gyi 'dzin stangs sbyor ba*
apprehended *gzung ba, grāhya*

apprehended and apprehender with different substances with respect to external objects *phyi rol gyi don la ltos pa'i gzung 'dzin rdzas gzhan*
apprehended and apprehender with different substances with respect to internal knowing *nang shes pa la ltos pa'i gzung 'dzin rdzas gzhan*
apprehended-aspect *gzung rnam, grāhyākāra*
apprehender *'dzin pa, grāhaka*
apprehender-aspect *'dzin rnam, grāhakākāra*
apprehender-imaginary nature *'dzin pa kun btags*
approximation-accomplishment *bsnyen bsgrub*
ārya bodhisattva *byang sems 'phags pa*
ārya grounds *'phags pa'i sa*
ascertain *nges pa*
aspect of the apprehender *'dzin pa'i rnam pa*
aspect *rnam pa, ākāra*
Aspectarian *rnam bcas pa, sākāra*
Aspectless Mind-Only *sems tsam rnam med pa,* Nirākāra Cittamātra
Assembly Dharma *tshogs chos*
auspicious restoration-purification *bkra shis pa'i gso sbyong*
Autonomists *rang rgyud pa,* *Svātantrika
autonomous reason *rang rgyud kyi gtan tshigs, svatantrahetu*
autonomous reasoning *rang rgyud kyi rigs pa*
basis *gzhi*
basis of emptiness *stong gzhi*
basis of intent *dgongs gzhi*
basis of negation *dgag gzhi*
basis of purification of stains *dri ma sbyang ba'i gzhi*
binding bodily functioning *lus kyi byed bcings*
bodhisattva ground *byang chub sems pa'i sa, bodhisattavabhūmi*
body maṇḍala *lus kyi dkyil 'khor*
body of union *zung 'jug gi sku*
boundaries of positing *'jog mtshams*
buddha-essence *sangs rgyas kyi snying po, buddhagarbha*
calm abiding *zhi gnas, śamatha*
calm abiding and special insight *zhi lhag, śamatha-vipaśyanā*
ceaseless continuity *rgyun mi 'chad pa*
center *dbus ma*
Central Channel *rtsa dbu ma, avadhūtī*
Cittamātra Followers *sems tsam pa*
clarity and cognition *gsal zhing rig pa*
clarity factor of primordial mind *ye shes kyi gsal cha*
Clear Realization of the Peak *rste mo'i mngon rtogs, mūrdhābhisamaya*
cognition *rig pa, vidya*

cognition of objects *yul rig pa*
cognizance *rnam par rig pa, vijñapti*
Cognizance-Only *rnam par rig pa tsam,* Vijñaptimātra
cognizing itself by itself *rang gis rang rig pa*
collection of primordial mind *ye shes kyi tshogs, jñānasaṃbhāra*
common locus *gzhi mthun*
completion stage *rdzogs pa'i rim pa, saṃpannakrama*
compounded *'dus byas, saṃskṛta*
concepts of superimposition and deprecation *sgro skur gyi rtog pa*
conceptual analysis *rtog dpyod*
conceptual mind *rtog pa*
conceptual mind apprehending sounds as meaning *sgra don 'dzin pa'i rtog pa*
conceptually superimposed through listening and thinking *thos bsam gyi rtog pas sgro btags pa*
concordant ultimate *mthun pa'i don dam*
consciousness *rnam par shes pa, vijñāna*
consciousness dualistically appearing as the apprehended and apprehender *gzung 'dzin gnyis su snang ba'i rnam shes*
consciousness empty of the apprehended and apprehender with different substances with respect to external objects *phyi rol gyi don la ltos pa'i gzung 'dzin rdzas gzhan gyis stong pa'i rnam par shes pa*
consciousness factor of the outward-looking apprehended-aspect *phyir blta gzung rnam rnam shes kyi cha*
consequence *thal 'gyur, prasaṅga*
consequence reasoning *thal 'gyur gyi rigs pa*
Consequentialists *thal 'gyur ba,* *Prāsaṅgika
continuum *rgyun*
conventions *tha snyad*
conventions of subsequent attainment *rjes thob kyi tha snyad*
damage to the explicit teaching *dngos la gnod byed*
definitive meaning *nges don, nītārtha*
definitive meaning implicitly taught by the middle pronouncement *bka' bar pa'i shugs bstan gyi nges don*
definitive meaning incorporated into experience through meditation *sgom pas nyams len gyi nges don*
definitive meaning of the explicit teachings of the last pronouncement *bka' tha ma'i dngos bstan gyi nges don*
definitive meaning of the explicit teachings of the middle pronouncement *bka' bar pa'i dngos bstan gyi nges don*
definitive meaning of the last pronouncement *bka' tha ma'i nges don*
dependent natures *gzhan dbang, paratantra*

dependent phenomenon *bltos chos*
dependently established *ltos grub, apekṣyasamutpāda*
deprecation *skur 'debs, apavāda*
determining appearances as mind *snang ba sems su thag gcod*
devoid of the apprehended *gzung ba med pa*
Dharma lineages *chos brgyud*
Dharma terminology *chos skad*
dharma-body *chos kyi sku, dharmakāya*
dharma-sphere *chos kyi dbyings, dharmadhātu*
direct object of cognition *dngos kyi rig bya*
direct perception *mngon sum, pratyakṣa*
direct seeing of the mode of being *gnas lugs mngon sum du mthong ba*
direct self-cognition of the outward-looking mind *kha phyir lta'i rang rig mngon sum*
direct self-cognition *rang rig pa'i mngon sum, svasaṃvedanapratyakṣa*
direct valid cognition *mngon sum tshad ma, pratyakṣapramāṇa*
divisions of reasoning and divisions of scriptural statements *rigs grwa dang lung grwa*
doxography *grub mtha', siddhānta*
dualistically appearing knowing *gnyis snang gi shes pa*
Early Dissemination *snga dar*
early Tibetans *bod snga rabs pa*
earth-rite dance *sa chog gi gar*
ecumenical movement *ris med*
effect of valid cognition *tshad 'bras, pramāṇaphala*
efficient ultimate truth *don dam bden pa go chod*
element of sugata-essence *khams bde bar gshegs pa'i snying po*
elimination of other isolates *ldog pa gzhan sel*
emanation-body *sprul pa'i sku, nirmāṇakāya*
empowerment *dbang, abhiṣeka*
empowerment of cognition-display *rig pa'i rtsal dbang*
empowerment stages *dbang gi rim pa*
emptiness *stong pa nyid, śūnyatā*
emptiness arrived at through severing superimpositions by listening and thinking *thos bsam gyi sgro 'dogs bcad pa'i stong pa nyid*
emptiness created by mind *blos byas stong pa*
emptiness of both *gnyis kas stong pa*
emptiness endowed with the supreme of all aspects *rnam pa kun gyi mchog dang ldan pa'i stong pa nyid*
emptiness experienced through meditation *nyams su myong bya'i stong nyid*
emptiness imputed by sounds and concepts which is renowned in tenets *sgra dang rtog pas btags pa'i stong nyid grub mtha' la grags pa*

emptiness in terms of non-findability at the time of examination by reasoning *rigs pas brtags pa'i tshe ma rnyed pa'i stong pa nyid*
emptiness in the face of reasoning *rigs ngo'i stong nyid*
emptiness in which the aggregates are excluded *phung po rnam bcad kyi stong pa nyid*
emptiness in which the apprehended and apprehender with different substances are negated *gzung 'dzin rdzas gzhan khegs pa'i stong nyid*
emptiness of duality of the apprehended and apprehender *gzung 'dzin gnyis stong*
emptiness realized through experience *nyams myong gi stong nyid*
emptiness related to searching for and not finding terminologically imputed meanings *tha snyad kyis btags don btsal bas ma rnyed pa'i stong pa nyid*
emptiness side *stong phyogs*
emptiness which is a non-affirming negation *med par dgag pa'i stong nyid*
emptiness which is beyond objects of mind *blo yi yul las 'das pa'i stong nyid*
empty phenomenon *stong pa'i dngos po*
engaging one's object in agreement with the object's way of being *yul gyi gnas tshul dang mthun par 'jug*
enjoyment-body *longs spyod rdzogs pa'i sku, saṃbhogakāya*
entity *ngo bo, bhāva*
entity of clarity *gsal ba'i ngo bo*
entity of dualistically appearing knowing *gnyis snang gi shes pa'i ngo bo*
entity of the dependent nature *gzhan dbang gi ngo bo*
entity of the thoroughly established nature, reality *chos nyid yongs grub kyi ngo bo*
entity-body *ngo bo nyid kyi sku, svābhāvikakāya*
Epistemology-Logic *tshad ma*, Pramāṇa
established by valid cognition *tshad mas grub pa*
establishing illusion as naturelessness *sgyu ma rang bzhin med par sgrub*
establishing mind as illusion *sems sgyu mar sgrub*
establishment of conventions by valid cognition *tha snyad tshad grub*
eternal *g.yung drung, śāśvatā*
eternalism *rtag mtha', śāśvatānta*
eternity *g.yung drung, śāśvatā*
excessive attachment to relative truth *kun rdzob kyi bden pa la lhag par zhen pa*
exclusion of other isolates *ldog pa gzhan sel*
experiencer *myong ba po*
experiencing *myong*
experiencing itself by itself *rang gis rang nyid nyams myong*
Explanation for Assembly *tshogs bshad*

Explanation for Disciples *slob bshad*
explanatory traditions of dialecticians *mtshan nyid pa'i bshad srol*
explanatory traditions of Mantra *sngags kyi bshad srol*
explicit teachings *dngos bstan*
explicit teachings of the last pronouncement *bka' tha ma'i dngos bstan*
explicit teachings of the middle pronouncement *bka' bar pa'i dngos bstan*
explicit teachings, the level of emptiness *dngos bstan stong nyid kyi rim pa*
expression of realizations *rtogs pa brjod pa, avadāna*
expressive sounds and concepts *rjod byed kyi sgra dang rtog pa*
external objects *phyi rol gyi don, bahirdhārtha*
extreme of deprecation *skur 'debs kyi mtha'*
extreme of superimposition *sgro 'dogs kyi mtha'*
extremes of proliferations *spros pa'i mtha', prapañcānta*
factor of non-affirming negation *med par dgag pa'i cha*
factor of the inward-looking apprehender-aspect *kha nang blta 'dzin rnam gyi cha*
factor of the outward-looking apprehended-aspect *kha phyir blta gzung rnam gyi cha*
False Aspectarian Followers of the Middle *rnam (b)rdzun dbu ma pa,* *Alīkākāravāda Mādhyamika
false *rdzun pa, alīka*
False Aspectarian Mind-Only *sems tsam rnam rdzun pa,* Alīkākāravāda Cittamātra
False Aspectarians *rnam rdzun pa,* Alīkākāravāda
False Aspectarians of Yogic Practice *rnal 'byor spyod pa'i rnam rdzun pa,* Alīkākāravāda Yogācāra
filling the role of nonexistence *med pa'i go chod pa*
final intent *mthar thug gi dgongs pa*
first Dharma-seal *chos kyi phyag rgya dang po*
five appropriated aggregates *nyer len gyi phung po, upādānaskandha*
Five Foremost Venerable Founders *rje btsun gong ma lnga*
Five Great Treasure Revealers *gter chen lnga*
fluctuating conceptual mentality *g.yo ba'i rtog yid*
Follower of Cognizance *rnam rig pa,* Vijñaptika
Follower of Other-Emptiness *gzhan stong pa*
Follower of Self-Emptiness *rang stong pa*
Follower of the Middle *dbu ma smra ba/ dbu ma pa,* Mādhyamika
Follower of the Middle of Proponents of Cognizance *rnam rig smra ba'i dbu ma pa,* *Vijñaptivāda Mādhyamika
Follower of the Middle of Proponents of Entitylessness *ngo bo nyid med par smra ba'i dbu ma pa,* Niḥsvabhāvavāda Mādhyamika
Follower of the Middle of Sūtra Followers *mdo sde spyod pa'i dbu ma pa* Sautrāntika Mādhyamika

Follower of the Middle of Yogic Practice *rnal 'byor spyod pa'i dbu ma pa*, Yogācāra Mādhyamika
Follower of Yogic Practice *rnal 'byor spyod pa pa*, Yogācāra
followers of explanatory and practice lineages *bshad rgyud pa dang sgrub rgyud pa*
form-body *gzugs kyi sku, rūpakāya*
fortunate instantanialists *skal ldan cig char ba*
Four Golden Dharmas of Shangpa *shangs pa'i gser chos bzhi*
four seals *phyag rgya bzhi, caturmudrā*
four stages of yoga *rnal 'byor gyi sa bzhi*
Fragmentation Period *sil bu'i dus*
freedom from proliferations *spros bral, aprapañca*
freedom from proliferations as the factor of non-affirming negation *spros bral med dgag gi cha*
freedom from proliferations taught in the third dharmacakra *'khor lo gsum pa'i spros bral*
fully ordained nun *dge slong ma, bhikṣuṇī*
functional thing *dngos po*
functional thing which is an affirming negation *ma yin par dgag pa'i dngos po*
fundamental mind *gnyug sems*
general meaning *spyi don*
generally characterized phenomenon *spyi mtshan, sāmānyalakṣaṇa*
generation stage *bskyed pa'i rim pa, utpattikrama*
generations of abbots *mkhan rabs*
genuine *mtshan nyid pa*
going on monastic rounds *grwa skor*
gradual engagement in the views *lta ba rim 'jug*
grasping at the self of the apprehended-phenomena *gzung ba chos kyi bdag 'dzin*
grasping at the self of the apprehender-phenomena *'dzin pa chos kyi bdag 'dzin*
Great Aspirational Prayers *smon lam chen mo*
great bliss *bde ba chen po, mahāsukha*
Great Madhyamaka *dbu ma chen po*
Great Mādhyamika *dbu ma pa chen po*
great monastic university *chos grwa chen mo*
Great One *chen po*
great paṇḍita *paṇ chen*
Great Perfection *rdzogs che*
great scriptures *gzhung chen*
Great Seal *phyag chen, mahāmudrā*
Great Seal Amulet Box *phyag chen ga'u ma*

gross objects *rags pa*
ground of dependence on which to depend *gang la ltos pa'i ltos sa*
guiding instructions on the Madhyamaka view *dbu ma'i lta khrid*
guiding mind instructions *sems khrid*
habitual tendencies *bag chags, vāsana*
harmonizing restoration-purification *mthun pa'i gso sbyong*
having a veiled intent *dgongs pa can*
having parts *cha bcas*
heretic *mu stegs, tīrthika*
hidden meaning, the level of clear realizations *sbas don mngon rtogs kyi rim pa*
hidden phenomenon *lkog gyur, parokṣa*
Higher Knowledge *mngon pa*, Abhidharma
Highest Yoga Tantra *bla med kyi rgyud, anuttarayogatantra*
illusion-like meditative concentration *sgyu ma lta bu'i ting nge 'dzin*
illusory body *sgyu lus, māyādeha*
illustration *mtshan gzhi*
imaginary apprehended and apprehender *gzung 'dzin kun btags*
imaginary form *kun brtags pa'i gzugs*
imaginary nature *kun btags/ kun brtags, parikalpita*
impermanence *mi rtag pa, anitya*
impure *ma dag, aśuddha*
impure-pure *ma dag dag pa, aśuddhaśuddha*
imputational form *rnam par brtags pa'i gzugs*
imputed *btags pa ba*
imputed uncompounded phenomenon *'dus ma byas btags pa ba*
in the face of conceptuality *rtog ngor*
in the face of meditative equipoise *mnyam gzhag gi ngor*
in the face of reasoning *rigs ngor*
in the face of the view *lta ba'i ngor*
inanimate emptiness *bems po'i stong pa nyid*
indestructible *gzhom du med pa*
indestructible mind-vajra *gzhom du med pa sems kyi rdo rje*
individual self-cognition *so so rang gis rig pa*
individually self-cognizing nonconceptual mind appearing as the illusion-like selfness *sgyu ma lta bu'i bdag nyid du snang ba'i blo rnam par mi rtog pa so sor rang gis rig pa*
individually self-cognizing primordial mind *so so(r) rang gis rig pa'i ye shes*
inducing ascertainment *nges pa 'dren pa*
inexpressible *brjod bral*
inexpressible knowing *brjod med kyi shes pa*

inexpressible primordial mind *brjod bral gyi ye shes*
inference *rjes dpag, anumāna*
inferential object of engagement *rjes dpag gi 'jug yul*
innate nature *rang bzhin lhan skyes*
innate primordial mind *lhan cig skyes pa'i ye shes*
Innate Union *lhan cig skyes sbyor*
Innate Union Great Seal *phyag chen lhan cig skyes sbyor*
innate worldly mind *'jig rten gyi blo lhan skyes*
inseparability of clarity and emptiness *gsal stong dbyer med*
instructional writings *khrid yig*
instructions *gdams pa*
intended meaning *dgongs don*
intended profound meaning *dgongs don zab mo*
intent *dgongs pa*
Intermediate Madhyamaka *dbu ma 'bring po*
interpretive and definitive *drang nges*
knowing *shes pa*
knowing and cognition *shes rig*
knowing at the present *da lta'i shes pa*
knowing devoid of duality of the apprehended and apprehender that does not have momentary parts *gzung 'dzin gnyis med kyi shes pa skad cig gi cha med*
knowing devoid of the apprehended and apprehender *gzung 'dzin med pa'i shes pa*
knowing that has dualistic appearance of the apprehended and apprehender *gzung 'dzin gnyis snang can gyi shes pa*
knowledge-seeing of āryas *'phags pa'i shes mthong*
lack of nature of the self of phenomena *chos kyi bdag rang bzhin med pa*
Later Dissemination *phyi dar*
later Tibetans *bod phyi ma*
Lesser Madhyamaka *dbu ma chung ngu*
level of incorporation into experience by wisdom arisen from meditation *sgom byung gis nyams su len pa'i tshe*
level of severing superimpositions by reasoning arisen from thinking *bsam byung gi rigs pas sgro 'dogs gcod pa'i tshe*
lifting restrictions set during the summer retreat *dgag dbye, prāraṇā*
lineage of bodhisattva vows *byang sems kyi sdom brgyud*
lineage of extensive deeds *rgya chen spyod brgyud*
lineage of profound view *zab mo lta brgyud*
lineage of Secret Mantra vows *gsang sngags kyi sdom brgyud*
lineage of vows of individual liberation *so thar gyi sdom brgyud*
luminosity *'od gsal, prabhāsvara*

luminous nature of mind *sems kyi rang bzhin 'od gsal ba*
luminous nature of mind free from all proliferations *spros pa thams cad dang bral ba sems kyi rang bzhin 'od gsal ba*
Madhyamaka Advocating Cognizance-Only *rnam par rig pa tsam du smra ba'i dbu ma*
Madhyamaka Advocating Interiority of Knowables *shes bya nang gir smra ba'i dbu ma*
Madhyamaka Asserted by Maitreya and Brothers Asaṅga and Vasubandhu *byams pa dang thogs med mched kyis bzhed pa'i dbu ma*
Madhyamaka Explained by the *Collection of Reasonings* with the Texts of Its Followers *rigs tshogs rjes 'brang dang bcas pas bshad pa'i dbu ma*
Madhyamaka of Pāramitāyāna Followers *phar phyin pa'i dbu ma*
Madhyamaka of the Highest Secret Mantra *gsang sngags bla na med pa'i dbu ma*
Madhyamaka view *dbu ma'i lta ba*
Madhyamaka with the Approach Advocating Thoroughly Established Phenomena as Entityness *yongs grub ngo bo nyid du smra ba'i tshul can gyi dbu ma*
Madhyamaka with the Approach of Entitylessness of All Phenomena *chos thams cad ngo bo nyid med pa'i tshul can gyi dbu ma*
Mādhyamika Utilizing Worldly Renown *'jig rten grags sde spyod pa'i dbu ma pa*
main topic *bstan bya'i gtso bo*
main topic of the middle pronouncement *bka' bar pa'i bstan bya'i gtso bo*
main types of Prāsaṅgika and Svātantrika *thal rang gi gtso bo*
manifest phenomena *mngon gyur, pratyakṣa*
Mantra *sngags*
Mantra system *sngags lugs*
Mantra texts *sngags gzhung*
Mantra Vehicle *sngags kyi theg pa*, Mantrayāna
Mantric Madhyamaka *sngags kyi dbu ma*
Master *slob dpon*
Master of Four Texts *bka' bzhi pa*
Master of Numerous Texts *rab 'byams pa*
Master of Ten Texts *bka' bcu pa/ ka bcu pa*
matter *gzugs, rūpa*
meaning-generality *don spyi, arthasāmānya*
meaning of the mode of being *gnas lugs kyi don*
means of accomplishment *sgrub thabs, sādhana*
measure *tshad*
meditation *sgom pa, bhāvanā*
meditative equipoise *mnyam gzhag, samāhita*

mental application of belief *mos pa yid byed, abhimuktimanaskāra*
mental isolation *sems dben, cittaviveka*
mental phenomenon *blo chos*
mere clarity *gsal ba tsam*
mere cognizance characterized by the aspect of the apprehender *'dzin pa'i rnam pa'i mtshan nyid rnam par rig pa tsam*
mere consciousness *rnam par shes pa tsam*
mere freedom from proliferations *spros pa bral tsam*
mere Mahāyāna *theg pa chen po tsam*
mere ultimate truth *don dam pa'i bden pa tsam*
metaphorical ultimate *rnam grangs pa'i don dam, paryāyaparamārtha*
middle *dbu ma*
Middle *dbu ma*, Madhyamaka
Middle of Cognizance *rnam rig gi dbu ma*, Vijñapti Madhyamaka
Middle of Proponents of Cognizance *rnam rig smra ba'i dbu ma*, *Vijñaptivāda Madhyamaka
mind *sems, citta*
mind luminous by nature *sems rang bzhin gyis 'od gsal ba*
mind of enlightenment *byang chub sems, bodhicitta*
mind possessing the aspect of the apprehender *'dzin pa'i rnam pa can gyi sems*
mind side *sems phyogs*
Mind Training *blo sbyong*
mind's clarity factor *sems kyi gsal cha*
mind's empty factor *sems kyi stong cha*
mind-only *sems tsam, cittamātra*
Mind-Only *sems tsam*, Cittamātra
mind-vajra *sems kyi rdo rje*
miracle aspirational prayers *cho 'phrul gyi smon lam*
mode *ji lta, yathā*
mode of apprehension of something as truly established *bden grub tu lta ba'i 'dzin stangs*
mode of being *gnas lugs*
mode of negating objects of negation *dgag bya 'gog pa'i tshul*
mode of proving objects being proven *bsgrub bya sgrub pa'i tshul*
mode of severing superimpositions *sgro 'dogs gcod pa'i tshul*
mode of the view *lta tshul*
momentarily disintegrating *skad cig gis 'jig pa*
momentariness *skad cig ma, kṣaṇika*
monastic examinations *blo gsar grwa skor*
Moral Discipline *'dul ba*, Vinaya
multiplicity *ji snyed, yāvat*

natural dharma-body *rang bzhin chos sku*
natural emptiness established as the mode of being which is experienced by yogis *gnas lugs su grub pa'i rang bzhin stong nyid rnal 'byor pas nyams su myong ba*
natural luminosity *rang bzhin 'od gsal, prakṛtiprabhāsvara*
natural nirvāṇa *rang bzhin gyi myang 'das*
natural permanence *rang bzhin rtag pa*
naturally luminous cognition *rig pa rang bzhin gyis 'od gsal ba*
naturally luminous mind free from proliferations *spros pa dang bral ba'i sems rang bzhin gyis 'od gsal ba*
negation of both the apprehended and apprehender *gzung 'dzin gnyis po bkag pa*
New and Old Secret Mantras *gsang sngags gsar rnying*
New Traditions *gsar ma*
nihilism *chad mtha', ucchedānta*
nihilist *chad par smra ba, ucchedavādin*
nihilistic emptiness *chad pa'i stong pa nyid*
Niḥsvabhāvavāda reasoning *ngo bo nyid med pa'i rigs pa*
non-affirming negation *med dgag, prasajyapratiṣedha*
non-affirming negation which is a mere negation of self of persons *gang zag gi bdag bkag tsam gyi med par dgag pa*
non-afflicted ignorance *nyon mongs pa can ma yin pa'i ma rig pa*
nonanalytical Madhyamaka experienced through meditation *rnam par ma brtags pa sgom pas nyams su myong bya'i dbu ma*
non-apprehension by a subject *yul can 'dzin med*
Non-Aspectarians *rnam med pa, nirākāra/ anākāra*
nonconceptual *rtog pa dang bral ba, kalpanāpoḍha*
nonconceptual knowing *rtog med kyi shes pa*
nonconceptual primordial mind *rnam par mi rtog pa'i ye shes, nirvikalpajñāna*
nonconceptual primordial mind of meditative equipoise *mnyam gzhag rnam par mi rtog pa'i ye shes*
non-deceptive *mi slu ba, avisaṃvādin*
non-dual knowing *gnyis med kyi shes pa*
non-dual primordial mind *gnyis su med pa'i ye shes, advayajñāna*
non-erroneous thoroughly established nature *phyin ci ma log pa'i yongs grub*
non-metaphorical ultimate *rnam grangs ma yin pa'i don dam, aparyāyaparamārtha*
non-mistaken *ma 'khrul ba, abhrānta*
non-observation of an object *yul dmigs med*
not having momentary parts *skad cig gi cha med*
not truly established *bden par ma grub*

novice monk's *dge tshul, śrāmaṇera*
object *yul*
object experienced by wisdom produced from meditation *sgom pa las byung ba'i shes rab kyis nyams su myong bya*
object of comprehension *gzhal bya, prameya*
object of engagement *'jug yul, pravṛttiviṣaya*
object of experience *nyams su myong bya*
object of experience of individually self-cognizing primordial mind *so sor rang gis rig pa'i ye shes kyi myong bya*
object of experience of wisdom arisen from meditation *sgom byung gi nyams su myong bya*
object of experience of yogic direct perception *rnal 'byor mngon sum gyi myong bya*
object of functioning of individually self-cognizing primordial mind *so so rang gis rig pa'i ye shes kyi spyod yul*
object of meditative experience *sgom pas nyams su myong bya*
object of negation *dgag bya*
object of observation *dmigs pa, ālambana*
object, freedom from proliferations *yul spros bral*
object, primordial mind free of proliferations *yul spros bral gyi ye shes*
objects of engagement *'jug pa'i yul*
objects of realization of Mantra *sngags kyi rtogs bya*
objects of sounds and concepts *sgra dang rtog pa'i yul*
obscurations of knowables *shes sgrib, jñeyāvaraṇa*
obscurations of knowables which are conceptions of the apprehended *shes bya'i sgrib pa gzung rtog*
Old Tradition *rnying ma*
omniscient primordial mind *thams cad mkhyen pa'i ye shes*
oral teachings *ngag sgros*
Ordinary Madhyamaka *dbu ma phal pa*
original primordial mind *gdod ma'i ye shes*
originally established primordial mind *gdod ma nas grub pa'i ye shes*
originally pure luminosity *gdod ma nas dag pa'i 'od gsal*
other entities *gzhan gyi ngo bo*
other-emptiness *gzhan stong/ gzhan gyis stong pa*
other-exclusion *gzhan sel, anyāpoha*
outward-looking knowing *kha phyir blta'i shes pa*
outward-looking stain factor *phyi blta dri ma'i cha*
overextended emptiness *thal byung gi stong pa nyid*
own entity *rang gyi ngo bo*
own final system *rang gi lugs mthar thug*
own system *rang lugs*

Pacification *zhi byed*
part of clarity and cognition *gsal rig gi cha*
part of dualistic appearance *gnyis snang gi cha*
partial concordance with definite discrimination *nges 'byed cha mthun, nirvedhabhāgiya*
path *lam, mārga*
Path and Result *lam 'bras*
Path and Result Explanations for the Assembly *lam 'bras tshogs bshad*
path of preparation *sbyor lam, prayogamārga*
path of seeing *mthong lam, darśanamārga*
peace *zhi ba, śānta*
perfection of wisdom *shes rab kyi pha rol tu phyin pa, prajñāpāramitā*
Perfection of Wisdom *shes rab kyi pha rol tu phyin pa,* Prajñāpāramitā
Perfection Vehicle *phar phyin theg pa,* Pāramitāyāna
permanence *rtag pa, nitya*
permanence of continuity *rgyun gyi(s) rtag pa*
permanent *rtag pa, nitya*
phenomenon *chos, dharma*
phenomenon whose continuity is not severed *rgyun mi 'chad pa yi dngos po*
physical isolation *lus dben, kāyaviveka*
pinnacle of all tenets, Madhyamaka which is the meaning expressed *grub mtha' kun gyi rtse mor gyur ba'i brjod bya don gyi dbu ma*
pointing-out instructions *mdzub khrid*
possessor of reality *chos can, dharmin*
postscripts *par byang*
practical incorporation into experience *spyod pa nyams len*
practice lineage *sgrub brgyud*
predispositions *bag chags, vāsana*
primordial mind *ye shes, jñāna*
primordial mind empty of duality *gnyis stong ye shes*
primordial mind factor of the inward-looking apprehender-aspect *nang blta 'dzin rnam ye shes kyi cha*
primordial mind free from the duality of the apprehended and apprehender *gzung 'dzin gnyis su med pa'i ye shes*
primordial mind free from the duality of the apprehended and apprehender in terms of self of persons *gang zag gi dbang du byas pa'i gzung 'dzin gnyis med kyi ye shes*
primordial mind free of proliferations *spros bral ye shes*
primordial mind of emptiness *stong pa nyid kyi ye shes*
primordial mind of the basis *gzhi dus kyi ye shes*
primordial mind of the dharma-sphere *chos kyi dbyings kyi ye shes, dharmadhatujñāna*

primordial mind of the great bliss *bde ba chen po'i ye shes*
primordial nature *gnyug ma'i rang bzhin*
primordial nature of phenomena *chos rnams kyi rang bzhin gnyug ma*
probandum *bsgrub bya, sādhya*
product *byas pa, kṛta*
production, disintegration, and abiding *skye 'jig gnas gsum*
profundity and extensiveness *zab rgyas*
progression of the four stages of yoga *rnal 'byor sa bzhi'i rim pa*
proponent of the extreme of eternalism as the middle *rtag mtha' la dbu mar smra ba*
proponent of the extreme of nihilism as the middle *chad mtha' la dbu mar smra ba*
Proponents of Cognizance *rnam rig smra ba,* Vijñaptivāda
Proponents of Entitylessness *ngo bo nyid med par smra ba/ ngo bo nyid med pa pa,* Niḥsvabhāvavāda
Proponents of Other-Emptiness *gzhan stong smra ba*
Proponents of Particulars *bye brag smra ba,* Vaibhāṣika
Proponents of Phenomenal Existence *dngos por smra ba, vastusatpadārthavāda*
Proponents of Self-Emptiness *rang stong smra ba*
provisionally Cittamātra Followers *gnas skabs sems tsam pa*
pure wordly primordial mind of subsequent attainment *rjes thob dag pa 'jig rten pa'i ye shes*
purificatory object of observation *rnam dag gi dmigs pa, viśuddhālambana*
purity from adventitious stains *glo bur rnam dag*
purpose *dgos pa*
quintessential instructions *man ngag, upadeśa*
reading transmission *lung*
reality *chos nyid, dharmatā*
reality-form *chos nyid kyi gzugs*
reality-limit *yang dag pa'i mtha', bhūtakoṭi*
realized by mind in an exclusionary way *blos rnam bcad du rtogs bya*
realizing *rtogs*
really existent entity *yang dag par yod pa'i ngo bo*
reason of ascertainment of simultaneous observation *lhan cig dmigs nges pa'i rtags*
reason of clarity and cognition *gsal zhing rig pa'i rtags*
reason of the lack of being one or many *gcig dang du bral gyi gtan tshigs / gcig dang du mar med pa'i gtan tshigs, ekānekaviyogahetu*
reasoning analyzing the ultimate *don dam dpyod byed kyi rigs pa*
reasoning negating elaborations apprehending signs *mtshan 'dzin gyi spros pa 'gog byed kyi rigs pa*
reasoning of listening and thinking *thos bsam gyi rigs pa*

reasonings used to negate concepts apprehending signs with respect to the mode of being *gnas lugs la mtshan 'dzin gyi rtog pa 'gog byed kyi rigs pa*
relative compounded phenomena *kun rdzob 'dus byas kyi dngos po*
relative existence *kun rdzob tu yod pa*
relative mind *kun rdzob pa'i sems*
relative truth *kun rdzob bden pa, saṃvṛtisatya*
relative truth of the world *'jig rten pa'i kun rdzob bden pa*
replenishing burnt offerings *kha gso'i sbyin sreg*
restoration-purification of vows *gso sbyong, poṣadha*
result *'bras bu, phala*
reverse of impermanence *mi rtag pa las log pa / mi rtag pa log pa*
rites of the three bases *gzhi gsum cho ga*
root guru *rtsa ba'i bla ma, mūlaguru*
Sakya Geshé *sa skya pa'i dge bshes*
scope of presumption *rlom tshod*
scope of reach *song tshod*
secret empowerment *gsang dbang, guhyābhiṣeka*
self of persons *gang zag gi bdag, pudgalātman*
self of phenomena *chos kyi bdag, dharmātman*
self of the apprehended-phenomena *gzung ba chos kyi bdag*
self-arisen innate primordial mind *rang byung lhan cig skyes pa'i ye shes*
self-blessings *rang byin rlabs*
self-characterized phenomenon *rang mtshan, svalakṣaṇa*
self-cognition *rang rig, svasaṃvedana/ svasaṃvitti*
self-cognition devoid of the duality of the apprehended and apprehender *gzung 'dzin gnyis med kyi rang rig*
self-cognition experiencing the apprehended-aspect *gzung rnam nyams su myong ba'i rang rig*
self-cognizing primordial mind of āryas *'phags pa rnams kyi rang rig pa'i ye shes*
self-emptiness *rang gis stong pa*
self-experiencing valid cognition *rang myong tshad ma*
self-illuminating self-cognition *rang rig rang gsal ba*
self-illuminating self-cognition of non-dual knowing *gnyis med kyi shes pa rang rig rang gsal ba*
selflessness *bdag med, nairātmya*
selflessness of persons *gang zag gi bdag med, pudgalanairātmya*
selflessness of phenomena *chos kyi bdag med, dharmanairātmya*
senior abbot *mkhan chen*
Seventy Meanings *don bdun cu*

severing proliferations by the view within meditative equipoise *mnyam gzhag tu lta bas spros pa gcod pa*
severing superimpositions by listening and thinking *thos bsam gyis sgro 'dogs gcod pa*
short-sighted ones *tshur rol mthong ba*
signs *mtshan ma*
signs of an object *yul gyi mtshan ma*
Six Applications *sbyor drug*
six collections of consciousness that are compounded *tshogs drug 'dus byas*
Six Dharmas of Nāro *nā ro chos drug*
Six Ornaments Beautifying the Snowy Land *gangs can mdzes pa'i rgyan drug*
something recognized as ultimate truth *don dam pa'i bden pa yin ngo shes pa zhig*
songs of contemplative experience *gsung mgur*
sounds and concepts *sgra rtog*
space *nam mkha'*
space-like non-affirming negation of all extremes of proliferations *spros pa'i mtha' thams cad bkag pa'i med dgag nam mkha' lta bu*
special deity *lhag pa'i lha*
special insight *lhag mthong, vipaśyanā*
sphere of mind *sems kyi dbyings*
śrāvaka schools *nyan thos sde pa*
stability *brtan pa, dhruva*
stable *brtan pa, dhruva*
stage of luminosity *'od gsal ba'i rim pa*
stage of self-blessings *rang byin gyis brlabs pa'i rim pa*
stage of yoga not realizing any extremes of proliferations *spros pa'i mtha' gang yang ma rtogs pa'i rnal 'byor gyi sa*
stage of yoga realizing the selflessness of persons *gang zag gi bdag med rtogs pa'i rnal 'byor gyi sa*
stage of yoga realizing the selflessness of the apprehended-phenomena *gzung ba chos kyi bdag med rtogs pa'i rnal 'byor gyi sa*
stage of yoga realizing the selflessness of the apprehender-phenomena *'dzin pa chos kyi bdag med rtogs pa'i rnal 'byor gyi sa*
stagnant calm abiding *ltengs po yi zhi gnas tsam*
stainless great bliss *zag med bde ba chen po*
stains *dri ma*
subject, primordial mind *yul can ye shes*
subject, supremely unchangeable bliss *yul can mchog tu mi 'gyur ba'i bde ba*

subject-basis for dispute *rtsod gzhi'i chos can*
subject-basis of emptiness *stong gzhi'i chos can*
subject-basis of other-emptiness *gzhan stong gi gzhi chos can*
subsequent attainment *rjes thob, pṛṣṭhalabdha*
subsequent conventions *rjes kyi tha snyad*
subsequent *Dharmas of Maitreya byams chos phyi ma*
subsequent permission *rjes gnang*
substance *rdzas, dravya*
substantially existent *rdzas su yod pa, dravyasat*
suchness *de bzhin nyid, tathatā*
sugata-essence *bde gshegs snying po, sugatagarbha*
summer retreat *dbyar gnas, vārṣika*
superimposed *sgro btags*
superimposition *sgro 'dogs, samāropa*
Sūtra Followers *mdo sde pa, sautrāntika*
synonymics *mngon brjod*
synonyms *mtshan gyi rnam grangs*
systems of methods of Followers of Self-Emptiness and Other-Emptiness *rang gzhan stong pa'i tshul lugs*
tantric skills in means *gsang sngags thabs la mkhas pa*
tathāgata-essence *de bshin gshegs pa'i snying po, tathāgatagarbha*
ten grounds *sa bcu, daśabhūmi*
tenets of cognizance *rnam rig grub pa'i mtha'*
tenets of the view and practice *lta spyod kyi grub mtha'*
textual systems *gzhung lugs*
that which has an appearance but does not ascertain it *snang la ma nges*
that which is cognized by mind *blos rig bya*
that which is determined by listening and thinking *thos bsam gyis gtan la dbab bya*
that which is experienced *nyams su myong bya*
thatness free from the duality of the apprehended and apprehender *gzung 'dzin gnyis med kyi de kho na nyid*
thatness of union *zung 'jug gi de kho na nyid*
thatness which is an object of experience *nyams su myong bya'i de kho na nyid*
third dharmacakra of perfect differentiation *legs par rnam par phye ba dang ldan pa'i chos kyi 'khor lo gsum pa*
third empowerment *dbang gsum pa*
thoroughly established nature *yongs grub, pariniṣpanna*
those with great desires *'dod chen, icchantika*
three characteristics *mtshan nyid gsum, trilakṣaṇa*
three natures *ngo bo nyid gsum, trisvabhāva*

Three Types of Vows *sdom gsum*
Transference *'pho ba*
Treasure *gter ma*
True Aspectarians *rnam bden pa,* Satyākāravāda
true establishment *bden par grub pa, satyasiddhi*
true self *bdag dam pa*
truly established *bden grub*
truly established atoms *rdul phran bden grub*
truly established moments *skad cig bden grub*
truth *bden pa, satya*
truthless *bden min*
truthlessness of external objects *phyi rol gyi don bden med*
truthlessness of the apprehended-aspects *gzung rnam bden med*
two extremes *mtha' gnyis, antadvaya*
two stages *rim pa gnyis, dvikrama*
two truths *bden pa gnyis, satyadvaya*
Types of Minds *blo rigs*
Types of Reasons *rtags rigs*
ultimate meaning *dam pa'i don, paramārtha*
ultimate mind *don dam pa'i sems*
ultimate mind of enlightenment *don dam byang chub kyi sems, paramārthabodhicitta*
ultimate nonbeing and ultimate nonexistence *don dam du ma yin pa dang med pa*
ultimate primordial mind *don dam pa'i ye shes*
ultimate truth *don dam pa'i bden pa, paramārthasatya*
ultimate truth on the level of the basis *gzhi dus kyi don dam bden pa*
ultimate way of being *don dam gyi gnas tshul*
ultimately Mādhyamika *mthar thug dbu ma pa*
unchangeable thoroughly established nature *'gyur ba med pa'i yongs grub*
uncompounded ultimate *don dam 'dus ma byas*
uninterrupted path of meditative equipoise *mnyam par gzhag pa'i bar chad med lam*
union *zung 'jug, yuganaddha*
union of non-observing compassion and emptiness *dmigs pa med pa'i snying rje dang stong pa nyid zung du 'jug pa*
unobservable *mi dmigs pa*
unreal ideation *yang dag pa ma yin pa'i kun tu rtog pa, abhūtaparikalpa*
utmost joy *rab tu dga' ba, pramuditā*
vajra of ultimate bodhicitta *don dam pa byang chub sems kyi rdo rje*
Vajra Vehicle, *rdo rje theg pa,* Vajrayāna
valid cognition *tshad ma, pramāṇa*

vase empowerment *bum dbang, kalaśābhiṣeka*
vehicle *theg pa, yāna*
verbal isolation *ngag dben, vāgviveka*
very pure *shin tu rnam dag, suviśuddha*
very subtle analysis *shin tu phra ba brtags pa*
view *lta ba, dṛṣṭi*
view and meditation *lta sgom*
view of the Middle *dbu ma'i lta ba*
view realized in Mantra *sngags kyi rtogs bya'i lta ba*
virtuous spiritual friend *dge ba'i bshes gnyen, kalyāṇamitra*
way of being *gnas tshul*
way of being empty *ji ltar stong pa'i tshul*
way of positing *'jog tshul*
wheel of teachings *chos 'khor,* dharmacakra
wisdom of individual analysis *so sor rtog pa'i shes rab*
wisdom-primordial mind empowerment *shes rab ye shes kyi dbang, prajñājñānābhiṣeka*
withstanding analysis by reasoning *rigs pas dpyad bzod*
word empowerment *tshig dbang*
Word of the Buddha *sangs rgyas kyi bka', buddhavacana*
worldly renown *'jig rten gyi grags pa*
yantra yoga *'khrul 'khor*
yogic direct perception *rnal 'byor mngon sum, yogipratyakṣa*
Yogic Practice *rnal 'byor spyod pa,* Yogācāra

Spellings of Tibetan Names and Terms

Amapel *a ma dpal*
Amgön Zangpo *a mgon zang po*
Baktön Shakya Özer *bag ston shākya 'od zer*
Baktön Zhönnu Gyeltsen *bag ston gzhon nu rgyal mtshan*
Belti Drachompa Khutön Tsöndrü Wangchuk *sbal ti dgra bcom pa khu ston brtson 'grus dbang phyug*
Belti Wangchuk Tsültrim *sbal ti dbang phyug tshul khrims*
Bodongpa *bo dong pa*
Bön *bon*
Butön Rinchendrup *bu ston rin chen grub*
Chakzang Rapjampa Sönam Pelden *lcags zangs rab 'byams pa bsod nams dpal ldan*
Changkya Rölpé Dorjé *lcang skya rol pa'i rdo rje*
Changlung Chödingpa Zhönnu Lodrö *spyang lung chos sdings pa gzhon nu blo gros*
Changlung Rinpoché *spyang lung rin po che*
Chapa Chökyi Senggé *phya pa chos kyi seng ge*
Chennga Ngakgi Wangpo *spyan snga ngag gi dbang po*
Chenpo *chen po*
Chesa Dakchen Lodrö Wangchuk *che sa bdag chen blo gros dbang phyug*
Chödrak Gyamtso *chos grags rgya mtsho*
Chödrak Yeshé *chos grags ye shes*
Choklé Namgyel *phyogs las rnam rgyal*
Chökyap Pelzang *chos skyabs dpal bzang*
Chökyi Gyeltsen *chos kyi rgyal mtshan*
Chölung *chos lung*
Chumik *chu mig*
Dalai Lama *tā la'i bla ma*
Dedünpa Wangchuk Gyeltsen *sde bdun pa dbang phyug rgyal mtshan*

Doklöpa Künga Zangpo *ldog lod pa' kun dga' bzang po*
Dölpopa Sherap Gyeltsen *dol po pa shes rab rgyal mtshan*
Döndrup Pelzang *don grub dpal bzang*
Dönyö Dorjé *don yod rdo rje*
Dönyö Druppa *don yod grub pa*
Dönyö Pelwa *don yod dpal ba*
Dönyöpa *don yod pa*
Doring Künpang *rdo rings kun dpangs*
Dorjé Gyelpo *rdo rje rgyal po*
Dorjechang Künga Zangpo *rdo rje 'chang kun dga' bzang po*
Dra Jampaling *grwa byams pa gling*
Drakkar *brag dkar*
Drakmar *brag dmar*
Drakmarwa *brag dmar ba*
Drakpa Gyeltsen *grags pa rgyal mtshan*
Drakpa Jungné *grags pa 'byung gnas*
Drakpa Özer *grags pa 'od zer*
Drakpa Zangpo *grags pa bzang po*
Drepung *'bras spungs*
Dreyül Kyetsel *'bras yul skyed tshal*
Drigung *'bri gung*
Drimé Lekpé Lodrö *dri med legs pa'i blo gros*
Drokmi Lotsawa *'brog mi lo tsā ba*
Dröpa Özer Gyelpo Pelwa *gros pa 'od zer rgyal po dpal ba*
Druk *'brug*
Dzongpa Künga Namgyel *rdzong pa kun dga' rnam rgyal*
Dzongsar *rdzong sar*
Gakhang *'ga' khang*
Gamo Dharma practitioner *dga' mo chos mdzad*
Ganden *dga' ldan*
Gartsa *mgar tsha*
Geluk *dge lugs*
Gendündrup *dge 'dun grub*
Geshé *dge bshes*
Gewa Gyeltsen *dge ba rgyal mtshan*
Gewé Shenyen *dge ba'i bshes gnyen*
Gö Lotsawa Zhönnupel *'gos lo tsā ba gzhon nu dpal*
Gönpa Shar *dgon pa shar*
Gorampa *go rams pa*
Gowo Rapjampa Sönam Senggé *go bo rab 'byams pa bsod nams seng ge*
Gugé *gu ge*
Gungru Gyeltsen Zangpo *gung ru rgyal mtshan bzang po*
Guru Trashi *guru bkra shis*

Gyama *rgya ma*
Gyeltsap Darma Rinchen *rgyal tshab dar ma rin chen*
Gyümé *rgyud smad*
Gyütö *rgyud stod*
Hor Shakya *hor shākya*
Jamchen Chöjé *byams chen chos rje*
Jamchen Rapjampa Sanggyepel *byams chen rab 'byams pa sangs rgyas 'phel*
Jamling *byams gling*
Jampel Gepé Shenyen *'jam dpal dges pa'i bshes gnyen*
Jamyang Chöjé *'jam dbyangs chos rje*
Jamyang Könchok Zangpo *'jam dbyang dkon mchog bzang po*
Jamyang Zhepa Ngakwang Tsöndrü *'jam dbyangs bzhad pa ngag dbang brtson grus*
Jang Ngamring *byang ngam rings*
Jé Khenpo *rje mkhan po*
Jonang Choklé Namgyel *jo nang phyogs las rnam rgyal*
Ju Mipam Jamyang Namgyel Gyamtso *'ju mi pham 'jam dbyangs rnam rgyal rgya mtsho*
Kachupa *bka' bcu pa/ ka bcu pa*
Kadam *bka' gdams*
Kadampa *bka' gdams pa*
Kagyü *bka' brgyud*
Kam *kam / skam*
Karma Kagyü *karma bka' brgyud*
Kazhipa *bka' bzhi pa*
Kelden Shingté Podrang Gyama Trikhang *skal ldan shing rta'i pho brang rgya ma khri khang*
Kelden Tsering *skal ldan tshe ring*
Kham *khams*
Khangsar *khang gsar*
Kharkha *mkhar kha*
Khartsé Changra *mkhar rtse lcang ra*
Khartsé Langtang *mkhar rtse glang thang*
Khedrup Gelek Pelzang *mkhas grub dge legs dpal bzang*
Khenpo *mkhan po*
Khoklung *khog lung*
Khyungpo Neljor *khyung po rnal 'byor*
Kirti Tsenzhap Rinpoché *kirti mtshan zhabs rin po che*
Könchok Gyeltsen *dkon mchog rgyal mtshan*
Könchok Rinchen *dkon mchog rin chen*
Kongtrül Yönten Gyamtso *kong sprul yon tan rgya mtsho*
Künga Chokdrup *kun dga' mchog grub*
Künga Döndrup *kun dga' don grub*

Künga Drölchok *kun dga' grol mchog*
Künga Gyeltsen *kun dga' rgyal mtshan*
Künga Lekpa *kun dga' legs pa*
Künga Penjor *kun dga dpal 'byor*
Künga Trashi *kun dga' bkra shis*
Künga Tsepel *kun dga' tshe 'phel*
Künga Wangchuk *kun dga' dbang phyug*
Kyormolung *skyor mo lung*
Langtang *glang thang*
Latö Lho *la stod lho*
Lekpa Rinchen *legs pa rin chen*
Lhayi Tsünpa *lha yi btsun pa*
Lhündrup Pelzang *lhun grub dpal bzang*
Lhündrup Trashi *lhun grub bkra shis*
Lingmé *gling smad*
Lingtö *gling stod*
Lodrö Chökyongwa *blo gros chos skyong ba*
Lodrö Gyeltsen *blo gros rgyal mtshan*
Lodrö Namgyel *blo gros rnam rgyal*
Lodrö Tayé *blo gros mtha' yas*
Lodrö Tenpa *blo gros brtan pa*
Lodrö Zangpo *blo gros bzang po*
Longchen Rapjam *klong chen rab 'byams*
Longchenpa *klong chen pa*
Loppön *slob dpon*
Lopzang Gyamtso *blo bzang rgya mtsho*
Loten *blo brtan*
Lotenpa *blo brtan pa*
Lowo Depa Tsangchen Trashi Gönpo *glo bo sde pa tshang chen bkra shis mgon po*
Lowo Khenchen Sönam Lhündrup *glo bo mkhan chen bsod nams lhun grub*
Mangkar *mang dkar*
Mapcha Jangchup Tsöndrü *rma bya byang chub brtson 'grus*
Marpa Lotsawa Chökyi Lodrö *mar pa lo tsā ba chos kyi blo gros*
Martön Gyamtso Rinchen *smar ston rgya mtsho rin chen*
Mati Penchen *ma ti paṇ chen*
Mikyö Dorjé *mi bskyod rdo rje*
Minyak *mi nyag*
Mipam Gyamtso *mi pham rgya mtsho*
Mü *mus*
Müpa Rapjampa *mus pa rab 'byams pa*
Mürampa Könchok Drakpa *mus ram pa dkon mchog grags pa*

Nakartsé *sna dkar rtse*
Nalendra *nā lendra*
Namgyel *rnam rgyal*
Namgyel Drakpa Zangpo *rnam rgyal grags pa bzang po*
Namgyel Pelzang *rnam rgyal dpal bzang*
Namkha Lhündrup *nam mkha' lhun grub*
Namkha Rapsel *nam mkha' rab gsal*
Namtseden *gnam rtse ldan*
Nang *nangs*
Nartang *snar thang*
Nego *gnas sgo*
Nenang *gnas nang*
Nenang Gyelwa *gnas snang rgyal ba*
Neudong *sne'u gdong*
Neudzong *sne'u rdzong*
Ngakwang Chödrak *ngag dbang chos grags*
Ngakwang Chögyel *ngag dbang chos rgyal*
Ngakwang Dorjé *ngag dbang rdo rje*
Ngari Lowo *mnga' ris glo bo*
Ngodro Rapjampa Wangchuk Pelwa *ngo gro rab 'byams pa dbang phyug dpal ba*
Ngödrup Pelbar *dngos grub dpal 'bar*
Ngok Lotsawa Loden Sherap *rngog lo tsā ba blo ldan shes rab*
Ngor *ngor*
Ngorchen Künga Zangpo *ngor chen kun dga' bzang po*
Norzang *nor bzang*
Nyangrampa *nyang ram pa*
Nyangtö Rapjampa Lhündrup Pel Zangpo *nyang stod rab 'byams pa lhun grub dpal bzang po*
Nyangtö Tsechen *nyang stod rtse chen*
Nyetang Chödzong *snye thang chos rdzong*
Nyimedrung *nyi ma'i drung*
Nyingma *rnying ma*
Ösel Tsemo *'od gsal rtse mo*
Öseltsé *'od gsal rtse*
Pajoding Okmin Nyipa *pha jo sdings 'og min gnyis pa*
Pakmo Drupa *phag mo gru pa*
Pakmodru *phag mo gru*
Pakpa Lodrö Gyeltsen *'phags pa blo gros rgyal mtshan*
Pangkha Chöding *spang kha chos sdings*
Patsap Nyimadrak *pa tshab nyi ma grags*
Pawo Tsuklak Trengwa *dpa' bo gtsug lag phreng ba*
Peltsek *dpal brtsegs*

Pelyül Chökhor Ling *dpal yul chos 'kbhor gling*
Pema Lingpa *padma gling pa*
Pema Zangpowa *padma bzang po ba*
penchen *paṇ chen*
Penyül *'phan yul*
Potopa Rinchensel *po to pa rin chen gsal*
Puchung Kachupa *phu chung ka bcu pa*
Püntsok Namgyel *phun tshogs rnam rgyal*
Purang *pu rangs*
Puyung *phu dbyung*
Ramdopa *rab mdo pa*
Ramoché *ra mo che*
Rangjung Dorjé *rang byung rdo rje*
Rapjampa *rab 'byams pa*
Rapsel Damgön *rab gsal zla mgon*
Rawa Dopa *ra ba mdo pa*
Renakara *ratna ka ra*
Rikden Namgyel Drakzang *rigs ldan rnam rgyal grags bzang*
Rinchen Gyeltsen *rin chen rgyal mtshan*
Rinchen Trashi *rin chen bkra shis*
Rinchen Zangpo *rin chen bzang po*
Rinpung *rin spungs*
Rinpung Norzang *rin spungs nor bzang*
Rinpungpa *rin spungs pa*
Rong *rong*
Rongtön Mawé Senggé *rong ston smra ba'i seng ge*
Rongtön Sheja Künrik *rong ston shes bya kun rig*
Sachen Künga Nyingpo *sa chen kun dga' snying po*
Sakya Pendita Künga Gyeltsen *sa skya paṇḍita kun dga' rgyal mtshan*
Sakya *sa skya*
Sakyapa *sa skya pa*
Samdruptsé *bsam grub rtse*
Sangda Bangrim *gsang mda' bang rim*
Sanggyé Chökyongwa *sangs rgyas chos skyong ba*
Sanggyé Lodrö *sangs rgyas blo gros*
Sanggyé Özer *sangs rgyas 'od zer*
Sanggyé Pel Zangpo *sangs rgyas dpal bzang po*
Sanggyé Zangpo *sangs rgyas bzang po*
Sangpu Neutok *gsang phu ne'u thog*
Serdok Penchen *gser mdog paṇ chen*
Serdok Penchen Shakya Chokden *gser mdog paṇ chen shākya mchog ldan*
Serdokchen *gser mdog can*

Serling *gser gling*
Shakya Gyeltsen *shākya rgyal mtshan*
Shakya Rinchen *shākya rin chen*
Shakya Zangmo *shākya bzang mo*
Shang *shangs*
Shangpa *shangs pa*
Shangpa Dubupa *shangs pa gdu bu pa*
Shangpa Kagyü *shangs pa bka' brgyud*
Sherap Ö *shes rab 'od*
Sherap Pelden *shes rab dpal ldan*
Sherap Penjor *shes rab dpal 'byor*
Sherap Senggé *shes rab seng ge*
Sönam Gyel *bsod nams rgyal*
Sönam Gyeltsen *bsod nams rgyal mtshan*
Sönam Tsemo *bsod nams rtse mo*
Sönam Tsültrim *bsod nams tshul khrims*
Tai Situ Jangchup Gyeltsen *tā'i si tu byang chub rgyal mtshan*
Taklung *stag lung*
Taktsang Lotsawa Sherap Rinchen *stag tshang lo tsā ba shes rab rin chen*
Tanak Tupten Namgyelling *rta nag thub bstan rnam rgyal gling*
Tangtong Gyelpo *thang stong rgyal po*
Taranatha *tā ra nā tha*
Tingkyé *gting skyes*
Tongwa Dönden *mthong ba don ldan*
Törawa *stod ra ba*
Trachar *khra char*
Trangpo Senggé Gang *'phrang po seng ge sgang*
Trangpowa *'phrang po ba*
Trapu *phra phu*
Trapuwa Sanggyé Zangpo *phra phu ba sangs rgyas bzang po*
Trashi Lhünpo *bkra shis lhun po*
Trashi Namgyel *bkra shis rnam rgyal*
Trashigön *bkra shis mgon*
Tsang *gtsang*
Tsangpo *gtsang po*
Tsel *tshal*
Tsel Chökhorling *tshal chos 'khor gling*
Tsewang Sönam *tshe dbang bsod nams*
Tsongkhapa Lopzang Drakpa *tsong kha pa blo bzang grags pa*
Tsungmé Chöjé *mtshungs med chos rje*
Tsurpu *mtshur phu*
Tuken Lopzang Chökyi Nyima *thu'u bkwan blo bzang chos kyi nyi ma*

Tukje Pelwa *thugs rje dpal ba*
Tupten Özer *thub bstan 'od zer*
Ü *dbus*
Ulek *dbu legs*
Ünyönpa *dbus smyon pa*
Ünyönpa Künga Zangpo *dbus smyon pa kun dga' bzang po*
Ütsang *dbus gtsang*
Wangchuk Pelwa *dbang phyug dpal ba*
Yakpa *g.yag pa*
Yaktön Sanggyepel *g.yag ston sangs rgyas dpal*
Yarlung *yar klungs*
Yeshé Dé *ye shes sde*
Yeshé Lhündrup *ye shes lhun grub*
Yönten Chömpel *yon tan chos 'phel*
Zangpa Lodrö Gyamtso *bzang pa blo gros rgya mtsho*
Zhalu Lotsawa Chökyong Zangpo *zha lu lo tsā ba chos skyong bzang po*
Zhamarpa *zhwa dmar pa*
Zhikatsé *gzhis ka rtse*
Zhönnu Chödrup *gzhon nu chos grub*
Zhu *gzhu*
Zhung Gyapa Ngödrup Pelbar *gzhung brgya pa dngos grub dpal 'bar*
Zilung *gzi lung*
Zurchepa *zur 'chad pa*

Notes

Introduction

1. Hereafter, I am using the simplified phonetic transcription of Tibetan based on the usage adopted by the Tibetan and Himalayan Library. For details, see http://www.thlib.org/reference/transliteration. When appropriate, it includes not only Tibetan words, but also Sanskrit words and names adopted by Tibetans, such as "Sakya Pendita" (*sa skya paṇḍita*), "Taranatha" (Tāranātha), and so forth, in order to approximate the way Tibetans themselves pronounce them. Also, depending on context, one and the same word or term can be rendered differently. For example, the phonetic transcription of *paṇ chen* is "penchen," but when the word is *translated* into English, it is spelled as "great paṇḍita," not "great pendita."

2. I am presently writing a manuscript in which I explore, among other topics, Buddhist challenges and contributions to the issue of (un)mediated mystical experience that occupies contemporary scholars of religion. In large part this manuscript focuses on the different approaches to the nature of ultimate reality and the process of its realization advocated by rival Tibetan thinkers. As my interpretive tools, I heavily rely on Shakya Chokden's ideas addressed in the current book.

3. For the discussion of life and teachings of this seminal Sakya thinker, see José Ignacio Cabezón and Geshe Lobsang Dargyay, *Freedom from Extremes: Gorampa's "Distinguishing the Views" and the Polemics of Emptiness* (Boston: Wisdom Publications, 2007). Hereafter, *Freedom from Extremes.*

4. See *The Buddha from Dölpo: A Study of the Life and Thought of the Tibetan Master Dölpopa Sherab Gyaltsen*, revised and enlarged edition (Ithaca, New York: Snow Lion Publications, 2010), 64 (hereafter, *The Buddha from Dölpo*) referring to Dongtok Tekchok Tenpé Gyeltsen (*gdong thog theg mchog bstan pa'i rgyal mtshan*), *Paṇḍi ta chen po shā kya mchog ldan dri med legs pa'i blo gros kyi gsung rab rin po che par du bskrun pa'i tshul las brtsams pa'i gleng ba bstan pa'i nyi gzhon yid srubs sprin las grol ba'i dga' ston tshangs pa'i bzhad sgra* (Thimphu: Kunzang Tobgey, 1976), 22–23. But Volker Caumanns mentions that "one informant, namely Ngor mKhan po bSod nams rgya mtsho,

denies that Shākya mchog ldan's writings were banned in Tibet. According to bSod nams rgya mtsho, copies of Shākya mchog ldan's works were kept in the libraries of Ngor Ewaṃ Chos ldan and rTa nag Thub bstan rnam rgyal monasteries, but scarcely anybody took an interest in these works." Volker Caumanns, "Tibetan Sources on the Life of Serdog Paṇchen Shākya Chogden (1428–1507)," in *Lives Lived, Lives Imagined: Biography in the Buddhist Traditions*, eds. Linda Covill, Ulrike Roesler, and Sarah Shaw (Boston: Wisdom Publications in collaboration with The Oxford Centre for Buddhist Studies, 2010), 207, note 8 (hereafter, "Tibetan Sources") referring to Ronald M. Davidson's "The Nor-pa Tradition," in *Wind Horse: Proceedings of the North American Tibetological Society*, ed. Ronald M. Davidson (Berkeley: Asian Humanities Press, 1981), 97. Hereafter, "Nor-pa Tradition."

5. This handwritten version was initially found in Bhutan in Pajoding Okmin Nyipa (*pha jo sdings 'og min gnyis pa*), the hermitage of Shakya Rinchen (*shākya rin chen*, 1710–1759), the ninth Jé Khenpo (*rje mkhan po*) of Bhutan. Leonard van der Kuijp, *Contributions to the Development of Tibetan Epistemology* (Wiesbaden: Franz Steiner, 1983), 9–10. Hereafter, *Contributions*. On Shakya Rinchen's role in preservation of Shakya Chokden writings in Bhutan, see Anne Burchardi, "Shakya mchog ldan's Literary Heritage in Bhutan," in John Ardussi and Sonam Tobgay (eds.), *Written Treasures of Bhutan: Mirror of the Past and Bridge to the Futue. Proceedings of the First International Conference on the Rich Scriptural Heritage of Bhutan* (Thimphu: The National Library of Bhutan, 2008), 25–34.

6. Chopgyé Trichen Ngakwang Khyenrap Tupten Lekshé Gyamtso (*bco brgyad khri chen ngag dbang mkhyen rab thub bstan legs bshad rgya mtsho*), *Feast for Minds of the Fortunate: Brief History of the Glorious Sakyapas—Chariot of the Teachings of Sūtras and Tantras of the Land of Snows* (*Gangs ljongs mdo sngags kyi bstan pa'i shing rta dpal ldan sa skya pa'i chos 'byung mdor bsdus skal bzang yid kyi dga' ston*, Dharamsala: Bod gzhung shes rig par khang, 1969), 47 (hereafter, *Feast for Minds of the Fortunate*). English translation in Chogay Trichen Rinpoche, *The History of the Sakya Tradition* (Bristol: Ganesha Press, 1983), 27.

7. For a brief biographical sketch of these five figures, see Migmar Tseten, "The History of the Sakya School," in *Treasures of the Sakya Lineage*, ed. Migmar Tseten (Boston: Shambhala, 2008), 233–249.

8. According to Künga Drölchok's (*kun dga' grol mchog*) *Detailed Analysis of the Liberation Story of the Great Paṇḍita Shakya Chokden* (*Paṇḍi ta chen po shākya mchog ldan gyi rnam par thar pa zhib mo rnam 'byed pa*), in Collected Writings of Gser-mdog paṇ-chen Śākya-mchog-ldan (Thimphu, Bhutan: Kunzang Tobgey, 1975), vol. 16, 18, 55, Shakya Chokden met Rongtön in 1437, and Künga Zangpo in 1451. According to the biography of Rongtön writtten by Shakya Chokden, viz. the *Enjoyment Ocean of Faith: Wondrous Liberation Story of the Foremost Venerable Omniscient Spiritual Friend Rongtön Shakya Gyeltsen* (*Rje btsun thams cad mkhyen pa bshes gnyen shākya rgyal mtshan gyi rnam thar ngo mtshar dad pa'i rol mtsho*), vol. 16, 306, 358, 361–362 (hereafter, *Enjoyment Ocean of Faith*), Rongtön was born in 1367 and passed away at dawn on the fourteenth day of the twelfth lunar month of the earth-male-dragon year (1448) at the age of eighty-three. The twelfth month should have fallen within

1449. Furthermore, Shakya Chokden himself acknowledges that according to the system of followers of treatises (*bstan bcos pa'i lugs*), the snake year (1449) began even prior to the twelfth month, i.e., at the beginning of the winter session (*dgun chos*) apparently during the 10th month and obviously not later than the eleventh month (ibid., 358). Nevertheless, according to the *Detailed Analysis*, vol. 16, pp. 50, 53, Rongtön passed away at dawn on the fourteenth day of the twelfth lunar month of the iron-male-horse year (1450). Its twelfth month should have fallen within 1451. Given the fact that Shakya Chokden knew Rongtön personally for many years and also that Drölchok was not always careful with dates (see p. 24 below), I think that the dates provided by Shakya Chokden are more reliable.

9. See pp. 50, 107, 168, and also Chapter 1 sections 2 and 3.

10. See Chapter 2 section 4 where I address the question of change of Shakya Chokden's views. See also p. 38 ff.

11. For example, Shakya Chokden himself admitted changes in his interpretation of the buddha-essence (*sangs rgyas kyi snying po, buddhagarbha*) or buddha-nature. See my article "Reburying the Treasure—Maintaining the Continuity: Two Texts by Shakya Chokden on the Buddha-Essence," *Journal of Indian Philosophy*, vol. 34, no. 6 (2006): 526, note 13. Hereafter, "Reburying the Treasure—Maintaining the Continuity."

12. Shakya Chokden's criticisms of the views of this thinker and his followers are not limited to interpretations of Madhyamaka only, but extend to the areas of Tantra, Yogācāra, epistemology, instructions on contemplation, and other topics.

13. See Jeffrey Hopkins (tr. and annotated in collaboration with Lama Lodrö Namgyel), *The Essence of Other-Emptiness by Tāranātha* (Ithaca, New York: Snow Lion Publications, 2007), 119–136 (hereafter *The Essence of Other-Emptiness*), as well as Klaus-Dieter Mathes, "Tāranātha's 'Twenty-One Differences with regard to the Profound Meaning'—Comparing the Views of the Two *gŹan stoṅ* Masters Dol po pa and Śākya mchog ldan," *Journal of the International Association of Buddhist Studies*, vol. 27, no. 2 (2004): 285–328, for a comparison of Shakya Chokden's and Dölpopa's views by Taranatha (*tā ra nā tha*, 1575–1634); Hopkins, *Tsong-kha-pa's Final Exposition of Wisdom* (Ithaca, New York: Snow Lion Publications, 2008), 271–362, for the comparison of Tsongkhapa's and Dölpopa's systems; and Hopkins, *Maps of the Profound: Jam-yang-shay-ba's Great Exposition of Buddhist and Non-Buddhist Views on the Nature of Reality* (Ithaca, New York: Snow Lion Publications, 2003), 526–694 (hereafter, *Maps of the Profound*), for criticisms of Tsongkhapa's views on Madhyamaka by Taktsang Lotsawa and refutations of those criticisms by Jamyang Zhepa Ngakwang Tsöndrü (*'jam dbyangs bzhad pa ngag dbang brtson grus*, 1648–1721/2). For the comparison and analysis of Tsongkhapa's and Gorampa's positions on reality, see Sonam Thakchoe, *The Two Truths Debate: Tsongkhapa and Gorampa on the Middle Way* (Boston: Wisdom Publications, 2007). See also p. 310 note 17 below.

14. On the nature of Buddhist scholastic commentaries, see Georges Dreyfus, *Recognizing Reality: Dharmakīrti's Philosophy and Its Tibetan Interpreters* (Albany, New York: State University of New York Press, 1997), 3–6. Hereafter, *Recognizing Reality*.

15. On the genre of doxography, see Jeffrey Hopkins, "The Tibetan Genre of Doxography: Structuring a Worldview," in *Tibetan Literature: Studies in Genre*, eds. José Ignacio Cabezón and Roger R. Jackson (Ithaca, New York: Snow Lion Publications, 1996), 170–186; and José Ignacio Cabezón, "The Canonization of Philosophy and the Rhetoric of Siddhānta in Tibetan Buddhism," in *Buddha Nature: A Festschrift in Honor of Minoru Kiyota*, ed. Paul J. Griffiths and John P. Keenan (Tokyo: Buddhist Books International, 1990), 7–26.

16. The term "Yogācāra" indicates the system of thought as well as its followers, that is, "Followers of Yogic Practice." When I use plural, i.e., "Yogācāras," it always indicates followers of Yogācāra.

17. For a survey of the Niḥsvabhāvavāda and Yogācāra systems, see Paul Williams, *Mahāyāna Buddhism: The Doctrinal Foundations*, 2nd ed. (London: Routledge, 2009), 63–102. Williams's interpretation of Madhyamaka is primarily informed by the Geluk views. Readers interested in learning more details of philosophical views of the Geluk tradition can refer to Jeffrey Hopkins's works on Cittamātra, the *Emptiness in the Mind-Only School of Buddhism: Dynamic Responses to Dzong-ka-ba's* The Essence of Eloquence: I (Los Angeles: University of California Press, 1999; hereafter, *Emptiness in the Mind-Only School of Buddhism*) and the *Reflections on Reality: The Three Natures and Non-Natures in Cittamātra School, Dynamic Responses to Dzong-ka-ba's* The Essence of Eloquence, Volume 2 (Berkeley: University of California Press, 2002; hereafter, *Reflections on Reality*), his multiple works on Madhyamaka, such as the *Meditation on Emptiness* (London: Wisdom Publications, 1983), as well as Thupten Jinpa's *Self, Reality and Reason in Tibetan Philosophy: Tsongkhapa's Quest for the Middle Way* (London: RoutledgeCurzon, 2002). For a very different perspective on Yogācāra and Madhyamaka that is particularly helpful in the context of this book, see Karl Brunnhölzl's *The Center of the Sunlit Sky: Madhyamaka in the Kagyü Tradition* (Ithaca, New York: Snow Lion Publications, 2004; hereafter, *The Center of the Sunlit Sky*).

18. Such an approach, where the Yogācāra system is relegated to the lineage of extensive deeds (*rgya chen spyod brgyud*), while the system of Niḥsvabhāvavāda is presented as the lineage of profound view (*zab mo lta brgyud*), is popular in the Tibetan intellectual world, but is delimiting, because it implies that the Yogācāra view of reality is insufficient in itself, and has to be substituted with that of Niḥsvabhāvavāda. Apparently, Shakya Chokden's teacher Rongtön Sheja Künrik also followed this widespread approach, as can be judged from his *Amassment of Jewels: Praise to the Six Ornaments and Two Supreme Ones* (*Rgyan drug mchog gnyis la bstod pa rin chen spungs pa*), in The Collected Works of Rong-ston Shak-kya Rgyal-mtsen, vol. B (*kha*), (Dehra Dun, India: Sakya College, 1999), 562–565, and other texts.

19. *Shing rta'i srol chen gnyis las 'byung ba'i dbu ma chen po'i lugs gnyis rnam par dbye ba/ nges don rgya mtsho'i sprin gyi 'brug sgra zab mo*, in *Two Controversial Mādhyamika Treatises*, 307–318 (Bir, India: Yashodhara Publications, 1996). Hereafter, *Profound Thunder*.

20. *Nges don rgya mtsho sprin gyi 'brug sgra zab mo'i rgyas 'grel bdud rtsi'i char 'bebs*, in *Two Controversial Mādhyamika Treatises*, 319–499 (Bir, India:

Yashodhara Publications, 1996). Hereafter, *Rain of Ambrosia*. With the exception of the *Rain of Ambrosia*, for all works of Shakya Chokden cited in this book I will be providing volume and page numbers from his collected works in twenty-four volumes. The *Rain of Ambrosia* is also contained in the second volume of his collected works, but when citing it, I am using the blockprint copy from the *Two Controversial Mādhyamika Treatises*. The *Profound Thunder* is included in the *Two Controversial Mādhyamika Treatises* but not found in the collected works separately, although its verses are contained in the *Rain of Ambrosia*. For the *Profound Thunder* and *Rain of Ambrosia*, I provide only page numbers based on the *Two Controversial Mādhyamika Treatises*. The *Profound Thunder* and *Rain of Ambrosia* are the only texts by Shakya Chokden I am aware of that survived in the blockprinted version. Apparently they were counted as one treatise by compilers of the *Two Controversial Mādhyamika Treatises* (Bir, India: Yashodhara Publications, 1996) that besides them also contains Rongtön Sheja Künrik's *Ascertainment of the Definitive Meaning: Explanation of [Candrakīrti's] 'Engaging in Madhyamaka' (Dbu ma la 'jug pa'i rnam bshad nges don rnam nges)*, 1–306.

21. *Zab zhi spros bral gyi bshad pa stong nyid bdud rtsi'i lam po che*, Collected Writings of Gser-mdog paṇ-chen Śākya-mchog-ldan, vol. 4, 107–207 (Thimphu, Bhutan: Kunzang Tobgey, 1975). Hereafter, *Great Path of Ambrosia of Emptiness*. I am currently working on the translation of the *Profound Thunder*, *Rain of Ambrosia*, and *Great Path of Ambrosia of Emptiness* that I am planning to publish as a separate volume.

22. See, for example, *Seventeen Wondrous Answers to the Questions of the Whole Monastic Community of Zi Samdrupling (Gzi bsam 'grub gling pa'i dge 'dun spyi'i dris lan ya mtshan bcu bdun pa)*, vol. 23, 466, and *Letter Pleasing Impartial Wise Ones on How Presentations of Turning Dharmacakras have been Accomplished (Chos kyi 'khor lo bskor ba'i rnam gzhag ji ltar grub pa'i yi ge gzu bor gnas pa'i mdzangs pa dga' byed)*, vol. 16, 478–479.

23. See Chapter 2 section 3, especially p. 100 ff.

Chapter 1

1. Dawa Norbu, *China's Tibet Policy* (Richmond, Surrey: Curzon Press, 2001), 55.

2. This term, used by David Ruegg, is discussed in Georges Dreyfus, *The Sound of Two Hands Clapping: The Education of a Tibetan Buddhist Monk* (Berkley and Los Angeles: University of California Press, 2003), 25. Hereafter, *The Sound of Two Hands Clapping*.

3. Sakya ascendance to power culminated in 1264 when Sakya Pendita's nephiew Pakpa Lodrö Gyeltsen was elevated to the religious and secular leadership of Tibet. See Matthew Kapstein, *The Tibetans* (Oxford: Blackwell Publishing, 2006), 112.

4. Particle "pa" added to "Pakmodru" to form the name "Pakmo Drupa," "Sakya" to form "Sakyapa," "Geluk" to form "Gelukpa," etc., indicates a follower or a member of those secular and religious institutions.

5. For the details of this administrative system, see *The Tibetans*, 114–115.

6. Giuseppe Tucci, *Tibet: Land of Snows*, tr. J. E. Stapleton Driver (London: Elek Books, 1967), 34.

7. Ibid., 35. Karmapas also took firm root in Kham (*khams*) and southeast Tibet, and were to occupy there a leading position for centuries.

8. Dan Martin, "A Brief Political History of Tibet by Gu-ru Bkra-shis," in *Tibetan History and Language: Studies Dedicated to Uray G'eza on His Seventieth Birthday*, ed. Ernst Steinkellner (Wien: Arbeitskreis für Tibetische und Buddhistische Studien, Universität Wien, 1991), 339–340.

9. *The Tibetans*, 122. Pakmo Drupa again began to reassert themselves in the first decades of the sixteenth century (ibid., 130).

10. Wangchuk Deden Shakabpa, *Tibet: A Political History* (New Haven and London: Yale University Press, 1967), 87–88.

11. *The Tibetans*, 129.

12. For details of Shakya Chokden's life, see the next section of this chapter. See also Künga Drölchok's *Detailed Analysis of the Liberation Story of the Great Paṇḍita Shakya Chokden* (*Paṇḍi ta chen po shākya mchog ldan gyi rnam par thar pa zhib mo rnam 'byed pa*), in Collected Writings of Gser-mdog paṇ-chen Śākya-mchog-ldan (Thimphu, Bhutan: Kunzang Tobgey, 1975), vol. 16, 94–97.

13. Norbu, *China's Tibet Policy*, 56.

14. *Sdom pa gsum gyi rab tu dbye ba*, Sa skya bka' 'bum, vol. 12 (na), 1a–48b. English translation by Jared Douglas Rhoton, *A Thorough Differentiation of the Three Types of Vows: Essential Distinctions among the Individual Liberation, Mahāyāna, and Tantric Systems* (Albany, New York: State University of New York Press, 2002).

15. On religious polemics in Tibet, see José Ignacio Cabezón and Geshe Lobsang Dargyay, *Freedom from Extremes*, 11–33.

16. As Leonard van der Kuijp puts it, "Bracketing the political and social motives that arose out of the special relationships that the leading figures of the Dga'-ldan-pa and Sa-skya-pa had formed with their patrons who usually consisted of influential families who were not always disinclined to mix power struggles and politics with religion, the attempts on the part of the Dga'-ldan-pa to create an aura of orthodoxy around their doctrines were vigorously opposed by the Sa-skya-pa of the 15th century" (*Contributions*, 8).

17. David Jackson, *The Early Abbots of 'Phan po Na-lendra* (Vienna: Arbeitkreis für Tibetische und Buddhistische Studien, 1989), 6. According to Jackson, "Rong-ston together with g.Yag-ston represented the main doctrinal alternative to the tradition of Tsong-kha-pa and his teacher Red-mda'-ba (1349–1412), though both pairs of savants were basically offshoots from a common trunk of the gSang-phu/Sa-skya scholarly and intellectual tradition" (ibid).

18. For details of Gorampa's criticisms of both Tsongkhapa and Dölpopa, see José Ignacio Cabezón and Geshe Lobsang Dargyay, *Freedom from Extremes*, 48 ff. For details of Taktsang's criticisms of Tsongkhapa's views see Jeffrey Hopkins, *Maps of the Profound*, 526–575.

19. *Sdom gsum rab dbye la dri ba legs pa*, vol. 17, 448–462. Hereafter, *Good Questions*.

20. David Jackson, "Birds in the Egg and Newborn Cubs: Metaphors for the Potentialities and Limitations of "All-at-once" Enlightenment," *Tibetan Studies: Proceedings of the 5th Seminar of the International Association for Tibetan Studies*, vol. 1 (1989): 95–114. Gorampa gave his response in his *Elimination of Mistakes about the Three Types of Vows: Answers to the Polemics and Questions Regarding the '[Thorough Differentiation of the] Three Types of Vows' Treatise* (*Sdom pa gsum gyi bstan bcos la dris shing rtsod pa'i lan sdom gsum 'khrul spong*), Collected Works of Kun-mkhyen Go-rams-pa Bsod-nams-seng-ge, vol. 9, 489–619 (Bir, India: Yashodhara Publications, 1995).

21. David Jackson, "Several Works of Unusual Provenance Ascribed to Sa Skya Paṇḍita," in *Tibetan History and Language: Studies Dedicated to Uray G'eza on His Seventieth Birthday*, ed. Ernst Steinkellner (Wien: Arbeitskreis für Tibetische und Buddhistische Studien, Universität Wien, 1991), 235–237. For details of life and works of Sönam Lhündrup, see Jowita Kramer, *A Noble Abbot from Mustang: Life and Works of Glo-bo Mkhan-chen (1456–1532)* (Wien: Arbeitskreis für Tibetische und Buddhistische Studien, Universität Wien, 2008). Hereafter, *A Noble Abbot from Mustang*.

22. *Sdom gsum gyi rab tu dbye ba'i bstan bcos kyi 'bel gtam rnam par nges pa legs bshad gser gyi thur ma*, vol. 6, 439–vol. 7, 229. Hereafter, *Golden Lancet*.

23. On Ngorchen Künga Zangpo and the Ngor tradition, see Davidson, "Nor-pa Tradition," 79–98.

24. For the history of this monastery, see David Jackson, *The Early Abbots of 'Phan po Na-lendra* (Vienna: Arbeitkreis für Tibetische und Buddhistische Studien, 1989).

25. According to Shakya Chokden's *Enjoyment Ocean of Faith*, vol. 16, 317, it was established in 1436 (the fire-male-dragon year) when Rongtön was seventy years old.

26. According to Dönyö Pelwa's biography written by Shakya Chokden, *Liberation Story of the Foremost Venerable Holy Amoghaśrībhadra That Induces Devotion of All Fortunate Beings* (*Rje btsun dam pa a mo gha shrī bha tra'i* [sic] *rnam par thar ba skal bzang skye rgu'i dang ba 'dren byed*), vol. 17, 56 (hereafter, *Liberation Story of the Foremost Venerable Holy Amoghaśrībhadra*), Dönyö Pelwa passed away at the age of eighty-seven on the fifteenth day of the twelfth lunar month of the hare year. This year started in 1483, but its last lunar month should have fallen within 1484.

27. For details see pp. 35 and 41.

28. Lozang Jamspal, "Zhalu Lotsava Chos skyong bZang po and His Literary Works," in *Tibetan Studies: Proceedings of the 5th Seminar of the International Association for Tibetan Studies*, vol. 1 (1989): 175–182.

29. *Deb ther sngon po*. See George Roerich (tr.), *Blue Annals* (Calcutta: Royal Asiatic Society of Bengal, 1949; reprint, Delhi: Motilal Banarasidas, 1996).

30. Gene Smith, *Among Tibetan Texts: History and Literature of the Himalayan Plateau* (Boston: Wisdom Publications, 2001), 16. For details of Gö Lotsawa Zhönnupel's life and works, see Klaus-Dieter Mathes, *A Direct Path to the Buddha Within: Gö Lotsāwa's Mahāmudrā Interpretation of the* Ratnagotravibhāga (Boston: Wisdom Publications, 2008). Hereafter, *A Direct Path to the Buddha Within*.

31. That is, rituals designed for accomplishing tantric deities in contemplative practice.

32. Chopgyé Trichen, *Feast for Minds of the Fortunate*, 46. English translation in Chogay Trichen Rinpoche, *The History of the Sakya Tradition*, 26.

33. His writing on Buddhist logic and epistemology—together with the writings of the Eighth Karmapa Mikyö Dorjé on other aspects of Buddhist learning—provide the core of the Kagyü curriculum.

34. See Michael Aris, *Hidden Treasures and Secret Lives* (London and New York: Kegan Paul International, 1989), 77; Karma Thinley, *The History of the Sixteen Karmapas of Tibet* (Boulder: Prajñā Press, 1980), 79–87. I discuss Chödrak Gyamtso's connection with Shakya Chokden below, pp. 43, 48–50, and 105.

35. *Paṇḍi ta chen po shākya mchog ldan gyi rnam par thar pa zhib mo rnam 'byed pa*, in Collected Writings of Gser-mdog paṇ-chen Śākya-mchog-ldan, vol. 16, 1–233 (Thimphu, Bhutan: Kunzang Tobgey, 1975). Hereafter, *Detailed Analysis*.

36. *Detailed Analysis*, 230. For the list of Shakya Chokden's disciples, see p. 328 note 192.

37. Ibid., 227.

38. Ibid., 230.

39. The *Detailed Analysis* also is the main source for several texts written in the twentieth century that address Shakya Chokden's biography. See, for example, Khetsun Sangpo, *Biographical Dictionary of Tibet and Tibetan Buddhism*, vol. 11 (Dharamsala, India: Library of Tibetan Works and Archives, 1979), 426–465. For further details, see Kuijp, *Contributions*, 10, and also Caumanns, "Tibetan Sources," that provides important details of the *Detailed Analysis* and other biographies of Shakya Chokden. In particular, see ibid., 214 ff. for the details of composition of the *Detailed Analysis*.

40. On problematic dates given by Drölchok in his *Detailed Analysis*, see also Caumanns, "Tibetan Sources," 219–220.

41. Note that Tibetans follow the lunar calendar. Tibetan year usually starts sometime in February, on different days of the solar year. When no months or other indicators are provided, it is difficult to figure out whether all events that are said to have happened in fire-female-hare year, for example, actually occurred in 1447 (to which it corresponds). To avoid confusion, I ignore this difference.

42. For the history of this monastrty, see Shunzo Onoda, "Abbatial Successions of the Colleges of Sangpu sNe'u thog Monastery," *Bulletin of the National Museum of Ethnology* (Osaka), vol. 15, no. 4 (1990): 1049–1071; and Leonard van der Kuijp, "The Monastery Gsang-phu ne'u-thog and Its Abbatial Succession from ca. 1073 to 1250," *Berliner Indologische Studien* 3 (1987): 103–127.

43. *Detailed Analysis*, vol. 16, 8–11.

44. Geshé (*dge bshes*) is an abbreviation of Gewé Shenyen (*dge ba'i bshes gnyen, kalyāṇamitra*), that can be translated as "virtuous spiritual friend." "Geshé" is commonly used as a title indicating scholarly achievements. In the present context, it should not be confused with the contemporary "Geshé"

title that can be received after years of study in Geluk or Bön (*bon*) monastic universities. It seems that back in the fifteenth century it did not necessarily indicate a sectarian affiliation, and could be applied to learned scholars as it had been done previously in the Kadam (*bka' gdams*) tradition as well. Notice also the expression "Sakya Geshé" mentioned below (32).

45. *Mahāyānasūtrālaṃkāra, Theg pa chen po mdo sde'i rgyan*, D4020, sems tsam, phi, 1a–39a. English translation in Lobsang Jamspal, R. Clark, J. Wilson, L. Zwilling, M. Sweet, and R. Thurman, *The Universal Vehicle Discourse Literature (*Mahāyānasūtrālaṁkāra*) By Maitreyanātha/Āryāsaṅga Together with its* Commentary *(*Bhāṣya*) By Vasubandhu* (New York: American Institute of Buddhist Studies, 2004).

46. *Mahāyānottaratantraśāstra, Theg pa chen po rgyud bla ma*, D4024, sems tsam, phi, 54b–73a. Edited Sanskrit text in Edward H. Johnston (ed.), *Ratnagotravibhāga Mahāyānottaratantraśāstra* (Patna: The Bihar Research Society, 1950). English translation in Jikido Takasaki, *A Study on the Ratnagotravibhāga* (Rome: Istituto Italiano per il Medio ed Estremo Oriente, 1966).

47. *Bodhisattvacaryāvatāra, Byang chub sems dpa'i spyod pa la 'jug pa*, D3871, dbu ma, la, 1a–40a. English translation: Kate Crosby and Andrew Skilton, *The Bodhicaryāvatāra* (Oxford: Oxford University Press, 1995).

48. See note 50 below.

49. *Detailed Analysis*, vol. 16, 13, 30–31.

50. According to Drölchok (*Detailed Analysis*, vol. 16, 18–19), Rongtön could not give him novice vows due to restrictions related to Geluk/Sakya sects issued by Pakmodru rulers from Neudong. It is not entirely clear what exactly those restrictions were, but it is clear that even such famous Sakya teachers as Rongtön could not freely give monastic ordination to monks of certain monasteries. Kyormolung monastery was founded in the eleventh century by a Kadampa (*bka' gdams pa*) lama Belti Drachompa Khutön Tsöndrü Wangchuk (*sbal ti dgra bcom pa khu ston brtson 'grus dbang phyug*)/ Belti Wangchuk Tsültrim (*sbal ti dbang phyug tshul khrims*, 1129–1215), and later was also associated with Tsongkhapa who stayed in that monastery. See Chömpel (*chos 'phel*), *New Guidebook Describing Pilgrimage Places of the Snowy Land of Tibet* (*Gangs can bod kyi gnas bshad lam yig gsar ma*, Pekin: Mi rigs dpe skrun khang, 2004), 96–98, and Gyurme Dorje, *Tibet Handbook* (England: Footprint Handbooks, 1999), 134. According to the *Tibet Handbook*, three colleges established in that university were Geluk colleges. Thus it is possible that by Shakya Chokden's time Kyormolung monastery was at least partly Geluk, which might be the reason why Rongtön could not freely give ordinations to its monks.

51. *Detailed Analysis*, vol. 16, 18.

52. *Abhisamayālaṃkāranāmaprajñāpāramitopadeśaśāstrakārikā, Shes rab kyi pha rol tu phyin pa'i man ngag gi bstan bcos mngon par rtogs pa'i rgyan zhes bya ba'i tshig le'ur byas pa*, D3786, shes phyin, ka, 1a–13a.

53. For more details on Tibetan monastic education, see Dreyfus, *The Sound of Two Hands Clapping*, especially pp. 101–110, 137–148; also 111–137 on different curricular models in contemporary Tibetan monastic universities.

54. See note 59.

55. *Detailed Analysis*, vol. 16, 19–20.

56. Ibid., 19–20.

57. *Detailed Analysis*, vol. 16, 20.

58. See pp. 36 and 47 below.

59. There are two important commentaries by Yakpa on the Prajñāpāramitā which are known as *Yakpa's Big and Small Commentaries* (*g.yag pa'i ṭī ka che chung*; see the *Detailed Analysis*, 34). They are the *Precious Treasury: Good Explanation of the 'Ornament of Clear Realizations' Treatise of Quintessential Instructions on the Perfection of Wisdom Together with Its Commentaries* (*Shes rab kyi pha rol tu phyin pa'i man ngag gi bstan bcos mngon par rtogs pa'i rgyan 'grel pa dang bcas pa legs par bshad pa rin po che'i bang mdzod*), vol. 1–2 (New Delhi: Ngawang Topgay, 1973) and the *King of Wish-Fulfilling Gems: Good Explanation of the 'Ornament of Clear Realizations' Treatise of Quintessential Instructions on the Perfection of Wisdom Together with Its Commentary 'Clear Meaning'* (*Shes rab kyi pha rol tu phyin pa'i man ngag gi bstan bcos mngon par rtogs pa'i rgyan dang de'i 'grel pa don gsal ba dang bcas pa legs par bshad pa rin chen bsam 'phel dbang gi rgyal po*, Zi ling: Mtsho sngon mi rigs dpe skrun khang, 2004). Darma Rinchen's commentary is the *Ornament of Essence: Explanation of [Haribhadra's] 'Clear Meaning' Commentary on the 'Ornament of Clear Realizations' Treatise of Quintessential Instructions on the Perfection of Wisdom* (*Shes rab kyi pha rol tu phyin pa'i man ngag gi bstan bcos mngon par rtogs pa'i rgyan gyi 'grel pa don gsal ba'i rnam bshad snying po'i rgyan*, Lan kru'u: Kan su'u mi rigs dpe skrun khang, 2000), also known as *Darma Rinchen's Commentary* (*Dar ṭik*). Rongtön's commentary is the *Thorough Clarification of Words and Meanings: Explanation of the Commentary on the Treatise of Quintessential Instructions on the Perfection of Wisdom Called 'Ornament of Clear Realizations'* (*Shes rab kyi pha rol tu phyin pa'i man ngag gi bstan bcos mngon par rtogs pa'i rgyan ces bya ba'i 'grel ba'i rnam bshad tshig don rab tu gsal ba*, New Delhi: Pal-ldan Sakya'i-sung-rab Book Publisher, 1989), also known as *Rongtön's Commentary* (*Rong ṭik*); hereafter, *Rongtön's Commentary*. (This commentary is still very popular in Sakya monastic universities, and its transmission continues unbroken into the present day).

60. *Detailed Analysis*, 16, 34.

61. According to Shakya Chokden's *Liberation Story of the Foremost Venerable Holy Amoghaśrībhadra*, vol. 17, 60, he studied with that teacher from the age of eleven until age sixteen, and then from age twenty until age twenty-three. Otherwise, in general he followed Dönyö Pelwa from age eleven until age fifty-seven (ibid., 62).

62. *Abhidharmasamuccaya*, *Chos mngon pa kun las btus pa*, D4053, sems tsam, li, 1a–117a.

63. See pp. 35 and 41 for details.

64. They are 1. *Ornament of Clear Realizations*, 2. *Ornament of Mahāyāna Sūtras*, 3. *Differentiation of the Middle and Extremes* (*Madhyāntavibhāga*, *Dbus dang mtha' rnam par 'byed pa*), D4021, sems tsam, phi, 40b–45a; 4. *Differentiation of Phenomena and the Nature of Phenomena* (*Dharmatadharmatāvibhaṅga*, *chos dang*

chos nyid rnam par 'byed pa), D4022, sems tsam, phi 46b1–49a6; and 5. *Sublime Continuum of Mahāyāna.*

65. *Detailed Analysis*, vol. 16, 21–23.

66. *Vinayasūtra, 'Dul ba'i mdo* by Guṇaprabha, D4117, 'dul ba, wu, 1b–100a.

67. *Detailed Analysis*, vol. 16, 25–26.

68. In Sakya Pendita, *Treasure of the Science of Valid Cognition: The Root Text and the [Auto-] Commentary* (*Tshad ma rigs pa'i gter gyi rtsa ba dang 'grel pa*, Bod ljongs mi dmangs dpe skrun khang, 1989).

69. *Abhidharmakośakārikā, Chos mngon pa'i mdzod kyi tshig le'ur byas pa*, D4089, mngon pa, ku, 1a–25a.

70. *Detailed Analysis*, vol. 16, 26.

71. *Clear Words: Commentary on [Nāgārjuna's] 'Root [Stanzas] on Madhyamaka' (Mūlamadhyamakavṛttiprasannapadānāma, Dbu ma rtsa ba'i 'grel pa tshig gsal ba zhes bya ba)*, D3860, dbu ma, 'a, 1a–200a.

72. This influential teacher, also known as Tsungmé Chöjé (Tib. *mtshungs med chos rje*), was an abbot of Sera monastery and had many disciples. He criticized and was criticized by Khedrup Gelek Pelzang with whom he disagreed regarding a correct interpretation of Tsongkhapa's views. According to Künga Drölchok (*Detailed Analysis*, 27), Gungru Gyeltsen Zangpo taught that the application of the mode of apprehension in remainder of negation of the object of negation (Tib. *dgag bya bkag shul gyi 'dzin stangs sbyor ba*) was specifically argued for by Khedrup Gelek Pelzang, and then spread by his followers. Otherwise, despite some subtle differences in their ways of identifying the object of negation, Tsongkhapa and Rendawa Zhönnu Lodrö's ways of approaching the mode of setting in meditative equipoise were similar. (Rendawa's approach is described below, pp. 84–85 The expression "the mode of apprehension in remainder of negation of the object of negation" refers to the Geluk approach to meditation on reality (see p. 338 note 79). Insisting on a direct connection between reality determined by reasoning and cultivated in meditation, Geluk thinkers argue that after the object of negation (such as true existence, etc.) had been negated through reasoning and one thereby arrived at the non-affirming negation of the object of negation, one has to retain and mentally cultivate that very negation in order to finally realize it directly in meditative equipoise, rather than leaving one's mind in the state free from any apprehension whatsoever, as many other Tibetan thinkers suggest.) Furthermore, Tuken Lopzang Chökyi Nyima (*thu'u bkwan blo bzang chos kyi nyi ma*) in his *Crystal Mirror of Good Explanations: Presentation of the Origins and Assertions of All Tenets* (*Grub mtha' thams cad kyi khungs dang 'dod tshul ston pa legs bshad shel gyi me long*, Kan su'u Mi rigs dpe skrun khang, 1984), 323–324, writes that when he was asked why his way of teaching disagrees with that of other direct disciples of Tsongkhapa, Gungru Gyeltsen Zangpo said: "I do not know what [Tsongkhapa] told those others. [But] this is how the Foremost Lama [Tsongkhapa] told me the way of meditating on emptiness [as] an affirming negation (*ma yin dgag, paryudāsa*)" (khong gzhan la ci gsungs

ma shes/ nged la rje bla mas stong pa nyid ma yin dgag gi sgom tshul 'di bzhin gsungs pa yin). Drölchok and Tuken thereby suggest that the Geluk way of meditation on ultimate reality as a non-affirming negation (*med dgag, prasajyapratiṣedha*) and its insistence on maintaining an apprehension of that negation in the actual meditative equipoise on emptiness—that became like trademarks of the Geluk approach to emptiness—were contested by direct disciples of Tsongkhapa himself. Nevertheless, it is unclear how faithful Drölchok's and Tuken's reports are and what the actual position of Gungru Gyeltsen Zangpo was. I did not find any substantial discrepancies with the "mainstream" Geluk position in Gungru Gyeltsen Zangpo's exposition of Madhyamaka views and contemplation in such recently published works as the *Stream of Nectar: Good Explanations [Based on] the Guru's Quintessential Instructions* (*Legs bshad bla ma'i man ngag bdud rtsi'i chu rgyun*), in Collected Works of Gungru Gyeltsen Zangpo (*Gung ru rgyal mtshan bzang po'i gsung'bum*), Mes po'i shul bzhag, vol. 37, 285–421 (Dpal brtsegs bod yig dpe rnying zhib 'jug khang, 2007), and the *Summarized Exposition of Madhyamaka* (*Dbu ma'i stong thun*), in Collected Works of Gungru Gyeltsen Zangpo (*Gung ru rgyal mtshan bzang po'i gsung'bum*), Mes po'i shul bzhag, vol. 38, 177–350 (Dpal brtsegs bod yig dpe rnying zhib 'jug khang, 2007).

73. *Prajñānāmamūlamadhyamakakārikā, Dbu ma rtsa ba'i tshig le'ur byas pa shes rab ces bya ba*), D3824, dbu ma, tsa, 1a–19a. English translation in Jay L. Garfield, *The Fundamental Wisdom of the Middle Way: Nāgārjuna's* Mūlamadhyamakakārikā (Oxford: Oxford University Press, 1995). Tsongkhapa's commentary on this text is the *Ocean of Reasoning: Explanation of [Nāgārjuna's] Wisdom: Root Stanzas on Madhyamaka (Dbu ma rtsa ba'i tshig le'ur byas pa shes rab ces bya ba'i rnam bshad rigs pa'i rgya mtsho,* Collected Works of Tsong kha pa Blo bzang grags pa, vol. 15 (ba), 1–583 (Sku 'bum: Sku 'bum byams pa gling par khang, 2000?). English translation: Geshe Ngawang Samten and Jay L. Garfield, *Ocean of Reasoning: A Great Commentary on Nāgārjuna's Mūlamadhyamakakārikā* (Oxford: Oxford University Press, 2006).

74. *Madhyamakāvatāra, Dbu ma la 'jug pa*, D3861, dbu ma, 'a, 201b–219a. Tsongkhapa's commentary on this text is the *Thorough Clarification of Intent: Extensive Explanation of [Candrakīrti's] 'Engaging in Madhyamaka'* (*Dbu ma la 'jug pa'i rgya cher bshad pa dgongs pa rab gsal*), Collected Works of Tsong kha pa Blo bzang grags pa, vol. 16 (ma), 7–612 (Sku 'bum: Sku 'bum byams pa gling par khang, 2000?).

75. *Detailed Analysis*, vol. 16, 26–27.

76. *Stong thun chung ba dbang po'i rdo rje zhes bya ba blo gsal mgu byed*, vol. 4, 433–605. Hereafter, *Smaller Summarized Exposition.*

77. *Theg pa chen po dbu ma rnam par nges pa'i bang mdzod lung dang rigs pa'i rgya mtsho*, vol. 14, 341–vol. 15, 695. Hereafter, *Ocean of Scriptural Statements and Reasoning.*

78. *Detailed Analysis*, vol. 16, 27–30.

79. Ibid., 32–33, 36.

80. *Detailed Analysis*, vol. 16, 38–42. Shakya Chokden calls him "Bodongpa" in the *Praise to the Great Paṇḍita Loten the Fourth* (*Paṇ chen blo brtan bzhi pa la bstod pa*), vol. 16, 267.

81. *Detailed Analysis*, vol. 16, 67–69, 94–97, 193–194.

82. Ibid., 48.

83. *Drumming Sounds amidst Wondrous Clouds: Liberation Story of Glorious Holy Lama Kumāramati* (*Dpal ldan bla ma dam pa ku ma ra ma ti'i rnam thar ngo mtshar sprin gyi rnga sgra*), vol. 16, 393–394.

84. See, for example, Ngawang Zangpo (tr. and introduction), *Jamgon Kongtrul's Retreat Manual* (Ithaca, New York: Snow Lion Publications, 1994), 24–31.

85. It appears that Sakya tantric teachings coming from this master were popular prior to the time when the Ngor system of Künga Zangpo became predominant (See the *Detailed Analysis*, vol. 16, 86–87). Shakya Chokden initially received many tantric teachings in the lineage of Künga Trashi, and kept practicing some of them personally. His closeness to this lineage was further augmented by the fact that Changlung Rinpoché was one of the main disciples of Künga Trashi, and transmitted Künga Trashi's teachings to Shakya Chokden (31). Künga Trashi was Rongtön's tantric teacher as well (see Shakya Chokden's *Enjoyment Ocean of Faith*, vol. 16, 309–310, and David Jackson and Shunzo Onoda, *Rong-ston on the Prajñāpāramitā Philosophy of the Abhisamayālaṃkāra: His Sub-commentary on Haribhadra's 'Sphuṭārthā'* (Kyoto: Nagata Bunshodo, 1988), III. b). Nevertheless, Künga Zangpo—who also practiced Künga Trashi's version of the Path and Result (*lam 'bras*) system personally—also became one of Shakya Chokden's main tantric teachers (31). It seems that later Shakya Chokden felt so responsible for the propagation of Künga Zangpo's version of the Path and Result system that he felt uncomfortable teaching Künga Trashi's Path and Result system in his own monastery Serdokchen (47). For a recent English translation of seminal texts of this core tantric system of Sakya, see Cyrus Stearns, *Taking the Result as the Path: Core Teachings of the Sakya Lamdre Tradition* (Boston: Wisdom Publications, 2006).

86. Ibid., 48–49, 53.

87. Ibid., 51–52, 70–71, 85–86, 92.

88. Ibid., 55, 57, 72, 79–80.

89. Ibid., 55–56.

90. *Shes rab kyi pha rol tu phyin pa'i man ngag gi bstan bcos mngon par rtogs pa'i rgyan 'grel pa dang bcas pa'i snga phyi'i 'brel rnam par btsal zhing/ dngos bstan gyi dka' ba'i gnas la legs par bshad pa'i dpung tshogs rnam par bkod pa/ bzhed tshul rba rlabs kyi phreng ba.* Collected Writings of Gser-mdog paṇ-chen Śākya-mchog-ldan, vol. 11, 157–587. Hereafter, *Garlands of Waves of Assertions*.

91. *Detailed Analysis*, vol. 16, 70. Also see the next section of this chapter.

92. *Mngon par rtogs pa'i rgyan 'grel pa don gsal ba dang bcas pa'i rnam par bshad pa shing rta'i srol gnyis gcig tu bsdus pa'i lam po che*, vol. 12, 1–319. Hereafter, *Great Path Compressing the Two Chariot Ways into One*.

93. *Byams chos lnga'i lam gyi rim pa gsal bar byed pa'i bstan bcos rin chen sgrom gyi sgo 'byed*, vol. 11, 39–149. Hereafter, *Opening Doors of a Chest of Gems*.

94. *Detailed Analysis*, vol. 16, 72–73, 103.

95. Mangtö Ludrup Gyamtso (*mang thos klu sgrub rgya mtsho*), *The Sun Illuminating Calculations of the Teachings* (*Bstan rtsis gsal ba'i nyin byed*, Bod ljongs mi dmangs dpe skrun khang, 1988), 228, mentions "hundred textual

systems" (*gzhung lugs brgya*) Shakya Chokden gave explanations on at that time.

96. *Rgyud sde spyi'i rnam par gzhag pa* (xylographic print, unknown publisher).

97. The *Three Hevajra Tantras* (*kye rdor rgyud gsum*) are (i) the root tantra *Two Chapters* (*rtsa ba'i rgyud brtag gnyis*), i.e., *Hevajratantrarājanāma, Kye'i rdo rje zhes bya ba rgyud kyi rgyal po*), D0417, rgyud, nga, 1b–30a, translated into English and edited by David Snellgrove in *The Hevajra Tantra: A Critical Study*, London Oriental Series, 6, parts 1–2 (London: Oxford University Press, 1959); (ii) the explanatory tantra *Vajra Canopy* (*bshad pa'i rgyud rdo rje gur*), i.e., *Āryaḍākinīvajrapañjaramahātantrarājakalpanāma, 'Phags pa mkha' 'gro ma rdo rje gur zhes bya ba'i rgyud kyi rgyal po chen po'i brtag pa*, D0419, rgyud, nga, 30a–65b; and (iii) the quintessential instructions tantra *Vajra Copulation* (*man ngag gi rgyud rdo rje saṃpuṭa*), i.e., *Saṃpuṭanāmamahātantra, Yang dag par sbyor ba zhes bya ba'i rgyud chen po*, D0381, rgyud, ga, 73b–158b.

98. The *Three Bodhisattva Commentaries* (*sems 'grel skor gsum*) are three commentaries written by ārya bodhisattvas: Puṇḍarīka's *Stainless Light* (*Vimalaprabhā, Dri ma med pa'i 'od*; the full title: *Vimalaprabhānāmamūlatantrānusāriṇīdvādaśasāhasrikālaghukālacakratantrarājaṭīkā, Bsdus pa'i rgyud kyi rgyal po dus kyi 'khor lo'i 'grel bshad rtsa ba'i rgyud kyi rjes su 'jug pa stong phrag bcu gnyis pa dri ma med pa'i 'od ces bya ba*), D1347, rgyud, tha, 107b–da, 297a; Vajragarbha's *Extensive Commentary on the 'Condensed Meaning of the Hevajra Tantra'* (*Hevajrapiṇḍārthaṭīkā, Kye'i rdo rje bsdus pa'i don gyi rgya cher 'grel pa*), D1180, rgyud, ka, 1–126a); Vajrapāṇi's *Meaning Commentary on the Cakrasaṃvara Tantra* (*Lakṣābhidhanāduddhṛtalaghutantrapiṇḍārthavivaraṇa, Mngon par brjod pa 'bum pa las phyung ba nyung ngu'i rgyud kyi bsdus pa'i don rnam par bshad pa*), D1402, rgyud, ba, 78b–141a.

99. *Detailed Analysis*, vol. 16, 76–77.

100. Those texts are grouped into six topics known as the "six great volumes" (*pod chen drug*): Prajñāpāramitā, Pramāṇa, Vinaya, Abhidharma, Madhyamaka, and the Three Types of Vows (*sdom gsum*). There are eighteen texts related to those topics known as the "eighteen [texts] of great renown" (*grags chen bco brgyad*): Vinaya contains the Buddha's *Individual Liberation Sūtra* (*Prātimokṣasūtra, So sor thar pa'i mdo*, D0002, 'dul ba, ca, 1b–20b) and Guṇaprabha's *Sūtra on Moral Discipline* (1–2); Pramāṇa contains Dignāga's *Compendium of Valid Cognition* and Dharmakīrti's *Commentary on Valid Cognition* and *Ascertainment of Valid Cognition* (3–5); Abhidharma contains Asaṅga's *Summary of Higher Knowledge* and Vasubandhu's *Treasury of Higher Knowledge* (6–7); Prajñāpāramitā contains the *Five Dharmas of Maitreya* and Śāntideva's *Engaging in the Bodhisattva Deeds* (8–13); Madhyamaka contains Nāgārjuna's *Wisdom: Root Stanzas on Madhyamaka*, Candrakīrti's *Engaging in Madhyamaka*, and Āryadeva's *Four Hundred* (14–16); the two remaining texts are Sakya Pendita's *Treasure of the Science of Valid Cognition* (17) and *Thorough Differentiation of the Three Types of Vows* (18). See Chopgyé Trichen, *Feast for Minds of the Fortunate*, 48–49; English translation: Chogay Trichen Rinpoche, *The History of the Sakya Tradition*, 27. See also Tarab Tulku, *A Brief History of Tibetan Academic Degrees*

in Buddhist Philosophy, NIAS Report Series, No. 43 (Copenhagen: Nordic Institute of Asian Studies, 2000), 12–17, for more details about the degrees mentioned above. (Tarab Tulku follows an alternative spelling of *bka' bcu pa*, etc., using *dka'* instead of *bka*.)

101. *Gsang ba 'dus pa, Guhyasamāja*. Full title: *Sarvatathāgatakāyavākcittarahasyoguhyasamājanāmamahākalparāja, De bzhin gshegs pa thams cad kyi sku gsung thugs kyi gsang chen gsang ba 'dus pa zhes bya ba brtag pa'i rgyal po chen po*, D0443, rgyud, ca, 90a–157b.

102. *Detailed Analysis*, vol. 16, 78–80. In the *Detailed Analysis*, vol. 16, 80, Drölchok identifies this text as the *Hundred Doors of Liberation: Explanation of the 'Secret Assembly'* (*Gsang 'dus rnam bshad rnam par thar pa'i sgo brgya pa*). I take it as an alternative title for the *Sevenfold Treasury of Gems: Explanation of the Glorious 'Secret Assembly'* (*Dpal gsang ba 'dus pa'i rnam bshad rin po che'i gter mdzod bdun pa*), vol. 7, 405–612, written in 1504. According to its colophon on p. 606, the text was written to fulfill wishes of Künga Zangpo. Also, a short supplementary text that immediately follows it mentions that the *Sevenfold Treasury of Gems* addresses hundred topics: gsang ba 'dus pa'i rnam bshad rin po che'i gter mdzod bdun pa zhes bya ba'i bstan bcos kyi brjod bya'i don gyi rnam grangs brgya tham ba (610).

103. *Detailed Analysis*, vol. 16, 98.

104. *Smaller Summarized Exposition*, vol. 4, 605.

105. The text of *Detailed Analysis*, vol. 16, 99, reads: dbu ma'i rnam thar nges pa che chung. I take *thar* as a misspelling of *par*. By the "*Big and Small Ascertainments of Madhyamaka*" Drölchok means what he also calls the "*Big and Small Summarized Expositions of Madhyamaka*" (*dbu ma'i stong thun che chung*) that according to him Shakya Chokden started writing in 1478 (*Detailed Analysis*, vol. 16, 125–126). The *Big Exposition/Ascertainment* is no doubt the *Ocean of Scriptural Statements and Reasoning*. As for the *Small Summarized Exposition*, unless Drölchok had in mind another text that is not available anymore, we should admit that he mistakenly assumed that both *Summarized Expositions/Ascertainments* were written at the same time. It is also possible that by the *Small Exposition/Ascertainment* Drölchok meant *not* the *Smaller Summarized Exposition* mentioned above (29) but the *Clear Identification of the Presence of the String of One Hundred and Eight Beads of Mistakes Conceived by [Wrong] Logic in Madhyamaka of the System of Others* (*Gzhan lugs kyi ni dbu ma la// rtog ges brtags pa'i nor ba'i phreng// brgya dang rtsa brgyad yod pa yi// ngos 'dzin gsal po*), vol. 4, 407–419. Such option is doubtful but plausible, because the latter text focuses on separating Shakya Chokden's own and others' systems through criticisms of Tsongkhapa's interpretation of Madhyamaka, while the *Smaller Summarized Exposition* focuses on difficult points of Candrakīrti's *Engaging in Madhyamaka*, although it does address the views of one's own and others' systems. No date of composition of the *Clear Identification* is provided in its colophon, but it does mention that the text was composed at Sangpu. Thus, it is also of an earlier date than the *Big Exposition/Ascertainment*.

106. *Detailed Analysis*, vol. 16, 100.

107. Ibid.

108. Ibid., 100.

109. Ibid., 103. The replenishing burnt offerings (*kha gso'i sbyin sreg*) ritual is usually performed at the end of retreats focusing on tantric deities in order to purify mistakes that might have been committed in recitation and other activities during the retreat, and so forth.

110. rang re'i gsang phu'i chen po'i khur de bzhag 'phral/ 'od gsal rtser kye rdo rje'i bsnyen bsgrub zla ba dgu pa cig mtshams bcad cha dam pa rang byas/ de dus sdig pa 'dra dag pa'i rtags yin yod/ tho rang 'od gsal gyi 'char sgo ya ma cha 'ga' re byung/ 'od gsal rtse mo ming don ldan yin. Ibid., 103–104.

111. Ibid., 104, 106, 108. Also see the next section of this chapter.

112. Ibid., 80.

113. See Chapter 5.

114. *Dbu ma'i lta khrid/ zhi gnas dang lhag mthong zung du 'jug pa ngo mtshar rgyan gyi phreng ba*, vol. 13, 190–202. Hereafter, *Guiding Instructions on the Madhyamaka View*.

115. For more details see p. 46.

116. *Detailed Analysis*, vol. 16, 108. I relied on this information in my somewhat immature *Three Texts on Madhyamaka by Shakya Chokden* (Dharamsala, India: Library of Tibetan Works and Archives, 2000), x. Hereafter, *Three Texts on Madhyamaka.* According to Shakya Chokden himself, he renamed this monastery in 1476 (see p. 41 below).

117. *Detailed Analysis*, vol. 16, 104–105.

118. They are the fundamental Vinaya rites of restoration-purification of vows (*gso sbyong, poṣadha*), summer retreat (*dbyar gnas, vārṣika*), and lifting restrictions set during the summer retreat (*dgag dbye, prāraṇā*).

119. *Detailed Analysis*, vol. 16, 108, 125.

120. For a description of this land and its people, see David P. Jackson, *The Mollas of Mustang: Historical, Religious and Oratorical Traditions of the Nepalese-Tibetan Borderland* (Dharamsala: Library of Tibetan Works and Archives, 1984), 1–12. See also Kramer, *A Noble Abbot from Mustang*, 13–35 for further historical details.

121. Künga Zangpo visited Lowo several times by invitation of its previous rulers, Amapel (*a ma dpal*, 1380–*c.* 1440) and Amgön Zangpo (*a mgon zang po*, b. 1420) who were Trashigön's grandfather and father, respectively. See Kramer, *A Noble Abbot from Mustang*, 21–23.

122. Ibid., 108–111.

123. They are included in a collection of texts found in vol. 17, 213–227. See the *Detailed Analysis*, vol. 16, 113–116, and section 3 of this chapter for details of the texts Shakya Chokden composed during his stay in Lowo.

124. *Detailed Analysis*, vol. 16, 114. This date is somewhat problematic, because in colophons of several texts composed at Sangpu Neutok Shakya Chokden already calls himself "Jampel Gepé Shenyen" or "Jampel Gawé Shenyen" (*'jam dpal dga' ba'i bshes gnyen*). See, for example, vol. 4, 399, 419. At the same time, Drölchok does not provide information about Shakya Chokden staying at Sangpu Neutok *after* his journey to Lowo.

125. *Sman bla'i mdo chog gi dri ba me tog mda' 'joms*, vol. 17, 319–324. Also, see the next section of this chapter.

126. See *Good Questions*, vol. 17, 461–462.

127. *Detailed Analysis*, vol. 16, 115–116.

128. Ibid., 117–118, 138–139.

129. Kramer, *A Noble Abbot from Mustang*, 62.

130. Ibid., 160–161. For details of Sönam Lhündrup's relationship with Shakya Chokden, see ibid., 66–67, 159–164.

131. *Byang pa bdag po rnam rgyal grags pa la bde gshegs snying po sman dpyad dus 'khor gsum gyi dri ba*, vol. 17, 325–329. According to Cyrus Stearns, "Namgyel Drakzang studied with many teachers of different traditions, but described himself as a follower of the Jonang (*jo nang*) teachings, especially those of the Kālacakra and the Six-branch Yoga, and considered Dölpopa to be the ultimate authority on these topics. . . . Namgyel Drakzang . . . wrote many important works, but very few seem to have survived. Shakya Chokden and Namgyel Drakzang corresponded by letter and met on several occasions. Their last meeting was in 1475 at the elderly ruler's residence near Ngamring, which Shakya Chokden visited on his return trip from a lengthy stay in Mustang, in present-day Nepal." *The Buddha from Dölpo*, 62–63. I altered only Stearns's way of transcribing personal names.

132. *Detailed Analysis*, vol. 16, 118–121.

133. *Rigs ldan chos kyi rgyal po rnam rgyal grags pa bzang po'i rnam par thar pa rab bsngags snyan pa'i 'brug sgra* (Kathmandu: Nepal-German Manuscript Preservation Project, Microfilm reel E–1872/6, Xylograph), folio 24b–25b. Hereafter, *Thunder of Melodious Praise*. I am very greateful to Cyrus Stearns who drew my attention to this text, generously provided me with relevant passages, and shared with me his ideas about their importance. See also *The Buddha from Dölpo*, 62–63.

134. This term can be translated as the name of a philosophical system, as I did here, or as the "mind-only," which is the main tenet of that system.

135. nged rang byis pa'i dus/ rje don yod dpal ba'i phyag phyi byas/ mkhan chen padma bzang po ba mjal ba la phyin pa'i gral la/ mkhan chen pa'i gsung nas/ slob dpon pa/ byams chos bar pa gsum gyi dgongs pa gang du gnas gsung gin yod gsungs pa la/ rje don yod dpal bas nged sems tsam du gnas zhu yin yod lags gsungs pa la/ de'i rgyu mtshan gang yin gsungs pa la/ sems las gzhan med par ni blos rig nas/ zhes lung 'dren mdzad kyin 'dug pa la/ 'o na de'i mjug rang na/ blo dang ldan pa gnyis ka med rig nas/ sogs shar te gsungs nas 'di rnams ci lags/ nged cag ni dus dang rnam pa thams cad du/ byams chos kyi dgongs don dbu ma chen po'i shing rta rma med pa nyid du 'grel ba yin gsungs shing. *Thunder of Melodious Praise*, 25a. Pema Zangpowa is known to have written a history of Buddhism and a large commentary on the *Kālacakra Tantra*. He was an important teacher of the Jonang abbot Jamyang Könchok Zangpo (*'jam dbyang dkon mchog bzang po*, 1398–1475)—a great Jonang master who is also present in the transmission lineage of the Path and Result teachings. See *The Buddha from Dölpo*, 68, 349 note 264; 348 note 252.

136. See the passage from the *Wish Fulfilling Meru* on the next page.

137. Shakya Chokden uses the widely accepted order of *listing* the *Five Dharmas of Maitreya* provided above, and applies the term "three intermediate Dharmas" to the *Ornament of Mahāyāna Sūtras* and the two *Differentiations.* Nevertheless, the order of their *composition* according to Shakya Chokden is different: 1. *Ornament of Clear Realizations,* 2. *Ornament of Mahāyāna Sūtras,* 3. *Sublime Continuum,* 4. *Differentiation of the Middle and Extremes,* 5. *Differentiation of Phenomena and the Nature of Phenomena.* For details, see the *Thorough Clarification of Definitive Meaning of the 'Five Dharmas of Maitreya,'* vol. 11, 11–12.

138. byang chub sems dpas bsod nams ye shes kyi// mtha' yas pha rol tshogs rnams legs bsags nas// chos la sems pa shin tu rnam nges phyir// don gyi rnam pa brjod pa'i rgyu can rtogs// de yis brjod pa tsam du don rig nas// der snang sems tsam la ni yang dag gnas// de nas chos dbyings gnyis kyi mtshan nyid dang// bral ba mngon sum nyid du rtogs par 'gyur// sems las gzhan med par ni blos rig nas// de nas sems kyang med pa nyid du rtogs// blo dang ldan pas gnyis po med rig nas// de mi ldan pa'i chos kyi dbyings la gnas. *Ornament of Mahāyāna Sūtras,* D4020, sems tsam, phi, 6b. Skt.: saṃbhṛtya saṃbhāram anantapāraṃ jñānasya puṇyasya ca bodhisatvaḥ/ dharmeṣu cintāsuviniśritatvāj jalpānvayām arthagatiṃ paraiti// arthān sa vijñāya ca jalpamātrān saṃtiṣṭhate tannibhacittamātre/ pratyakṣatāmeti ca dharmadhātus tasmād viyukto dvayalakṣaṇena// nāstīti cittāt parametya buddhyā cittasya nāstitvam upaiti tasmāt/ dvayasya nāstitvam upetya dhīmān saṃtiṣṭhate 'tad gatidharmadhātau. In Sylvain Lévi, *Mahāyāna-sūtrālaṃkāra: exposé de la doctrine du grand véhicule selon le systéme Yogācāra* (Paris: Bibliothéque de l'École des Hautes Études, 1907), vol. 1, pp. 23–24. Tibetan version has *shin tu rnam nges,* reading *viniścita* instead of *viniśrita.* Ibid., vol. 2, p. 52.

139. See p. 146 ff.

140. bod phyi ma dag las/ la la ni/ lnga char yang sems tsam pa nyid du nges'/ zhes dang/ kha cig ni/ thams cad dbu mar nges zhes dang/ phyi dus 'di na/ thog mtha' gnyis dbu ma dang/ bar pa gsum sems tsam du nges sam [*sic*] zhes dbyangs gcig tu smra bar byed mod/ kho bo cag ni/ byams pa'i gzhung thog mtha' gnyis kyang sher phyin gyi mdo'i dgongs pa 'khor lo gsum pas bkral ba de nyid kyi dbu ma bstan bya'i gtso bo nyid du mdzad par gzhung nyid kyi bshad tshul mngon sum gyis grub par khas len to. *Dbu ma'i byung tshul rnam par bshad pa'i gtam yid bzhin lhun po,* vol. 4, 225. (Hereafter, *Wish Fulfilling Meru.*) See also my *Three Texts on Madhyamaka,* 15 ff. for a slightly different translation and further details. Note that Shakya Chokden interprets the meaning of the *Ornament of Clear Realizations* slightly differently from that of the other four *Dharmas of Maitreya* (see p. 204 ff.).

141. nged la gzigs nas/ dbon chung shes rab 'dug pa 'di 'dra'i skor la gzhig pa chug cig ces ja'i gsol ras kyang gnang ba de dus man nas nges don la gzhig 'brel chug pa yin kyang grub mtha'i gzhung shin tu bsgril ba'i bstan bcos su zhib rgyas rang 'khod pa med/ than thun ngag nas smras pa tsam yin/ slar nas rigs ldan chen po ba'i bka'i bsgo ba thob phyir rtsal 'don du bskyangs pa yin no. *Thunder of Melodious Praise,* 25a. I retained Stearns's translation in *The Buddha from Dölpo,* 64, altering only the transcription of personal names.

142. *Thunder of Melodious Praise*, 25a–b.

143. *'Dul ba mdo'i dka' ba'i gnas rnam par bshad pa mdo'i snang byed nyi ma'i shing rta*, vol. 22, 1–265. *Detailed Analysis*, vol. 16, 121.

144. Ibid., 122–124.

145. See the first page of a nameless text by Shakya Chokden contained in vol. 17, 307–309 of his collected works. See Kuijp, *Contributions*, 8–9, and 261, note 24, who addresses this text and provides further details.

146. *Dharmadhātustotra, Chos kyi dbyings su bstod pa*, D1118, bstod tshogs, ka, 63b–67b. For English translation and analysis, see Karl Brunnhölzl (tr. and introduction), In Praise of Dharmadhātu *by Nāgārjuna, Commentary by the Third Karmapa* (Ithaca, New York: Snow Lion Publications, 2007).

147. See the next section of this chapter.

148. This date accords with the colophon of the *Golden Lancet*, vol. 7, 222.

149. *Detailed Analysis*, vol. 16, 138–140. According to a postscript of the *Golden Lancet*, vol. 7, 229, carving of woodblocks of this text started in the first half of the first lunar month of 1483 and was completed in the ninth lunar month at a special time of the Buddha's Descent from the Divine Realm (*lha las babs pa'i dus khyad par chen*) festival. According to the *Detailed Analysis*, vol. 16, 138, Shakya Chokden composed the *Golden Lancet* in 1483. I wonder whether this particular discrepancy is based on the fact that Drölchok took the printing date for the writing date.

150. According to Drölchok it happened on the tenth lunar month. This date is questionable, because on the seventh lunar month of that year Shakya Chokden was already in Penyül (*phan yul*; I take *phan yul* as an alternative spelling of *'phan yul* in Ü) where he composed such texts as the *Harbor of the Ocean of Faith: Extensive Explanation of the 'King of Aspirational Prayers of Deeds of Ārya Samantabhadra'* (*'Phags pa kun tu bzangs po'i spyod pa'i smon lam gyi rgyal po'i rgya cher bshad pa dad pa rgya mtsho'i 'jug ngogs*), vol. 8, 352–403 (see vol. 8, 403, and the next section of this chapter). I doubt that he traveled back and forth between Tsang and Ü within those three months.

151. Ibid., 134, 136.

152. Ibid., 136. In other words, even though he did not despise the *Collected Topics* in general, he strongly resisted interpretations of certain elements related to that literature that were popularized by later interpreters.

153. *Tshad ma rigs pa'i gter gyi rnam par bshad pa sde bdun ngag gi rol mtsho*, vol. 19, 447–749. Hereafter, *Enjoyment Ocean of the Speech of the 'Seven Works.' Detailed Analysis*, vol. 16, 138.

154. Should be Dönyö Dorjé.

155. *Detailed Analysis*, vol. 16, 138, 156.

156. *Detailed Analysis*, vol. 16, 141–142, 144.

157. This text does not seem to be extant anymore.

158. *Detailed Analysis*, vol. 16, 148–149.

159. In general, subsequent permissions form a part of different tantric empowerments. But they can also be transmitted separately after one has received related empowerments. Subsequent permissions also can be given alone, without any connection to empowerments, especially for those deities that do not have complete empowerments.

160. *Detailed Analysis*, vol. 16, 151–153.

161. *Detailed Analysis*, vol. 16, 154–156, 170–174.

162. *Rgyas pa'i bstan bcos tshad ma rnam 'grel gyi rnam bshad kun bzang chos kyi rol mtsho*, vol. 18, 189–693. Hereafter, *Enjoyment Ocean of the Entirely Good Dharma*.

163. *Detailed Analysis*, vol. 16, 157–158.

164. Some of these texts are contained in a small collection called "Prayers and Numerous Songs of Contemplative Experience" (*Gsol 'debs dang mgur 'bum gyi skor*), vol. 17, 463–472. But note that the last text in that collection ([Nameless], vol. 17, 471–472) was composed when Shakya Chokden was eighty years old.

165. *Detailed Analysis*, vol. 16, 161–162.

166. Ibid., 162–164.

167. *Detailed Analysis*, vol. 16, 164–165. For more details see *A Means to Achieve Bhikṣuṇī Ordination*, p. 4. No author mentioned. Downloadable from: http://www.thubtenchodron.org/BuddhistNunsMonasticLife/a_means_to_achieve_bhiksuni_ordination.pdf. On the issue of the *bhikṣuṇī* ordination, see Thea Mohr and Jampa Tsedroen (ed.), *Dignity and Discipline: Reviving Full Ordination for Buddhist Nuns* (Boston: Wisdom Publications, 2010).

168. In this context, I take it as the same as the Explanation for Assembly (*tshogs bshad*). The formal division of the Path and Result teachings into the Explanation for Assembly and the Explanation for Disciples (*slob bshad*) started from Künga Zangpo's immediate successor Müchen Sempa Chenpo Könchok Gyeltsen (*mus chen sems pa chen po dkon mchog rgyal mtshan*, 1388–1469), and reflected the separation of teachings by Künga Zangpo who would give the Explanation for Disciples to a few close disciples and the Explanation for Assembly to the assembly of students gathering annually at Ngor. Davidson, "Nor-pa Tradition," 89.

169. *Detailed Analysis*, vol. 16, 165.

170. *Thub pa'i dgongs pa rab tu gsal ba* (xylographic print, unknown publisher).

171. *Detailed Analysis*, vol. 16, 169.

172. *Brtag gnyis kyi bsdus don// bshad rgyud kyi rgyud pa'i rim pa rnams*, vol. 13, 463–467.

173. *Lam skor brgyad kyi gsal byed bdud rtsi'i thig pa*, vol. 13, 630–640.

174. *Detailed Analysis*, vol. 16, 173, 178–179.

175. grub mtha' smra ba rnam bzhi yi// rtse gyur ngo bo nyid med du// smra ba'i dbu ma chen po pa. *Guiding Instructions on the Madhyamaka View*, vol. 13, 190.

176. For the discussion of the issue of change of Shakya Chokden's views see Chapter 2 section 4.

177. *Detailed Analysis*, vol. 16, 180–185.

178. *Chos kyi 'khor lo bskor ba'i rnam gzhag ji ltar grub pa'i yi ge gzu bor gnas pa'i mdzangs pa dga' byed*, vol. 16, 474 ff. Hereafter, *Letter Pleasing Impartial Wise Ones*.

179. *Detailed Analysis*, vol. 16, 189–190.

180. *Detailed Analysis*, vol. 16, 200–202.

181. According to the *Detailed Analysis*, 202–203, the letter came in 1502. This date conflicts with the date given in the history of Pramāṇa called the *Appearance of the Sun Pleasing All Thinkers: Discussion of the History of the Chariot Ways of [Dignāga's] 'Sūtra on Valid Cognition' and [Its] Treatises* (*Tshad ma'i bstan bcos kyi shin rta'i srol rnams ji ltar 'byung ba'i tshul gtam du bya ba nyin byed snang ba*), vol. 19, 137, whose colophon states that Shakya Chokden composed that text in 1501 in Serdokchen by request of the "Lord of Enlightened Activities of all Buddhas of Three Times, the Self-Arisen Omniscient King of Dharma" (dus gsum gyi sangs rgyas thams cad kyi phrin las dbang po/ rang byung kun mkhyen chos kyi rgyal po), i.e., Karmapa. The history of Madhyamaka is the *Wish Fulfilling Meru*. It does not mention in its colophon (vol. 4, p. 248) the date of composition, but says that it was composed in Serdokchen and offered by Shakya Chokden to Karmapa whom he addresses as the "Lord of Enlightened Activities of all Victors of Three Times who embraces [everything] with [the look of his] compassionate eyes, as he sits firmly on the lion throne of the Dharma seat among the ocean-like gathering of disciples in the great temple of Rasa Trülnang" (dus gsum rgyal ba mtha' dag gi phrin las dbang po/ 'dus pa rgya mtsho'i tshogs dang bcas pa/ ra sa 'phrul snang gi gtsug lag khang chen por chos kyi gdan seng ge'i khri la zhabs zung brtan par gdan chags pa'i thugs rje'i spyan zung gis nye bar khyab pa). If we agree with Drölchok that Shakya Chokden met Karmapa in Lhasa in 1502, and if we assume that Shakya Chokden either sent both histories to Karmapa before going to Lhasa or offered them to Karmapa on his visit there, then we will have to agree that Karmapa's letter came not later than 1501, and the history of Madhyamaka was written not later than 1502. Most probably it was written in 1501, together with the history of Pramāṇa.

182. *Detailed Analysis*, vol. 16, 203–204.

183. *Tshad ma legs par bshad pa thams cad kyi chu bo yongs su 'du ba rigs pa'i gzhung lugs kyi rgya mtsho* (Sarnath, Varanasi: Central Institute of Higher Tibetan Studies, 1999). Hereafter, *Ocean of Textual Systems of Reasoning*. For more on that text, see p. 81.

184. Ibid., 205–206.

185. *Chos byung mkhas pa'i dga' ston* (Delhi, India: Karmapae Chodhey Gyalwae Sungrab Partun Khang), vol. 2, 259–260. Hereafter, *Feast for Scholars*. For details see Stearns, *The Buddha from Dölpo*, 61–62. For more on the three meetings between Chödrak Gyamtso and Shakya Chokden, including translations of relevant passages from the *Feast for Scholars*, see Anne Burchardi, "The Logic of Liberation: Epistemology as a Path to the Realization of Mahāmudrā," forthcoming in *Proceedings of the 7th Nordic Tibet Research Conference* (Helsinki, 2009).

186. *Dpal gsang ba 'dus pa'i rnam bshad rin po che'i gter mdzod bdun pa*, vol. 7, 405–612. Hereafter, *Sevenfold Treasury of Gems*.

187. *Dpal dang po'i sangs rgyas rab tu grub pas bka' 'khor lo gsum pa'i mdo dang rgyud sde kun gyi snying po bsdus pa*, vol. 8, 10–183. Hereafter, *Thorough Establishment of the Glorious Original Buddha*.

188. See the next section of this chapter and the *Detailed Analysis*, vol. 16, 208–209.

189. Ibid., 209–215.

190. Ibid., 218–219.

191. Ibid., 233.

192. Ibid., 136. Drölchok provides a list of Shakya Chokden's disciples in ibid., 228–230. Most names on that list have place names appended to them in small letters, most probably penned by Künga Drölchok himself. They can indicate places of origin of those individuals (such as "Lowo," for example) or places and monasteries they came to be affiliated with (such as "Nartang"). In Tibetan they are usually followed by particles *pa* or *ba*, and I translate most of them into English preceded by the preposition "from." Some of them—such as "Drakmarwa" (*brag dmar ba*), for example—might have been used more often than the person's actual name. According to the list, Shakya Chokden's disciples included Künga Gyeltsen (*kun dga' rgyal mtshan*) from Tingkyé (*gting skyes*); Künga Tsepel (*kun dga' tshe 'phel*) from Drakmar (*brag dmar*); Lodrö Gyeltsen (*blo gros rgyal mtshan*) from Lowo; Namgyel Pelzang (*rnam rgyal dpal bzang*) from Gugé (*gu ge*); Chödrak Pelzang (*chos grags dpal bzang*) from Minyak (*mi nyag*); Rinchen Gyeltsen (*rin chen rgyal mtshan*) from Tsel (*tshal*); Sanggyé Zangpo (*sangs rgyas bzang po*) from Trapu (*phra phu*); Gartsa (*mgar tsha*) scholar from Khangsar (*khang gsar*) monastic college; Lhayi Tsünpa (*lha yi btsun pa*); master Nyangrampa (*nyang ram pa*) Lhündrup Pelzang (*lhun grub dpal bzang*; this can be read as the "holder of 'Rapjampa' degree from Nyangtö," and he must be the same individual as Nyangtö Rapjampa Lhündrup Pel Zangpo mentioned on p. 50); master Sanggyé Lodrö (*sangs rgyas blo gros*) from Nang (*nangs*); master Drakpa Zangpo (*grags pa bzang po*) from Nartang (*snar thang*); Sönam Gyeltsen (*bsod nams rgyal mtshan*) from Drakkar (*brag dkar*); Künga Trashi (*kun dga' bkra shis*) from Serling (*gser gling*); Ngakwang Chögyel (*ngag dbang chos rgyal*) from Langtang; chief (*rje dpon*) Shakya Gyeltsen (*shākya rgyal mtshan*); Trachar (*khra char*) abbot from Purang (*pu rangs*); Jamling (*byams gling*) abbot from Lowo; Drakkar (*brag dkar*) abbot from Lowo; Ulek (*dbu legs*) abbot from Ngari; foremost venerable Künga Chokdrup (*kun dga' mchog grub*); Zhönnu Chödrup from Changlung; Lodrö Namgyel (*blo gros rnam rgyal*) from Purang; Sherap Penjor (*Sherap Penjor*) from Lowo; yogin Ünyönpa Künga Zangpo; Sönam Gyel (*bsod nams rgyal*)—great yogin from Ulek; Gamo Dharma practitioner (*dga' mo chos mdzad*) from Penyül; Namkha Rapsel (*nam mkha' rab gsal*) from Khoklung (*khog lung*); Lodrö Zangpo (*blo gros bzang po*) from Khartsé Changra (*mkhar rtse lcang ra*); Dorjé Gyelpo (*rdo rje rgyal po*) from Nyangtö Tsechen (*nyang stod rtse chen*); Dönyö Druppa (*don yod grub pa*) from Ngari Lowo; Yeshé Lhündrup (*ye shes lhun grub*) from Puyung (*phu dbyung*); Rapsel Damgön (*rab gsal zla mgon*) from Mangkar (*mang dkar*); Tukje Pelwa (*thugs rje dpal ba*) from Mü (*mus*); Mürampa Könchok Drakpa (*mus ram pa dkon mchog grags pa*; similar to *nyang ram pa* above, here *mus ram pa* also can be read as a "holder of 'Rapjampa' degree from Mü," that is, "Müpa Rapjampa," *mus pa rab 'byams pa*); Rinchen Trashi (*rin chen bkra shis*) from Samdruptsé; Könchok Gyeltsen (*dkon mchog rgyal mtshan*)—Puchung Kachupa (*phu chung ka bcu pa*; this name can be read

as the "holder of Kachupa degree [nicknamed] 'kid' [due to his young age]"); Nartang abbot Sherap Pelden (*shes rab dpal ldan*); Yönten Chömpel (*yon tan chos 'phel*) from Ramoché (*ra mo che*); Dedünpa Wangchuk Gyeltsen (*sde bdun pa dbang phyug rgyal mtshan*; "Dedünpa" indicates either his degree—if there was such a degree at the time—or just the fact that he mastered the *Seven Works* (*sde bdun*) of Dharmakīrti; for the list of those works, see p. 336 note 64 below); Sanggyé Özer (*sangs rgyas 'od zer*); Choklé Namgyel (*phyogs las rnam rgyal*); Doring Künpang (*rdo rings kun dpangs*); Wangchuk Pelwa (*dbang phyug dpal ba*) from Lowo; Rawa Dopa (*ra ba mdo pa*) from Trangpo Senggé Gang (*'phrang po seng ge sgang*; I presume that he is the same person as Ramdopa mentioned above (47) who in 1496 persuaded Shakya Chokden to give the Path and Result teachings in the system of Künga Trashi); commander (*sde pa sgar pa*) Dönyö Dorjé; descendant of Khön lineage (*'khon gyi gdung brgyud*) Shakya Gyeltsen (*shākya rgyal mtshan*); Lingmé (*gling smad*) abbot Künga Penjor (*kun dga' dpal 'byor*); Chölung's senior abbot Sanggyé Pel Zangpo (*sangs rgyas dpal bzang po*); senior abbot Namkha Lhündrup (*nam mkha' lhun grub*); Törawa (*stod ra ba*); and six generations of abbots (*mkhan rabs*)—senior abbots (*mkhan chen*) Lotenpa (*blo brtan pa*), Lhündrup Trashi (*lhun grub bkra shis*), Lekpa Rinchen (*legs pa rin chen*), Künga Penjor (*kun dga dpal 'byor*), Drakpa Gyeltsen (*grags pa rgyal mtshan*), and Trashi Namgyel (*bkra shis rnam rgyal*). See also Kuijp, *Contributions*, 11–13.

193. Might be the same individual as Wangchuk Pelwa mentioned in the list of Shakya Chokden's disciples in the previous note.

194. *Detailed Analysis*, vol. 16, 5.

195. nged dang chos rje chen po sems gcig yin pas gang gi zhabs thegs kyang bsam pa yongs su rdzogs. Ibid., 6.

Chapter 2

1. David Seyfort Ruegg, *The Literature of the Madhyamaka School of Philosophy in India* (Wiesbaden: Harrassowitz, 1981), 1–2. Hereafter, *The Literature of the Madhyamaka School*. The terms "Niḥsvabhāvavāda" and "Śūnya(tā)vāda" refer to the system that advocates the view of all phenomena being empty of their own nature or entity.

2. For example, Taranatha speaks of two subdivisions of Madhyamaka into the Ordinary Madhyamaka (*dbu ma phal pa*, translated by Hopkins as "Ordinary Middle Way") and the Great Madhyamaka (*dbu ma chen po*, translated by Hopkins as "Great Middle Way"), and treats only the former one as the Niḥsvabhāvavāda system. He identifies the Great Madhyamaka as the system of Vijñapti Madhyamaka (*rnam rig gi dbu ma*, "Middle of Cognizance," translated by Hopkins as the "Middle Way School of Cognition"), arguing that it is known in Tibet as Other-Emptiness. See Hopkins, *The Essence of Other-Emptiness*, 13–16, 55, 62, 92.

3. See C.W. Huntington, Jr, "Was Candrakīrti a Prāsaṅgika?" in *The Svātantrika-Prāsaṅgika Distinction: What a Difference does a Difference Make?* eds.

Georges B. J. Dreyfus and Sara L. McClintock (Boston: Wisdom Publications, 2003), 74.

4. Most dates provided in this section are based on *The Literature of the Madhyamaka School*.

5. Ruegg, *The Literature of the Madhyamaka School*, 4. It should be noted that Shakya Chokden ascribes the origins of Madhyamaka to an earlier master, namely Saraha, whom he places shortly before Nāgārjuna. Shakya Chokden does admit that Niḥsvabhāvavāda Madhyamaka originated from Nāgārjuna. See the *Three Texts on Madhyamaka by Shakya Chokden*, 9–10.

6. The *Collection of Reasonings* (*Rigs tshogs*) consists of *Wisdom: Root Stanzas on Madhyamaka*; *Sixty Stanzas of Reasoning* (*Yuktiṣaṣṭikākārikā, Rigs pa drug cu pa'i tshig le'ur byas pa zhes bya ba*), D3825, dbu ma, tsa, 20b–22b; *Treatise Called the 'Finely Woven'* (*Vaidalyasūtranāma, Zhib mo rnam par 'thag pa zhes bya ba'i mdo*), D3826, dbu ma, tsa, 22b–24a; *Seventy Stanzas on Emptiness* (*Śūnayatāsaptatikārikā, Stong pa nyid bdun cu pa'i tshig le'ur byas pa*), D3827, dbu ma, tsa, 24a–27a; and *Refutation of Objections* (*Virgrahavyāvartanīkārikā, Rtsod pa bzlog pa'i tshig le'ur byas pa*), D3828, dbu ma, tsa, 27a–29a.

7. *Treatise of Four Hundred Stanzas* (*Catuḥṣatakaśāstranāmakārikā, Bstan bcos bzhi brgya pa zhes bya ba'i tshig le'ur byas pa*), D3846, dbu ma, tsha, 1a–18a.

8. Maitreya is traditionally seen by Tibetans as a bodhisattva and a future Buddha, and by some contemporary scholars—as a human teacher of Asaṅga.

9. According to Shakya Chokden, the Yogācāra system was pioneered by Asaṅga, or more generally—by Asaṅga and Vasubandhu. See the *Three Texts on Madhyamaka*, 10, 14. Also, see p. 183 ff. below. Vasubandhu's dates are not more precise than his older brother's.

10. *Mahāyānasaṃgraha, Theg pa chen po bsdus pa*, D4048, sems tsam, ri, 1a–43a.

11. *Yogācārabhūmi, Rnal 'byor spyod pa'i sa*, D4035, sems tsam, tshi, 1a–D4037, sems tsam, wi, 213a.

12. *Mahāyānasaṃgrahabhāṣya, Theg pa chen po bsdus pa'i 'grel pa*, D4050, sems tsam, ri, 121–190.

13. *Madhyāntavibhāgaṭīkā, Dbus dang mtha' rnam par 'byed pa'i 'grel pa*, D4027, sems tsam, bi, 1a1–27a7.

14. Here, I am taking "mental states" broadly, referring to all types of mental processes, including those that are given names of wisdom, primordial mind, non-dual wisdom, etc., as well as those that according to some thinkers transcend mind.

15. See 127 ff. for details.

16. See my *Three Texts on Madhyamaka*, 12, 45–46. For an explanation of this debate, as well as different positions on the nature and origins of Prāsaṅgika and Svātantrika, see *The Center of the Sunlit Sky*, 333–444, and the collection of excellent essays on the topic in Georges Dreyfus and Sara L. McClintock (ed.), *The Svātantrika-Prāsaṅgika Distinction: What a Difference does a Difference Make?* (Boston: Wisdom Publications, 2003). Hereafter *The Svātantrika-Prāsaṅgika Distinction*.

17. See, for example, Drakpa Gyeltsen's (*grags pa rgyal mtshan*) *Precious Tree: Clear Realizations of Tantras* (*Rgyud kyi mngon par rtogs pa rin po che'i ljon shing*), in Sa-skya lam 'bras literature series, vol. 23 (Dehradun, U.P., India: Sakya Centre, 1985), 47–48. In general, Sautrāntika and Yogācāra are "Aspectarians" in terms of admitting that mind perceives its objects via a mental image or an aspect (*rnam pa, akāra*). Vaibhāṣika is "Non-Aspectarian" because it accepts that perception occurs without the medium of a mental image. The views of Niḥsvabhāvavāda are of two types, at least according to some thinkers. (For details, see Yuichi Kajiyama, "Controversy between the sākāra- and nirākāra-vadins of the yogācāra school—some materials," *Indogaku Bukkyōgaku Kenkyū*, vol. 14, no. 1 (1965): 429–418; hereafter "Controversy between the sākāra- and nirākāra-vadins.") The views of Aspectarians and Non-Aspectarians as subdivisions of Yogācāra system have a more specific meaning, being synonymous with the views of Satyākāravāda and Alīkākāravāda, respectively. In the Yogācāra context, the two pairs can be used interchangeably, although some thinkers prefer the one over the other. For example, discussing Śāntarakṣita's analysis of Yogācāra, Kajiyama says that Satyākāravādin is also called Sākāravādin, while Alīkākāravādin is also called Anākāravādin (Yuichi Kajiyama, "Later Mādhyamikas on Epistemology and Meditation," in *Mahāyāna Buddhist Meditation: Theory and Practice*, ed. Minoru Kiyota (Honolulu: The University of Hawaii, 1978), 125), but further notes that Śantarakṣita himself uses the terms "Sākāravādin" and "Anākaravādin" more frequently (ibid., 142, note 20). On the other hand, Shakya Chokden—as well as the majority of other Tibetan thinkers—prefer to use the terminology of "*rnam rdzun pa/ rnam bden pa*" instead of "*rnam med pa/ rnam bcas pa*," possibly in order to avoid making a wrong impression that some Yogācāras do not accept aspects at all.

18. As Yuichi Kajiyama explains in the "Controversy between the sākāra- and nirākāra-vadins," "Dharmapāla's theory is similar to *sākāravāda* of Jñānaśrīmitra and Ratnakīrti, while Sthiramati's to the *nirākāravāda* of Ratnākaraśānti." Kazufumi Oki also sees Sthiramati's theory as nirākāravijñānavāda, and Dharmapāla's as a sākāravijñānavāda ("Musōyuishiki to Usōyuishiki," in *Kōza Daijō Bukkyō 8 Yuishiki Shisō* (Tokyo: Shunjūsha, 1982), 179. Also, as Kajiyama shows, Bodhibhadra (*c.* 1000) considered Dignāga with his followers as proponents of *sākāra* and Asaṅga with his followers as proponents of *nirākāra* ("Controversy between the sākāra- and nirākāra-vadins," 424). Ruegg too mentions that Dignāga was regarded as belonging to the Satyākāravāda or Sākāravāda branch of the Vijñānavāda school (*The Literature of the Madhyamaka School*, 61). Nevertheless, this classification of Yogācāra thinkers into two groups faces certain problems. See Chapter 3 section 6, and p. 357 note 116.

19. See p. 157 ff. for details. On different interpretations of the individually self-cognizing primordial mind, see "We Are All Gzhan stong pas," *Journal of Buddhist Ethics*, vol. 7 (2000): 110 ff. Hereafter, "We Are All Gzhan stong pas." On the question of whether self-cognition cognizes itself according to Shakya Chokden, see Chapter 5 section 4.

20. See the *Three Texts on Madhyamaka*, 16.

21. It should be noted that even Bhāviveka used reasoning derived from works on logic by Dignāga and Dharmakīrti. In that way, Bhāviveka was different from Buddhapālita who resisted the adoption of the logical and epistemological ideas of Dignāga. See *The Literature of the Madhyamaka School*, 60.

22. *The Literature of the Madhyamaka School*, 62. The two texts are respectively *Madhyamakahṛdayakārikā, Dbu ma'i snying po'i tshig le'ur byas pa*, D3855, dbu ma, dza, 1a–40b and *Madhyamakahṛdayavṛttitarkajvālā, Dbu ma'i snying po'i 'grel pa rtog ge 'bar ba*, D3856, dbu ma, dza, 40b–329b. For an English translation and edition of Bhāviveka's crtitique of Yogācāra in both texts, see Malcolm David Eckel, *Bhāviveka and His Buddhist Opponents*, Harvard Oriental Series, 70 (Cambridge, Massachusetts: Department of Sanskrit and Indian Studies, Harvard University, 2009), 213ff.

23. *Madhyamakāvatārabhāṣya, Dbu ma la 'jug pa'i bshad pa*, D3862, dbu ma, 'a, 220a–349a.

24. *The Literature of the Madhyamaka School*, 61–62.

25. It is unclear which praises (or "hymns") the *Collection of Praises* (*bstod tshogs*) actually consists of (*The Literature of the Madhyamaka School*, 31). It seems that during Shakya Chokden's time, this Collection was more or less formalized, because Shakya Chokden received a reading transmission (*lung*) of the *Collection of Praises* from Rongtön Sheja Künrik at the age of eighteen according to Künga Drölchok's *Detailed Analysis*, vol. 16, 35. One of the most well-known praises allegedly composed by Nāgārjuna is the *Praise of the Dharma-Sphere*, commented upon in Shakya Chokden's *Ascertainment of the Dharma-Sphere: Explanation of [Nāgārjuna's] Treatise 'Praise of the Dharma-Sphere'* (*Chos kyi dbyings su bstod pa zhes bya ba'i bstan bcos kyi rnam par bshad pa chos kyi dbyings rnam par nges pa*), vol. 7, 303–346.

26. See p. 195 ff.

27. *Bodhicittavivaraṇa, Byang chub sems kyi 'grel pa*, D1800, rgyud, ngi, 38a–42b.

28. *Rain of Ambrosia*, 340–342.

29. Ibid., 343.

30. This problem was noticed by contemporary scholars as well. See *The Literature of the Madhyamaka School*, 35, where Ruegg addresses the issue of criticizing Nāgārjuna's view as negativistic on the basis of only the *Wisdom: Root Stanzas on Madhyamaka*, and judging authenticity of his writings based on that text only, rather than the whole corpus of his works.

31. For details, see Chapter 3 sectrion 4.

32. *The Literature of the Madhyamaka School*, 59.

33. *Lta ba'i khyad par*, D4360, sna tshogs, jo, 213b–228a. This division is mentioned on p. 213b: "ātsārya bhavyas mdzad pa la ni mdo sde pa'i dbu ma zhes btags/ ātsārya shāntarakṣitas mdzad pa la ni rnal 'byor spyod pa'i dbu ma zhes btags so."

34. *Lta ba'i rim pa'i man ngag snang ba bcu bdun*, P4728, rgyud grel, bu, 424b–425a. In the later translation period too, Butön Rinchendrup (*bu ston rin chen grub*, 1290–1364) classified Śāntarakṣita and Kamalaśīla as Yogācāra Mādhyamikas and Bhāviveka and Jñānagarbha as Sautrāntika Mādhyamikas.

See Eugéne Obermiller (tr.), *History of Buddhism by Bu-ston* (Heidelberg: Otto Harrassowitz, 1932), 135. Shakya Chokden agrees with this classification (see p. 139 ff.). On the problem of classification of Jñānagarbha as a Sautrāntika Mādhyamika or Jñānagarbha's system as Yogācāra Mādhyamika, see Malcolm David Eckel, *Jñānagarbha's Commentary on the Distinction Between the Two Truths* (Albany, New York: State University of New York Press, 1987), 19–23.

35. *Explanation of the Stages of the Views* (*Lta ba'i rim pa bshad pa*), D4356, sna tshogs, co, 237a.

36. Kevin A. Vose, *Resurrecting Candrakīrti: Disputes in the Tibetan Creation of Prāsaṅgika* (Boston: Wisdom Publications, 2009), 20. (Hereafter, *Resurrecting Candrakīrti.*)

37. Shakya Chokden also acknowledges this distinction. See the *Three Texts on Madhyamaka*, 12. When addressing the *Differences of the Views*, he usually calls it *Notes on the Views* (*Lta ba'i brjed byang*).

38. For an excellent analysis of Candrakīrti's posthumous rise to power in the Tibetan intellectual world, see Vose, *Resurrecting Candrakīrti.*

39. *Three Texts on Madhyamaka*, 22–24.

40. Vose, *Resurrecting Candrakīrti*, 20.

41. Ibid., 36, 57, and 188 note 119.

42. *Grub mtha' so so'i bzhed gzhung gsal bar ston pa chos 'byung grub mtha' chen mo bstan pa'i sgron me* (Nemo Leh, Ladakh: Tshul-khrims-'jam-dbyangs, 1977), 165–193. Sherap Ö treats autonomous reasons and consequences as two subdivisions of inferential objects of engagement (*rjes dpag gi 'jug yul*, ibid., 189–190). Neither does he use them as a basis of the Svātantrika/Prāsaṅgika distinction per se, nor does he make that distinction in his analysis of Madhyamaka textual systems (ibid., 166 ff.). An English translation of this important text by José Ignacio Cabezón is forthcoming in 2011.

43. Georges Dreyfus, "Would the True Prāsaṅgika Please Stand? The Case and View of 'Ju Mi pham," in Dreyfus and McClintock (ed.), *The Svātantrika-Prāsaṅgika Distinction*, 318.

44. For the discussion of interpretations of the Svātantrika/Prāsaṅgika distinction by different thinkers in the eleventh to fourteenth centuries, see Helmut Tauscher, "Phya pa chos kyi seng ge as a Svātantrika," in Dreyfus and McClintock (ed.), *The Svātantrika-Prāsaṅgika Distinction*, 209–213; José Ignacio Cabezón, "Two Views on the Svātantrika-Prāsaṅgika Distinction in Fourteenth-Century Tibet," in ibid., 294–296. See also Kevin Vose, "Making and Remaking the Ultimate in Early Tibetan Readings of Śāntideva," *Journal of the International Association of Buddhist Studies*, vol. 32, no. 2 (2009, released 2011): 285–318; Georges Dreyfus and Drongbu Tsering, "Pa tshab and the Origin of Prāsaṅgika," ibid.: 387–418; and Thomas Doctor, "In Pursuit of Transparent Means of Knowledge, "The Madhyamaka Project of rMa bya Byaṅ chub brtson grus," ibid.: 419–442.

45. Shakya Chokden also mentions that according to Tsongkhapa's teacher Rendawa, on the Mahāyāna path, the Svātantrika view has to be abandoned from the first bodhisattva ground (*byang chub sems pa'i sa, bodhisattavabhūmi*),

while the Prāsaṅgika view has to be abandoned in the state of buddhahood. See the *Letter Pleasing Impartial Wise Ones on How Presentations of Turning Dharmacakras have been Accomplished* (*Chos kyi 'khor lo bskor ba'i rnam gzhag ji ltar grub pa'i yi ge gzu bor gnas pa'i mdzangs pa dga' byed*), vol. 16, 472.

46. For details of refutations of Tsongkhapa's take on the Svātantrika/ Prāsaṅgika distinction and his interpretation of the view of Prāsaṅgika by his critics, see Georges Dreyfus, "Would the True Prāsaṅgika Please Stand? The Case and View of 'Ju Mi pham," in Dreyfus and McClintock (ed.), *The Svātantrika-Prāsaṅgika Distinction*, 317–347. On Rongtön's and Gorampa's positions see José Ignacio Cabezón, "Two Views on the Svātantrika-Prāsaṅgika Distinction in Fourteenth-Century Tibet," in ibid., 289–315.

47. dbu ma rtsa ba'i dgongs pa thal 'gyur dang rang rgyud du 'chad pa'i bye brag gis/ thal rang gnyis su gyes par bshad pa'i don ma rtogs par lta ba bzang ngan gyi bye brag gis 'byed pa ni 'phags pa'i yul gyi dbu ma smra ba chen po dag gi lta ba la sgro 'dogs skur 'debs su smra ba yin pas/ mchil ma'i thal ba bzhin du dor bar bya'o. *Dbu ma rtsa ba'i rnam bshad zab mo'i de kho na nyid snang ba* (Sarnath: Central Institute of Higher Tibetan Studies, 1988), 40.

48. Articles by several contributors to *The Svātantrika-Prāsaṅgika Distinction* point in that direction. For example, William L. Ames in his "Bhāvaviveka's Own View of His Differences with Buddhapālita," in Dreyfus and McClintock (ed.), *The Svātantrika-Prāsaṅgika Distinction*, 56, comes to a conclusion that "in Bhāvaviveka's own view, his differences with Buddhapālita were almost entirely methodological rather than substantive."

49. For details of Shakya Chokden's approach, see Chapter 3 section 4. For Gorampa's position, see for example the *Distinguishing the Views: Moonrays of Essential Points of the Supreme Vehicle* (*Lta ba'i shan 'byed theg mchog gnad kyi zla zer*), Collected Works of Kun-mkhyen Go-rams-pa Bsod-nams-seng-ge, vol. 5 (Bir, India: Yashodhara Publications, 1995), 420 (hereafter, *Distinguishing the Views*), translated into English in José Ignacio Cabezón and Geshe Lobsang Dargyay, *Freedom from Extremes*, 71. See also *Freedom from Extremes*, p. 278, note 8.

50. See Georges Dreyfus, "Would the True Prāsaṅgika Please Stand? The Case and View of 'Ju Mi pham," in Dreyfus and McClintock (ed.), *The Svātantrika-Prāsaṅgika Distinction*, 322.

51. For example, in his *Commentary on Difficult Points of [Śāntarakṣita's] 'Compendium of Principles'* (*Tattvasaṃgrahapañjikā, De kho na nyid bsdus pa'i dka' 'grel*), D4267, tshad ma, ze 133b-'e-331a, Kamalaśīla distinguishes between two types of Vijñānavādins: Sākāravādins and Nirākāravādins, but at the same time speaks just of undifferentiated Mādhyamikas (*The Literature of the Madhyamaka School*, 58).

52. On the category of tantric Madhyamaka, see p. 254 ff.

53. This pertains to the level of sūtric teachings only. As I demonstrate on pp. 254–255, Shakya Chokden posits a separate category of tantric Madhyamaka.

54. I use the word "explicitly" because according to Shakya Chokden himself, his harmonizing approach was shared by important Indian and Tibetan thinkers.

55. It is clear in such famous works he wrote as the *Distinguishing the Views*, and *General Presentation of Madhyamaka: Thorough Clarification of Definitive Meaning* (*Dbu ma'i spyi don nges don rab gsal*), Collected Works of Kunmkhyen Go-rams-pa Bsod-nams-seng-ge, vol. 5, 1–415 (Yashodhara Publications, 1995).

56. In support of his harmonizing approach that emphasizes the compatibility of the views of Alīkākāravāda and Niḥsvabhāvavāda, Shakya Chokden usually quotes an opening verse from Ratnākaraśānti's *Quintessential Instructions on the 'Ornament of Madhyamaka'* (*Madhyamakālaṃkāropadeśa, Dbu ma rgyan gyi man ngag*), D4085, sems tsam, hi, 223b (see p. 155). Outside that context, in his *Ocean of Scriptural Statements and Reasoning*, vol. 14, 384, Shakya Chokden also quotes Ratnākaraśānti's *Quintessential Instructions on the Perfection of Wisdom* (*Prajñāpāramitopadeśa, Shes rab kyi pha rol tu phyin pa'i man ngag*), D4079, sems tsam, hi, 133b–162b, in support of his position that the final view of ultimate reality in Yogācāra system is an affirming negation. Overall, Shakya Chokden quotes Ratnākaraśānti much less than one would expect, given the similarity of their approaches to the Mahāyāna systems. In my opinion, it is due to the fact that Ratnākaraśānti was relatively less popular than Śāntarakṣita and other thinkers whose authority Shakya Chokden also resorts to in support of his position.

57. Ruegg mentions that Ratnākaraśānti followed Alīkākāra- or Nirākāra-Vijñānavāda and held his views to be the true Madhyamaka called "Vijñapti-Madhyamaka" (*The Literature of the Madhyamaka School*, 110). These features make Ratnākaraśānti's approach similar to that of Shakya Chokden.

58. 'di ltar rnal 'byor spyod pa pa ni chos rnams kyi rang bzhin gnyug ma gsal ba tsam ni rdzas su yod par 'dod pa yin la/ dbu ma pa ni rdzas de yang mi 'dod de/ khyad par 'di yang ming tsam du rtogs so// des na rtsa ba med par rnal 'byor spyod pa pa rnams dang/ dbu ma pa rnams lhan cig tu rtsod pa ni skye bo shin tu gnas ngan pa nyid. *Prajñāpāramitopadeśa, Shes rab kyi pha rol tu phyin pa'i man ngag*, D4079, 149b–150a.

59. Ibid., 143a.

60. See, for example, his *'Gateway to Scholarship' Treatise* (*Mkhas pa'i tshul la 'jug pa'i sgo zhes bya ba'i bstan bcos*, Mtsho sngon mi rigs dpe skrun khang, 1988), 149–151, and *Oral Instructions of Delighted Guru Mañjughoṣa: Explanation of [Śāntarakṣita's] 'Ornament of Madhyamaka'* (*Dbu ma rgyan gyi rnam bshad 'jam dbyangs bla ma dgyes pa'i zhal lung*, in Thomas H. Doctor (tr.), *Speech of Delight: Mipham's Commentary on Śāntarakṣita's* Ornament of the Middle Way *by Mipham Jamyang Namgyal Gyatso* (Ithaca, New York: Snow Lion Publications, 2004), 358–407 (hereafter, *Speech of Delight*).

61. de tlar na gzung ba dang 'dzin pa gnyis kyi rnam pa thams cad dang bral te yul dang yul can med pa'i rig pa rang bzhin gyis 'od gsal ba brjod du med pa tsam ni bdag gnyis kyis stong pa'i yongs grub de bzhin

nyid dang tha mi dad pa de ni sems tsam pas kyang rtogs dgos na dbu ma pas lta ci smos so// sems tsam pa ltar na de'i rang bzhin la stong nyid bcu drug gi don yongs su rdzogs te phyi dang nang la sogs pa gzung 'dzin gyi chos gang du yang bsam pa dang brjod par bya ba ma yin pas spros bral du 'dod do// 'on kyang brjod med kyi shes pa de yi ngo bo la bden grub tu 'jog tshul gyi grub mtha' phra mo tsam zhig lhag mar lus pa de nyid rigs pas sun phyungs te gzung 'dzin med pa'i shes pa nyid kyang bden pa med pa'i stong pa dang zung du zhugs pa'i rang sems gdod ma nas dag pa'i 'od gsal nyid du 'dod na dbu ma yang dag pa yin te des na theg chen dbu sems 'di gnyis zhen pa'i gnad phra mo zhig chod ma chod kyi khyad par las/mnyam rjes kyi nyams len phyogs 'dra ba lta bur 'ong bas 'phags yul gyi paṇ grub chen po rnams kyang theg pa chen po nyams su len pa la 'di gnyis khyad med lta bur mdzad pa'ang don de lta bu'i phyir yin no. *Chos dang chos nyid rnam par 'byed pa'i tshig le'ur byas pa'i 'grel ba ye shes snang ba rnam 'byed,* Sde-dge dgon-chen Printings of the Writings of 'Jam-mgon 'Ju Mi-pham-rgya-mtsho, vol. 4 (pa), pp. 626–627.

62. "[S]ince the genuine proponents of Cittamātra are the Proponents of True Features, their proposition is of solid bearing. [Yet,] by not holding external objects to be true as mind, the Proponents of False Features are a bit closer to the emptiness of truth, and so they form, as it were, a connecting link to the Middle Way." Translation by Thomas H. Doctor in the *Speech of Delight*, 381, 383; Tibetan text, ibid., 380, 382. (Doctor translates *rnam bden pa* and *rnam brdzun pa* as "Proponents of True Features" and "Proponents of False Features," respectively.)

63. The *Sūtra on Valid Cognition* (*Tshad ma'i mdo*) is a popular title for Dignāga's *Compendium of Valid Cognition* (*Pramāṇasamuccaya, Tshad ma kun las btus pa*), D4203, tshad ma, ce, 1b–13a.

64. These *Seven Works* (*sde bdun*) are the *Analysis of Relations* (*Sambandhaparīkṣa, 'Brel ba brtag pa*), D4214, tshad ma, ce, 255a–256a, *Ascertainment of Valid Cognition* (*Pramāṇaviniścaya, Tshad ma rnam par nges pa*), D4211, tshad ma, ce, 152b–230a, *Commentary on Valid Cognition* (*Pramāṇavārttikakārikā, Tshad ma rnam 'grel gyi tshig le'ur byas pa*), D4210, tshad ma, ce, 94b–151a, *Drop of Reasoning* (*Nyāyabinduprakaraṇa, Rigs pa'i thigs pa zhes bya ba'i rab tu byas pa*), D4212, tshad ma, ce, 231b–238a, *Drop of Reasons* (*Hetubindunāmaprakaraṇa, Gtan tshigs kyi thigs pa zhes bya ba'i rab tu byas pa*), D4213, tshad ma, ce, 238a–255a, *Science of Debate* (*Vādanyāya, Rtsod pa'i rigs pa*), D4218, tshad ma, che, 326b–355b, and *Proof of Other Continua* (*Saṃtānāntarasiddhināmaprakaraṇa, Rgyud gzhan grub pa zhes bya ba'i rab tu byed pa*), D4219, tshad ma, che, 355b–359a.

65. *Ocean of Textual Systems of Reasoning*, vol. 1, 348.

66. Ibid., vol. 1, 352–353.

67. de ltar lung dang rigs pa mtha' yas pa'i sgo nas shin rta'i srol 'byed gnyis kyi mthar thug gi lta ba'i zab gnad dang dgongs pa gcig tu shes par bya'o. Ibid., vol. 1, 354.

68. Ibid., vol. 2, 271.

69. Cf. Shakya Chokden's interpretation of Vijñaptivāda as synonymous with Yogācāra but not synonimous with Cittamātra (see p. 355 note 88 below).

70. Apparently, Rangjung Dorjé was taken as a source of the other-emptiness view in the Karma Kagyü tradition by those whom Mikyö Dorjé argued against. Some Tibetan sources speak of Rangjung Dorjé as an adherent of the other-emptiness view (Mathes, *A Direct Path to the Buddha Within*, 54 ff.), and even as its first adherent in Tibet (Stearns, *The Buddha from Dolpo*, 49). For an excellent analysis of of Rangjung Dorjé's views and English translation of some of his key writings, see Karl Brunnhölzl, *Luminous Heart: The Third Karmapa on Consciousness, Wisdom, and Buddha Nature* (Ithaca, New York: Snow Lion Publications, 2009), hereafter *Luminous Heart*. See also Mathes, *A Direct Path to the Buddha Within*, 51–75.

71. For details, see the *Ocean of Textual Systems of Reasoning*, vol. 2, 272–278.

72. *'Jig rten gsum gyi sgron me*. To my knowledge, this text is not extant anymore.

73. phar tshad 'di gnyi ga lta ba gzhan stong gtso cher bkral mod kyang sems tsam gyi lta ba la gzhan stong du ming btags pa bod kha cig gi 'dod pa ltar bkral ba ni ma yin la/ spyir rje 'di sems kyi bshis stong nyid gtso bor ston pa zab mo lta rgyud/ rang bzhin 'od gsal gtso bor ston pa rgya chen spyod rgyud ste sems kyi zab pa dang gsal ba ni gnyis su mi phyed pas na shing rta'i srol gnyis dgongs pa gcig tu bzhed pa yin no. *Feast for Scholars*, vol. 2, 265.

74. See p. 118 ff.

75. For details see Chapter 4 section 4.

76. See pp. 111–112.

77. See, for example, Lambert Schmithausen, "On Some Aspects of Descriptions or Theories of 'Liberating Insight' and 'Enlightenment' in Early Buddhism," in *Studien zum Jainismus und Buddhismus: Gedenkschrift für Ludwig Alsdorf*, eds. Klaus Bruhn und Albrecht Wezler (Wiesbaden: Steiner, 1981), 199–250, for the discussion of two currents in early Buddhist thought that Schmithausen calls "intellectual" and "mystical."

78. See, for example, Gorampa's *Distinguishing the Views*, 432, 494–495, translated in José Ignacio Cabezón and Geshe Lobsang Dargyay, *Freedom from Extremes*, 93–95, 217; and Mipam's *Precious Lamp of Definitive Knowledge* (*Nges shes rin po che'i sgron me*), Sde-dge dgon-chen Printings of the Writings of 'Jam-mgon 'Ju Mi-pham-rgya-mtsho, vol. 9, 71–123, translated in John Whitney Pettit, *Mipham's* Beacon of Certainty*: Illuminating the View of Dzogchen, the Great Perfection* (Boston: Wisdom Publications, 1999), topics three and four.

79. *Dbu ma la 'jug pa'i rnam bshad de kho na nyid gsal ba'i sgron ma* (Sarnath, Varanasi: Central Institute of Higher Tibetan Studies, 1995), 91–93. Rendawa is usually treated as one of the main teachers of Tsongkhapa. At the same time, Rendawa's approach to Madhyamaka is very different from Tsongkhapa's, as is clear from the above passage and further comparison of

their commentaries on Candrakīrti's *Engaging in Madhyamaka* (*Madhyamakāvatāra, Dbu ma la 'jug pa*), D3861, dbu ma, 'a, 201b–219a: Rendawa's *Lamp Illuminating Thatness: Explanation of [Candrakīrti's] 'Engaging in Madhyamaka'* and Tsongkhapa's *Thorough Clarification of Intent*. It is possible that some Geluk thinkers, such as Gungru Gyeltsen Zangpo, believed that Rendawa's and Tsongkhapa's approaches to the process of meditation on emptiness are similar (see p. 317 note 72 above). Nevertheless, judging from Rendawa's and Tsongkhapa's writings alone, their positions appear to be very different. Tsongkhapa and his followers emphasize a direct connection between the reality determined through conceptual reasoning and the reality realized nonconceptually, directly. Tsongkhapa formulates this view in the *'Stages of the Path to Enlightenment' Teaching in Their Entirety All Stages Incorporated into Experience by the Three Beings / Great Stages of the Path to Enlightenment* (*Skyes bu gsum gyi nyams su blang ba'i rim pa thams cad tshang bar ston pa'i byang chub lam gyi rim pa/ Byang chub lam rim che ba*, Mtsho sngon mi rigs dpe skrun khang), translated into English by The Lamrim Chenmo Translation Committee as *The Great Treatise on the Stages of the Path to Enlightenment*, vol. 3 (Ithaca, New York: Snow Lion Publications, 2002), 331–350. According to the majority of Geluk thinkers, the difference between the two lies in the presence or absence of the conceptual generic image or "meaning-generality" (*don spyi, arthasāmānya*) through which reality is realized, not in reality itself. (See p. 317 note 72 on a different view attributed to Gungru Gyeltsen Zangpo.) Consequently, the transition from conceptual to nonconceptual understanding of reality lies in the weakening and eventual disappearance of the conceptual image of reality accompanied by the simultaneous increase in vividness of reality itself.

80. For a relevant comparison of different approaches to ultimate reality, see my "Encountering Ineffability—Counting Ineffability: On Divergent Verbalizations of the Ineffable in 15th Century Tibet," *Acta Tibetica et Buddhica*, vol. 1 (2008): 1–15. Hereafter, "Encountering Ineffability—Counting Ineffability."

81. Shakya Chokden treats reality realized on the tantric path as more profound but compatible with the sūtric one (see Chapter 5 section 5).

82. This is true for the tantric path as well (see pp. 249–252).

83. This reason alone is not sufficient for a system to be Madhyamaka: as Shakya Chokden himself asserts (p. 116), every Buddhist system sees itself as Madhyamaka. This is why I am using the word "complementary" here.

84. Allegedly, this is how some contemporary Tibetan teachers present systems of self-emptiness and other-emptiness in general, and those of Shakya Chokden in particular. Mistaken interpretations of Shakya Chokden's views will be addressed at different points of this study.

85. See the next section for details.

86. *Shes bya mtha' yas pa'i rgya mtsho*, vols. 1–3 (Peking: Mi rigs pe skrun khang, 1982).

87. For the relevant passages see the *Limitless Ocean of Knowables*, vol. 2, 544–546, 553–557; and vol. 3, 58–62. Thanks to Michelle Martin for drawing my attention to these passages.

88. See the next section for details.

89. 'di dag la tsong kha pa yab sras gsum zhes grags pa des/ sngon bod kyi bshad rgyud pa dang sgrub rgyud pa mtha' dag las logs shig tu mdo sngags gnyis ka'i shing rta'i srol chen po dang por byed pa dang/ bar du 'dzin pa dang/ tha mar lugs snga ma dag khyad du bsad pa'i gtam chen pos mthar phyin par mdzad. *Letter Pleasing Impartial Wise Ones*, vol. 16, 473.

90. Ibid., 460.

91. *Gzi bsam 'grub gling pa'i dge 'dun spyi'i dris lan ya mtshan bcu bdun pa*, vol. 23, 418–419. Hereafter, *Seventeen Wondrous Answers.*

92. de dag ni/ 'phags yul nas grub thob kyi rgyun ma chad/ bden gnyis dang lta sgom dang zhi lhag gi 'jog lugs rnams kyi rtsa ba ' 'thun pa kho na yin la/ dus phyis gangs can du/ de dang de dag gi rnam par bzhag pa/ sngon bod yul du byon pa'i bshad brgyud pa dang/ sgrub brgyud pa kun dang phyogs gcig tu mi mthun pa'i glegs bam gyi tshogs gsar byung gi smra ba rab tu mang po dag gis/ chos brgyud snga ma de dag gi rjes 'brang du khas 'che ba'i phyis byon bshad nyan pa dag gi thugs rgyud rnam par bslad nas/ rang rang gi brgyud pa la med pa'i gtam chos skad du smra ba dag la zur za ba'o// de dag kyang gang zhe na/ gtso bor kun rdzob kyi bden pa la lhag par zhen pa'i grub mtha' gzhung shing du btsugs pa las 'phros pa'i glegs bam gyi tshogs rnams. Ibid., 419.

93. Tsongkhapa outlines this position in *The Great Treatise on the Stages of the Path to Enlightenment*, vol. 3 (Ithaca, New York: Snow Lion Publications, 2002), 163–183. See p. 125 ff. below for more details.

94. See for example, a very early text he wrote at Sangpu called *Clear Identification of the Presence of the String of One Hundred and Eight Beads of Mistakes Conceived by [Wrong] Logic in Madhyamaka of the System of Others* (*Gzhan lugs kyi ni dbu ma la// rtog ges brtags pa'i nor ba'i phreng// brgya dang rtsa brgyad yod pa yi// ngos 'dzin gsal po*), vol. 4, 414–415.

95. The topic of "establishment of conventions by valid cognition" seems to have been a hot issue when Shakya Chokden taught at Sangpu. It is clear from Drölchok's description of a debate that happened between representatives of Lingtö (*gling stod*) and Lingmé (*gling smad*) colleges during the winter session some time at the end of 1465—beginning of 1466. (Such debates might have been a common practice at Sangpu.) Drölchok's *Detailed Analysis*, vol. 16, 98. See also page 98 ff. below.

96. See my "Reburying the Treasure—Maintaining the Continuity," 521–570, and "Shakya Chokden's Interpretation of the *Ratnagotravibhāga*: "Contemplative" or "Dialectical?"" *Journal of Indian Philosophy*, vol. 38, no. 8 (2010): 441–452 (hereafter, "Shakya Chokden's Interpretation of the *Ratnagotravibhāga*"). For a recent study of Ngok Loden Sherap's interpretation of the buddha-essence, see Kazuo Kano, *rNgog Blo-ldan-shes-rab's Summary of the* Ratnagotravibhāga (Ph.D. Dissertation, University of Hamburg, 2006).

97. For example, in the *Appearance of the Sun Pleasing All Thinkers: Discussion of the History of the Chariot Ways of [Dignāga's] 'Sūtra on Valid Cognition' and [Its] Treatises* (*Tshad ma'i bstan bcos kyi shin rta'i srol rnams ji ltar 'byung ba'i tshul gtam du bya ba nyin byed snang ba*), vol. 19, 28–42, Shakya Chokden outlines three valid (*tshad ldan*) explanatory systems of Pramāṇa developed in

Tibet: that of Ngok Lotsawa, Chapa Chökyi Senggé, and Sakya Pendita. He contrasts them with the views of later Tibetans—those of Darma Rinchen in particular—that lack authentic origins (*khungs med*). Ibid., 42–83.

98. See p. 131 ff. In his choice of Dölpopa and Tsongkhapa as the objects of his criticisms, Shakya Chokden is similar to Gorampa who criticizes them together in one and the same *Distinguishing the Views* as the "proponent of the extreme of eternalism as the middle" (*rtag mtha' la dbu mar smra ba*) and "proponent of the extreme of nihilism as the middle" (*chad mtha' la dbu mar smra ba*), respectively. Also similar to Gorampa, Shakya Chokden does not level as many criticisms at Dölpopa as at Tsongkhapa, partly because Dölpopa's views were most likely somewhat obscured by the popularity of the Geluk system by Shakya Chokden's time.

99. *Letter Pleasing Impartial Wise Ones*, vol. 16, 469.

100. phyi rabs pa ni/ mdo sngags kyi mthar thug gi lta ba'i yul/ slob dpon zla bas bshad pa'i stong nyid de las gzhan ngos 'dzin rgyu med cing/ de las gzhan pa'i don dam bden pa'i mtshan gzhi yang ngos 'dzin med par 'dod la/ 'dod pa de deng sang rang phyogs pa kun la 'dres byung/ sa skya pa ni/ ngo bo nyid med smra'i gzhung nas don dam bden pa go chod ma bshad par bzhed pa dang/ lugs de'i stong pa nyid ni spyi don dang rnam grangs pa'i don dam tsam dang/ thos pa dang/ bshad pas go ba'i lta bar bzhed kyi/ mthar thug gi dang sgom pas nyams myong gi lta ba ni/ rang byung lhan cig skyes pa'i ye shes las gzhan du mi bzhed. *Seventeen Wondrous Answers*, vol. 23, 420–421. When Shakya Chokden distinguishes between the views of sūtric and tantric Madhyamaka, he explains that the cultivation of the innate primordial mind—which is a type of but is not synonymous with primordial mind—is a unique feature of tantric practice (see p. 255).

101. Teaching lineages and sects that developed during the period of Later Dissemination (*phyi dar*) of Buddhism in Tibet are "new" in contrast to the early or "old" systems whose origins go back to the period of Early Dissemination (*snga dar*) during the Tibetan Imperial Period (*c.* 600–*c.* 920). The period in between the Early and Later Disseminations that followed the disintegration of the Tibetan empire is known as the "Fragmentation Period" (*sil bu'i dus*). The old/new distinction is primarily based on early and late translations of tantric teachings made in Tibet during the two periods. As Shakya Chokden explains in the *Letter Pleasing Impartial Wise Ones*, vol. 16, 462, the beginning of the Later Dissemination was marked by works of the great translator Rinchen Zangpo (*rin chen bzang po*, 958–1055), who also authored a treatise called *Refutation of Wrong Mantra [Teachings]* (*Sngags log sun 'byin*), and it is from that time that the terms "New and Old Secret Mantras" (*gsang sngags gsar rnying*) emerged in Tibet.

102. I.e., *zhi byed*, *phyag chen/ phyag rgya chen po*, and *rdzogs chen/ rdzogs pa chen po*, respectively.

103. *Seventen Wondrous Answers*, vol. 23, 422–423. The "subsequent *Dharmas*" in this context are the *Dharmas of Maitreya* other than the *Ornament of Clear Realizations*.

104. mtha' bral du gtan la phab nas/ zung 'jug tu nyams su len. *Seventen Wondrous Answers*, vol. 23, 422.

105. Ibid., 423.

106. *Zab rgya'i snying po bsdus pa rin chen gter mdzod chos tshan brgyad pa*, in *'Hundred and Eight Dharma Sections' Treatise* (*Chos tshan brgya dang brgyad pa zhes bya ba'i bstan bcos*), vol. 13, 181–186. Hereafter, *Precious Treasury of the Condensed Essence*.

107. Ibid., vol. 13, 181–182.

108. *Ocean of Scriptural Statements and Reasoning*, vol. 15, 505–506.

109. Ibid., 506.

110. *Madhyamakopadeśa, Dbu ma'i man ngag*, D3929, dbu ma, ki, 95b1–96a7.

111. *Ocean of Scriptural Statements and Reasoning*, vol. 15, 506–507.

112. See Kamalaśīla, *Stages of Meditation* (*Bhāvanākrama, Sgom pa'i rim pa*), D3917, dbu ma, ki, 55b–68b.

113. See Kamalaśīla, *Stages of Meditation* (*Bhāvanākrama, Sgom pa'i rim pa*), D3915, dbu ma, ki, 42a–55b.

114. *Ocean of Scriptural Statements and Reasoning*, vol. 15, 505–508. On Haribhadra's interpretation of the four stages, see p. 151 ff.

115. See, for example, his *Moonrays of Essential Points: Abridged Essence of Incorporation into Experience* (*Nyams su len pa'i rim pa snying po mdor bsdus pa gnad kyi zla zer*), in The Collected Works of Rong-ston Shak-kya Rgyal-mtsen, vol. B, *kha* (Dehra Dun, India: Sakya College, 1999), 562–565, and other meditative instructions in the same volume.

116. Further details of Rendawa's view in Shakya Chokden's description can be found in the *Letter Pleasing Impartial Wise Ones*, vol. 16, 472. See also the *Three Texts on Madhyamaka*, 23 ("Dokdokpa" (*mdog ldog pa*) mentioned in that text as the name of one of Rendawa's teachers is a misspelled name of Doklöpa Künga Zangpo (*ldog lod pa' kun dga' bzang po*); thanks to Jonang abbot Ngakwang Dorjé (*ngag dbang rdo rje*) for the identification). For more on this thinker, see Carola Roloff, *Red mda' ba. Buddhist Yogi-Scholar of the Fourteenth Century: The Forgotten Reviver of Madhyamaka Philosophy in Tibet* (Wiesbaden: Ludwig Reichert Verlag, 2009).

117. "Luminosity" is one of the several stages of the *Guhyasamāja Tantra* practice that is further elaborated upon by Nāgārjuna and Āryadeva. These stages are usually counted as six—physical isolation (*lus dben, kāyaviveka*), verbal isolation (*ngag dben, vāgviveka*), mental isolation (*sems dben, cittaviveka*), illusory body (*sgyu lus, māyādeha*), luminosity, and union (*zung 'jug, yuganaddha*)—or five, when the first stage is included into the second one. For details of the *Guhyasamāja* thought and practice, see Shakya Chokden's *Sevenfold Treasury of Gems*, vol. 7, 405–612 mentioned above. See also Christian K. Wedemeyer, *Āryadeva's* Lamp that Integrates the Practices (Caryāmelāpakapradīpa*): The Gradual Path of Vajrayāna Buddhism According to the Esoteric Community Noble Tradition* (New York: American Institute of Buddhist Studies, 2008), Daniel Cozort, *Highest Yoga Tantra: An Introduction to the Esoteric Buddhism of Tibet* (Ithaca, New York: Snow Lion Publications, 1986), and Yangchen Gawai

Lodoe, *Paths and Grounds of Guhyasamaja [sic]* (Dharamsala, India: Library of Tibetan Works and Archives, 1995).

118. nub pa'i rgyu mtshan yang rje btsun red mda' bas/ ji skad du/ sems tsam pa'i grub pa'i mtha' ji lta ba bzhin du shes pa gzhan mi snang ngo// zhes dang/ 'phags pa yab sras kyi bzhed pa'i 'od gsal ji lta ba bzhin du ngos zin pa ni gangs can 'di na gzhan mi snang ngo// zhes gsungs la/ gsung des ni zhi phyag rdzogs gsum dang lam 'bras kyi lta ba sems tsam du sgrub pa dang/ dgyes rdor nas bshad pa'i rang rig pa'i dag pa sems tsam du sgrub pa dang/ don dam bden pa dang shes pa'i gzhi mthun 'gog par bzhed nas bshad pa yin pas na/ rang gzhan gyi grub pa'i mtha' shan phyed par gal che'o. *Bshes gnyen mus pa rab 'byams pa'i dri lan mthong ba don ldan*, vol. 23, 368–369. Hereafter, *Meaningful to Behold.*

119. See pp. 158 ff. and 239 ff.

120. ye shes su gang bshad pa de ni rnam shes su 'gal. *Tshad ma'i bstan bcos kyi shin rta'i srol rnams ji ltar 'byung ba'i tshul gtam du bya ba nyin mor byed pa'i snang bas dpyod ldan mtha' dag dga' bar byed pa*), vol. 19, 117. Hereafter, *Appearance of the Sun.* In his distinction between consciousness and primordial mind Shakya Chokden is similar to such thinkers as Rangjung Dorjé. See the latter's *Treatise Differentiating beween Consciousness and Primordial Mind* (*Rnam par shes pa dang ye shes 'byed pa'i bstan bcos*, Rumtek blockprint, n.d.), translated in Brunnhölzl, *Luminous Heart*, 361–366. In my previous works on Shakya Chokden, I did not clearly distinguish between *shes pa* and *rnam shes*, translating both as "consciousness." In this book, I use the term "consciousness" only for *rnam shes*, and translate *shes pa* exclusively as "knowing."

121. phyis byung gi chos skad rgya cher 'dres pa'i nongs pa mang pos deng sang kun la khyab pa yin no// 'di ltar don dam pa'i bden pa khas blangs nas bden par ma grub zer ba dang/ kun rdzob tu yod pas yod pa'i go chod cing/ don dam du ma yin pa dang med pas de dang de'i go mi chod par 'dod pa dang/ rnam mkhyen dang lhan cig skyes pa'i ye shes sogs shes pa mtha' dag kun rdzob kyi bden pa nyid du khas blangs nas/ gzung 'dzin gnyis su med pa'i ye shes kho na/ gnas lugs dang don dam pa'i bden par bshad na sems tsam las ma 'das so// zhes bla ma red mda' bas bshad la/ 'di'i rgyab brten dbu ma 'jug par thug cing/ rang gzhan gyi phyi rabs pa dag la ni/ 'jug par bshad pa las ma gtogs pa'i don dam bden pa'i ngos 'dzin mi 'dug pas rdo rje theg pa'i lam srol mtha' dag las nyams te/ kun rdzob kyi bden pa gang yin mtha' dag ni ma rig pa kho na'i 'khrul snang du mi 'chad pa'i mdo sngags kyi gzhung med cing/ de ltar mi 'chad pa'i bod snga rabs pa su yang med do// de'i phyir bden grub la 'jigs mi dgos te/ yod na bden dgos pa'i phyir ro// de lta mod kyi yod 'dzin gyi rtog pa spang byar mi 'dod pa'i dbu ma dang sngags kyi gzhung lugs yod pa ma yin no. *Seventen Wondrous Answers*, vol. 23, 419–420.

122. See pp. 208–209. See also the *Rain of Ambrosia*, 339–340.

123. Note that when Shakya Chokden goes into a more detailed analysis of Niḥsvabhāvavāda teachings, he distinguishes between some Niḥsvabhāvavāda texts—such as Candrakīrti's *Engaging in Madhyamaka*—that

did not teach the authentic ultimate reality versus those that did teach it, such as Śāntarakṣita's and Kamalaśīla's works. For details, see page 201 ff.

124. As we have seen, Shakya Chokden was already criticizing Tsongkhapa's views on Madhyamaka in the *Smaller Summarized Exposition*, written when he was thirty-two years old.

125. See p. 312 note 17.

126. *Garlands of Waves of Assertions*, vol. 11, 536.

127. This date is given in the colophon of the *Ocean of Scriptural Statements and Reasoning*, vol. 15, 692. According to Künga Drölchok's *Detailed Analysis*, vol. 16, 125–126, Shakya Chokden only started writing this text in the earth-male-dog year (1478).

128. They are, respectively, the *Harbor for Fortunate Ones: Explanation of [Nāgārjuna's 'Wisdom:] Root [Stanzas] on Madhyamaka' (Dbu ma rtsa ba'i rnam bshad bskal bzangs kyi 'jug ngogs)*, vol. 5, 1–280, and *Commentary on Essentials of Definitive Meaning: Explanation of [Candrakīrti's] 'Engaging in Madhyamaka Way' (Dbu ma la 'jug pa'i rnam par bshad pa nges don gnad kyi ṭī ka)*, vol. 5, 281–457.

129. I use the word "complete" because Shakya Chokden's collected works contain such undated writings as the *Beautiful Garland of Water-Lilies: Explanation of Several Difficult Points of [Candrakīrti's] 'Engaging in Madhyamaka' (Dbu ma la 'jug pa'i dka' ba'i gnas 'ga' zhig rnam par bshad pa ku mud kyi phreng mdzes)*, vol. 5, 459–497. There is no clear indication that this text was *not* composed after 1477 (although I do presume that such is the case).

130. The *Garlands of Waves of Assertions* composed in 1454 was the first major commentary written by Shakya Chokden.

131. *Essence of Sūtras and Tantras: Explanation of the Buddha-Essence (Sangs rgyas kyi snying po'i rnam bshad mdo rgyud snying po)*, vol. 13, 124–136, written in 1474.

132. *Drop of Ambrosia: Differentiation of Classes of Tantras (Rgyud sde'i rnam par phye ba bdud rtsi'i thig pa)*, vol. 13, 467–478, written in 1456.

133. A good example is Shakya Chokden's commentaries on the *Sublime Continuum* written during different periods of his life, addressed in my "Reburying the Treasure—Maintaining the Continuity." (Note 41 of that article has "Satyākāravāda Madhyamaka"; it should read instead "Satyākāravāda Yogācāra." Line fifteen on p. 558 has "*rnam shes, jñāna*"; it should read "*rnam shes, vijñāna*." My translation of some text titles in that article also varies slightly. Most notably, I translate *Gser gyi thur ma* there as the *Golden Spoon*, while in this book I translate it as the *Golden Lancet*.)

134. *Seventeen Wondrous Answers*, vol. 23, 466.

135. According to one tradition Sakya Pendita wrote his *Thorough Differentiation of the Three Types of Vows* in 1232, when he was about fifty. See Jared Douglas Rhoton (tr.), *A Clear Differentiation of the Three Codes: Essential Distinctions among the Individual Liberation, Mahāyāna, and Tantric Systems* (Albany, New York: State University of New York Press, 2002), 4. Hereafter, *A Clear Differentiation of the Three Codes.*

136. See Georges Dreyfus, *Recognizing Reality*, 28–29; Stearns, *The Buddha from Dölpo*, 61–64; Kuijp, *Contributions*, 13–14; D. S. Ruegg, "The Jo nan pas: A School of Buddhist Ontologists According to the *Grub mtha' śel gyi me long*," *Journal of the American Oriental Society*, vol. 83 (1963): 89–90.

137. *Grub mtha' thams cad kyi khungs dang 'dod tshul ston pa legs bshad shel gyi me long* (Kan su'u Mi rigs dpe skrun khang, 1984), 199.

138. Ibid., 231.

139. See p. 119 ff.

140. *Bod kyi mkhas pa snga phyi dag gi grub mtha' shan 'byed mtha' dpyod dang bcas pa'i 'bel ba'i gtam* (Thimphu, Bhutan: Kunzang Tobgyal, 1984), 244–245. (Hereafter, *Abundant Discourse on Distinguishing and Decisive Analysis*.) For more details see Kuijp, *Contributions*, 13–15.

141. khyed kyis 'dod pa 'di ni rnam brdzun pa'i lta ba las gong du cung zad kyang ma 'phags pa yin. *Dbu ma chen po'i sgom rim la 'khrul pa spong shing thal rang gi grub pa'i mtha' dang lta ba'i gnas rnam par bshad pa tshangs pa'i dbyangs kyi rnga sgra*, vol. 4, 340. Hereafter, *Drumming Sounds of the Melodious Voice of Brahma*.

142. mdor na gangs can gyi ljongs 'dir/ sems tsam rnam rdzun gyi lta ba la dbu mar 'dod pa gzhan stong par grags pa dang/ grub mtha' bzhi ka dang mi mthun pa stong nyid la mtshan mar 'dzin pa'i blo dbu mar 'dod pa rang stong gi lugs su rlom pa gnyis so. Ibid., 340. Criticisms in this passage are aimed at Dölpopa and Tsongkhapa respectively. In such expressions and terms used by Shakya Chokden as "does not apprehend any signs of being empty, not being empty, and so forth" (*stong mi stong la sogs pa'i mtshan ma gang du yang mi 'dzin; Rain of Ambrosia*, 328), "proliferations apprehending signs" (*mtshan 'dzin gyi spros pa*; ibid., 372), "faults of apprehending the non-dual primordial mind as signs" (*gnyis med kyi ye shes la mtshan 'dzin gyi nyes pa*; ibid., 369), and so forth, the word "signs" (*mtshan ma*) indicates any referents of knowing that is other than the non-dual primordial mind or the direct realization of reality. To apprehend something as signs means to apprehend it in a way other than it really is. In this particular context the term refers to the emptiness described as a non-affirming negation, which according to Tsongkhapa can be an object of the direct realization of reality, but according to Shakya Chokden is an object of conceptual minds only.

143. Ibid., 303–304.

144. dbu ma pa'i nang na med de/ thal 'gyur ba'i nang na yang med/ rang rgyud pa'i nang na yang med pa'i phyir. Ibid., 341.

145. *Abundant Discourse on Distinguishing and Decisive Analysis*, 236–239. For details of Shakya Chokden's view of the buddha-essence see pp. 187–189 below, as well as my two articles: "Reburying the Treasure—Maintaining the Continuity," and "Shakya Chokden's Interpretation of the *Ratnagotravibhāga*."

146. *Abundant Discourse on Distinguishing and Decisive Analysis*, 234–235.

147. *Chos kyi dbyings su bstod pa zhes bya ba'i bstan bcos kyi rnam par bshad pa chos kyi dbyings rnam par nges pa*, vol. 7, 336. Hereafter, *Ascertainment of the Dharma-Sphere*.

148. See p. 81 ff.

149. Ibid.

150. See Dreyfus, *Recognizing Reality*, 28; and Stearns, *The Buddha from Dölpo*, 61–62.

151. Stearns, *The Buddha from Dolpo*, 62.

152. See Chapter 1 section 3.

153. *Rgyud sde'i rnam par phye ba bdud rtsi'i thig pa*, vol. 13, 467–478.

154. *Zab mo nang (gi) don* (Mtsho sngon mi rigs dpe skrun khang, 2001). Some parts of this text with the auto-commentary are translated in Brunnhölzl, *Luminous Heart*, 129–169.

155. *Drop of Ambrosia: Differentiation of Classes of Tantras*, vol. 13, 469.

Chapter 3

1. For the relevant passages, see the *Great Path of Ambrosia of Emptiness*, vol. 4, 110–113; *Wish Fulfilling Meru*, vol. 4, 212–213; *Ocean of Scriptural Statements and Reasoning*, vol. 15, 441–442, 447; and *Rain of Ambrosia*, 323–326. Because my objective is to clarify Shakya Chokden's ideas, I am also using the categories of "higher" and "lower" tenets in this study, although I am aware of their artificiality.

2. *Rain of Ambrosia*, 325–326.

3. grub mtha' bzhi'i rim pas bstan pa la 'jug pa na/ bsgrub bya sgrub pa'i tshul la snga mas bsgrubs pa de nyid phyi mas 'gog dgos pa yod kyang/ dgag bya 'gog pa'i tshul la snga mas bkag pa de nyid phyi mas kyang thad sor 'jog dgos pa yin te/ dper na nyan thos sde pas gang zag gi bdag bkag pa dang/ sems tsam pas gzung ba chos kyi bdag bkag pa bzhin no. *Ocean of Scriptural Statements and Reasoning*, vol. 14, 555.

4. *Ocean of Scriptural Statements and Reasoning*, vol. 15, 451. See also the *Discourse Eliminating Mistakes with Regard to the Teachings of Scriptural Collections: Fourteen Dharma Sections* (*Sde snod kyi chos la 'khrul pa sel ba'i gtam chos tshan bcu bzhi pa*), vol. 13, 209.

5. gang zag gi bdag med ni yongs su rdzogs par bye brag tu smra ba'i gzhung las kyang bstan na/ mdo sde pas khas len pa lta ci smos/ de'i phyir bye mdo gnyis kyi gzhung gis gtan la phab pa'i gang zag gi bdag med de goms par byas pas de mngon sum du mthong ba dang/ de nyid goms par byas pas gang zag gi bdag tu 'dzin pa'i sa bon spangs pa'i myang 'das mngon du byed par nus so. *Great Path of Ambrosia of Emptiness*, vol. 4, 110–111. Note that in the same text (pp. 124–125), Shakya Chokden also discusses differences in the way of positing (*'jog tshul*) that selflessness as primordial mind free from the duality of the apprehended and apprehender in terms of self of persons (*gang zag gi dbang du byas pa'i gzung 'dzin gnyis med kyi ye shes*), a non-affirming negation which is a mere negation of self of persons (*gang zag gi bdag bkag tsam gyi med par dgag pa*), etc., depending on different systems. Nevertheless, different descriptions of selflessness of persons do not prevent followers of all four Buddhist tenets from accessing the same realizations of that selflessness. As I demonstrate below, Shakya Chokden approaches the

Niḥsvabhāvavāda and Alīkākāravāda tenets in the same way: different ways of positing emptiness and different descriptions of its realization do not prevent their advocates from accessing the same direct realization of emptiness and achieving the same result of buddhahood.

6. de ltar bye mdo gnyis kyi lta ba ni theg pa gsum gyi nang nas nyan thos kyi theg pa pa dag gi lta ba go chod po dang/ sems tsam gyi lta ba 'di ni rang sangs rgyas kyi theg pa pa dag gi lta ba go chod po nyid du bshad pa ltar khas len nus pa yin te/ lta ba de dang de dag gi don la mnyam par gzhag pa'i bar chad med lam gyis nyon mongs pa dang shes bya'i sgrib pa gzung rtog ces pa theg pa gnyis po'i lam gyi spang byar bshad pa de dag gi sa bon drungs 'byin nus par bshad pa'i phyir ro. *Rain of Ambrosia*, 325.

7. gzugs su snang ba'i rnam rig las ma gtogs pa'i gzugs khas len pa theg pa chen po'i chos la med do. *Sevenfold Treasury of Gems*, vol. 7, 562.

8. phyi rol gyi don bden med du sgrub pa'i rigs pa la/ dbu sems gnyis khyad par ci yang yod pa ma yin pa dang/ gzung rnam bden med du sgrub pa'i rigs pa la/ rnam brdzun pa dang/ ngo bo nyid med par smra ba dag zab mi zab kyi khyad par ci yang yod pa ma yin pa. *Ocean of Scriptural Statements and Reasoning*, vol. 15, 436. The "apprehended-aspects" are minds projecting dualistic appearances. For details, see p. 161 ff.

9. Attainment of the pratyekabuddha nirvāṇa requires a partial abandonment of obscurations of knowables, more specifically—conceptions of the apprehended.

10. gal te sems can yod min na// su la snying rje bya zhe na// 'bras bu'i don du khas blangs pa'i// rmongs pas brtags pa gang yin pa'o// sems can med 'bras su yi yin// bden te 'on kyang rmongs las 'dod. *Engaging in the Bodhisattva Deeds*, 33b. Skt: yadi sattvo na vidyeta kasyopari kṛpeti cet/ kāryārtham abhyupetena yō mōhena prakalpitaḥ// kāryaṃ kasya na cet satvaḥ satyam īhā tu mohataḥ. In Parmananda Sharma, *Śāntideva's* Bodhicharyāvatāra *[sic]: Original Sanskrit text with English Translation and Exposition Based on Prajnākarmati's* [sic] *Panjikā* [sic] (New Delhi: Aditya Prakashan, 1990), vol. 2, 422–423 (*Śāntideva's* Bodhicharyāvatāra). For an alternative English translation, see also Kate Crosby and Andrew Skilton, *The Bodhicaryāvatāra* (Oxford: Oxford University Press, 1995), 122–123.

11. *Rain of Ambrosia*, 324.

12. phyi don dang de snang ba'i bzung rnam bden med du bsgrub byed kyi rigs pa la gcig dang du bral gyi gtan tshigs zhes bya ba zhig bshad la/ de'i tshul la ni dbu sems gnyis la zab mi zab kyi khyad par cung zad kyang ma dmigs pa. *Shes rab kyi pha rol tu phyin pa'i man ngag gi bstan bcos mngon par rtogs pa'i rgyan 'grel pa dang bcas pa'i dka' ba'i gnas rnams rnam par bshad pa rang gzhan gyi grub mtha' rnam par dbye ba lung rigs kyi rol mtsho*, vol. 2, 333. Hereafter, *Enjoyment Ocean of Scriptural Statements and Reasoning*. For more references to the reason of the lack of being one or many see pp. 154, 225, and 236 ff. This reason focuses on the relationship between phenomena and their parts, and demonstrates that phenomena do no really exist as either singular or manifold entities. For details, see Jan Westerhoff, *Nāgārjuna's Madhyamaka: A Philosophical Investigation* (Oxford: Oxford University Press, 2009), 36–38;

Tom Tillemans, "The 'Neither One Nor Many' Argument for *Śūnyatā* and Its Tibetan Interpretations," in *Contributions on Tibetan and Buddhist Religion and Philosophy*, eds. Ernst Steinkellner and Helmut Tauscher (Arbeitskreis für Tibetische und Buddhistische Studien, Universität Wien, Vienna, 1983), 305–320; and Tom Tillemans, "Two Tibetan Texts on the 'Neither One Nor Many' Argument for *Śūnyatā*," *Journal of Indian Philosophy*, vol. 12 (1984): 357–388.

13. *Ocean of Scriptural Statements and Reasoning*, vol. 15, 451.

14. Ibid., 450.

15. Ibid., 451.

16 chos la ltos pa'i mtha' gnyis sel tshul yongs su ma rdzogs pa de srid du dbu ma par mi bzhag go. *Ocean of Scriptural Statements and Reasoning*, vol. 15, 451.

17. Ibid.

18. mdor na sems tsam pa la rnam bden rdzun dang/ dbu ma pa la thal rang gnyis su 'byed pa ni 'phags yul gyi grub mtha' rnam dbye la yod pa ma yin te/ lung gis ma dmigs pa'i phyir dang/ rigs pas kyang mi 'thad pa ni grub mtha'i rnam dbye byed pa ni lta ba'i cha nas yin pa las/ dbu ma thal rang gnyis la/ lta ba'i khyad par ma dmigs pa'i phyir/ de lta mod kyi dbu ma la rang gzhan stong pa'i tshul lugs gnyis su 'byed pa ni shin rta'i srol chen gnyis kyi gzhung na legs par gsal lo. *Thorough Clarification of Definitive Meaning of the 'Five Dharmas of Maitreya'* (*Byams chos lnga'i nges don rab tu gsal ba zhes bya ba'i bstan bcos*), vol. 11, 18. Emphasis mine.

19. rnam rdzun pa 'di la sems tsam par 'chad pa'i khungs thub kyi lung med cing/ dbu ma par ston pa'i lung ni dbus dang mtha' rnam par 'byed pa 'di yod pa. *Thorough Clarification of Definitive Meaning of the 'Five Dharmas of Maitreya,'* vol. 11, 10. Here, Shakya Chokden refers to the appproach of the *Differentiation of the Middle and Extremes* in general, and in particular to the first two lines of its second verse discussed below, pp. 132–133 and 146.

20. rnal 'byor spyod pa'i gzhung lugs su// sems tsam pa dang dbu ma pa// gnyis su dbye ba byams pa'i gzhung// 'gral par bcas pa dag na bzhugs// bod du grags pa sems tsam pa// rnam bden rnam rdzun zhes byar 'chad. *Tshul gnyis rnam 'byed las 'phros pa'i dris lan*, vol. 17, 414.

21. *Ocean of Scriptural Statements and Reasoning*, vol. 15, 461.

22. See p. 141 below.

23. See pp. 161–163 for details.

24. For more on this subject, see Chapter 3 section 4.

25. *Wish Fulfilling Meru*, vol. 4, 212–214. Shakya Chokden develops this approach in a large number of writings. Chapter 4 of this book deals exhaustively with this topic and related issues.

26. spyir dbu ma chung ngu ni nyan thos sde pa'i nges don gyi lta ba la 'chad par kun la grags shing// dbu ma chen po ni grub mtha' smra ba bzhi'i ya mthar gyur pa'i dbu ma de nyid yin la/ de'i ngos 'dzin la mi 'dra ba gnyis te/ rnal 'byor spyod pa'i gzhung las 'byung ba dang/ ngo bo nyid med par smra ba'i gzhung las 'byung ba'o// gnyis ka chen po kho nar 'jog gam zhe na/ de la gnas skabs gnyis te/ phar phyin theg pa rkyang pa'i skabs dang/ sngags kyi theg pa dang zung du sbrel ba'i tshe'o// dang

po'i dbang du byas na ngo bo nyid med pa pa'i dbu ma nyid chen po ste mtshan 'dzin gyi spros pa 'gog byed kyi rigs pa snga ma las ches zab pa'i phyir/ de'i tshe cig shos dbu ma 'bring por bzhag go/ gnyis pa'i dbang du byas pa la'ang gnyis te/ bka' tha ma'i dngos bstan dang 'brel ba dang/ bar pa'i dngos bstan dang 'brel ba'o// dang po ni/ dbu ma chen po kho nar nges te/ gzung 'dzin gnyis su med pa'i ye shes de nyid sgom pas nyams su myong bya nyid du nges pa'i dbu ma yin pa'i phyir/ de'i 'brel pa yang/ theg pa 'dir so sor rtog pa'i shes rab kyi dpyad pa sngon du song ba gtso mi che la sgom pas nyams su myong ba gtso che ba'i phyir/ de'i shugs la rigs tshogs kyi dngos bstan dbu ma 'bring por grub bo// rigs tshogs kyi dngos bstan gyi dbu ma de yang bstod tshogs kyi nyams su myong bya dang 'brel na ni/ sngags kyi theg pa 'dir dbu ma chen po nyid du nges pas srol gnyis ka yang dbu ma chen por bzhag dgos te/ 'dir mtshan 'dzin gyi spros pa 'gog byed thos bsam gyi rigs pa kho na la rag ma las pa'i phyir. *Rain of Ambrosia*, 378–379.

27. I explain details of the nature and relationship of the two pronouncements and the two *Collections*, and related issues, in Chapter 4 section 3.

28. For details of this technique, see Chapter 4 section 4.

29. See p. 329 note 2 above.

30. Chapter 5 section 5.

31. Vol. 13, 166–171.

32. See p. 324 note 137 above.

33. spyir gzhan stong gi rnam par gzhag pa ni/ rnal 'byor spyod pa'i gzhung las 'byung la/ rang stong gi rnam par bzhag pa ni/ ngo bo nyid med par smra ba'i gzhung las 'byung ngo. *Ocean of Scriptural Statements and Reasoning*, vol. 15, 514. Note that Shakya Chokden does not limit the origins of the above views to those sources only. Nor does he argue that Nāgārjuna or Maitreya taught only those views. I discuss these issues in Chapter 4.

34. See, for example, the *Great Path of Ambrosia of Emptiness*, vol. 4, 114, where Asaṅga's system is described as that of Proponents of Other-Emptiness, while Prāsaṅgika and Svātantrika systems are described as those of Proponents of Self-Emptiness.

35. Jonang abbot Ngakwang Dorjé, personal communication.

36. For an excellent survey of the other-emptiness views in Tibet, see Stearns, *The Buddha from Dolpo*, 41–110.

37. *Rdzogs pa chen po sems nyid ngal gso* (California: Yeshe De Project, 1994), 168–174.

38. Although persons *are* phenomena too, in the twofold division into persons and phenomena, persons are treated separately.

39. rang stong smra bas . . . gang zag gi bdag med kyi 'jog tshul ni gzhan stong gi tshul du 'chad pa yin te/ dgag gzhi nyer len gyi phung po lnga dgag bya gang zag gi bdag gis stong pa la gang zag gi bdag med pa'i don du 'chad pa'i phyir/ de nyid rang stong gi 'chad tshul ma yin te. *Great Path of Ambrosia of Emptiness*, vol. 4, 116.

40. Although there is more than one type of the thoroughly established nature (see p. 366 note 44), when it is understood as the ultimate reality underlying all phenomena (as in the present context), I use singular, not plural.

41. See pp. 171, 224, 226–227 below. See also the *Appearance of the Sun*, vol. 19, 118, and *Garlands of Waves of the Ocean of Yogācāras' Scriptures: Explanation of the Holy Dharma of [Asaṅga's] 'Summary of Higher Knowledge'* (*Dam pa'i chos ngon pa kun las btus pa'i rnam par bshad pa rnal 'byor spyod gzhung rgya mtsho'i rlabs kyi phreng ba*), vol. 14, 169.

42. Shakya Chokden views Nāgārjuna, Āryadeva, and Candrakīrti, who authored tantric treatises, as the same individuals who authored Niḥsvabhāvavāda texts. From this perspective, Nāgārjuna appears to be the most diverse writer: on the non-tantric level he authored separate texts on self-emptiness and other-emptiness, as well as presented both types of emptiness in the same text, and furthermore taught other-emptiness in his tantric works.

43. *Pañcakrama*, *Rim pa lnga pa*, D1802, rgyud, ngi, 45a–57a.

44. *Pradīpodyotana*, *Sgron ma gsal bar byed pa*, D1785, rgyud, ha, 1–201b.

45. In this context, they are synonymous, because emptiness is treated as negation.

46. Note that persons empty of themselves is a type of selflessness of phenomena, *not* selflessness of persons.

47. gang stong pa'i gzhi ni shes bya la gang ji snyed cig srid pa'i chos thams cad do// gang gis stong pa'i dgag bya yang dgag gzhi gang yin pa de nyid do/ mdor na gang zag dang/ chos gnyis so// ji ltar stong pa'i tshul ni/ dgag gzhir gzung pa'i chos gang yin pa de nyid de nyid kyis stong pa yin te/ don dam dpyod byed kyi rigs pas dpyad pa gang gi tshe de nyid de nyid du ma grub pa'i phyir ro// dper na bum pa de gcig dang du ma gang du grub dpyad pa'i tshe bum par ma grub pa bzhin no. *Great Path of Ambrosia of Emptiness*, vol. 4, 115–116.

48. rang stong gi 'chad tshul la/ chos can gang dang gang yin pa de rang rang gis stong par 'chad pa'i lugs dang/ de ltar bshad na chad stong du song bas/ chos can tshad grub kyi steng du dgag bya gzhi ma grub kyis stong pa la rang stong du 'chad pa'i lugs gnyis bod du byung yang/ phyi ma de ngo bo nyid med pa pa'i lugs su ni lung dang rigs pas mi 'thad do. *Rain of Ambrosia*, 380.

49. Shakya Chokden does not address Tsongkhapa by name in this passage. He does call Tsongkhapa by name in other texts, where he either openly criticizes Tsongkhapa's views or just describes them as one of many systems developed by Tibetans. See, respectively, the *Precious Treasury of the Condensed Essence*, vol. 13, 181–186; and the *Mirror Clarifying Individual Texts: Presentation of the Views, Meditations, and Actions of Earlier and Later Great Beings of the Land of Snows* (*Gangs can gyi chen po snga phyir byon pa'i lta sgom spyod pa'i rnam bzhag rang gzhung gsal ba'i me long*), vol. 23, 94–96 (hereafter, *Mirror Clarifying Individual Texts*).

50. They are the relative truth (*kun rdzob bden pa, saṃvṛtisatya*) and ultimate truth (*don dam bden pa, paramārthasatya*).

51. gangs can du phyis byon pa'i rang stong smra bar khas len pa dag na re/ rang stong gi don bden pa gnyis kyi chos rnams ji snyed pa de dang de de nyid yin pa 'gog pa ni ma yin te/ yin na bden pa gnyis po mtha' dag la skur pa btab par 'gyur ba'i phyir ro// dper na myu gu myu gu ma yin na myu gu med par khas len dgos pa dang/ myu gu bden stong yang rang

nyid ma yin na de med par thal ba'i skyon 'byung ba bzhin no// des na rang stong 'jog pa la chos can tshad mas grub pa rnams kyi steng du dgag bya bden grub kyi tshad dang/ bdag gnyis kyi 'jog mtshams ngos zin par byas nas de nyid 'gog dgos pa yin. *Great Path of Ambrosia of Emptiness*, vol. 4, 119.

52. Tsongkhapa discusses these elements of his view in *The Great Treatise on the Stages of the Path to Enlightenment*, vol. 3 (Ithaca, New York: Snow Lion Publications, 2002), 125–223.

53. This is a part of the following passage from Candrakīrti's *Engaging in Madhyamaka* (*Madhyamakāvatāra, Dbu ma la 'jug pa*), D3861, dbu ma, 'a, 213a–b: gang phyir de yi rang bzhin de// yin phyir mig ni mig gis stong// de bzhin rna ba sna dang lce// lus dang yid kyis bsnyad par bya.

54. ji skad du/ gang phyir mig ni mig gis stong/ zhes sogs su rtsod gzhi'i chos can gang dang gang yin pa de de dang de nyid kyis stong pa la rang stong gi don du bshad pa yin gyi/ rang gi ngo bo yin pa lta zhog// rang dang 'brel ba gang yang ma grub pa zhig bkag pa la rang stong gi don du bshad pa med pa'i phyir. *Great Path of Ambrosia of Emptiness*, vol. 4, 119.

55. gzhan stong gi 'chad tshul de rigs pa ma yin par khyed cag gis 'dod bzhin du don de nyid khas blangs nas de la rang stong gi ming gis btags nas bshad par song ba yin te/ dgag gzhi gzhan dbang tshad grub kyi steng du dgag bya kun brtags tshad mas ma grub pa zhig gis stong par bshad nas/ de des stong pa'i stong nyid de don dam pa'i bden pa mthar thug tu khas len cing/ stong nyid de yod pa ma yin par khas blangs na skur 'debs kyi lta bar 'gyur ro zhes gzhan stong pa dag gis khas blangs la/ khyed kyis kyang khas blangs pa'i phyir ro. *Great Path of Ambrosia of Emptiness*, vol. 4, 121–122. See also the *Rain of Ambrosia*, 380, for a similar passage. Tsongkhapa himself is aware of both the approach to self-emptiness that Shakya Chokden allies with and the fact that from the standpoint of that approach his own position can be criticized as that of other-emptiness. Nevertheless, he treats such as an approach as a misunderstanding of the correct Madhyamaka view. In his *Thorough Clarification of Intent: Extensive Explanation of [Candrakīrti's] 'Engaging in Madhyamaka'* (*Dbu ma la 'jug pa'i rgya cher bshad pa dgongs pa rab gsal*), Collected Works of Tsong kha pa Blo bzang grags pa, vol. 16 (ma) (Sku 'bum: Sku 'bum byams pa gling par khang, 2000?), 137b–138a, he makes a well-known statement: "It is absolutely unreasonable to say that a pot not being empty of a pot but being empty of truth is the other-emptiness, and therefore a pot being empty of a pot is the self-emptiness. If a pot were empty of a pot, then there will have to be no pot in pot. In that case, if [a pot] itself did not exist in itself, then because [it] would not exist in anything else, a pot will turn out to be totally nonexistent. Because in that [context] all other things are [also] like that, the advocate of such [position] also will turn out to be nonexistent, and no presentations at all of 'being empty of this' and 'this not being empty' will be possible" (bum pa bum pas mi stong bar bden pas stong pa ni/ gzhan stong yin pas bum pa bum pas stong pa ni rang stong yin no zhes smra ba ni gtan nas mi rigs te/ bum pa bum pas stong na bum pa la bum pa med dgos na/ rang la rang med na gzhan su la yang med pas bum pa gtan med par 'gyur ro/ de'i tshe dngos po gzhan thams cad kyang de

dang 'dra bas/ de ltar smra mkhan yang med par 'gyur zhing/ 'dis stong pa dang ' 'di mi stong zhes pa'i rnam gzhag gang yang mi srid par 'gyur ro). The first line of this passage became like a logo of Tsongkhapa's view of emptiness known to virtually all its critics and advocates.

56. Such is accepted only by Satyākāravāda, not by Alīkākāravāda. For details see Chapter 4 section 1.

57. gang stong pa'i gzhi ni gzhan dbang ste gzung 'dzin gnyis snang can gyi shes pa mtha' dag go// dgag bya ni kun brtags pa ste/ gzung ba dang 'dzin pa'i dbye bas gnyis yin la/ de re re la'ang gang zag gi dbang du byas pa dang/ chos kyi dbang du byas pa'i gzung 'dzin gnyis gnyis so . . . ji ltar stong pa'i tshul ni/ dgag bya des dgag gzhi de gzhan stong gi tshul gyis stong pa yin gyi/ rang stong gi tshul gyis ni ma yin te/ dgag bya gzung 'dzin gnyis po de dgag gzhi gnyis snang gi shes pa gnyis po de la ltos pa'i gzhan gyi ngo bo yin gyi/ de'i rang gi ngo bor mi 'jog pa'i phyir. *Great Path of Ambrosia of Emptiness,* vol. 4, 114–115. See also the *Rain of Ambrosia,* 377–378, 387, etc.

58. See pp. 164–166 for details.

59. Shakya Chokden treats the *Sublime Continuum* also as a Yogācāra Madhyamaka treatise of other-emptiness. Nevertheless, he discusses it separately because he believes that all definitive meanings of the three dharmacakras are condensed in it (*Rain of Ambrosia,* 418), because it provides unique teachings on the tathāgata-essence (*de bshin gshegs pa'i snying po, tathāgatagarbha*), and so forth.

60. *Conquest Over Objections about the Three Mother Scriptures: Extensive Explanation of the Superior 'One Hundred Thousand Stanza,' 'Twenty-five Thousand Stanza,' and 'Eighteen Thousand Stanza Perfection of Wisdom' Sūtras* (*Āryaśatasāhasrikāpañcaviṃsatisāhasrikāṣṭadaśasāhasrikāprajñāpāramitābṛhaṭṭīkā, 'Phags pa shes rab kyi pha rol tu phyin pa 'bum pa dang nyi khri lnga stong pa dang khri brgyad stong pa'i rgya cher bshad pa/ yum gsum gnod 'joms*), D3808, shes phyin, pha, 1a–292b. Hereafter, *Conquest over Objections.*

61. gzhan stong gi gzhi chos can ngos 'dzin tshul la mi 'dra ba gnyis byung ste/ rnal 'byor spyod pa'i gzhung du/ stong gzhi gzhan dbang dgag bya kun btags kyis stong pa'i chos nyid yongs grub tu bshad pa dang/ rgyud bla ma dang yum gyi gnod 'joms su chos nyid yongs grub dgag bya kun btags kyis stong par bshad pa'o// gnyis po yang shes bya thams cad kun btags dang yongs grub gnyis su bsdus pa dang/ gzhan dbang dang gsum du phye ba'i khyad par las yin gyi 'gal ba ni ma yin no. *Rain of Ambrosia,* 379–380.

62. *Explanation of [Maitreya's] 'Sublime Continuum of Mahāyāna'* (*Mahāyānottaratantraśāstravyākhyā, Theg pa chen po'i rgyud bla ma'i bstan bcos kyi rnam par bshad pa*), D4025, sems tsam, phi, 74b–129a. Edited Sanskrit text in Edward H. Johnston (ed.), *Ratnagotravibhāga Mahāyānottaratantraśāstra* (Patna: The Bihar Research Society, 1950). English translation in Jikido Takasaki, *A Study on the Ratnagotravibhāga* (Rome: Istituto Italiano per il Medio ed Estremo Oriente, 1966).

63. *Rain of Ambrosia,* 408. As Shakya Chokden himself explains, Asaṅga interpreted other-emptiness differently in his commentary on the *Sublime Continuum* and the *Summary of Higher Knowledge.* Among other differences, in

the commentary on the *Sublime Continuum* Asaṅga did *not* explain the three characteristics (*mtshan nyid gsum, trilakṣaṇa*), i.e., the three natures. These interpretive differences stem from different sūtras explored in those texts (*Rain of Ambrosia*, 407).

64. *Rain of Ambrosia*, 419. Details of Shakya Chokden's approach to the *Sublime Continuum* can be found in the *Rain of Ambrosia*. See also the *Essence of Sūtras and Tantras: Explanation of the Buddha-Essence* (*Sangs rgyas kyi snying po'i rnam bshad mdo rgyud snying po*), vol. 13, 124–136, and the *Previously Unseen Sun: The Definitive Meaning of the 'Sublime Continuum' Treatise* (*Rgyud bla ma'i bstan bcos kyi nges don sngon med nyi ma*), vol. 13, 113–124, both translated in their entirety into English in my "Reburying the Treasure—Maintaining the Continuity." Besides that, almost all commentaries written by Shakya Chokden on the *Ornament of Clear Realizations* heavily rely on the *Sublime Continuum* when commenting on the tathāgata-essence and related topics.

65. *Great Path of Ambrosia of Emptiness*, vol. 4, 139.

66. kun rdzob kyi bden pa thams cad rang stong du gtan la phab nas/ don dam pa'i ye shes 'ba' zhig lhag par 'jog pa. *Gzi bsam 'grub gling pa'i dge 'dun spyi'i dris lan ya mtshan bcu bdun pa*, vol. 23, 440.

67. *Seventeen Wondrous Answers*, vol. 23, 439.

68. *Great Path of Ambrosia of Emptiness*, vol. 4, 136 ff.

69. Ibid., 139. Note that in the *Rain of Ambrosia*, 484–485, Shakya Chokden writes that the *Conquest over Objections* teaches the final Yogācāra Madhyamaka view (i.e., the Alīkākāravāda view)—that very view which has been intended by Maitreya. Thus, when in the *Great Path of Ambrosia of Emptiness* he writes that the mode of emptiness (*stong tshul*) explained in the *Conquest over Objections* does not accord with either Yogācāra or Niḥsvabhāvavāda, he is referring to the way of positing or determining emptiness—not to emptiness itself.

70. In contrast to Shakya Chokden, Tsongkhapa—himself a strong critic of the other-emptiness view of Dölpopa—denies Vasubandhu's authorship of this text, and attributes it to Daṃṣṭasena. See, Jeffrey Hopkins, *Emptiness in the Mind-Only School of Buddhism*, 231–233.

71. gangs can du byon pa'i gzhan stong smra ba dag na re/ kun rdzob 'dus byas kyi dngos po thams cad rang stong dang/ don dam 'dus ma byas rnams gzhan stong du 'chad pa 'di ni dbu ma pa chen po dbyig gnyen gyi bzhed pa yin te/ yum gyi gnod 'joms las de ltar bshad pa'i phyir/ zhes 'chad pa ni rigs pa ma yin te/ rje btsun gyi gzhung rtsa ba dang mi mthun zhing/ thogs med sku mched kyi gzhung rtsod med rnams dang/ phyogs glang yab sras kyi gzhung lugs las gzhan stong gyi 'chad tshul gsal bar gsungs pa rnams dang 'gal ba'i phyir ro// ji ltar zhe na/ gang yang khyed kyi ltar na/ chos can gzhan dbang dgag bya kun brtags kyis stong pa la gzhan stong gi don du mi 'chad par chos nyid yongs grub de chos can gzhan dbang dang kun brtags kyis stong pa ni gzhan stong gi don du khas blangs la/ 'chad tshul de 'dra de gzhung lugs de dang de dag na med do. *Great Path of Ambrosia of Emptiness*, vol. 4, 116–117. Shakya Chokden does not address Dölpopa by name in this passage. He does mention Dölpopa's name when discussing

his views in the *Mirror Clarifying Individual Texts*, vol. 23, 89–91. Dölpopa's view criticized by Shakya Chokden is explained in Jeffrey Hopkins (tr. and introduction), *Mountain Doctrine: Tibet's Fundamental Treatise on Other-Emptiness and the Buddha-Matrix* (Ithaca, New York: Snow Lion Publications, 2006), 210–230. Dölpopa himself is aware of objections his view of other-emptiness provokes, and as if answering Shakya Chokden's criticisms, explains that Asaṅga treated the dependent natures as bases of emptiness only tentatively, but in the end asserted the thoroughly established nature itself as the basis of emptiness (ibid., 218).

72. yang dag ma yin kun rtog yod// de la gnyis po yod ma yin. *Differentiation of the Middle and Extremes* (*Madhyāntavibhāga, Dbus dang mtha' rnam par 'byed pa*), D4021, sems tsam, phi, 40b. Skt.: abhūtaparikalpo 'sti dvayaṃ tatra na vidyate. In Thomas E. Wood, *Mind Only: A Philosophical and Doctrinal Analysis of the Vijñānavāda*, Monographs of the Society for Asian and Comparative Philosophy, 9 (Honolulu: University of Hawaii Press, 1991), 10. See also Gadjin M. Nagao's *Madhyāntavibhāga-Bhāṣya: A Buddhist Philosophical Treatise Edited for the First Time from a Sanskrit Manuscript* (Tokyo: Suzuki Research Foundation, 1964), 17. Hereafter, *Madhyāntavibhāga-Bhāṣya: A Buddhist Philosophical Treatise*.

73. 'o na ci zhig yod ce na/ ji skad du/ yang dag ma yin kun rtog yod// de la gnyis po yod ma yin/ zhes 'byung ba ltar/ gzhan dbang stong gzhi'i chos can dang/ gzung 'dzin kun brtags gnyis po gang gis stong pa'i dgag bya dang/ gzung 'dzin gnyis med kyi ye shes la stong pa'i dngos por bshad pa zhes bya ba zhig yod pa yin. *Great Path of Ambrosia of Emptiness*, vol. 4, 117.

74. stong gzhi'i chos can du 'jog pa ma yin te/ de la sgrub byed med cing gnod byed yod pa'i phyir/ sgrub byed med pa ni de ltar 'chad byed kyi gzhung med pa dang/ gnod byed ni stong nyid sgrub byed kyi rigs pas chos can yongs grub kyi steng du dgag chos kun brtags dang gzhan dbang gis stong par sgrub dgos na rtsod gzhi'i chos can nges pa'i dus su bsgrub bya grub zin par thal ba dang/ yang na rtsod gzhi'i chos can ma nges par bsgrub bya sgrub pa'i gtan tshigs yang dag srid par 'gyur ro. *Great Path of Ambrosia of Emptiness*, vol. 4, 117–118.

75. gzhan dbang gi dngos po rang stong du 'chad pa la'ang sgrub byed med cing gnod byed yod do// sgrub byed med pa ni/ gzhung lugs de dang de dag nas de ltar ma bshad pa'o// gnod byed yod pa ni gzhan dbang gi ngo bo bden par ma grub na chos nyid yongs grub kyi ngo bo bden par med pa nyid du 'gyur te/ gzung 'dzin gnyis med kyi de kho na nyid ni gnyis snang gi shes pa'i ngo bor bzhed pa'i phyir te/ ji skad du/ de ni de yi de nyid yin/ zhes pa'i gzhung gis de'i ngo bor bstan pa'i phyir. *Great Path of Ambrosia of Emptiness*, vol. 4, 118. The passage Shakya Chokden is referring to is found in the *Commentary on Valid Cognition* (*Pramāṇavārttikakārikā, Tshad ma rnam 'grel gyi tshig le'ur byas pa*), D4210, tshad ma, ce, 126b: de la gcig ni med pas kyang// gnyis ka'ang nyams par 'gyur ba yin// de phyir gnyis stong gang yin pa// de ni de yi'ang de nyid yin. Skt.: tatraikasyāpy abhāvena dvayam apy avahīyate/ tasmāt tad eva tasyāpi tattvaṃ yā dvayaśūnyatā. In

Yūsho Miyasaka (ed.), "Pramāṇavārttika-kārikā (Sanskrit and Tibetan)," *Acta Indologica,* vol. 2 (1971/72): 68.

76. See also the *Ocean of Scriptural Statements and Reasoning,* vol. 14, 381–383.

77. The following remark by Matthew Kapstein is right to the point: "I would suggest, therefore, that given our present knowledge of Tibetan doctrinal history doxographic labels such as *gzhan stong pa* and *rang stong pa* are best avoided, except of course where they are used within the tradition itself. Our primary task must be to document and interpret precise concepts and arguments, and in many cases the recourse to overly broad characterizations seems only to muddy the waters" ("We Are All Gzhan stong pas," 121).

78. See, for example, the *Ocean of Scriptural Statements and Reasoning,* vol. 15, 494–505, 512–524. He uses the same technique also in his earlier texts, such as the *Drumming Sounds of the Melodious Voice of Brahma,* written before he developed his unique approach to the classification of tenets.

79. On the differences between Alīkākāravāda and Satyākāravāda views on the three natures, see pp. 164–166.

80. gzhan dbang rang bzhin gyis yod pa dang/ bden med sgyu ma lta bur 'chad pa mi 'gal ba ni gzhan stong smra ba'i gzhung gi de kho na nyid 'byed pa'i lde mig tu shes par bya'o. *Great Path of Ambrosia of Emptiness,* vol. 4, 115.

81. gzhan dbang bden grub ni thogs med zhabs kyi grub pa'i mtha' ma yin te/ de'i gzhung du de sgyu ma lta bur bshad pa'i phyir/ de'i ngo bo bden par bshad pas de bden par mi 'gyur te/ bum sogs kyi ngo bo chos nyid du 'chad pa'i skabs bzhin no. *Rain of Ambrosia,* 388.

82. For example, his *Great Ship of Discrimination that Sails into the Ocean of Definitive Meaning: Treatise Differentiating the Tenets of Prāsaṅgika and Svātantrika Madhyamaka* (*Dbu ma thal rang gi grub pa'i mtha' rnam par dbye ba'i bstan bcos nges don gyi rgya mtshor 'jug pa'i rnam dpyod kyi gru chen*), vol. 4, 399–407, is dedicated entirely to the Prāsaṅgika/Svātantrika distinctions that Shakya Chokden presents in six steps: (1) the difference in their interpretations of the reason, that which establishes; (2) the difference in their interpretations of the thesis, that which is established; (3) the difference in their interpretations of valid cognition, that which measures; (4) the difference in their interpretations of the object, that which is measured; (5) the mode of existence of temporal difference in their views; (6) conclusion by showing that the their final views are in agreement. Hereafter, *Great Ship.* See my translation in the *Three Texts on Madhyamaka,* 43–51. Also, see the *Wish Fulfilling Meru,* vol. 4, 219–224, translated in the *Three Texts on Madhyamaka,* 10–14.

83. *Great Ship,* vol. 4, 405.

84. Note that technically speaking, such phenomena as reasoning, thesis, etc., mentioned in the note 82 above, as well as the very process of moving from the relative to the ultimate level dicussed in this section, are subsumed under the category of relative truth. But these types of relative truth are not counted as the relative truth *of the world,* because instead of being posited without analysis by ordinary wordly minds, they are posited by minds

articulating Buddhist philosophical tenets. Therefore, although Prāsaṅgika and Svātantrika Mādhyamikas are not different in their ways of positing the relative truth of the world, they *are* different in their ways of positing those elements of their tenets that are subsumed under the category of relative truth.

85. *Satyadvayavibhaṅga, Bden pa gnyis rnam par 'byed pa,* D3881, dbu ma, sa, 1a–3b. English translation in Eckel, *Jñānagarbha's Commentary on the Distinction Between the Two Truths.*

86. *Madhyamakālaṃkārakārikā, Dbu ma'i rgyan gyi tshig le'ur byas pa,* D3884, dbu ma, sa, 53a1–56b3. Edited Tibetan and English translation in Masamichi Ichigō, "Śāntarakṣita's Madhyamakālaṃkāra," in *Studies in the Literature of the Great Vehicle,* Michigan Studies in Buddhist Literature No. 1, edited by Luis O. Gómez and Jonathan A. Silk, 141–240 (Ann Arbor: Collegiate Institute for the Study of Buddhist Literature and Center for South and Southeast Asian Studies, The University of Michigan, 1989).

87. dbu ma thal rang du grags pa'i slob dpon rnams 'jig rten gyi kun rdzob bden pa rigs pas ma dpyad par 'jog tshul la khyad par ci yang mi snang ste/ grub mtha' smra ba'i rigs pas mi dpyod par 'jig rten gyi blo lhan skyes la ji ltar snang zhin grags pa bzhin du de'i rnam gzhag zhal gyis bzhes par mthun pa'i phyir/ slob dpon de dag mthar thug gi don dam pa'i bden pa ngos 'dzin lugs la'ang mi 'dra ba'i khyad par cung zad kyang mi snang ste/ spros pa'i tshogs mtha' dag dang bral ba'i sgra rtog gi yul las 'das pa zhig la don dam pa'i bden pa zhes tha snyad 'dogs par zhal 'cham pa'i phyir/ de lta na yang don dam pa'i bden pa de gtan la 'bebs byed kyi rigs pa dang/ rigs pa de la dang por 'jug pa'i sgo mi 'dra ba yin te/ rang rgyud kyi rigs pa dang thal 'gyur gyi rigs pas gtan la 'bebs tshul so sor nges pa'i phyir dang/ kun rdzob kyi bden pa ma dor bar don dam pa'i bden pa la 'jug pa'i cha [*sic,* should read *tshe*] grub mtha' 'og ma la rim gyis zhugs nas dbu ma la 'jug pa'i tshul dang/ 'og ma la ma zhugs par 'jig rten gyi grags pa nyid nas dbu ma la 'jug pa'i tshul rnam pa gnyis mthong pa'i phyir/ dang po la'ang gnyis te/ rnam par rig pa tsam gyi grub pa'i mtha' la'ang mi 'jug par thog mar mdo sde pa'i grub mtha' la zhugs nas/ de nas dbu ma nyid la 'jug pa dang/ mdo sems gnyis la rim gyis zhugs nas de nas dbu ma la 'jug pa'i tshul lo// dang po ni slob dpon ye shes snying po'i bden gnyis rnam par 'byed pa las 'byung la/ gnyis pa ni/ byang chub sems dpa' zhi ba mtsho'i dbu ma'i rgyan las 'byung ngo. *Ocean of Scriptural Statements and Reasoning,* vol. 14, 422–423.

88. Shakya Chokden treats "Vijñaptimātra" and "Yogācāra" as synonymous. He also calls them "Vijñaptika" (*rnam rig pa,* "Followers of Cognizance"), and "Vijñaptivāda." See the *Discourse Eliminating Mistakes with Regard to the Teachings of Scriptural Collections: Fourteen Dharma Sections* (*Sde snod kyi chos la 'khrul pa sel ba'i gtam chos tshan bcu bzhi pa*), in *'Hundred and Eight Dharma Sections' Treatise* (*Chos tshan brgya dang brgyad pa zhes bya ba'i bstan bcos*), vol. 13, 208–209 (hereafter, *Discourse Eliminating Mistakes*), the *Answers to Questions Issuing from the 'Differentiation of the Two Modes,'* vol. 17, 414–416, and especially a nameless text, vol. 17, 416–417 where he explains that according to Indian texts and early Tibetan thinkers, Vijñaptivāda is not

subsumed under the category of Cittamātra, while Cittamātra is subsumed under the categories of both Vijñaptivāda and Yogācāra. See also pp. 159 ff. below. Although in the above passage Shakya Chokden mentions first Vijñaptimātra in general and then Cittamātra in particular, this does not imply that in his opinion Śāntarakṣita with his followers do not negate the Alīkākāravāda view by reasoning. But it does imply that while in their system the Cittamātra view is completely disposed with after having been refuted, the Alīkākāravāda view of primordial mind is first negated in the conceptual process of Niḥsvabhāvavāda reasoning, but then accepted as the ultimate view experienced through meditation. I clarify this issue in the next section, p. 142 ff.

89. *Wish Fulfilling Meru*, vol. 4, 221.

90. *Ocean of Scriptural Statements and Reasoning*, vol. 14, 436–438. In the *Explanation of [Sakya Pendita's] 'Entrance into Scholarship' Together with Answers to Questions* (*Mkhas pa la 'jug pa'i sgo'i rnam bshad dri lan dang bcas pa*), vol. 24, 147, Shakya Chokden explains that the term "mdo sde spyod pa'i dbu ma pa" derives from the *Notes on the View* by the great translator Yeshé Dé, and "rnal sbyor spyod pa'i dbu ma pa" is clearly explained in Śāntarakṣita's *Ornament of Madhyamaka*. Nevertheless, " 'jig rten grags sde spyod pa'i dbu ma pa" was coined by Tibetan masters after Candrakīrti's works had been translated into Tibetan.

91. *Ocean of Scriptural Statements and Reasoning*, vol. 14, 438.

92. Their mutual debates are discussed in detail in the *Ocean of Scriptural Statements and Reasoning*, vol. 14, 438–467.

93. *Rain of Ambrosia*, 378.

94. *Great Ship*, vol. 4, 401.

95. In his writings in general, Shakya Chokden prefers to use the terms "Yogācāra Madhyamaka" and "Sautrāntika Madhyamaka" over "Yogācāra Svātantrika Madhyamaka" and "Sautrāntika Svātantrika Madhyamaka."

96. *Rain of Ambrosia*, 370; *Ocean of Scriptural Statements and Reasoning*, vol. 15, 461.

97. *Condensed Essence of Madhyamaka: Explanation of [Nāgārjuna's] 'Commentary on the Ultimate Mind of Enlightenment'* (*Don dam byang chub sems 'grel gyi bshad pa dbu ma'i snying po bsdus pa*), vol. 7, 361.

98. *Previously Unseen Sun: The Definitive Meaning of the 'Sublime Continuum' Treatise* (*Rgyud bla ma'i bstan bcos kyi nges don sngon med nyi ma*), vol. 13, 121; *Meaningful to Behold*, vol. 23, 364.

99. *Discourse Eliminating Mistakes*, vol. 13, 209.

100. *Meaningful to Behold*, vol. 23, 388.

101. See p. 75 above.

102. des na rnal 'byor spyod pa'i dbu ma la/ byams chos nas bshad pa dang/ byang chub sems pa zhi ba 'tsho yab sras kyis bzhed pa dang gnyis 'dug pa de'i khyad par ni/ gnas lugs la mtshan 'dzin gyi rtog pa 'gog byed kyi rigs pa mi 'dra ba yin gyi/ don dam gyi gnas tshul dang nyams su myong bya la khyad par med . . . lugs 'dir rigs ngo'i stong nyid med dgag tu 'chad kyang/ sgom pas nyams su myong bya'i stong nyid med dgag tu mi 'chad

pas thal rang gi gtso bo nyid dang khyad par phyed dgos so. *Meaningful to Behold*, vol. 23, 389–390.

103. nges don gyi mthar thug ye shes la 'chad pa 'di ni 'phags pa thog med bzhed pa'i dbu ma 'dir ma zad/ ngo bo nyid med par smra ba'i nang gi rnal 'byor spyod pa'i dbu ma pa dag kyang bzhed pa yin te/ dper na slob dpon 'phags seng bzhin no. *Rain of Ambrosia*, 399. For more on Haribhadra's approach, see p. 151 ff.

104. zhi ba 'tsho'i rjes su 'brang ba gcig ni slob dpon seng ge bzang po ste/ 'dis yum gyi don 'grel tshul/ rnal ' 'byor spyod pa'i tshul ltar 'grel bas/ mtshan 'dzin 'gog tshul ngo bo nyid med pa'i rigs pa dang/ sgom pas nyams su myong bya rnal 'byor spyod pa'i lugs su bshad par ni gangs can pa mtha' dag 'thun pa yin no. *Wish Fulfilling Meru*, vol. 4, 223.

105. See p. 124 above.

106. See right below.

107. dbu ma pa ni gnyis te/ rnal 'byor spyod pa'i dbu ma pa dang/ ngo bo nyid med par smra ba'i dbu ma pa'o/ dang po la rang stong du smra ba dang/ gzhan stong du smra ba'o// ngo bo nyid med pa pa de la'ang/ gnyis te/ thal 'gyur ba dang/ rang rgyud pa'o/ de la'ang gnyis te/ gnas skabs mdo sde pa ltar khas len pa dang/ sems tsam pa ltar khas len pa'o. *Rain of Ambrosia*, 326.

108. rnal 'byor spyod pa par bshad pa tsam gyis sems tsam par 'grub na ni/ zhi ba 'tsho dpon slob la sogs rnal 'byor spyod pa'i dbu ma pa mtha' dag sems tsam pa nyid du thal bar 'gyur ro. *Thorough Clarification of Definitive Meaning of the 'Five Dharmas of Maitreya,'* vol. 11, 10.

109. I also discuss it in detail in Chapter 4 section 1.

110. rnam rdzun gyi lta ba dbu mar khas len na/ sems tsam pa'i slob dpon dang gzhung mi rnyed par 'gyur. *Meaningful to Behold*, vol. 23, 361.

111. byams chos dang thogs med kyi shin rta'i srol dbu ma yin na/ sems tsam gyi gzhung dang slob dpon gyi mtshan gzhi gang yin gsung ba. *Seventeen Wondrous Answers*, vol. 23, 421.

112. See Jeffrey Hopkins, *Maps of the Profound*, 419 ff., and Üpa Losel (*dbus pa blo gsal*, 14th century CE), *Treasury of Explanations of Tenets* (*Grub pa'i mtha' rnam par bshad pa'i mdzod*), in Katsumi Mimaki (ed. with partial translation into French and introduction), *Blo gsal grub mtha'* (Kyoto: Université de Kyoto, 1982), 99 ff.

113. *Meaningful to Behold*, vol. 23, 363–364.

114. Note that Shakya Chokden does not say that the views of those tenets *derive* from those texts or are *created* by those authors. This analogy, therefore, does not correspond to what it exemplifies in all respects.

115. *Triṃśikākārikā, Sum cu pa'i tshig le'ur byas pa*, D4055, sems tsam, shi, 1a–3a.

116. See also the *Ocean of Scriptural Statements and Reasoning*, 382. Note that other leading Tibetan thinkers, such as the Geluk polymath Jamyang Zhepa, argued that according to all Indian and Tibetan scholars, each text authored by Asaṅga, Dignāga, and Dharmakīrti, etc., such as the *Grounds of Yogācāra*, *Sūtra on Valid Cognition*, and *Seven Works on Valid Cognition*, contains

presentations of both Satyākāravāda and Alīkākāravāda views (Hopkins, *Maps of the Profound*, 310–311). Another seminal Geluk thinker Changkya Rölpé Dorjé (*lcang skya rol pa'i rdo rje*, 1717–1786) agreed with this position, and further argued that although such scholars as Bodhibhadra treated Asaṅga with his followers as Alīkākāravādins and Dignāga with his followers as Satyākāravādins, the final views of the former and the latter group cannot be decisively ascertained as Alīkākāravāda and Satyākāravāda, respectively. This is because in his criticism of Yogācāra, Bhāviveka presented the former group's position as Satyākāravāda, while Prajñākaragupta and Dharmottara presented the position of the *Commentary on Valid Cognition* as Alīkākāravāda (in contrast to Devendrabuddhi and Śākyabuddhi who presented it as Satyākāravāda). See Changkya's *Ornament Beautifying the Meru of Muni's Teachings: Presentation of Tenets* (*Grub pa'i mtha' rnam par gzhag pa thub bstan lhun po'i mdzes rgyan*, Krung go bod kyi shes rig dpe skrun khang, 1989), 144. (Shakya Chokden understood Śākyabuddhi's interpretation of Dharmakīrti differently; see p. 154.) This ambiguity and the fact that the seminal Yogācāra texts allowed for alternative interpretations of their final views no doubt played to the advantage of Shakya Chokden, who presented the ultimate view of all leading Yogācāra thinkers as Alīkākāravāda.

117. As I show in the next section, Shakya Chokden puts Buddhist logicians Dharmakīrti, etc., into the same category of Alīkākāravādins as Maitreya, Asaṅga, etc.

118. For the full passage, see p. 39 above.

119. See p. 132–133 above.

120. yang sde bdun gyi mthar thug sems tsam du gnas zhes zer ba yang/ shing rta'i srol chen so so'i dbye ba ma phyed pa yin te/ byams pa'i gzhung rjes 'brang dang bcas pa 'di dag na sems tsam ston pa'i gzhung dang/ de bkag nas de las gong mar gyur pa'i lugs dang gnyis gnyis su phye nas bshad pa yin la de'i tshe phyi ma de sems tsam du gnas pa dang/ lugs phyi ma de las gong na dbu ma'i grub mtha' yod par 'chad byed kyi yi ge 'bru gcig kyang ston rgyu med la/ gnyis gnyis su ji ltar phye ba'i tshul yang dper mthson na/ mdo sde'i rgyan du/ der snang sems tsam la ni yang dag gnas// zhes dang/ de nas sems kyang med pa nyid du rtogs// zhes dang/ dbus mthar/ yang dag ma yin kun rtog yod// ces dang/ de la gnyis po yod ma yin// zhes pa lta bu shin tu mang . . . las/ rkang pa dang pos gzung ba med pa sems tsam pa'i gzhung dang/ rkang pa gnyis pa rnams kyis sems tsam bkag nas gzung 'dzin gnyis po bkag pa'i bshul na gnas lugs su gyur pa'i ye shes zhig lus pa de dbu ma/ rigs pa de dang rjod byed kyi sgras yul du ma byas pa'i de bzhin nyid mthar thug tu bzhed pa yin. *Appearance of the Sun*, vol. 19, 92–93. See also the *Rain of Ambrosia*, 325–326, and the *Seventeen Wondrous Answers*, vol. 23, 423–424, for similar citations and interpretations.

121. *Vimalaprabhā*, *Dri ma med pa'i 'od*, D1347, rgyud, da, 26a.

122. *Jñānasārasamuccaya*, *Ye shes snying po kun las btus pa*, D3851, dbu ma, tsha, 27b.

123. *Sugatamatavibhaṅgakārikā*, *Bde bar gshegs pa'i gzhung rnam par 'byed pa'i tshig le'ur byas pa*, D3899, dbu ma, a, 8a.

124. gzung dang 'dzin pa las grol ba'i// rnam par shes pa don dam yod// ces pa rnal 'byor spyod pa'i gzhung// rgya mtsho'i pha rol phyin rnams sgrogs. Skt.: grāhyagrāhakavaidhuryāt vijñānaṃ paramārthasat/ yogācāramatāmbhodhipāragair iti gīyate. In Jagannāth Upādhyāya (ed. and annotated), *Vimalaprabhā: śrīmañjuśrīyaśoviracitasya paramādibuddhoddhṛtasya śrīlaghukālacakratantrarājasya kalkinā śrīpuṇḍarīkeṇa viracitā ṭīkā*, vol. 1, Bibliotheca Indo-Tibetica Series, 11 (Sarnath, Varanasi: Central Institute of Higher Tibetan Studies, 1986), 266. Hereafter, *Vimalaprabhā ṭīkā*. For an alternative translation, see Vesna A. Wallace, *The Kālacakratantra: The Chapter on the Individual together with the* Vimalaprabhā (New York: American Institute of Buddhist Studies at Columbia University, 2004), 244. Hereafter, *The Kālacakratantra*.

125. rkan pa dang po ni gzung 'dzin gnyis kyis stong pa'i tshul dang/ rkang pa gnyis pas ni de'i shul na yod pa'i ye shes de don dam pa'i dben par dang/ de nas rkang pa gnyis kyis ni de ltar 'chad pa de rnal 'byor spyod pa pa la gnas skabs sems tsam pa dang/ mthar thug dbu ma pa gnyis las/ phyi ma'i lugs so zhes 'chad pa'o// 'dir rnam par shes pa zhes bya ba ye shes kyi zlas phye ba de la zer ba ma yin te/ de yin na gzung 'dzin las grol bar 'gal bas so. *Rain of Ambrosia*, 365.

126. rnam bden brdzun zhes bya ba ni rnal 'byor spyod pa pa dag gi nges don gyi rgya mtshor 'jug pa'i them skas kyi rim pa kho na yin gyi/ grub mtha' so so ba ma yin. *Mkhas pa la 'jug pa'i sgo'i rnam bshad dri lan dang bcas pa*, vol. 24, 141. Hereafter, *Explanation of the 'Entrance into Scholarship.'*

127. Ibid., 140–142.

128. See the passages preceding and following after that very quote, as well as Chapter 4 section 1 below.

129. *Explanation of the 'Entrance into Scholarship,'* vol. 24, 140–141.

130. Ibid., 141–142.

131. sems tsam pa ni rnal 'byor spyod pa pa yin mod/ de'i gzhung rgya mtsho'i pha rol tu son pa ma yin. *Rain of Ambrosia*, 370. Emphasis mine.

132. See p. 357 note 116 above.

133. See p. 112. See also p. 167 below.

134. See p. 189.

135. In my *Three Texts on Madhyamaka* (p. 59 note 27), I wrote that according to Shakya Chokden, Yogācāra is identical with Alīkākāravāda, and Cittamātra is identical with Satyākāravāda. I thereby treated Yogācāra in general as a subdivision of Madhyamaka. That was an oversimplification of his position caused by an insufficient reading of his corpus. As I demonstrate in this study, Shakya Chokden argues that while Cittamātra is indeed identical with Satyākāravāda, it is nevertheless a type of Yogācāra too, although it is not Madhyamaka; only Alīkākāravāda Yogācāra is Madhyamaka alongside with Niḥsvabhāvavāda. However, given the fact that at times Shakya Chokden himself discusses Alīkākāravāda under the generic name of Yogācāra (143, 171–172, 186, 257 ff., etc.)—no doubt because according to him the fully understood Yogācāra view is necessarily that of Alīkākāravāda—my treatment of Yogācāra in general as Madhyamaka in the *Three Texts on Madhyamaka* was not very far from Shakya Chokden's position.

136. Also, by cultivating the Satyākāravāda view, practitioners can proceed as far as the Mahāyāna path of preparation (*sbyor lam, prayogamārga*). See also p. 167 below.

137. When referring to Ratnākaraśānti's views, Shakya Chokden persistently cites the introductory verse of the *Quintessential Instructions on the 'Ornament of Madhyamaka'* (see p. 155).

138. byang chub sems dpa' zhi ba 'tsho dang slob dpon seng ge bzang po dang rtsod dus kyi thams cad mkhyen pa ratna ā ka ra shanti pa ni lugs gnyis po dgongs pa mthun zhes 'chad pa ltar legs pas phyogs su lhung bar mi bya'o. *Appearance of the Sun*, vol. 19, 7.

139. 'o na slob dpon 'dis/ de yang rten cing 'brel bar 'byung ba yin pa'i phyir/ zhes gnyis med kyi ye shes rang stong du bsgrubs pa ma yin nam zhe na/ bsam byung gi rigs pas sgro 'dogs gcod pa'i tshe de ltar bshad mod sgom byung gis nyams su len pa'i tshe ye shes de nyid myong byar bshad pa yin te/ ji skad du/ sgyu ma lta bu'i bdag nyid du snang ba'i blo rnam par mi rtog pa so sor rang gis rig pa ci zhig ltar yang dag par skyes na/ zhes bshad la/ ye shes de nyid nyams su ma myong na skabs de'i rang rig de 'byung sa med pa'i phyir. *Rain of Ambrosia*, 364.

140. *Sphuṭārthā, Don gsal*; full title is *Abhisamayālaṃkāranāmaprajñāpāramitopadeśaśāstravṛtti, Shes rab kyi pha rol tu phyin pa'i man ngag gi bstan bcos mngon par rtogs pa'i rgyan ces bya ba'i 'grel pa*), D3793, shes phyin, ja, 78b–140a.

141. The names of these four stages provided by Shakya Chokden in his commentaries on the *Ornament of Clear Realizations* vary slightly from commentary to commentary. Here, I follow the names given in one of his latest commentaries on this text written in 1499, the *Great Path Compressing the Two Chariot Ways into One: Explanation of [Maitreya's] 'Ornament of Clear Realizations' Together with [Haribhadra's] 'Clear Meaning' Commentary* (*Mngon par rtogs pa'i rgyan 'grel pa don gsal ba dang bcas pa'i rnam par bshad pa shing rta'i srol gnyis gcig tu bsdus pa'i lam po che*), vol. 12, 257.

142. As will be explained below (p. 161 ff.), Shakya Chokden differentiates between the apprehended-aspect (*gzung rnam, grāhyākāra*)/apprehender-aspect (*'dzin rnam, grāhakākāra*) pair on the one hand and the apprehended (*gzung ba, grāhya*)/apprehender (*'dzin pa, grāhaka*) pair on the other. What Haribhadra in the above passage calls "aspect of the apprehender" (*'dzin pa'i rnam pa*) is taken by Shakya Chokden to refer to the apprehender, *not* the apprehender-aspect, as is clear from the *Rain of Ambrosia* where Shakya Chokden writes, commenting on "also eliminates that mere cognizance characterized by the aspect of the apprehender" and other similar passages: "[Those passages] clearly taught the hierarchical difference between the views of mind-only and truthlessness of the apprehender (sems tsam dang 'dzin pa bden med kyi lta ba la gong 'og gi khyad par gsal bar gsungs). *Rain of Ambrosia*, 326.

143. In the passage cited above, Shakya Chokden provides a slightly different version of this line that does not affect its meaning.

144. *Clear Meaning*, 124b–125a: sngon po dang de'i blo dag lhan cig dmigs pa nges pa'i phyir 'di ni sems tsam kho na yin gyi/ phyi rol gyi don med do zhes bya ba yid la byed cing 'dzin pa'i rnam pa can gyi sems la

mngon par zhen pa yongs su ma bor bas phyi rol gyi don du mngon par zhen pa spangs te/ gzung ba med na 'dzin pa med do snyam du nges par sems pas 'dzin pa'i rnam pa'i mtshan nyid rnam par rig pa tsam de yang bsal te/ gnyis su med pa'i ye shes 'ba' zhig 'di yang dag par yod pa'i ngo bo yin no snyam du nges par byas nas/ de yang rten cing 'brel par 'byung ba yin pa'i phyir/ sgyu ma bzhin du ngo bo nyid med pa ste/ yang dag par ni gcig tu dngos po dang dngos po med pa la sogs par brtag pa'i ngo bo dang bral ba yin no snyam du bsgoms pas bsgom pa'i stobs grub pa na kha cig la nor bu dang dngul la sogs pa'i shes pa bzhin du 'khrul pa'i mtshan ma mtha' dag spangs pa sgyu ma lta bu'i bdag nyid du snang ba'i blo rnam par mi rtog pa so so rang gis rig par bya ba ci zhig ltar yang dag par skyes na/ rnal 'byor pas shes bya'i sgrib pa yang dag par spong ngo.

145. *Madhyamakālaṃkārakārikā, Dbu ma'i rgyan gyi tshig le'ur byas pa*, D3884, dbu ma, sa, 56a; *Dharmadhātudarśanagīti, Chos kyi dbyings su lta ba'i glu*, D2314, rgyud, zhi, 256b.

146. nyams su myong bya'i de kho na nyid kyi ngos 'dzin gnyis med kyi ye shes la 'chad pa 'di ni/ byang chub sems pa zhi ba 'tsho dang/ jo bo a ti sha gnyis kas bzhed pa yin te/ dbu ma rgyan dang jo bos mdzad pa'i chos kyi dbyings su lta ba'i glu gnyis ka las/ tshul gnyis shing rta zhon nas su// rigs pa'i srab skyogs 'ju byed pa// de dag de phyir ji bzhin don// theg pa chen po pa nyid 'thob// ces 'byung la/ tshul gnyis ni rnal 'byor spyod pa pa dang ngo bo nyid med par smra ba'i tshul lo. *Rain of Ambrosia*, 364.

147. Consider, for example, the famous statement by Atiśa in his *Engaging in the Two Truths* (*Satyadvayāvatāra, Bden pa gnyis la 'jug pa*), D3902, bdu ma, a, 72b: "[The one prophesied by Tathāgata,]// the seer of reality// [is] Nāgārjuna. [His] disciple is Candrakīrti.// With the quintessential instructions passed down from him,// the truth of reality is realized (de bzhin gshegs pas lung bstan zhing// chos nyid bden pa gzigs pa yi// klu sgrub slob ma zla grags yin// de las brgyud pa'i man ngag gis// chos nyid bden pa rtogs par 'gyur), quoted by Shakya Chokden in the *Rain of Ambrosia*, 382.

148. *Appearance of the Sun*, vol. 19, 9.

149. *Pramāṇavārttikālaṃkāra, Tshad ma rnam 'grel gyi rgyan*, D4221, tshad ma, te 1b–the 282a.

150. *Appearance of the Sun*, vol. 19, 11.

151. Ibid., 27.

152. Ibid.

153. Ibid., 85.

154. Ibid., 23.

155. Ibid., 24, 93–94.

156. Candrakīrti, *Extensive Commentary on [Āryadeva's] 'Four Hundred Stanzas on the Yogic Deeds of Bodhisattvas'* (*Bodhisattvayogacaryācatuḥśatakaṭīkā, Byang chub sems dpa'i rnal 'byor spyod pa bzhi brgya pa'i rgya cher 'grel pa*), D3865, dbu ma, ya, 30b–239a.

157. This verse can be found in two texts by Ratnākaraśānti: *Establishment of the Middle Way: Commentary on the 'Ornament of Madhyamaka'* (*Madhyamakālaṃkāravṛttimadhyamapratipadāsiddhināma, Dbu ma rgyan gyi 'grel ba dbu*

ma'i lam grub pa zhes bya ba), D4072, sems tsam, hi, 102a, and *Quintessential Instructions on the 'Ornament of Madhyamaka'* (*Madhyamakālaṃkāropadeśa, Dbu ma rgyan gyi man ngag*), D4085, sems tsam, hi, 223b. In other texts too, Shakya Chokden says that this verse comes from Ratnākaraśānti's *Ornament of Madhyamaka*. See *Wish Fulfilling Meru*, vol. 4, 227, and *Appearance of the Sun*, vol. 19, 133–134. While both Ratnākaraśānti's texts have *yis* as the last syllable in the third line of the Tibetan text, all three Shakya Chokden's texts when he cites this verse have *yi* (see the next note). My translation is based on Shakya Chokden's reading.

158. mdor na thogs med sku mched dang/ phyogs glang yab sras kyi gzhung du/ dbu ma'i tshul bshad ma thag pa 'di las gzhan mi 'byung zhing/ klu sgrub zhabs kyi dgongs pa yang/ de ltar du gnas so zhes shing rta chen po dpal ldan chos skyong zhabs kyis bzhed do zhes bzhi brgya pa'i 'grel par 'byung ngo// don de dag kyang ji skad du/ shan ti pas mdzad pa'i dbu ma'i rgyan zhes bya ba'i bstan bcos las/ byams pa thogs med kyis gsungs shing// klu sgrub kyang ni bzhed pa yi// tshad ma lung dang ldan pa yi// bden pa gnyis po 'dir bshad bya// zhes dang/ jo bo mar me mdzad kyis/ klu sgrub dang ni thogs med kyang// grub pa'i mtha' yang mtshungs so zhes// rin chen 'byung gnas zhi ba smra// zhes 'byung ba yin no. *Ocean of Scriptural Statements and Reasoning*, vol. 15, 456–457.

159. *Ocean of Scriptural Statements and Reasoning*, vol. 15, 456–457.

Chapter 4

1. *Ocean of Scriptural Statements and Reasoning*, vol. 15, 460–461.

2. According to Shakya Chokden, no Buddhist tenets, Madhyamaka or other, accept relative phenomena as the mode of being and as truly established. *Ocean of Scriptural Statements and Reasoning*, vol. 15, 461.

3. Ibid., 462.

4. Ibid., 462–463.

5. kun rdzob kyi snang ba mtha' dag sems su khas len zhin/ gzung 'dzin gnyis med kyi ye shes khas mi len pa de la sems tsam pa zhes ming 'dogs pa de dang/ gnyis med kyi ye shes las ma gtogs pa'i don dam pa'i bden pa khas mi len pa de la rnam rdzun dbu ma pa zhes bya zhing/ de gnyis ka yang shes bya nang gir smra ba dang/ rnam par rig pa tsam du smra ba la khyad par med do. *Meaningful to Behold*, vol. 23, 364.

6. See the *Enjoyment Ocean of the Speech of the 'Seven Works,'* vol. 19, 474–476. Both reasons demonstrate that the apprehended and apprehender are of one substance, or, to put it differently, that whatever appears to mind has to be mind. The reason of simultaneous observation demonstrates that because objects and subjective minds that cognize them are always observed simultaneously, they are not two different substances. The reason of clarity and cognition demonstrates that all appearances have the entity of clarity and cognition—the two main charachteristics of knowing or mind. For details, see

Mipam, *Oral Instructions of Delighted Guru Mañjughoṣa*, in Doctor (tr.), *Speech of Delight*, 322 ff. Both of these two reasons can also be applied on the second of the four stages of yoga mentioned above (152), when all appearances are established as consciousness, but they will not be applicable on the level of the third stage, when the consciousness itself is negated.

7. chos kyi dbyings las ma gtogs pa// gang phyir chos med de yi phyir. *Ornament of Mahāyāna Sūtras*, D4020, sems tsam, phi, 18a. Skt.: dharmadhātu vinirmukto yasmād dharmo na vidyate. Sylvain Lévi, *Mahāyāna-sūtrālaṃkāra: exposé de la doctrine du grand véhicule selon le systéme Yogācāra*, vol. 1, p. 87.

8. chos kyi dbyings ni ma gtogs par// 'di ltar chos yod ma yin te. *Differentiation of the Middle and Extremes*, D4021, sems tsam, phi, 44b. The Sanskrit version of this passage provided in Gadjin M. Nagao's *Madhyāntavibhāga-Bhāṣya: A Buddhist Philosophical Treatise*, 67, is virtually identical to the one from the *Ornament of Mahāyāna Sūtras* in the previous note.

9. lugs 'di'i dbu ma ni/ gzung 'dzin gyi mtha' gnyis las grol ba'am rang rig rang gsal ba'o// lugs 'dir chos kyi dbyings las ma gtogs pa'i chos gzhan khas mi len pas na/ sems tsam pa dang khyad par shin tu che'o. *Wish Fulfilling Meru*, vol. 4, 213. For the fuller citation, see pp. 216 below.

10. spyir ni rnam par rig ces pa// rnam par rig las ma gtogs pa'i// bden pa gnyis po mi 'jog cing// gnyis su shes bya thams cad 'du// rnam rig smra la sems tsam dang// dbu mar smra ba'i dbye bas gnyis// sems tsam pas ni phyi rol don// med dang kun rdzob bden par 'chad// bag chags dbang gi der snang ba'i// rnam shes yod dang don dam bden// . . . rnam rig smra ba'i dbu ma pas// phyi rol don dang der snang gi// rnam shes gnyis ka kun rdzob bden// gnyis stong ye shes dam pa'i don. *Discourse Eliminating Mistakes*, vol. 13, 209. I cite the lines skipped in this passage and the lines that immediately follow it on p. 167–168 ff. where I am discussing how Shakya Chokden treats Satyākāravāda and Alīkākāravāda in the context of the Buddhist paths and stages.

11. See immedidately below. See also Chapter 5 section 3 for details of relationship between primordial mind and consciousness.

12. 'dzin pa zhes bya ba'i sgra ni gzung bar snang zhing de 'dzin pa'i blo nyid la bshad pa yin gyi gnyis med kyi ye shes la 'dzin pa'i tha snyad gsung rab nas mi 'byung ba. *Rain of Ambrosia*, 326. See also the *Appearance of the Sun*, vol. 19, 94.

13. See p. 163 below.

14. I take *gzugs 'dzin gnyis med* in the text as a misspelling of *gzung 'dzin gnyis med*.

15. theg pa chen po pa dag gis ni rnam shes la srid pa'i bde sdug tu snang ba'i rnam rig las ma gtogs pa'i bde sdug yod pa grub pa'i mthar mi 'chad la/ de'i tshe rnam rig la gnyis te/ kha phyir blta gzung rnam gyi cha dang/ nang blta 'dzin rnam gyi cha'o// dang po de shes rig tu khas len pa sems tsam pa'i grub mtha' la yin te/ gzugs 'dzin mig shes kyis gzugs mthong bar 'chad pa'i tshe/ gzugs med kyang mthong ba po sems nyid du khas len pa bzhin no// rnam brdzun dbu ma pa yan chad kyi ni/ gzugs

'dzin gnyis med ces bya ba grub pa'i mthar 'chad dgos pas 'dzin pa po shes pa lta ci smos/ dngos por 'dod pa ma yin no. *Rgyud bla ma'i bstan bcos kyi nges don sngon med nyi ma*, vol. 13, 120–121. Hereafter, *Previously Unseen Sun*.

16. *Enjoyment Ocean of the Speech of the 'Seven Works,'* vol. 19, 632.

17. rnam rdzun pa la ni 'dzin rnam las gzhan pa'i shes pa mi srid la/ de'i phyir gzung rnam nyams su myong ba'i 'dzin rnam mi srid/ rnam bden pa la srid pa de'i tshe na 'dzin rnam dang rang rig kho [*sic*] nang kho nar phyogs pa yin min gyi khyad par cung zad 'byed dgos par gsal lo. *Enjoyment Ocean of the Entirely Good Dharma*, vol. 18, 524–525.

18. rnam bden pa ltar na/ kha phyir blta'i shes pa rnams kyang/ rang gi gzung rnam la ma 'khrul ba nyid kyi phyir rang rig pa'i mngon sum yin la . . . rnam rdzun pa ltar na/ de 'dra de yang/ skra shad 'dzag snang gi dbang shes ltar/ 'khrul pa'i phyir mngon sum du mi rung bas/ rang rig ni gnyis med kyi shes pa kho na'o. Ibid., 477–478.

19. See Chapter 5 section 4 for more details on self-cognition, such as whether it should be understood as the "cognition of itself," etc.

20. For more details on this topic, see p. 214 ff.

21. *Enjoyment Ocean of the Speech of 'Seven Works,'* vol. 19, 646.

22. See also the *Appearance of Reasoning Defeating Bad Systems: Commentary on Difficult Points of the Extensive Treatise 'Commentary on Valid Cognition'* (*Rgyas pa'i bstan bcos tshad ma rnam 'grel gyi dka' 'grel rigs pa'i snang ba lugs ngan pham byed*), vol. 19, 309–310, 312; and the *Essence of Logic: Condensed Thatness of [Dignāga's] 'Sūtra on Valid Cognition' and [Dharmakīrti's] Textual System in the 'Seven Works'* (*Tshad ma'i mdo dang gzhung lugs sde bdun gyi de kho na nyid bsdus pa rtog ge'i snying po*), vol. 18, 111.

23. *'Phags pa thogs med zhabs kyi rtogs pa brjod pa nges don zla zer dkar po'i phreng bas snying gi gdung ba 'phrog byed*, vol. 16, 569–570. Hereafter, *Snatching Away the Heart's Torments*.

24. *Snatching Away the Heart's Torments*, vol. 16, 569.

25. Ibid., 569.

26. Ibid., 570.

27. In the *Ocean of Scriptural Statements and Reasoning*, vol. 15, 448, for example, Shakya Chokden treats the terms "dependent nature," "dualistically appearing consciousness," and "apprehended-aspect" together as synonyms.

28. *Ocean of Scriptural Statements and Reasoning*, vol. 14, 381, 388–389. Shakya Chokden provides the same explanation based on the *Summary of Mahāyāna* in his *Answers to Three Universally Known Questions from the 'One Hundred and Eight Questions on the 'Thorough Differentiation of the Three Types of Vows''* (*Sdom pa gsum gyi rab dbye'i dri ba brgya dang brgyad las kun la grags che ba'i dri ba gsum gyi lan gdabs pa*), vol. 17, 396. See also the *Appearance of the Sun*, vol. 19, 91–92, where Shakya Chokden argues that the clarity and cognition part of the dependent nature is not the dependent nature but the thoroughly established nature. The *Summary of Mahāyāna* passage reads: "The imaginary nature present in the dependent nature belongs to the thoroughly afflicted part. The thoroughly established nature present [in the dependent nature] belongs to the very purified part. As for the dependent nature itself, it

belongs to both parts (gzhan gya [*sic*] dbang gi ngo bo nyid la kun tu brtags pa'i ngo bo nyid yod pa ni kun nas nyon mongs pa'i char gtogs pa'o// yongs su grub pa'i ngo bo nyid yod pa ni rnam par byang ba'i char gtogs pa'o// gzhan gyi dbang de nyid ni de gnyi ga'i char gtogs pa)." *Mahāyānasaṃgraha, Theg pa chen po bsdus pa*, D4048, sems tsam, ri, 19b.

29. *Snatching Away the Heart's Torments*, vol. 16, 570.

30. That is, those obscurations of knowables which are conceptions of the apprehended (*shes bya'i sgrib pa gzung rtog*). This is contrasted to grasping at the self of the apprehender-phenomena (*'dzin pa chos kyi bdag 'dzin*) that can be eliminated only by the Madhyamaka view.

31. phyi rol don gyis stong pa yi// gsal rig dmigs par byas goms pas// ran sangs rgyas kyi lta thob ste// gzung ba chos kyi bdag 'dzin sel// lta ba de dang byang chub sems// zung du sbrel bas theg chen gyi// nges 'byed cha 'thun [*sic*, should read *mthun*] thob par gsungs. *Discourse Eliminating Mistakes*, vol. 13, 209. "Partial concordance with definite discrimination" is synonymous with the path of preparation.

32. gnyis stong ye shes rnam dag gi// dmigs par byas nas ring goms pa// byang chub sems dang zung 'brel las// sa bcu po ni mthar phyin byed. *Discourse Eliminating Mistakes*, vol. 13, 209.

33. srol gnyis po gnas skabs su rigs pas gtan la 'bebs tshul gyi khyad par yod pa dang/ sgom pas nyams su myong bya'i nges don zhig ngos 'dzin pa'i tshe 'dzin tshul la khyad par med pa'i tshul bshad par 'dod pas. *Rain of Ambrosia*, 390.

34. As will be demonstrated below, Shakya Chokden argues that not all Niḥsvabhāvavādins identify the definitive meaning experienced through meditation: Prāsaṅgika and Sautrāntika Mādhyamikas do not. Those who *do* identify it, i.e., Yogācāra Mādhyamikas on the Niḥsvabhāvavāda side, do it in agreement with Alīkākāravāda.

35. More specifically, on the level of the subsequent attainment, it is the descriptions provided by Prāsaṅgika and Svātantrika that differ from those of Alīkākāravāda. The Yogācāra Madhyamaka system on the Niḥsvabhāvavāda side agrees with the description given by Alīkākāravāda. See Chapter 3 section 5 and pp. 203–206 for details.

36. gnyis kas kyang mnyam gzhag tu lta bas spros pa gcod pa'i tshe mtshan ma gang yang yid la mi byed cing/ so sor rtog pa'i shes rab nyid kyang ye shes kyi mes bsreg dgos pa nyid du bzhed par mtshungs kyang/ rjes thob tu rang lugs su grub pa'i mtha' smra ba na/ gnyis med kyi ye shes yod par khas len pa dang/ de mi len pa'o// de bas na mnyam gzhag tu spros pa gcod tshul la khyad par med pa de'i phyir lugs gnyis ka'i lta ba la shes sgrib kyi bag chags spong nus mi nus kyi khyad par dbye nus pa ma yin no. *Thorough Clarification of Definitive Meaning of the 'Five Dharmas of Maitreya,'* vol. 11, 19–20.

37. See pp. 200–201, p. 374 note 118, as well as pp. 176–177 and 261.

38. That is, conventions applied in subsequent attainment after meditative equipoise. Shakya Chokden also calls them "subsequent conventions" (*rjes kyi tha snyad*; see *Rain of Ambrosia*, 335).

39. *Rain of Ambrosia*, 334–335.

40. As I show below (p. 210 ff.), this distinction is also important for explaining why adherents of the two systems do not treat each other as Mādhyamikas.

41. *Rain of* Ambrosia, 379.

42. dbu ma smra ba gnyis po'i gzhung las 'byung ba'i lta bas sgro 'dogs gcod pa'i tshul la ni/ gzhi chos can rgya che chung gyi khyad par shin tu che ba yin te/ ngo bo nyid med pa pas ni/ kun btags gzhan dbang yongs grub gsum ka ngo bo nyid kyis stong par gtan la phab nas/ de'i shul du stong pa nyid ces bya ba'i chos kyang khas mi len te/ de yang rang gi ngo bos stong par 'chad pa'i phyir ro// rnal 'byor spyod pa pas ni/ kun btags rang gi ngo bos stong pa dang/ gzhan dbang gzhan gi ngo bos stong pa dang/ de'i shul du rang gi ngo bos mi stong par lus pa ni/ gzhan dbang gi ngo bo'am yongs grub ces bya ba de nyid do// zhes 'chad pa'am yang na stong gzhi'i chos can ni gzhan dbang/ de gang gis stong pa'i dgag bya ni kun btags/ chos can de dgag bya des stong pa'i dngos po ni yongs grub ces 'chad do. *Rain of Ambrosia*, 333–334.

43. This should not be confused with the mode of severing proliferations within meditative equipoise in the citation on p. 169, which is the same in both Madhyamaka systems, and is just another term indicating the direct realization of ultimate reality.

44. The unchangeable thoroughly established nature is the ultimate reality underlying all phenomena. In the *Ocean of Scriptural Statements and Reasoning*, vol. 14, 385, Shakya Chokden describes it as the self-illuminating self-cognition of non-dual knowing (*gnyis med kyi shes pa rang rig rang gsal ba*) characterized by the dependent natures being empty of the imaginary natures. It is one of the two types of the thoroughly established nature, the other one being the non-erroneous thoroughly established nature (*phyin ci ma log pa'i yongs grub*). In the *Enjoyment Ocean of Scriptural Statements and Reasoning*, vol. 2, 134, Shakya Chokden identifies the former as "the factor of experience, clarity, and cognition characterized by the negation of that [imaginary nature on the basis of the dependent nature]" (*de bkag pas khyad par du byas pa'i myong ba gsal rig gi cha*). He identifies the latter as "the primordial mind of the meditative equipoise of āryas that directly realizes that [unchangeable thoroughly established nature]" (*de mngon sum du rtogs pa'i 'phags pa'i mnyam gzhag ye shes*).

45. That is, after the meditative equipoise directly realizing the ultimate view.

46. dbu ma de gnyis ka yang 'phags pa'i mnyam gzhag gis bsgom bya'am nyams su myons bya zhig khas len pa'i tshe na ngos 'dzin tshul ni mthun pa yin te/ rnal 'byor spyod pa pas ni 'gyur ba med pa'i yongs grub ces bya ba'i ming can chos dbyings ye shes sam gnyis su med pa'i ye shes de nyid don dam pa'i bden pa dngos dang/ bdag dam pa dang/ rtag brtan zhi ba g.yung drung dang/ bden par grub pa nyid du tha snyad 'dogs par byed la// cig shos kyis ni lta ba mthar thug gi rjes thob tu dgag bya bden grub med pa'i phyir bden med kyang yod pa ma yin no// zhes 'chad pas

dbu ma pa gnyis ka yang mnyam gzhag tu lta tsul ni mthun pa yin te/ rnal 'byor spyod pa'i lugs la yang lta ba'i ngor ni des gang la dmigs pa'i chos dbyings de yod med dang bden brdzun la sogs pa gang du yang mi 'dzin zhing/ mi 'dzin pa ltar de dan der ma grub pa'i phyir ro. *Rain of Ambrosia*, 334.

47. *Wish Fulfilling Meru*, vol. 4, 215–216.

48. Ibid., 216.

49. mtshan gyi rnam grangs snga ma can de dag ni/ bka' 'khor lo gsum pa'i mdo dang/ theg pa kun gyi rtse mor gyur pa'i rgyud sde dag las gsungs la/ mtshan gyi rnam grangs phyi ma can de dag ni/ gtso bor bka' 'khor lo bar par grags pa sher phyin gyi mdo'i dngos bstan dang/ gzhan yang mdo sde du ma dag las lan gcig ma yin par gsungs so. *Wish Fulfilling Meru*, vol. 4, 216.

50. gnyis ka yang khungs thub pa'i lung las gsungs shing/ mtha' yas pa'i yon tan gyi rten du 'gyur ba la snga ma de med du mi rung zhing de yang kun rdzob bden par khas len na/ ma rig pas bslad pa'i chos su thal bar 'gyur la/ med par dgag pa stong pa nyid rigs tshogs nas bshad pa'i rigs pas gtan la ma phebs na/ ji skad du/ de nyid mi shes 'khor ba dang// mya ngan 'das par rlom sems te// de nyid mthong na 'khor ba dang// myang ngan 'das par rlom sems med// ces bshad pa ltar mtshan 'dzin gyi rtog pa bzlog dka' ba'i phyir/ des na 'dir yang dbu ma'i tshul snga ma des skur 'debs kyi mtha' sel bar byed la/ phyi mas sgro 'dogs kyi mtha' sel bar byed do. *Wish Fulfilling Meru*, vol. 4, 216–217. My translation of the citation from the *Sixty Stanzas of Reasoning* is based on Shakya Chokden's text. For a slightly different version see *Yuktiṣaṣṭikākārikā*, *Rigs pa drug cu pa'i tshig le'ur byas pa zhes bya ba*, D3825, dbu ma, tsa, 20a: de nyid ma mthong 'jig rten dang// mya ngan 'das par rlom sems te// de nyid gzigs rnams 'jig rten dang// mya ngan 'das par rlom sems med. Skt.: saṃsāraṃ caiva nirvāṇaṃ manyante 'tattvadarśinaḥ/ na saṃsāraṃ na nirvāṇaṃ manyante tattvadarśinaḥ. In Christian Lindtner, *Nagarjuniana: Studies in the Writings and Philosophy of Nāgārjuna*, Indiske Studier 4 (Copenhagen: Akademisk Forlag, 1982), 104. For Lindtner's translation, see ibid., 105.

51. In this text, Shakya Chokden also calls them, respectively, "emptiness [arrived at] through severing superimpositions by listening and thinking" (*thos bsam gyis sgro 'dogs bcad pa'i stong nyid*) and "emptiness [realized through] experience" (*nyams myong gi stong nyid*). See the *Rain of Ambrosia*, 362.

52. stong pa nyid kyi ming can ni gnyis te/ sgra dang rtog pas btags pa'i stong nyid grub mtha' la grags pa dang/ gnas lugs su grub pa'i rang bzhin stong nyid rnal 'byor pas nyams su myong ba'o// dang po ni/ med par dgag pa dang blo chos dang ldog pa gzhan sel dang spyi mtshan du bzhag dgos pa nyid kyi phyir/ don dam pa'i bden par mi rung ste/ rnal 'byor mngon sum gyi myong byar mi rigs pa'i phyir yang ngo// gnyis pa de ni don dam pa'i bden par 'jog dgos te/ sangs rgyas kyi ye shes kyis kyang don de nyid gzigs pas don chos dang rtog pas gzhom par mi nus pas rdo rje dang don dam par don byed nus pas rang mtshan dang mi slu bas bden pa nyid kyi phyir. *Rain of Ambrosia*, 361–362. See also the *Appearance of the Sun*, vol. 19, 84.

53. med par dgag pa ni spyi mtshan nyid las ma 'das la/ de dngos yul du byed pa'i blo ni sgra don 'dzin pa'i rtog pa las gzhan med pas so so rang rig pa'i ye shes kyi spyod yul du 'gal. *Appearance of the Sun*, vol. 19, 92. See also the *Rain of Ambrosia*, 394.

54. According to the abbot Püntsok Namgyel (*phun tshogs rnam rgyal*) of Dzongsar (*rdzong sar*) monastery in Kham (*khams*), this refers to such special body-related advanced techniques mentioned in the *Hevajra* teachings as pressing points of the neck, yantra yoga (*'khrul 'khor*), and so forth. (Personal communication.)

55. gnas tshul de rtogs pa'i thabs ni gnyis te/ phar phyin pas thos bsam gyi sgo nas dang/ gsang sgnags pas rang byin rlabs dang lus kyi byed bcings dang dbang gi rim pa sogs las so// dang po la yang gnyis te/ rnal 'byor spyod pa pas gzung 'dzin gnyis po rang gi ngo bos stong zhing gnyis med kyi ye shes gzhan gyis stong par gtan la phab nas dang/ ngo bo nyid med pa pas shes bya thams cad rang gi ngo bos stong par gtan la phab nas so// tshul de gnyis ka yang 'jug yul don dam pa'i bden pa la mi slu ba yin te/ de ltar gtan la phab nas zhugs pas don dam pa de nyid nyams su myong ba'i rnal 'byor mngon sum mngon du 'gyur ba'i phyir. *Rain of Ambrosia*, 362.

56. rnal 'byor spyod pa pa ltar na/ dgag bya bdag gnyis bkag pa'i dngos po kho na la 'chad la/ rang stong du smra ba ltar na/ dbag gnyis bkag tsam gyi med par dgag pa'i cha'o. *Great Path of Ambrosia of Emptiness*, vol. 4, 114.

57. 'dir nges don mthar thug pa ni bde bar gshegs pa'i snying po zhes bya ba'i ming can sems rang bzhin gyis 'od gsal ba de nyid yin la/ 'di yang ma yin par dgag pa yin gyi/ med par dgag pa ni ma yin. *Ocean of Scriptural Statements and Reasoning*, vol. 14, 393.

58. *Appearance of the Sun*, vol. 19, 85.

59. *Ocean of Scriptural Statements and Reasoning*, vol. 15, 461.

60. On the twofold division of mind into the ultimate and relative mind, see p. 158 above.

61. *Rain of Ambrosia*, 348.

62. *Rain of Ambrosia*, 334.

63. mdor na dbu ma gnyis ka'i lugs la yang don dam pa la smra bsam brjod med kyis khyab par ni rang rang gi gzhung na gsal zhing/ de ltar gsal ba de'i phyir don dam pa'i bden pa yin ngo shes pa zhig 'phags pa rnams kyi rang rig pa'i ye shes kyis myong yang/ rjod byed kyi sgra dang rtog pas ni 'di zhes ngos bzung bar mi nus. *Rain of Ambrosia*, 335.

64. de ltar na'ang tha snyad la ma brten par rtogs mi nus pas/ tha snyad kyi dus su bden pa de'i mtshan gzhi lung rigs dang mi 'gal ba zhig ngos 'dzin na gzung 'dzin gnyis su med pa'i ye shes de nyid la ngos 'dzin dgos pa yin te/ dbu ma thal rang gi gzhung du ni/ don dam bden pa mtshan nyid pa de'i mtshan gzhi ngos bzung ba med cing/ byams chos rjes 'brang dang bcas par ni/ de yin ngo shes pa'i mtshan gzhi ye shes de nyid la gsal bar bshad pa'i lung las dang/ rigs pa yang/ tshad mas ma gzhal ba na don dam pa'i bden par mi rung la/ tshad ma la yang rjes dpag gis gzhal ba ni/ spyi mtshan du 'chad pa'i phyir don dam pa'i bden par mi rung zhing/ mngon sum gyis gzhal bya la ni rang mtshan gyis khyab pa'i phyir snga ma kho na'o. *Rain of Ambrosia*, 335–336.

65. *Rain of Ambrosia*, 377.

66. There are no influential sūtric works on Madhyamaka attributed to Mañjuśrī, the embodiment of wisdom. This divine figure rather operates "behind the scenes," so to say, appearing in visions to different thinkers, such as Shakya Chokden himself, and encouraging their understanding of Madhyamaka.

67. See, for example, Nāgārjuna's *Praise of the Mind-Vajra* (*Cittavajrastava, Sems kyi rdo rje'i bstod pa*), D1121, bstod tshogs, ka, 69b–70a.

68. srol 'byed snga phyi gnyis kas bka' tha ma'i nges don don dam pa'i bden pa de ngos 'dzin pa na/ theg chen 'phags pa'i mnyam gzhag ye shes kyi myong byar gyur ba'i gzhom du med pa sems kyi rdo rje de nyid la 'chad par mthun la. *Rain of Ambrosia*, 390.

69. 'khor lo bar pa'i dngos bstan gyi stong pa nyid ni/ srol dan pos mthar kun rdzob kho nar bshad pas don dam pa'i bden pa dang mnyam gzhag gi myong byar 'chad pa lta ci smos/ lugs der 'khor lo bar pa'i dngos bstan gyi sgom 'chad pa na/ sems kyi rdo rje la sgom bya nyid du mi 'chad par/ sgom rgyu ci yang med pa la sgom du btags pa'o. *Rain of Ambrosia*, 390. For more details, see the *Rain of Ambrosia*, 329, 340, 380–381.

70. That is, the metaphorical ultimate.

71. srol 'byed gnyis pas kyang/ 'khor lo bar ba'i bstan bya'i gtso bor gyur pa'i stong nyid ni 'khor lo phyi mas gtan la phab pa'i ye shes de nyid yin la/ bar pa'i dngos bstan la yod pa'i gzhan dbang kun dtags kyis stong pa'i med dgag gi cha de ni myong bya lta ci smos/ don dam pa'i bden pa tsam du'ang mi bzhed de/ spyi mtshan yin pa dang/ thos bsam gyi rtog pas sgro btags pa'i phyir/ des na don dam pa'i bden pa zhig ngos 'dzin pa'i tshe na srol gnyis ka mthun no. *Rain of Ambrosia*, 390–391.

72. For more details on how, in Nāgārjuna's system, one and the same phenomenon can be gradually posited first as ultimate and then as relative truth, see the *Drop of Ambrosia of Definitive Meaning: Entering Essential Points of the Two Truths* (*Bden pa gnyis kyi gnad la 'jug pa nges don bdud rtsi'i thigs pa*), vol. 4, 376–381, translated in the *Three Texts on Madhyamaka*, 37–41.

73. Shakya Chokden is aware that Tsongkhapa's followers treat Asaṅga as a Prāsaṅgika on grounds that in his commentary on the *Sublime Continuum*, Asaṅga interpreted the intent (*dgongs pa*) of the *Sublime Continuum* as the Prāsaṅgika view (*Meaningful to Behold*, vol. 23, 360). Nevertheless, Shakya Chokden strongly disagrees with such an approach, arguing that neither did Asaṅga express the Prāsaṅgika view in that commentary nor could he be a Prāsaṅgika Mādhyamika because of any other reasons. For details, see the *Rain of Ambrosia*, 419–421, where Shakya Chokden also explains that Asaṅga cannot be a Prāsaṅgika because his life predated the formation of the Prāsaṅgika system by Candrakīrti.

74. See p. 127 ff. above.

75. It is interesting to note that this position runs contrary to Tsongkhapa's approach in his *Essence of Good Explanations: Treatise Differentiating the Interpretive and the Definitive Meaning* (*drang ba dang nges pa'i don rnam par 'byed pa'i bstan bcos legs bshad snying po*, Mundgod: Drepung Loseling Library, 1991), where Tsongkhapa tries to prove exactly the opposite—that the

ultimate reality in both Niḥsvabhāvavāda and Yogācāra/Cittamātra systems has to be identified as a non-affirming negation, and in the latter case that non-affirming negation is the thoroughly established nature described as the dependent natures being empty of the imaginary natures. For more details, see Hopkins, *Emptiness in the Mind-Only School of Buddhism*, 377 ff. (for the critical Tibetan edition) and 92 ff. (for the annotated English translation). Tsongkhapa's position in its turn was at least partly formed in response to the interpretation of Yogācāra philosophy by Dölpopa criticized in the same text. For an exhaustive analysis of Tsongkhapa's interpretation of Yogācāra/Cittamātra, see Hopkins, *Reflections on Reality*. For the complete English translation of the *Essence of Good Explanations*, see Robert Thurman, *Central Philosophy of Tibet: A Study and Translation of Jey Tsongkhapa's Essence of True Eloquence* (Princeton: Princeton University Press, 1984).

76. *Rain of Ambrosia*, 387.

77. Ibid., 327.

78. rnal 'byor spyod pa pas ni/ bka' tha ba'i [*sic*] dngos bstan gyi nges don ni gzhan dbang kun btags kyis stong pa'i ye shes de nyid yin la/ de nyid bka' bar pa'i bstan bya'i gtso bo nyid du yang dag par rdzogs pa'i sangs rgyas nyid kyis gsungs so. *Rain of Ambrosia*, 336.

79. *Rain of Ambrosia*, 337.

80. *Ocean of Scriptural Statements and Reasoning*, vol. 15, 521–522.

81. thogs med zhabs kyis spros pa kun bral ba'i// gnyis med ye shes rang rig rang gsal ba// don dam mthar thug sangs rgyas snying po zhes// chos 'khor gnyis kyi nges don yin par bkral. *Profound Thunder*, 310. As the following discussion will make clear, according to Shakya Chokden, primordial mind is not equivalent with the buddha-essence: while all beings have the former, only Mahāyāna āryas have the latter.

82. *Rain of Ambrosia*, 398.

83. *Āryasaṃdhinirmocananāmamahāyānasūtra*, *'Phags pa dgongs pa nges par 'grel pa zhes bya ba theg pa chen po'i mdo*, D0106, mdo sde, ca, 1b–55b.

84. *Āryasarvabuddhaviśayāvatārajñānālokālaṃkāranāmamahāyānasūtra*, *'Phags pa sangs rgyas thams cad kyi yul la 'jug pa'i ye shes snang ba'i rgyan ces bya ba theg pa chen po'i mdo*, D100, mdo sde, ga, 276a–305a.

85. *Āryamahāparinirvāṇanāmamahāyānasūtra*, *'Phags pa yongs su mya ngan las 'das pa chen po'i mdo*, D119, mdo sde, nya-ta.

86. *Rain of Ambrosia*, 399.

87. *Sangs rgyas kyi snying po'i rnam bshad mdo rgyud snying po*, vol. 13, 124–136. Hereafter, *Essence of Sūtras and Tantras*.

88. *Golden Lancet*, vol. 6, 510.

89. For further details, see my "Reburying the Treasure—Maintaining the Continuity."

90. de bzhin gshegs pa'i rang bzhin gang// 'gro ba 'di yi rang bzhin yin// de bzhin gshegs pa'i rang bzhin med. *Wisdom: Root Stanzas on Madhyamaka*, D3824, dbu ma, tsa, 13b. See *Rain of Ambrosia*, 399. Skt.: tathāgato yatsvabhāvas tatsvabhāvam idaṃ jagat/ tathāgato niḥsvabhāvo. In Jan W.

de Jong (ed.), *Nāgārjuna Mūlamadhyamakakārikāḥ* (Madras: India, The Adyar Library and Research Centre, 1977), 31.

91. That is, the *Dharmas of Maitreya* other than the *Ornament of Clear Realizations*.

92. These two are the enjoyment-body (*longs spyod rdzogs pa'i sku, saṃbhogakāya*) and the emanation-body (*sprul pa'i sku, nirmāṇakāya*).

93. lta ba gzhan stong gi rigs pas sgro 'dogs bcad cing/ sgom pa so sor rang gis rig pa'i ye shes la mnyam par gzhag nas/ spyod pa bsod nams kyi tshogs dang zung du sbrel bas 'bras bu ngo bo nyid kyi sku yon tan kun tshang dang/ gzhan snang du gzugs kyi sku gnyis lhun gyis grub bo zhes 'chad pa ni/ gsal stong gzung 'dzin bral ba'i rig pa tsam// chos rnams kun gyi gnas lugs yin shes nas// mtha' yas bsod nams tshogs dang zung 'brel bas// sku gsum lhun gyis grub pa thogs med gzhung// ces pa'o. *Rain of* Ambrosia, 391–392; *Profound Thunder*, 309. Emphasis mine.

94. This approach does not undermine the sharp distinction between the views posited through reasoning and realized directly that has been addressed above.

95. rigs tshogs su ni thos bsam gyi sgro 'dogs gcod pa'i dbang du byas la/ bstod pa'i tshogs su ni sgom pas nyams su blang ba'i dbang du byas pa'o. *Rain of Ambrosia*, 331.

96. 'phags mchog de yi bshad tshul rnam gnyis po// rigs pa'i tshogs kyis 'khor lo gnyis pa'i mdo// ji bzhin sgra yis bshad dang bstod tshogs su// 'khor lo tha ma'i ngas [*sic*] don 'chad tshul gyis// rnam par phye'o. *Profound Thunder*, 309. *ngas* in the root text is a misspelling of *nges*, which is spelled correctly in the *Rain of Ambrosia*, 396.

97. klu sgrub zhabs kyi gzhung nas 'byung ba'i stong pa nyid dang/ de bzhin nyid dang/ chos nyid ces bya ba'i ming can ni gnyis te/ spros pa'i tshogs mtha' dag rigs pas bkag pa'i med par dgag pa dang/ spros pa'i mtha' gang du yang mi 'dzin pa'i ye shes gzhi lam 'bras bu'i gnas skabs thams cad du rgyun chags pa'o// dang po ni/ 'khor lo bar pa'i dngos bstan yin la/ de sgrub byed kyi rigs pa mtha' yas pa ni rigs tshogs kyi dngos bstan yin no// phyi ma de la'ang gnyis te/ spros pa'i mtshan ma 'gog byed kyi rigs pa sngon du btang nas de mi 'dzin pa dang/ dbang dang byin rlabs sogs kyi nus pas spros med du song ba'o// de gnyis ni go rim bzhin du/ 'khor lo tha ma la'ang phar phyin theg pa'i dbang du byas pa dang/ sngags lugs kyi dbang du byas pa'i cha de so so'i nges don du bshad do. *Rain of Ambrosia*, 396. This division of primordial mind into two types should not be taken as exhaustive. In general, emptiness or reality cannot be created anew. In particular, according to Shakya Chokden, primordial mind persists throughout *all* levels of the basis, path, and result, and it never grasps at extremes of proliferations because it is always nonconceptual. Therefore, the two divisions of primordial mind provided in the passage indicate only those types of primordial mind that are "made manifest," i.e., actually realized by Mahāyāna practitioners.

98. For more details on how Shakya Chokden matches the views of Alīkākāravāda and Tantra, see Chapter 5 section 5.

99. *Rain of Ambrosia*, 327.

100. Ibid.

101. rnal 'byor spyod pa pa ltar/ stong pa nyid ces bya ba'i chos rnal 'byor pa'i mngon sum gyis nyams su myong bya zhig tha snyad du'ang khas len pa ma yin te/ med par dgag pa ni ldog pa gzhan sel las ma 'das pas mngon sum lta zhog// rtog med kyi shes pa tsam gyi'ang yul du mi rung ba'i phyir/ des na stong pa nyid thos bsam gyis gtan la phab pa'i don la mnyam par gzhag pa'i shes rab kyis ni stong mi stong la sogs pa'i mtshan ma gang du yang mi 'dzin no. *Rain of Ambrosia*, 327–328.

102. mnyam gzhag tu yul gyi mtshan ma ci yang ma mthong ba la don dam pa mthong ngo zhes tha snyad btags pa yin gyi/ rang gi lugs mthar thug pa na don dam pa'i bden pa zhes bya ba'i mtshan gzhi yang khas mi len na/ de mngon sum du rtogs pa lta ga la yod/ de'i shes byed kyang/ stong pa nyid dang/ rang bzhin gyi myang 'das dang/ chos kyi dbyings sogs sgra dang rtog pa'i yul du byar rung ba de thams cad ni kun rdzob kyi bden pa kho na ste/ rnam par dpyad pa'i dpung mi bzod pa'i phyir dang/ sgra rtog gi yul las ma 'das pa'i phyir. *Rain of Ambrosia*, 328.

103. gnas skabs su bden pa gnyis kyi rnam gzhag 'jog pa'i tshe don dam pa'i bden par bshad pa de dag kyang rnam grangs pa dang mthun pa don dam tsam du 'chad kyi/ rnam grangs pa ma yin pa'i don dam zhes bya ba ni rigs pa'i tshogs 'grel ba dang bcas pa nas mi 'chad do// mthar de rtogs pa'i ye shes kyang khas mi len. *Rain of Ambrosia*, 328–329.

104. lta ba rang stong gi rigs pas sgro 'dogs bcad cing/ sgom pa yul dmigs med dang yul can 'dzin med kyi ngang la mnyam par bzhag nas rjes thob sa bcu'i rim pas sbyin sogs bsod nams kyi tshogs la 'grus par byas pa las/ 'bras bu spros pa thams cad nye bar zhi ba'i chos kyi sku dang/ gzhan snang du gzugs kyi sku lhun gyis grub bo zhes 'chad pa ni/ rgya chen bsod nams tshogs la mi lhod par// chos kun ngo bos stong pa'i rigs pa yis// 'dzin med ngang la mnyam par gzhag byas pas// sku gsum lhun gyis grub pa klu sgrub gzhung// zhes pa'o. *Rain of Ambrosia*, 391; *Profound Thunder*, 309. Emphasis mine.

105. *Rain of Ambrosia*, 330.

106. de nyid tha snyad du don dam pa'i bden pa mtshan nyid par khas len dgos pa yin te/ 'phags mchog rnams kyi rnal 'byor mngon sum gyi myong bya yin pa'i phyir dang/ chos kyi dbyings dang/ khams bde bar gshegs pa'i snying po dang/ sems kyi rdo rje nyid du 'chad dgos pa'i phyir. *Rain of Ambrosia*, 330. Note the difference between the buddha-essence/sugata-essence on the one hand and the element of sugata-essence on the other. We know already that according to Shakya Chokden, only Mahāyāna āryas have the buddha-essence or sugata-essence. On the other hand, he argues that *all* sentient beings have the element of sugata-essence. For details, see the *Ascertainment of the Dharma-Sphere*, vol. 7, 310.

107. lta ba rang stong gi rigs pas sgro 'dogs bcad pa mthar thug pa'i 'og tu/ sgom pa spros bral rtogs pa'i ye shes kyis don dam byang chub kyi sems dri ma sbyang ba'i gzhir bzhag nas thabs shes zung 'brel du nyams su blangs pas sbyangs 'bras sku gsum lhun gyis grub pa yang klu sgrub yab

sras kyi dgongs pa gnyis pa yin no zhes 'chad pa ni/ chos kun spros dang bral ba'i rigs pa la// ma rmongs mkhas pa rnams la sems kyi dbyings// don dam sems kyi rdo rjer 'chad pa yang// klu sgrub zhabs kyi 'chad tshul gnyis pa yin// zhes pa. *Rain of* Ambrosia, 392; *Profound Thunder*, 309.

108. bstod pa'i tshogs kyi lung tshad mar byas nas/ ngo bo nyid med par smra ba'i gzhung du yang/ chos kyi dbyings kyi ye shes nyid rnal 'byor pa'i mngon sum gyi myong byar gyur pa'i nges pa'i don nyid du bsgrub par bya ba yin no. *Rain of Ambrosia*, 323.

109. sa skya pa ni/ ngo bo nyid med smra'i gzhung nas don dam bden pa go chod ma bshad par bzhed pa. *Seventeen Wondrous Answers*, vol. 23, 421.

110. *Rain of Ambrosia*, 393. As we know already, these different modes of setting in equipoise do not affect the possibility of accessing the same nondual primordial mind, which is beyond all sounds and concepts.

111. *Rain of Ambrosia*, 394.

112. spros bral med dgag gi cha dang/ spros pa dang bral ba'i sems rang bzhin gyis 'od gsal ba gnyis las/ dang po 'khor lo bar ba'i dngos bstan dang/ gnyis pa de 'khor lo phyi ma'i bstan bya'i gtso bo yin pas/ don dam pa'i mtshan gzhi mi 'dzin pa'i skabs phar zhog// 'dzin phyin chad phyi ma kho nar nges te/ dang po de ni ldog pa gzhan sel dang/ spyi mtshan dang/ blos rnam bcad du rtogs bya kho nar nges pas sangs rgyas kyi ye shes kyis mngon sum du ma gzigs pa'i phyir. *Rain of Ambrosia*, 394–395.

113. Literally, "there will be no confusion with respect to contradiction" (*'gal ba la mi 'khrul bar 'gyur*). *Rain of Ambrosia*, 395.

114. rigs tshogs su rang bzhin gyi myang 'das lta bu kun rdzob tu bshad pa de/ rlom tshod la rang bzhin myang 'das dngos su rlom yang/ song tshod de'i gzhan sel nyid yin te/ sgra rtog gis tha snyad du byas pa'i phyir/ des na sgra rtog gi dngos yul zhig kun rdzob tu 'chad pa dang/ mngon sum gyi myong bya gcig don dam par bshad pa gnyis la ni 'gal ba ci yang yod pa ma yin te/ rang bzhin myang 'das zhes pa lta bu ming gcig kyang don so sor nges pa'i phyir. *Rain of Ambrosia*, 395.

115. de ltar na 'phags pas rigs tshogs sngar mdzad cing/ de'i rjes su bstod pa'i tshogs mdzad par grub pa yin te/ lta ba la sgro 'dogs gcod byed kyi rigs pa sngon du song nas/ des gtan la phab pa'i don nyams su len rigs pa'i phyir dang/ rigs tshogs ni bka' bar pa'i dngos bstan sgra ji bzhin pa nyid du rigs pas gtan la 'bebs byed yin la/ bstod tshogs ni bka' 'khor lo tha ma nas 'byung ba'i nges don de nyid chos kyi sku sgrub pa'i gzhir bshad nas/ rnal 'byor pas nyams su blangs bya'i yul du 'chad pa'i phyir. *Rain of Ambrosia*, 332.

116. rigs tshogs su thos bsam gyi shes pas sgro 'dogs bcad pa de ni/ nyams su myong bya la mtshan 'dzin gyi rtog pa 'gog pa'i ched yin la/ de ltar bkag nas chos kyi dbyings nyams su myong byar bstan pa la nyes pa ci yang yod pa ma yin. *Rain of Ambrosia*, 331.

117. 'o na lta bas gzhan zhig gtan la phab nas sgom pas gzhan zhig nyams su blangs par 'gyur ba ma yin nam zhe na ma yin te/ lta bas spros pa'i tshogs mtha' dag bkag nas bsgoms pa na/ goms byed kyi blos chos kyi dbyings kyi ye shes nyid las gzhan nyams su myong byar rigs pa ci yang yod pa ma yin pa'i phyir. *Rain of Ambrosia*, 332.

118. rigs pas gtan la gang phab pa// de nyid nyams su myong bya zhes// zer ba 'di pa'i lugs min te// de'i gsung kun dang 'gal phyir ro. *Mirror Clarifying Individual Texts*, vol. 23, 84–89. See also the *Appearance of the Sun*, vol. 19, 95, where Shakya Chokden objects to Tsongkhapa's criticism of positing one thing through listening and then meditating on something else (that criticism being backed with the example given by Potopa Rinchensel (*po to pa rin chen gsal*, 1027–1105) about heading in one direction but riding the horse in another). See also the *Great Path Compressing the Two Chariot Ways into One*, vol. 12, 262, where Shakya Chokden explains that this position criticized by Potopa is not treated as faulty in the system of Haribhadra, because Haribhadra accepts it.

119. *Rain of Ambrosia*, 377–378.

120. See also the *Rain of Ambrosia*, 329, 348, 390, etc.

121. rigs tshogs kyi dngos bstan la nges don med dgag gi cha las gzhan du ma bshad pas ci yang mi sgom pa la stong nyid sgom pa dang/ ci yang ma mthong ba la de kho na nyid mthong bar 'chad pa yin gyi de las gzhan du mi 'chad la/ de nyid legs ldan 'byed dang zla ba'i gzhung dang spyod 'jug na gsal lo. *Rain of Ambrosia*, 380–381.

122. so sor rang rig pa'i ye shes spyod yul dang bcas pa ni legs ldan 'byed dang/ zla ba gnyis kas 'bad nas bkag pa. *Rain of Ambrosia*, 331.

123. ngo bo nyid med par smra ba'i slob dpon kha cig lta ba rang stong du bshad nas/ sgom pa so sor rang rig gi ye shes khas len pa ji snyed yod pa de dag gis ni bka' tha ma nges don mthar thug tu khas blangs pa yin te/ bka' bar pa'i dngos bstan gyi nges don ni rnal 'byor mngon sum gyi nyams su myong byar mi 'thad pa'i phyir. *Rain of Ambrosia*, 381.

124. nges don gyi mthar thug ye shes la 'chad pa 'di ni 'phags pa thogs med bzhed pa'i dbu ma 'dir ma zad/ ngo bo nyid med par smra ba'i nang gi rnal 'byor spyod pa'i dbu ma pa dag kyang bzhed pa yin te/ dper na slob dpon 'phags seng bzhin no. *Rain of Ambrosia*, 399.

125. 'phags seng gnyis ka yang lta ba gtan la 'bebs tshul thal rang ltar bzhed kyang/ bka' bar pa'i shugs bstan gyi nges don dang sgom pas nyams len gyi nges don ye shes la 'chad pa yin. *Rain of Ambrosia*, 399–400.

126. *Seventeen Wondrous Answers*, vol. 23, 422.

127. de nyid rje btsun gyi dgongs par gnas pa yin te/ rgyan gyis sher phyin gyi mdo'i brjod bya'i gtso bo sbas don mngon rtogs kyi rim pa de dngos bstan stong nyid kyi rim pa dang sbyar nas bshad pa'i phyir. *Rain of Ambrosia*, 400.

128. thogs med mched kyis thal rang gi// lugs de dbu mar mi 'chad cing// des kyang de lugs der mi 'chad. *Sngags lugs kyi zab rgya'i gnad rnam par gtan la dbab pa rdo rje 'chang gi dgongs pa rab gsal chos mtshan nyi shu rtsa gcig pa*, in *'Hundred and Eight Dharma Sections' Treatise* (*Chos tshan brgya dang brgyad pa zhes bya ba'i bstan bcos*), vol. 13, 331. Hereafter, *Thorough Clarification of Vajradhara's Intent*. Shakya Chokden is well aware that the Prāsaṅgika system developed *after* Asaṅga's time, and furthermore uses this fact in his argument against Geluk's opinion that Asaṅga held the Prāsaṅgika view (see p. 369 note 73). Therefore, in contexts like this one, "that system of

Prāsaṅgikas and Svātantrikas" refers to the Niḥsvabhāvavāda system based on the explicit teachings of the second dharmacakra that only later developed into Prāsaṅgika and Svātantrika.

129. *Wish Fulfilling Meru*, vol. 4, 216, 228.

130. gal te gzhung lugs de dag nas byung ba'i nges don rje btsun byams pas dbu mar bshad kyang/ legs ldan 'byed dang/ zla grags kyis dbu ma'i lugs ma yin par bshad pa de gnyis dbang btsan no snyam na ni/ 'o na de dag gi bshad pa la yang thogs med zhabs kyis mdo drangs nas/ skur 'debs kyi lta bar bshad cing/ rgya gar ba'i man ngag gi gzhung dang/ mdo sde dag na ngo bo nyid med par smra bas 'chad pa'i stong pa nyid de la/ bems po'i stong pa nyid dang/ chad pa'i stong pa nyid dang/ thal byung gi stong pa nyid ces/ nges don gyi ngos 'dzin tshul phyogs gnyis ka la/ tshad ldan gyi gzhung dag na dgag pa phyogs re ba re mdzad yod pas na dgongs don zab mo dag la ma brtags par phan tshun du gcig gis cig shos 'gog par nus pa ma yin no. *Wish Fulfilling Meru*, vol. 4, 244.

131. That is, non-tantric Mahāyāna systems.

132. shing rta'i srol mi cig pa gzhan gyis gzhan du bshad pas der khas len dgos pa ma yin te de lta na shing rta'i srol so so ba dag 'chol bar thal ba'i phyir dang/ theg pa chen po tsam dang rdo rje'i theg pa sas [*sic*] rgyas kyi bka' ma yin par smra ba dag kyang yod pa'i phyir dang/ rnal 'byor gong mas 'og ma la gnod ces zer mod kyang dbu ma'i tshul 'di gnyis la gong 'og gi khyad par dbye dka' ba yin. *Appearance of the Sun*, vol. 19, 94.

133. See pp. 110 and 137 ff. See also p. 262 ff.

134. de la 'jig rten phal pa ni// rnal 'byor 'jig rten gyis gnod cing// rnal 'byor pa yang blo khyad kyis// gong ma gong ma rnams kyis gnod. *Engaging in the Bodhisattva Deeds*, D3871, dbu ma, la, 31a. Skt.: tatra prākṛtako loko yogilokena bādhyate// bādhyante dhīviśeṣeṇa yogino 'py uttarottaraiḥ. In Sharma, *Śāntideva's* Bodhicharyāvatāra, 368–369. English translation from Sanskrit: Kate Crosby and Andrew Skilton, *The Bodhicaryāvatāra* (Oxford: Oxford University Press, 1995), 115.

135. *Ocean of Scriptural Statements and Reasoning*, 14, 381–382.

136. [Nameless], vol. 17, 417.

137. On the term "nirākāra," see p. 331 note 17.

138. Note at the same time that it is true only for earlier thinkers. In the *Answers to Questions Issuing from the 'Differentiation of the Two Modes,'* vol. 17, 414–416, Shakya Chokden criticizes what he sees as misinterpretations of Cittamātra and Alīkākāravāda by Rendawa. Also, it should be mentioned that Shakya Chokden does not share opinions of *all* early thinkers on this matter. For example, in the *Meaningful to Behold*, vol. 23, 388, he explains that although the system described by Puṇḍarīka's *Stainless Light*'s words "Free from the apprehended and apprehender// Consciousness exists [as] the ultimate" (cited on p. 147) is not Cittamātra within the four types of proponents of tenets, earlier Tibetan thinkers explained it as Cittamātra because that system accepts primordial mind as true and does not accept reasoning positing it as truthless. As we know already, Shakya Chokden himself does not share this view.

139. *Meaningful to Behold*, vol. 23, 366.

140. gal te 'o na dbu ma 'di gnyis la zab rgyas kyi khyad par ci zhe na/ chos thams cad ngo bo nyid med par gtan la 'bebs pa'i rigs pa ni cig shos rgyas la bsgom pas nyams su myong bar bya ba'i nges don ni lugs 'dir zab pa yin te/ gnyis su med pa'i ye shes kho na bsgom byung gi nyams su myong bya nyid du 'chad pa ni rdo rje'i theg pa dag dang ches shin tu mthun pa'i phyir lugs 'di zab pa yin no. *Appearance of the Sun*, vol. 19, 95.

141. de de ltar 'grel ba ni thos bsam gyis sgro 'dogs gcod pa'i dbang du byas la/ sgom byung gi myong byar 'chad pa de ni spyod pa nyams len gyi dbang du byas pa yin pas lta spyod kyi grub mtha' 'jog lugs mi mtshungs. *Rain of Ambrosia*, 337–338.

142. As has been explained above (201 ff.), what distinguishes Candrakīrti and Bhāviveka from Yogācāra Mādhyamikas on the Niḥsvabhāvavāda side is that the latter accept the non-dual primordial mind when describing ultimate reality experienced through meditation, while the former do not accept it because they do not give any descriptions of such reality in their sūtric writings.

143. mdo 'ga zhig dang thogs med mched kyis ngo bo nyid med pa pa la chad smra ba zer ba yang/ sgom pas nyams su myong bya zhig ngos ma bzung ba la bsams pa yin gyi/ rigs pas gtan la 'bebs tshul la klan ka mdzad pa ma yin te/ rigs pa ni chos kyi graga pa yang ngo bo nyid med pa pa ltar bzhed pa'i phyir ro. *Meaningful to Behold*, vol. 23, 364.

144. As has been mentioned above (p. 115), Shakya Chokden believes that this reasoning is the same for both Alīkākāravāda and Niḥsvabhāvavāda, and was used by Dharmakīrti (p. 154).

Chapter 5

1. See p. 369 note 75 above. The view of Changkya Rölpé Dorjé is an exception from this "rule." As Jeffrey Hopkins demonstrates in his *Reflections on Reality*, 246 ff., Changkya treats ultimate reality in Cittamātra as an affirming negation.

2. For the comparison and analysis of divergent positions on the relationship between ultimate reality and mental states, see my "Encountering Ineffability—Counting Ineffability."

3. See, for example, his *Moonrays of Essential Points: Abridged Essence of Incorporation into Experience* (*Nyams su len pa'i rim pa snying po mdor bsdus pa gnad kyi zla zer*), in The Collected Works of Rong-ston Shak-kya Rgyal-mtsen, vol. B, *kha*, Dehra Dun, India: Sakya College, 1999), 562–565, and other meditative instructions in the same volume.

4. mdor na theg pa chen po pa dag las/ rnal 'byor spyod pa pa dag dang/ ngo bo nyid med pa pa dang/ rdo rje theg pa pa rnams su'i lugs yin kyang rung ste/ chos kyi bdag med rtogs pa'i lta ba de'i dngos kyi rig byar gyur pa'i nges don zhig khas len phyin chad stong pa nyid kyi ngo bo ye shes la ngos 'dzin pas khyab pa yin. *Rain of Ambrosia*, 374.

5. yod na chos dbyings yin pas khyab pa 'di ngo bo nyid med par smra ba kho na'i lugs sam zhe na/ de kho nar ma zad/ sems tsam rnam rdzun par grags pa de'i yang mthar thug gi lugs te/ ji skad du/ chos kyi dbyings las ma gtogs pa// 'di ltar chos yod ma yin te// zhes rgyan dang/ dbus mtha' gnyis ka las 'byung bas so. *Sdom pa gsum gyi rab dbye'i dri ba brgya dang brgyad las kun la grags che ba'i dri ba gsum gyi lan gdabs pa*, vol. 17, 396. The actual passage referred to here varies slightly between the *Ornament of Mahāyāna Sūtras* and the *Differentiation of the Middle and Extremes*. See p. 160 above.

6. theg pa chen po'i dbu ma 'chad tshul la gnyis te/ rang stong gi sgo nas dang/ gzhan stong gi sgo nas 'chad tshul lo// dang po ni/ spros pa'i mtha' thams cad bkag pa'i shul na dbus ma zhes bya ba'i dngos po ci yang lus pa med pa zhig la dbu ma zhes bya ba'i tha snyad btags pa tsam yin te/ rang gi ngo bos mi stong pa'i shes bya mi srid pa'i phyir/ gnyis pa ni/ gzung 'dzin gnyis med pa dang/ gnyis med kyi ye shes yod pa ste de lta bu'i sgro skur gyi mtha' gnyis bsal ba'i shul na yod pa'i dngos po zhig la ni dbu ma zhes bya. *Thorough Clarification of Definitive Meaning of the 'Five Dharmas of Maitreya,'* vol. 11, 15–16.

7. See p. 232 ff.

8. See also the *Appearance of the Sun*, vol. 19, 24, for the same statement about the system of Dharmakīrti.

9. In this context, the two terms stand for ultimate and conventional phenomena, respectively.

10. grub mtha' bzhi pa'i mtha' gnyis sel tshul la gnyis te/ rnal 'byor spyod pa'i dang/ ngo bo nyid med par smra ba'o// dang po ni byams pa'i chos las gsungs pa ltar/ bzung ba dang/ 'dzin pa'i dngos po ni/ gdod ma nas yod ma myong ba'i phyir yod mtha' sel/ de yang rigs pa yang dag gam rgyu rkyen gzhan gyis med par byas pa ma yin pas na med mtha' sel lo// de'i shes byed kyang/ sngar yod pa zhig phyis med par song ba nyid du khas blangs na med pa'i mtha' la gnas pa ste/ 'jig rten pas ni sngar nor rdzas yod pa la phyis zad pa'i tshe nor med du khas blangs pas rtag chad gnyis ka'i mtha' la gnas pa'o// lugs 'di'i dbu ma ni/ gzung 'dzin gyi mtha' gnyis las grol ba'am rang rig rang gsal ba'o// lugs 'dir chos kyi dbyings las ma gtogs pa'i chos gzhan khas mi len pas na/ sems tsam pa dang khyad par shin tu che'o// gnyis pa ni/ ji lta ba dang ji snyed pa'i shes bya mtha' dag gdod ma nas yod ma myong bas na yod pa'i mtha' sel/ sngar yod pa zhig rigs pa'am 'phags pa'i shes mthong gis med par byas pa ma yin pas na med pa'i mtha' sel/ su yang yod ma myong bas na gnyis ka yin pa'i mtha' sel/ gang la ltos pa'i ltos sa gnyis ka yin pa mi srid na/ bltos chos gnyis ka ma yin pa'ang khas len par mi nus te/ ltos grub ma yin pa'i chos khas blangs na bden grub las ma 'das pa'i phyir. *Wish Fulfilling Meru*, vol. 4, 213–214.

11. der med pas med pa'i go chod pa ni thal rang gi gtso bo'i lugs yin gyi/ rnal 'byor spyod pa pa la med do// 'o na kun rdzob dbang btsan par thal lo// zhe na/ ma yin te/ don dam dpyod byed kyi rigs pa'i ngor med na/ don dam du med pas khyab pa ma nges pa'i phyir. *Meaningful to Behold*, 23, 389. See also *Meaningful to Behold*, 23, 415.

12. An exception to this "rule" is the position of Dharmakīrti who, according to Shakya Chokden, is similar to Niḥsvabhāvavādins in negating even primordial mind in the face of reasoning. Nevertheless, in Dharmakīrti's system such negation does not entail the nonexistence of primordial mind. For details, see the section 2 of this chapter.

13. rigs ngor ma grub pas gnas tshul la yang ma grub pa'i go chod pa dang/ der ma grub kyang mnyam gzhag gi ngor grub pas grub pa'i go chod par 'dod pa 'di ni mdo sde dang grags sde spyod pa'i dbu ma pa gnyis kyi dang/ rnal 'byor spyod pa'i dbu ma pa'i srol so so ba dag go. *Great Path Compressing the Two Chariot Ways into One,* vol. 12, 263–264.

14. 'o na rigs pas dpyad bzod du khas len nam zhe na/ ma yin te/ don dam dpyod byed kyi rigs pa'i don ni gcig dang du ma sogs mtha' gang du yang grub par khas mi len pa'i phyir/ 'o na gzhom du med par 'gal lo zhe na/ ma yin te rtog pas gzhom du yod pa dang/ ye shes kyi ngor gzhom du med pa mi 'gal ba'i phyir. *Rain of Ambrosia,* 375–376.

15. *Sevenfold Treasury of Gems,* vol. 7, 566–567.

16. klu sgrub zhabs kyis bshad pa'i rigs pas rigs pa de'i ngor gnyis med kyi ye shes yod par khegs mod/ spyir yod pa mi khegs te/ sgra rtog gi yul las 'das pa'i phyir dang/ rang rig pa'i ye shes kyis nyams su myong ba'i phyir. *Appearance of the Sun,* vol. 19, 90.

17. On Dharmakīrti's position, see the section 2 of this chapter.

18. See p. 191 ff. above.

19. don dam bden min du shad pa yang rnam dpyod kyi rigs pa de'i ngor yin gyi spyir btang nas ma yin te/ don dam du khas len pa dang bden min du khas len pa mi 'grig pa'i phyir. *Appearance of the Sun,* vol. 19, 91.

20. The Tibetan word *bden par grub pa* can be translated both as "truly established" and "established as truth," and the word *bden pa* itself can be translated either as the noun "truth" or the adjective "true." When the case particle *ra* is added to it to connect it with *grub pa* and thereby form the suchness (*de nyid*) subdivision of the accusative case (*las su bya ba*), *bden pa* can either retain its meaning as a noun (and thereby *bden par* can be translated as "as truth") or become an adjectival basis for a new adverb (*bden par* thereby will be translated as "truly"). To a native Tibetan speaker, both readings would sound the same, but to English readers used to translations of Geluk works, the adverbial reading will immediately sound an alarm, indicating the object of negation; according to Tsongkhapa and his followers, *dben par grub pa* is the object of negation through Madhyamaka reasoning, while *bden pa* is not. Tsongkhapa's critics who were native Tibetan speakers—Shakya Chokden included—dealt with only a single reading of the term, and challenged Tsongkhapa, asking: why can a pot be established as a pot but truth cannot be established as truth?

21. *Meaningful to Behold,* vol. 23, 388.

22. ye shes de la bden 'dzin spang byar mi 'dod pa ma yin te/ 'dzin pa kun btags ngo bos stong pa dang/ gzhan dbang spang byar khas len pas so. *Meaningful to Behold,* vol. 23, 388.

23. de bden par grub na de la bden 'dzin gyi rtog pa spong mi nus pa'i phyir na/ bden grub khas len gyi dbu ma pa ni mo sham gyi bu dang mtshungs. *Appearance of the Sun*, vol. 19, 117–118.

24. chos kyi dbyings kyi ye shes bden par grub kyang/ de la mtshan mar 'dzin pa'i rtog pa ni/ gzhan gyi dbang nyid kyi phyir spang bya dang/ kun tu brtags pa nyid du nges pa'i phyir spong bar nus so. *Appearance of the Sun*, vol. 19, 118. Emphasis mine. As has been mentioned above (p. 166), both the apprehended and the apprehender parts of dualistic appearances ultimately boil down to being the imaginary natures, while their underlying nature of clarity and cognition is the thoroughly established nature.

25. zhen blo bag chags dang bcas pa// 'gog byed rigs pa'i rnam grangs gnyis// rtog ngor de yul bkag pa yis// de 'dzin 'gog pa'i rigs pa dang// yang na 'dzin pa kun btags nyid// gcig dang du bral rigs pas so. *Precious Treasury of the Condensed Essence*, vol. 13, 174.

26. yul chos dbyings rang stong du gtan la ma phab na/ de la mtshan mar 'dzin pa'i blo ldog mi nus zhes pa ni zla ba'i zhabs sogs kyi bzhed pa yin mod/ thogs med zhabs kyis byams pa'i gzhung 'grel ba na ni/ 'dzin pa kun btags rang stong du gtan la phab nas goms par byas pa nyid kyis mnyam gzhag tu 'dzin pa rang gi ngang gis zhi bar nus. *Rain of Ambrosia*, 415. See also the *Appearance of the Sun*, vol. 19, 118–119 for more details.

27. In the *Appearance of the Sun*, vol. 19, 119, Shakya Chokden uses the famous example of the mind seeing magic appearances of horses, etc. By realizing that this mind is mistaken, one abandons grasping at reality of its appearances. To realize that the mind is mistaken, one does not have to first realize the nonexistence of the hallucinatory horses, and so forth.

28. de bden med du gtan la 'bebs byed kyi rigs pa sngon du ma song ba'i phyir de la bden 'dzin ldog mi nus so snyam na/ rigs pa des der gtan la 'bebs mi nus te/ de'i yul las 'das pa'i phyir/ bden 'dzin gyis kyang der 'dzin mi nus te/ de'i yul las 'das pa'i phyir/ yongs grub la bden par 'dzin pa'i rtog pa de'i yul ni de'i don spyi'am gzhan sel las ma 'das la/ de ni kun btags pa nyid yin pas rang gi ngo bos stong par gtan la phab zin no. *Rain of Ambrosia*, 388–389.

29. yongs grub bden par khas blangs na rtag pa'i mthar 'gyur ba ma yin nam ji ltar na lta ba 'dis mtha' gnyis sel zhe na/ nyes pa med de mtha' gnyis sel byed kyi lta ba la bden grub tu lta ba'i 'dzin stangs med pa'i phyir dang/ de bden no zhes pa ni lta sgom gnyis ka'i rjes kyi tha snyad yin pa'i phyir. *Rain of Ambrosia*, 388.

30. The other three seals are: all contaminated phenomena are suffering (*zag bcas thams cad sdug bsngal ba*), all phenomena are empty and selfless (*chos thams cad stong zhing bdag med pa*), and nirvāṇa is peace and bliss (*myang ngan las 'das pa zhi zhing bde ba*).

31. Geluk thinkers do not follow this "rule." With the exception of the aforementioned Changkya Rölpé Dorjé (p. 376 note 1), the majority of Geluk thinkers argue that ultimate reality in both Madhyamaka and Cittamātra is a non-affirming negation which is subsumed under the category of permanence

in the permanence/impermanence pair due to the following reasons: whatever exists—including ultimate reality—has to be either permanent or impermanent; because non-affirming negations are not impermanent but exist, they should be permanent.

32. *De bzhin gshegs pa'i snying po bstan pa zhes bya ba'i bstan bcos* (xylographic print from blocks preserved at Rum-btegs Karma-chos-sgar in Sikkim), 8a. This text is translated in Brunnhölzl, *Luminous Heart*, 352–360.

33. *Golden Lancet*, vol. 6, 498. For details of the question of compoundedness of primordial mind, see my "Reburying the Treasure—Maintaining the Continuity," note 39.

34. See *Zab don nyer gcig pa*, in Collected Works of Jo-naṅ rJe-btsun Tāranātha, vol. 4, *nga* (Leh, Ladakh: Smanrtsis Shesrig Dpemzod, 1985), 792. For an English translation see Hopkins, *The Essence of Other-Emptiness*, 132.

35. *Zab don nyer gcig pa*, in Collected Works of Jo-naṅ rJe-btsun Tāranātha, vol. 4, *nga* (Leh, Ladakh: Smanrtsis Shesrig Dpemzod, 1985), 787–788. For an English translation of the passage see Hopkins, *The Essence of Other-Emptiness*, 126.

36. *Tshad ma rigs pa'i gter gyi rtsa ba dang 'grel* pa (Bod ljongs mi dmangs dpe skrun khang, 1989), 100–101. Hereafter, *Treasure of the Science of Valid Cognition*.

37. dngos med kyi yod pa de ci/ don byed nus na dngos por 'gyur la/ mi nus na ci'ang med pas yod par ming btags kyang med pa nyid yin no. Ibid., 145.

38. de'i phyir mi rtag par yang khas len dgos pa yin te/ dngos po yin pas skad cig gis 'jig par khas len dgos pa'i phyir/ de lta na yang/ skabs gzhan du rtag par bshad pa dang mi 'gal te/ rgyun gyi rtag pa la bsams nas de ltar 'chad pa'i phyir. *Golden Lancet*, vol. 6, 498. For further details, see my "Reburying the Treasure—Maintaining the Continuity," note 39.

39. de yang rgyun gyi dbang du mdzad la/ skad cig las ni de ma thag pa'i rkyen can nyid kyi phyir mi rtag ste. *Previously Unseen Sun*, vol. 13, 117.

40. gzung 'dzin gnyis ka med pa de lta na/ lhag ma ci zhig yod ce na/ gzung 'dzin gnyis med kyi shes pa skad cig gi cha med pa cig kho na yod do. *Enjoyment Ocean of the Speech of the 'Seven Works,'* vol. 19, 475–476.

41. *Precious Treasury of the Condensed Essence*, vol. 13, 171.

42. Ibid., 171, 173.

43. Ibid., 171, 172.

44. As Shakya Chokden explains, according to Dharmakīrti, on the level of conventions (*tha snyad*), i.e., on the level of relative truth, the production, disintegration, and abiding of things are accepted as they are accepted in the world. This coarse type of impermanence is used in order to establish the subtle impermanence—the non-abiding of phenomena even for a moment—which is explained in terms of the ultimate meaning (*dam pa'i don*). Thereby the hidden phenomenon (*lkog gyur, parokṣa*), the ultimate truth, is established by using as the reason the manifest phenomenon (*mngon gyur, pratyakṣa*), a conventional truth. This is similar to establishing something as impermanent

on the basis of its being a product (*byas pa, kṛta*). Ibid., 173. It should be noted that Shakya Chokden is not denying that according to Dharmakīrti, phenomena do abide only for only one moment and do not abide for a second moment. The point he is making is that the abiding of phenomena does not precede their disintegration but is simultaneous with it; "coming into being," "abiding," and "disintegration" are different descriptions of one and the same process. Thus, when Shakya Chokden writes regarding all phenomena produced from their causes that their "abiding [even] for a moment is negated" (skad cig tu// gnas pa bkag pa) and that they "do not abide anywhere" (gang du'ang gnas pa med pa, ibid., 171), what he refutes is the abiding of phenomena *that is separate from* their coming into existence and disintegration. This is made clear in ibid., 173.

45. Ibid., 173.

46. Ibid.

47. yong grub bden par mi 'chad pa// byams pa'i gzhung dang 'gal zhe na// sems kyi rdo rje'ang thos bsam gyi// rigs pas brtags pa'i ngor med kyang// med par bzhag nus ma yin te// sgra rtog yul las 'das phyir ro// 'o na rang stong rigs pa la// rtsal du bton pas ci bya na// yongs grub sems kyi rdo rje la// zhen pa spong ba'i phyir yin no. Ibid., 173–174.

48. In this context "early Tibetan thinkers" refers to Tibetan writers prior to Sakya Pendita.

49. 'di la bod snga ma na re/ rdul phran bden grub dang skad cig bden grub 'gog pa'i rigs pa mtshungs so zhes zer/ mtshungs pa ma yin te/ rags pa rtsoms pa'i tshe/ phyogs drug gi rdul gyis cig char du bskor bas na/ dbus kyi rdul phran cha bcas su 'gyur la/ dus gsum cig char mi skye bas da lta'i shes pa skad cig gi cha med yin pa'i phyir ro// de la 'di skad ces/ gnyis med ye shes rtog dpyod kyis// dpyad na gnas med rang stong gi// tshul yin rtog dpyod las 'das par// gnas pa gzhan stong smra ba'i lugs// zhes so. *Enjoyment Ocean of the Speech of the 'Seven Works,'* vol. 19, 476. Emphasis mine.

50. See Sakya Pendita's *Treasure of the Science of Valid Cognition*, 54–57.

51. shes pa'i sgo nas rang rig gcig. *Treasure of the Science of Valid Cognition*, 58.

52. Ibid.

53. *Previously Unseen Sun*, vol. 13, 121. This passage has already been cited on p. 162.

54. rnam shes 'khrul pa'i chos ji nyid [*sic*, should read *snyed*] pa la nang blta ye shes kyi cha re re yod kyang/ ye shes kyi gsal cha rnam shes kyi ngo bor 'gyur srid pa dang/ cig shos kyang der 'gyur srid pa ni ma yin te/ gzhan du na/ ye shes srid pa'i bde sdug myong ba por thal ba dang/ rnam shes kyi ming can yang dag pa ma yin pa'i kun tu rtog pa de dag zag med kyi yon tan mtha' dag gi sgrub gzhi nyid du thal bar 'gyur pa'i phyir ro// gdod ma'i ye shes de med par blo bur gyi rnam shes 'khrul snang du mi 'byung mod/ gnyis po'i gzhi mthun srid par 'dod pa ni ma yin te/ nam mkha' la sprin dang/ gser la g.ya' dang/ chu dangs ba la rnyog pa bzhin no. *Previously Unseen Sun*, vol. 13, 121. See also the *Appearance of the Sun*, vol. 19, 117.

55. In his *Ocean of Scriptural Statements and Reasoning*, vol. 14, 410, distinguishing between consciousness and primordial mind, Shakya Chokden provides a somewhat limited description of the latter: "Then what is the distinction between consciousness and primordial mind? The former one is [the mind] dualistically appearing as the apprehended and apprehender due to the pollution of ignorance. The latter is the mind correctly realizing the mode of being due to the separation from that [pollution of ignorance]. That [primordial mind] is also of two [types]: the nonconceptual primordial mind of meditative equipoise and the pure worldly primordial mind of subsequent attainment" ('o na rnam shes dang/ ye shes kyi khyad par ci zhe na/ dang po ni ma rig pa'i bslad pa zhugs pa'i dbang gis gzung 'dzin gnyis su snang ba'o// gnyis pa ni/ de dang bral ba'i dbang gis gnas tshul ji lta ba bzhin rtogs pa'i blo'o// de la'ang gnyis te/ mnyam gzhag rnam par mi rtog pa'i ye shes dang/ rjes thob dag pa 'jig rten pa'i ye shes so). This distinction is not exhaustive: as my overall study demonstrates, Shakya Chokden treats ultimate reality as primordial mind and vice versa. In particular, he treats primordial mind as ultimate reality in the same *Ocean of Scriptural Statements and Reasoning*, vol. 15, 461–2 (see also p. 158 above). It is clear that primordial mind in his system is not limited to meditative equipoise or subsequent attainment only, but is treated as the everpresent ultimate reality. This particular distinction, therefore, is made in terms of not merely having but actually manifesting and cognizing the two types of knowing with their appearances. While ordinary beings can always cognize consciousness with its appearances, it is only āryas in meditative equipoise and subsequent attainment who can manifest and cognize primordial mind with its appearances. (For more details, see the next section.)

56. rnam shes rang gi ngo bo gsal rig tu khas mi len na/ bems po nyid kyi phyir yul ma rig par 'gyur ro zhe na/ ha cang thal ba nyid du mi 'gyur te/ spyir rnam shes ni tshad mas mi 'grub kyang/ 'khrul pas yod par sgro btags pa nyid du khas len gyi/ rig pa lta ci smos/ yod par yang khas mi len te/ kun rdzob bden pa nyid kyi phyir ro. *Previously Unseen Sun*, vol. 13, 121–2.

57. I am omitting a part of the passage and cite it below (p. 250).

58. de lta na 'khrul pa la gzhi med pa'i phyir ye shes la rag ma las par yang ' 'khrul snang skye bar 'gyur ro// zhe na/ ma yin te/ mtho yor med na mir 'dzin gyi rtog pa mi 'byung ba bzhin no// gdod ma nas grub pa'i ye shes med par 'khrul snang mi 'char zhing/ 'khrul snang gi kha nang blta 'dzin rnam gyi cha de gdod ma'i ye shes su nges par gnas shing/ . . . dper na nam mkha' med par bum pa dang khang pa sogs kyi snang ba mi 'char mod/ nam mkha' nyid bum sogs kyi ngo bor song ba ma yin pa bzhin no. *Previously Unseen Sun*, vol. 13, 122.

59. "Basis" (*gzhi*) refers to those conditions that are naturally present even in ordinary life and can serve as the basis for practicing the path and achieving its result.

60. gzhi dus kyi don dam bden pa ye shes su khas len na/ tshur rol mthong bas kyang/ don dam pa'i bden pa dang/ bde bar gshegs pa'i snying po mngon gsum [*sic*] du mthong bar thal ba ma yin nam zhe na/ tshur

mthong gi tshe ni/ rang nyid gsal ba'i ngo bor skyes tsam la rang rig par tha snyad 'dogs pa yod kyang/ de la nges pa 'dren mi nus pas na/ rang gis rang rig pa zhes mi bya la/ 'phags pa'i sar ni/ de la nges pa 'dren nus pa'i phyir/ so so rang gis rig pa'i ye shes kyi spyod yul zhes bshad do. *Sevenfold Treasury of Gems*, vol. 7, 435.

61. See the *Treasure of the Science of Valid Cognition*, 64–65. For details of Shakya Chokden's approach to the question of inducing ascertainment, see his *Dispelling Mental Darkness: Abridgement of the Modes of Inducing Ascertainment by Valid Cognition* (*Tshad mas nges pa 'dren pa'i tshul nyung ngur bsdus pa yid kyi mun sel*), vol. 19, 146–155.

62. gzhan yang gzhi dus ye shes de// 'dzin rnam nyid kyis myong zhes pa// rnam 'grel mdzad pa'i gzhung chen las// gsal bar gsungs mod rgyud bla mar// bde gshegs sning po mthong ba la// so so'i skye bo la sogs pa// mig dang mi ldan rnam pa gzhi// bshad pa de ma nges la dgongs. *Skye 'phags snang ba 'thun pa la brtsad pa rdo rje'i gseng lam chos tshan bcu bdun pa*, in *'Hundred and Eight Dharma Sections' Treatise* (*Chos tshan brgya dang brgyad pa zhes bya ba'i bstan bcos*), vol. 13, 390.

63. That is, the four individuals discussed in the *Sublime Continuum*, verses 32–33, with the subsequent commentary by Asaṅga (following the verse order given in Jikido Takasaki, *A Study on the Ratnagotravibhāga* (Rome: Istituto Italiano per il Medio ed Estremo Oriente, 1966)).

64. As will become clear below, this is not what Shakya Chokden himself accepts. He accepts that self-cognition experiences itself without necessarily cognizing or realizing itself.

65. sems kyi rang bzhin 'od gsal ba// rang myong tshad mas rig pa'i phyir// 'gro ba kun gyis rang rang gi// snying po rtogs par thal zhe na// sems kyi rang bzhin 'od gsal ba// rang gis rang nyid nyams myong nas// de la nges pa 'dren pa ni// theg chen 'phags pa min la med. *Precious Treasury of the Condensed Essence*, vol. 13, 187.

66. As an analogy, we might think of our day-to-day perception: myriads of thoughts rush through our mind every moment, but how many of them are ascertained and acknowledged?

67. 'o na rang blo rang la ni// lkog tu gyur par thal zhe na// 'od gsal ba yi sems de nyid// rang la mngon sum tshad yin phyir// rang blo rang la lkog gyur du// thal bar 'gyur ba ma yin no// de la mngon sum tshad yin na// de ma rtogs par 'gal zhe na// mngon sum thams cad rang rang gi// 'jug pa'i yul la tshad yin kyang// de rtogs mdzad pa'i nges med par// rnam 'grel mdzad pas bshad pa yin. *Precious Treasury of the Condensed Essence*, vol. 13, 187.

68. rang gis rang nyid rig min pa// rang rig nyid du 'gal zhe na// 'od gsal ba yi sems gang la// rtog dang bral zhing ma 'khrul bar// song na de la mngon sum ste// de yang rang rig las gzhan med// rang nyid yul du byed pa ni// rang rig pa la spyir mi 'thad// khyad par gnyis med ye shes la// yul med rig pa'i gter las bshad// spyir yang theg pa chen po las// so sor rang rig ces bya ba// rang nyid rig par skyes tsam las// rtogs bya gzhan med pa la bshad. Ibid.

69. As we will see below, in general, cognizing itself by itself does not necessarily imply taking itself as an object according to Shakya Chokden.

70. As Shakya Chokden stated in the preceding quote, self-cognition has an object of engagement. Having an object of engagement, therefore, does not entail having an object.

71. *Treasure of the Science of Valid Cognition*, 58.

72. rang rig pa'ang rig bya rig byed du phye ba'i rang rig pa ma yin gyi/ bems po las logs nas rig pa skyes pa tsam de nyid yin. *Treasure of the Science of Valid Cognition*, 233–234. The discussion of whether self-cognition has an object or not is relevant because in the *Treasure of the Science of Valid Cognition*, 40, Sakya Pendita defines the "object" (*yul*) as "that which is cognized by mind" (*blos rig bya*). To accept cognition of itself by itself *might* imply that self-cognition takes itself as the object, unless clearly explained. In that case, it will contradict the statement that self-cognition does not have an object.

73. *Enjoyment Ocean of the Speech of the 'Seven Works,'* vol. 19, 479. See also the *Essence of Logic: Condensed Thatness of [Dignāga's] 'Sūtra on Valid Cognition' and [Dharmakīrti's] Textual System of 'Seven Works'* (*Tshad ma'i mdo dang gzhung lugs sde bdun gyi de kho na nyid bsdus pa rtog ge'i snying po*), vol. 18, 110.

74. spyir ni so so skye bo la rnal 'byor mngon sum med kyang/ gnas lugs mngon sum du mthong ba zhig yod. *Dri ba lhag bsam rab dkar gyi dris lan man ngag gi dgongs rgyan*, vol. 23, 353.

75. shes pa thams cad kyi steng na yul gyi kha ma sgyur ba'i gsal rig gi cha re re yod la/ de yod pa tsam gyis shes pa thams cad rang gis rang rig pa. *Tshad ma'i mdo dang gzhung lugs sde bdun gyi de kho na nyid bsdus pa rtog ge'i snying po*, vol. 18, 110.

76. spyir shes pa rang gis rang rig pa mi srid na/ thams cad mkhyen pa'i ye shes thams cad mkhyen pa'i ye shes kho na'i spyod yul ma yin par 'gyur. *Ocean of Scriptural Statements and Reasoning*, vol. 14, 559.

77. As has been mentioned previously, such practices related to conventional phenomena as cultivation of compassion and so forth can and have to be used on the path to enlightenment. Nevertheless, they cannot become *actual direct* antidotes of ignorance.

78. See pp. 190, 192 ff., and 195.

79. 'khrul snang gi kha nang blta 'dzin rnam gyi cha de gdod ma'i ye shes su nges par gnas shing/ gnas pa de nyid gsang sngags pas nyon mongs pa dang rnam rtog lam du byed pa'i thabs mkhas kyi tshe/ thog mar skyed rdzogs gnyis ka'i sgrub gzhi dang/ bar du de gnyis ka'i ngo bo nyid du lhun gyis grub nas spang bya de dag gi kha phyir blta'i cha nam mkha' la sprin dengs pa bzhin du rang zhi rang dag tu 'gro ba yin gyi/ nang blta skyed rdzogs kyi ngo bo nyid du song ba de las logs shig tu kha phyir blta'i cha lam du byas nas spang dgos pa ni ma yin no. *Previously Unseen Sun*, vol. 13, 122.

80. *Thorough Establishment of the Glorious Original Buddha*, vol. 8, 32–33.

81. phyi blta dri ma'i cha de rang zhi nas nang blta ye shes kyi cha de don dam pa'i dkyil 'khor dang sangs rgyas nyid du gyur pa zhes bya ba de mngon du byed pa nyid do// 'di kho nar ma zad rnam shes kyi dri ma thams cad la sbyong tshul de bzhin no. Ibid., 33.

82. sngags gzhung thun mong min dag na// lta bas nyams su myong bya ba// byams pa'i gzhung dang mi mthun par// bshad pa 'ga' yang yod ma yin. *Sngags la 'jug pa'i mun pa sel bar byed pa'i chos kyi sgron me gzhung tshan bcu bdun* pa, in *'Hundred and Eight Dharma Sections' Treatise* (*Chos tshan brgya dang brgyad pa zhes bya ba'i bstan bcos*), vol. 13, 230. Hereafter, *Lamp of Dharma*.

83. sde bdun mdzad pas gtan la phab pa'i nges don 'di dag ni/ rje btsun byams pas gtan la phab pa'i shing rta'i srol nyid las byung ba ste/ 'di yang theg pa chen po spyi dang khyad par gsang sngags la 'jug pa'i sgo tsam du ma zad rdo rje theg pa'i lam gyi gzhung shing du gyur pa'i rtsa ba mthar thug pa'o. *Appearance of the Sun*, vol. 19, 100. See also pp. 99–100 of the same text for more details.

84. pha rol phyin pa'i spros bral las// lhag pa'i lta ba yod na ni// lta de spros pa can du 'gyur// spros bral yin na khyad par med// des na bshad pas go ba yi// thos pa'i lta ba gcig nyid yin// 'on kyang spros bral rtogs pa yi// thabs la gsang sgnags khyad par 'phags. See Rhoton, *A Clear Differentiation of the Three Codes*, for the Tibetan text (p. 308) and alternative translation (p.129)

85. See, for example, Kelden Tsering (*skal ldan tshe ring*), *Presentation of Tenets of Glorious Sakyapas* (*Dpal sa skya pa'i grub mtha'i rnam bzhag*, Zhang kang then mā dpe skrun khang, 2001), 98.

86. lta ba'i ming yul spros bral la bshad pa dang yul can ye shes la bshad pa gnyis las/ snga ma'i dbang du byas na de las lhag pa sngags su ma bshad mod/ phyi ma'i dbang du byas na snga ma las lhag par grub ste yul can mchog tu mi 'gyur ba'i bde bas yul spros bral gyi ye shes de nyid nyams su myong ba'i phyir. *Rain of Ambrosia*, 376. See also ibid., 361.

87. *Wish Fulfilling Meru*, vol. 4, 230. For a further discussion of this issue in connection to the above passage from the *Thorough Differentiation of the Three Types of Vows* and other texts, see the *Wish Fulfilling Meru*, vol. 4, 227–232, translated in the *Three Texts on Madhyamaka*, 17–20 (I provide a slightly different translation of the *Thorough Differentiation of the Three Types of Vows*'s passage there).

88. spyir ni dbu ma rnam gsum ste// shing rta'i srol gnyis las byung ba'i// dbu ma gnyis dang sngags kyi'o. *Thorough Clarification of Vajradhara's Intent*, vol. 13, 331.

89. *Wish Fulfilling Meru*, vol. 4, 217. For more details, see the *Three Texts on Madhyamaka*, 8–9, 17–20, 29–30.

90. *Appearance of the Sun*, vol. 19, 133.

91. For details, see the *Lamp of Dharma*, vol. 13, 229–231, 257–260; *Appearance of the Sun*, vol. 19, 133–135; *Rain of Ambrosia*, 356–361. Also, see the *Rain of Ambrosia*, 343–348 for more parallels between the views of Alīkākāravāda and Tantra.

92. *Wish Fulfilling Meru*, vol. 4, 227–232, translated in the *Three Texts on Madhyamaka*, 17–20.

93. sngags kyi thun mong min pa yi// lta ba lhan cig skyes ye shes// rtogs byed thabs dang rtogs bya ba// gnyis ka pha rol phyin la med// pha rol phyin pa'i spros bral tsam// sngags kyis ye shes kyis mi rtogs// sngags

kyis rtogs pa'i stong pa nyid// zag med bde ba chen por 'dus. *Thorough Clarification of Vajradhara's Intent*, vol. 13, 328.

94. *Precious Treasury of the Condensed Essence*, vol. 13, 178. On the same page, Shakya Chokden writes that the tantric view does not surpass the "freedom from proliferations [taught] in the third [dharma]cakra" (*'khor lo gsum pa'i spros bral*), although according to Prāsaṅgika and Svātantrika there is a Madhyamaka view (i.e., their own view) that surpasses that type of freedom from proliferations.

95. rdo rje theg pa'i lta ba ni gzung 'dzin gnyis su med pa'i ye shes 'ba' zhig gi nang tshan du snang ba. *Meaningful to Behold*, vol. 23, 364.

96. des na sngags lugs kyi lta ba thun mong ba rnams ni rnal 'byor spyod pa dang mthun zhing/ thal rang dang mi mthun la/ thun mong ma yin pa ni phar phyin pa'i dbu ma gsum ka las khyad par du 'phags so. Ibid., 364–365.

97. khyad par thal rang dbu ma pa'i// stong pa nyid dang sngags lugs kyi// rtogs bya la ni gzhi mthun kyang// srid pa min zhes shes par bya// rnal 'byor spyod pa'i stong nyid dang// sngags kyi rang bzhin lhan skyes la// gzhi mthun yod phyir gnyis ka la// so sor rang rig ye shes zer. *Thorough Clarification of Vajradhara's Intent*, vol. 13, 329.

98. *Appearance of the Sun*, 114–115.

99. rdo rje theg pa ba kun gyis bsgom pas nyams su myong bar bya ba'i nges don mthar thug pa ni/ legs par rnam par phye ba dang ldan pa'i chos kyi 'khor lo gsum pa 'di nyid las 'byung ba yin. *Appearance of the Sun*, vol. 19, 115.

100. *Appearance of the Sun*, vol. 19, 115–116.

101. bka' 'khor lo tha ma'i mdo ni bka' bar pa la ltos nas kyang nges pa'i don can nyid du grub ste/ bka' bar pas sgro skur gyi rtog pa mtha' dag bsal zin pa gzhir byas kyi steng du sgom pas nyams su blangs bya'i nges don mthar thug pa de nyid ni 'di yin no zhes gsal bar gtan la phab pa'i phyir/ mdo gang du na/ mdo sde dgongs pa nges 'grel lta bu phar phyin theg pa'i dbang du byas pa'i bka' tha ma rnams su so sor rang gis rig pa'i ye shes kyi myong byar rang bzhin chos sku dang bde bar gshegs pa'i snying po'i ming can de nyid gsal ba'i phyir dang/ bka' tha ma nyid kyi dbang du byas pa'i sngags kyi theg par yang nges don mthar thug pa ni dgag bya gzung 'dzin gyi spros pa mtha' dag bkag pa'i chos dbyings ye shes nyid gsal bar bstan pa yin la/ de ni bka' bar par sgra ji bzhin pa nyid kyis ma bstan cing/ ji srid chos kyi dbyings 'di tha na'ang mos pa yid byed tsam gyis ma rtogs pa de srid du lam rim pa gnyis kyi nyams len byed shes pa mi 'byung ba'i phyir. *Rain of Ambrosia*, 351–352.

102. *Lamp of Dharma*, vol. 13, 230.

103. byams pa'i chos las gzung 'dzin gyi// chos rnams stong par rtogs rjes su// gnyis med ye shes de kho na// rtogs byar bzhed pas sngags dang mthun. Ibid., 230.

104. *Appearance of the Sun*, vol. 19, 119–120.

105. *Rain of Ambrosia*, 392.

106. lta sgom gyi rim pa 'di ni mdo sngags gnyis ka'i lugs su shin tu 'bral chags pa yin te/ mdo lugs kyi lam rkyang pas bgrod pa'i tshe na mtshan 'dzin gyi rtog pa 'gog pa'i shes rab kyi skye tshul rnal 'byor spyod pa pa'i mthar thug gi lugs las kyang ches shin tu zab cing/ sngags lugs su 'brel ba'i tshe mtshan 'dzin gyi rtog pa 'gog byed kyi rigs pa zab shos de sngon du song ba gzhir bzhag gi steng du/ don dam byang chub kyi sems de lhag pa'i lha dang/ de'i rig pa dang/ bde ba chen po'i ye shes sogs kyi sgrub gzhir bzhag pa'i phyir. *Rain of Ambrosia*, 392–393.

107. *Appearance of the Sun*, vol. 19, 120.

108. It is counted as third in the popular set of the four empowerments. The first two are the vase empowerment (*bum dbang, kalaśābhiṣeka*) and secret empowerment (*gsang dbang, guhyābhiṣeka*), the fourth is the word empowerment (*tshig dbang*). This set of four is used in the majority of Highest Yoga tantras practiced by Tibetan Buddhist traditions other than Nyingma.

109. brjod bral nyams su myong ba la der gtan la 'bebs byed kyi rigs pa sngon du 'gro mi dgos te/ gsang sngags thabs la mkhas pa'i khyad par gyis brjod bral gyi ye shes mngon du gyur pa de nyid kyis bsam med dang brjod med du grub zin pa'i phyir/ dper na dbang gsum pa'i ye shes bzhin no. *Rain of Ambrosia*, 376.

110. *rang byin gyis brlabs pa'i rims pa* in the text.

111. *Appearance of the Sun*, vol. 19, 102.

112. sngags kyi theg par ni mtshan 'dzin gyi spros pa gcod pa tsam gyi dbang du byas na ngo bo nyid med par smra ba'i lta ba rigs tshogs nas bshad pa des kyang go chod mod/ zung 'jug gi sku bsgrub pa la de tsam gyis chog pa ma yin. *Rain of Ambrosia*, 348–349.

113. *Seventeen Wondrous Answers*, vol. 23, 439–440.

114. dgyes pa rdo rje las/ ji skad du/ rnal 'byor spyod pa de las phyis// de rjes dbu ma bstan par bya// sngags kyi rim pa kun shes nas// de rjes kyee'i rdo rje bstan// zhes lta ba rim 'jug 'chad pa'i skabs der go rim bzhin du/ gzung 'dzin gnyis su med pa'i ye shes dang/ chos thams cad rang gi ngo bos stong ba'i med par dgag pa dang/ dmigs pa med pa'i snying rje dang stong pa nyid zung du 'jug pa'i lta ba gsum rim par bshad do. *Wish Fulfilling Meru*, vol. 4, 227–228. ("Non-observing compassion" is compassion towards sentient beings combined with non-observation of their nature, i.e., realization of their emptiness.) A slightly different Tibetan version of the *Hevajra* passage is provided in Snellgrove, *The Hevajra Tantra: A Critical Study*, part 2, p. 91: de nas rnal 'byor spyod pa nyid// de yi rjes su dbu ma bstan// sngags kyi rim pa kun shes nas// de rjes kye'i rdo rje brtsam. Skt.: yogācāraṃ tataḥ paścāt · tadanu madhyamakaṃ diśet// sarvamantranayaṃ jñātvā · tadanu hevajram ārabhet (ibid, 90). For Snellgrove's translation, see ibid., part 1, p.116.

115. This gradual process is contrasted with another mode of realizing the view which is opened to "fortunate instantanialists" (*skal ldan cig char ba*). These capable individuals can realize the thatness of union (*zung 'jug gi de kho na nyid*) from the very beginning, by receiving tantric empowerments.

Shakya Chokden adds that, in that case, there is no need for teaching and realizing the views of Madhyamaka of Svātantrika and Prāsaṅgika. *Meaningful to Behold*, vol. 23, 365.

116. *Meaningful to Behold*, vol. 23, 364.

117. *Mngon par rtogs pa rin po che'i ljon shing zhes bya ba'i dngos bstan gyi dka' gnas la som nyi'i mtha' rnam par dpyad nas/ gsang sngags bla na med pa'i yid bzhin gyi rgya mtshor 'jug pa/ nges don rin po che'i 'jug ngogs*, vol. 17, 435–436. Hereafter, *Precious Harbor of Definitive Meaning*.

118. *Appearance of the Sun*, vol. 19, 90. Also see pp. 134–135 of the same text for more details on this passage.

119. I have already cited this passage on p. 147.

120. ye shes de yang don dam du// yod par mkhas rnams mi 'dod de. *Appearance of the Sun*, vol. 19, 90. Derge provides a slightly different version: rnam par shes pa don dam yod// de yang mkhas rnam mi 'dod de. *Vimalaprabhā, Dri ma med pa'i 'od*, D1347, rgyud 'grel, da, 26b. Skt.: neṣṭaṃ tadapi dhīrāṇāṃ vijñānaṃ paramārthasat. In Upādhyāya, *Vimalaprabhā ṭīkā*, 267. My translation is based on on the citation from the *Appearance of the Sun*. For an alternative translation, see Vesna Wallace, *The Kālacakratantra*, 246.

121. *Appearance of the Sun*, vol. 19, 89–90.

122. *Lamp of Dharma*, vol. 13, 260–261.

123. *Precious Treasury of the Condensed Essence*, vol. 13, 175.

124. byams chos bar pa'i lta bas nyon mongs pa can ma yin pa'i ma rig pa drung 'byin par mi nus na/ rdo rje theg pa'i lta bas ji ltar nus te/ de dang de'i khyad par dbye dka' ba'i phyir. *Appearance of the Sun*, vol. 19, 89.

125. *Rgyud kyi mngon par rtogs pa rin po che'i ljon shing*, in Sa-skya lam 'bras literature series, vol. 23, 1–277 (Dehradun, U.P., India: Sakya Centre).

126. rnal 'byor spyod pa'i lta ba la// dbu ma sems tsam gnyis yod kyang// ljon shing nang du sems tsam pa'i// lta ba las lhag mi 'chad pa// rnam rdzun zhes grags lta ba ni// sngags kyi rtogs byar 'dus la dgongs. *Nges don rin po che'i 'jug ngogs*, vol. 17, 435.

127. Ibid.

128. ngo bo nyid med par smra ba'i slob dpon de dag gis mdzad pa'i sngags kyi bstan chos su yul can lta ba dang/ lta ba de'i yul chos dbyings dang don dam bden pa'i ngos 'dzin ni/ 'phags pa thogs med sku mched sogs rnal 'byor spyod pa pa'i slob dpon rnams kyi gzhung las ji ltar 'byung ba de dang mthun pa kho na yin te/ sems kyi rdo rje dang/ sems kyi rang bzhin 'od gsal ba nyid la don dam pa'i bden par bshad cing/ de mngon sum du rtogs pa'i ye shes nam skyes pa de'i tshe lta ba rtogs par 'jogs pa'i phyir. *Rain of Ambrosia*, 338.

129. See p. 341 note 117.

130. thogs med zhabs kyis thugs su chud pa'i gzung 'dzin gnyis med kyi ye shes zhes bya ba de dang/ zla ba'i zhabs rang nyid kyis gsang ba 'dus par bshad pa'i 'od gsal ba'i rim pa dang/ sems kyi rdo rje zhes bya ba'i ngos 'dzin la khyad par ci yang mi snang. *Meaningful to Behold*, vol. 23, 359–360.

131. nges pa'i don du gang 'gyur rdo rje theg pa'i rgyud dang man ngag rnams tshad mar byas nas brtag par bya. *Appearance of the Sun*, vol. 19, 7.

Conclusion

1. This passage has been addressed on p. 208.

Bibliography

Sūtras and Tantras

Copulation Tantra (*Saṃpuṭanāmamahātantra, Yang dag par sbyor ba zhes bya ba'i rgyud chen po*). D0381, rgyud, ga, 73b–158b.

Great Nirvāṇa Sūtra (*Āryamahāparinirvāṇanāmamahāyānasūtra, 'Phags pa yongs su mya ngan las 'das pa chen po'i mdo*). D119, mdo sde, nya-ta.

Hevajra Tantra (*Hevajratantrarājanāma, Kye'i rdo rje zhes bya ba rgyud kyi rgyal po*). D0417, rgyud, nga, 1b–30a. Translated into Enlish and edited by Snellgrove, David L. *The Hevajra Tantra: A Critical Study*, London Oriental Series, 6, parts 1–2. London: Oxford University Press, 1959.

Individual Liberation Sūtra (*Prātimokṣasūtra, So sor thar pa'i mdo*). D0002, 'dul ba, ca, 1b–20b.

Root Tantra of Mañjuśrī (*Āryamañjuśrīmūlatantra, 'Phags pa 'jam dpal gyi rtsa ba'i rgyud*). D0543, rgyud, na, 105a–351a.

Secret Assembly Tantra (*Sarvatathāgatakāyavākcittarahasyoguhyasamājanāmamahākalparāja, De bzhin gshegs pa thams cad kyi sku gsung thugs kyi gsang chen gsang ba 'dus pa zhes bya ba brtag pa'i rgyal po chen po*). D0443, rgyud, ca, 90a–157b.

Sūtra of the Ornament of Appearances of Primordial Mind (*Āryasarvabuddhaviśayāvatārajñānālokālaṃkāranāmamahāyānasūtra, 'Phags pa sangs rgyas thams cad kyi yul la 'jug pa'i ye shes snang ba'i rgyan ces bya ba theg pa chen po'i mdo*). D100, mdo sde, ga, 276a–305a.

Sūtra Unraveling the Intent (*Āryasaṃdhinirmocananāmamahāyānasūtra, 'Phags pa dgongs pa nges par 'grel pa zhes bya ba theg pa chen po'i mdo*). D0106, mdo sde, ca, 1b–55b.

Ten Grounds Sūtra (*Daśabhūmikasūtra, Mdo sde sa bcu pa*). P761.31, vol. 25.

Vajra Canopy Tantra (*Āryaḍākinīvajrapañjaramahātantrarājakalpanāma, 'Phags pa mkha' 'gro ma rdo rje gur zhes bya ba'i rgyud kyi rgyal po chen po'i brtag pa*). D0419, rgyud, nga, 30a–65b.

Indian and Tibetan Buddhist Works in Tibetan

Āryadeva. *Four Hundred/Treatise of Four Hundred Stanzas* (*Catuḥṣatakaśāstranāmakārikā, Bstan bcos bzhi brgya pa zhes bya ba'i tshig le'ur byas pa*). D3846, dbu ma, tsha, 1a–18a.

———. *Summary of Primordial Mind's Essence* (*Jñānasārasamuccaya, Ye shes snying po kun las btus pa*). D3851, dbu ma, tsha, 26b–28a.

Asaṅga. *Explanation of [Maitreya's] 'Sublime Continuum of Mahāyāna'* (*Mahāyānottaratantraśāstravyākhyā, Theg pa chen po'i rgyud bla ma'i bstan bcos kyi rnam par bshad pa*). D4025, sems tsam, phi, 74b–129a. Edited Sanskrit text in Johnston, Edward H. (ed.). *Ratnagotravibhāga Mahāyānottaratantraśāstra.* Patna: The Bihar Research Society, 1950. English translation in Takasaki, Jikido. *A Study on the Ratnagotravibhāga.* Rome: Istituto Italiano per il Medio ed Estremo Oriente, 1966.

———. *Grounds of Yogācāra* (*Yogācārabhūmi, Rnal 'byor spyod pa'i sa*). D4035, sems tsam, tshi, 1a– D4037, sems tsam, wi, 213a.

———. *Summary of Higher Knowledge* (*Abhidharmasamuccaya, Chos mngon pa kun las btus pa*). D4053, sems tsam, li, 1a–117a.

———. *Summary of Mahāyāna* (*Mahāyānasaṃgraha, Theg pa chen po bsdus pa*). D4048, sems tsam, ri, 1a–43a.

Atiśa Dīpaṃkara. *Engaging in the Two Truths* (*Satyadvayāvatāra, Bden pa gnyis la 'jug pa*). D3902, bdu ma, a, 72a–73a. English translation in Lindtner, Christian. "Atiśa's Introduction to the Two Truths, and Its Sources." *Journal of Indian Philosophy*, vol. 9, no. 2 (1981): 161–214.

———. *Song of the View of the Dharma-Sphere* (*Dharmadhātudarśanagīti/ -saragīta, Chos kyi dbyings su lta ba'i glu*). D2314, rgyud, zhi, 254b–260b.

———. *Quintessential Instructions on Madhyamaka* (*Madhyamakopadeśa, Dbu ma'i man ngag*). D3929, dbu ma, ki, 95b1–96a7.

Bhāviveka. *Blaze of Reasoning: Commentary on the 'Heart of Madhyamaka'* (*Madhyamakahṛdayavṛttitarkajvālā, Dbu ma'i snying po'i 'grel pa rtog ge 'bar ba*). D3856, dbu ma, dza, 40b–329b. Its part dealing with the critique of Bhāviveka's Buddhist opponents is edited and translated into English in Eckel, Malcolm David. *Bhāviveka and His Buddhist Opponents.* Harvard Oriental Series, 70. Cambridge, Massachusetts: Department of Sanskrit and Indian Studies, Harvard University, 2009.

———. *Stanzas on the Heart of Madhyamaka* (*Madhyamakahṛdayakārikā, Dbu ma'i snying po'i tshig le'ur byas pa*). D3855, dbu ma, dza, 1a–40b. Its part dealing with the critique of Bhāviveka's Buddhist opponents is edited and translated into English in Eckel, Malcolm David. *Bhāviveka and His Buddhist Opponents.* Harvard Oriental Series, 70. Cambridge, Massachusetts: Department of Sanskrit and Indian Studies, Harvard University, 2009.

Candrakīrti. *Clear Lamp* (*Pradīpodyotana, Sgron ma gsal bar byed pa*). D1785, rgyud, ha, 1–201b.

———. *Clear Words: Commentary on [Nāgārjuna's] 'Root [Stanzas] on Madhyamaka'* (*Mūlamadhyamakavṛttiprasannapadānāma, Dbu ma rtsa ba'i 'grel pa tshig gsal ba zhes bya ba*). D3860, dbu ma, 'a, 1a–200a.

———. *Engaging in Madhyamaka* (*Madhyamakāvatāra, Dbu ma la 'jug pa*). D3861, dbu ma, 'a, 201b–219a.

———. *Explanation of the 'Engaging in Madhyamaka'* (*Madhyamakāvatārabhāṣya, Dbu ma la 'jug pa'i bshad pa*). D3862, dbu ma, 'a, 220a–349a.

———. *Extensive Commentary on [Āryadeva's] 'Four Hundred Stanzas on the Yogic Deeds of Bodhisattvas' (Bodhisattvayogacaryācatuḥśatakaṭīkā, Byang chub sems dpa'i rnal 'byor spyod pa bzhi brgya pa'i rgya cher 'grel pa)*. D3865, dbu ma, ya, 30b–239a.

Changkya Rölpé Dorjé (*lcang skya rol pa'i rdo rje*). *Ornament Beautifying the Meru of Muni's Teachings: Presentation of Tenets (Grub pa'i mtha' rnam par gzhag pa thub bstan lhun po'i mdzes rgyan)*. Krung go bod kyi shes rig dpe skrun khang, 1989.

Chödrak Gyamtso (*chos grags rgya mtsho*, the Seventh Karmapa). *Ocean of Textual Systems of Reasoning Entirely Condensing Streams of All Good Explanations of Valid Cognition (Tshad ma legs par bshad pa thams cad kyi chu bo yongs su 'du ba rigs pa'i gzhung lugs kyi rgya mtsho)*. Sarnath, Varanasi: Central Institute of Higher Tibetan Studies, 1999.

Chömpel (*chos 'phel*). *New Guidebook Describing Pilgrimage Places of the Snowy Land of Tibet (Gangs can bod kyi gnas bshad lam yig gsar ma)*. Pekin: Mi rigs dpe skrun khang, 2004.

Chopgyé Trichen Ngakwang Khyenrap Tupten Lekshé Gyamtso (*bco brgyad khri chen ngag dbang mkhyen rab thub bstan legs bshad rgya mtsho*). *Feast for Minds of the Fortunate: Brief History of Glorious Sakyapas—Chariot of the Teachings of Sūtras and Tantras of the Land of Snows (Gangs ljongs mdo sngags kyi bstan pa'i shing rta dpal ldan sa skya pa'i chos 'byung mdor bsdus skal bzang yid kyi dga' ston)*. Dharamsala: Bod gzhung shes rig par khang, 1969. English translation in Chogay Trichen Rinpoche. *The History of the Sakya Tradition*. Bristol: Ganesha Press, 1983.

Darma Rinchen (*dar ma rin chen*)/ Gyeltsap Darma Rinchen (*rgyal tshab dar ma rin chen*). *Ornament of Essence: Explanation of [Haribhadra's] 'Clear Meaning' Commentary on the 'Ornament of Clear Realizations' Treatise of Quintessential Instructions on the Perfection of Wisdom (Shes rab kyi pha rol tu phyin pa'i man ngag gi bstan bcos mngon par rtogs pa'i rgyan gyi 'grel pa don gsal ba'i rnam bshad snying po'i rgyan)*. Lan kru'u: Kan su'u mi rigs dpe skrun khang, 2000

Dharmakīrti. *Analysis of Relations (Sambandhaparīkṣa, 'Brel ba brtag pa)*. D4214, tshad ma, ce, 255a–256a.

———. *Ascertainment of Valid Cognition (Pramāṇaviniścaya, Tshad ma rnam par nges pa)*. D4211, tshad ma, ce, 152b–230a.

———. *Commentary on Valid Cognition (Pramāṇavārttikakārikā, Tshad ma rnam 'grel gyi tshig le'ur byas pa)*. D4210, tshad ma, ce, 94b–151a. Also in Miyasaka, Yūsho (ed.). "Pramāṇavārttika-kārikā (Sanskrit and Tibetan)." *Acta Indologica*, vol. 2 (1971/72): 1–206.

———. *Drop of Reasoning (Nyāyabinduprakaraṇa, Rigs pa'i thigs pa zhes bya ba'i rab tu byas pa)*. D4212, tshad ma, ce, 231b–238a.

———. *Drop of Reasons (Hetubindunāmaprakaraṇa, Gtan tshigs kyi thigs pa zhes bya ba'i rab tu byas pa)*. D4213, tshad ma, ce, 238a–255a.

———. *Proof of Other Continua (Saṃtānāntarasiddhināmaprakaraṇa, Rgyud gzhan grub pa zhes bya ba'i rab tu byed pa)*. D4219, tshad ma, che, 355b–359a.

———. *Science of Debate* (*Vādanyāya, Rtsod pa'i rigs pa*). D4218, tshad ma, che, 326b–355b.

Dignāga. *Compendium of Valid Cognition* (*Pramāṇasamuccaya, Tshad ma kun las btus pa*). D4203, tshad ma, ce, 1b–13a.

Drakpa Gyeltsen (*grags pa rgyal mtshan*). *Precious Tree: Clear Realizations of Tantras* (*Rgyud kyi mngon par rtogs pa rin po che'i ljon shing*), 1–277. In Sa-skya lam 'bras literature series, vol. 23. Dehradun, U.P., India: Sakya Centre, 1985.

Gorampa Sönam Senggé (*go rams pa bsod nams seng ge*). *Distinguishing the Views: Moonrays of Essential Points of the Supreme Vehicle* (*Lta ba'i shan 'byed theg mchog gnad kyi zla zer*). Collected Works of Kun-mkhyen Go-rams-pa Bsod-nams-seng-ge, vol. 5, 417–510. Bir, India: Yashodhara Publications, 1995. English translation in Cabezón, José Ignacio and Geshe Lobsang Dargyay. *Freedom from Extremes: Gorampa's "Distinguishing the Views" and the Polemics of Emptiness*. Boston: Wisdom Publications, 2007.

———. *Elimination of Mistakes about the Three Types of Vows: Answers to the Polemics and Questions Regarding the '[Thorough Differentiation of the] Three Types of Vows' Treatise* (*Sdom pa gsum gyi bstan bcos la dris shing rtsod pa'i lan sdom gsum 'khrul spong*). Collected Works of Kun-mkhyen Go-rams-pa Bsod-nams-seng-ge, vol. 9, 489–619. Bir, India: Yashodhara Publications, 1995.

———. *General Presentation of Madhyamaka: Thorough Clarification of Definitive Meaning* (*Dbu ma'i spyi don nges don rab gsal*). Collected Works of Kun-mkhyen Go-rams-pa Bsod-nams-seng-ge, vol, 5, 1–415. Bir, India: Yashodhara Publications, 1995.

Guṇaprabha. *Sūtra on Moral Discipline* (*Vinayasūtra, 'Dul ba'i mdo*). D4117, 'dul ba, wu, 1b–100a.

Gungru Gyeltsen Zangpo (*gung ru rgyal mtshan bzang po*). *Stream of Nectar: Good Explanations [Based on] the Guru's Quintessential Instructions* (*Legs bshad bla ma'i man ngag bdud rtsi'i chu rgyun*). Collected Works of Gungru Gyeltsen Zangpo (*Gung ru rgyal mtshan bzang po'i gsung'bum*), in Mes po'i shul bzhag, vol. 37, 285–421. Dpal brtsegs bod yig dpe rnying zhib 'jug khang, 2007.

———. *Summarized Exposition of Madhyamaka* (*Dbu ma'i stong thun*). Collected Works of Gungru Gyeltsen Zangpo (*Gung ru rgyal mtshan bzang po'i gsung'bum*), in Mes po'i shul bzhag, vol. 38, 177–350. Dpal brtsegs bod yig dpe rnying zhib 'jug khang, 2007.

Haribhadra. *Clear Meaning* (*Sphuṭārthā, Don gsal*; full title: *Abhisamayālaṃkāranāmaprajñāpāramitopadeśaśāstravṛtti, Shes rab kyi pha rol tu phyin pa'i man ngag gi bstan bcos mngon par rtogs pa'i rgyan ces bya ba'i 'grel pa*). D3793, shes phyin, ja, 78b–140a.

Jetāri. *Differentiation of Sugata's Texts* (*Sugatamatavibhaṅgakārikā, Bde bar gshegs pa'i gzhung rnam par 'byed pa'i tshig le'ur byas pa*). D3899, dbu ma, a, 7b–8a.

Jñānagarbha. *Differentiation of the Two Truths* (*Satyadvayavibhaṅga, Bden pa gnyis rnam par 'byed pa*). D3881, dbu ma, sa, 1a–3b. English translation in Eckel, Malcolm David. *Jñānagarbha's Commentary on the Distinction*

Between the Two Truths. Albany, New York: State University of New York Press, 1987.

Kamalaśīla. *Commentary on Difficult Points of [Śāntarakṣita's] 'Compendium of Principles' (Tattvasaṃgrahapañjikā, De kho na nyid bsdus pa'i dka' 'grel)*. D4267, tshad ma, ze 133b–'e 331a.

———. *Stages of Meditation (Bhāvanākrama, Sgom pa'i rim pa)*. D3915, dbu ma, ki, 22a–41b; D3916, dbu ma, ki, 42a–55b; D3917, dbu ma, ki, 55b–68b.

Kelden Tsering (*skal ldan tshe ring*). *Presentation of Tenets of Glorious Sakyapas (Dpal sa skya pa'i grub mtha'i rnam bzhag)*. Zhang kang then mā dpe skrun khang, 2001.

Kongtrül Yönten Gyamtso (*kong sprul yon tan rgya mtsho*)/ Lodrö Tayé (*blo gros mtha' yas*). *Limitless Ocean of Knowables (Shes bya mtha' yas pa'i rgya mtsho)*, vol. 1–3. Peking: Mi rigs pe skrun khang, 1982.

Künga Drölchok (*kun dga' grol mchog*). *Detailed Analysis of the Liberation Story of the Great Paṇḍita Shakya Chokden (Paṇḍi ta chen po shākya mchog ldan gyi rnam par thar pa zhib mo rnam 'byed pa)*. In Collected Works of Shakya Chokden, vol. 16, 1–233. Thimphu, Bhutan: Kunzang Tobgey, 1975.

———. *Thunder of Melodious Praise: Liberation Story of the Dharma King Rikden Namgyel Drakpa Zangpo (Rigs ldan chos kyi rgyal po rnam rgyal grags pa bzang po'i rnam par thar pa rab bsngags snyan pa'i 'brug sgra)*. Kathmandu: Nepal-German Manuscript Preservation Project. Microfilm reel E–1872/6. Xylograph, 39 fols.

Longchen Rapjam (*klong chen rab 'byams*). *Great Chariot: [Auto-]Commentary on the 'Mind Nature Revitalization of the Great Perfection' (Rdzogs pa chen po sems nyid ngal gso)*. California: Yeshe De Project, 1994.

Maitreya. *Differentiation of Phenomena and the Nature of Phenomena (Dharmadharmatāvibhāga, Chos dang chos nyid rnam par 'byed pa)*. D4022, sems tsam, phi, 46b–49a.

———. *Differentiation of the Middle and Extremes (Madhyāntavibhāga, Dbus dang mtha' rnam par 'byed pa)*. D4021, sems tsam, phi, 40b–45a. Edited Sanskrit text: Nagao, Gadjin M. *Madhyāntavibhāga-Bhāṣya: A Buddhist Philosophical Treatise Edited for the First Time from a Sanskrit Manuscript*. Tokyo: Suzuki Research Foundation, 1964. Sanskrit text and English translation of the first chapter in Wood, Thomas E. *Mind Only: A Philosophical and Doctrinal Analysis of the Vijñānavāda*. Monographs of the Society for Asian and Comparative Philosophy, 9. Honolulu: University of Hawaii Press, 1991.

———. *Ornament of Clear Realizations (Abhisamayālaṃkāranāmaprajñāpāramitopadeśaśāstrakārikā, Shes rab kyi pha rol tu phyin pa'i man ngag gi bstan bcos mngon par rtogs pa'i rgyan zhes bya ba'i tshig le'ur byas pa)*. D3786, shes phyin, ka, 1a–13a.

———. *Ornament of Mahāyāna Sūtras (Mahāyānasūtrālaṃkāra, Theg pa chen po mdo sde'i rgyan)*. D4020, sems tsam, phi, 1a–39a. Sanskrit text and French translation: Lévi, Sylvain. *Mahāyāna-sūtrālaṃkāra: exposé de la doctrine du grand véhicule selon le systéme Yogācāra*. 2 vols. Paris: Bibliothéque de l'École des Hautes Études, 1907, 1911. English translation: Lobsang

Jamspal, R. Clark, J. Wilson, L. Zwilling, M. Sweet, and R. Thurman. *The Universal Vehicle Discourse Literature (*Mahāyānasūtrālaṁkāra*) By Maitreyanātha/Āryāsaṅga Together with its* Commentary *(*Bhāṣya*) By Vasubandhu.* New York: American Institute of Buddhist Studies, 2004.

———. *Sublime Continuum of Mahāyāna* (*Mahāyānottaratantraśāstra, Theg pa chen po rgyud bla ma*). D4024, sems tsam, phi, 54b–73a. Edited Sanskrit text in Johnston, Edward H. (ed.). *Ratnagotravibhāga Mahāyānottaratantraśāstra.* Patna: The Bihar Research Society, 1950. Translated in Takasaki, Jikido. *A Study on the Ratnagotravibhāga.* Rome: Istituto Italiano per il Medio ed Estremo Oriente, 1966.

Mangtö Ludrup Gyamtso (*mang thos klu sgrub rgya mtsho*). *The Sun Illuminating Calculations of the Teachings* (*Bstan rtsis gsal ba'i nyin byed.* Bod ljongs mi dmangs dpe skrun khang, 1988.

Mikyö Dorjé (*mi bskyod rdo rje*, the Eighth Karmapa). [Addendum to Chödrak Gyamtso's *Ocean of Textual Systems of Reasoning.*] In the *Ocean of Textual Systems of Reasoning Entirely Condensing Streams of All Good Explanations of Valid Cognition* (*Tshad ma legs par bshad pa thams cad kyi chu bo yongs su 'du ba rigs pa'i gzhung lugs kyi rgya mtsho*), vol. 2, 270–279. Sarnath, Varanasi: Central Institute of Higher Tibetan Studies, 1999.

Mipam Gyamtso (*mi pham rgya mtsho*). *Differentiation of Primordial Mind and Appearances: Commentary on Maitreya's Stanzas of 'Differentiation of Phenomena and the Nature of Phenomena'* (*Chos dang chos nyid rnam par 'byed pa'i tshig le'ur byas pa'i 'grel ba ye shes snang ba rnam 'byed*). Sde-dge dgon-chen Printings of the Writings of 'Jam-mgon 'Ju Mi-pham-rgya-mtsho, vol. 4, 609–657.

———. *'Gateway to Scholarship' Treatise* (*Mkhas pa'i tshul la 'jug pa'i sgo zhes bya ba'i bstan bcos*). Mtsho sngon mi rigs dpe skrun khang, 1988.

———. *Oral Instructions of Delighted Guru Mañjughoṣa: Explanation of [Śāntarakṣita's] 'Ornament of Madhyamaka'* (*Dbu ma rgyan gyi rnam bshad 'jam dbyangs bla ma dgyes pa'i zhal lung*). Sde-dge dgon-chen Printings of the Writings of 'Jam-mgon 'Ju Mi-pham-rgya-mtsho, vol. 13, 1–358. English translation in Thomas H. Doctor (tr.), *Speech of Delight: Mipham's Commentary on Śāntarakṣita's* Ornament of the Middle Way *by Mipham Jamyang Namgyal Gyatso.* Ithaca, New York: Snow Lion Publications, 2004.

———. *Precious Lamp of Definitive Knowledge* (*Nges shes rin po che'i sgron me*). Sde-dge dgon-chen Printings of the Writings of 'Jam-mgon 'Ju Mi-pham-rgya-mtsho, vol. 9, 71–123. English translation in Pettit, John Whitney. *Mipham's* Beacon of Certainty*: Illuminating the View of Dzogchen, the Great Perfection.* Boston: Wisdom Publications, 1999.

Nāgārjuna. *Commentary on the Mind of Enlightenment* (*Bodhicittavivaraṇa, Byang chub sems kyi 'grel pa*). D1800, rgyud, ngi, 38a–42b.

———. *Five Stages* (*Pañcakrama, Rim pa lnga pa*). D1802, rgyud, ngi, 45a–57a.

———. *Praise of the Dharma-Sphere* (*Dharmadhātustotra, Chos kyi dbyings su bstod pa*). D1118, bstod tshogs, ka, 63b–67b. English translation in Brunnhölzl, Karl. In Praise of Dharmadhātu *by Nāgārjuna, Commentary by the Third Karmapa,* 117–129. Ithaca, New York: Snow Lion Publications, 2007.

———. *Praise of the Mind-Vajra* (*Cittavajrastava, Sems kyi rdo rje'i bstod pa*). D1121, bstod tshogs, ka, 69b–70a.
———. *Refutation of Objections* (*Virgrahavyāvartanīkārikā, Rtsod pa bzlog pa'i tshig le'ur byas pa*). D3828, dbu ma, tsa, 27a–29a.
———. *Seventy Stanzas on Emptiness* (*Śūnayatāsaptatikārikā, Stong pa nyid bdun cu pa'i tshig le'ur byas pa*). D3827, dbu ma, tsa, 24a–27a.
———. *Sixty Stanzas of Reasoning* (*Yuktiṣaṣṭikākārikā, Rigs pa drug cu pa'i tshig le'ur byas pa*). D3825, dbu ma, tsa, 20b–22b. Edited Tibetan with Sanskrit fragments and English translation in Lindtner, Christian. *Nagarjuniana: Studies in the Writings and Philosophy of Nāgārjuna*. Indiske Studier 4, 100–119. Copenhagen: Akademisk Forlag, 1982.
———. *Treatise Called 'Finely Woven'* (*Vaidalyasūtranāma, Zhib mo rnam par 'thag pa zhes bya ba'i mdo*). D3826, dbu ma, tsa, 22b–24a.
———. *Wisdom: Root Stanzas on Madhyamaka* (*Prajñānāmamūlamadhyamakakārikā, Dbu ma rtsa ba'i tshig le'ur byas pa shes rab ces bya ba*). D3824, dbu ma, tsa, 1a–19a. Edited Sanskrit: de Jong, Jan W. (ed.). *Nāgārjuna Mūlamadhyamakakārikāḥ*. Madras: India, The Adyar Library and Research Centre, 1977. English translation: Garfield, Jay L. *The Fundamental Wisdom of the Middle Way: Nāgārjuna's* Mūlamadhyamakakārikā. Oxford: Oxford University Press, 1995.
Ngakwang Chödrak (*ngag dbang chos grags*). *Abundant Discourse on Distinguishing and Decisive Analysis of Tenets of Early and Late Tibetan Scholars* (*Bod kyi mkhas pa snga phyi dag gi grub mtha' shan 'byed mtha' dpyod dang bcas pa'i 'bel ba'i gtam*). Thimphu, Bhutan: Kunzang Tobgyal, 1984.
Pawo Tsuklak Trengwa (*dpa' bo gtsug lag phreng ba*). *Feast for Scholars: Buddhist History* (*Chos byung mkhas pa'i dga' ston*), 2 vols. Delhi, India: Karmapae Chodhey Gyalwae Sungrab Partun Khang.
Peltsek (*dpal brtsegs*). *Explanation of the Stages of the Views* (*Lta ba'i rim pa bshad pa*). D4356, sna tshogs, co, 236b–238b.
———. *Quintessential Instructions on the Stages of the Views: Seventeen Visions* (*Lta ba'i rim pa'i man ngag snang ba bcu bdun*). P4728, rgyud grel, bu, 424a–426b.
Prajñākaragupta. *Ornament of [Dharmakīrti's] 'Commentary on Valid Cognition'* (*Pramāṇavārttikālaṃkāra, Tshad ma rnam 'grel gyi rgyan*). D4221, tshad ma, te, 1b-the, 282a.
Puṇḍarīka. *Stainless Light* (*Vimalaprabhā, Dri ma med pa'i 'od*; the full title: *Vimalaprabhānāmamūlatantrānusāriṇīdvādaśasāhasrikālaghukālacakratantrarājaṭīkā, Bsdus pa'i rgyud kyi rgyal po dus kyi 'khor lo'i 'grel bshad rtsa ba'i rgyud kyi rjes su 'jug pa stong phrag bcu gnyis pa dri ma med pa'i 'od ces bya ba*). D1347, rgyud, tha, 107b- da, 297a. Edited and annotated Sanskrit text of the first two chapters: Upādhyāya, Jagannāth (edited and annotated). *Vimalaprabhā: śrīmañjuśrīyaśoviracitasya paramādibuddhoddhṛtasya śrīlaghukālacakratantrarājasya kalkinā śrīpuṇḍarīkeṇa viracitā ṭīkā*, vol. 1. Bibliotheca Indo-Tibetica Series, 11. Sarnath, Varanasi: Central Institute of Higher Tibetan Studies, 1986. English translation of the second chapter: Wallace, Vesna A. (tr.). *The Kālacakratantra: The Chapter on the*

Individual together with the Vimalaprabhā. New York: American Institute of Buddhist Studies at Columbia University, 2004.

Rangjung Dorjé (*rang byung rdo rje*, the Third Karmapa). *Profound Inner Meaning* (*Zab mo nang (gi) don*). Mtsho sngon mi rigs dpe skrun khang, 2001.

———. *Treatise Called 'Explanation of the Tathāgata-Essence'* (*De bzhin gshegs pa'i snying po bstan pa zhes bya ba'i bstan bcos*). Xylographic print from blocks preserved at Rum-btegs Karma-chos-sgar in Sikkim. English translation in Brunnhölzl, Karl. *Luminous Heart: The Third Karmapa on Consciousness, Wisdom, and Buddha Nature*, 352–360. Ithaca, New York: Snow Lion Publications, 2009.

———. *Treatise Differentiating beween Consciousness and Primordial Mind* (*Rnam par shes pa dang ye shes 'byed pa'i bstan bcos*, Rumtek blockprint, n.d.). English translation in Brunnhölzl, Karl. *Luminous Heart: The Third Karmapa on Consciousness, Wisdom, and Buddha Nature*, 361–366. Ithaca, New York: Snow Lion Publications, 2009.

Ratnākaraśānti. *Establishment of the Middle Way: Commentary on the 'Ornament of Madhyamaka'* (*Madhyamakālaṃkāravṛttimadhyamapratipadāsiddhināma, Dbu ma rgyan gyi 'grel ba dbu ma'i lam grub pa zhes bya ba*). D4072, sems tsam, hi, 102a–120b.

———. *Quintessential Instructions on the 'Ornament of Madhyamaka'* (*Madhyamakālaṃkāropadeśa, Dbu ma rgyan gyi man ngag*). D4085, sems tsam, hi, 223b–231a.

———. *Quintessential Instructions on the Perfection of Wisdom* (*Prajñāpāramitopadeśa, Shes rab kyi pha rol tu phyin pa'i man ngag*). D4079, sems tsam, hi, 133b–162b.

Rendawa Zhönnu Lodrö (*red mda' ba gzhon nu blo gros*). *Lamp Illuminating Thatness: Explanation of [Candrakīrti's] 'Engaging in Madhyamaka'* (*Dbu ma la 'jug pa'i rnam bshad de kho na nyid gsal ba'i sgron ma*). Sarnath, Varanasi: Central Institute of Higher Tibetan Studies, 1995.

Rongtön Sheja Künrik (*rong ston shes bya kun rig*). *Amassment of Jewels: Praise to the Six Ornaments and Two Supreme Ones* (*Rgyan drug mchog gnyis la bstod pa rin chen spungs pa*). The Collected Works of Rong-ston Shak-kya Rgyal-mtsen, vol. B (*kha*), 392–394. Dehra Dun, India: Sakya College, 1999.

———. *Ascertainment of the Definitive Meaning: Explanation of [Candrakīrti's] 'Engaging in Madhyamaka'* (*Dbu ma la 'jug pa'i rnam bshad nges don rnam nges*). In *Two Controversial Mādhyamika Treatises*, 1–305. Bir, India: Yashodhara Publications, 1996.

———. *Moonrays of Essential Points: Abridged Essence of Incorporation into Experience* (*Nyams su len pa'i rim pa snying po mdor bsdus pa gnad kyi zla zer*). The Collected Works of Rong-ston Shak-kya rgal-mtsen, vol. B (*kha*), 562–565. Dehra Dun, India: Sakya College, 1999.

———. *Thorough Clarification of Words and Meanings: Explanation of the Commentary on the Treatise of Quintessential Instructions on the Perfection of Wisdom Called 'Ornament of Clear Realizations'* (*Shes rab kyi pha rol *tu phyin pa'i man ngag gi bstan bcos mngon par rtogs pa'i rgyan ces bya ba'i 'grel ba'i rnam bshad tshig don rab tu gsal ba*). New Delhi: Pal-ldan Sakya'i-sung-rab Book Publisher, 1989.

———. *Vision of Profound Thatness: Explanation of [Nāgārjuna's 'Wisdom:] Root [Stanzas on] Madhyamaka' (Dbu ma rtsa ba'i rnam bshad zab mo'i de kho na nyid snang ba)*. Sarnath: Central Institute of Higher Tibetan Studies, 1988.

Sakya Pendita Künga Gyeltsen (*sa skya paṇḍita kun dga' rgyal mtshan*). *Thorough Clarification of Muni's Intent (Thub pa'i dgongs pa rab tu gsal ba)*. Xylographic print. Unknown publisher.

———. *Thorough Differentiation of the Three Types of Vows (Sdom pa gsum gyi rab tu dbye ba)*. Sa skya bka' 'bum, vol. 12 (na), 1a–48b. English translation by Rhoton, Jared Douglas. *A Clear Differentiation of the Three Codes: Essential Distinctions among the Individual Liberation, Mahāyāna, and Tantric Systems*. Albany, New York: State University of New York Press, 2002.

———. *Treasure of the Science of Valid Cognition: The Root Text and the [Auto-] Commmentary (Tshad ma rigs pa'i gter gyi rtsa ba dang 'grel pa)*. Bod ljongs mi dmangs dpe skrun khang, 1989.

Śāntarakṣita. *Ornament of Madhyamaka (Madhyamakālaṃkārakārikā, Dbu ma'i rgyan gyi tshig le'ur byas pa)*. D3884, dbu ma, sa, 53a1–56b3. English translation and edited Tibetan in Ichigō, Masamichi. "Śāntarakṣita's Madhyamakālaṃkāra." In *Studies in the Literature of the Great Vehicle*. Michigan Studies in Buddhist Literature No. 1, edited by Luis O. Gómez and Jonathan A. Silk, 141–240. Ann Arbor: Collegiate Institute for the Study of Buddhist Literature and Center for South and Southeast Asian Studies, The University of Michigan, 1989.

Śāntideva. *Engaging in the Bodhisattva Deeds (Bodhisattvacaryāvatāra, Byang chub sems dpa'i spyod pa la 'jug pa)*. D3871, dbu ma, la, 1a–40a. Edited and translated in Sharma, Parmananda. *Śāntideva's* Bodhicharyāvatāra *[*sic*]: Original Sanskrit text with English Translation and Exposition Based on Prajnākarmati's [*sic*] Panjikā [*sic*]*, vols. 1–2. New Delhi: Aditya Prakashan, 1990. Also translated in Crosby, Kate and Andrew Skilton. *The Bodhicaryāvatāra*. Oxford: Oxford University Press, 1995.

Shakya Chokden (*shākya mchog ldan*). *Abbreviated Meaning of the '[Hevajra in] Two Chapters': Transmission Stages of the Explanatory Lineage (Brtag gnyis kyi bsdus don// bshad rgyud kyi rgyud pa'i rim pa rnams)*. Collected Writings of Gser-mdog paṇ-chen Śākya-mchog-ldan, vol. 13, 463–467. Thimphu, Bhutan: Kunzang Tobgey, 1975.

———. *Answer to the Inquiry Regarding Identification of the Support and Supported [Maṇḍala] of Raktayamāri (Gshed dmar gyi rten dang brten par bcas pa'i ngos 'dzin gyi zhus lan)*. Collected Writings of Gser-mdog paṇ-chen Śākya-mchog-ldan, vol. 17, 606–608. Thimphu, Bhutan: Kunzang Tobgey, 1975.

———. *Answers to Questions Issuing from the 'Differentiation of the Two Modes' (Tshul gnyis rnam 'byed las 'phros pa'i dris lan)*. Collected Writings of Gser-mdog paṇ-chen Śākya-mchog-ldan, vol. 17, 414–416. Thimphu, Bhutan: Kunzang Tobgey, 1975.

———. *Answers to Three Universally Known Questions from the 'One Hundred and Eight Questions on the 'Thorough Differentiation of the Three Types of Vows''* (*Sdom pa gsum gyi rab dbye'i dri ba brgya dang brgyad las kun la grags che ba'i dri ba gsum gyi lan gdabs pa*). Collected Writings of Gser-mdog paṇ-chen Śākya-mchog-ldan, vol. 17, 381–401. Thimphu, Bhutan: Kunzang Tobgey, 1975.

———. *Appearance of Reasoning Defeating Bad Systems: Commentary on Difficult Points of the Extensive Treatise 'Commentary on Valid Cognition'* (*Rgyas pa'i bstan bcos tshad ma rnam 'grel gyi dka' 'grel rigs pa'i snang ba lugs ngan pham byed*). Collected Writings of Gser-mdog paṇ-chen Śākya-mchog-ldan, vol. 19, 169–445. Thimphu, Bhutan: Kunzang Tobgey, 1975.

———. *Appearance of the Sun Pleasing All Thinkers: Discussion of the History of the Chariot Ways of [Dignāga's] 'Sūtra on Valid Cognition' and [Its] Treatises* (*Tshad ma'i bstan bcos kyi shin rta'i srol rnams ji ltar 'byung ba'i tshul gtam du bya ba nyin mor byed pa'i snang bas dpyod ldan mtha' dag dga' bar byed pa*). Collected Writings of Gser-mdog paṇ-chen Śākya-mchog-ldan, vol. 19, 1–137. Thimphu, Bhutan: Kunzang Tobgey, 1975.

———. *Ascertainment of Intents of Mighty Lords: [Treatise in] Eleven Dharma Sections Eliminating Mistakes Regarding Hidden Meanings of Oral Lineages* (*Snyan rgyud gyi sbas don la 'khrul pa spong ba mthu stobs dbang phyug gi dgongs pa rnam nges chos tshan bcu gcig pa*). In *'Hundred and Eight Dharma Sections' Treatise* (*Chos tshan brgya dang brgyad pa zhes bya ba'i bstan bcos*). Collected Writings of Gser-mdog paṇ-chen Śākya-mchog-ldan, vol. 13, 274–300. Thimphu, Bhutan: Kunzang Tobgey, 1975.

———. *Ascertainment of Intents of Supreme Accomplished Ones: Treatise on Differentiation of the Great Seal* (*Phyag rgya chen po'i shan 'byed kyi bstan bcos grub pa mchog gi dgongs pa rnam nges*). Collected Writings of Gser-mdog paṇ-chen Śākya-mchog-ldan, vol. 17, 346–355. Thimphu, Bhutan: Kunzang Tobgey, 1975.

———. *Ascertainment of Secrecy of the Three Tantras: Extensive Explanation of the 'Sūtra on Taking the Result as the Path'* (*'Bras bu lam byed kyi mdo'i rgya cher bshad pa rgyud gsum gyi gsang ba rnam nges*). Collected Writings of Gser-mdog paṇ-chen Śākya-mchog-ldan, vol. 13, 485–521. Thimphu, Bhutan: Kunzang Tobgey, 1975.

———. *Ascertainment of the Dharma-Sphere: Explanation of [Nāgārjuna's] Treatise 'Praise of the Dharma-Sphere'* (*Chos kyi dbyings su bstod pa zhes bya ba'i bstan bcos kyi rnam par bshad pa chos kyi dbyings rnam par nges pa*). Collected Writings of Gser-mdog paṇ-chen Śākya-mchog-ldan, vol. 7, 303–346. Thimphu, Bhutan: Kunzang Tobgey, 1975.

———. *Beautiful Garland of Water-Lilies: Explanation of Several Difficult Points of [Candrakīrti's] 'Engaging in Madhyamaka'* (*Dbu ma la 'jug pa'i dka' ba'i gnas 'ga' zhig rnam par bshad pa ku mud kyi phreng mdzes*), Collected Writings of Gser-mdog paṇ-chen Śākya-mchog-ldan, vol. 5, 459–497. Thimphu, Bhutan: Kunzang Tobgey, 1975.

———. *Beautifully Woven Garlands of Wondrous Deeds of Glorious Atiśa with His [Spiritual] Sons and Lineage* (*Dpal ldan a ti sha sras dang brgyud par bcas pa'i ngo mtshar mdzad pa'i phreng ba spel legs*). Collected Writings of Gser-mdog paṇ-chen Śākya-mchog-ldan, vol. 16, 538–550. Thimphu, Bhutan: Kunzang Tobgey, 1975.

———. *Beautifying Ornament of the Lord of Speech: Decisive Analysis in Consequences of the Twenty Kinds of Saṅgha* (*Dge 'dun nyi shu'i mtha' rnam par dpyad pa'i thal 'gyur ngag gi dbang po'i mdzes rgyan*). Collected Writings of Gser-mdog paṇ-chen Śākya-mchog-ldan, vol. 13, 1–111. Thimphu, Bhutan: Kunzang Tobgey, 1975.

———. *Chariot of the Sun Illuminating the 'Sūtra': Explanation of Difficult Points of the 'Sūtra on Moral Discipline'* (*'Dul ba mdo'i dka' ba'i gnas rnam par bshad pa mdo'i snang byed nyi ma'i shing rta*). Collected Writings of Gser-mdog paṇ-chen Śākya-mchog-ldan, vol. 22, 1–265. Thimphu, Bhutan: Kunzang Tobgey, 1975.

———. *Clarification of Acceptance and Rejection Regarding the Profound Path: [Treatise in] Thirteen Dharma Sections on Differentiation of Incorporation into Experience of Mantra by Outsiders [non-Buddhists] and Insiders [Buddhists]* (*Phyi nang gi sngags kyi nyams len so sor phye ba zab lam blang dor gsal byed chos tshan bcu gsum*). In *'Hundred and Eight Dharma Sections' Treatise* (*Chos tshan brgya dang brgyad pa zhes bya ba'i bstan bcos*). Collected Writings of Gser-mdog paṇ-chen Śākya-mchog-ldan, vol. 13, 428–458. Thimphu, Bhutan: Kunzang Tobgey, 1975.

———. *Clear Identification of the Presence of the String of One Hundred and Eight Beads of Mistakes Conceived by [Wrong] Logic in Madhyamaka of the System of Others* (*Gzhan lugs kyi ni dbu ma la// rtog ges brtags pa'i nor ba'i phreng// brgya dang rtsa brgyad yod pa yi// ngos 'dzin gsal po*). Collected Writings of Gser-mdog paṇ-chen Śākya-mchog-ldan, vol. 4, 407–419. Thimphu, Bhutan: Kunzang Tobgey, 1975.

———. *Commentary on Essentials of Definitive Meaning: Explanation of [Candrakīrti's] 'Engaging in Madhyamaka'* (*Dbu ma la 'jug pa'i rnam par bshad pa nges don gnad kyi ṭī ka*). Collected Writings of Gser-mdog paṇ-chen Śākya-mchog-ldan, vol. 5. 281–457. Thimphu, Bhutan: Kunzang Tobgey, 1975.

———. *Condensed Essence of Madhyamaka: Explanation of [Nāgārjuna's] 'Commentary on the Ultimate Mind of Enlightenment'* (*Don dam byang chub sems 'grel gyi bshad pa dbu ma'i snying po bsdus pa*). Collected Writings of Gser-mdog paṇ-chen Śākya-mchog-ldan, vol. 7, 346–391. Thimphu, Bhutan: Kunzang Tobgey, 1975.

———. *Continuous Meter Praise of the Gathering of Deities of the Support and Supported [Maṇḍala] of Cakrasaṃvara* (*Rten dang brten par bcas pa'i 'khor lo bde mchog gi lha tshogs la rgyun chags pa'i sdeb sbyor gyi sgo nas bstod pa*). Collected Writings of Gser-mdog paṇ-chen Śākya-mchog-ldan, vol. 8, 1–10. Thimphu, Bhutan: Kunzang Tobgey, 1975.

———. *Defeater of Flower Arrows: Questions on the 'Bhaiśajyaguru Sūtra' Ritual* (*Sman bla'i mdo chog gi dri ba me tog mda' 'joms*). Collected Writings of Gser-mdog paṇ-chen Śākya-mchog-ldan, vol. 17, 319–324. Thimphu, Bhutan: Kunzang Tobgey, 1975.

———. *Discourse Eliminating Mistakes with Regard to Teachings of Scriptural Collections: Fourteen Dharma Sections* (*Sde snod kyi chos la 'khrul pa sel ba'i gtam chos tshan bcu bzhi pa*). In *'Hundred and Eight Dharma Sections' Treatise* (*Chos tshan brgya dang brgyad pa zhes bya ba'i bstan bcos*). Collected Writings of Gser-mdog paṇ-chen Śākya-mchog-ldan, vol. 13, 202–229. Thimphu, Bhutan: Kunzang Tobgey, 1975.

———. *Dispelling Mental Darkness: Abridgement of the Modes of Inducing Ascertainment by Valid Cognition* (*Tshad mas nges pa 'dren pa'i tshul nyung ngur bsdus pa yid kyi mun sel*). Collected Writings of Gser-mdog paṇ-chen Śākya-mchog-ldan, vol. 19, 146–155. Thimphu, Bhutan: Kunzang Tobgey, 1975.

———. *Divine Drum Melody: Praise of the Great Kashmiri Paṇḍita Śākyaśri* (*Kha che paṇ chen shākya shri'i bstod pa lha'i rnga dbyangs*). Collected Writings of Gser-mdog paṇ-chen Śākya-mchog-ldan, vol. 16, 556–557. Thimphu, Bhutan: Kunzang Tobgey, 1975.

———. *Drop of Ambrosia: Clarification of the Eight Path Cycles* (*Lam skor brgyad kyi gsal byed bdud rtsi'i thig pa*). Collected Writings of Gser-mdog paṇ-chen Śākya-mchog-ldan, vol. 13, 630–640. Thimphu, Bhutan: Kunzang Tobgey, 1975.

———. *Drop of Ambrosia: Differentiation of Classes of Tantras* (*Rgyud sde'i rnam par phye ba bdud rtsi'i thig pa*). Collected Writings of Gser-mdog paṇ-chen Śākya-mchog-ldan, vol. 13, 467–478. Thimphu, Bhutan: Kunzang Tobgey, 1975.

———. *Drop of Ambrosia of Definitive Meaning: Entering Essential Points of the Two Truths* (*Bden pa gnyis kyi gnad la 'jug pa nges don bdud rtsi'i thigs pa*). Collected Writings of Gser-mdog paṇ-chen Śākya-mchog-ldan, vol. 4, 375–381. Thimphu, Bhutan: Kunzang Tobgey, 1975. English translation in Komarovski, Yaroslav (tr.). *Three Texts on Madhyamaka by Shakya Chokden*. Dharamsala, India: Library of Tibetan Works and Archives, 2000.

———. *Drumming Sounds amidst Wondrous Clouds: Liberation Story of Glorious Holy Lama Kumāramati* (*Dpal ldan bla ma dam pa ku ma ra ma ti'i rnam thar ngo mtshar sprin gyi rnga sgra*). Collected Writings of Gser-mdog paṇ-chen Śākya-mchog-ldan, vol. 16, 379–401. Thimphu, Bhutan: Kunzang Tobgey, 1975.

———. *Drumming Sounds from the Treasury of Immortality: Explanation of the Texts of the 'Extensive Sūtra on Differences between Former Aspirational Prayers of Seven Tathāgatas' and [Related] Rituals* (*De bzhin gshegs bdun gyi sngon gyi smon lam gyi khyad par rgyas pa'i mdo dang cho ga'i gzhung gi rnam bshad 'chi med mdzod kyi rnga sgra*). Collected Writings of Gser-mdog paṇ-chen Śākya-mchog-ldan, vol. 8, 426–445. Thimphu, Bhutan: Kunzang Tobgey, 1975.

———. *Drumming Sounds of the Melodious Voice of Brahma: Refutation of Mistakes About Meditative Stages of the Great Madhyamaka and Explanation of Tenets and Topics of the Views of Prāsaṅgika and Svātantrika* (*Dbu ma chen po'i sgom rim la 'khrul pa spong shing thal rang gi grub pa'i mtha' dang lta ba'i gnas rnam par bshad pa tshangs pa'i dbyangs kyi rnga sgra*). Collected Writings of Gser-mdog paṇ-chen Śākya-mchog-ldan, vol. 4, 249–373. Thimphu, Bhutan: Kunzang Tobgey, 1975.

———. *Enjoyment Ocean of Faith: Wondrous Liberation Story of the Foremost Venerable Omniscient Spiritual Friend Rongtön Shakya Gyeltsen* (*Rje btsun thams cad mkhyen pa bshes gnyen shākya rgyal mtshan gyi rnam thar ngo mtshar dad pa'i rol mtsho*). Collected Writings of Gser-mdog paṇ-chen Śākya-mchog-ldan, vol. 16, 299–377. Thimphu, Bhutan: Kunzang Tobgey, 1975.

———. *Enjoyment Ocean of Scriptural Statements and Reasoning Differentiating One's Own and Others' Tenets: Explanation of Difficult Points of the 'Ornament of Clear Realizations' Treatise of Quintessential Instructions on the Perfection of Wisdom Together with Its Commentaries* (*Shes rab kyi pha rol tu phyin pa'i man ngag gi bstan bcos mngon par rtogs pa'i rgyan 'grel pa dang bcas pa'i dka' ba'i gnas rnams rnam par bshad pa rang gzhan gyi grub mtha' rnam par dbye ba lung rigs kyi rol mtsho*). Collected Works, vol. 1, 9-vol. 2, 469. Thimphu, Bhutan: Kunzang Tobgey, 1975.

———. *Enjoyment Ocean of the Altruistic Melody: Explanation of [Parahita-ghoṣāraṇyaka's] Treatise Called 'Seventy Stanzas on Aspirational Prayers'* (*Smon lam bdun cu pa zhes pa'i bstan bcos kyi rnam par bshad pa gzhan phan pa'i dbyangs kyi rol mo*). Collected Writings of Gser-mdog paṇ-chen Śākya-mchog-ldan, vol. 24, 151–232. Thimphu, Bhutan: Kunzang Tobgey, 1975.

———. *Enjoyment Ocean of the Entirely Good Dharma: Explanation of the Extensive Treatise 'Commentary on Valid Cognition'* (*Rgyas pa'i bstan bcos tshad ma rnam 'grel gyi rnam bshad kun bzang chos kyi rol mtsho*). Collected Writings of Gser-mdog paṇ-chen Śākya-mchog-ldan, vol. 18, 189–693. Thimphu, Bhutan: Kunzang Tobgey, 1975.

———. *Enjoyment Ocean of the Speech of the 'Seven Works': Explanation of the 'Treasure of the Science of Valid Cognition'* (*Tshad ma rigs pa'i gter gyi rnam par bshad pa sde bdun ngag gi rol mtsho*). Collected Writings of Gser-mdog paṇ-chen Śākya-mchog-ldan, vol. 19, 447–749. Thimphu, Bhutan: Kunzang Tobgey, 1975.

———. *Entrance into Scholarship* (*Chos la 'jug pa'i sgo*). Collected Writings of Gser-mdog paṇ-chen Śākya-mchog-ldan, vol. 24, 309–320. Thimphu, Bhutan: Kunzang Tobgey, 1975.

———. *Entrance into the 'Dharmas of Maitreya': Explanation of the Aspirational Prayer Made by Ārya Maitreya* (*'Phags pa byams pas btab pa'i smon lam gyi rnam par bshad pa byams pa'i chos la 'jug pa'i sgo*). Collected Writings of Gser-mdog paṇ-chen Śākya-mchog-ldan, vol. 8, 403–426. Thimphu, Bhutan: Kunzang Tobgey, 1975.

———. *Essence of Logic: Condensed Thatness of [Dignāga's] 'Sūtra on Valid Cognition' and [Dharmakīrti's] Textual System of 'Seven Works'* (*Tshad ma'i mdo dang gzhung lugs sde bdun gyi de kho na nyid bsdus pa rtog ge'i snying po*). Collected Writings of Gser-mdog paṇ-chen Śākya-mchog-ldan, vol. 18, 1–187. Thimphu, Bhutan: Kunzang Tobgey, 1975.

———. *Essence of Sūtras and Tantras: Explanation of the Buddha-Essence* (*Sangs rgyas kyi snying po'i rnam bshad mdo rgyud snying po*). Collected Writings of Gser-mdog paṇ-chen Śākya-mchog-ldan, vol. 13, 124–136. Thimphu, Bhutan: Kunzang Tobgey, 1975. English translation in Komarovski, Yaroslav. "Reburying the Treasure—Maintaining the Continuity: Two Texts by Shakya Chokden on the Buddha-Essence." *Journal of Indian Philosophy*, vol. 34, no. 6 (2006): 521–570.

———. *Essence of the Ocean of Scriptural Teachings: Condensation of Desiderata of General Meaning of the 'Ornament of Clear Realizations' with Its Commentaries* (*Mngon par rtogs pa'i rgyan 'grel pa dang bcas pa'i spyi'i don nyer mkho bsdus pa lung chos rgya mtsho'i snying po*). Collected Writings of Gser-mdog paṇ-chen Śākya-mchog-ldan, vol. 3, 163–561. Thimphu, Bhutan: Kunzang Tobgey, 1975.

———. *Explanation of [Sakya Pendita's] 'Entrance into Scholarship' Together with Answers to Questions* (*Mkhas pa la 'jug pa'i sgo'i rnam bshad dri lan dang bcas pa*). Collected Writings of Gser-mdog paṇ-chen Śākya-mchog-ldan, vol. 24, 67–149. Thimphu, Bhutan: Kunzang Tobgey, 1975.

———. *Explanation of the First Level—[Vows of] Individual Liberation; from the Extensive Explanation of the Presentation of the Three Types of Vows* (*Sdom gsum gyi rnam par bzhag pa rgya cher bshad pa las/ so sor thar pa'i rim pa dang po rnam par bshad pa*). Collected Writings of Gser-mdog paṇ-chen Śākya-mchog-ldan, vol. 6, 285–342. Thimphu, Bhutan: Kunzang Tobgey, 1975.

———. *Feast for the Lord of Speech: Praise to Glorious Places and Persons of Sakya Issuing from [Meanings Expressed by] the Sound [of Its First Letter "Sa"]* (*Dpal ldan sa skya'i gnas dang gang zag la sgra las drangs pa'i bstod pa ngag gi dbang po'i dga' ston*). Collected Writings of Gser-mdog paṇ-chen Śākya-mchog-ldan, vol. 17, 28–30. Thimphu, Bhutan: Kunzang Tobgey, 1975.

———. *Fifty-One Sections of Definitive Meaning: Abbreviated Meaning of the 'Thorough Establishment of the Glorious Original Buddha' Treatise* (*Dpal dang po'i sangs rgyas rab du grub pa zhes bya ba'i bstan bcos kyi bsdus pa'i don nges don gyi tshoms lnga bcu rtsa gcig zhes bya ba*). Collected Writings of Gser-mdog paṇ-chen Śākya-mchog-ldan, vol. 8, 187–193. Thimphu, Bhutan: Kunzang Tobgey, 1975.

———. *Garland of Trees Fulfilling All Wishes: Explanation of [Ngok Loden Sherap's] Letter 'Drop of Ambrosia'* (*Spring yig bdud rtsi'i thigs pa'i rnam bshad dpag bsam yongs 'du'i ljon phreng*). Collected Writings of Gser-mdog paṇ-chen Śākya-mchog-ldan, vol. 24, 320–348. Thimphu, Bhutan: Kunzang Tobgey, 1975.

———. *Garland of White Lotuses: Agreeing with Sūtras Description of the Array of Positive Qualities of the Land of Bliss and Pure Aspirational Prayers* (*Bde ba can gyi zhing gi yon tan gyi bkod pa dang smon lam rnam par dag pa mdo dang 'thun par brjod pa padma dkar po'i phren ba*). Collected Writings of Gser-mdog paṇ-chen Śākya-mchog-ldan, vol. 7, 284–301. Thimphu, Bhutan: Kunzang Tobgey, 1975.

———. *Garlands of Waves of Assertions: Investigation of Connections of Former and Later [Elements in] the 'Ornament of Clear Realizations' Treatise of Quintessential Instructions on the Perfection of Wisdom Together with Its Commentaries, and Placement of the Army of Good Explanations on Difficult Points of Explicit Teachings* (*Shes rab kyi pha rol tu phyin pa'i man ngag gi bstan bcos mngon par rtogs pa'i rgyan 'grel pa dang bcas pa'i snga phyi'i 'brel rnam par btsal zhing/ dngos bstan gyi dka' ba'i gnas la legs par bshad pa'i dpung tshogs rnam par bkod pa/ bzhed tshul rba rlabs kyi phreng ba*). Collected Writings of Gser-mdog paṇ-chen Śākya-mchog-ldan, vol. 11, 157–587. Thimphu, Bhutan: Kunzang Tobgey, 1975.

———. *Garlands of Waves of the Ocean of Yogācāras' Scriptures: Explanation of the Holy Dharma of [Asaṅga's] 'Summary of Higher Knowledge'* (*Dam pa'i chos ngon pa kun las btus pa'i rnam par bshad pa rnal 'byor spyod gzhung rgya mtsho'i rlabs kyi phreng ba*). Collected Writings of Gser-mdog paṇ-chen Śākya-mchog-ldan, vol. 14, 1–339. Thimphu, Bhutan: Kunzang Tobgey, 1975.

———. *Garlands of Wondrous Ornaments of the Union of Calm Abiding and Special Insight: Guiding Instructions on the Madhyamaka View* (*Dbu ma'i lta khrid / zhi gnas dang lhag mthong zung du 'jug pa ngo mtshar rgyan gyi phreng ba*). In *'Hundred and Eight Dharma Sections' Treatise* (*Chos tshan brgya dang brgyad pa zhes bya ba'i bstan bcos*), Collected Writings of Gser-mdog paṇ-chen Śākya-mchog-ldan, vol. 13, 190–202. Thimphu, Bhutan: Kunzang Tobgey, 1975.

———. *Golden Lancet: Resolved Abundant Discourse on the 'Thorough Differentiation of the Three Types of Vows' Treatise* (*Sdom gsum gyi rab tu dbye ba'i bstan bcos kyi 'bel gtam rnam par nges pa legs bshad gser gyi thur ma*). Collected Writings of Gser-mdog paṇ-chen Śākya-mchog-ldan, vol. vol. 6, 439–vol. 7, 229. Thimphu, Bhutan: Kunzang Tobgey, 1975.

———. *Good Questions about the 'Thorough Differentiation of the Three Types of Vows'* (*Sdom gsum rab dbye la dri ba legs pa*). Collected Writings of Gser-mdog paṇ-chen Śākya-mchog-ldan, vol. 17, 448–462. Thimphu, Bhutan: Kunzang Tobgey, 1975.

———. *Great Ocean of Particularized Explanations: Treatise Explaining Difficult Points of [Vasubandhu's] 'Treasury of Higher Knowledge'* (*Chos mngon pa'i mdzod kyi dka' ba'i gnas rnam par bshad pa'i bstan bcos bye brag tu bshad pa'i mtsho chen po*). Collected Writings of Gser-mdog paṇ-chen Śākya-mchog-ldan, vol. 20, 1–vol. 21, 355. Thimphu, Bhutan: Kunzang Tobgey, 1975.

———. *Great Path Compressing the Two Chariot Ways into One: Explanation of [Maitreya's] 'Ornament of Clear Realizations' Together with [Haribhadra's] 'Clear Meaning' Commentary* (*Mngon par rtogs pa'i rgyan 'grel pa don gsal ba dang bcas pa'i rnam par bshad pa shing rta'i srol gnyis gcig tu bsdus pa'i lam po che*). Collected Writings of Gser-mdog paṇ-chen Śākya-mchog-ldan, vol. 12, 1–319. Thimphu, Bhutan: Kunzang Tobgey, 1975.

———. *Great Path of Ambrosia of Emptiness: Explanation of Profound Pacification Free from Proliferations* (*Zab zhi spros bral gyi bshad pa stong nyid bdud rtsi'i lam po che*). Collected Writings of Gser-mdog paṇ-chen Śākya-mchog-ldan, vol. 4, 107–207. Thimphu, Bhutan: Kunzang Tobgey, 1975.

———. *Great Ship of Discrimination that Sails into the Ocean of Definitive Meaning: Treatise Differentiating the Tenets of Prāsaṅgika and Svātantrika Madhyamaka* (*Dbu ma thal rang gi grub pa'i mtha' rnam par dbye ba'i bstan bcos nges don gyi rgya mtshor 'jug pa'i rnam dpyod kyi gru chen*). Collected Writings of Gser-mdog paṇ-chen Śākya-mchog-ldan, vol. 4, 399–407. Thimphu, Bhutan: Kunzang Tobgey, 1975. English translation in Komarovski, Yaroslav (tr.). *Three Texts on Madhyamaka by Shakya Chokden*. Dharamsala, India: Library of Tibetan Works and Archives, 2000.

———. *Harbor for Fortunate Ones: Explanation of [Nāgārjuna's 'Wisdom:] Root [Stanzas] on Madhyamaka'* (*Dbu ma rtsa ba'i rnam bshad bskal bzangs kyi 'jug ngogs*). Collected Writings of Gser-mdog paṇ-chen Śākya-mchog-ldan, vol. 5, 1–280. Thimphu, Bhutan: Kunzang Tobgey, 1975.

———. *Harbor of the Ocean of Faith: Extensive Explanation of the 'King of Aspirational Prayers of Deeds of Ārya Samantabhadra'* (*'Phags pa kun tu bzangs po'i spyod pa'i smon lam gyi rgyal po'i rgya cher bshad pa dad pa rgya mtsho'i 'jug ngogs*). Collected Writings of Gser-mdog paṇ-chen Śākya-mchog-ldan, vol. 8, 352–403. Thimphu, Bhutan: Kunzang Tobgey, 1975.

———. *'Hundred and Eight Dharma Sections' Treatise* (*Chos tshan brgya dang brgyad pa zhes bya ba'i bstan bcos*). Collected Writings of Gser-mdog paṇ-chen Śākya-mchog-ldan, vol. 13, 159–462. Thimphu, Bhutan: Kunzang Tobgey, 1975.

———. *Intensive Expansion of Fortune: Praise of the Wondrous Outstanding Munīndra* (*Ngo mtshar rmad du byung ba'i thub pa'i dbang po'i bstod pa bkra shis rab rgyas*). Collected Writings of Gser-mdog paṇ-chen Śākya-mchog-ldan, vol. 16, 491–494. Thimphu, Bhutan: Kunzang Tobgey, 1975.

———. *Key to Essential Points of Definitive Meaning: Modes of Identification of Individual Views—Answers to the Questions of the Great Meditator Yeshé Zangpo* (*Sgom chen ye shes bzang po'i dris lan lta ba so so'i ngos 'dzin tshul nges don gnad kyi lde mig*). Collected Writings of Gser-mdog paṇ-chen Śākya-mchog-ldan, vol. 23, 99–104. Thimphu, Bhutan: Kunzang Tobgey, 1975.

———. *Lamp of Dharma Eliminating Obscurity with regard to Engaging in Mantra: Seventeen Textual Sections* (*Sngags la 'jug pa'i mun pa sel bar byed pa'i chos kyi sgron me gzhung tshan bcu bdun pa*). In *'Hundred and Eight Dharma Sections' Treatise* (*Chos tshan brgya dang brgyad pa zhes bya ba'i bstan bcos*). Collected Writings of Gser-mdog paṇ-chen Śākya-mchog-ldan, vol. 13, 229–274. Thimphu, Bhutan: Kunzang Tobgey, 1975.

———. *Letter Pleasing Impartial Wise Ones on How Presentations of Turning Dharmacakras have been Accomplished* (*Chos kyi 'khor lo bskor ba'i rnam gzhag ji ltar grub pa'i yi ge gzu bor gnas pa'i mdzangs pa dga' byed*). Collected Writings of Gser-mdog paṇ-chen Śākya-mchog-ldan, vol. 16, 457–482. Thimphu, Bhutan: Kunzang Tobgey, 1975.

———. *Liberation Story of the Foremost Venerable Holy Amoghaśrībhadra That Induces Devotion of All Fortunate Beings* (*Rje btsun dam pa a mo gha shrī *bha tra'i rnam par thar ba skal bzang skye rgu'i dang ba 'dren byed*). Collected Writings of Gser-mdog paṇ-chen Śākya-mchog-ldan, vol. 17, 43–62. Thimphu, Bhutan: Kunzang Tobgey, 1975.

———. *Meaningful to Behold: Answers to the Questions of Spiritual Friend Müpa Rapjampa* (*Bshes gnyen mus pa rab 'byams pa'i dri lan mthong ba don ldan*). Collected Writings of Gser-mdog paṇ-chen Śākya-mchog-ldan, vol. 23, 297–418. Thimphu, Bhutan: Kunzang Tobgey, 1975.

———. *Mirror Captivating Clear-Minded Ones That Clarifies Ornaments of Meaning: Praise to the Teacher Munīndra* (*Ston pa thub pa'i dbang po la bstod pa don rgyan gsal ba'i me long blo gsal yid 'phrog*). Collected Writings of Gser-mdog paṇ-chen Śākya-mchog-ldan, vol. 16, 495–500. Thimphu, Bhutan: Kunzang Tobgey, 1975.

———. *Mirror Clarifying Individual Texts: Presentation of the Views, Meditations, and Actions of Earlier and Later Great Beings of the Land of Snows* (*Gangs can gyi chen po snga phyir byon pa'i lta sgom spyod pa'i rnam bzhag rang gzhung gsal ba'i me long*). Collected Writings of Gser-mdog paṇ-chen Śākya-mchog-ldan, vol. 23, 78–99. Thimphu, Bhutan: Kunzang Tobgey, 1975.

———. *Moon Chariot: Treatise Clarifying Individual Meanings of Difficult Points of Hundred and One Activities [of Moral Discipline]* (*Las brgya rtsa gcig gi dka' gnas so so'i don gsal bar byed pa'i bstan bcos zla ba'i shing rta*). Collected Writings of Gser-mdog paṇ-chen Śākya-mchog-ldan, vol. 22, 311–525. Thimphu, Bhutan: Kunzang Tobgey, 1975.

———. *Music of a Wondrous Discourse: Summary of the Ways of Maintaining the Teachings by the Great Ngok Lotsawa [Loden Sherap]* (*Rngog lo tsā ba chen pos bstan pa ji ltar bskyangs tshul mdo tsam du bya ba ngo mthsar gtam gyi rol mo*). Collected Writings of Gser-mdog paṇ-chen Śākya-mchog-ldan, vol. 16, 443–456. Thimphu, Bhutan: Kunzang Tobgey, 1975.

———. [Nameless]. Collected Writings of Gser-mdog paṇ-chen Śākya-mchog-ldan, vol. 17, 111–113. Thimphu, Bhutan: Kunzang Tobgey, 1975.

———. [Nameless]. Collected Writings of Gser-mdog paṇ-chen Śākya-mchog-ldan, vol. 17, 116–117. Thimphu, Bhutan: Kunzang Tobgey, 1975.

———. [Nameless]. Collected Writings of Gser-mdog paṇ-chen Śākya-mchog-ldan, vol. 17, 204–207. Thimphu, Bhutan: Kunzang Tobgey, 1975.

———. [Nameless]. Collected Writings of Gser-mdog paṇ-chen Śākya-mchog-ldan, vol. 17, 307–309. Thimphu, Bhutan: Kunzang Tobgey, 1975.

———. [Nameless]. Collected Writings of Gser-mdog paṇ-chen Śākya-mchog-ldan, vol. 17, 416–417. Thimphu, Bhutan: Kunzang Tobgey, 1975.

———. [Nameless]. Collected Writings of Gser-mdog paṇ-chen Śākya-mchog-ldan, vol. 17, 471–472. Thimphu, Bhutan: Kunzang Tobgey, 1975.

———. *Necklace for Clear-Minded Ones: Description of Parts of Realizations of the Lord of Reasoning Gewa Gyeltsen and His Veneration* (*Rigs pa'i dbang phyug dge ba rgyal mtshan gyi rtogs pa'i cha shas brjod cing 'dud pa blo gsal gyi mgul rgyan*). Collected Writings of Gser-mdog paṇ-chen Śākya-mchog-ldan, vol. 16, 258–260. Thimphu, Bhutan: Kunzang Tobgey, 1975.

———. *Necklace for Clear-Minded Ones: Presentation of Time Periods* (*Dus tshigs kyi rnam par bzhag pa blo gsal gyi mgul rgyan*). Collected Writings of

Gser-mdog paṇ-chen Śākya-mchog-ldan, vol. 6, 231–283. Thimphu, Bhutan: Kunzang Tobgey, 1975.

———. *Ocean of Ambrosia: Treatise Clarifying Words of the Three Bases [of Moral Discipline]* (*Gzhi gsum gyi tshig gsal bar byed pa'i bstan 'chos bdud rtsi'i rol mtsho*). Collected Writings of Gser-mdog paṇ-chen Śākya-mchog-ldan, vol. 22, 267–302. Thimphu, Bhutan: Kunzang Tobgey, 1975.

———. *Ocean of Faith: Ascertainment of the Akaniṣṭhaghanavyūha Realm* (*'Og min stug po bkod pa'i zhing khams kyi rnam par nges pa dad pa'i rgya mtsho*). Collected Writings of Gser-mdog paṇ-chen Śākya-mchog-ldan, vol. 7, 231–264. Thimphu, Bhutan: Kunzang Tobgey, 1975.

———. *Ocean of Meaning of Scriptural Statements: Extensive Explanation of the Body and Branches of the 'Perfection of Wisdom' Sūtras and the 'Ornament of Clear Realizations' Together with Commentaries* (*Shes rab kyi pha rol tu phyin pa'i mdo dang mngon par rtogs pa'i rgyan 'grel dang bcas pa'i lus dang yan lag rgyas par bshad pa lung don rgya mtsho*). Collected Writings of Gser-mdog paṇ-chen Śākya-mchog-ldan, vol. 3, 1–161. Thimphu, Bhutan: Kunzang Tobgey, 1975.

———. *Ocean of Scriptural Statements and Reasoning: Treasury of Ascertainment of Mahāyāna Madhyamaka* (*Theg pa chen po dbu ma rnam par nges pa'i bang mdzod lung dang rigs pa'i rgya mtsho*). Collected Writings of Gser-mdog paṇ-chen Śākya-mchog-ldan, vol. 14, 341–vol. 15, 695. Thimphu, Bhutan: Kunzang Tobgey, 1975.

———. *Opening Doors of a Chest of Gems: Treatise Elucidating Stages of the Path of the 'Five Dharmas of Maitreya'* (*Byams chos lnga'i lam gyi rim pa gsal bar byed pa'i bstan bcos rin chen sgrom gyi sgo 'byed*). Collected Writings of Gser-mdog paṇ-chen Śākya-mchog-ldan, vol. 11, 39–149. Thimphu, Bhutan: Kunzang Tobgey, 1975.

———. *Ornament of Intent of the 'Treasure of the Science of Valid Cognition' [Called] 'Defeater of Bad Systems with the Wheel of Scriptural Statements and Reasonings'; Also Called 'Great Destroyer of Mistakes about Logic'* (*Tshad ma rigs pa'i gter gyi dgongs rgyan lung dang rigs pa'i 'khor los lugs ngan pham byed pa'am/ ming gzhan rtog ge'i 'khrul 'joms chen mo*). Collected Writings of Gser-mdog paṇ-chen Śākya-mchog-ldan, vol. 9, 1–vol. 10, 587. Thimphu, Bhutan: Kunzang Tobgey, 1975.

———. *Ornament of Intents of Quintessential Instructions: Answers to the Questions from [Tsongkhapa's] 'Questions [Based on] Purely White Supreme Motivation'* (*Dri ba lhag bsam rab dkar gyi dris lan man ngag gi dgongs rgyan*). Collected Writings of Gser-mdog paṇ-chen Śākya-mchog-ldan, vol. 23, 297–358. Thimphu, Bhutan: Kunzang Tobgey, 1975.

———. *Praise to Mañjuśrī Which Agrees with Clear Realizations [of the 'Litany of Ultimate Names of Mañjuśrī']* (*'Jam dpal gyi bstod pa mngon rtogs dang mthun pa*). Collected Writings of Gser-mdog paṇ-chen Śākya-mchog-ldan, vol. 16, 501–503. Thimphu, Bhutan: Kunzang Tobgey, 1975.

———. *Praise to the Great Paṇḍita Loten the Fourth* (*Paṇ chen blo brtan bzhi pa la bstod pa*). Collected Writings of Gser-mdog paṇ-chen Śākya-mchog-ldan, vol. 16, 266–267. Thimphu, Bhutan: Kunzang Tobgey, 1975.

———. *Prayers and Numerous Songs of Contemplative Experience (Gsol 'debs dang mgur 'bum gyi skor)*. Collected Writings of Gser-mdog paṇ-chen Śākya-mchog-ldan, vol. 17, 463–472. Thimphu, Bhutan: Kunzang Tobgey, 1975.

———. *Precious Harbor of Definitive Meaning [for] Entering into the Wish Fulfilling Ocean of the Highest Secret Mantra upon Analysis of Doubts Regarding Difficult Points of Explicit Teachings of [Drakpa Gyeltsen's] 'Precious Tree: Clear Realizations [of Tantras]' (Mngon par rtogs pa rin po che'i ljon shing zhes bya ba'i dngos bstan gyi dka' gnas la som nyi'i mtha' rnam par dpyad nas/ gsang sngags bla na med pa'i yid bzhin gyi rgya mtshor 'jug pa/ nges don rin po che'i 'jug ngogs)*. Collected Writings of Gser-mdog paṇ-chen Śākya-mchog-ldan, vol. 17, 432–448. Thimphu, Bhutan: Kunzang Tobgey, 1975.

———. *Precious Treasury of the Condensed Essence of the Profound and Extensive in Eight Dharma Sections (Zab rgya'i snying po bsdus pa rin chen gter mdzod chos tshan brgyad pa)*. In *'Hundred and Eight Dharma Sections' Treatise (Chos tshan brgya dang brgyad pa zhes bya ba'i bstan bcos)*. Collected Writings of Gser-mdog paṇ-chen Śākya-mchog-ldan, vol. 13, 166–190. Thimphu, Bhutan: Kunzang Tobgey, 1975.

———. *Previously Unseen Sun: The Definitive Meaning of the 'Sublime Continuum' Treatise (Rgyud bla ma'i bstan bcos kyi nges don sngon med nyi ma)*. Collected Writings of Gser-mdog paṇ-chen Śākya-mchog-ldan, vol. 13, 113–124. Thimphu, Bhutan: Kunzang Tobgey, 1975. English translation in Komarovski, Yaroslav. "Reburying the Treasure—Maintaining the Continuity: Two Texts by Shakya Chokden on the Buddha-Essence." *Journal of Indian Philosophy*, vol. 34, no. 6 (2006): 521–570.

———. *Profound Thunder amidst the Clouds of the Ocean of Definitive Meaning: Differentiation of the Two Systems of the Great Madhyamaka Deriving from the Two Great Chariot Ways (Shing rta'i srol chen gnyis las 'byung ba'i dbu ma chen po'i lugs gnyis rnam par dbye ba/ nges don rgya mtsho'i sprin gyi 'brug sgra zab mo)*. In *Two Controversial Mādhyamika Treatises*, 301–318. Bir, India: Yashodhara Publications, 1996.

———. *Questions to the Jang Ruler Namgyel Drakpa about Three [Topics of] the Sugata-Essence, [Four Tantras of] Medical Analysis, and Kālacakra (Byang pa bdag po rnam rgyal grags pa la bde gshegs snying po sman dpyad dus 'khor gsum gyi dri ba)*. Collected Writings of Gser-mdog paṇ-chen Śākya-mchog-ldan, vol. 17, 325–329. Thimphu, Bhutan: Kunzang Tobgey, 1975.

———. *Quintessential Instructions on the Correct Reading of the 'Litany of Ultimate Names of the Foremost Venerable [Mañjuśrī]jñānasattva' (Rje btsun ye shes sems dpa'i don dam pa'i mtshan yang dag par brjod pa tshul bzhin du klag pa'i man ngag)*. Collected Writings of Gser-mdog paṇ-chen Śākya-mchog-ldan, vol. 8, 275–320. Thimphu, Bhutan: Kunzang Tobgey, 1975.

———. *Rain of Ambrosia: Extensive [Auto-]Commentary on the 'Profound Thunder amidst the Clouds of the Ocean of Definitive Meaning' (Nges don rgya mtsho sprin gyi 'brug sgra zab mo'i rgyas 'grel bdud rtsi'i char 'bebs)*. In *Two Controversial Mādhyamika Treatises*, 319–499. Bir, India: Yashodhara Publications, 1996; also in Collected Writings of Gser-mdog paṇ-chen

Śākya-mchog-ldan, vol. 2, 471–616. Thimphu, Bhutan: Kunzang Tobgey, 1975.

———. *Register of Printing [Dharmakīrti's] 'Commentary on Valid Cognition' Text* (*Rnam 'grel gyi gzhung par du bsgrub pa'i dkar chag*). Collected Writings of Gser-mdog paṇ-chen Śākya-mchog-ldan, vol. 17, 216–220. Thimphu, Bhutan: Kunzang Tobgey, 1975.

———. *Register of Printing [Sakya Pendita's] 'Thorough Differentiation of the Three Types of Vows' Text* (*Sdom gsum rab dbye'i gzhung par du bsgrub pa'i dkar chag tu gnang ba*). Collected Writings of Gser-mdog paṇ-chen Śākya-mchog-ldan, vol. 17, 222–226. Thimphu, Bhutan: Kunzang Tobgey, 1975.

———. *Register of Printing [Sakya Pendita's] 'Treasure of the Science of Valid Cognition' Text* (*Rigs gter gyi gzhung par du sgrub pa'i dkar chag*). Collected Writings of Gser-mdog paṇ-chen Śākya-mchog-ldan, vol. 17, 220–222. Thimphu, Bhutan: Kunzang Tobgey, 1975.

———. *Register of Printing the 'Litany of [Ultimate] Names [of Mañjuśrī]* (*Mtshan brjod kyi par sgrub pa'i dkar chag*). Collected Writings of Gser-mdog paṇ-chen Śākya-mchog-ldan, vol. 17, 226–227. Thimphu, Bhutan: Kunzang Tobgey, 1975.

———. *Register of Printing the 'Perfection of Wisdom' [Sūtra] in Lowo* (*Glo bo phar phyin gyi par bzhengs pa'i dkar chag tu gnang ba*). Collected Writings of Gser-mdog paṇ-chen Śākya-mchog-ldan, vol. 17, 213–214. Thimphu, Bhutan: Kunzang Tobgey, 1975.

———. *Sarasvatī's Enjoyment Ocean: Commentary on [Daṇḍin's] 'Mirror of Poetry'* (*Snyan ngag me long gi 'grel pa dbyangs can gyi rol mtsho*). Collected Writings of Gser-mdog paṇ-chen Śākya-mchog-ldan, vol. 24, 1–67. Thimphu, Bhutan: Kunzang Tobgey, 1975.

———. *Sevenfold Treasury of Gems: Explanation of the Glorious 'Secret Assembly' [Tantra]* (*Dpal gsang ba 'dus pa'i rnam bshad rin po che'i gter mdzod bdun pa*). Collected Writings of Gser-mdog paṇ-chen Śākya-mchog-ldan, vol. 7, 405–612. Thimphu, Bhutan: Kunzang Tobgey, 1975.

———. *Seventeen Wondrous Answers to the Questions of the Whole Monastic Community of Zi Samdrupling* (*Gzi bsam 'grub gling pa'i dge 'dun spyi'i dris lan ya mtshan bcu bdun pa*). Collected Writings of Gser-mdog paṇ-chen Śākya-mchog-ldan, vol. 23, 418–475. Thimphu, Bhutan: Kunzang Tobgey, 1975.

———. *Shakwangma* (*Shāk dbang ma*). Collected Writings of Gser-mdog paṇ-chen Śākya-mchog-ldan, vol. 8, 448–450. Thimphu, Bhutan: Kunzang Tobgey, 1975.

———. *Smaller Summarized Exposition [of Madhyamaka] Called 'Vajra of the Lord [of Gods]' Pleasing Clear-Minded Ones* (*Stong thun chung ba dbang po'i rdo rje zhes bya ba blo gsal mgu byed*). Collected Writings of Gser-mdog paṇ-chen Śākya-mchog-ldan, vol. 4, 433–605. Thimphu, Bhutan: Kunzang Tobgey, 1975.

———. *Snatching Away the Heart's Torments with the Garland of the White Moonrays of Definitive Meaning: Expression of Realizations of Honorable Ārya Asaṅga* (*'Phags pa thogs med zhabs kyi rtogs pa brjod pa nges don zla zer dkar po'i phreng bas snying gi gdung ba 'phrog byed*). Collected Writings of Gser-mdog paṇ-chen Śākya-mchog-ldan, vol. 16, 566–573. Thimphu, Bhutan: Kunzang Tobgey, 1975.

———. *Sounds of Brahma's Drum: Praise to the Lord of Dharma [Sakya Pendita] Himself as Superior to Other Teaching Holders* (*Chos kyi rje nyid la bstan 'dzin gzhan las khyad par du 'phags par bstod pa tshangs pa'i rnga sgra*). Collected Writings of Gser-mdog paṇ-chen Śākya-mchog-ldan, vol. 17, 23–28. Thimphu, Bhutan: Kunzang Tobgey, 1975.

———. *Stanzas for Offering Seven Royal Attributes and Seven Gems* (*Rgyal srid sna bdun dang/ rin chen sna bdun 'bul ba'i tshigs bcad*). Collected Writings of Gser-mdog paṇ-chen Śākya-mchog-ldan, vol. 17, 314–317. Thimphu, Bhutan: Kunzang Tobgey, 1975.

———. *Sun Benefiting Others That Dispels External and Internal Darkness: Notes Thoroughly Clarifying the Five Stages of the Glorious 'Secret Assembly' [Tantra]* (*Dpal gsang ba 'dus pa'i rim pa lnga rab tu gsal bar byed pa'i brjed byang phyi nang gi mun pa sel byed gzhan la phan pa'i nyi ma*). Collected Writings of Gser-mdog paṇ-chen Śākya-mchog-ldan, vol. 23, 496–518. Thimphu, Bhutan: Kunzang Tobgey, 1975.

———. *Thorough Clarification of Definitive Commitments: Answers to Objections to [Drakpa Gyeltsen's] 'Elimination of Mistakes [Regarding Root Downfalls]'* (*'Khrul spong gi brgal lan rnam par nges pa'i dam tshig rab tu gsal ba*). Collected Writings of Gser-mdog paṇ-chen Śākya-mchog-ldan, vol. 23, 105–295. Thimphu, Bhutan: Kunzang Tobgey, 1975.

———. *Thorough Clarification of Definitive Meaning of the 'Five Dharmas of Maitreya'* (*Byams chos lnga'i nges don rab tu gsal ba zhes bya ba'i bstan bcos*). Collected Writings of Gser-mdog paṇ-chen Śākya-mchog-ldan, vol. 11, 1–37. Thimphu, Bhutan: Kunzang Tobgey, 1975.

———. *Thorough Clarification of Vajradhara's Intent: Ascertainment of Profound and Extensive Points of the Mantra System in Twenty-One Dharma Sections* (*Sngags lugs kyi zab rgya'i gnad rnam par gtan la dbab pa rdo rje 'chang gi dgongs pa rab gsal chos mtshan nyi shu rtsa gcig pa*). In *'Hundred and Eight Dharma Sections' Treatise* (*Chos tshan brgya dang brgyad pa zhes bya ba'i bstan bcos*). Collected Writings of Gser-mdog paṇ-chen Śākya-mchog-ldan, vol. 13, 301–345. Thimphu, Bhutan: Kunzang Tobgey, 1975.

———. *Thorough Establishment of the Glorious Original Buddha: [Treatise] Condensing the Essence of All Sūtras and Tantras of the Pronouncement of the Third Dharmacakra* (*Dpal dang po'i sangs rgyas rab tu grub pas bka' 'khor lo gsum pa'i mdo dang rgyud sde kun gyi snying po bsdus pa*). Collected Writings of Gser-mdog paṇ-chen Śākya-mchog-ldan, vol. 8, 10–183. Thimphu, Bhutan: Kunzang Tobgey, 1975.

———. *Treasury of Immortality: Praise to the Teacher Munīndra in Agreement with His Teachings* (*Ston pa thub pa'i dbang po la bstan pa dang mthun par bstod pa 'chi med kyi mdzod*). Collected Writings of Gser-mdog paṇ-chen Śākya-mchog-ldan, vol. 16, 487–490. Thimphu, Bhutan: Kunzang Tobgey, 1975.

———. *Vajra Shortcut: Disputes about Common Appearances of Ordinary Beings and Āryas in Seventeen Dharma Sections* (*Skye 'phags snang ba 'thun pa la brtsad pa rdo rje'i gseng lam chos tshan bcu bdun pa*). In *'Hundred and Eight Dharma Sections' Treatise* (*Chos tshan brgya dang brgyad pa zhes bya ba'i bstan bcos*). Collected Writings of Gser-mdog paṇ-chen Śākya-mchog-ldan, vol. 13, 386–428. Thimphu, Bhutan: Kunzang Tobgey, 1975.

———. *White Lotus Garland of Ascertainment of Oral Instructions of the Pervasive Lord Vajrasattva: [Treatise Providing] an Easy Understanding of the 'Praise of Nairātmyā''s Commentary* (*Bdag med bstod 'grel gyi go sla khyab bdag rdo rje sems dpa'i zhal lung rnam par nges pa padma dkar po'i 'phreng ba*). In *'Hundred and Eight Dharma Sections' Treatise* (*Chos tshan brgya dang brgyad pa zhes bya ba'i bstan bcos*). Collected Writings of Gser-mdog paṇ-chen Śākya-mchog-ldan, vol. 13, 345–386. Thimphu, Bhutan: Kunzang Tobgey, 1975.

———. *Wish Fulfilling Meru: Discourse on the History of Madhyamaka* (*Dbu ma'i byung tshul rnam par bshad pa'i gtam yid bzhin lhun po*). Collected Writings of Gser-mdog paṇ-chen Śākya-mchog-ldan, vol. 4, 209–248. Thimphu, Bhutan: Kunzang Tobgey, 1975. English translation in Komarovski, Yaroslav (tr.). *Three Texts on Madhyamaka by Shakya Chokden*. Dharamsala, India: Library of Tibetan Works and Archives, 2000; French translation of its concluding part in Tillemans, Tom and Toru Tomabechi. "Le *dBu ma'i byung tshul de Śākya mchog-ldan*." *Asiatische Studien*, vol. 49, no. 4 (1995): 891–918.

———. *Wondrous Divine Drum Melody: Exposition of the Bodhisattva Dwelling in the Land of Tuṣita* (*Byang chub sems dpa' dga' ldan gyi gnas na bzhugs pa'i bkod pa ngo mtshar lha'i rnga dbyangs*). Collected Writings of Gser-mdog paṇ-chen Śākya-mchog-ldan, vol. 7, 265–284. Thimphu, Bhutan: Kunzang Tobgey, 1975.

Sherap Ö (*shes rab 'od*/ Lama Rokgi Bende Sherap Ö, *bla ma rog gi ban dhe shes rab 'od*). *Lamp Demonstrating Great Tenets: Buddhist History Clearly Teaching Texts Asserted by Individual Tenets* (*Grub mtha' so so'i bzhed gzhung gsal bar ston pa chos 'byung grub mtha' chen mo bstan pa'i sgron me*). Nemo Leh, Ladakh: Tshul-khrims-'jam-dbyangs, 1977.

Sönam Tsemo (*bsod nams rtse mo*). *General Presentation of Tantras* (*Rgyud sde spyi'i rnam par gzhag pa*). Xylographic print. Unknown publisher.

Tāranātha. *Twenty-One Differences Regarding the Profound Meaning* (*Zab don nyer gcig pa*). Collected Works of Jo-naṅ rJe-btsun Tāranātha, vol. 4 (*nga*). Leh, Ladakh. Smanrtsis Shesrig Dpemzod, 1985. English translation in Hopkins, Jeffrey. *The Essence of Other-Emptiness*. Ithaca, New York: Snow Lion Publications, 2007. Also translated in Mathes, Klaus-Dieter. "Tāranātha's 'Twenty-One Differences with regard to the Profound Meaning'—Comparing the Views of the Two *gŹan stoṅ* Masters Dol po pa and Śākya mchog ldan." *Journal of the International Association of Buddhist Studies*, vol. 27, no. 2 (2004): 285–328.

Tsongkhapa Lopzang Drakpa (*tsong kha pa blo bzang grags pa*). *Essence of Good Explanations: Treatise Differentiating the Interpretive and the Definitive Meaning* (*drang ba dang nges pa'i don rnam par 'byed pa'i bstan bcos legs bshad snying po*). Mundgod: Drepung Loseling Library, 1991. English translation in Thurman, Robert. *Central Philosophy of Tibet: A Study and Translation of Jey Tsongkhapa's Essence of True Eloquence*. Princeton: Princeton University Press, 1984. Critical edition and annotated English translation of the prologue and the Cittamātra section: Hopkins, Jeffrey. *Emptiness in the Mind-Only School of Buddhism: Dynamic Responses to Dzong-ka-ba's* The Essence of Eloquence: I. Los Angeles: University of California Press, 1999.

———. *Ocean of Reasoning: Explanation of [Nāgārjuna's] Wisdom: Root Stanzas on Madhyamaka* (*Dbu ma rtsa ba'i tshig le'ur byas pa shes rab ces bya ba'i rnam bshad rigs pa'i rgya mtsho*, Collected Works of Tsong kha pa Blo bzang grags pa, vol. 15 (ba), 1–583 (Sku 'bum: Sku 'bum byams pa gling par khang, 2000?). English translation: Geshe Ngawang Samten and Jay L. Garfield, *Ocean of Reasoning: A Great Commentary on Nāgārjuna's* Mūlamadhyamakakārikā. Oxford: Oxford University Press, 2006.

———. *'Stages of the Path to Enlightenment' Teaching in Their Entirety All Stages Incorporated into Experience by the Three Beings / Great Stages of the Path to Enlightenment* (*Skyes bu gsum gyi nyams su blang ba'i rim pa thams cad tshang bar ston pa'i byang chub lam gyi rim pa/ Byang chub lam rim che ba*). Mtsho sngon mi rigs dpe skrun khang. Translated into English by The Lamrim Chenmo Translation Committee as *The Great Treatise on the Stages of the Path to Enlightenment*, vols. 1–3. Ithaca, New York: Snow Lion Publications, 2002.

———. *Thorough Clarification of Intent: Extensive Explanation of [Candrakīrti's] 'Engaging in Madhyamaka'* (*Dbu ma la 'jug pa'i rgya cher bshad pa dgongs pa rab gsal*). Collected Works of Tsong kha pa Blo bzang grags pa, vol. 16 (ma), 7–612 (Sku 'bum: Sku 'bum byams pa gling par khang, 2000?).

Tuken Lopzang Chökyi Nyima (*thu'u bkwan blo bzang chos kyi nyi ma*). *Crystal Mirror of Good Explanations: Presentation of Origins and Assertions of All Tenets* (*Grub mtha' thams cad kyi khungs dang 'dod tshul ston pa legs bshad shel gyi me long*). Kan su'u Mi rigs dpe skrun khang, 1984.

Üpa Losel (*dbus pa blo gsal*). *Treasury of Explanations of Tenets* (*Grub pa'i mtha' rnam par bshad pa'i mdzod*). Edited and partly translated into French in Mimaki, Katsumi. *Blo gsal grub mtha'*. Kyoto: Université de Kyoto, 1982.

Vajragarbha. *Extensive Commentary on the 'Condensed Meaning of the Hevajra Tantra'* (*Hevajrapiṇḍārthaṭīkā, Kye'i rdo rje bsdus pa'i don gyi rgya cher 'grel pa*). D1180, rgyud, ka, 1–126a).

Vajrapāṇi. *Meaning Commentary on the Cakrasaṃvara Tantra* (*Lakṣābhidhanādud-dhṛtalaghutantrapiṇḍārthavivaraṇa, Mngon par brjod pa 'bum pa las phyung ba nyung ngu'i rgyud kyi bsdus pa'i don rnam par bshad pa*). D1402, rgyud, ba, 78b–141a.

Vasubandhu. *Commentary on [Asaṅga's] 'Summary of Mahāyāna'* (*Mahāyānasaṃ-grahabhāṣya, Theg pa chen' po bsdus pa'i 'grel pa*). D4050, sems tsam, ri, 121–190.

———. *Commentary on [Maitreya's] 'Differentiation of the Middle and Extremes'* (*Madhyāntavibhāgaṭīkā, Dbus dang mtha' rnam par 'byed pa'i 'grel pa*). D4027, sems tsam, bi, 1a1–27a7.

———. *Conquest over Objections about the [Three] Mother Scriptures*. Full title: *Conquest Over Objections about the Three Mother Scriptures: Extensive Explanation of the Superior 'One Hundred Thousand Stanza,' 'Twenty-five Thousand Stanza,' and 'Eighteen Thousand Stanza Perfection of Wisdom' Sūtras* (*Āryaśatasāhasrikāpañcaviṃsatisāhasrikāṣṭadaśasāhasrikāprajñāpāramitābṛhaṭṭīkā*, *'Phags pa shes rab kyi pha rol tu phyin pa 'bum pa dang nyi khri lnga stong pa dang khri brgyad stong pa'i rgya cher bshad pa/ yum gsum gnod 'joms*). D3808, shes phyin, pha, 1a–292b.

———. *Thirty Stanzas* (*Triṃśikākārikā*, *Sum cu pa'i tshig le'ur byas pa*). D4055, sems tsam, shi, 1a–3a.

———. *Treasury of Higher Knowledge* (*Abhidharmakośakārikā*, *Chos mngon pa'i mdzod kyi tshig le'ur byas pa*). D4089, mngon pa, ku, 1a–25a.

Yaktön Sanggyepel (*g.yag ston sangs rgyas dpal*). *King of Wish-Fulfilling Gems: Good Explanation of the 'Ornament of Clear Realizations' Treatise of Quintessential Instructions on the Perfection of Wisdom Together with Its Commentary 'Clear Meaning'* (*Shes rab kyi pha rol tu phyin pa'i man ngag gi bstan bcos mngon par rtogs pa'i rgyan dang de'i 'grel pa don gsal ba dang bcas pa legs par bshad pa rin chen bsam 'phel dbang gi rgyal po*. Zi ling: Mtsho sngon mi rigs dpe skrun khang, 2004

———. *Precious Treasury: Good Explanation of the 'Ornament of Clear Realizations' Treatise of Quintessential Instructions on the Perfection of Wisdom Together with Its Commentaries* (*Shes rab kyi pha rol tu phyin pa'i man ngag gi bstan bcos mngon par rtogs pa'i rgyan 'grel pa dang bcas pa legs par bshad pa rin po che'i bang mdzod*), vol. 1–2. New Delhi: Ngawang Topgay, 1973.

Yeshé Dé (*ye shes sde*). *Differences of the Views* (*Lta ba'i khyad par*)/*Notes on the Views* (*Lta ba'i rjed byang*). D4360, sna tshogs, jo, 213b–228a.

Contemporary Scholarship

Ames, William L. "Bhāvaviveka's Own View of His Differences with Buddhapālita." In *The Svātantrika-Prāsaṅgika Distinction: What a Difference does a Difference Make?*, edited by Georges B. J. Dreyfus and Sara L. McClintock, 41–66. Boston: Wisdom Publications, 2003.

Ardussi, John, and Sonam Tobgay. *Written Treasures of Bhutan: Mirror of the Past and Bridge to the Futue. Proceedings of the First International Conference on the Rich Scriptural Heritage of Bhutan*. Thimphu: The National Library of Bhutan, 2008.

Aris, Michael. *Hidden Treasures and Secret Lives*. London and New York: Kegan Paul International, 1989.

Brunnhölzl, Karl. In Praise of Dharmadhātu *by Nāgārjuna, Commentary by the Third Karmapa*. Ithaca, New York: Snow Lion Publications, 2007.

———. *Luminous Heart: The Third Karmapa on Consciousness, Wisdom, and Buddha Nature*. Ithaca, New York: Snow Lion Publications, 2009.

———. *The Center of the Sunlit Sky: Madhyamaka in the Kagyü Tradition*. Ithaca, New York: Snow Lion Publications, 2004.

Burchardi, Anne. "Shakya mchog ldan's Literary Heritage in Bhutan." In *Written Treasures of Bhutan: Mirror of the Past and Bridge to the Futue. Proceedings of the First International Conference on the Rich Scriptural Heritage of Bhutan*, edited by John Ardussi and Sonam Tobgay, 25–74. Thimphu: The National Library of Bhutan, 2008.

———. "The Logic of Liberation: Epistemology as a Path to the Realization of Mahāmudrā." Forthcoming in *Proceedings of the 7th Nordic Tibet Research Conference*. Helsinki, 2009.

Cabezón, José Ignacio. "The Canonization of Philosophy and the Rhetoric of Siddhānta in Tibetan Buddhism." In *Buddha Nature: A Festschrift in Honor of Minoru Kiyota*, edited by Paul J. Griffiths and John P. Keenan, 7–26 (Tokyo: Buddhist Books International, 1990).

———. "Two Views on the Svātantrika-Prāsaṅgika Distinction in Fourteenth-Century Tibet." In *The Svātantrika-Prāsaṅgika Distinction: What a Difference does a Difference Make?*, edited by Georges B.J. Dreyfus and Sara L. McClintock, 289–315. Boston: Wisdom Publications, 2003.

Cabezón, José Ignacio, and Geshe Lobsang Dargyay. *Freedom from Extremes: Gorampa's "Distinguishing the Views" and the Polemics of Emptiness*. Boston: Wisdom Publications, 2007.

Cabezón, José Ignacio, and Roger R. Jackson (ed.). *Tibetan Literature: Studies in Genre*. Ithaca, New York: Snow Lion, 1996.

Caumanns, Volker. "Tibetan Sources on the Life of Serdog Paṇchen Shākya Chogden (1428–1507)." In *Lives Lived, Lives Imagined: Biography in the Buddhist Traditions*, edited by Linda Covill, Ulrike Roesler, and Sarah Shaw, 205–239. Boston: Wisdom Publications in collaboration with The Oxford Centre for Buddhist Studies, 2010.

Conze, Edward. *Prajñāpāramitā Literature*. Tokyo: Reiyukai, 1978.

Cozort, Daniel. *Highest Yoga Tantra: An Introduction to the Esoteric Buddhism of Tibet*. Ithaca, New York: Snow Lion Publications, 1986.

Crosby, Kate, and Andrew Skilton. *The Bodhicaryāvatāra*. Oxford: Oxford University Press, 1995.

Davidson, Ronald M. "The Ṅor-pa Tradition." In *Wind Horse: Proceedings of the North American Tibetological Society*, edited by Ronald M. Davidson, vol. 1, pp. 79–98. Berkeley: Asian Humanities Press, 1981.

de Jong, Jan W. (ed.). *Nāgārjuna Mūlamadhyamakakārikāḥ*. Madras: India, The Adyar Library and Research Centre, 1977.

Doctor, Thomas H. "In Pursuit of Transparent Means of Knowledge: The Madhyamaka Project of rMa bya Byaṅ chub brtson grus." *Journal of the International Association of Buddhist Studies*, vol. 32, no. 2 (2009, released 2011): 419–442.

——— (tr.). *Speech of Delight: Mipham's Commentary on Śāntarakṣita's* Ornament of the Middle Way *by Mipham Jamyang Namgyal Gyatso*. Ithaca, New York: Snow Lion Publications, 2004.

Dreyfus, Georges B. J. *Recognizing Reality: Dharmakīrti's Philosophy and Its Tibetan Interpreters*. Albany, New York: State University of New York Press, 1997.

———. *The Sound of Two Hands Clapping: The Education of a Tibetan Buddhist Monk.* Berkley and Los Angeles, University of California Press, 2003.

———. "Would the True Prāsaṅgika Please Stand? The Case and View of 'Ju Mi pham." In *The Svātantrika-Prāsaṅgika Distinction: What a Difference does a Difference Make?*, edited by Georges B.J. Dreyfus and Sara L. McClintock, 317–347. Boston: Wisdom Publications, 2003.

Dreyfus, Georges B. J., and Drongbu Tsering. "Pa tshab and the Origin of Prāsaṅgika." *Journal of the International Association of Buddhist Studies*, vol. 32, no. 2 (2009, released 2011): 387–418.

Dreyfus, Georges B. J., and Sara L. McClintock (ed.). *The Svātantrika-Prāsaṅgika Distinction: What a Difference does a Difference Make?* Boston: Wisdom Publications, 2003.

Eckel, Malcolm David. *Bhāviveka and His Buddhist Opponents.* Harvard Oriental Series, 70. Cambridge, Massachusetts: Department of Sanskrit and Indian Studies, Harvard University, 2009.

———. *Jñānagarbha's Commentary on the Distinction Between the Two Truths.* Albany, New York: State University of New York Press, 1987.

Garfield, Jay L. *The Fundamental Wisdom of the Middle Way: Nāgārjuna's* Mūlamadhyamakakārikā. Oxford: Oxford University Press, 1995.

Geshe Ngawang Samten, and Jay L. Garfield. *Ocean of Reasoning: A Great Commentary on Nāgārjuna's* Mūlamadhyamakakārikā. Oxford: Oxford University Press, 2006.

Griffiths, Paul J., and John P. Keenan (ed.). *Buddha Nature: A Festschrift in Honor of Minoru Kiyota.* Tokyo: Buddhist Books International, 1990.

Gyurme Dorje. *Tibet Handbook.* England: Footprint Handbooks, 1999.

Hopkins, Jeffrey. *Emptiness in the Mind-Only School of Buddhism: Dynamic Responses to Dzong-ka-ba's* The Essence of Eloquence: I. Los Angeles: University of California Press, 1999.

———. *Maps of the Profound: Jam-yang-shay-ba's Great Exposition of Buddhist and Non-Buddhist Views on the Nature of Reality.* Ithaca, New York: Snow Lion, 2003.

———. *Meditation on Emptiness.* London: Wisdom Publications, 1983.

———. (tr. and introduction). *Mountain Doctrine: Tibet's Fundamental Treatise on Other-Emptiness and the Buddha-Matrix.* Ithaca, New York: Snow Lion Publications, 2006.

———. *Reflections on Reality: The Three Natures and Non-Natures in Cittamātra School, Dynamic Responses to Dzong-ka-ba's* The Essence of Eloquence, Volume 2. Berkeley: University of California Press, 2002.

———. (tr. and annotated in collaboration with Lama Lodrö Namgyel). *The Essence of Other-Emptiness by Tāranātha.* Ithaca, New York: Snow Lion Publications, 2007.

———. "The Tibetan Genre of Doxography: Structuring a Worldview." In *Tibetan Literature: Studies in Genre*, edited by José Ignacio Cabezón and Roger R. Jackson, 170–186. Ithaca, New York: Snow Lion, 1996.

———. *Tsong-kha-pa's Final Exposition of Wisdom.* Ithaca, New York: Snow Lion Publications, 2008.

Huntington, C. W. "Was Candrakīrti a Prāsaṅgika?" In *The Svātantrika-Prāsaṅgika Distinction: What a Difference does a Difference Make?*, edited by Georges B. J. Dreyfus and Sara L. McClintock, 67–91. Boston: Wisdom Publications, 2003.

Ichigō, Masamichi. "Śāntarakṣita's Madhyamakālaṃkāra." In *Studies in the Literature of the Great Vehicle*. Michigan Studies in Buddhist Literature No. 1, edited by Luis O. Gómez and Jonathan A. Silk, 141–240. Ann Arbor: Collegiate Institute for the Study of Buddhist Literature and Center for South and Southeast Asian Studies, The University of Michigan, 1989.

Jackson, David. "Birds in the Egg and Newborn Cubs: Metaphors for the Potentialities and Limitations of "All-at-once" Enlightenment." *Tibetan Studies: Proceedings of the 5th Seminar of the International Association for Tibetan Studies*, vol. 1 (1989): 95–114.

———. "Several Works of Unusual Provenance Ascribed to Sa Skya Paṇḍita." In *Tibetan History and Language: Studies Dedicated to Uray G'eza on His Seventieth Birthday*, edited by Ernst Steinkellner, 233–254. Wien: Arbeitskreis für Tibetische und Buddhistische Studien, Universität Wien, 1991.

Jackson, David, and Shunzo Onoda. *Rong-ston on the Prajñāpāramitā Philosophy of the Abhisamayālaṃkāra: His Sub-commentary on Haribhadra's 'Sphuṭārthā.'* Kyoto: Nagata Bunshodo, 1988.

———. *The Early Abbots of 'Phan po Na-lendra*. Vienna: Arbeitkreis für Tibetische und Buddhistische Studien, 1989.

———. *The Mollas of Mustang: Historical, Religious and Oratorical Traditions of the Nepalese-Tibetan Borderland*. Dharamsala: Library of Tibetan Works and Archives, 1984.

Kajiyama, Yuichi. "Controversy between the sākāra- and nirākāra-vadins of the yogācāra school—some materials." *Indogaku Bukkyōgaku Kenkyū*, vol. 14, no. 1 (1965): 429–418.

———. "Later Mādhyamikas on Epistemology and Meditation." In *Mahāyāna Buddhist Meditation: Theory and Practice*, edited by Minoru Kiyota, 114–143. Honolulu: The University of Hawaii, 1978.

Kano, Kazuo. *rNgog Blo-ldan-shes-rab's Summary of the* Ratnagotravibhāga. Ph.D. Dissertation, University of Hamburg, 2006.

Kapstein, Matthew. *The Tibetans*. Malden, MA; Oxford: Blackwell Publishing, 2006.

———. "We Are All Gzhan stong pas." *Journal of Buddhist Ethics*, vol. 7 (2000): 105–125.

Karma Thinley. *The History of the Sixteen Karmapas of Tibet*. Boulder: Prajñā Press, 1980.

Khetsun Sangpo. *Biographical Dictionary of Tibet and Tibetan Buddhism*. Dharamsala, India: Library of Tibetan Works and Archives, 1979.

Komarovski, Yaroslav. "Encountering Ineffability—Counting Ineffability: On Divergent Verbalizations of the Ineffable in 15th Century Tibet." *Acta Tibetica et Buddhica*, vol. 1 (2008): 1–15.

———. "Reburying the Treasure—Maintaining the Continuity: Two Texts by Shakya Chokden on the Buddha-Essence." *Journal of Indian Philosophy*, vol. 34, no. 6 (2006): 521–570.

———. "Shakya Chokden's Interpretation of the *Ratnagotravibhāga*: "Contemplative" or "Dialectical?"" *Journal of Indian Philosophy*, vol. 38, no. 4 (2010): 441–452.

———. (tr.). *Three Texts on Madhyamaka by Shakya Chokden*. Dharamsala, India: Library of Tibetan Works and Archives, 2000.

Kramer, Jowita. *A Noble Abbot from Mustang: Life and Works of Glo-bo Mkhan-chen (1456–1532)*. Wien: Arbeitskreis für Tibetische und Buddhistische Studien, Universität Wien, 2008.

Lévi, Sylvain. *Mahāyāna-sūtrālaṃkāra: exposé de la doctrine du grand véhicule selon le systéme Yogācāra*. 2 vols. Paris: Bibliothéque de l'École des Hautes Études, 1907, 1911.

Lindtner, Christian. "Atiśa's Introduction to the Two Truths, and Its Sources." *Journal of Indian Philosophy*, vol. 9, no. 2 (1981): 161–214.

———. *Nagarjuniana: Studies in the Writings and Philosophy of Nāgārjuna*. Indiske Studier 4. Copenhagen: Akademisk Forlag, 1982.

Lobsang Jamspal, R. Clark, J. Wilson, L. Zwilling, M. Sweet, and R. Thurman. *The Universal Vehicle Discourse Literature (*Mahāyānasūtrālaṁkāra*) By Maitreyanātha/Āryāsaṅga Together with its* Commentary *(*Bhāṣya*) By Vasubandhu*. New York: American Institute of Buddhist Studies, 2004.

Lozang Jamspal. "Zhalu Lotsava Chos skyong bZang po and His Literary Works." *Tibetan Studies: Proceedings of the 5th Seminar of the International Association for Tibetan Studies*, vol. 1 (1989): 175–182.

Martin, Dan. "A Brief Political History of Tibet by Gu-ru Bkra-shis." In *Tibetan History and Language: Studies Dedicated to Uray G'eza on His Seventieth Birthday*, edited by Ernst Steinkellner, 329–351. Wien: Arbeitskreis für Tibetische und Buddhistische Studien, Universität Wien, 1991.

Mathes, Klaus-Dieter. *A Direct Path to the Buddha Within: Gö Lotsāwa's Mahāmudrā Interpretation of the* Ratnagotravibhāga. Boston: Wisdom Publications, 2008.

———. "Tāranātha's 'Twenty-One Differences with regard to the Profound Meaning'—Comparing the Views of the Two *gŹan stoṅ* Masters Dol po pa and Śākya mchog ldan." *Journal of the International Association of Buddhist Studies*, vol. 27, no. 2 (2004): 285–328.

Migmar Tseten, "The History of the Sakya School." In *Treasures of the Sakya Lineage*, edited by Migmar Tseten, 233–249. Boston: Shambhala, 2008.

————(ed.). *Treasures of the Sakya Lineage*. Boston: Shambhala, 2008.

Mimaki, Katsumi. *Blo gsal grub mtha'*. Kyoto: Université de Kyoto, 1982.

Miyasaka, Yūsho (ed.). "Pramāṇavārttika-kārikā (Sanskrit and Tibetan)." *Acta Indologica*, vol. 2 (1971/72): 1–206.

Mohr, Thea, and Jampa Tsedroen (ed.). *Dignity and Discipline: Reviving Full Ordination for Buddhist Nuns*. Boston: Wisdom Publications, 2010.

Nagao, Gadjin M. *Madhyāntavibhāga-Bhāṣya: A Buddhist Philosophical Treatise Edited for the First Time from a Sanskrit Manuscript*. Tokyo: Suzuki Research Foundation, 1964.

Ngawang Zangpo (tr. and introduction). *Jamgon Kongtrul's Retreat Manual*. Ithaca, New York: Snow Lion Publications, 1994.

[No author mentioned]. *A Means to Achieve Bhikṣuṇī Ordination*, http://www.thubtenchodron.org/BuddhistNunsMonasticLife/a_means_to_achieve_bhiksuni_ordination.pdf

Norbu, Dawa. *China's Tibet Policy*. Richmond, Surrey: Curzon Press, 2001.

Obermiller, Eugéne (tr.). *History of Budhism by Bu-ston*. Heidelberg: Otto Harrassowitz, 1932.

Oki, Kazufumi. "Musōyuishiki to Usōyuishiki." In *Kōza Daijō Bukkyō 8 Yuishiki Shisō*, 178–209. Tokyo: Shunjūsha, 1982.

Onoda, Shunzo. "Abbatial Successions of the Colleges of gSang phu sNe'u thog Monastery." *Bulletin of the National Museum of Ethnology* (Osaka), vol. 15, no. 4 (1990): 1049–1071.

Pettit, John Whitney. *Mipham's* Beacon of Certainty*: Illuminating the View of Dzogchen, the Great Perfection*. Boston: Wisdom Publications, 1999.

Rhoton, Jared Douglas (tr.). *A Clear Differentiation of the Three Codes: Essential Distinctions among the Individual Liberation, Mahāyāna, and Tantric Systems*. Albany, New York: State University of New York Press, 2002.

Roerich, George (tr.). *Blue Annals*. Calcutta: Royal Asiatic Society of Bengal, 1949; reprint, Delhi: Motilal Banarasidas, 1996.

Roloff, Carola. *Red mda' ba. Buddhist Yogi-Scholar of the Fourteenth Century: The Forgotten Reviver of Madhyamaka Philosophy in Tibet*. Wiesbaden: Ludwig Reichert Verlag, 2009.

Ruegg, David Seyfort. "The Jo naṅ pas: A School of Buddhist Ontologists According to the *Grub mtha' śel gyi me long*." *Journal of the American Oriental Society*, vol. 83 (1963): 73–91.

———. *The Literature of the Madhyamaka School of Philosophy in India*. Wiesbaden: Harrassowitz, 1981.

Schmithausen, Lambert. "On Some Aspects of Descriptions or Theories of 'Liberating Insight' and 'Enlightenment' in Early Buddhism." In *Studien zum Jainismus und Buddhismus: Gedenkschrift für Ludwig Alsdorf*, edited by Klaus Bruhn und Albrecht Wezler, 199–250. Wiesbaden: Steiner, 1981.

Shakabpa, Wangchuk Deden. *Tibet: A Political History*. New Haven and London: Yale University Press, 1967.

Sharma, Parmananda. *Śāntideva's* Bodhicharyāvatāra *[sic]: Original Sanskrit text with English Translation and Exposition Based on Prajnākarmati's [sic] Panjikā [sic]*, vols. 1–2. New Delhi: Aditya Prakashan, 1990.

Smith, Gene. *Among Tibetan Texts: History and Literature of the Himalayan Plateau*. Boston: Wisdom Publications, 2001.

Snellgrove, David L. *The Hevajra Tantra: A Critical Study*, London Oriental Series, 6, parts 1–2. London: Oxford University Press, 1959.

Sonam Thakchoe. *The Two Truths Debate: Tsongkhapa and Gorampa on the Middle Way*. Boston: Wisdom Publications, 2007.

Stearns, Cyrus. *Taking the Result as the Path: Core Teachings of the Sakya Lamdre Tradition*. Boston: Wisdom Publications, 2006.

———. *The Buddha from Dölpo: A Study of the Life and Thought of the Tibetan Master Dölpopa Sherab Gyaltsen*, revised and enlarged edition. Ithaca, New York: Snow Lion Publications, 2010.

Tarab Tulku. *A Brief History of Tibetan Academic Degrees in Buddhist Philosophy*. NIAS Report Series, No. 43. Copenhagen: Nordic Institute of Asian Studies, 2000.

Tauscher, Helmut. "Phya pa chos kyi seng ge as a Svātantrika." In *The Svātantrika-Prāsaṅgika Distinction: What a Difference does a Difference Make?*, edited by Georges B. J. Dreyfus and Sara L. McClintock, 207–255. Boston: Wisdom Publications, 2003.

Thupten Jinpa. *Self, Reality and Reason in Tibetan Philosophy: Tsongkhapa's Quest for the Middle Way*. London: RoutledgeCurzon, 2002.

Thurman, Robert. *Central Philosophy of Tibet: A Study and Translation of Jey Tsongkhapa's Essence of True Eloquence*. Princeton: Princeton University Press, 1984.

Tillemans, Tom. "The 'Neither One Nor Many' Argument for *Śūnyatā* and Its Tibetan Interpretations." In *Contributions on Tibetan and Buddhist Religion and Philosophy*, edited by Ernst Steinkellner and Helmut Tauscher, 305–320. Arbeitskreis für Tibetische und Buddhistische Studien, Universität Wien, Vienna, 1983.

———. "Two Tibetan Texts on the 'Neither One Nor Many' Argument for *Śūnyatā*." *Journal of Indian Philosophy*, vol. 12 (1984): 357–388.

Tillemans, Tom, and Toru Tomabechi. "Le *dBu ma'i byung tshul de Śākya mchog-ldan*," *Asiatische Studien*, vol. 49, no. 4 (1995): 891–918.

Tucci, Giuseppe. *Tibet: Land of Snows* (tr. J.E. Stapleton Driver). London: Elek Books, 1967.

Upādhyāya, Jagannāth (edited and annotated). *Vimalaprabhā: śrīmañjuśrīyaśo-viracitasya paramādibuddhoddhṛtasya śrīlaghukālacakratantrarājasya kalkinā śrīpuṇḍarīkeṇa viracitā ṭīkā*, vol. 1. Bibliotheca Indo-Tibetica Series, 11. Sarnath, Varanasi: Central Institute of Higher Tibetan Studies, 1986.

van der Kuijp, Leonard. *Contributions to the Development of Tibetan Epistemology*. Wiesbaden: Franz Steiner, 1983.

———. "The Monastery Gsang-phu ne'u-thog and Its Abbatial Succession from ca. 1073 to 1250." *Berliner Indologische Studien* 3 (1987): 103–127.

Vose, Kevin A. "Making and Remaking the Ultimate in Early Tibetan Readings of Śāntideva." *Journal of the International Association of Buddhist Studies*, vol. 32, no. 2 (2009, released 2011): 285–318.

_______. *Resurrecting Candrakīrti: Disputes in the Tibetan Creation of Prāsaṅgika*. Boston: Wisdom Publications, 2009.

Wallace, Vesna A. (tr.). *The Kālacakratantra: The Chapter on the Individual together with the* Vimalaprabhā. New York: American Institute of Buddhist Studies at Columbia University, 2004.

Wedemeyer, Christian K. *Āryadeva's* Lamp that Integrates the Practices (Caryāmelāpakapradīpa)*: The Gradual Path of Vajrayāna Buddhism According to the Esoteric Community Noble Tradition.* New York: American Institute of Buddhist Studies, 2008.

Westerhoff, Jan. *Nāgārjuna's Madhyamaka: A Philosophical Investigation.* Oxford: Oxford University Press, 2009.

Williams, Paul. *Mahāyāna Buddhism: The Doctrinal Foundations,* 2nd ed. London: Routledge, 2009.

Wood, Thomas E. *Mind Only: A Philosophical and Doctrinal Analysis of the Vijñānavāda.* Monographs of the Society for Asian and Comparative Philosophy, 9. Honolulu: University of Hawaii Press, 1991.

Yangchen Gawai Lodoe. *Paths and Grounds of Guhyasamaja [*sic*].* Dharamsala, India: Library of Tibetan Works and Archives, 1995.

Index

abandonment, 114
  of afflictions, 113
  of obscurations, 114
    of knowables, 113, 346n.9
  See also object
Abhayākāragupta, 92
Abhidharma, 22, 25–27, 36, 44, 47, 230, 320n.100
affirmation, 8, 114
  by reasoning, 227
Alīkākāravāda. *See* Yogācāra, Cittamātra
Alīkākāravādin, 13–14, 83, 85–87, 118, 141, 144–45, 149–50, 154–55, 161, 169, 171–72, 179, 182, 186–87, 189, 195, 207–209, 211–12, 216, 218, 224–25, 227, 233, 237, 248, 258, 265, 267, 273, 331n.17, 358n.116–17
Anākāra. *See* Non-Aspectarians
analysis, 84, 177, 194, 220–23, 233, 235, 248, 354n.48
  by reasoning, 137, 220–23
  by the reasonings of the proponents of tenets, 137
  by the wisdom of individual analysis, 120
  Madhyamaka analysis, 222, 235
  of intended profound meanings, 208
  very subtle, 79
  See also wisdom
antidote
  of ignorance, 111
    direct, 85, 384n.77
  to obscurations, direct, 170
  to obscurations of knowables, 153, 189
appearance, 8, 39, 73, 97, 158, 162–64, 214, 239, 241, 243, 268, 362–63n.6, 379n.27, 382n.55
  and emptiness, union of, 214
  dualistic, 14, 78, 128, 158–59, 166, 239, 346n.8, 379n.24
    of persons and phenomena, 128
    of the apprehended and apprehender, 128
  external, 163
  magic, 379n.27
  mental, 73
  mistaken, 99, 239, 241, 249–51
  of external phenomena, 162, 165
  of luminosity, 26, 34
  of others, 190, 195
  relative, 159
apprehended, 128, 152, 158–59, 161, 165
  conceptions of, 112, 346n.9, 365n.30
  See also apprehended and apprehender, four stages of yoga, mind, mind-only, negation, obscurations, phenomenon
apprehended and apprehender, 80, 128, 133, 147, 154, 159, 161–62, 166, 168, 177, 216, 231, 246, 259, 263, 360n.142, 362n.6, 375n.138, 379n.24
  imaginary, 165
  non-duality of, 162, 239

apprehended and apprehender (*continued*)
  parts of dualistic appearances, 379n.24 and n.27
  two types of, 128
  with different substances, 166
    with respect to external objects, 157, 166
    with respect to internal knowing, 158, 166
  See also appearance, apprehender-aspect, cognition, consciousness, emptiness, extreme, knowing, mind, negation, phenomenon, primordial mind, proliferations, remainder, self, self-cognition, thatness
apprehended-aspect, 115, 118, 158, 161–63, 165, 168, 250, 346n.8, 360n.142, 364n.27
  See also apprehender-aspect, cognition, consciousness, existence, negation, self-cognition, truthlessness
apprehender, 152, 159, 161–62, 165–66, 239, 360n.142
  aspect of, 152, 360n.142
  See also appearance, apprehended and apprehender, apprehender-aspect, cognizance, duality, extreme, four stages of yoga, knowing, mind, self, three natures, truthlessness
apprehender-aspect, 115, 117, 161–64, 168, 226, 243, 248–50, 360n.142
  comprehending the apprehended-aspect, 164
  devoid of the apprehended and apprehender, 164
  experiencing the apprehended-aspect, 163
  inward-looking, 162
    factor of, 162, 241, 249
  of self-cognition, 164
  See also cognition, primordial mind
arhat, 110, 189
ārya, 196, 266, 382n.55
  ārya bodhisattva, 188–89, 238, 320n.98
  knowledge-seeing of āryas, 217
  Mahāyāna ārya, 150, 189–90, 238, 243–44, 247, 370n.81, 372n.106
  See also ground, meditative equipoise, object, primordial mind
Āryavimuktisena, 143, 202–205
Asaṅga, 13, 26, 27, 32, 38, 41, 47, 72, 81–83, 92, 101, 103, 127, 129–30, 132, 134, 136, 141–42, 144–46, 154–55, 166, 183–87, 189–91, 203–207, 211–12, 226, 230, 254–55, 266, 275, 320n.100, 330n.8–9, 331n.18, 348n.34, 351–52n.63, 353n.71, 357–58n.116–17, 369n.73, 374n.128, 383n.63
Aspectarians, 73, 331n.17
Aspectless Mind-Only. *See* Nirākāra Cittamātra *under* Cittamātra
Atiśa (Dīpaṃkara), 92, 96–97, 101, 150, 153–55, 252, 361n.147
atom, 235–37
  partless, 111, 113, 234–37
  truly established, 235
Autonomists. *See* Svātantrika *under* Madhyamaka

Baktön Shakya Özer. *See* Baktön Zhönnu Gyeltsen
Baktön Zhönnu Gyeltsen, 25–26, 50
basis, 129, 187, 192, 241, 250, 371n.97, 382n.59
  for determining emptiness, 130
  level of, 242–43
  of accomplishing the dharma-body, 200
  of accomplishment of all stainless positive qualities, 239
  of accomplishment of the generation and completion stages, 250, 259–60
  of accomplishment of the special deity, 260

of cyclic existence and nirvāṇa, 251, 258
of dispute, 133
of emptiness, 124, 128–31, 135, 280, 353n.71
of intent, 188
of limitless positive qualities, 174
of negation, 123–28, 219
of purification of stains, 196
that is empty, 124, 128
See also primordial mind, subject
Bhāviveka, 72–75, 90, 139, 142, 189, 202–203, 205, 207, 209, 212, 218–19, 223, 233–34, 237–38, 248, 332n.21–22 and n.34, 358n.116, 376n.142
bliss, 379n.30
great, 257
arisen from empowerments, 253
stainless great, 255
supremely unchangeable, 253
See also primordial mind
bodhisattva, 39, 146, 189, 271, 330n.8
See also ārya, ground
Bodongpa, 29, 271, 318n.80
body maṇḍala, 250
body of union, 261
buddha, 113, 188–89, 202
major and minor marks of, 104
qualities of a, 188
ultimate, 251
See also nirvāṇa, primordial mind
buddha-essence, 36, 85, 94, 101, 104, 187–90, 231, 243–44, 309n.11, 339n.96, 344n.145, 370n.81, 372n.106
characterized by the purity from adventitious stains, 150, 189
endowed with all positive qualities of a buddha, 188
ornamented with major and minor marks of a buddha, 104
ornamented with the positive qualities of a buddha, 189
buddhahood, 7, 10, 15, 76, 83, 85–87, 106, 112, 115, 117, 150, 153, 167–69, 171, 175, 183, 211, 238, 249–50, 254, 262, 264–65, 269, 334n.45, 346n.5
See also obscurations
Buddhapālita, 73–74, 139, 332n.21
Butön Rinchendrup, 332n.34

Cakrasaṃvara, 29–31, 33, 250
calm abiding, 93, 96
Candrakīrti, 28, 34–35, 42, 46, 73–76, 78, 90, 95, 99–101, 103, 124, 126, 139, 142, 154–55, 188–89, 202, 205, 207–209, 211–12, 218–19, 223, 226, 233–34, 237–38, 248, 266–67, 273, 275, 320n.100, 321n.123, 333n.38, 338n.79, 342n.123, 349n.42, 350n.53, 356n.90, 361n.147 and n.156, 369n.73, 376n.142
Changkya Rölpé Dorjé, 358n.116, 376n.1, 379n.31
Changlung Chödingpa Zhönnu Lodrö. *See* Changlung Rinpoché
Changlung Rinpoché, 30–31, 43, 45, 47, 97, 319n.85
Chapa Chökyi Senggé, 27, 48, 340n.97
Chennga Ngakgi Wangpo, 22
Chesa Dakchen Lodrö Wangchuk, 33, 36, 43
Chödrak Gyamtso (the Seventh Karmapa), 19, 22–23, 43, 48–50, 81–82, 105, 314n.34, 327n.181 and n.185
Chödrak Yeshé (the Fourth Zhamarpa), 22
Chödrup Pelmotso, 45
Chökyap Pelzang, 25
Chölung, 42, 329n.192
Chumik, 33, 36, 43–44
Cittamātra, 7–10, 13, 38–40, 79–83, 91, 97–99, 101, 103–104, 109–10, 112–13, 115, 117–19, 137, 140, 144–49, 157, 160, 162, 167, 209, 213–14, 217, 236, 265, 310n.17, 336n.62, 337n.69, 356n.88,

Cittamātra *(continued)*
359n.135, 370n.75, 375n.138, 376n.1, 379n.31
Alīkākāravāda Cittamātra, 104, 215
Nirākāra Cittamātra, 209
Cittamātra Followers, 80, 89, 110, 118, 144–45, 149, 159–60, 162, 208
provisionally, 147
Yogācāra Cittamatra Followers, 118
clarity, 82, 214, 242, 366n.44
and cognition, 166–67, 240–41, 248, 364n.28, 379n.24
and emptiness, inseparability of, 85
and emptiness, union of, 214
clarity factor of primordial mind, 239–40
factor of, 240
mere clarity, 79
See also cognition, entity, mind, mind's clarity factor, reason
clinging, 80
to external objects, 152
to mind possessing the aspect of the apprehender, 152
cognition, 80, 160, 162, 162, 213–14, 241, 246, 260, 267, 366n.44
appearing as matter, 112
itself as, 247
mere cognition of clarity-emptiness free from the apprehended and apprehender, 190
naturally luminous, 80
of itself, 246–48, 364n.19, 384n.72
of objects, 85
of primordial mind, 238, 244
of the apprehended-aspect by the apprehender-aspect, 248
of the buddha-essence, 243
See also clarity, entity, knowing, object, reason, self-cognition, valid cognition
cognizance, 160–61
cognizance-only, 159
mere cognizance characterized by the aspect of the apprehender, 152, 360n.142
tenets of, 81
Cognizance-Only. *See* Vijñaptimātra
completion stage. *See* two stages
concepts, 85–86, 181, 200–201, 218, 221, 225, 241, 250, 260, 263, 272–73
apprehending signs, 260
with respect to the mode of being, 141
regarding the object of experience, 200
grasping at the extremes, 263
of superimposition and deprecation, 258
See also emptiness, object, sounds and concepts
conceptuality, 86, 89, 176, 220–23, 225, 234, 261
consciousness, 14, 73, 98, 147, 157–58, 160–62, 214, 226, 239–41, 263, 342n.120, 363n.6 and n.11, 375n.138, 382n.55
adventitious, 239
appearing as external objects, 161
conceptual consciousness grasping at existence, 99
consciousness factor of the outward-looking apprehended-aspect, 250
distorted sensory, 163
dualistic, 14, 77, 135, 162, 202, 238, 241
dualistically appearing, 161, 164, 166, 364n.27
as the apprehended and apprehender, 158
empty of the apprehended and apprehender with different substances, 166
with respect to external objects, 158
eye consciousness, 162
grasping at the true existence of primordial mind, 227

mistaken, 239
outward-looking, 163–64
six collections of, 229
stains of, 251
with dualistic appearances, 128, 159
See also entity
consequence, 36, 73, 77, 138–39, 240, 276, 333n.42
See also reasoning
Consequentialists. *See* Prāsaṅgika *under* Madhyamaka
conventions, 172, 179, 181, 193–94, 199, 232, 242, 339n.95, 380n.44
of meditative equipoise, 179
of subsequent attainment, 170, 179, 187, 365n.38
subsequent, 170, 228, 339, 365n.38
worldly, 138, 269, 274
See also establishment
cyclic existence, 239
cause of, 186, 251
liberation from, 76, 83, 111
path out of, 251
rebirth in, 111
thoughts fancying cyclic existence and nirvāṇa, 174
See also basis, phenomena, proliferations

Darma Rinchen. *See* Gyeltsap Darma Rinchen
dependent nature. *See* three natures
deprecation, 77, 96, 127, 208, 258
See also extreme
definitive meaning, 40, 48, 95, 97, 119, 130, 142, 165, 183, 187, 189, 192, 200, 202–203, 207–208, 215, 258, 267
determined by the author of the *Seven Works*, 251
experienced through meditation, 168, 210, 258, 365n.34
final, 178, 183, 203, 208, 258
of the ocean of Yogācāras' texts, 165
incorporated into experience through meditation, 258
incorporated into experience through meditation, 204
of the *Five Dharmas of Maitreya*, 38
of Yogācāra teachings, 41, 106
of Yogācāras' texts, 148
of the mode of being, 170
which is the object of experience of yogic direct perception, 197
See also dharmacakra, pronouncement
Devendrabuddhi, 358n.116
dharma-body, 195, 200, 229
natural, 258
Dharma lineages, 93
dharmacakra, 40, 47, 351n.59
definitive meaning of the three dharmacakras, 351n.59
second (middle) dharmacakra, 40, 92, 121, 174, 183–88, 191, 206, 257, 259
definitive meaning of, 203
explicit teachings of, 95, 184–86 192, 195, 198, 201, 203, 205–206, 259, 375n.128
explicit teachings of the second dharmacakra and the *Collection of Reasonings*, 197
main topic of, 184–87, 193, 206
second and third (last two) dharmacakras, 174, 183, 186–87, 202, 205, 207
definitive meaning of, 187
main topics of both, 186–87
third (last, final) dharmacakra, 40, 92, 95–96, 101, 104, 121, 174, 178, 183, 185–89, 192, 200, 203, 206–207, 211, 231, 257–59
definitive meaning of, 96, 186, 191–93, 197, 201
definitive teachings of, 183–84, 192, 197, 203, 205–206
explicit teachings of, 130
main topic of, 186–87, 198, 211
See also emptiness, meaning, meditation, pronouncement, ultimate reality

Dharmakīrti, 26, 50, 73, 81, 101, 132, 134, 141, 145, 149–50, 154–55, 178, 205, 212, 216, 223, 225, 230–33, 236–38, 243, 245, 248, 251, 273, 275, 320n.100, 329n.192, 332n.21, 357–58n.116–17, 376n.144, 377n.8, 378n.12 and n.17, 380–81n.44
Dharmapāla, 73–75, 155, 202, 205, 331n.18
dharma-sphere, 39, 158, 160, 173, 178, 194, 196, 215, 217, 258, 266
See also entity, grasping, primordial mind
Dharmottara, 358n.116
Dignāga, 26, 50, 73, 81, 132, 149, 154–55, 205, 230, 232, 320n.100, 331n.18, 332n.21, 336n.63, 357–58n.116
Dīpaṃkara, 22
Dokham, 50
Doklöpa Künga Zangpo, 341n.116
Dölpopa Sherap Gyeltsen, 5–6, 8, 11–12, 94, 103–104, 122, 131–32, 135–36, 213, 229–30, 309n.13, 312n.18, 323n.131, 340n.98, 344n.142, 352–53n.70–71, 370n.75
Döndrup Pelzang, 25
Dönyö Dorjé, 19, 325n.154, 329n.192
Dönyö Pelwa, 21, 26–28, 35–36, 38–39, 41, 43–44, 49, 313n.26, 316n.61
Dönyöpa, 49
Dorjechang Künga Zangpo. *See* Künga Zangpo
doxography, 7–8, 72, 74
Drakpa Gyeltsen, 4, 265, 329n.192, 331n.17
Drakpa Jungné, 22
Drakpa Özer, 29
Drepung, 21
Dreyül Kyetsel, 21, 37
Drigung. *See* Kagyü
Drokmi Lotsawa, 93, 97
Drölchok. *See* Künga Drölchok
Dröpa Özer Gyelpo Pelwa, 27
Druk. *See* Kagyü
Dzongpa Künga Namgyel, 4

early Tibetans, 90, 101–102, 248
ecumenical movement, 30, 79, 87–88
emanation-body, 229, 371n.92
empowerment, 19, 23–24, 29–31, 33, 35, 38, 44–45, 48–49, 96, 106, 177, 192, 247, 253, 255, 325n.159, 387n.115
empowerment of cognition-display, 273
empowerment stages, 177
four empowerments, 387n.108
secret empowerment, 387n.108
vase empowerment, 387n.108
wisdom-primordial mind empowerment, 261
word empowerment, 273, 387n.108
See also bliss, primordial mind
emptiness, 4, 6, 8–9, 36, 72, 80, 85, 95, 103–105, 107–108, 114–15, 122–27, 130–31, 133, 136, 138, 142–44, 147, 153, 165, 170–80, 184, 191–94, 199–202, 210–12, 216, 221, 235–36, 255, 257, 260–62, 270–71, 317–18n.72, 346n.5, 349n.42 and n.45, 351n.55, 352n.69, 371n.97, 387n.114
accessed conceptually, 124
arrived at through searching for and not finding phenomena under analysis, 221
arrived at through severing superimpositions by listening and thinking, 173, 367n.51
conceptually understood, 184
created by mind, 229
described as a non-affirming negation, 192–93, 344n.142
described as negation of all phenomena, 198

described as the negation of reality of all phenomena, 184
determined by reasoning, 124, 176, 179, 259
related to listening and thinking, 186
determined through listening and thinking, 176, 179, 193–94, 197, 259
directly experienced by yogic direct perception, 176
directly realized in meditative equipoise, 179
emptiness side, 81
endowed with the supreme of all aspects, 173
experienced in meditative equipoise, 142
directly, 178
experienced through meditation, 142
explicitly taught by the middle (second) dharmacakra, 184–86
imputed by sounds and concepts which is renowned in tenets, 175
in terms of non-findability at the time of examination by reasoning, 221
in the face of reasoning, 141
in which the aggregates are excluded, 174
in which the apprehended and apprehender with different substances are negated, 164–66
inanimate, 208
natural emptiness established as the mode of being which is experienced by yogis, 175
nihilistic, 103, 125, 208
of all phenomena, 72, 111, 232
of both, 122
of duality, 134
of the apprehended and apprehender, 164–66
of the apprehended and apprehender, 154
of true existence, 126
of truth, 336n.62
other-emptiness, 3, 6, 12, 43, 46, 72, 82, 87, 94, 102–108, 122–24, 126–29, 131–32, 134–36, 165, 171, 175–77, 180, 182, 185, 190, 210, 215, 218–19, 223, 261, 270–71, 273, 337n.70, 338n.84, 348n.36, 349n.42, 350n.55, 351n.59 and n.63, 352n.70, 353n.71
overextended, 208
posited through reasoning, 142, 181, 184
realized by the path of Mantra, 255
realized in meditative experience, 186
realized in the meditative equipoise of Mahāyāna āryas, 124
realized through experience, 367n.51
related to searching for and not finding terminologically imputed meanings, 174
self-emptiness, 3, 12, 43, 46, 72, 87, 94, 103–104, 107–108, 122–29, 135–36, 143, 165, 171, 175–77, 180, 182, 185, 195–96, 203, 210, 215, 219, 223, 232–33, 235, 260–62, 264, 270–71, 273, 338n.84, 350n.55
sixteen types of, 80
taught in Nāgārjuna's *Collection of Praises*, 192
taught in the definitive teachings of the third dharmacakra, 192
taught in the explicit teachings of the second dharmacakra, 185, 192
which is a non-affirming negation, 174
which is beyond objects of mind, 174

emptiness *(continued)*
which is cognized conceptually, 176
which is the main topic of the middle dharmacakra, 185
See also basis, clarity, cognition, entity, explicit teachings, meditation, mode, subject, reasoning
enjoyment-body, 229, 371n.92
entity, 129, 131, 136, 152, 166, 171, 221, 227, 240–41, 246–47, 249–51, 271
nonexistent, 129
of clarity, 242
and cognition, 362n.6
of consciousness, 239–40
of dualistically appearing knowing, 134
of emptiness, 215
of inexpressible knowing, 80
of negation, 8
of the dependent nature, 129, 134, 166, 171, 240
of the dharma-sphere, 231
of the generation and completion stages, 250
of the non-dual primordial mind, 172
of the thoroughly established nature, 134, 165–66, 240
own entity, 126, 131, 134, 171, 224, 240, 329n.1
possessor of, 129
real, 129, 234
really existent, 152
self-cognizing, 221, 238
single, 234, 238, 240, 271
truly established, 135, 234
truly existent, 129, 238
unreal, 129
See also nonexistence
entity-body, 190
Epistemology-Logic. *See* Pramāṇa
establishment, 219
of conventional phenomena by conventional valid cognition, 93
of conventions by valid cognition, 93, 339n.95
of relative phenomena by valid cognition, 88, 93
true, 99, 126, 172, 225
existence, 98, 100, 161–62, 213, 215–16, 228, 232, 237, 253, 381n.44
as different substances, 165
conventional, 10, 100
external, 110, 235
in the face of reasoning, 219
lack of, 217–18
of an external material world, 73
of cognition, 160
of external objects, 8, 110
of objective phenomena, 218
of partless atoms, 111, 236
of partless moments of knowing, 236
of phenomena, 216–17
of primordial mind, 215
beyond sounds and concepts, 233
directly experienced in meditative equipoise, 223
of relative, conventional phenomena, 215
of subjective phenomena, 218
of the apprehended, 158
real, 73, 159
of dualistically appearing mind, 159
relative, 98, 100
substantial, 158
true, 82, 86–87, 214, 223–25, 317n.72
lack of, 82
of primordial mind, 224
of the apprehended-aspects, 113
of ultimate reality, 14
ultimate existence of primordial mind, 14
See also consciousness, cyclic existence, emptiness, extreme, grasping, object, reasoning
explanatory traditions of dialecticians, 93

explanatory traditions of Mantra, 93
explicit teachings
  explicit teachings, the level of emptiness, 204
  damage to, 188
  of the *Collection of Reasonings*, 120, 192, 202
  of the *Perfection of Wisdom* sūtras, 174
  See also dharmacakra, pronouncement
extreme, 74, 117, 212, 216–18, 220, 226, 228, 254
  freedom from extremes, 95
  of being both, 217
  of deprecation, 174
  of eternalism, 116, 187, 217, 228
  of existence, 217, 263
  of nihilism, 116, 217
  of nonexistence, 217, 263
  of superimposition, 175
  two extremes, 117, 216–17, 227–28
    of superimposition and deprecation, 216
    of the apprehended and apprehender, 160, 217
  See also four stages of yoga, luminosity, middle, mode, negation, primordial mind, proliferations, proponent of the extreme of eternalism as the middle, proponent of the extreme of nihilism as the middle, remainder

False Aspectarian Followers of the Middle. *See* Alīkākāravāda Mādhyamika *under* Mādhyamika
False Aspectarian Mind-Only. *See* Alīkākāravāda Cittamātra *under* Cittamātra
False Aspectarians. *See* Alīkākāravāda *under* Yogācāra
Five Foremost Venerable Founders, 4
Followers of Cognizance. *See* Vijñaptika
Followers of the Middle. *See* Mādhyamika
Followers of the Middle of Proponents of Cognizance. *See* Vijñaptivāda Mādhyamika *under* Mādhyamika
Followers of the Middle of Proponents of Entitylessness. *See* Niḥsvabhāvavāda Mādhyamika *under* Mādhyamika
Followers of the Middle of Sūtra Followers. *See* Sautrāntika Mādhyamika *under* Mādhyamika
Followers of the Middle of Yogic Practice. *See* Yogācāra Mādhyamika *under* Mādhyamika
Followers of Other-Emptiness, 87, 102, 117, 127, 135, 212
Followers of Self-Emptiness, 102, 117, 135
Followers of Yogic Practice. *See* Yogācāra
form-body, 190, 195
Four Golden Dharmas of Shangpa, 31, 45
four stages of yoga, 97, 152, 341n.114, 360n.141, 363n.6
  stage of yoga not realizing any extremes of proliferations, 152
  stage of yoga realizing the selflessness of persons, 152
  stage of yoga realizing the selflessness of the apprehended-phenomena, 152
  stage of yoga realizing the selflessness of the apprehender-phenomena, 152
functional thing, 162, 178, 230–31, 239
  qualified by negation of the objects of negation, 177–78
  which is an affirming negation, 178

Gakhang, 25, 29

Ganden, 21
Gelek Pelzang. *See* Khedrup Gelek Pelzang
Geluk, 3, 5, 7, 18–21, 23, 25, 28, 30, 33–34, 43, 47, 77, 88, 90, 92, 94–97, 100, 103, 214, 225, 310n.17, 311n.4, 315n.44 and n.50, 317–18n.72, 338n.79, 340n.98, 357–58n.116, 374n. 128, 378n.20, 379n.31
Gelukpa, 29, 271, 311n.4
Gendündrup, 21–22
generation stage. *See* two stages
Gewa Gyeltsen, 27
Gö Lotsawa Zhönnupel, 22, 313n.30
Gönpa Shar, 43
Gorampa Sönam Senggé, 3–6, 11, 20–22, 77–78, 83–84, 100, 104, 122, 209, 309n.13, 312n.18, 313n.20, 334n.46 and n.49, 337n.78, 340n.98
Gowo Rapjampa Sönam Senggé. *See* Gorampa Sönam Senggé
grasping, 14, 192, 214, 223–27, 379n.27
  as true, 224
  at existence, 99
  at objects, 225–26
  at primordial mind as true, 228
  at signs, 143
  at the dharma-sphere, 226
  at the self of persons, 112
  at the self of the apprehended-phenomena , 167
  at the self of the apprehender-phenomena, 365n.30
  at the true existence of primordial mind, 223–24, 226
  at true establishment, 225
  at true existence, 87, 224–28
  at truth, 227
  See also consciousness, object
Great Perfection, 87, 95, 98, 214, 267, 273
Great Seal, 31, 87, 95, 98, 273
  Great Seal Amulet Box, 31
  Innate Union Great Seal, 45
  Nāro's Great Seal, 45
ground
  bodhisattva ground, 189, 243, 247, 333n.45
  for arising of self-cognition, 151
  Mahāyāna ārya grounds, 242
  of dependence on which to depend, 217
  See also ten grounds
Guhyasamāja
  Akṣobhya Guhyasamāja, 31
  Mañjuśrīvajra Guhyasamāja, 30
Gungru Gyeltsen Zangpo, 28, 317–18n.72, 338n.79
Gyama, 43, 45, 48
Gyeltsap Darma Rinchen, 20, 22, 27, 92, 97, 316n.59, 340n.97
Gyümé, 21
Gyütö, 21, 300

Haribhadra, 27, 97, 141, 143, 150–53, 203–205, 219, 341n.114, 357n.103, 360n.142, 374n.118
Hevajra, 30, 34, 49, 96, 262–63
Higher Knowledge. *See* Abhidharma
Highest Secret Secret Mantra. *See* Mantra
Highest Yoga Tantra, 30, 249, 252–53, 264, 273

ignorance, 85, 99, 111, 113–14, 170, 249, 382n.55
  non-afflicted, 264
  See also antidote, phenomenon
illusory body, 341n.117
image
  conceptual, 227, 261
  dream, 227
  generic, 338n.79
  mental, 331n.17
imaginary nature. *See* three natures
impermanence, 133, 228–34, 237–38, 271, 380n.31 and n.44
  reverse of, 230, 232

India, xi, 22, 83, 87, 89–90, 92, 102, 109, 117–18, 270, 276
Innate Union, 45
Innate Union Great Seal. *See* Great Seal

Jamchen Chöjé, 21
Jamchen Rapjampa Sanggyepel, 20–21, 37
Jamyang Chöjé, 21
Jamyang Könchok Zangpo, 323n.135
Jamyang Zhepa Ngakwang Tsöndrü, 309n.13, 357n.116
Jang Ngamring, 38
Jayānanda, 76
Jetāri, 147, 154
Jñānagarbha, 138–39, 332–33n.34
Jñānaśrīmitra, 331n.18
Jonang, 323n.131 and n.135
Jonang Choklé Namgyel, 94
Jonangpa, 103, 271
Ju Mipam Jamyang Namgyel Gyamtso. *See* Mipam Gyamtso

Kadam, 27, 315n.44
Kadampa, 315n.50
Kagyü, 23, 29–31, 45, 82, 96, 314n.33
  Drigung, 31
  Druk, 31
  Karma, 18–19, 21–22, 29–31, 106, 337n.70
  Shangpa, 29–31
  Taklung, 29, 31
Kālacakra, 29–31, 38, 323n.131
  Mahāsaṃvara form of, 38
Kam, 30
Kamalaśīla, 27, 74–75, 78, 97, 139, 141, 145, 205, 332n.34, 334n.51, 341n.112–13, 343n.123
Karma. *See* Kagyü
Kham, 25, 37, 312n.7, 368n.54
Khartsé Langtang, 44
Khedrup Gelek Pelzang, 20, 22, 92, 97, 317n.72
Khyungpo Neljor. *See* Shangpa Dubupa
knowing, 84–85, 98–99, 158, 162–64, 214, 231, 238–39, 248, 342n.120, 344n.142, 362n.6, 382n.55
  and cognition, 162
  at the present, 235
  devoid of duality of the apprehended and apprehender that does not have momentary parts, 231, 235
  devoid of the apprehended and apprehender, 80
  dualistically appearing, 98, 128, 134, 158
  free from dualistic appearances, 158
  incorporating into experience the path of the two stages, 259
  inexpressible, 80
  mistaken, 152
  non-conceptual, 193
  non-dual, 163
  outward-looking types of, 163
  that has dualistic appearance of the apprehended and apprehender, 128
  with dualistic appearances, 158
  without dualistic appearances, 158
  See also apprehended, entity, mode, moment, negation, self-cognition
Kongtrül Yönten Gyamtso (Lodrö Tayé), 87
Künga Döndrup, 21
Künga Drölchok, 24–26, 28, 31, 34–36, 38, 40–42, 45, 103, 105–106, 308–309n.8, 312n.12, 314n.40, 315n.50, 317–18n.72, 321n.102 and n.105, 322n.124, 325n.149–50, 327n.181, 328n.192, 332n.25, 339n.95, 343n.127
Künga Lekpa, 22
Künga Trashi, 30–31, 45, 47–48, 319n.85, 329n.192
Künga Zangpo, 4, 21, 31–33, 35–36, 38, 43, 47–48, 271, 308n.8, 313n.23, 319n.85, 321n.102, 322n.121, 326n.168

Kurukullā, 31
Kyormolung, 25, 315n.50

Langtang, 45–46, 48, 328n.192
later Tibetans, 40, 47, 88, 95–96, 99, 102, 104, 209, 225, 340n.97
Lesser Madhyamaka. *See* Madhyamaka
Lhasa, 19, 48, 327n.181
lineage of bodhisattva vows, 92
lineage of extensive deeds, 82, 310n.18
lineage of profound view, 82, 310n.18
lineage of Secret Mantra vows, 92
lineage of vows of individual liberation, 92
Lodrö Chökyongwa, 30
Lodrö Tenpa (Loten the Fourth), 29
Longchen Rapjam. *See* Longchenpa
Longchenpa, 122, 213–14
Lord of Dharma Namgyel, 28
Loten the Fourth. *See* Lodrö Tenpa
Lowo, 36–38, 41, 104, 322n.121 and n.123–24, 328n.192
Lowo Depa Tsangchen Trashi Gönpo. *See* Trashigön
Lowo Khenchen Sönam Lhündrup, 20, 37–38, 313n.21, 323n.130
luminosity, 26, 34, 158, 213, 274, 341n.117
  empty, 268
  natural luminosity free from all extremes of proliferations, 188
  originally pure, 80
  primordially pure, 80
  stage of, 97, 266

Madhyamaka, xi, 2, 4–14, 20, 22–23, 26–27, 29, 31–32, 34, 38, 40–44, 48–50, 68, 71–72, 74–92, 96–97, 99–101, 103–104, 106–109, 112–13, 115–22, 131, 136–42, 145–48, 150, 154–57, 159, 166–75, 181, 183, 185–86, 188, 201, 203–205, 207–12, 214–16, 218, 220–23, 254–57, 259, 262–66, 269–72, 274–77, 309n.12–13, 310n.17, 318n.72, 320n.100, 321n.105, 327n.181, 329n.2, 330n.5, 333n.42, 335n.57, 337n.79, 338n.83, 340n.100, 343n.124, 350n.55, 359n.135, 362n.2, 365n.30, 366n.43, 369n.66, 379n.31, 386n.94, 388n.115
  analytical Madhyamaka accessed by severing superimpositions apprehending signs, 173
  Great Madhyamaka, 39–41, 46, 103, 116, 119–21, 329n.2
  Intermediate Madhyamaka, 120
  Lesser Madhyamaka, 119–20
  Madhyamaka Advocating Cognizance-Only, 141
  Madhyamaka Advocating Interiority of Knowables, 141
  Madhyamaka Asserted by Maitreya and Brothers Asaṅga and Vasubandhu, 255
  Madhyamaka Explained by the *Collection of Reasonings* with the Texts of Its Followers, 255
  Madhyamaka of Pāramitāyāna Followers, 257
  Madhyamaka of the Highest Secret Mantra, 255
  Madhyamaka with the Approach Advocating Thoroughly Established Phenomena as Entityness, 255
  Madhyamaka with the Approach of Entitylessness of All Phenomena, 255
  Mahāyāna Madhyamaka, 216
  Mantric Madhyamaka, 96
  Niḥsvabhāvavāda Madhyamaka, 8–13, 35, 40–43, 46–47, 50–51, 71–75, 77–79, 82–88, 91–92, 95, 99–101, 103, 105, 107–108, 113, 115–17, 119, 121–22, 124, 126–27, 131, 135–36, 138–40, 142–44, 150–51, 153, 155–57, 168–73, 175–87, 191, 197, 199, 201–10,

212–17, 219, 222–23, 226, 229, 235, 251, 253, 256–57, 259–64, 266, 270, 272, 274–76, 310n.17–18, 329n.1–2, 330n.5, 331n.17, 335n.56, 342n.123, 346n.5, 349n.42, 352n.69, 359n.135, 365n.34 and n.35, 370n.75, 375n.128, 376n.142 and n.144
nonanalytical Madhyamaka experienced through meditation, 173
non-tantric Madhyamaka, 78, 140
Ordinary Madhyamaka, 329n.2
Prāsaṅgika Madhyamaka, 13, 26, 47, 73, 76–78, 83, 91, 96, 100, 104, 110, 117–19, 124, 136–40, 142–44, 154, 171, 179, 180, 197, 202–203, 206–207, 218, 232, 257, 269, 274–75, 330n.16, 333n.42 and n.44, 334n.45 and n.46, 348n.34, 354n.82, 365n.35, 369n.73, 374–75n.128, 386n.94, 388n.115
Sautrāntika Madhyamaka, 75–76, 140, 148, 179–80, 206, 356n.95
sūtric Madhyamaka, 254, 256–57, 340n.100
Svātantrika Madhyamaka, 12–13, 26, 47, 68, 73, 76–78, 83, 96, 100, 104, 117–19, 124, 136–44, 148, 171, 197, 202–203, 207, 218, 232, 257, 269, 274–75, 330n.16, 333n.42 and n.44, 333–34n.45–46, 348n.34, 354n.82, 365n.35, 375n.128, 386n.94, 388n.115
Sautrāntika Svātantrika Madhyamaka, 140, 356n.95
Yogācāra Svātantrika Madhyamaka, 140, 356n.95
tantric Madhyamaka, 14, 254–57, 259, 264, 274, 334n.52–53, 340n.100
Vijñapti Madhyamaka, 329n.2, 335n.57
Vijñaptivāda Madhyamaka, 141
Yogācāra Madhyamaka, 13, 75–76, 119–20, 140–42, 144–45, 154, 173, 175, 179–80, 205–206, 219, 222, 251, 351n.59, 352n.69, 356n.95, 365n.35
See also analysis, reasoning, Niḥsvabhāvavāda, Vijñaptivāda, Yogācāra
Mādhyamika, 79–83, 85–87, 89, 103–104, 115, 118, 132, 138–39, 141–45, 150, 154–55, 160, 162, 171–72, 189, 201–203, 205, 207, 211–12, 215, 223–25, 228, 239, 270, 272, 334n.51, 366n.40
Alīkākāravāda Mādhyamika, 118, 141, 148, 159, 162, 239
Great Mādhyamika, 103, 132
Mādhyamika Utilizing Worldly Renown, 139, 219
Niḥsvabhāvavāda Mādhyamika, 143–44
Prāsaṅgika Mādhyamika, 137, 181, 205, 257, 355n.84, 365n.34, 369n.73
Sautrāntika Mādhyamika, 139, 205, 219, 332–33n.34, 365n.34
sūtric Mādhyamika, 272
Svātantrika Mādhyamika, 137, 181, 257, 355n.84
tantric Mādhyamika, 272
ultimately Mādhyamika, 147
Vijñaptivāda Mādhyamika, 161
Yogācāra Mādhyamika, 118, 139, 141, 143–45, 178, 182–83, 203–205, 211, 219, 223, 273, 332–33n.34, 365n.34, 376n.142
See also Prāsaṅgikas, Svātantrikas
Mahāmudrā. *See* Great Seal
Mahāyāna, 2, 4, 6–14, 35, 46, 71–72, 80–82, 84–85, 87–89, 91–92, 95, 100–101, 110–13, 116–17, 120–21, 129, 145, 148, 150, 153, 157, 162, 167, 189, 208–209, 213–14, 229, 235, 246–47, 249–53, 267–69, 271–72, 274–77, 335n.56, 371n.97, 375n.131
See also ārya, emptiness, ground, path
Maitreya, 12, 25–27, 32, 40, 44, 72, 81–83, 101, 117–18, 122, 124,

Maitreya *(continued)*
132, 134, 136, 141, 145–46, 154–55, 160, 178, 183, 186–87, 190–91, 201, 204–205, 207, 215, 226, 230, 233, 243, 251, 255, 264–65, 275, 330n.8, 348n.33, 352n.69, 358n.117
Mañjuśrī, 37, 44, 183, 369n.66
White Mañjuśrīvajra, 37
Mantra, 177, 192, 250–55, 257, 259–60, 262, 265
See also explanatory traditions of Mantra, lineage of Secret Mantra vows, object
Mantra Vehicle. *See* Mantrayāna
Mantrayāna, 119–21, 255–56, 258, 261
See also object
Mapcha Jangchup Tsöndrü, 36–37, 50
Marpa Lotsawa Chökyi Lodrö, 93
Martön Gyamtso Rinchen, 27
Mati Penchen, 94
meaning
general, 36, 95
hidden meaning, the level of clear realizations, 204
intended meaning of the *Five Dharmas of Maitreya*, 39–40
intended profound meaning, 208
interpretive, 188
of the mode of being, 170
ultimate, 161, 164, 263, 380n.44
See also definitive meaning, dharmacakra, pronouncement
meaning-generality, 227, 338n.79
meditation, 84, 88, 92–93, 152–53, 155, 170, 184, 190–91, 195–96, 200–201, 203, 221, 228, 247, 254, 258–60, 274, 317n.72, 356n.88
explicitly taught by the middle dharmacakra, 184
on emptiness, 202, 338n.79
on reality, 35, 317n.72
on tantric deities, 250
on the conventional maṇḍala, 250
on ultimate reality, 143, 318n.72
tantric, 50, 262
See also definitive meaning, emptiness, Madhyamaka, object, ultimate reality, ultimate view, wisdom
meditative equipoise, 80, 84–86, 96, 112, 114, 131, 142–44, 154–55, 159, 169–70, 172–73, 175, 178–79, 181–82, 184–85, 187, 191–97, 200, 202, 204–205, 210–13, 219, 223, 226, 228, 249, 254, 259–60, 262–63, 270, 274–75, 317n.72, 365n.38, 366n.43 and n.45, 382n.55
of āryas, 172, 366n.44
of Mahāyāna āryas 124, 169–70, 172–73, 175–76, 178, 219
on emptiness, 318n.72
on the meaning of emptiness determined by listening and thinking, 193
on ultimate reality, 86
view of, 75, 114, 170, 194
See also convention, object, primordial mind, wisdom
meditative experience, 2, 25, 35, 51, 85–86, 89, 96, 120, 131, 142, 169, 184, 201, 203, 214, 260, 270, 276
direct, 13, 86, 173, 274
of reality, 14, 86, 271–74
of the ultimate, 273
of ultimate reality, 35, 86
of primordial mind free from proliferations, 261
of reality, 89, 202
of ultimate reality, 35
See also emptiness, object, ultimate reality
middle, 72, 83, 104, 147, 160, 216–17
between the two extremes of eternalism and nihilism, 116
free from extremes, 85, 216
See also proponent of the extreme of eternalism as the middle,

proponent of the extreme of nihilism as the middle
Middle of Cognizance. *See* Vijñapti Madhyamaka *under* Madhyamaka
Middle of Proponents of Cognizance. *See* Vijñaptivāda Madhyamaka *under* Madhyamaka
Middle of Yogic Practice. *See* Yogācāra Madhyamaka *under* Madhyamaka
Mikyö Dorjé (the Eighth Karmapa), 77, 81–82, 105–106, 314n.33, 337n.70
mind, 8, 39, 50, 73, 80, 84, 88, 94, 96–98, 105, 110–11, 113, 123, 141, 146–47, 149, 158–59, 161–63, 165–66, 168–69, 176, 178, 209, 213–14, 226–27, 238, 242, 244–46, 248–50, 258, 271, 317n.72, 330n.14, 331n.17, 336n.62, 354n.84, 362n.6, 368n.60, 379n.27, 383n.66, 384n.72
adhering, 225
appearing as external world, 152
appearing as the apprehended-phenomena, 162
apprehending emptiness as signs, 104
conceptual, 179, 193, 199, 221–22, 227, 250, 256, 344n.142
apprehending signs, 174
apprehending sounds as meaning, 176
conventional, 250
correctly realizing the mode of being, 382n.55
devoid of dualistic appearances, 78
dualistic, 239
dualistically appearing, 134, 159
as the apprehended and apprehender, 382n.55
empty character of, 82
familiarizing, 201
fundamental, 213
individually self-cognizing non-conceptual, 153
appearing as the illusion-like selfness, 151–52
innate worldly, 137
luminous, 178, 244–45
luminous by nature, 178, 289
luminous nature of, 244, 266
mind side, 81
mind's clarity factor, 82
mind's empty factor, 82
naturally luminous mind free from proliferations, 198
non-dual, 164
of enlightenment, 167–68
ultimate, 196, 198, 260
of listening and thinking, 200
possessing the aspect of the apprehender, 152
profundity and clarity of, 82
projecting appearances of external phenomena, 165
projecting dualistic appearances, 346n.8
relative, 158, 368n.60
self-experiencing, 243
sphere of, 196
subjective, 153, 362n.6
subliminal, 274
that appears as external objects, 158
ultimate, 14, 158, 178, 200, 222, 239, 368n.60
worldly, 137, 139, 354n.84
innate, 137
See also clinging, emptiness, mind-only, self-cognition, primordial mind
mind-only, 39, 146–47, 152, 323n.134, 360n.142
devoid of the apprehended, 146
mind-only view of Cittamātra, 147
Mind-Only. *See* Cittamātra
Mind Training, 31, 48

mind-vajra, 184, 196, 233, 266
  indestructible, 184, 286
  ultimate, 196
Mipam Gyamtso, 79–81, 84, 214, 337n.78, 363n.6
mode, 137
  and multiplicity, 217
  explanatory, 191, 196
    by way of other-emptiness, 216
    by way of self-emptiness, 216
    of other-emptiness, 126
  meditative equipoise and subsequent attainment modes of positing the final view, 179–81
  of apprehension, 317n.72
    of something as truly established, 228
  of being, 99, 147, 158, 170, 190, 219, 247, 362n.2, 382n.55
    which is experienced by yogis, 175
  of determining the ultimate, 139
    by autonomous reasoning, 137
    by consequence reasoning, 137
  of eliminating the two extremes with respect to phenomena, 116
  of emptiness explained in the *Conquest over Objections*, 131, 352n.69
  of engagement, 238
  of entering into Madhyamaka, 137
  of explaining Mahāyāna Madhyamaka, 216
  of explaining self-emptiness, 125
  of explaining the definitive meaning of the last dharmacakra, 191
  of explanation of other-emptiness, 132
  of explanation of self-emptiness, 123
  of generating wisdom that ceases concepts apprehending signs, 260
  of gradually entering Sautrāntika and Cittamātra, 137
  of identifying an object of meditation, 172
  of identifying the subject-basis of other-emptiness, 129
  of initially entering Sautrāntika, 137
  of introducing students to Madhyamaka tenets, 138–39
  of knowing, 221
  of negating objects of negation, 110, 289
  of positing the reason of the lack of being one or many, 115
  of positing the selflessness of persons, 123
  of positing the ultimate, 139
  of positing without analysis by reasoning the relative truth of the world, 137
  of proving objects being proven, 110
  of realizing the view, 387n.115
  of setting in meditative equipoise, 197, 317n.72, 373n.110
  of severing proliferations within meditative equipoise, 169, 366n.43
  of severing superimpositions, 171
  of temporarily positing views through reasoning, 168
  of the view within meditative equipoise, 172
  of upholding the ultimate view, 168
  See also concepts
moment, 228, 231–33, 236–38, 380–81n.44
  mental, 237
  of knowing, 236–37
  of primordial mind, 232–33
  of the non-dual primordial mind, 236
  partless, 234–35, 237
    of knowing, 234–37
    of primordial mind, 237
  truly established, 235
Moral Discipline. *See* Vinaya

Nāgārjuna, 12–13, 26–28, 35, 41–42, 71–72, 75, 81–82, 92, 96, 98, 101, 104, 117, 120, 122, 124, 155, 174, 183–85, 188–89, 191–97, 199–200, 202, 204–205, 218, 222–23, 254, 260, 266, 275, 320n.100, 330n.5, 332n.25 and n.30, 341n.117, 348n.33, 349n.42, 361n.147, 369n.67 and n.72
Nalendra, 21, 26, 28–29, 45
Namgyel. *See* Lord of Dharma Namgyel
Namgyel monastic university, 36
Namgyel Drakpa Zangpo. *See* Namgyel Drakzang
Namgyel Drakzang (Rikden Namgyel Drakzang), 38, 41, 106, 323n.131
Nāro Ḍākiṇī, 49
negation, 110, 113–15, 125–26, 129, 153, 165, 177–79, 184, 195, 198, 220, 223–24, 234, 237–38, 317–18n.72, 349n.45, 366n.44, 378n.12
  affirming, 177–80, 182, 188–89, 193, 220, 253, 256, 317n.72, 335n.56, 376n.1
  by reasoning, 227
  non-affirming, 142, 154, 174–80, 182, 185–86, 188–89, 192–94, 196, 198, 201–202, 202, 214, 220, 253, 258, 262, 318n.72, 344n.142, 370n.75, 379–80n.31
    of all extremes of proliferations, space-like, 178
    of all proliferations, 256
    which is a mere negation of self of persons, 345n.5
  of all external phenomena, 113
  of all phenomena in the face of reasoning, 143
  of entity, 8, 153, 172
  of external material things, 113
  of external things, 115
  of impermanence of primordial mind, 238
  of momentary knowing, 236
  of nature, 8
  of partless atoms, 235
  of partless moments of knowing, 235
  of phenomena extended in space and time, 113
  of primordial mind, 224, 238
  of both the apprehended and apprehender, 147, 290
  of the apprehended-aspects, 113, 115
  of the imaginary nature on the basis of the dependent nature, 185, 190, 366n.44
  of the reality of the dualistic consciousness, 77
  of the self of persons, 110
  of the self of the apprehended-phenomena, 110
  of the two types of self, 113–14, 178
  See also basis, emptiness, entity, functional thing, object, primordial mind, remainder, subject
Nego, 19, 26, 29, 34
Nenang, 29
Nenang Gyelwa, 106
Neudong, 18–19, 25, 28, 315n.50
Neudzong. *See* Neudong
New Traditions, 93, 95
Ngakwang Chödrak, 103–105
Ngari, 50, 328n.192
Ngari Lowo. *See* Lowo
Ngok Lotsawa Loden Sherap, 50, 93–94, 155, 339n.96, 340n.97
Ngor, 21, 45, 47, 313n.23, 319n.85
Ngor monastery, 21, 31, 33, 308n.4, 326n.168
Ngorchen Künga Zangpo. *See* Künga Zangpo
Niguma cycle, 44
Niguma's empowerment, 45
nihilism, 126–27
  See also extreme, proponent of the extreme of eternalism as the middle, proponent of the extreme of nihilism as the middle

nihilist, 207, 209, 211
Niḥsvabhāvavāda. *See* Madhyamaka
Niḥsvabhāvavādin, 13–14, 46, 72–75, 79, 83, 85–87, 100, 103, 117, 122–25, 136, 138–39, 141, 143–44, 154–55, 169, 171–72, 177, 179, 182–83, 186–87, 189, 191, 197, 202–204, 207–209, 211–12, 214, 216, 224–27, 229, 233–34, 236, 265–67, 273, 365n.34, 378n.12
Nirākāra. *See* Non-Aspectarians
Nirākāra Cittamātra, 209
Nirākāravāda, 77, 331n.18
Nirākāravādin, 334n.51
nirvāṇa, 112–13, 150, 170, 199, 379n.30
  natural, 194, 199, 223
  of buddhas, 113, 167
  of pratyekabuddhas, 113, 150, 167, 346n.9
  of Pratyekabuddhayāna, 112
  of śrāvakas, 113
  of Śrāvakayāna, 112
  See also basis, cyclic existence, path, proliferations
Non-Aspectarians, 73, 331n.17
nonexistence, 10, 14, 39, 98, 100, 216, 218–20, 234, 253, 379n.27
  in a true or ultimate way, 100
  in the face of reasoning, 218–20
  of entity, 134
  of phenomena, 127, 217, 234, 237
  of primordial mind, 378n.12
    in the face of reasoning, 14, 219
  of the thoroughly established nature, 134
  ultimate, 98
  See also extreme
Norzang, 18–19
Nyetang Chödzong, 29
Nyimedrung, 42
Nyingma, xi, 22, 30, 79, 214, 387n.108

object, 8, 80, 84, 128, 147, 152, 160, 167–68, 170, 176, 193–95, 201, 214, 225–27, 238, 240, 243, 245–49, 252–53, 256, 258–60, 266, 331n.17, 354n.82, 362n.6, 384n.69–70 and n.72
  being proven, 110
  conceptual, 186
  directly experienced in meditative equipoise, 212
  experienced by wisdom produced from meditation, 173
  experienced through meditation, 204, 211
  external, 8, 39, 112, 115, 146, 152, 158–61, 165–67, 336n.62
  gross, 235
  incorporated into experience by yogis, 200
  material, 241
  non-observation of, 195
  of abandonment, 99, 112, 224–25, 227, 250, 258
    by Madhyamaka reasoning, 225
    outward-looking factors of, 250
  of actual tantric meditation of the two stages, 260
  of cognition, direct, 215
  of comprehension, 182
  of concepts, 178, 185, 193, 253–54
  of conceptual mind, 176, 179, 185, 193, 227, 256, 344n.142
  of desire, 226
  of direct experience, 179, 184, 199
  of direct perception, 193
  of direct yogic experience, 175
  of engagement, 177, 245, 384n.70
    inferential, 333n.42
    of primordial mind, 247
  of experience, 120, 141, 151, 200, 210, 251, 259
    by the view, 251
    of meditative equipoise, 184
      of the generation and completion stages, 262
  of individually self-cognizing primordial mind, 188, 258

of primordial mind of the meditative equipoise of Mahāyāna āryas, 184
of wisdom arisen from meditation, 211
of yogic direct perception, 176, 193, 197, 203
of foremost āryas, 196
of functioning, 203, 247–48
of primordial mind, 247
of individually self-cognizing primordial mind, 173, 176, 242–43, 247
of the omniscient primordial mind, 248
of grasping, 227
at true existence, 227
of incorporation into experience by the meditative equipoise of āryas, 172
of observation, 167
purificatory, 168
of meditation, 184, 212
on ultimate reality, 143
by the meditative equipoise of āryas, 172
on ultimate truth, 213
of meditative equipoise of the generation and completion stages, 262
of meditative experience, 103, 120, 143, 151, 153, 182, 185, 203, 210, 259–60
of negation, 110, 123–30, 132–33, 136, 171–72, 219, 222, 317n.72, 378n.20
by reasoning, 219, 222
through Madhyamaka reasoning, 378n.20
of realization, 259
common to both sūtras and tantras, 256
in Tantra, 265
of the view common to both sūtras and tantras, 256
of the uncommon tantric view, 256
of the uncommon view of Mantrayāna, 255–56
of the Mantra system, 257
of Mantra, 265
of reasoning, 227
of self-cognition, 246
of sounds and concepts, 137, 175, 181, 194, 199, 222, 233
of the direct realization of reality, 344n.142
of the final view of sūtras and tantras, 95
of yogic direct perception, 176, 198
realized by mind in an exclusionary way, 198
realized in meditative equipoise, 193–94
See also apprehended, cognition, consciousness, emptiness, grasping, negation, reasoning, remainder, thatness
obscurations, 9, 117, 169, 171, 226, 257
afflictive, 112–13
of knowables, 115, 152, 169–70, 264–65
which are conceptions of the apprehended, 112, 365n.30
predispositions of, 169
to buddhahood, 86
See also abandonment, antidote
Old Tradition, 93, 95
See also Nyingma
Ösel Tsemo, 34
Öseltsé. *See* Ösel Tsemo
other-emptiness. *See* emptiness
other-exclusion, 199, 227, 232, 261

Pacification, 95, 98
Padampa Sanggyé, 93
Padmasambhava, 93
Pakmo Drupa, 18–19, 21, 28, 311n.4, 312n.9
Pakmodru, 18, 22, 28, 311n.4, 315n.50
Pakpa Lodrö Gyeltsen, 4, 33, 311n.3

Pangkha Chöding, 25
Pāramitāyāna, 119–20, 177, 188, 192, 252, 255–58
path, 9, 80, 112, 114, 150, 167, 186–87, 192, 249–51, 250, 363n.10, 371n.97, 382n.59, 384n.77
  five paths, 167
  Mahāyāna path, 85–86, 167, 249, 333n.45
    of preparation, 360n.136
    of seeing, 189, 238, 243–44
  of Mantra, 255
  of meditative equipoise, uninterrupted, 112
  of preparation, 167, 365n.31
  of the two stages, 259
  Sūtra path, 260
  sūtric or non-tantric path of Mahāyāna, 85
  tantric, 252, 338n.81–82
  three Buddhist paths, 150
  to the nirvāṇa of pratyekabuddhas, 149
  Vajrayāna path, 99, 251
Path and Result, 31, 45–49, 87, 98, 319n.85, 323n.135, 326n.168, 329n.192
Patsap Nyimadrak, 76
Pawo Tsuklak Trengwa, 49, 82, 105
Peltsek, 76
Pema Lingpa, 23
Pema Zangpowa, 38–41, 106, 323n.135
Penyül, 21, 325n.150, 328n.192
perception, 19, 159, 331n.17, 383n.66
  direct, 40, 163, 182, 242–43, 245–47
  yogic, 176–77, 193, 247
  See also object
Perfection Vehicle. *See* Pāramitāyāna
Perfection of Wisdom. *See* Prajñāpāramitā
permanence, 172, 228–30, 232, 271, 379–80n.31
  natural, 229
  of continuity, 229, 231–33
phenomenon, 8, 72, 79, 84, 123–29, 131, 133, 135–36, 138, 158, 160–61, 163–64, 168, 171–72, 182, 185, 187, 190, 193–95, 199, 201–202, 215–17, 219, 221, 229–34, 236–39, 249–51, 260, 262, 264, 270, 329n.1, 346n.12, 348n.38 and n.40, 354n.84, 366n.44, 369n.72, 379n.30, 380–81n.44
  actual, 176
  apprehended-, 162
    and apprehender-, 187, 216, 259
  compounded, 229
    relative, 132
  contaminated, 379n.30
  conventional, 93, 126, 130, 135, 137, 139, 215, 234, 377n.9, 384n.77
  dependent, 217
  empty, 133
  established by valid cognition, 136
  extended in space and time, 113, 237
  external, 72–73, 110, 113, 161–65
  generally characterized, 176, 182, 185, 198
  hidden, 244–45, 380n.44
  impermanent, 10, 14, 228, 230
  knowable, 193
  manifest, 245, 380n.44
  mental, 164, 175, 213, 243
  momentary, 232, 236
  objective, 218
  of cyclic existence and nirvāṇa, 82
  of the apprehended and apprehender, 80
  polluted by ignorance, 174
  partless, 236
  relative, 88, 93, 127, 135, 196, 362n.2
  self-characterized, 176, 182, 261
  subjective, 218

ultimate, 377n.9
uncompounded, 230
imputed, 230
whose continuity is not severed, 232
See also appearance, emptiness, establishment, existence, grasping, mind, mode, negation, nonexistence, self, selflessness, four stages of yoga
possessor of reality, 132, 158, 187, 196
Potopa Rinchensel, 374n.118
practice lineages, 10, 29–30, 45, 51, 87–88, 96–97
Prajñākaragupta, 154–55, 358n.116
Prajñāpāramitā, 22, 26–27, 32, 37, 42, 44, 47, 82, 316n.59, 320n.100
Pramāṇa, 22–23, 26–28, 32, 36–37, 42, 44, 46, 48–49, 82, 101, 230, 268, 320n.100, 327n.181, 339n.97
Prāsaṅgika. *See* Madhyamaka
Prāsaṅgikas (as followers of the Prāsaṇgika system), 139, 143–44, 203, 207, 375n.129
pratyekabuddha, 149, 167, 189, 244
See also nirvāṇa, path
Pratyekabuddhayāna, 112
See also nirvāṇa
primordial mind, 11, 14, 39, 74, 86, 98, 133, 142, 147, 151, 153, 157–63, 169–70, 173, 176, 179, 181–82, 185–87, 190–92, 194, 196, 198, 201–204, 210, 213–16, 218–24, 226–34, 237–71, 273–74, 330n.14, 340n.100, 342n.120, 356n.88, 363n.11, 366n.44, 370n.81, 371n.97, 375n.138, 378n.12, 380n.33, 382n.55
characterized by the dependent natures being empty of the imaginary natures, 186
collection of, 39, 262
devoid of duality of the apprehended and apprehender, 165
devoid of subjective-objective duality, 153
directly experienced in meditative equipoise, 223
empty of duality, 161, 168, 292
free from proliferations, 253, 255–56, 261
free from the apprehended and apprehender, 99
free from the duality of the apprehended and apprehender, 99, 120, 154, 159, 181, 231, 257–58, 262, 265–66
in terms of self of persons, 345n.5
innate, 99, 255–56, 340n.100
self-arisen, 95
inexpressible, 261
in the mental streams of Mahāyāna āryas, 243
in the mental streams of ordinary beings, 243
inward-looking, 239
inward-looking primordial mind factor, 250–51
luminous, 35
nonconceptual, 85
of meditative equipoise, 382n.55
non-dual, 40, 86, 96, 98, 131, 143, 151–54, 158–62, 164–66, 168–69, 172, 175, 177, 178, 180–84, 186–87, 189, 191–93, 197–99, 201–204, 210–11, 215–16, 219, 222–23, 225, 228, 232, 235–37, 241, 246, 251, 255, 259, 264, 271, 344n.142, 366n.44, 373n.110, 376n.142
free from all proliferations, 187
qualified by negation of other phenomena, 195
not apprehending any extremes of proliferations, 192
of buddhas, 176, 198
of emptiness, 221
of non-duality of the apprehended and apprehender, 133

primordial mind *(continued)*
of the basis, 243
of the dharma-sphere, 172–73, 197, 201, 221, 225, 258
of the great bliss, 260
of the third empowerment, 261
omniscient, 248, 291
original, 239, 241, 249–50
originally established, 241
primordial mind factor of the inward-looking apprehender-aspect, 239, 250
pure worldly primordial mind of subsequent attainment, 382n.55
qualified by negation of the imaginary natures on the basis of the dependent natures, 185
self-cognizing, 13, 14, 153, 178, 244, 255, 257
individually, 74, 85, 186, 190, 203, 248, 255, 258, 331n.19
of āryas, 181
transcending sounds and concepts, 223, 234
ultimate, 130, 196
See also clarity, cognition, empowerment, entity, existence, moment, nonexistence, object, self-cognition
primordial nature, 79
probandum, 133–34
proliferations, 80, 84, 137, 169, 172, 175, 177, 183, 192, 195–96, 200, 222, 225, 252, 259–61, 263–64
apprehending signs, 259, 261, 344n.142,
conceptual, 86, 222, 259, 261
extremes of, 152, 178, 188, 192, 216, 371n.97
freedom from, 196, 198, 252–56, 273, 386n.94
of cyclic existence and nirvāṇa, 82
of the apprehended and apprehender, 258
See also four stages of yoga, luminosity, mind, mode, negation, primordial mind, reasoning
pronouncement, 348n.27
last, 203, 211, 258
definitive meaning of, 183, 211
definitive meaning of the explicit teachings of, 186
explicit teachings of, 120
middle, 258
and last pronouncements, 121
definitive meaning implicitly taught by, 204
definitive meaning of the explicit teachings of, 203
explicit teachings of, 120, 200
main topic of, 186
of the middle dharmacakra, 174
of the last (third) dharmacakra, 174, 200, 258
See also dharmacakra
proponent of the extreme of eternalism as the middle, 340n.98
proponent of the extreme of nihilism as the middle, 340n.98
Proponents of Cognizance. *See* Vijñaptivāda
Proponents of Emptiness. *See* Śūnyatāvāda
Proponents of Entitylessness. *See* Niḥsvabhāvavāda *under* Madhyamaka
Proponents of Other-Emptiness, 104, 122, 124, 127, 131–32, 135, 143–44, 235, 348n.34
Proponents of Particulars. *See* Vaibhāṣika
Proponents of Phenomenal Existence. *See* Vastusatpadārthavāda
Proponents of Self-Emptiness, 122–25, 143–44, 178, 348n.34
Puṇḍarīka, 147, 320n.98, 375n.138
purity
from adventitious stains, 150, 189
self-cognizing, 98

Raktayamāri, 30
Ramdopa, 47, 329n.192
Rangjung Dorjé (the Third Karmapa), 81, 106, 229, 337n.70, 342n.120

Ratnākaraśānti, 50, 74, 78–79, 92, 101, 150–51, 155, 331n.18, 335n.56–57, 360n.137, 361–62n.157
Ratnakīrti, 331n.18
reality-limit, 129
reason, 87, 101, 133, 147, 159, 174, 177, 233–34, 236, 257–58, 272, 346n.12, 354n.82, 380n.44
  autonomous, 73, 77, 138–39, 333n.42
  of ascertainment of simultaneous observation, 153, 159
  of clarity and cognition, 159, 362–63n.6
  of simultaneous observation, 362–63n.6
  of the lack of being one or many, 115, 165, 235–37, 346n.12
  See also reasoning
reasoning, 32, 34, 42, 75, 80–81, 84, 86, 88–89, 97, 111, 115, 117, 120, 124–25, 131, 133, 137–38, 142–44, 151, 153, 155, 169–70, 175, 177, 179–82, 185, 187, 190–92, 195, 197, 199–201, 203–205, 208, 210, 212, 216–24, 227, 233–38, 245, 254, 259–61, 263–64, 266, 273–74, 317n.72, 332n.21, 338n.79, 354n.84, 356n.88, 371n.94, 376n.144, 378n.12
  Alīkākāravāda reasoning of other-emptiness, 261
  analytical, 224
  analyzing the ultimate, 97, 125, 218, 220, 223
  arisen from thinking, 151
  autonomous, 137–38
  consequence reasoning, 137
  determining primordial mind as truthless, 227
  establishing
    emptiness, 133
    external things and the apprehended-aspects as empty, 115
    primordial mind as truthless, 224
    truthlessness of external objects, 112
    truthlessness of the apprehended-aspects, 112–13
  Madhyamaka reasoning, 218, 220, 222, 225, 234
  negating
    adhering minds together with habitual tendencies, 225
    all signs of proliferations, 192
    concepts apprehending signs with respect to the mode of being, 141
    elaborations apprehending signs, 119
    grasping at objects, 225
    indestructible moments of knowing, 237
    only the apprehender-imaginary nature by the reason of the lack of being one or many, 225
    temporal partlessness, 236
    true existence, 227
    truly established atoms, 235
    truly established moments, 235
    partless atoms, 236–37
    partless moments of knowing, 237
    proliferations, 260
  Niḥsvabhāvavāda reasoning, 143, 201, 261, 263, 273–74, 356n.88
    of self-emptiness, 261
  of all phenomena being empty of their own entities, 195
  of all phenomena being free from proliferations, 196
  of impermanence, 232
  of listening and thinking, 120, 233
  of other-emptiness, 177, 182, 190, 218, 223, 261, 273
  of phenomena being free from proliferations, 196
  of self-emptiness, 177, 182, 195–96, 223, 233, 235, 260, 264, 273
  of the lack of being one or many, 154, 212

reasoning *(continued)*
positing all phenomena as entityless, 210
positing primordial mind as truthless, 375n.138
positing selflessness, 212
severing proliferations, 263
severing superimpositions, 200, 263
that ceases concepts apprehending signs, 260
Yogācāra reasoning, 259
See also analysis, emptiness, existence, mode, negation, nonexistence, object
remainder, 147, 171, 190, 201, 216
of negation, 171–72, 201, 216, 218, 219
of all extremes of proliferations, 216
of both the apprehended and apprehender, 147
of extremes, 216
of the object of negation, 177, 317n.72
Renakara, 42
Rendawa Zhönnu Lodrö, 30–31, 84–85, 97–99, 209, 317n.72, 333n.45, 337–38n.79, 341n.116, 375n.138
Rikden Namgyel Drakzang. *See* Namgyel Drakzang
Rinpung, 18–19, 21, 23, 42–44, 49, 105–106
Rinpung Norzang. *See* Norzang
Rongtön Mawé Senggé. *See* Rongtön Sheja Künrik
Rongtön Sheja Künrik, 3–4, 20–23, 25–29, 36, 38, 43, 47–49, 76, 97, 100, 214, 271, 308–309n.8, 310n.18, 311n.20, 313n.25, 315n.50, 316n.59, 319n.85, 332n.25, 334n.46

Sachen Künga Nyingpo, 4, 23
sādhana, 22
Sākāra. *See* Aspectarians
Sākāravāda, 77, 331n.18
Sākāravādin, 334n.51
Sakya, xi, 3–4, 7, 10, 17–21, 23–30, 32–33, 37–38, 43, 45–48, 51, 78, 90, 94–101, 103, 155, 201, 214, 238, 252, 270–72, 307n.3, 311n.3–4, 315n.50, 316n.59, 319n.85
Sakya Pendita Künga Gyeltsen, 3–4, 20, 27–28, 33, 37, 93–94, 102, 209, 230, 236, 238, 242–43, 246, 252, 254, 269, 307n.1, 311n.3, 317n.68, 320n.100, 340n.97, 343n.135, 381n.48 and n.50, 384n.72
Śākyabuddhi, 154, 358n.116
Sakyapa, 24, 43, 91, 94–95, 98, 106, 197, 311n.4
Sangda Bangrim, 25
Sanggyé Chökyongwa, 27
Sangpu Neutok, 19, 25–29, 33–34, 94, 321n.105, 322n.124, 339n.94–95
Śāntarakṣita, 74–75, 78, 92, 101, 138–39, 141–45, 150–51, 153, 155, 204–205, 331n.17, 332n.34, 335n.56, 343n.123, 356n.88 and n.90
Śāntideva, 25, 114, 202, 208–209, 320n.100
Satyākāravāda. *See* Yogācāra
Sautrāntika, 7, 75, 83, 109, 111–13, 119–20, 137–38, 140, 144–46, 148, 150, 167, 229, 331n.17
Sautrāntika Madhyamaka. *See* Madhyamaka
Sautrāntika Mādhyamika. *See* Mādhyamika
Sautrāntikas (as followers of the Sautrāntika system), 117
scope of presumption, 199
scope of reach, 199
Secret Mantra. *See* Mantra
self, 123
of persons, 110, 116, 123
of phenomena, 81, 116
true, 172

two types of, 113–14, 126, 178
See also grasping, negation, primordial mind
self-cognition, 9, 14, 74, 79, 151, 153, 161–64, 168, 214, 238, 242–43, 245–49, 331n.19, 364n.19, 383n.64, 384n.70 and n.72
devoid of the duality of the apprehended and apprehender, 164
direct, 163
of the outward-looking mind, 163
experiencing the apprehended-aspect, 164
free from both the apprehended and apprehender, 159
individual, 79, 246, 247
of dualistically appearing consciousness, 164
of ordinary beings, 245
of primordial mind, 243
of the non-dual knowing, 163
self-illuminating, 160, 164, 187, 217
of non-dual knowing, 366n.44
See also apprehender-aspect, ground, object
self-emptiness. *See* emptiness
selflessness, 36, 114, 116, 123, 345n.5
view of, 116
of persons, 110–12, 116, 123, 273, 345n.5, 349n.46
of phenomena, 110, 112, 116–17, 123–24, 215, 349n.46
See also four stages of yoga, mode, reasoning
Sera, 21, 28, 317n.72
Serdokchen, 19, 21, 26–27, 33, 35–36, 38, 41, 43–44, 46–47, 49–50, 91, 271, 319n.85, 327n.181
Shangpa. *See* Kagyü
Shangpa Dubupa, 93
Sherap Ö, 76, 333n.42
Sherap Senggé, 21
Six Dharmas of Nāro, 31
Six Ornaments Beautifying the Snowy Land, 3–4
Sönam Lhündrup. *See* Lowo Khenchen Sönam Lhündrup
Sönam Tsemo, 4, 32, 76, 265
Sönam Tsültrim, 25, 29
sounds and concepts, 170, 181–82, 187, 199, 222–23, 231, 233, 373n.110
expressive, 181
See also emptiness, object, existence, primordial mind
special insight, 93, 96, 280, 295
śrāvaka, 113, 189, 236, 244, 271
See also nirvāṇa
śrāvaka schools, 110–11, 119–20
Śrāvakayāna, 112
See also nirvāṇa
stain factor, outward-looking, 250
stains, 189, 229, 251
See also basis, buddha-essence, consciousness, purity
Sthiramati, 73, 75, 331n.18
subject, 80, 85, 126, 214, 226, 246, 249, 253, 256, 266
apprehending objects, 128
-basis for dispute, 126, 133–34
-basis of emptiness, 126, 129–30, 133, 171
established by valid cognition, 126
-basis of other-emptiness, 129
established by valid cognition, 125
non-apprehension by, 195
of a non-affirming negation, 179
of emptiness, 125, 172, 221
substance, 79, 159, 165, 230, 362n.6
and isolates, 42
See also apprehended, consciousness, emptiness, existence
suchness, 147, 174, 192, 230
subsequent attainment, 80, 84, 114, 169, 172, 179, 182, 187, 193–95, 228, 365n.35, 382n.55
See also conventions, mode, primordial mind
sugata-essence, 178, 242–43, 258, 372n.106
element of, 173, 196, 372n.106

Śūnyatāvāda, 71, 329n.1
superimposition, 77, 151, 153, 190–91, 195–96, 200, 204, 211
  See also concept, emptiness, extreme, Madhyamaka, mode
Sūtra Followers. *See* Sautrāntika
Svātantrika. *See* Madhyamaka
Svātantrikas (as followers of the Svātantrika system), 138–39, 143–44, 203, 207, 375n.128

Tai Situ Jangchup Gyeltsen, 17–18
Taklung. *See* Kagyü
Taktsang Lotsawa Sherap Rinchen, 8, 20, 309n.13, 312n.18
Tanak Tupten Namgyelling, 21
Tangtong Gyelpo, 23
Tantra, 14, 20, 22–23, 33, 42, 44, 91–92, 99, 101, 121, 209, 214, 249, 251–54, 256–57, 259–65, 267–68, 309n.12, 371n.98, 385n.91
  See also Highest Yoga Tantra, object
Tārā, 30, 49
Taranatha, 121, 229–30, 307n.1, 309n.13, 329n.2
tathāgata, 189–90
tathāgata-essence, 351n.59, 352n.64
ten grounds, 167–68, 195
thatness, 134, 202
  free from the duality of the apprehended and apprehender, 134
  of union, 387n.115
  of the texts of Proponents of Other-Emptiness, 135
  which is an object of experience, 153
thoroughly established nature. *See* three natures
three bodies, 190, 195–96
  See also dharma-body, emanation-body, enjoyment-body
three natures, 123–24, 127–28, 130, 134, 136, 164, 168, 171, 352n.63, 354n.79
  dependent, 123, 127–36, 164–66, 171–72, 185–86, 190, 224–25, 240, 353n.71, 364n.27–28, 366n.44, 370n.75
  imaginary, 123–24, 127–33, 136, 164–66, 171–72, 185–86, 190, 225, 227, 364n.28, 366n.44, 370n.75, 379n.24
    apprehender-imaginary, 224–26
  thoroughly established, 80, 123, 129–34, 136, 164–66, 171–72, 186, 211, 224–28, 232–33, 240, 348n.40, 353n.71, 364n.28, 366n.44, 370n.75, 379n.24
    non-erroneous, 366n.44
    unchangeable, 366n.44
  See also entity
three types of form, 131
  imaginary, 131
  imputational, 131
  reality-, 131
  See also three natures
Tibet, 8, 20, 22, 26, 30, 45, 72, 75–78, 83, 88–90, 92–93, 97, 101, 109, 118, 125, 252, 308n.4, 311n.3, 312n.15, 329n.2, 337n.70, 340n.97 and n.101, 348n.36
  Central, 3, 17–18, 25
  fifteenth-century, 3, 6, 10–11, 17, 20, 23, 264, 275–76
  Lower, 50
  Middle, 50
  Post-Sakya, 17
  southeast, 312n.7
  Upper, 50
  See also Tsang, Ü, Ütsang Ruzhi
Tongwa Dönden (the Sixth Karmapa), 22
Trangpowa, 47
Trashi Lhünpo, 21
Trashigön, 36–37, 42, 48, 322n.121
truth, 79–80, 115, 136, 176, 181, 224, 227–28, 350n.55, 378n.20
  conventional, 94, 214, 380n.44
  of reality, 361n.147
  relative, 93–94, 99, 130, 137, 158, 160–61, 174, 184–85, 194, 241,

349n.50, 354–55n.84, 369n.72, 380n.44
of the world, 137, 354–55n.84
ultimate, 10, 95, 98–99, 137–38, 147, 158–59, 161, 164, 166, 172, 176–77, 181–86, 189, 194, 198, 213, 214, 218, 220–21, 223–24, 229, 231–33, 241–43, 247, 266, 349n.50, 380n.44
directly experienced in meditative equipoise, 213
efficient, 95, 99, 197
experienced in the meditative equipoise of Mahāyāna āryas, 219
final, 127, 137, 187, 219, 258
genuine, 181, 194, 196–97, 199, 215
mere, 185
non-metaphorical, 99, 215
on the level of the basis, 242
See also emptiness, grasping, two truths
truthlessness, 172
of external objects, 112
of the apprehended-aspects, 112–13
of the apprehender, 360n.142
primordial mind's, 227
Tsang, 17–19, 21, 27, 37, 41–43, 106, 325n.150
See also Ütsang *and* Ütsang Ruzhi
Tsangpo, 18
Tsel Chökhorling, 28
Tsongkhapa Lopzang Drakpa, 3, 5–6, 8, 11–12, 19–21, 28–30, 76, 83, 88, 90, 92–98, 100, 122, 125–27, 135–36, 209, 275, 309n.13, 312n.18, 315n.50, 317–18n.72, 318n.73–74, 321n.105, 333n.45, 334n.46, 337–38n.79, 339n.93, 340n.98, 343n.124, 344n.142, 349n.49, 350–51n.52 and n.55, 352n.70, 369–70n.73 and n.75, 374n.118, 378n.20
Tsungme Chojé. *See* Gungru Gyeltsen Zangpo
Tsurpu, 106
Tuken Lopzang Chökyi Nyima, 103, 305, 317–18n.72
two natures, 129–30, 134, 136, 240
See also three natures
two stages, 249, 255, 260
completion stage, 249
generation stage, 249
generation and completion stages, 260–61
See also basis, entity, object, path
two truths, 93, 125–26, 155, 160, 168, 194
See also truth

ultimate, 86, 97, 125, 137–39, 147, 166, 177, 181, 192, 194–95, 198–99, 218, 220, 224, 229, 247, 263, 271, 273–74, 375n.138
concordant, 194
metaphorical, 95, 184, 194, 221, 369n.70
non-metaphorical, 194, 220
uncompounded, 132
See also reasoning
ultimate reality, 4, 6, 10–11, 13–14, 35, 74–75, 84–88, 91, 110, 130, 133, 136–40, 149, 154, 158, 166, 169, 171, 173, 177–79, 181–85, 190–91, 196, 201, 211, 213–14, 220, 222–23, 229, 232, 238, 242, 244, 247–48, 258, 261, 263, 266–67, 270–71, 273–74, 276, 307n.2, 338n.80, 343n.123, 348n.40, 366n.44, 370n.75, 376n.1–2, 379–80n.31, 382n.55
directly experienced in the meditative equipoise of Mahāyāna āryas, 202
directly realized in meditative experience, 185
experienced in meditative equipoise, 131, 142, 196, 254
directly, 154, 223
experienced through meditation, 376n.142
directly, 183
realization of, 85, 138, 214

ultimate reality *(continued)*
direct, 169, 183, 196, 222, 269, 366n.43
realized in meditative equipoise, 212
directly, 210
realized within the meditative equipoise of Mahāyāna āryas, 195
view of, 7, 14, 84, 137, 140, 154, 211, 264, 267, 273, 335n.56
See meditation, meditative equipoise, meditative experience, realization
ultimate view, 73, 75–76, 83, 85, 138, 142, 153–54, 166, 168, 182–83, 186, 191, 198, 202, 204, 213, 254, 273–74, 358n.116, 366n.45
directly realized in meditative equipoise, 270
directly realized through meditative experience, 169
experienced in meditation, 155, 212, 356n.88
experienced in meditative equipoise, 143
of Alīkākāravāda and Madhyamaka, 38
of sūtric and tantric systems of Madhyamaka, 269
of Niḥsvabhāvavāda, 75, 78
of Prāsaṅgika, 137
of Sautrāntika, 75
of Svātantrika, 137
of the non-dual primordial mind, 191
of Yogācāra, 75, 142
Ünyönpa Künga Zangpo, 35, 46, 328n.192
Ütsang, 48
Ütsang Ruzhi, 50

Vaibhāṣika, 7, 83, 109–13, 119–20, 140, 145, 150, 167, 229–30, 331n.17
Vaibhāṣikas (as followers of the Vaibhāṣika system), 110, 117
vajra, 173
indestructible, 198
of ultimate bodhicitta, 176
See also mind-vajra
Vajrabhairava, 30
Vajrapāṇi, 44, 320n.98
Vajravārāhī, 29
Vajrayāna, 208, 210, 215, 257–59, 264–65, 267
See also path
Vajrayoginī, 33
Vajrayoginī Central Channel, 31
valid cognition, 94, 115, 126–27, 158, 182, 240, 245, 247, 354n.82
conventional, 93
direct, 244–45
effect of, 164
self-experiencing, 244
ultimate, 154
See also establishment, three natures, phenomenon, subject
Vastusatpadārthavāda, 119
Vasubandhu, 28, 32, 72, 81, 103, 130–32, 144, 146, 154, 204–205, 207, 211, 255, 266, 320n.100, 330n.9, 352n.70
Vijñaptika, 355n.88
Vijñaptimātra, 137–38, 355–56n.88
Vijñaptivāda, 81–82, 161, 209, 337n.69, 355–56n.88
Vijñaptivāda Mādhyamika, 161
Vijñaptivādin, 160–61
Vikramaśīla, 79
Vinaya, 22–23, 25–28, 36–37, 42, 45–46, 48, 67, 320n.100, 322n.118

way of being, 177, 219
object's, 170
ultimate way of being, 141
way of being empty, 124
wisdom, 330n.14
arisen from meditation, 151
embodiment of, 369n.66

method and, 196
non-dual, 330n.14
of individual analysis, 169
of meditative equipoise on the meaning of emptiness determined by listening and thinking, 193
perfection of, 84
that ceases concepts apprehending signs, 260
See also analysis, empowerment, mode, object

Yakpa, 3–4, 26–27, 36, 50, 316n.59
Yaktön Sanggyepel. *See* Yakpa
Yamāntaka, 32
Yarlung, 18
Yeshé Dé, 75, 141, 356n.90
Yogācāra, xi, 2, 4–6, 8–14, 20, 26, 41, 43–44, 47–48, 50, 71–75, 77–79, 81–84, 87–88, 91, 99, 101, 106, 109, 118–19, 122–24, 127–31, 133, 135–36, 138–45, 148–51, 153–55, 157, 159, 161, 183, 187, 191, 193, 202, 209, 214, 216, 219, 226–27, 230, 249, 253, 257–58, 262–67, 269–71, 273, 275–77, 309n.12, 310n.16–18, 330n.9, 331n.17–18, 332n.22, 335n.56, 337n.69, 343n.133, 352n.69, 355–56n.88, 358n.116, 359n.135, 370n.75
Alīkākāravāda, 8–14, 38, 40–43, 50, 73–74, 77–79, 81–83, 85–88, 90, 100–101, 103–108, 112–13, 115–19, 121–22, 128, 130–31, 133–35, 139–41, 143–51, 154–73, 175–81, 183–87, 190–91, 193, 197, 202–206, 208–12, 214–15, 217–19, 222–24, 226–27, 231, 235, 246, 251–53, 256–62, 264–70, 272–76, 331n.17, 335n.56, 346n.5, 351n.56, 352n.69, 354n.79, 356n.88, 358n.116, 359n.135, 363n.10, 365n.34 and n.35, 371n.98, 375n.138, 376n.144, 385n.91
Satyākāravāda, 8–10, 12–13, 73–74, 77–79, 81, 83, 99–100, 104, 110, 112, 116–18, 128, 140, 143–46, 148–50, 157–68, 209, 246, 269, 275, 331n.17 and n.18, 343n.133, 351n.56, 354n.79, 358n.116, 359n.135, 360n.136, 363n.10
See also Cittamātra, Madhyamaka, reasoning
Yogācāra Madhyamaka. *See* Madhyamaka
Yogācāra Mādhyamika. *See* Mādhyamika
Yogācāras (as followers of the Yogācāra system), 72–75, 79, 83, 87, 122–24, 127, 132, 141, 144, 147–49, 154–55, 161, 165, 177, 183, 191, 202, 207, 218, 260, 263, 274, 310n.16, 331n.17
Alīkākāravāda Yogācāras, 171–72, 186, 214

Zangpa Lodrö Gyamtso, 27
Zhalu Lotsawa Chökyong Zangpo, 22
Zhönnu Chödrup, 31, 328n.192
Zilung, 21, 27, 35–36